Dina Tsagari and Jayanti Banerjee (Eds.)
Handbook of Second Language Assessmen

MW00805479

Handbooks of Applied Linguistics

Communication Competence
Language and Communication Problems
Practical Solutions

Edited by
Karlfried Knapp
Gerd Antos
Daniel Perrin
Marjolijn Verspoor

Volume 12

Handbook of Second Language Assessment

Edited by
Dina Tsagari and Jayanti Banerjee

DE GRUYTER
MOUTON

The hardcover edition of this book was published in 2016.

ISBN 978-1-61451-624-8
e-ISBN (PDF) 978-1-61451-382-7
e-ISBN (EPUB) 978-1-5015-0086-2

Library of Congress Cataloging-in-Publication Data
A CIP catalog record for this book has been applied for at the Library of Congress.

Bibliographic information published by the Deutsche Nationalbibliothek
The Deutsche Nationalbibliothek lists this publication in the Deutsche Nationalbibliografie;
detailed bibliographic data are available on the Internet at http://dnb.dnb.de.

© 2017 Walter de Gruyter Inc., Boston/Berlin
Typesetting: Meta Systems Publishing & Printservices GmbH, Wustermark
Printing and binding: CPI books GmbH, Leck
♾ Printed on acid-free paper
Printed in Germany

www.degruyter.com

MIX
Papier aus verantwor-
tungsvollen Quellen
FSC
www.fsc.org   FSC® C083411

Preface

The present volume constitutes another addition to the De Gruyter Mouton *Handbooks of Applied Linguistics*. As the reader can see from our subsequent *Introduction to the Handbook Series* on the next pages, the founding editors originally intended to comprise nine books only. However, various developments led us to abandon this self-imposed restriction, the most important ones being those in Applied Linguistics itself.

When we began planning this series in the late 1990s, the disciplinary status and scope of Applied Linguistics was less clear than it appears to be today. At that time, intensive debates were going on as to whether Applied Linguistics should be restricted to applying methods and findings from linguistics only, whether it should be regarded as a field of interdisciplinary synthesis drawing on psychology, sociology, ethnology and similar disciplines that are also dealing with aspects of language and communication, whether it should be regarded as an independent discipline in its own right, whether it was restricted to foreign language teaching, etc. Thus, what "Applied Linguistics" is and what an Applied Linguist does was highly controversial.

Against that backdrop, we felt that a series of Handbooks of Applied Linguistics could not simply be an accidental selection of descriptions of research findings and practical activities that were or could be published in books and articles labeled as "applied linguistic". Rather, for us such a series had to be based on an epistemological concept that frames the status and scope of our concept of Applied Linguistics. Departing from contemporary Philosophy of Science which sees academic disciplines under the pressure to successfully solve practical everyday problems encountered by the societies which aliment them, we emphasized the view that was at that time only emerging – the programmatic view that Applied Linguistics means the solving of real-world problems with language and communication. This concept appears to have become mainstream since.

In line with our conviction that Applied Linguistics is for problem solving, we decided to compile a series of books which aimed at giving representative descriptions of the ability of this field of academic inquiry of providing accounts, analyses, explanations and, where possible, solutions of everyday problems with language and communication. To delimit the range of topics to be dealt with, we planned a set of nine volumes which were intended to present findings and applications of Applied Linguistics in concentric circles, as it were, departing from aspects of the communication competence of the individual via those of interpersonal, intergroup, organizational, public, multilingual, foreign language, intercultural, and technical communication ultimately to the level of society at large.

From the reception this series received in the academic community, among practitioners, and on the market, the underlying concept was a complete success.

In fact, this success even triggered competitive handbook series by other publishers.

It has to be admitted, though, that the selection of topic areas for these nine volumes more than ten years ago was guided by what were key issues in Applied Linguistics at that time. Meanwhile, however, further problems with language and communication have come to the fore, and also some topics which were dealt with in individual chapters of the previous nine volumes meanwhile have attracted so much attention, generating so much new insights, that they merit an in-depth treatment in individual volumes devoted solely to these. This development, the fact that repeatedly distinguished colleagues approached us with proposals to edit further volumes in this handbook series and the market success convinced both De Gruyter Mouton publishers and the series editors to continue the *Handbooks of Applied Linguistics* beyond the initial nine.

Meanwhile, this is an open-ended series. It will publish individual, self-contained volumes that depart from the view that Applied Linguistics is problem solving and that give a coherent and representative account of how the respective area of practical problems with language and communication is dealt with in this field of inquiry.

The present volume is an example of this. It also marks a change in the series editorship, with Daniel Perrin and Marjolijn Verspoor succeeding the founding editors.

Karlfried Knapp (Erfurt)
Gerd Antos (Halle/Saale)
Daniel Perrin (Zürich)
Marjolijn Verspoor (Groningen)

Karlfried Knapp and Gert Antos
Introduction to the handbook series

Linguistics for problem solving

1 Science and application at the turn of the millennium

The distinction between "pure" and "applied" sciences is an old one. According to Meinel (2000), it was introduced by the Swedish chemist Wallerius in 1751, as part of the dispute of that time between the scholastic disciplines and the then emerging epistemic sciences. However, although the concept of "Applied Science" gained currency rapidly since that time, it has remained problematic.

Until recently, the distinction between "pure" and "applied" mirrored the distinction between "theory" and "practice". The latter ran all the way through Western history of science since its beginnings in antique times. At first, it was only philosophy that was regarded as a scholarly and, hence, theoretical discipline. Later it was followed by other leading disciplines, as e.g., the sciences. However, as academic disciplines, all of them remained theoretical. In fact, the process of achieving independence of theory was essential for the academic disciplines to become independent from political, religious or other contingencies and to establish themselves at universities and academies. This also implied a process of emancipation from practical concerns – an at times painful development which manifested (and occasionally still manifests) itself in the discrediting of and disdain for practice and practitioners. To some, already the very meaning of the notion "applied" carries a negative connotation, as is suggested by the contrast between the widely used synonym for "theoretical", i.e. "pure" (as used, e.g., in the distinction between "Pure" and "Applied Mathematics") and its natural antonym "impure". On a different level, a lower academic status sometimes is attributed to applied disciplines because of their alleged lack of originality – they are perceived as simply and one-directionally applying insights gained in basic research and watering them down by neglecting the limiting conditions under which these insights were achieved.

Today, however, the academic system is confronted with a new understanding of science. In politics, in society and, above all, in economy a new concept of science has gained acceptance which questions traditional views. In recent philosophy of science, this is labelled as "science under the pressure to succeed" – i.e. as science whose theoretical structure and criteria of evaluation are increasingly conditioned by the pressure of application (Carrier, Stöltzner, and Wette 2004):

Whenever the public is interested in a particular subject, e.g., when a new disease develops that cannot be cured by conventional medication, the public requests science to provide new insights in this area as quickly as possible. In doing so, the public is less interested in whether these new insights fit seamlessly into an existing theoretical framework, but rather whether they make new methods of treatment and curing possible. (Institut für Wirtschafts- und Technikforschung 2004, our translation).

With most of the practical problems like these, sciences cannot rely on knowledge that is already available, simply because such knowledge does not yet exist. Very often, the problems at hand do not fit neatly into the theoretical framework of one particular "pure science", and there is competition among disciplines with respect to which one provides the best theoretical and methodological resources for potential solutions. And more often than not the problems can be tackled only by adopting an interdisciplinary approach.

As a result, the traditional "Cascade Model", where insights were applied top-down from basic research to practice, no longer works in many cases. Instead, a kind of "application oriented basic research" is needed, where disciplines – conditioned by the pressure of application – take up a certain still diffuse practical issue, define it as a problem against the background of their respective theoretical and methodological paradigms, study this problem and finally develop various application oriented suggestions for solutions. In this sense, applied science, on the one hand, has to be conceived of as a scientific strategy for problem solving – a strategy that starts from mundane practical problems and ultimately aims at solving them. On the other hand, despite the dominance of application that applied sciences are subjected to, as sciences they can do nothing but develop such solutions in a theoretically reflected and methodologically well founded manner. The latter, of course, may lead to the well-known fact that even applied sciences often tend to concentrate on "application oriented basic research" only and thus appear to lose sight of the original practical problem. But despite such shifts in focus both the boundaries between disciplines and between pure and applied research are getting more and more blurred.

Today, after the turn of the millennium, it is obvious that sciences are requested to provide more and something different than just theory, basic research or pure knowledge. Rather, sciences are increasingly being regarded as partners in a more comprehensive social and economic context of problem solving and are evaluated against expectations to be practically relevant. This also implies that sciences are expected to be critical, reflecting their impact on society. This new "applied" type of science is confronted with the question: Which role can the sciences play in solving individual, interpersonal, social, intercultural, political or technical problems? This question is typical of a conception of science that was especially developed and propagated by the influential philosopher Sir Karl Popper – a conception that also this handbook series is based on.

2 "Applied Linguistics": Concepts and controversies

The concept of "Applied Linguistics" is not as old as the notion of "Applied Science", but it has also been problematical in its relation to theoretical linguistics since its beginning. There seems to be a widespread consensus that the notion "Applied Linguistics" emerged in 1948 with the first issue of the journal *Language Learning* which used this compound in its subtitle *A Quarterly Journal of Applied Linguistics*. This history of its origin certainly explains why even today "Applied Linguistics" still tends to be predominantly associated with foreign language teaching and learning in the Anglophone literature in particular, as can bee seen e.g., from Johnson and Johnson (1998), whose *Encyclopedic Dictionary of Applied Linguistics* is explicitly subtitled *A Handbook for Language Teaching*. However, this theory of origin is historically wrong. As is pointed out by Back (1970), the concept of applying linguistics can be traced back to the early 19th century in Europe, and the very notion "Applied Linguistics" was used in the early 20th already.

2.1 Theoretically Applied vs. Practically Applied Linguistics

As with the relation between "Pure" and "Applied" sciences pointed out above, also with "Applied Linguistics" the first question to be asked is what makes it different from "Pure" or "Theoretical Linguistics". It is not surprising, then, that the terminologist Back takes this difference as the point of departure for his discussion of what constitutes "Applied Linguistics". In the light of recent controversies about this concept it is no doubt useful to remind us of his terminological distinctions.

Back (1970) distinguishes between "Theoretical Linguistics" – which aims at achieving knowledge for its own sake, without considering any other value –, "Practice" – i.e. any kind of activity that serves to achieve any purpose in life in the widest sense, apart from the striving for knowledge for its own sake – and "Applied Linguistics", as being based on "Theoretical Linguistics" on the one hand and as aiming at usability in "Practice" on the other. In addition, he makes a difference between "Theoretical Applied Linguistics" and "Practical Applied Linguistics", which is of particular interest here. The former is defined as the use of insights and methods of "Theoretical Linguistics" for gaining knowledge in another, non-linguistic discipline, such as ethnology, sociology, law or literary studies, the latter as the application of insights from linguistics in a practical field related to language, such as language teaching, translation, and the like. For Back, the contribution of applied linguistics is to be seen in the planning of practical action. Language teaching, for example, is practical action done by practitioners, and what applied linguistics can contribute to this is, e.g., to provide contrastive descriptions of the languages involved as a foundation for teaching methods. These contrastive descriptions in turn have to be based on the descriptive methods developed in theoretical linguistics.

However, in the light of the recent epistemological developments outlined above, it may be useful to reinterpret Back's notion of "Theoretically Applied Linguistics". As he himself points out, dealing with practical problems can have repercussions on the development of the theoretical field. Often new approaches, new theoretical concepts and new methods are a prerequisite for dealing with a particular type of practical problems, which may lead to an – at least in the beginning – "application oriented basic research" in applied linguistics itself, which with some justification could also be labelled "theoretically applied", as many such problems require the transgression of disciplinary boundaries. It is not rare that a domain of "Theoretically Applied Linguistics" or "application oriented basic research" takes on a life of its own, and that also something which is labelled as "Applied Linguistics" might in fact be rather remote from the mundane practical problems that originally initiated the respective subject area. But as long as a relation to the original practical problem can be established, it may be justified to count a particular field or discussion as belonging to applied linguistics, even if only "theoretically applied".

2.2 Applied linguistics as a response to structuralism and generativism

As mentioned before, in the Anglophone world in particular the view still appears to be widespread that the primary concerns of the subject area of applied linguistics should be restricted to second language acquisition and language instruction in the first place (see, e.g., Davies 1999 or Schmitt and Celce-Murcia 2002). However, in other parts of the world, and above all in Europe, there has been a development away from aspects of language learning to a wider focus on more general issues of language and communication.

This broadening of scope was in part a reaction to the narrowing down the focus in linguistics that resulted from self-imposed methodological constraints which, as Ehlich (1999) points out, began with Saussurean structuralism and culminated in generative linguistics. For almost three decades since the late 1950s, these developments made "language" in a comprehensive sense, as related to the everyday experience of its users, vanish in favour of an idealised and basically artificial entity. This led in "Core" or theoretical linguistics to a neglect of almost all everyday problems with language and communication encountered by individuals and societies and made it necessary for those interested in socially accountable research into language and communication to draw on a wider range of disciplines, thus giving rise to a flourishing of interdisciplinary areas that have come to be referred to as hyphenated variants of linguistics, such as sociolinguistics, ethnolinguistics, psycholinguistics, conversation analysis, pragmatics, and so on (Davies and Elder 2004).

That these hyphenated variants of linguistics can be said to have originated from dealing with problems may lead to the impression that they fall completely into the scope of applied linguistics. This the more so as their original thematic focus is in line with a frequently quoted definition of applied linguistics as "the theoretical and empirical investigation of real world problems in which language is a central issue" (Brumfit 1997: 93). However, in the recent past much of the work done in these fields has itself been rather "theoretically applied" in the sense introduced above and ultimately even become mainstream in linguistics. Also, in view of the current epistemological developments that see all sciences under the pressure of application, one might even wonder if there is anything distinctive about applied linguistics at all.

Indeed it would be difficult if not impossible to delimit applied linguistics with respect to the practical problems studied and the disciplinary approaches used: Real-world problems with language (to which, for greater clarity, should be added: "with communication") are unlimited in principle. Also, many problems of this kind are unique and require quite different approaches. Some might be tackled successfully by applying already available linguistic theories and methods. Others might require for their solution the development of new methods and even new theories. Following a frequently used distinction first proposed by Widdowson (1980), one might label these approaches as "Linguistics Applied" or "Applied Linguistics". In addition, language is a trans-disciplinary subject par excellence, with the result that problems do not come labelled and may require for their solution the cooperation of various disciplines.

2.3 Conceptualisations and communities

The questions of what should be its reference discipline and which themes, areas of research and sub-disciplines it should deal with, have been discussed constantly and were also the subject of an intensive debate (e.g., Seidlhofer 2003). In the recent past, a number of edited volumes on applied linguistics have appeared which in their respective introductory chapters attempt at giving a definition of "Applied Linguistics". As can be seen from the existence of the Association Internationale de Linguistique Appliquée (AILA) and its numerous national affiliates, from the number of congresses held or books and journals published with the label "Applied Linguistics", applied linguistics appears to be a well-established and flourishing enterprise. Therefore, the collective need felt by authors and editors to introduce their publication with a definition of the subject area it is supposed to be about is astonishing at first sight. Quite obviously, what Ehlich (2006) has termed "the struggle for the object of inquiry" appears to be characteristic of linguistics – both of linguistics at large and applied linguistics. Its seems then, that the meaning and scope of "Applied Linguistics" cannot be taken for granted, and this is why a wide variety of controversial conceptualisations exist.

For example, in addition to the dichotomy mentioned above with respect to whether approaches to applied linguistics should in their theoretical foundations and methods be autonomous from theoretical linguistics or not, and apart from other controversies, there are diverging views on whether applied linguistics is an independent academic discipline (e.g., Kaplan and Grabe 2000) or not (e.g., Davies and Elder 2004), whether its scope should be mainly restricted to language teaching related topics (e.g., Schmitt and Celce-Murcia 2002) or not (e.g., Knapp 2006), or whether applied linguistics is a field of interdisciplinary synthesis where theories with their own integrity develop in close interaction with language users and professionals (e.g., Rampton 1997 [2003]) or whether this view should be rejected, as a true interdisciplinary approach is ultimately impossible (e.g., Widdowson 2005).

In contrast to such controversies Candlin and Sarangi (2004) point out that applied linguistics should be defined in the first place by the actions of those who practically *do* applied linguistics:

> [...] we see no especial purpose in reopening what has become a somewhat sterile debate on what applied linguistics is, or whether it is a distinctive and coherent discipline. [...] we see applied linguistics as a many centered and interdisciplinary endeavour whose coherence is achieved in purposeful, mediated action by its practitioners. [...] What we want to ask of applied linguistics is less what it is and more what it does, or rather what its practitioners do. (Candlin and Sarangi 2004: 1–2)

Against this background, they see applied linguistics as less characterised by its thematic scope – which indeed is hard to delimit – but rather by the two aspects of "relevance" and "reflexivity". Relevance refers to the purpose applied linguistic activities have for the targeted audience and to the degree that these activities in their collaborative practices meet the background and needs of those addressed – which, as matter of comprehensibility, also includes taking their conceptual and language level into account. Reflexivity means the contextualisation of the intellectual principles and practices, which is at the core of what characterises a professional community, and which is achieved by asking leading questions like "What kinds of purposes underlie what is done?", "Who is involved in their determination?", "By whom, and in what ways, is their achievement appraised?", "Who owns the outcomes?".

We agree with these authors that applied linguistics, in dealing with real world problems, is determined by disciplinary givens – such as e.g., theories, methods or standards of linguistics or any other discipline – but that it is determined at least as much by the social and situational givens of the practices of life. These do not only include the concrete practical problems themselves but also the theoretical and methodological standards of cooperating experts from other disciplines, as well as the conceptual and practical standards of the practitioners who are confronted with the practical problems in the first place. Thus, as Sarangi and van Leeuwen (2003) point out, applied linguists have to become part of the respective "community of practice".

If, however, applied linguists have to regard themselves as part of a community of practice, it is obvious that it is the entire community which determines what the respective subject matter is that the applied linguist deals with and how. In particular, it is the respective community of practice which determines which problems of the practitioners have to be considered. The consequence of this is that applied linguistics can be understood from very comprehensive to very specific, depending on what kind of problems are considered relevant by the respective community. Of course, following this participative understanding of applied linguistics also has consequences for the Handbooks of Applied Linguistics both with respect to the subjects covered and the way they are theoretically and practically treated.

3 Applied linguistics for problem solving

Against this background, it seems reasonable not to define applied linguistics as an autonomous discipline or even only to delimit it by specifying a set of subjects it is supposed to study and typical disciplinary approaches it should use. Rather, in line with the collaborative and participatory perspective of the communities of practice applied linguists are involved in, this handbook series is based on the assumption that applied linguistics is a specific, problem-oriented way of "doing linguistics" related to the real-life world. In other words applied linguistics is conceived of here as "linguistics for problem solving".

To outline what we think is distinctive about this area of inquiry: Entirely in line with Popper's conception of science, we take it that applied linguistics starts from the assumption of an imperfect world in the areas of language and communication. This means, firstly, that linguistic and communicative competence in individuals, like other forms of human knowledge, is fragmentary and defective – if it exists at all. To express it more pointedly: Human linguistic and communicative behaviour is not "perfect". And on a different level, this imperfection also applies to the use and status of language and communication in and among groups or societies.

Secondly, we take it that applied linguists are convinced that the imperfection both of individual linguistic and communicative behaviour and language based relations between groups and societies can be clarified, understood and to some extent resolved by their intervention, e.g., by means of education, training or consultancy. Thirdly, we take it that applied linguistics proceeds by a specific mode of inquiry in that it mediates between the way language and communication is expertly studied in the linguistic disciplines and the way it is directly experienced in different domains of use. This implies that applied linguists are able to demon-

Karlfried Knapp and Gert Antos

strate that their findings – be they of a "Linguistics Applied" or "Applied Linguistics" nature – are not just "application oriented basic research" but can be made relevant to the real-life world.

Fourthly, we take it that applied linguistics is socially accountable. To the extent that the imperfections initiating applied linguistic activity involve both social actors and social structures, we take it that applied linguistics has to be critical and reflexive with respect to the results of its suggestions and solutions.

These assumptions yield the following questions which at the same time define objectives for applied linguistics:

1. Which linguistic problems are typical of which areas of language competence and language use?
2. How can linguistics define and describe these problems?
3. How can linguistics suggest, develop, or achieve solutions of these problems?
4. Which solutions result in which improvements in speakers' linguistic and communicative abilities or in the use and status of languages in and between groups?
5. What are additional effects of the linguistic intervention?

4 Objectives of this handbook series

These questions also determine the objectives of this book series. However, in view of the present boom in handbooks of linguistics and applied linguistics, one should ask what is specific about this series of thematically different volumes.

To begin with, it is important to emphasise what it is not aiming at:

- The handbook series does not want to take a snapshot view or even a "hit list" of fashionable topics, theories, debates or fields of study.
- Nor does it aim at a comprehensive coverage of linguistics because some selectivity with regard to the subject areas is both inevitable in a book series of this kind and part of its specific profile.

Instead, the book series will try

- to show that applied linguistics can offer a comprehensive, trustworthy and scientifically well-founded understanding of a wide range of problems,
- to show that applied linguistics can provide or develop instruments for solving new, still unpredictable problems,
- to show that applied linguistics is not confined to a restricted number of topics such as, e.g., foreign language learning, but that it successfully deals with a wide range of both everyday problems and areas of linguistics,
- to provide a state-of-the-art description of applied linguistics against the background of the ability of this area of academic inquiry to provide descriptions, analyses, explanations and, if possible, solutions of everyday problems. On the

one hand, this criterion is the link to trans-disciplinary co-operation. On the other, it is crucial in assessing to what extent linguistics can in fact be made relevant.

In short, it is by no means the intention of this series to duplicate the present state of knowledge about linguistics as represented in other publications with the supposed aim of providing a comprehensive survey. Rather, the intention is to present the knowledge available in applied linguistics today firstly from an explicitly problem solving perspective and secondly, in a non-technical, easily comprehensible way. Also it is intended with this publication to build bridges to neighbouring disciplines and to critically discuss which impact the solutions discussed do in fact have on practice. This is particularly necessary in areas like language teaching and learning – where for years there has been a tendency to adopt fashionable solutions without sufficient consideration of their actual impact on the reality in schools.

5 Criteria for the selection of topics

Based on the arguments outlined above, the handbook series has the following structure: Findings and applications of linguistics will be presented in concentric circles, as it were, starting out from the communication competence of the individual, proceeding via aspects of interpersonal and inter-group communication to technical communication and, ultimately, to the more general level of society. Thus, the topics of the first nine volumes are as follows:
1. Handbook of Individual Communication Competence
2. Handbook of Interpersonal Communication
3. Handbook of Communication in Organisations and Professions
4. Handbook of Communication in the Public Sphere
5. Handbook of Multilingualism and Multilingual Communication
6. Handbook of Foreign Language Communication and Learning
7. Handbook of Intercultural Communication
8. Handbook of Technical Communication
9. Handbook of Language and Communication: Diversity and Change

This thematic structure can be said to follow the sequence of experience with problems related to language and communication a human passes through in the course of his or her personal biographical development. This is why the topic areas of applied linguistics are structured here in ever-increasing concentric circles: in line with biographical development, the first circle starts with the communicative competence of the individual and also includes interpersonal communication as belonging to a person's private sphere. The second circle proceeds to the everyday environment and includes the professional and public sphere. The third circle extends to the experience of foreign languages and cultures, which at least in officially monolingual societies, is not made by everybody and if so, only later in life. Technical communication as the fourth circle is even more exclusive and restricted to a more special professional clientele. The ninth volume extends this process to focus on more general, supra-individual national and international issues.

For almost all of these topics, there already exist introductions, handbooks or other types of survey literature. However, what makes the present volumes unique is their explicit claim to focus on topics in language and communication as areas of everyday problems and their emphasis on pointing out the relevance of applied linguistics in dealing with them.

6 References

Back, Otto. 1970. Was bedeutet und was bezeichnet der Begriff ,angewandte Sprachwissenschaft'? *Die Sprache* 16: 21–53.

Brumfit, Christopher. 1997. How applied linguistics is the same as any other science. *International Journal of Applied Linguistics* 7(1): 86–94.

Candlin, Chris N. and Srikant Sarangi. 2004. Making applied linguistics matter. *Journal of Applied Linguistics* 1(1): 1–8.

Carrier, Michael, Martin Stöltzner and Jeanette Wette. 2004. *Theorienstruktur und Beurteilungsmaßstäbe unter den Bedingungen der Anwendungsdominanz*. Universitat Bielefeld: Institut fur Wissenschafts- und Technikforschung, http://www.uni-bielefeld.de/iwt/projekte/wissen/anwendungsdominanz.html (accessed 5 January 2007).

Davies, Alan. 1999. *An Introduction to Applied Linguistics. From Practice to Theory*. Edinburgh: Edinburgh University Press.

Davies, Alan and Catherine Elder. 2004. General introduction – Applied linguistics: Subject to discipline? In: Alan Davies and Catherine Elder (eds.). *The Handbook of Applied Linguistics*, 1–16. Malden etc.: Blackwell.

Ehlich, Konrad. 1999. Vom Nutzen der „Funktionalen Pragmatik" für die angewandte Linguistik. In: Michael Becker-Mrotzek and Christine Doppler (eds.). *Medium Sprache im Beruf. Eine Aufgabe für die Linguistik*, 23–36. Tubingen: Narr.

Ehlich, Konrad. 2006. Mehrsprachigkeit für Europa – öffentliches Schweigen, linguistische Distanzen. In: Sergio Cigada, Jean-Francois de Pietro, Daniel Elmiger and Markus Nussbaumer (eds.). *Öffentliche Sprachdebatten – linguistische Positionen. Bulletin Suisse de Linguistique Appliquée/VALS-ASLA-Bulletin* 83(1): 11–28.

Johnson, Keith and Helen Johnson (eds.). 1998. *Encyclopedic Dictionary of Applied Linguistics. A Handbook for Language Teaching*. Oxford: Blackwell.

Kaplan, Robert B. and William Grabe. 2000. Applied linguistics and the Annual Review of Applied Linguistics. In: W. Grabe (ed.). *Applied Linguistics as an Emerging Discipline. Annual Review of Applied Linguistics* 20: 3–17.

Knapp, Karlfried. 2006. Vorwort. In: Karlfried Knapp, Gerd Antos, Michael Becker-Mrotzek, Arnulf Deppermann, Susanne Göpferich, Joachim Gabowski, Michael Klemm and Claudia Villiger (eds.). *Angewandte Linguistik. Ein Lehrbuch*. 2nd ed., xix–xxiii. Tübingen: Francke UTB.

Meinel, Christoph. 2000. Reine und angewandte Wissenschaft. *Das Magazin*. Ed. Wissenschaftszentrum Nordrhein-Westfalen 11(1): 10–11.

Rampton, Ben. 1997 [2003]. Retuning in applied linguistics. *International Journal of Applied Linguistics* 7(1): 3–25, quoted from Seidlhofer (2003), 273–295.

Sarangi, Srikant and Theo van Leeuwen. 2003. Applied linguistics and communities of practice: Gaining communality or losing disciplinary autonomy? In: Srikant Sarangi and Theo van Leeuwen (eds.). *Applied Linguistics and Communities of Practice*, 1–8. London: Continuum.

Schmitt, Norbert and Marianne Celce-Murcia. 2002. An overview of applied linguistics. In: Norbert Schmitt (ed.). *An Introduction to Applied Linguistics*. London: Arnold.

Seidlhofer, Barbara (ed.). 2003. *Controversies in Applied Linguistics*. Oxford, UK: Oxford University Press.

Widdowson, Henry. 1984 [1980]. Model and fictions. In: Henry Widdowson (ed.). *Explorations in Applied Linguistics* 2: 21–27. Oxford, UK: Oxford University Press.

Widdowson, Henry. 2005. Applied linguistics, interdisciplinarity, and disparate realities. In: Paul Bruthiaux, Dwight Atkinson, William G. Egginton, William Grabe and Vaidehi Ramanathan (eds.). *Directions in Applied Linguistics. Essays in Honor of Robert B. Kaplan*, 12–25. Clevedon: Multilingual Matters.

To our families
and our friends

Contents

Dina Tsagari and Jayanti Banerjee
1 The handbook of second language assessment

1 Introduction

In stating the aims and scope of the series of which this volume is a part, the series editors describe Applied Linguistics as a field that "deals with the theoretical and empirical investigation of real world problems in which language and communication are a central issue" (Brumfit 1997: 93). They view it as a "problem-oriented and problem-solving activity" (Brumfit 1997: 93). These statements encapsulate the work of researchers and practitioners of second language assessment as it helps to solve various real world problems. For example, at the level of individuals such work identifies and certifies degrees of second language competence that can be used for decisions on further educational or professional careers. At the level of institutions like the education system it evaluates teachers. At the level of organizations it helps to select or promote staff with the necessary foreign language and communication skills. Finally, at the level of states it helps in the development of language tests as a basis for granting citizenship to immigrants. In many cases, assessment has a gatekeeping function. It therefore has to be done responsibly and with care.

Arguably, there is nothing more 'real world' than a second language assessment tool. For second language assessment is a process of gathering information about how much language a learner knows and can use. The first step in designing a language test is the definition of what it means to be proficient in the language (be it English, German, Korean, Igbo, or Bengali) and, as such, both language and communication are central to language testers' work. As a result, language testing researchers are often at the leading edge of investigations into second language ability.

2 History of second language assessment

The professional roots of the field of second language assessment can be traced to the publication of Robert Lado's (1961) book *Language Testing*. At that time the approach to assessment was primarily structural. It reflected the way that language was taught – as a set of discrete elements. As views of language teaching and language use have evolved, the approach to language assessment has also changed. The psycholinguistic-sociolinguistic approach resulted in integrative, global measures such as cloze passages and dictation. These assessments required test takers to demonstrate their ability to use, in combination, the different aspects of language knowledge (grammar, vocabulary, spelling, etc.).

However, both the structuralist and psycholinguistic-sociolinguistic approaches to language and language learning were criticized for their restrictive view of how language works. Canale and Swain (1980) presented an alternative, the communicative approach. They showed how language is used to communicate meaning. This involves: knowledge of vocabulary, morpho-syntax, and phonology (grammatical knowledge); knowledge of the rules of language use, as demonstrated by register choice, and pragmatic inferences, and knowledge of the rules of discourse (sociolinguistic competence); and, knowledge of strategies, such as gestures, that can maintain communication (strategic competence). For the last thirty-five years, this view of language has informed approaches to language teaching and assessment. Tests are generally expected to provide context for the tasks and to engage the test takers in processing and producing realistic discourse.

As well as representing a long-standing approach to second language teaching and assessment, Canale and Swain's (1980) paper is important because of the explicit way in which it draws in detail on major thought trends in linguistics at the time including Hymes' (1972) discussion of language use as encompassing both grammaticality and sociolinguistic appropriacy as well as van Ek's (1976) notion of language functions. This reflects a persistent relationship between linguistics and second language assessment. As Davies (1990) comments, language assessment is a "chief way of applying linguistics, perhaps more so than most other activities in applied linguistics, in that the selection of material for language tests and the statements made in terms of the results achieved [a]re always of linguistic import, making statements about the nature of language and language learning (p. 74)."

3 Aims of the volume

Indeed, second language assessment is a transdisciplinary field that is influenced certainly by linguistics but also by politics, philosophy, psychology, sociology and psychometrics. For instance, in order to make a judgment about a learner's vocabulary proficiency, we need to understand how words and formulaic phrases are learned, particularly learners' sensitivity to patterns and sequences (Ellis, 2002) and the principles of Zipfian distribution (Sorrell, 2013). This seemingly straightforward aim of assessing vocabulary draws on lessons learned from psychology and mathematics.

In a very different example, the fields of politics and philosophy illuminate the agendas that motivate second language testing practices and show their consequences. McNamara and Roever (2006) expose in detail how language assessments can perpetuate unquestioned social values and policies. They show how language tests are used to exclude asylum seekers and to deny immigrants access to work opportunities.

The central aim of this volume is to capture the main debates and research advances in second language assessment over the last fifty or so years, showing the influence of linguistics, politics, philosophy, psychology, sociology and psychometrics. It provides:

- an overview of current theories and research of language assessment by considering the philosophical and historical underpinnings of assessment practices,
- a balanced evaluation of the major positions and approaches, including the examination of the increasingly important social and political context of language assessment,
- practical applications of language assessment theory for practitioners, and
- a theoretical basis for considering and analyzing language tests and understanding administration and training issues involved.

As such, the volume charts the new avenues that second language assessment has moved into by considering not only issues of design, administration and training involved in the assessment of second language but also the growing range of public policy, social and ethical issues. It also considers the various assessment and linguistic contexts while emphasis is put on the need for a careful consideration of various groups of test takers, e.g., young, adult and those with learning and other disabilities as well consideration of subtle dimensions of language proficiency such as the assessment of pragmatic competence.

The authors bring to their topics a high level of expertise and represent diverse methodological approaches, and geographic regions of the world. Each chapter includes a brief history of the topic to provide the context, discusses the major key issues, research approaches and findings, and ends with a forward-looking section where authors discuss what they view to be the most important challenges and research steps that their fields need to take.

4 Overview of the volume

The volume is organized around four parts each comprising five to eight chapters. Part I, entitled 'Conceptual foundations of second language assessment' contains four chapters focusing on the history of language assessment, purposes, standards, frameworks and approaches and other characteristics of assessment such as quality, in terms of reliability, validity and impact.

Part II 'Assessing second language skills/areas' includes eight chapters focusing on the assessment of traditional skills such as listening, reading, speaking and writing as well as emerging language areas such as the assessment of pragmatic and intercultural competence, fluency and translation and interpretation. The five chapters in Part III, 'Second language assessment contexts', address exciting areas in the field such as learning-oriented assessment, dynamic assessment, assessment for the workplace and immigration, citizenship and asylum. Part IV explores new avenues by bringing together a collection of six chapters that draw on research and developments in a multitude of areas such as aligning language assessments to frameworks, using technology, assessing young learners and students with learning and other disabilities, the importance of 'voice' in second language assessment and teachers' assessment literacy and professional development.

Part I begins with Liz Hamp-Lyon's contribution (Chapter 2), which shows how, in recent years, the terms assessment, testing, examining, and evaluation have become increasingly intertwined. New terms such as alternative assessment, [X]-based assessment, and related concepts/terms such as learning-oriented language assessment, dynamic assessment and peer feedback have come to the fore. In her chapter Hamp-Lyons maintains a diachronic cast to these issues and builds up a picture of the present expanding view of the purposes of language assessment. Her chapter closes with a consideration of the opportunities and challenges for the future offered by these broader views of the purposes of language assessment for research and practice in language testing/assessment.

Given their increasing use by governments and international agencies as policy instruments, the need for clarity of 'standards' and 'frameworks' in language assessment is ever more pressing. This is the motivation behind the next chapter (Chapter 3) written by Glenn Fulcher entitled 'Standards and frameworks'. Fulcher defines the terms, explores the relationship between models and frameworks, discusses standards-based testing as a new social phenomenon, and calls for a return to validation research that focuses on scores from tests and assessments, rather than standard-setting procedures.

In Chapter 4, Yasuyo Sawaki provides an overview of two key frames of reference for language test-score interpretation: 'norm-referenced' and 'criterion-referenced' testing (NRT and CRT respectively). Sawaki starts with a definition of the frames and their historical development. She then discusses aspects of measurement and quality through the provision of concrete examples and concludes with a discussion of issues, challenges, and future directions of language assessment research related to NRT and CRT.

The next two chapters in the volume (Chapters 5 and 6) focus on quality and impact in language assessment. Xiaoming Xi and Larry Davis (Chapter 5) begin by exploring the different ways in which test quality has been conceptualized such as validity, fairness, and test usefulness. They discuss frameworks for test validation, focusing particularly on the argument-based approach to test validation developed by Kane (2013).

Nick Saville and Hanan Khalifa (Chapter 6) explore the notion of impact by design in language assessment. They consider the effects and consequences resulting from the development and use of language assessments in societal contexts. Their discussion encompasses washback but expands the notion to deal with the wider effects and consequences which assessments have in society. Several recent case studies are used to illustrate the discussion and to present ways in which impact-related research can be integrated into operational validation procedures. The concluding section considers future challenges and ways in which this aspect of language assessment might develop in the future.

Part II presents eight impressive accounts of the assessment of language skills and areas. In the first of these chapters, Tineke Brunfaut (Chapter 7) describes the listening construct, a highly complex process, and gives an overview of different approaches to measuring listening ability. Different test techniques are illustrated with reference to existing listening tests, and factors that influence listening task difficulty such as text characteristics, task procedures and the interaction between listening texts and task responses as well as cognitive, affective and linguistic characteristics of the listener. The chapter concludes by discussing implications for listening assessment of the role of task- and listener-related characteristics, their interaction, and the resulting challenges for listening assessment practice and research.

In the following chapter, Fabiana MacMillan (Chapter 8), addressing the topic of assessing reading, draws on studies in written discourse analysis and second language reading and suggests a framework for the analysis of reading assessment items in terms of what specific reading skills are essential to successfully complete such tasks. MacMillan then discusses results of research applying this model to the analysis of large-scale standardized reading assessments. Her chapter concludes by showing that examining the number and type of lexical connections between reading comprehension questions and their keys is a helpful tool in evaluating the effectiveness of reading assessments.

In Chapter 9, Talia Isaacs discusses the challenges and inevitable trade-offs involved in assessing speech in ways that simulate test takers' real world oral communication demands. Isaacs focuses particularly on how the construct of speaking ability has been defined and operationalized in assessment instruments, paying particular attention to sources of variability in L2 speaking performances as well as to the validity of human judgments and technology-mediated assessments.

Chapter 10, by Thomas Eckes, Anika Müller-Karabil and Sonja Zimmermann, provides a thorough review of the key conceptual and methodological issues involved in writing assessment. The chapter introduces basic concepts, components, and challenges of writing assessment, highlights a range of assessment purposes and settings, and discusses perspectives on issues of assessment design of the complex, multidimensional nature of the writing construct. The authors pay particular attention to the measurement issues concerning the role of human raters in scoring writing performances.

In Chapter 11, Kirby Grabowski presents several strands of the literature relevant to the assessment of pragmatic competence, a key aspect of communicative language ability. The chapter begins with an overview of the ways in which pragmatic competence has been conceptualized in the second language (L2) literature, including perspectives from both early language testing theory and the broader field of pragmatics, which emerged in parallel. This is followed by a survey of the empirical research in the assessment of pragmatic competence which highlights important contributions and limitations from the studies reviewed. Grabowski highlights the central role of context in the evolution of meaning in interaction which is seen as particularly crucial to the validity of the inferences made based on test scores in L2 pragmatics assessment. The chapter closes with a brief discussion of the advantages and disadvantages of the instruments available for measuring pragmatic competence.

Gila Schauer opens her chapter (Chapter 12) on assessing intercultural competence with a discussion of different definitions of the term "culture". She then presents the concepts of culture and communicative competence which are necessary prerequisites for understanding intercultural competence and presents intercultural competence models that are suitable for second language assessment research. Subsequent to this, Schauer compares and contrasts different instruments that are used to assess intercultural competence in educational settings. The chapter concludes by discussing the research challenges and future directions in this field.

In Chapter 13, Nivja de Jong initially reviews research that has investigated how aspects of fluency are related to proficiency and draws conclusions about how and which measures of fluency are indicative of L2 proficiency. She evaluates the different types of measures put forward by researchers to measure fluency objectively, such as speech rate and pausing. De Jong concludes her chapter by presenting theoretical and practical arguments to enable researchers and language testing practitioners to make well-informed choices between the many fluency measures.

In Chapter 14, the final chapter of Part II, June Eyckmans, Philippe Anckaert and Winibert Segers focus on the assessment of translation and interpretation skills in professional as well as educational contexts. Throughout the chapter the emphasis is placed on translation and interpretation products rather than on translation or interpretation processes. Eyckmans, Anckaert, and Segers introduce readers to the origins of translation and interpretation assessment leading readers to the definition of the constructs of translation and interpretation competence. They review current assessment practices in terms of reliability and validity criteria for translation and interpretation. Finally, Eyckmans et al. propose ways to optimize the reliable assessment of translation and interpretation skills. They also argue for the creation of a common framework of reference for translation and interpretation competences.

Part III begins with a chapter by Karmen Pižorn and Ari Huhta (Chapter 15) that discusses formal and summative national foreign language assessment schemes and other standardized national and international high-stakes foreign language examinations. Pižorn and Huhta consider these examinations in terms of purpose, testing practices, and the wider social, cultural and educational contexts. They highlight various factors from the wider social, cultural and educational contexts which affect the structure, administration and use of the assessment instruments. Pižorn and Huhta also stress the development phases and administration issues, the sustainability of good testing practice, the influence of politics and the washback effect of these assessments on teaching and learning.

In Chapter 16, Carolyn E. Turner and James E. Purpura propose an initial working framework for learning-oriented assessment in second and foreign language classrooms that explores, from a number of different theoretical and empirical perspectives, whether, when, and how planned and unplanned L2 assessments contribute to learning in L2 instructional settings. The chapter begins with a brief history of classroom-based assessment and then presents a working definition of Turner and Purpura's framework i.e. Learning-oriented Assessment (LOA), relating it to learning theory and a proficiency framework. Three perspectives of LOA (teacher, student, interactional) are considered in detail and the authors illustrate their discussions with case study data. The chapter concludes by examining key issues that affect LOA and future directions, both in practice and research.

In a similar vein, Matthew E. Poehner and Paolo Infante (Chapter 17) introduce the concept of Dynamic Assessment (DA). DA departs from the assessment convention of examining individuals' independent performance in favor of the inclusion of mediation which, according to Poehner and Infante, yields a more comprehensive diagnosis of language development. The chapter reviews the forms and functions of mediation in second language DA research to date before considering how material and dialogic mediation may function in tandem. The authors tie their discussion to a recent project involving adult second language learners of English in a writing-intensive course through close analysis of mediator-learner interaction. Poehner and Infante conclude their chapter by discussing the feasibility of implementing DA in second language educational contexts.

In Chapter 18, Ute Knoch and Susy Macqueen provide a definition and a historical overview of language assessment for the workplace. They then discuss the different types of assessment approaches for and in workplaces focusing on three types of assessments (e.g., professional English exit tests from tertiary institutions, generic assessments of language for the workplace and profession-specific approaches). The authors illustrate their discussion through well-known examples of each of these types of assessments (e.g., GSLPA, TOEIC, BULATS and OET). Knoch and Macqueen provide a detailed discussion of some of the key issues involved in developing and validating tests for the workplace and outline some of the results of current research in this area.

In the last chapter of Part III (Chapter 19), Kerry Ryan discusses the development and use of language assessments for immigration, citizenship, and asylum, with a particular focus on the role of language assessment professionals in such practices. Ryan first clarifies the differences between language assessment in the three contexts in terms of historical background and contemporary practices. He also discusses key research, researchers and research groups in each of the three areas and identifies the main theoretical and practical challenges, as well as opportunities, for the profession leading into the future.

The final six chapters, in Part IV of the volume, begin with a chapter by Spiros Papageorgiou (Chapter 20) that discusses the alignment of language assessments to standards and frameworks. This chapter is the result of increased interest in aligning curricula, textbooks and, in particular, assessments to external standards. Papageorgiou focuses in particular on the alignment of tests to the CEFR and other educational standards and frameworks. He also elaborates on how such alignment is placed within theories of validation, in particular those that follow an argument-based approach.

The next chapter (Chapter 21), by Alistair Van Moere and Ryan Downey, examines the utilization of technology to provide or enhance the assessment of learners' language abilities. The chapter begins with a historical look at the use of technology in language assessment. It then focuses on state-of-the-art automated scoring systems, and describes in plain terminology the complex techniques for assessing both written and spoken language. Finally, the chapter concludes with an exploration of the future of the use of technology in service to language assessment.

The next two chapters deal with sensitive areas. Yuko Goto Butler (Chapter 22) describes the characteristics of young learners and discusses how language assessment should conceptualize the constructs of assessment among such learners so that they target the appropriate knowledge and skills. Butler covers key issues (e.g., washback and ethical issues) related to practices and consequences for classroom-based and large-scale assessments. Butler concludes by suggesting topics for future research such as the need for building theories of L2 development among young learners, the role of teachers in assessment and the use of computers, multimedia and games for the assessment of young learners.

In Chapter 23, Lynda Taylor and Natalie Nordby Chen draw our attention to issues of equity, ethics, principles, and the practice of test modifications or testing accommodations as they relate to tests of language proficiency for students with learning and other disabilities/special needs. Taylor and Chen discuss the key characteristics of test takers with a permanent or temporary disability that should be considered when designing a language test. They draw our attention to the nature and extent of any modifications that may need to be made to standard language test content and delivery to accommodate the needs of students with disabilities. Other than the ethical, logistical and measurement challenges involved in meeting the special requirements of such learners, the chapter also explores the role that research can play in this area.

Given the cultural and linguistic diversity of student populations in writing classrooms the aspect of authorial voice is now regarded as an important concept in teaching as well as in language assessment at both secondary and postsecondary levels. In Chapter 24, Cecilia Guanfang Zhao addresses the concept of "authorial voice" in language assessment. Zhao provides an overview of the issues associated with the instruction and assessment of this subtle dimension of the construct of writing. Based on a review of the relevant literature, Zhao presents the most up-to-date theoretical conceptions of voice, frameworks and empirical results in second language writing instruction and assessment research. In its final part, the chapter highlights avenues for future research into the topic in the assessment of second language proficiency in general and second language writing competence in particular.

In the final chapter of the volume (Chapter 25), Luke Harding and Benjamin Kremmel write about teachers' "language assessment literacy" (LAL) an important new research area which is receiving increasing attention in the field. This chapter presents a survey of current research and practice in the area of teacher assessment literacy as well as current approaches to pre- and in-service instruction in language assessment across a range of international contexts. Harding and Kremmel discuss the most pressing challenges which exist for fostering teacher assessment literacy, and suggest directions for future research and professional development activities which will address these challenges.

We most sincerely thank our authors for sharing their expertise and experience. We also hope that this volume will be useful to its readers.

5 References

Brumfit, Christopher. 1997. How applied linguistics is the same as any other science. *International Journal of Applied Linguistics* 7(1): 86–94.

Canale, Michael and Merrill Swain. 1980. Theoretical bases of communicative approaches to second language teaching and testing. *Applied Linguistics* 1(1): 1–47.

Hymes, Dell. 1972. On communicative competence. In: John B. Pride and Janet Holmes (Eds.), *Sociolinguistics*, 269–293. Harmondsworth: Penguin Books.

Davies, Alan. 1990. *Principles of language testing*. Oxford: Basil Blackwell Ltd.

Ellis, Nick C. 2002. Frequency effects in language processing: A review with implications for theories of implicit and explicit language acquisition. *Studies in Second Language Acquisition* 24: 143–188.

Kane, Michael. 2013. Validating the interpretations and uses of test scores. *Journal of Educational Measurement*. 50(1): 1–73.

Lado, Robert. 1961. *Language Testing: The construction and use of foreign language tests*. London: Longman.

McNamara, Tim and Carsten Roever. 2006. *Language testing: The social dimension*. Malden, MA: Blackwell Publishing, Ltd.

Sorrell, C. Joseph. 2013. Zipf's law and vocabulary, In: Carol A. Chapelle (Ed.), *The Encylopedia of Applied Linguistics*. Blackwell Publishing Ltd. DOI: 10.1002/9781405198431.wbeal1302.

van Ek, Jan A. 1976. *Significance of the threshold level in the early teaching of modern language*. Strasbourg: Council of Europe.

I. Conceptual foundations of second language assessment

Liz Hamp-Lyons

2 Purposes of assessment

1 Introduction

In the world of the 21st century, assessments have taken on many purposes and many shapes, and the assessment of language is no exception. The language for talking about language assessment is, therefore, also becoming more nuanced. As will be seen in other chapters in this collection, language testing in its current research and practice concerns itself with a much wider set of issues than ever before, encompassing considerations of construct validity (in the sense of seeking construct representativeness and coverage), test impact and consequences, as well as with the reliability and practicality of various forms of tests and assessments. One of the directions which modern language testing/assessment has taken is a concern with test purpose, the need to ensure that a test or assessment instrument is fit for purpose.

The simple term *test* is often thought of as the root term in the field, but the use of this term was itself a kind of signal for a change in attitude and theory that took place in the early decades of the 20th century. Montgomery (1965) dates the beginning of examinations in any form we would recognize to England during the second half of the 19th century, specifically the *University Locals* introduced by the Universities of Oxford and Cambridge (Montgomery 1965: 1). The purpose of these examinations was the selection of candidates for entrance to the university, and this is a purpose that endures today. But this selection process involved judging a person's proficiency or achievement in a language or a body of knowledge, or (as often mentioned in critiques of the practice of the time) some less immediately relevant quality such as physical presentation and evidence of *being a gentleman* (Stray 2001). Examinations were originally oral, later written, and tied to a very specific context and purpose such as entrance to a university or decisions about certification at the end of a programme of instruction. Also, due to their fundamentally performative nature, they were usually small-scale. The use of the term test became common with the development of intelligence testing and *mental testing* in the early decades of the 20th century (Binet 1916; Thorndike 1904) and grew rapidly, propelled, as Spolsky (1995: 36) describes, by the influence of Yerkes on the large-scale testing of military recruits for "mental fitness" during 1917–18.

In the field of what for its earlier years was simply called *language testing*, the term *assessment* has only come into common use more recently. In education, assessment refers to "all activities teachers use to help students learn and to gauge student progress" (Black and Wiliam 1998: 143) – that is, an assessment implied a different purpose than a test, a more learner-oriented and learning-centred purpose. However, it has gradually shifted its connotation to something more like a kinder, gentler sort of test; and may be applied not only to tests, but also to all the other things we can do to learn about someone's abilities.

The term *evaluation* now appears in another form in the increasingly common use of the phrase test validation, which also relates to judging the value/worth of something. Specifically, validation as a test purpose is "the accumulation of evidence to support the argument that scores derived from a given test yield accurate inferences to support intended interpretations and uses" (Herman and Choi 2012: 1).

It has been common to distinguish two key purposes for assessing language: achievement and proficiency. Language achievement tests are backward-looking, in that they aim to measure the specific content that has been covered in a course or programme of language instruction. Language proficiency tests are different in that they measure general language command and make no assumptions about a relationship with the content of a teaching sequence. A third distinction that has often been made is assessing for language aptitude, that is, to assess whether or not an individual has the potential to learn [a] language well. These three are separated in their relationship to time: backward-looking, present-focused, and forward-looking. A test purpose that has come much more to our attention in the last 20 years is the diagnostic purpose; this relates to another forward-looking purpose: the need to identify and record a learner's (or a group's) strengths and weaknesses within the context of a set of specific needs. As greater attention has been given to diagnostic forms of assessment, what used to be called progress tests have taken on more meaning and value as their purpose shifts further away from a box-ticking or cumulative score-giving exercise and becomes part of a more coherent approach to understanding the learner's needs and development along hypothesized continua of language ability and performance.

At this point we need to acknowledge another dimension to our picture of test purposes the distinction between large-scale, externally agented tests, and small(er)-scale, internally oriented, classroom/learning-focused and teacher-made tests. This division has long existed, but in the last quarter century the reach and power of language tests – and of English language tests particularly – has grown dramatically (Kirkpatrick and Zang 2011; Li 1990; Shohamy 2001; Weir 2013b) and the impact of language tests has reached worrying proportions. Teachers in their classrooms and their principals and school boards test/assess because they want to ensure that students are mastering the curriculum they have been instructed in. Almost without exception, then, teacher-made tests are achievement-oriented in purpose; some of them may also have a diagnostic function. In contrast, while achievement tests developed and delivered by testing bodies do exist, most of the work of these bodies relates to assessment of proficiency or to aptitude. I will return to this bifurcation of context and consequently of purposes later, for it is important. But it should be noted here that these two fundamentally different needs/purposes for assessment in the context of second language testing have had a major role in the proliferation of new terms such as alternative assessment, [X]-based assessment (where X equals, for example, classroom-based, school-based, teacher-based, etc) as well as related concepts/terms such as dynamic assessment and peer feedback. Each of these terms signals a distinct purpose perceived by some group engaged, in some way, in work we can refer to as language testing or language assessment.

2 A brief history

The rise of formal large-scale examinations of (modern) languages other than one's own began only a century or so ago, and is often ascribed to the development of mental testing techniques in the US during and after the First World War (Spolsky 1995: 33–34), which greatly facilitated the development of so-called objective tests. Although this research and the associated testing techniques were originally designed for intelligence testing, they soon became adapted for use in language testing, specifically for tests that would improve selection of candidates with strong potential for learning a new language with the needs of governmental and military roles in mind (the Modern Language Aptitude Test). Testing for language aptitude has been far more prevalent in the US than in other countries, presumably because of its far greater self-consciousness about its security and military roles, together with the very poor uptake of foreign language study in that country.

However, in Britain there was little evidence of the influence of such mental testing. Modern foreign languages were examined as Greek and Latin had been examined in the previous two hundred years, and for the same purpose: assessment of achievement. But a change in purpose came when in 1911 the Cambridge University Senate proposed the formation of a committee to develop a teaching certificate in Modern Foreign Languages. This was quickly followed by Certificates of Proficiency in French, German, English for Foreign Students, and Religious Knowledge (Weir, Vidaković and Galaczi 2013: 14–16). The Cambridge Certificate of Proficiency (CPE) was introduced in 1913: language proficiency was at that time seen as the main requirement for teaching the language. In two years, the original test purpose of teacher certification had been adapted to one of language proficiency assessment. The 1913 CPE paper is reprinted in Weir, Vidaković and Galaczi 2013 (Appendix A). The paper comprised translation (French or German), a grammar test, a phonetic transcription, an essay, and an oral test that involved a dictation, reading aloud and a conversation (the oral test paper has not survived). Throughout its history, the CPE (as well as the other members of the test suite that was gradually developed) has always included both speaking and writing. In this it was very different from the US model: as Spolsky has noted (1995: 53) examinations in Britain as a whole were much less influenced by the psychometric hegemony that was happening in the US between the 1920s and the 1970s, and continued to favour more subjective measures of language. This can be explained by the different test purpose that dominated education and testing in Britain: during that period Britain was eager to develop its relationships with its colonies and former colonies, and to strengthen its influence around the world through education. If it was concerned with selection, it was less with selecting out and more with attracting in international students. Davies (2008) describes the early approach of the British Council, which at that time was almost the sole access point for those seeking to enter the UK for academic study: "The British ... had by 1954 developed a test instrument to measure the adequacy in English of the growing number of overseas candidates for official scholarships and fellowships. This was ... a rating form, the Knowledge of English Form; it was issued to guide Council offers in making their subjective judgments in-country" (Davies 2008: 9).

This historical point, the late 1950s and the early 1960s, marks the beginning in the US and Britain of the modern era of language testing. This was a time when in the US work in aptitude testing, or the search for reliable predictions of how well an individual will able to master a new language, was being structured and formalized through the work of John Carroll and others for the US army and air force on the development of the Foreign Language Aptitude Battery (Carroll 1962). It was also the era of the influential work of Robert Lado at the University of Michigan on the *Michigan tests*, particularly the Certificate of Proficiency in English (ECPE), and of David Harris at the American University Language Center in Washington D.C. which led ultimately to the TOEFL. These were proficiency tests, in that they made no assumptions about material studied in a previous course of study, in contrast to the British CPE. These tests were influenced by the psychometric advances that had been and were being made and, as with the aptitude tests the search for objectivity was dominant.

Change was beginning too in Britain, not only because of dissatisfaction with the "British Council subjective test", which was found not to reflect closely the actual language competence of entrants, as Davies (2008: 9–11) explains, but also because of the rapid increase in the number of overseas applicants to UK universities from the mid-1960s. English was taking off as the language of advanced education because of its growing role in international commerce and politics (Phillipson 1992, 2010; Weir 2013b). It was no longer a matter of choosing the best of the few, but of catering to much larger numbers seeking advanced education, whose need for language support was more varied than ever before. As competition for university (mainly postgraduate) places became greater, several new tests owing more to the Lado tradition than to "British subjectivity" were developed. Best-known among them were the English Proficiency Test Battery (EPTB: Davies 2008), and the Test in English-Overseas (TEO: McEldowney 1976). These new tests had the mixed purposes of selection, diagnosis and, in the cases of borderline candidates, placement into English language courses in the UK pre- or within-study. For the first time in Britain, the use of language tests for complex purposes emerged: not only was it necessary to assess applicants' existing proficiency more accurately in order to find those most likely to do well, but also to judge how much more they had to do before they would be ready for academic study in English.

The next major change in approaches in language testing was inspired by the seminal work on communicative competence of Hymes (1972), Widdowson (1978) and Canale and Swain's influential article in the first issue of Applied Linguistics (1980: 1–46). In Britain, communicative language teaching took off (Munby 1978; Brumfit and Johnson 1979) and with it attention to communicative language testing (Morrow 1979). Davies (2008) comments: "The new paradigm of communicative language teaching and testing required that the British Council, as a leading exponent of professionalism in ELT, should furnish itself with a new test in order to keep itself publicly in the lead" (2008: 29). Working with the University of Cambridge Local Examinations Syndicate (UCLES), the British Council made plans for a completely new test (Carroll 1978) which would be "communicative", and would also be tied directly to the British Council's purpose in testing: assessing proficiency in an academic study context.

In 1979, the new test, the English Language Testing Service (ELTS) replaced the EPTB; but Davies calls the next few years a "communicative interlude" (2008: 28). ELTS was a difficult and expensive test to develop, to deliver, and to score, but it attracted substantial interest internationally. Over the following ten years, research was carried out (Clapham 1996; Hamp-Lyons 1986) showing that ELTS could not achieve its purpose of assessing individual university applicants on the basis of their disciplinary background or intended course of study (a "specific academic purpose" test: Hamp-Lyons 1986: 375) either more reliably or more validly than could a "general academic purpose" test. ELTS became IELTS, a much simpler form of academic purpose assessment (Clapham and Alderson 1997). But the ambitious initiative represented by ELTS remains a significant influence in bringing the need for tests that are sensitive to test-taker purposes to the attention of the field. Canadian universities use the CAEL (Canadian Academic English Language assessment), which is an integrated test drawing on activities typical of a first year course. In the US, the present TOEFL iBT uses task-types more like early academic language-using activities. In Australia, the MASUS procedure (Bonnano and Jones 2007) is an excellent example of a diagnostic assessment tailored to students' academic contexts and needs.

The next major watershed in the developing sophistication of concepts of test purpose in language testing came with the publication of Lyle Bachman's Fundamental Considerations in Language Testing (1990) and the presentation of his model of communicative language ability (developed from work with Adrian Palmer). A large-scale study funded by UCLES enabled Bachman to develop and test out his Communicative Language Ability (CLA) model to the full, in carrying out a comparability study of the First Certificate in English (FCE) and the TOEFL (Davidson and Bachman 1990; Bachman, Davidson, Ryan and Choi 1995). Weir comments that the Bachman model proved to be extremely difficult to use because of its complexity and detail, which left unclear which of its many parameters should be considered criterial for language testing purposes, especially for *test development*, when it is necessary to define and test at different levels of language proficiency (Weir 2013a: 77–78).

The Bachman model proved not to help us much with test purposes, but the FCE-TOEFL Comparability Study did have an indirect and positive effect in alerting UCLES to the need for professionalization of its work by showing that the FCE was not reliable enough to be useable for comparison purposes. Around the same time, an influential movement was beginning within Europe, funded and supported by the Council of Europe, to develop a common European framework for languages, which became the Common European Framework of Reference (CEFR). The key purposes of this major project were "provid[ing] a common basis for the elaboration of language syllabuses, curriculum guidelines, examinations, textbooks, etc. across Europe" and to "overcome the barriers to communication among professionals working in the field of modern languages arising from the different educational systems in Europe" (Council of Europe 2001: 1). It was asserted that "[t]he provision of objective criteria for describing language proficiency will facilitate the mutual recognition of qualifications gained in different learning contexts, and accordingly will aid European mobility" (Council of Europe 2001: 1). Discussion of the CEFR is beyond the reach and purpose of this chapter: suffice it to say that among the welter of publications on the CEFR there has been some controversy over its usefulness, the purposes for which it has proved useful, and its impact (see, for example, Alderson 2007).

Quite separately, it seems, we can see from the distance of about 20 years that this was also a period of heightened awareness of the importance of the construct in test design. More thought was being given to the meaning of proficiency, and it was acknowledged that if the purpose of a test is to assess a learner's language proficiency, the assessment must assess that proficiency in all four skills. Jacobs et al. (1981) produced the first practical guide to evaluating student essays; the TOEFL for the first time introduced a direct test of writing and Stansfield and Ross (1988) developed a research agenda for the (TOEFL) Test of Written English. Hamp-Lyons (1986) had completed the first detailed study of a test of direct writing in the UK and published the first book-length research on writing assessment (1991). Direct assessment of speaking was also under the spotlight, as shown by Chalhoub-Deville and Fulcher (2003), who provide an interesting history of oral proficiency testing in the period when the ACTFL and FSI interviews were being adapted to non-government purposes in the US. Chalhoub-Deville and Fulcher critique the quality of the then-available evidence for these OPIs as they were revised and renamed to correspond more closely to the needs and purposes of the academic community. The increased attention given to the development and validation of direct tests of speaking and writing from the late 1970s represented increasing acceptance of the fact that the majority of tests and assessments, whether they are thought of as proficiency, achievement or diagnosis, aim to have as a purpose the obtaining of the clearest and fullest possible picture of what the learner or test taker can do.

In the 1990s language testers also became much more aware of the work on validity in psychological and educational measurement, particularly that of Messick (1989; 1996) and Kane (1992). This heightened understanding of the importance of validity may not have changed tests' purposes: but it certainly placed greater demands on language testers for self-awareness in their work, and for accountability in the profession (Hamp-Lyons 2000; McNamara 2006), including the expectation that tests will be fit for purpose. This was also a time when language testers' concerns were turning to the effects of tests. The work of Messick and of Kane continues to strongly influence research in language testing today, and the present concern with the assessment use argument (AUA) emphasizes the centrality of test purpose to the validity argument: for example, Kane (2012: 16) states: "In developing a test, we typically have some purpose in mind, and this purpose guides the development of both the test and the interpretation/use argument."

An inevitable effect of the use of language tests, and sometimes an intended consequence – a specified purpose – of their existence, is to influence what is taught and how it is taught. Hughes (1988) had argued for the potential for beneficial backwash/washback from tests, while Li (1990) protested the negative effects of China's National Higher Education Entrance Examination (*gao kao*). Since Alderson and Wall's seminal paper (1993), and further influenced by Messick's (1996) application of his model of construct validity to language testing, a large body of work has appeared (Alderson and Hamp-Lyons 1996; Bachman 2000; Bailey 1996; Cheng and Curtis 2004; Green 2007; Hamp-Lyons 1997; Hawkey 2006), and a major series of studies of the effects of the changes to the TOEFL (Wall and Horak, 2006, 2008, 2011). The debate over whether it is desirable, or possible, to design and implement tests specifically with the purpose of *creating beneficial washback* onto teaching and learning is one that still has some way to run. The longitudinal study by Dianne Wall and Tania Horák of the implementation of the new TOEFL (TOEFL iBT®) is particularly interesting in this regard: this exemplary study, despite lasting for 5 years and with four rounds of ETS funding, was able to clearly identify only some areas of change resulting from the ambitious changes to the test itself from those that had been hypothesized, and was not able to establish consistent "evidential links" (Wall and Horák 2011: 122) between changes to the test and consistent changes in how teachers taught. The study of earlier stages of washback in the run-up to the introduction of the TOEFL iBT® from 2005 carried out by Shohamy and Hamp-Lyons (2003) in Stage 1 and then by Hamp-Lyons and Brown (2005) in Stage 2, was not able to provide any conclusions as it was not further funded; but it did find that by 2004–2005 many students were very aware of the coming change and very concerned about it, while teachers' levels of awareness and concern seemed more varied. It would seem then that we must question whether it would be of any value to make beneficial washback itself a test purpose.

The TOEFL iBT® development and validation project proved to be a significant step for language testing, and has had tremendous influence on a number of fronts. One of these has been the increasing attention to construct theory, that is, to defining what should be tested, and why (see Chapelle, Enright and Jamieson 2008: 1– 26). An area of agreement among the large group involved in developing the blueprint for the TOEFL iBT® was that the focus should now be on *assessing performance*. There was also agreement within the TOEFL project team, as there increasingly was among language testers as a whole, that a test itself cannot be validated unless it is validated from the perspective of the appropriacy of its score interpretations. In other words, questions of *test use* were becoming increasingly important. This shift of emphasis is reflected in Bachman and Palmer's book *Language assessment in practice: Developing language assessments and justifying their use in the real world* (2010), in which the authors devote the first chapter to describing language use and justifying the use of language assessments. Note that tests have become assessments; and the focus on test *use* takes us close to issues of test purposes.

3 Language test purposes in the 21st century

3.1 Assessments with diagnostic purposes

There have been language tests and assessments with diagnostic purposes and uses as long as there have been tests. But Alderson & Huhta (2005: 301) claim that DIALANG is "the first major testing system that is oriented towards diagnosing language skills and providing feedback to users rather than certifying their proficiency." DIALANG is a European Union-funded computer-based diagnostic testing project that not only exemplifies the diagnostic purpose of an assessment, but also implements self-assessment and allows users to benchmark their own performance against standards in 14 European languages. This is an ambitious project, but seems to have been hampered by the instability of its computer interface[1]. There are many much smaller-scale projects with the intention of diagnosing learners' strengths and weaknesses in a foreign language. Here is a point where classroom teachers should have a greater voice than they have usually had. Teachers are in the best position to be able to identify what kinds of information are needed for and by each learner for the purposes of planning curriculum, and for learners to plan their language learning strategies. The movement from diagnosis to provide information on learner strengths and weaknesses to developing tools to help

---

1 DIALANG is (Oct 2015) housed on the Lancaster University server: http://www.lancaster.ac.uk/researchenterprise/dialang/about. "Lancaster University is currently working to try to find a sustainable future for DIALANG."

learners benefit from such information through their learning takes us to formative assessment.

3.2 Beyond diagnosis: formative assessment and assessment for learning

Here we must return to the distinction made earlier between large-scale, externally agented tests, and small(er)-scale, internally oriented, classroom/learning-focused and teacher-made assessments. Among several important differences between these – not two kinds of tests but two ends of a continuum of possible test types – a key one is usually the stakes of the test. Test stakes may be very high, as in the case of a medical doctor's qualifying exams, for instance, or a Chinese high school student preparing for the *gao kao*, the major English test that plays a large part in decisions about who can enter university; or stakes can be very low, for example when teachers set progress checks and "pop quizzes" during a sequence of instruction. The higher the stakes, the more likely it is that formal tests will be used, and reported in summary numerical form; the lower the stakes, the more likely it is that classroom assessment or teacher-made tests will be used, and that they will include descriptive commentary as well as number scores. These distinctions are characterized by the terms summative and formative assessment purposes. Harlen (2005) argues that formative assessment cannot be differentiated from summative assessment purely on the grounds of the type or form of the assessment tool being used to gather evidence of learning, but by the purpose to which such assessment tools are put; to help learning, or to summarise learning. Large-scale tests, or large systems of testing, usually have as their purpose the provision of reports to official bodies on the performance, progress or achievement of groups of learners, or of a school system, or of the implementation of new testing systems. Summative tests provide numbers but do not look into teaching and learning, and so they cannot be used to inform instruction. Formative assessment usually has as its core purpose the provision of information (usually in the form of feedback) to the learner in a form that the learner can use to extend and improve their own learning. Carless (2011) argues for the "formative use of summative tests" (FUST) as a bridge between the aims of formative assessment and the realities of summative testing, although he carefully acknowledges its limitations. The teacher data he reports shows that, for teachers, the summative purpose of the test is dominant even when they value the strategies of using summative information for formative purposes.

An important development in the last 15 years is the *Assessment for Learning* movement (Black and Wiliam 1998; Black et al. 2004). The concept of AfL is somewhat ambiguous, sometimes being considered as very specific, at other times being equated with formative assessment, and at still others being used more widely to suggest a contrast to traditional norm-referenced examination-dominated assessment systems. Thus, assessment for learning (AfL) can relate to formative assessment, self and peer assessment, classroom assessment, dynamic assessment, student-oriented assessment and several other assessment terms that have emerged recently enough to still be in flux at this point. But Black et al. (2004: 3) make clear early in this book that assessment for learning is a "third purpose" and define AfL as "any assessment for which the first priority is to serve the purpose of promoting students' learning." The fundamental principles of AfL are that teachers work with learners to ensure each learner perceives a gap between their current and desired knowledge or ability; that then the learner must actively work to close that gap and reach the desired goal; and importantly, that learners receive appropriate and timely feedback on their active efforts. Clearly there is a shift in assessment purpose away from score reporting, certification, and creating league tables and towards the learner.

3.3 Dynamic assessment and learning-oriented [language] assessment

Dynamic assessment has emerged in second/foreign language learning and assessment only recently, appearing originally in psychological assessment and in assessment of special needs learners, where assessments must be flexible and tailored to individual needs (e.g., Nicholls n.d.). Lantolf and Poehner (2004) describe the key belief behind dynamic assessment as being "that a full picture requires two additional bits of information: the person's performance with assistance from someone else and the extent to which the person can benefit from this assistance not only in completing the same task or test, but in transferring this mediated performance to different tasks or tests" (see also Poehner and Infante, this volume).

Another quite new assessment term to have emerged recently is *learning-oriented assessment* (Carless, Joughin, Liu and associates 2007), which like AfL puts student learning at the heart of the assessment. Purpura (2004) discusses learning-oriented assessment in the context of assessing grammar, and points out that construct definition is just as important in learning-oriented assessment as in traditional large-scale testing. Green and Hamp-Lyons (2015) expand on the LOA foci of learner-oriented tasks, self and peer engagement in assessment, and feedback as feed-forward in the specific context of language learning. They introduce a model that they refer to as "learning-oriented language assessment" (LOLA), which adds emphasis on the essential interactivity implicit in using language as both the vehicle for and the content of the assessment, plus a greater awareness of the role of the teacher or interlocutor in creating language learning opportunities, and they apply this model to oral proficiency interviews in Cambridge English Language Assessment tests.

Developments in language testing in the early 21st century have tended to focus around understanding learners and their needs as people, not only as test consumers. Testing bodies have increasingly embraced these more social and educational purposes, and are being aided by the development of more sophisticated measurement tools and approaches, so that there are more and better tools available for a wider range of purposes than ever before.

4 Present issues and future directions

Undoubtedly there are multiple other purposes for language tests: these include assessing the language of students with learning and other disabilities/special needs; assessing the effects of non-language variables such as motivation, self-efficacy and extra/introversion on language learning; and assessing intercultural linguistic competence. They include assessing language for academic purposes as well as for the workplace and for very specific purposes such as English in international aviation and English in doctor-patient communication. In some contexts, such as Hong Kong, tests/assessments are used for the purpose of assessing language teachers' competence in the language they teach; at a meta-level, we must not forget the importance of language teacher assessment literacy if teachers are to choose, use and understand the results of assessments of their students. These and other purposes are discussed in later chapters. Importantly, in a book such as this we must not forget that tests and assessments are also often used as tools in language research, particularly language learning research. This purpose is important because very often a potentially good research project is marred by the uncritical use of a language test, for example, in pre-/post-instruction studies.

But the future direction in language assessments, and increasingly evident at the present, is the much greater awareness of the use of language tests for purposes unintended at the time of their development and validation, or by their developers. The encroachment of language tests into unintended purposes is particularly visible in their use in assessing a person's language for immigration, citizenship, or asylum purposes (see Ryan this volume). Another area at the front of many people's attention is the use of language standards, in the sense of officially-approved and perhaps prescribed language standards or performance standards for various (not always clearly stated) purposes (see Fulcher this volume). The growing use of the Common European Framework of Reference (CEFR), the emergence of the CEFR-Japanese and the prospect of a Common Frame for Chinese have all led to questions as to whether a focus on establishing common standards *as a purpose in itself* is the way our profession should be heading.

An increasingly explicit move toward using language tests for fundamentally bureaucratic and political purposes is an inevitable characteristic of the increasingly globalizing world of the 21st century. In proceeding cautiously when faced with demands for tests to be used as instruments for decisions about access to certain goods and rights about which conflicting moral position are held, such as prestigious and valuable fellowships and other awards, or the more urgent purposes of migration, citizenship and asylum, we are best advised to refer to relevant codes of ethics, such as the ILTA Code of Ethics 2000 (http://www.iltaonline.com/index.php/en/resources/ilta-code-of-ethics). As conflicts between and within countries increase, the movement of people seeking safety and a livelihood is becoming a major concern for all developed countries as well as for the conflict-affected countries they hope to leave. These problems will not leave language testers unaffected, and can be expected to be a major future issue but also, one may hope, a direction for both research and concrete action. We cannot expect easy solutions, nor to be left untouched by these concerns. One thing we may hold on to, however, when trying to decide what is right for us to do or say as professionals, is the question of purpose: what is the purpose to which this test, my work, my advice, will be put? The last principle (Principle 9) of the ILTA Code of Ethics states: Language testers shall regularly consider the potential effects, both short and long term, on all stakeholders of their projects, reserving the right to withhold their professional services on the grounds of conscience.

5 References

Alderson, J. Charles. 2007. The CEFR and the need for more research. *The Modern Language Journal* 91(4): 659–663.

Alderson, J. Charles and Liz Hamp-Lyons. 1996. TOEFL preparation courses: A case study. *Language Testing* 13(3): 280–297.

Alderson, J. Charles and Ari Huhta. 2005. The development of a suite of computer-based diagnostic tests based on the Common European Framework. *Language Testing* 22(3): 301–320.

Alderson, J. Charles and Dianne Wall. 1993. Does washback exist? *Applied Linguistics* 14(2): 115–29.

Bachman, Lyle F. 1990. *Fundamental considerations in language testing*. Oxford, UK: Oxford University Press.

Bachman, Lyle F. 2000. Modern language testing at the turn of the century: assuring that what we count counts. *Language Testing* 17(1): 1–42.

Bachman, Lyle F., Fred Davidson, Katherine Ryan and Inn Chull Choi. 1995. *An Investigation into the Comparability of Two Tests of English as a Foreign Language*. Cambridge, UK: UCLES/Cambridge University Press.

Bachman, Lyle F. and Adrian S. Palmer. 2010. *Language Assessment in Practice: Developing Language Assessments and Justifying their Use in the Real World*. Oxford, UK: Oxford University Press.

Bailey, Kathleen M. 1996. Working for washback: A review of the washback concept in language testing. *Language testing* 13(3): 257–279.

Binet, Alfred. 1916. *The Development of Intelligence in Children*. Baltimore: Williams and Wilkins.

Black, Paul and Dylan Wiliam. 1998. Inside the black box: Raising standards through classroom assessment. *Phi Delta Kappan* (October): 139–148.

Black, Paul, Christine Harrison, Clare Lee, Bethan Marshall and Dylan Wiliam. 2004. Working inside the black box: Assessment for learning in the classroom. *Phi Delta Kappan* (September): 8–21.

Bonnano, Helen and Janet Jones. 2007. *The MASUS Procedure: Measuring the Academic Skills of University Students: A Diagnostic Assessment. Revised Edition 2007.* http://sydney.edu.au/stuserv/documents/learning_centre/MASUS.pdf (accessed 26 July 2014).

Brumfit, Christopher J. and Keith Johnson (eds.). 1979. *The communicative approach to language teaching.* Oxford, UK: Oxford University Press.

Canale, Michael and Merrill Swain. 1980. Theoretical Bases of Communicative Approaches to Second Language Teaching and Testing. *Applied Linguistics* 1(1): 1–47.

Carless, David 2011. *From testing to productive student learning: Implementing formative assessment in Confucian-heritage settings.* Abingdon UK: Routledge/Taylor and Francis.

Carless, David, Gordon Joughin, Ngar-Fun Liu, and associates. 2007. *How assessment supports learning: learning-oriented assessment in Action.* Hong Kong: Hong Kong University Press.

Carroll, John B. 1962. The prediction of success in intensive foreign language training. In: Robert Glaser (ed.), *Training Research and Evaluation,* 87–136. Pittsburgh PA: University of Pittsburgh Press.

Carroll, John B. 1978. *An English Language Testing Service: Specifications.* London: British Council.

Chalhoub-Deville, Micheline and Glenn Fulcher. 2003. The Oral Proficiency Interview: A Research Agenda. *Foreign Language Annals* 36(4): 498–506.

Chapelle, Carol A., Mary K. Enright and Joan M. Jamieson, 2008. (eds.). *Building a validity argument for the Test of English as a Foreign Language*ᵀᴹ. Routledge.

Cheng, Liying and Andy Curtis. 2004. Washback or backwash: A review of the impact of testing on teaching and learning. In: Liying Cheng, Yoshinori Watanabe and Andy Curtis (eds.). *Washback in language testing: Research contexts and methods,* 3–17. Mahwah, NJ: Lawrence Erlbaum Associates.

Clapham, Caroline. 1996. *The development of IELTS: A study of the effect of background knowledge on reading comprehension.* Cambridge, UK: Cambridge University Press/UCLES.

Clapham, Caroline and J. Charles Alderson (eds.). 1997. *IELTS Research Report 3: Constructing and trialling the IELTS test.* Cambridge: The British Council/UCLES/IDP.

Council of Europe. 2001. *Common European Framework of Reference for Languages: Learning, teaching, assessment.* Cambridge, UK: Cambridge University Press.

Davidson, Fred, and Lyle F. Bachman. 1990. The Cambridge-TOEFL comparability study: An example of the cross-national comparison of language tests. *AILA Review* 7: 24–45.

Davies, Alan. 2008. *Assessing Academic English: Testing English Proficiency 1950–1989 – The IELTS Solution.* Cambridge, UK: UCLES/Cambridge University Press.

Fulcher, Glenn. This volume. Standards and frameworks. In: Dina Tsagari and Jayanti Banerjee (eds.). *Handbook of Second Language Assessment.* Berlin: DeGruyter Mouton.

Green, Anthony. 2007. *IELTS washback in context: Preparation for academic writing in higher education.* Cambridge: University of Cambridge ESOL Examinations/Cambridge University Press.

Green, Anthony and Liz Hamp-Lyons. 2015. Introducing opportunities for learning-oriented assessment to large-scale speaking tests. Final project report for Cambridge English Language Assessment research funding Round 4, 2012.

Hamp-Lyons, Liz. 1986. *Assessing second language writing in academic settings.* Edinburgh: University of Edinburgh dissertation.

Hamp-Lyons, Liz. 1997. Washback, impact and validity: ethical concerns. *Language Testing* 14(3): 295–303.

Hamp-Lyons, Liz. 2000. Social, professional and individual responsibility in language testing. *System* 28(4): 579–591.

Hamp-Lyons, Liz and Annie Brown. 2005. *The effect of changes in the new TOEFL format on the teaching and learning of EFL/ESL: Stage 2 (2003–05): Entering innovation* Report presented to the TOEFL Committee of Examiners.

Harlen, Wynne. 2005. Formative and summative assessment a harmonious relationship? Paper given at an ASF Seminar. http://wikieducator.org/images/d/d7/Arlen_-_Formative_and_summative_assessment.pdf (accessed 10 November 2013).

Hawkey, Roger. 2006. *The Theory and Practice of Impact Studies: Studies of the IELTS Test and Progetto Lingue 2000*. Cambridge: Cambridge University Press/UCLES.

Herman, Joan and Kilchan Choi. 2012. *Validation of ELA and mathematics assessments: A general approach. National Center for Research on Evaluation, Standards and Student Testing*. http://www.cse.ucla.edu/products/states_schools/ValidationELA_FINAL.pdf (accessed 28 October 2013).

Hughes, Arthur. 1988. Introducing a needs-based test of English for study in an English medium university in Turkey. In: Arthur Hughes (ed.). *Testing English for university study*, ELT Documents 127: 134–157. Oxford UK: Modern English Press.

Hymes, Dell H. 1972. On communicative competence. In: Janet Pride and John Holmes (eds.). *Sociolinguistics: Selected Readings*, 269–293. Harmondsworth: Penguin.

Jacobs, Holly, Stephen Zinkgraf, Deanne Wormuth, V. Faye Hartfiel and Jane Hughey. 1981. *Testing ESL composition: A practical approach*. Rowley, MA: Newbury House.

Kane, Michael. 1992. An argument-based approach to validity. *Psychological Bulletin* 112(3): 527–535.

Kane, Michael. 2012. Validating score interpretations and uses. *Language Testing* 29(1): 3–17.

Kirkpatrick, Robert and Yuebin Zang. 2011. The Negative Influences of Exam-Oriented Education on Chinese High School Students: Backwash from Classroom to Child. *Language Testing in Asia* 1(3): 36–45.

Lantolf, James and Matthew Poehner. 2004: Dynamic assessment of L2 development: bringing the past into the future. *Journal of Applied Linguistics* 1(1): 49–72.

Li, Xiaoju. 1990. How powerful can a language test be? The MET in China. *Journal of Multilingual and Multicultural Development* 11(5): 393–404.

McEldowney, Patricia. 1976. *Test in English (overseas): the position after ten years*. Manchester: Joint Matriculation Board Occasional Publications.

McNamara, Tim. 2006. Validity in Language Testing: The Challenge of Sam Messick's legacy. *Language Assessment Quarterly* 3(1): 31–51.

Messick, Samuel. 1989. Validity. In: Robert L. Linn (ed.). *Educational Measurement* 3 edn., 13–103. New York: Macmillan.

Messick, Samuel. 1996. Validity and washback in language testing. *Language Testing* 13(3): 243–256.

Montgomery, Robert J. 1965. *Examinations: An account of their evolution as administrative Devices in England* London: Longman.

Morrow, Keith. 1979. Communicative language testing: Revolution or evolution? In: Christopher J. Brumfit and Keith Johnson (eds.). 1979. *The communicative approach to language teaching*, 143–159. Oxford, UK: Oxford University Press.

Munby, John L. 1978. *Communicative syllabus design*. Cambridge, UK: Cambridge University Press.

Nicholls, Eva. 'Dynamic' Assessment'. Presentation, Department of Education and Training, Northern Territory Government. http://www.education.nt.gov.au/__data/assets/pdf_file/0020/20648/DynamicAssessment.pdf (accessed 26 July 2014).

Phillipson, Robert. 1992. *Linguistic Imperialism*. London: Routledge.

Phillipson, Robert. 2010. *Linguistic Imperialism Continued*. London: Routledge.

Poehner, E. Matthew and Paolo Infante. This volume. Dynamic assessment in the language classroom. In: Dina Tsagari and Jayanti Banerjee (eds.). *Handbook of Second Language Assessment*. Berlin: DeGruyter Mouton.

Purpura, James. 2004. *Assessing Grammar*. Cambridge, UK: UCLES/Cambridge University Press.

Ryan, Kerry. This volume. Language assessment and analysis for immigration, citizenship and asylum. In: Dina Tsagari and Jayanti Banerjee (eds.). *Handbook of Second Language Assessment*. Berlin: DeGruyter Mouton.

Shohamy, Elana. 2001. *The power of tests: A critical perspective of the uses of language tests*. Harlow, Essex: Longman.

Shohamy, Elana and Liz Hamp-Lyons. 2003. *The effect of changes in the new TOEFL format on the teaching and learning of EFL/ESL: Stage 1 (2002–03): Instrument development and validation*. Report presented to the TOEFL Committee of Examiners.

Spolsky, Bernard. 1995. *Measured Words*. Oxford, UK: Oxford University Press.

Stray, Christopher. 2001. The shift from oral to written examination: Cambridge and Oxford 1700– 1900. *Assessment in Education: Principles, Policy & Practice* 8(1): 33–50.

Stansfield, Charles and Jacqueline Ross. 1988. A long-term research agenda for the Test of Written English. *Language Testing* 5(2): 160–186.

Thorndike, Edward L. 1904. *An Introduction to the Theory of Mental and Social Measurements*. New York, NY: The Science Press.

Wall, Dianne, and Tania Horák 2006. *The impact of changes in the TOEFL examination on teaching and learning in Central and Eastern Europe – Phase 1: The baseline study* (TOEFL Monograph Series, MS-34). Princeton, NJ: Educational Testing Service.

Wall, Dianne, and Tania Horák 2008. *The impact of changes in the TOEFL examination on teaching and learning in Central and Eastern Europe – Phase 2, coping with change*. Princeton, NJ: Educational Testing Service.

Wall, Dianne and Tania Horák 2011. *The Impact of Changes in the TOEFL® Exam on Teaching in a Sample of Countries in Europe: Phase 3, The Role of the Coursebook and Phase 4, Describing Change*. TOEFL iBT Research Report 17. Princeton, NJ: Educational Testing Service.

Weir, Cyril J. 2013a. An overview of the influences on English language testing in the United Kingdom 1913–2012. In: Cyril J. Weir, Ivana Vidakovic and Evelina Galaczi (eds.). Measured Constructs: *A History of Cambridge English Examinations, 1913–2012*, 1–102. Cambridge, UK: Cambridge University Press.

Weir, Cyril J. 2013b. Conclusions and recommendations. In: Cyril J. Weir, Ivana Vidakovic and Evelina Galaczi (eds.). *Measured Constructs: A History of Cambridge English Examinations, 1913–2012*, 420–444. Cambridge, UK: Cambridge University Press.

Weir, Cyril J., Ivana Vidaković and Evelina D. Galaczi (eds.). 2013. *Measured Constructs: A History of Cambridge English Examinations, 1913–2012*. Cambridge, UK: UCLES/Cambridge University Press.

Widdowson, Henry G. 1978. *Teaching language as communication*. Oxford, UK: Oxford University Press.

Glenn Fulcher

3 Standards and frameworks

1 Introduction

The terms "standards" and "frameworks" are controversial, and subject to differential interpretation throughout the language testing and educational measurement literature. This frequently obfuscates important issues (Davidson et al. 1995: 15). An urgent need for clarity arises because standards-based assessment is increasingly being used by governments and international agencies as policy and accountability instruments (Hudson 2012). Only through transparency can we evaluate contemporary standards-based social practices.

Our stance towards standards-based practices is also ambivalent. On the one hand, language testers adopt the language of critical theory to critique the institutional appropriation of assessment terms and practices (McNamara 2007). The entire raison d'être for such enquiry is a piercing analysis of the utilization of power and control through unchallenged practice. On the other hand, much technical research demonstrates high levels of acquiescence in developing methodologies to ensure conformity with political mandates.

Perhaps neither the observation that assessment serves policy, nor the claim that language testers are frequently complicit, should be quite as shocking as they appear when presented in such a stark manner. Although the current usage of the term "standards" is but a few decades old, the concept appears to be universal, and endemic to human society. It is also essentially political in the sense that some notion of standards is required to actualize a vision of utopia. The educational system is the engine by which the desired society is constructed, and assessment is the toolkit that maintains the engine in working order.

This is clear from the earliest text on education, which is also a treatise in political philosophy. In *The Republic* (380 BC [1955]), Plato sets out clear standards to guide teaching and learning, and which must be assessed to select the most suitable to become Guardians. From poetry to music, mathematics, geometry, astronomy, dialectics, and physical education, the content and standards are set out as requirements for young people to meet if they are going to be successful in Platonic society. Progress is dependent upon passing sequences of trials and tests (Plato 380 BC [1955]: 178–180). Only those who continually meet the standard may enter high office.

To whichever period of history we turn, a similar story is found. Miyazaki (1981) describes the standards for anyone wishing to enter the Chinese civil service, and Roach (1971) retells the story of the introduction of public examinations in the United Kingdom within the context of a new vision of civil society and participatory democracy. The standards are those required by the decision makers for individuals to obtain rights, social advancement, further education, or employment opportunities. If there are standards, they have to be set by someone, and that is inevitably someone in authority. Foucault's (1975) critique of testing as the exercise of power by an elite is somewhat banal partly because it is obviously true, but more importantly because it denies the possibility of altruistic motive. For example, John Stuart Mill was an ardent supporter of testing and assessment throughout school life; but the purpose was to endow the population with the knowledge required to justify universal suffrage (Mill 1873: 257).

Our response to standards and their use is therefore largely conditioned by the degree to which we share the vision of society which the standards serve, or find ourselves sympathetic to the ideals of whoever is driving the agenda. Whether the standards have any purchase on reality is a secondary question. Our primary, visceral reaction depends on the values that we bring to the evaluation of the envisioned utopia (Fulcher 2009).

Half the question of complicity has thus been addressed. Many testing practitioners will welcome the policy and eagerly await the society it is designed to create. Others will not, and tensions emerge. Davies (2008: 438) provides an analysis of the Common European Framework of Reference (CEFR) as a tool for manipulation by "juggernaut-like centralizing institutions", whereas Jones (2013: 108) advises us not to take such views seriously. When powerful institutions push well-resourced agendas, fund confirmatory research, and implement recognition schemes, we should also expect high levels of amenability from test producers. Such is the nature of visionary test-driven education policy, and ever was it so.

The other half of the question is answered by the measurement inheritance of language testing. This comes from the endeavour to produce standard weights and measures for commerce (Fulcher 2010: 32–34; Jones 2012a: 350–351), extended to educational "products". In an age where statistical data is the battleground of evidence-based decision making (Blastland and Dilnot 2010), everything must be quantified and compared. Crease (2011) calls this the "modern metroscape". In our metroscape the notion of a "common" framework that can be used to compare competence across languages and contexts, and translate the meaning of a score from one test to another, has always been just too seductive to resist (Clark 1980). Trim (2012: 20) points to the need for portable qualifications across international boundaries that "provide[s] the driving force behind the worldwide interest in levels and frameworks – a need for objective international standards, which will not go away."

In order to further explore standards and frameworks, this chapter will proceed in the following order. The next section will deal with nomenclature. I then describe three of the most influential frameworks. I then consider issues of enduring concern, and provide a brief account of related research. I conclude with some crystal ball gazing.

2 Terminology

The use of the term "standard" originated in the criterion-referenced testing movement, whose primary purpose was to interpret score meaning in terms of performance rather than relative position on a scale. Glaser (1963: 519) explained: "What I shall call criterion-referenced measures depend upon an absolute standard of quality ..." "Standard" was used interchangeably with "criterion", which referred to whether a test taker could perform tasks modelled on critical domain (job) specific tasks. The notion of a cut score to determine mastery or lack of mastery on an external "standard" was introduced by Mager (1962). Quickly taken up by psychometricians and policy makers, the term morphed into its common use today, with a focus upon mapping cut scores to external standards documents (Fulcher and Svalberg 2013). This reinterpretation has moved language testing away from making decisions based on scores that are related to specific contexts of interaction, to making "context free" decisions about the place of test takers on abstract sets of levels.

The second common confusion relates to the distinction between "models" and "frameworks". Fulcher and Davidson (2007: 36–37) argue that a model is an "overarching and relatively abstract theoretical description of what it means to be able to communicate in a second language", whereas a framework is "a selection of skills and abilities from a model that are relevant to a specific assessment context." A framework mediates between a model and a test specification that determines the content and format of a particular test. A framework provides the rationale for the selection of constructs and content for a specific decision-making context. However, in modern standards-based assessment "framework" has been confounded with "model". The origin of this corruption can be traced to the early development of the Common European Framework of Reference (CEFR). Trim recounts that the term "model" was used for the CEFR, but because the term implied "perfection" for the French, the term "framework" was adopted (Saville 2005: 282). The disastrous consequence has been the tendency to ignore the mediating step between model and test; hence the fallacious claim that it is possible to have a test of a model (a "CEFR test").

The confusion between models and frameworks also blurs the distinction between rating scales used for scoring test performances, and performance level descriptors (PLDs). The former are sets of descriptors designed to rate performances on test tasks. The latter are level labels designed as a reporting tool (see Alderson 1991). Cut scores are set on individual tests that reflect boundaries in PLD levels (Cizek and Bunch 2007: 44–48). The PLDs therefore operate as a means for policy makers to set performance standards for a variety of purposes, and test providers may report the outcomes of test performance as PLD levels. When the scoring and reporting functions are confounded the resulting circularity makes test-score validation impossible. Yet, as Green (2012: 65) states with reference to the CEFR, "The vertical dimension represented by the reference levels and illustrative descriptors was not primarily designed as a rating instrument for use in language assessment."

Standard-setting methodologies were originally designed to establish cut-scores on tests for decision-making purposes in specific assessment contexts. In standards-based testing, however, standard setting is practiced "... to link performances on assessments to extant descriptors that have currency and meaning outside of the assessment and to which multiple assessments may be linked" (Kenyon 2012: 28). It is for this reason that scoring and reporting functions must be kept separate, and test frameworks distinguished from the reporting function of the PLDs in models.

3 History

3.1 American Council on the Teaching of Foreign Languages (ACTFL)

The ACTFL Guidelines were designed for use in schools and colleges. They grew out of the Foreign Service Institute (FSI) and Interagency Language Roundtable (ILR) scales, which were designed for use in the US military. Each ACTFL level is illustrated with sample performances for speaking and writing, and typical task types for listening and speaking. As Liskin-Gasparro (2003: 484) says of the Guidelines, they have been "institutionalized" through their use in textbooks and teacher training, as well as through their use in creating national standards.

ACTFL and its predecessors are different from other models, guidelines or frameworks, because it is associated with a particular test (the Oral Proficiency Interview). Clifford (2012: 53) describes ACTFL as being "task-centric". The scales describe not only the tasks, but also the conditions under which they are to be performed, and the accuracy with which they must be accomplished. Furthermore, it is non-compensatory (or "conjunctive", Cizek and Bunch (2007: 20)). A learner must accomplish all tasks for a particular level to be awarded that level (Lowe 2012: 103).

The evolution of ACTFL into a standards-based framework is part of the growing accountability agenda. For example, Deville and Chalhoub-Deville (2011) set out the history of the No Child Left Behind reforms and place the development of standards within the context of a system that holds schools and teachers accountable for student progress. Penalties are in place for schools and districts that do not meet the required standards. This has evolved into the establishment of national common core standards (CCS) to guide teaching and assessment (http://www.core standards.org/). Alignment of state standards to CCS is required to attract federal funding, thus forcing compliance. As the production of tests that assess progress against standards is expensive, states often join consortia to drive down their costs (see Bunch 2011). As states start to use the same tests, the performance of their schools can also be compared.

This demonstrates that accountability agendas quickly require comparison across larger units, for which harmonization of practice is required. With regard to English language learners Maxwell (2013) argued that *Toward a Common definition of English Learner* (Linquanti and Cook 2013) is designed to get states to agree on criteria for the definition of an English learner, how to assess English language learners (ELLs) in ways that make it possible to compare progress, and establish identical criteria for reclassifying ELLs as "fluent". When accountability agendas become established, harmonization across the educational system becomes an absolute requirement to identify compliance and failure (Fulcher 2004).

3.2 Canadian Language Benchmarks (CLB)

The CLB is a descriptive scale developed to assess the English ability of adult immigrants in Canada. It plays a dual role as a set of standards as well as scoring criteria. As Pawlikowska-Smith (2000: 7) states, the CLB acts as "... a national standard for planning second language curricula for a variety of contexts, and a common 'yardstick' for assessing the outcomes." The framework has three levels (basic, intermediate and advanced) divided into four sub-levels for each of the skills (speaking, writing, reading and listening). This generates a 12-level descriptive system, each with a "standard" that sets out what a "satisfactory learner" must be able to do to be placed at the level. Sample tasks and performance conditions are also provided. Where the CLB excels is the detailed description of tasks, conditions, discourse and social interaction that is expected at each level. While this is not empirically founded, it provides the basis for extensive empirical validation within the context of the needs of adult immigrants.

3.3 Common European Framework of Reference (CEFR)

Like the CLB, the CEFR is a three level system (basic, independent and proficient), each split into two sub-levels, generating a six level system. Each level is characterized by a set of "can do" statements that are indicative of what a learner at a particular level may be able to do. It is a model rather than a framework. The level descriptors were generated by creating a corpus of some 200 existing rating scales, extracting and rewriting their descriptors to make them positive, and scaling them using Rasch to produce new sets of "illustrative" scales (North 1996/2000; Fulcher 2003: 107–112).

Nowhere in the CEFR is it claimed that the scales can (or should) be used for rating. It is suggested that they can be used to state "the criteria for the attainment of a learning objective", and compare systems of qualifications (Council of Europe

2001: 19). For example, Saville (2012: 66) says that "... the scales and related descriptors are not operationally adequate as they stand, but need to be adapted or developed further for specific contexts and uses, for example, for rating purposes within a testing system."

The scales cannot be used for scoring partly because they are a patchwork quilt of existing descriptors. But it is also acknowledged that a broad model of language competence cannot capture individual profiles, just as it cannot describe domain specific language use beyond a "common core" of linguistic knowledge (North 2011: 38–39). Indeed, it is argued that the scales and descriptors are relevant only to the original intended use as a heuristic in guiding the teaching and learning of adults in Europe (North 2011: 50–51).

4 Issues

4.1 Ontology

The most pressing problem is the ontological status of the levels and descriptors in standards documents. At one extreme, the levels are seen as a "ladder" to be climbed, reflecting stages of universal second language acquisition. At the other, they are merely heuristics that make policy implementation a practical proposition, even if the processes of "mapping" or "linking" tests to standards are completely arbitrary (Glass 2011). As Jones (2012b) explained with regard to the comparison of levels and specific tests "... the location of a language qualification in a qualifications framework is an attribution of social value, and has nothing intrinsically to do with proficiency." The outcome can only be validated in terms of processes. Using a legal analogy, Cizek and Bunch (2007: 15) state "According to the relevant legal theory, important decisions about a person's life, liberty, or property must involve due process – that is, a process that is clearly articulated in advance, is applied uniformly, and includes an avenue for appeal."

Statistically elegant mapping studies give a spurious impression of scientific description and measurement. Despite the façade, they remain constructions erected to satisfy the erratic exigencies of social policy.

4.2 Validation

Validation is increasingly being interpreted as standard setting by following the procedures as set out in some authoritative text. This has the effect of subverting the primary requirement of validation theory, which is the specification of test purpose, and the provision of evidence to support score meaning for intended decisions. Thus, if policy makers specify that B2 on the CEFR is the required standard for university entrance, linking a university entrance test to the CEFR at level B2 becomes the de facto requirement for "recognition". "Validation" and "recognition" become synonymous. Standard-setting researchers know what the outcome must be before they begin if the test is to be recognised (see Fulcher 2010: 244–248 for examples and discussion).

While test providers are urged to investigate the validity of their tests for purpose prior to engaging in standard setting, the requirements for recognition often simply take over. For example, if the primary purpose of standards is to enhance the "portability" of qualifications across national boundaries, social value can become more important than substantive validation. In this vein, Trim (2012: 19) stresses the benefits to individual mobility, and the "ministries, employers and university authorities, called on to interpret qualifications from diverse sources and to make administrative decisions on that basis."

Test purpose is lost in the social vision and bureaucratic process. Test scores gain their meaning not through substantive inferences to real-world performance, but by the association between a score boundary and a standard required by policy makers to trigger a high-stakes decision. The first victim is content relevance and representativeness. Tests of academic English can be used to certify readiness for medical practice, or general tests for school learners to issue work visas. As Little (2012: 75) correctly says: "Lawyers will master the lexicon and discourse of the law, but not of nuclear physics; economists will be able to debate the finer points of economic policy, but not of animal husbandry; and so on." Validation for primary purpose should always precede standard setting.

4.3 Hooks

A recurring problem is how to anchor the scale at the top and bottom. The traditional answer is to make the top level equivalent to a "well-educated native speaker" (WENS). At the other end is "no practical ability" (Lowe 1983: 231). Lowe (2012: 100) states that "... the presence of a 'highly articulate well-educated native speaker' at the top of the scale affects the whole nature of the scale below", which articulates "what non-native speakers cannot do." The top level descriptor therefore acts as the hook upon which to hang the levels below. Each of these levels is not exhaustively defined in the descriptors, but is said to provide a "gestalt" description to facilitate level interpretation.

While the use of the WENS is still prominent, the first attempt to remove it as a hook came from data-driven scale development. In this approach the descriptors at the top and bottom of a scale are derived from the most and least proficient performances of typical test takers for whom the test was designed (Fulcher 1996). This has been taken up in standards documents more widely since its inception. For example, Jones (2013: 111) notes that C2 on the CEFR is termed 'mastery', but this is not associated with a native speaker. Rather, it is language use by an extremely successful learner. In principle, it is possible to have performances higher than C2.

The concept of the native speaker remains controversial, but it has had a lasting influence on language testing. Davies (2004) charts the issues, showing that while it is difficult to define the native speaker, it still has a resonance for language testers as a practical concept for establishing standards.

4.4 Compliance

It is the use of standards and frameworks for compliance that frequently leads to conflict. In order to force compliance, recognition needs to usurp validation. The Standards documents become the primary tool for achieving policy aims. Language testers then see their task as ensuring that those who use tests are working to implement policy. In the CEFR context, Kaftandjieva (2007: 35) argues approvingly, "the main goal of this linking exercise is to demonstrate compliance with a mandate." The compliance agenda is frequently welcomed by those who approve of the centralization and harmonization of educational systems, such as that proposed for Europe in the Bologna Declaration of 1999. Hehl and Kruczek (2013), for example, advocate collaboration between Universities "... to further promote the CEFR as our common framework of reference ... and prevent the development of idiosyncratic uses which might be counter-productive as they would impede communication." The purpose of collaboration is normally to achieve some goal beyond institutionalizing an endorsed interpretation the tool used for encouraging collaboration. As standards become embedded in a compliance agenda, the next step is to monitor and control that compliance. Poszytek (2013: 72), for example, describes the main aim of the Language Rich Europe (LRE) project as developing "... a pioneering new tool for monitoring the level of adherence of national multilingual policies and practices to European recommendations and resolutions ..."

McNamara (2007: 281) argues that our current concept of test consequences as part of validity "... did not seem to have envisaged the situation in which the values implicit in tests would be imposed from outside, and validation of test constructs would be reduced to negotiating their acceptability to stakeholders." This echoes Fulcher (2004; 2009) who also provides a social critique of the use of standards by powerful institutions to enforce compliance with political goals. Inevitably, such social critiques receive rebuttals from the institutions that use the policy framework to extend the use of tests to potentially new uses (e.g., Jones and Saville 2009).

This is the point at which the standards and frameworks are subsumed into politics and economics. It has become, and will remain, a fertile ground for profound disagreement.

5 Research

5.1 Alignment of tests to standards

There is no one correct way to link a test to standards. Many methods for conducting alignment studies have been proposed, and each may result in a different outcome. The only implication of the legal analogy is that the researcher can defend the consistent application of the method selected. Research into alignment is not the primary focus of this chapter (see Papageorgiou this volume). However, the development of new alignment methods (see Cizek 2012) and the evaluation of alignment studies (Davis-Becker and Buckendahl 2013), remain high priority areas for continued research.

5.2 Assessment for learning

When standards documents are not associated with policy agendas many of the contentious issues evaporate. For example, they have been successfully used as heuristics to plan language learning, as is the case with the Language Portfolio. Little (2012: 75) is particularly perceptive in this context. He argues that while politicians may have a policy that learners will achieve B2 by the end of high school, this ignores learning reality: "The ability to perform these and related tasks spontaneously, however, is not something that teachers can transmit to their learners in so many hours of instruction; rather, it develops gradually over time as learners repeatedly engage with the tasks in question." Little (2009) documents the success achieved by the contextual interpretation of standards documents to enhance learner autonomy, and enrich the language learning process. Further research into such deregulated uses in teaching and learning is to be welcomed.

5.3 Migration

The use of standards in immigration policy is growing quickly around the world (Kunnan 2012). While language testers are deeply divided on the suitability of language testing for this purpose (see the special issue of Language Assessment Quarterly 6(1) for 2009), there is no clear way to adjudicate the ethical issues that are raised by emerging practices (Bishop 2004). Saville (2009) describes the migration journey and attempts to draft an agenda for language testing research and practice relevant to each stage.

Van Avaermat and Rocca (2013: 15) address a number of pertinent issues including who is to be tested, when and where they are to be tested, the maintenance of test security and appropriate administration, communicating results to decision makers, and the decision-making process. The most important question in their list is "what features of the language will be covered and what is the justification for this?" This is the critical validation question if we are to move from score to sound inferences about an individual's ability to use the language for work and social integration. That is, foregrounding the investigation of the language contexts immigrants operate within on arrival in a country, and the linguistic and communicative skills that will be essential for them to survive. However, this is undermined by the next question: "What proficiency level (e.g., CEFR level) is realistic for different groups?" This question focuses upon the policies that are being served and encourages validation by standard setting.

As a result, off-the-peg tests are frequently repurposed for immigration without required retrofits (Fulcher and Davidson 2009). Specially designed tests reveal item types that do not appear to have any relevance to the language needs of immigrants (e.g., de Jong et al. 2009). There is therefore a very real need for effect-driven studies into the language needs of immigrants to inform appropriate test design.

5.4 Comparability of frameworks

There has recently been an interest in comparing standards in the search for a "Universal Model". The assumption underlying this endeavor is that there is a "true" and "complete" description of language competence that is only partially realized in existing standards documents. As Lowe (2012: 94) puts it: "An ultimate, but distant goal would allow the resultant ratings, even assessment instruments, to be interchangeable." Here we are firmly in the realm of Arthurian legend.

Research generally does not have such grandiose ambitions. It addresses the issue by looking at how standards documents may relate to each other by comparing tests that have been mapped to them. Kenyon (2012: 23) argues: "From a psychometric perspective, creating links between any assessment and verbally-defined proficiency levels (such as the ACTFL proficiency levels or the CEFR levels) is ultimately a socially-moderated procedure of great complexity ... Given this reality, creating links between two verbally-defined sets of proficiency levels in any psychometrically satisfactory manner will necessarily be a socially-moderated endeavor of even greater complexity."

Kenyon identifies five "issue sets". The first is whether there is validation evidence for the intended inferences of a test that is to be linked to a framework. The second is the extent to which two tests are comparable in terms of content, tasks, and language elicited. The third is the extent to which they generate similar scores. The fourth is whether standard-setting procedures could be used to arrive at interpretations of a validated, linked test, from one framework to the other framework. Fifthly, there needs to be evidence that decisions made on the basis of test scores are valid. Finally, and perhaps most importantly, it would be necessary that similar decisions could be made on the basis of scores from either test. This is where the argument breaks down. As Kenyon (2012: 31) states: "These decisions generally take place in a very specific and local context; for example, do these language learners have the language proficiency required to do this job, or is this class of language learners making as much progress as they should?" However, the validation work for interpretation to a specific context is done in the primary validation research for test inferences – or Kenyon's first set of issues. If this validation evidence is convincing, there is no further advantage to interpreting scores in terms of more general descriptors that do not relate to the primary inferences to be made from the test – unless there is a political mandate to do so, for purposes of recognition and "portability".

Another approach is represented by Chapelle (2012). This involves the analysis of scale descriptors across standards to see which reflect similar constructs at particular levels. She does this in terms of the theoretical approach to language (psycholinguistic, communicative, structural and functional), approaches to construct definition (trait, processing, task-based, contexts of use, interactionalist, sociocultural), and approaches to language learning (using the same categories as the theoretical approach to language). Even though the CEFR descriptors are parasitical on other rating scales and frameworks (36 descriptors were taken from ACTFL), Chapelle is unable to match them up using any of these criteria. I agree with Clifford (2012: 52) who argues that "Without a clear alignment of both testing purpose and test type, attempts to align the ACTFL and CEFR tests based on similar wording in the rating scales they use will be a feckless exercise." I should also add that ACTFL is regularly updated, whereas the CEFR relies on descriptors borrowed from the 1986 version of ACTFL. Furthermore, with regard to the critical area of construct definition, Chapelle (2012: 42) concludes that "It is not immediately evident from the scale language of ACTFL and the example CEFR-based scale what the intended approaches to construct definition are." I agree, because neither are theoretically driven or data-based. This is why it is quite misleading to talk about the levels representing "acquisition" in anything but the grossest sense of "language use improves with study". And no one would deny that it is possible to generate small numbers of levels that are socially useful, and function as abstractions of our experience of language learning trajectories.

5.5 Policy

Inevitably there is a growth in policy related research because of the role played by standards in implementing national and international political agendas. This is mostly policy analysis, rather than empirical studies of the impact of policy implementation. There is no funding available for policy research that is not likely to be confirmatory. It therefore covers areas like the potential relationship of testing to political philosophy (Fulcher 2009), harmonizing transnational educational systems (Fulcher 2004), and the poverty of standards-based constructs for decision making in specific contexts (McNamara 2011).

6 Future directions

The explicit aim of a universal metroscape is to create a "common currency" in test-score meaning. Certificates issued on any test can therefore report score meaning in the common currency, thus achieving worldwide portability. Despite the subversion of validation that this has brought in its wake, there is little likelihood that it will be reversed, even if the reversal only requires the political will to recognize the qualifications of other jurisdictions. Secondly, standards provide politicians with a tool to use language for policy implementation along a wide range of fronts, from controlling University entry to immigration. Language is too useful a surrogate measure to be abandoned. Thirdly, there is a strong economic incentive. As standard setting studies are a matter of "social moderation" and "assigning social value" to test scores, it is a game that anyone can play; and the extremely flexible rules always assure the required outcome. Test recognition is therefore guaranteed for a variety of purposes without users having to provide validation evidence to support each separate claim.

Given that testing and assessment has always served political ideology, it is highly unlikely that the current situation will change. It is a feature of globalization. The role of independent language testers will be to continually call attention to the importance of validation evidence for the meaning of scores for stated purposes, prior to seeking standards-based interpretations. This is elegantly stated in Standard 1.1 of the *Standards for Educational and Psychological Testing*: "A rationale should be presented for each recommended interpretation and use of test scores, together with a comprehensive summary of the evidence and theory bearing on the intended use of interpretation" (APA 1999: 17). In an accountability culture, holding institutions to account is a valuable role to play.

We must also be careful not to create economic monopolies that lead to hermetically sealed systems with an interest in stasis. For example, Little (2012: 76) suggests of the CEFR that: "The action-oriented approach offers to bring curriculum, pedagogy and assessment into closer interdependence than has traditionally been the case: each "can do" descriptor may be used to (i) define a learning target, (ii) select and/or develop learning activities and materials, and (iii) guide the selection and design of assessment tasks." Such an argument can be used by a test producer to justify expanding into the production of textbooks that prepare learners for the test, and providing training for teachers who will use the textbooks. In the market economy that the framework is designed to serve, there is a strong argument that these functions should be kept separate in order to avoid predictability of test content, cheating, or the monopoly that comes from having "insider information" for sale. Similar conflicts of interest are legislated against in other industries.

While policy analysis and institutional accountability will become ever more important, we should also recognize the need to continually improve standards documents, frameworks, PLDs and descriptors for scoring rubrics. A range of approaches to scale development have been described and illustrated (Fulcher 2003; Fulcher, Davidson, and Kemp 2011), some of which hold out the possibility of improving the inferential link between score and likely performance in the real world. We should not lose sight of the original insights from criterion-referenced assessment. Finally, it is important to recognize the need for a balance between the abstraction required for multinational standardized systems, and the equally important need for indigenous ecologically sensitive assessment that serves local needs.

The tensions and issues outlined in this chapter are far from new; but they take on a fresh form with each incarnation. Critical awareness and engagement is the only way forward, for the world will not change at the bidding of language testers.

7 References

Alderson, J. Charles. 1991. Bands and Scores. In: J. Charles Alderson and Brian North (eds.). *Language Testing in the 1990s*, 71–86. London: Modern English Publications and the British Council.

American Council on the Teaching of Foreign Languages. 2012. *ACTFL Proficiency Guidelines*. Alexandria, VA: ACTFL.

American Psychological Association. 1999. *Standards for Educational and Psychological Testing*. Washington D.C.: AERA, APA, NCME.

Bishop, Sharon. 2004. Thinking About a Professional Ethics. *Language Assessment Quarterly* 1(2–3): 109–122.

Blastland, Michael and Andrew Dilnot. 2010. *The Numbers Game: The Commonsense Guide to Understanding Numbers in the News, in Politics, and in Life*. London: Gotham Books.

Bunch, Michael B. 2011. Testing English Language Learners Under No Child Left Behind. *Language Testing* 28(3): 323–341.

Chapelle, Carol. 2012. Seeking Solid Theoretical Ground for the ACTFL-CEFR Crosswalk. In: Erwin Tschirner (ed.). *Aligning Frameworks of Reference in Language Testing: The ACTFL Proficiency Guidelines and the Common European Framework of Reference for Languages*, 35–48. Tübingen: Stauffenburg Verlag.

Cizek, Gregory J. 2012. *Setting Performance Standards: Foundations, Methods, and Innovations. Second Edition*. New York: Routledge.

Cizek, Gregory J. and Michael B. Bunch. 2007. *Standard Setting: A Guide to Establishing and Evaluating Performance Standards on Tests*. London: Sage.

Clark, John L. D. 1980. Toward a Common Measure of Speaking Proficiency. In: James R. Frith (ed.). *Measuring Spoken Language Proficiency*, 15–26. Washington D.C.: Georgetown University Press.

Clifford, Ray T. 2012. It is Easier to Malign Tests Than It is to Align Tests. In: Erwin Tschirner (ed.). *Aligning Frameworks of Reference in Language Testing: The ACTFL Proficiency Guidelines and the Common European Framework of Reference for Languages*, 49–56. Tübingen: Stauffenburg Verlag.

Council of Europe. 2001. *Common European Framework of Reference for Languages: Learning, Teaching, Assessment*. Cambridge, UK: Cambridge University Press.

Crease, Robert P. 2011. *World in the Balance. The Historic Quest for an Absolute System of Measurement*. New York and London: W. W. Norton and Company.

Davidson, Fred, J. Charles Alderson, Dan Douglas, Ari Huhta, Carolyn Turner and Elaine Wylie. 1995. *Report of the Task Force on Testing Standards (TFTS) to the International Language Testing Association (ILTA)*. International Language Testing Association.

Davis-Becker, Susan L. and Chad W. Buckendahl. 2013. A Proposed Framework for Evaluating Alignment Studies. *Educational Measurement: Issues and Practice* 32(1): 23–33.

Davies, Alan. 2004. The Native Speaker in Applied Linguistics. In: Alan Davies and Cathie Elder (eds.). *The Handbook of Applied Linguistics*, 431–450. London: Blackwell.

Davies, Alan. 2008. Ethics, Professionalism, Rights and Codes. In: Nancy Hornberger and Elana Shohamy (eds.). *Language Testing and Assessment*, Encyclopedia of Language and Education. Vol. 7, 429–443. New York: Springer.

De Jong, John H. A. L., Matthew Lennig, Anne Kerkhoff and Petra Poelmans. 2009. Development of a Test of Spoken Dutch for Prospective Immigrants. *Language Assessment Quarterly* 6(1): 41–60.

Deville, Craig and Micheline Chalhoub-Deville. 2011. Accountability-assessment Under No Child Left Behind: Agenda, Practice, and Future. *Language Testing* 28(3): 307–321.

Foucault, Michel. 1975. *Discipline and Punish. The Birth of the Prison*. London: Penguin.

Fulcher, Glenn. 1996. Does Thick Description Lead to Smart Tests? A data-based approach to rating scale construction. *Language Testing* 13(2): 208–238.

Fulcher, Glenn. 2003. *Testing Second Language Speaking*. Harlow: Longman.

Fulcher, Glenn. 2004. Deluded by Artifices? The Common European Framework and Harmonization. *Language Assessment Quarterly* 1(4): 253–266.

Fulcher, Glenn. 2009. Test Use and Political Philosophy. *Annual Review of Applied Linguistics* 29. 3–20.

Fulcher, Glenn. 2010. *Practical Language Testing*. London: Hodder Education.

Fulcher, Glenn and Fred Davidson. 2007. *Language Testing and Assessment: An Advanced Resource Book*. London and New York: Routledge.

Fulcher, Glenn and Fred Davidson. 2009. Test Architecture, Test Retrofit. *Language Testing* 26(1): 123–144.

Fulcher, Glenn, Fred Davidson and Jenny Kemp. 2011. Effective rating scale development for speaking tests: Performance Decision Trees. *Language Testing* 28(1): 5–29.

Fulcher, Glenn and Agneta Svalberg. 2013. Limited Aspects of Reality: Frames of reference in language assessment. *International Journal of English Studies* 13(2): 1–20.

Glaser, Robert. 1963. Instructional Technology and the Measurement of Learning Outcomes: some Questions. *American Psychologist* 18: 519–521.

Glass, Gene V. 2011. Standards and Criteria. *Journal of MultiDisciplinary Evaluation* 7(15): 227–257. (Originally published in 1977 as an Occasional Paper).

Green, Anthony. 2012. CEFR and ACTFL Crosswalk: A Text Based Approach. In: Erwin Tschirner (ed.). *Aligning Frameworks of Reference in Language Testing: The ACTFL Proficiency Guidelines and the Common European Framework of Reference for Languages*, 82–92. Tübingen: Stauffenburg Verlag.

Hehl, Ursula and Nicole Kruczek. 2013. The Impact of the Common European Framework of Reference for Languages on Teaching and Assessment at the Language Centres of the Universities of Bonn and Göttingen. In: Evelina D. Galaczi and Cyril J. Weir (eds.). *Exploring Language Frameworks. Proceedings of the ALTE Kraków Conference*, July 2011, Studies in Language Testing 36: 164–186. Cambridge, UK: Cambridge University Press.

Hudson, Thom. 2012. Standards-based Testing. In: Glenn Fulcher and Fred Davidson (eds.). *The Routledge Handbook of Language Testing*, 479–494. London and New York: Routledge.

Jones, Neil. 2012a. Reliability and Dependability. In: Glenn Fulcher and Fred Davidson (eds.). *The Routledge Handbook of Language Testing*, 350–363. London and New York: Routledge.

Jones, Neil. 2012b. CEFR Qualification. Posted on Language Testing Research and Practice (LTEST-L), 23 August.

Jones, Neil. 2013. Defining an Inclusive Framework for Languages. In: Evelina D. Galaczi and Cyril J. Weir (eds.). *Exploring Language Frameworks Proceedings of the ALTE Kraków Conference*, July 2011, Studies in Language Testing 36, 105–117. Cambridge, UK: Cambridge University Press.

Jones, Neil and Nick Saville. 2009. European Language Policy: Assessment, Learning and the CEFR. *Annual Review of Applied Linguistics* 29: 51–63.

Kaftandjieva, Felianka. 2007. Quantifying the Quality of Llinkage between Language Examinations and the CEF. In: Cecilie Carlsen and Eli Moe (eds.). *A Human Touch to Language Testing*, 33–43. Oslo: Novus Press.

Kenyon, Dorry. 2012. Using Bachman's Assessment Use Argument as a Tool in Conceptualizing the Issues Surrounding Linking ACTFL and CEFR. In: Erwin Tschirner (ed.). *Aligning Frameworks of Reference in Language Testing: The ACTFL Proficiency Guidelines and the Common European Framework of Reference for Languages*, 23–34. Tübingen: Stauffenburg Verlag.

Kunnan, Antony J. 2012. Language Assessment for Immigration and Citizenship. In: Glenn Fulcher and Fred Davidson (eds.). *The Routledge Handbook of Language Testing*, 162–177. London and New York: Routledge.

Linquanti, Robert and Gary Cook. 2013. *Toward a Common Definition of English Learner: Guidance for States and State Assessment Consortia in Defining and Addressing Policy.* http://www.ccsso.org/Resources/Publications/Toward_a_Common_Definition_English_Learner_.html (accessed 31 August 2013). Washington D.C.: Council of Chief State School Officers.

Liskin-Gasparro, Janet. 2003. The ACTFL Proficiency Guidelines and the Oral Proficiency interview: A Brief History and Analysis of their Survival. *Foreign Language Annals* 36(4): 483–490.

Little, David. 2009. Language Learner Autonomy and the European Language Portfolio: Two L2 English examples. *Language Teaching* 42(2): 222–233.

Little, David. 2012. Elements of L2 Proficiency: The CEFR's Action-Oriented Approach and Some of Its Implications. In: Erwin Tschirner (ed.). *Aligning Frameworks of Reference in Language Testing: The ACTFL Proficiency Guidelines and the Common European Framework of Reference for Languages*, 71–82. Tübingen: Stauffenburg Verlag.

Lowe, Pardee. 1983. The ILR Oral Interview: Origins, Applications, Pitfalls, and Implications. *Die Unterrichtspraxis* 16(2): 230–244.

Lowe, Pardee. 2012. Understanding "Hidden Features" of the ACTFL Speaking Guidelines as an Intermediate Step to Comparing the ACTFL Guidelines and the CEFR for Speaking Assessment. In: Erwin Tschirner (ed.). *Aligning Frameworks of Reference in Language Testing: The ACTFL Proficiency Guidelines and the Common European Framework of Reference for Languages*, 93–106. Tübingen: Stauffenburg Verlag.

Mager, Robert F. 1962. *Preparing Instructional Objectives*. Palo Alto, CA: Feardon Publishers.

McNamara, Tim F. 2007. Language Assessment in Foreign Language Education: The Struggle Over Constructs. *The Modern Language Journal* 91(2): 280–282.

McNamara, Tim F. 2011. Managing learning: Authority and Language Assessment. *Language Teaching* 44(4): 500–15.

Maxwell, Lesli. 2013. New Guide to Help States Commonly Define English-Learners. *Education Week*, 30th August. from http://blogs.edweek.org/edweek/learning-the-language/2013/08/new_guide_for_states_on_how_to.html (accessed 31 August 2013).

Mill, John S. 1873. *Autobiography*. London: Longmans, Green, Reader and Dyer.

Miyazaki, Ichisada. 1981. *China's Examination Hell: The Civil Service Examinations of Imperial China*. New Haven and London: Yale University Press.

North, Brian. 1996/2000. *The Development of a Common Framework Scale of Descriptors of Language Proficiency based on a Theory of Measurement*. PhD Thesis. Thames Valley University/New York: Peter Lang.

North, Brian. 2011. Describing Language Levels. In: Barry O'Sullivan (ed.). *Language Testing: Theories and Practice*, 33–59. Basingstoke: Palgrave Macmillan.

Papageorgiou, Spiros. This volume. Aligning language assessments to standards and frameworks. In: Dina Tsagari and Jayanti Banerjee (eds.). *Handbook of Second Language Assessment*. Berlin: DeGruyter Mouton.

Pawlikowska-Smith, Grazyna. 2000. *Canadian Language Benchmarks 2000: English as a Second Language – for Adults*. Toronto: Centre for Canadian Language Benchmarks.

Plato. 380 BC [1955]. *The Republic*. Tr. by Desmond Lee. London: Penguin Books.

Poszytek, Pawel. 2013. European Index of Multilingual Policies and Practices. In: Evelina D. Galaczi and Cyril J. Weir (eds.). *Exploring Language Frameworks. Proceedings of the ALTE Kraków Conference*, July 2011, Studies in Language Testing 36, 72–84. Cambridge, UK: Cambridge University Press.

Roach, John. 1971. *Public Examinations in England 1850–1900*. Cambridge, UK: Cambridge University Press.

Saville, Nick. 2005. An Interview with John Trim at 80. *Language Assessment Quarterly* 2(4): 263–288.

Saville, Nick. 2009. Language Assessment in the Management of International Migration: A Framework for Considering the Issues. *Language Assessment Quarterly* 6(1): 17–29.

Saville, Nick. 2012. The CEFR: An Evolving Framework of Reference. In: Erwin Tschirner (ed.). *Aligning Frameworks of Reference in Language Testing: The ACTFL Proficiency Guidelines and the Common European Framework of Reference for Languages*, 57–69. Tübingen: Stauffenburg Verlag.

Trim, John. 2012. Provo Address. In: Erwin Tschirner (ed.). *Aligning Frameworks of Reference in Language Testing: The ACTFL Proficiency Guidelines and the Common European Framework of Reference for Languages*, 19–22. Tübingen: Stauffenburg Verlag.

Van Avermaet, Piet and Lorenzo Rocca. 2013. Language Testing and Access. In: Evelina D. Galaczi and Cyril J. Weir (eds.). *Exploring Language Frameworks. Proceedings of the ALTE Kraków Conference*, July 2011, Studies in Language Testing 36, 11–44. Cambridge, UK: Cambridge University Press.

Yasuyo Sawaki

4 Norm-referenced vs. criterion-referenced approach to assessment

1 Introduction

The purpose of this chapter is to provide a nontechnical overview of two key frames of reference for language test-score interpretation. One is norm-referenced testing, where a test taker's performance is interpreted with respect to the performance of other test takers. The other is criterion-referenced testing, a situation where test takers' performance is compared against pre-determined assessment criteria, regardless of how other test takers do. Section 2 will illuminate key features of the two types of testing, giving examples of testing situations depicting both types of test-score interpretation, followed by their definitions and a synopsis of their history. Section 3 will focus on measurement issues. Specifically, classical test theory and generalizability theory, two major analytic approaches to analyzing language tests for both types of testing, will be introduced. Key measurement concepts such as test-score reliability and dependability will also be explained. Section 4 will present illustrative examples of previous language assessment studies on norm-referenced and criterion-referenced testing. Finally, the chapter will conclude with a brief discussion of future directions of language assessment research related to norm-referenced and criterion-referenced testing.

2 Key features of norm-referenced and criterion-referenced testing

2.1 Illustrative examples of different types of language assessment score interpretation

Language assessments are administered for different purposes, and their scores are interpreted and used for making various types of decisions about language learners, teachers, and educational programs. For example, suppose that an international studies program of a university in Japan admits 200 students every year. Candidates applying for this program, where English is the medium of instruction, are required to take an English exam. While other pieces of information such as high school grade point average (GPA) and a statement of purpose are also taken into consideration, a relatively large weight is given to the English exam score in making admission decisions. In another example, suppose that a teacher administers end-of-unit tests throughout a language course. Each test covers materials related to specific instructional goals of each unit, and the test results are used to monitor students' achievement in a given unit and inform planning of subsequent classes.

Note that the test scores are being interpreted in different ways in the two examples above. The type of test-score interpretation illustrated in the first scenario for an admission test is norm-referenced. This is because a given examinee's score is interpreted with reference to a norm, namely, performance of all other examinees. Whether or not an examinee is admitted to the program depends on how well he/she performs relative to others. So, even if an examinee felt confident that he/she did fairly well on the exam, he/she would not be admitted unless ranked among the top 200 on the test score, everything else being equal. By contrast, the second example of end-of-unit tests during the course of a semester depicts a case of criterion-referenced test-score interpretation. In this case, a student's relative standing in class is irrelevant. Instead, the teacher's assessment about his/her students' achievement levels is based solely on the degree to which they demonstrate mastery of the unit content by earning high enough scores.

2.2 Definitions

Popham (1981: 26) provides a common definition of a norm-referenced test, which is "used to ascertain an individual's status with respect to the performance of other individuals on the test." Thus, tests where scores are used to rank-order examinees for making selection decisions are typical norm-referenced tests. In the admission test example above, the group against which a given examinee's score is compared (the reference group) was the group of all examinees who took the same test. However, the reference group can be defined as an external group as well. For example, a large-scale national Grade 8 standardized English test may define the entire Grade 8 population (14 year olds) in the country as the reference group. In this case, a representative sample of Grade 8 students would be tested prior to the test administration. Once the score distribution for this reference group is obtained, a given examinee's test score is interpreted by identifying his/her relative standing in the reference group. As for criterion-referenced assessment, this chapter adopts Brown and Hudson's (2002: 5) definition of a criterion-referenced test, which "is primarily designed to describe the performance of examinees in terms of the amount that they know of a specific domain of knowledge or set of objectives." It should be noted that the word "criterion" in criterion-referenced assessment has two meanings. One is the amount of knowledge of a specific domain as in the case of the end-of-unit assessment example above. The other is the level of performance as, for example, in a second language test for certification where a minimally acceptable level of speaking performance is required to pass the test.

While many similarities and differences between norm-referenced and criterion-referenced tests can be noted, differences in test design principles are particularly important. On the one hand, norm-referenced tests are often designed to assess a broad range of language ability. For this reason, a norm-referenced test often comprises multiple sections containing items of different types that tap into different aspects of language ability. On the other hand, criterion-referenced tests are typically designed to assess the degree of mastery of specific content, so tests are relatively short and contain a limited number of item types covering a narrow range of clearly defined content. Teacher-made tests designed to test students' mastery of course content are common examples of the latter type. Norm-referenced and criterion-referenced tests differ from each other not only in the test design but also in measurement properties, which will be discussed in Section 3.

2.3 Historical perspective

Today the terms norm-referenced and criterion-referenced tests are part of language testers' everyday vocabulary as this distinction is commonly discussed in language assessment textbooks. Testing abilities of individuals has centuries of history, and Popham (1981: 13–22) notes that many traditional tests are considered to be norm-referenced in nature because many of them were designed to spread examinees across a scale for selection purposes (e.g., large-scale intelligence testing for the selection of military official candidates during the World War I). However, it has only been about 50 years since the two terms – norm-referenced assessment and criterion-referenced assessment – were introduced to the measurement literature. In his seminal paper on the interpretation of achievement test scores, Glaser (1963: 520) criticized the then-current test theory for focusing on norm-referenced testing; it was preoccupied with aptitude testing as well as rank-ordering candidates for selection and prediction purposes. Glaser (1963: 520) suggested the need for criterion-referenced achievement tests that are sensitive to instructional outcomes.

Despite Glaser's (1963) insightful proposal, the discussion on criterion-referenced assessment was rather sporadic in the rest of the 1960s. However, this was followed by a proliferation of research and discussion on criterion-referenced tests in the 1970s, resulting in the publication of well-cited volumes specializing in criterion-referenced testing such as Popham's (1978) and Berk's (1980), which laid a foundation for the design, development, and analysis of criterion-referenced tests. Popham (1981: 29) stated that a predicted major contribution of criterion-referenced tests was "their increased descriptiveness" of the target construct. Popham's (1978) proposal of test specification, a document that provides a test blueprint, has offered a basis for criterion-referenced test design. Meanwhile, analytic approaches for analyzing criterion-referenced tests were proposed as well. Prime examples of those include classical methods of criterion-referenced test item analysis as well as generalizability theory (G theory; Brennan 2001; Cronbach et al. 1972; Shavelson and Webb, 1991), which can handle analyses of both norm-referenced and criterion-referenced tests. Popham (1981: 25) notes that, at one point, the view of criterion-referenced assessment as a panacea in the 1970s went so far as to suggest that norm-referenced assessment could be discarded entirely. The current view, however, is that both norm-referenced and criterion-referenced tests are necessary because they serve different purposes (Popham 1981: 25; Brown and Hudson 2002: 9).

The distinction between norm-referenced and criterion-referenced tests was introduced to the field of applied linguistics and language assessment only in the early 1980s. Cziko (1981, 1982) discussed the distinction between psychometric vs. edumetric tests, which corresponded to norm-referenced and criterion-referenced tests, respectively. This was followed by the publication of empirical application studies that examined the reliability and validity of institutional language tests (e.g., Bachman, Lynch, and Mason 1995; Brown 1989; Hudson and Lynch 1984; Kunnan 1992; Sawaki 2007) as well as large-scale tests such as the Test of English as a Foreign Language™ (e.g., Brown 1999; Lee 2006; Xi 2007). Meanwhile, concerning the design of criterion-referenced language tests, Lynch and Davidson (1994) and Davidson and Lynch (2002) introduced the notion of test specifications based on Popham (1978), the discussion of which has now become an integral part of language assessment textbooks.

3 Key issues

3.1 Measurement properties of norm-referenced and criterion-referenced tests

As briefly noted above, a main difference between norm-referenced and criterion-referenced tests lies in their measurement properties. On the one hand, the primary purpose of administering a norm-referenced test is to rank-order examinees and to select those who have earned relatively high scores. To meet this goal, it is important to secure sufficient score variability, so that the test scores are spread across the scale widely. Moreover, a norm-referenced test assumes the score distribution to be normal. On the other hand, the assumptions of norm-referenced tests above do not necessarily hold for criterion-referenced tests, the purpose of which is to test mastery of a specific, clearly defined domain or to classify test takers into different ability levels. First, the criterion-referenced test-score distribution cannot be assumed to be normal. If, for example, the test is administered to a group of students who have not received instruction on which the test is based, the score distribution would be positively skewed with a majority of test takers scoring low, although some may manage to earn higher scores due to their previous knowledge.

If, however, the same test is administered to the same group of students after instruction, we may observe a negatively skewed distribution with a majority of the students scoring quite high, while some others may still score relatively low. Second, sufficient score variability assumed in a norm-referenced test may not be present in a criterion-referenced test. Consider an ideal situation where a group of students mastered the instructional content extremely well. In this case, many students, if not all, would score similarly with a majority of their scores clustering around the top of the scale. We can expect the opposite case to happen as well, where a group of students' mastery of the instructional content is so low that you see most of their scores clustering around the bottom of the scale. (Of course, we never want to face this situation as teachers!)

Traditionally, analytic approaches to test-score analysis, including classical test theory (CTT), which has a history of over 100 years now, relied on the assumption of normal score distribution and the presence of sufficient score variability. The distinction between norm-referenced and criterion-referenced assessment recognized in the early 1960s led to the development of analytic approaches that are better suited for handling criterion-referenced test data that have different measurement properties from norm-referenced tests. In the subsequent sections, I will first describe classical test item analysis procedures and the notion of score reliability for norm-referenced and criterion-referenced tests. Then, based on a discussion of some limitations of these traditional analytic approaches, I will provide a brief introduction to generalizability theory (G theory) as an example of more recently developed measurement models that address some of the limitations of the traditional methods.

3.2 Classical item analysis

3.2.1 Classical item analysis in norm-referenced assessment

Statistical analysis of individual test items that are normally obtained from piloting is an integral part of test development. In norm-referenced assessment, statistical data required to examine how items are functioning can be obtained from a single pilot test administration. In such a pilot test for a norm-referenced test, two types of indices – item facility (IF) and item discrimination (ID) indices – are often calculated. The item facility index indicates the difficulty of a given item for a group of examinees and is defined as the proportion of examinees who have answered a given item correctly. If 60 out of 100 examinees have answered an item correctly, the IF value for this item is $60 / 100 = 0.60$. The IF value ranges from 0 to 1.00. An item with a high IF value is easy, while an item with a low IF value is difficult. The item discrimination index provides information about the degree to which a given item distinguishes examinees at higher ability levels from those at lower ability levels. While there are a few different ways to obtain an ID value, below I will describe a simple method that helps the reader understand the underlying logic.

In this method, all examinees are rank-ordered according to the test total score first in order to identify the high-scoring and low-scoring groups. While the upper and lower 27 % are often designated as the high- and low-scoring groups for large samples, the upper and lower 33 % is used for smaller samples (Bachman, 2004: 123). Next, the IF value for a given item is calculated separately for the upper and lower groups. The ID value for the item is then obtained by subtracting the IF value for the lower group from that for the upper group. For instance, if the IF value of a given item for the upper group is .80 and that for the lower group is .30, then the ID value for this item is ID = .80 − .30 = .50. While the procedure above is easy to implement with small samples, correlation between the score on a given item and the test total score is often used as an item discrimination index for larger samples as well. Two commonly used indices are the point-biserial correlation coefficient and the biserial correlation coefficient. While they are both item-total correlations, there are important differences in the assumptions between the two. For further details, see Bachman (2004: 129) and Brown and Hudson (2002: 118).

Item statistics such as those introduced above are useful for assembling test forms and revising tests. Given the goal of a norm-referenced test to rank-order examinees, maximizing score variability is critical. Since it is known that score variability of a given item is maximized when the IF value is 0.50, many items having IF values around .50 are often selected for norm-referenced assessment. However, it is also important to have a sufficient number of more difficult items and easier items to ensure discrimination among examinees at higher and lower ability levels as well. Thus, it is normally the case that items with IF values between 0.30 and 0.70 are selected. In terms of item discrimination, the higher the ID value, the better. Ebel and Frisbie (1991: 232) suggest that items with ID values of 0.4 or above are very good, while items with ID values of below 0.19 should be rejected or revised.

3.2.2 Classical item analysis in criterion-referenced assessment

Similar to the item analysis in norm-referenced assessment discussed above, the item facility (IF) index plays an important role in the development of criterion-referenced tests. However, it is obtained as part of the calculation of the difference (DI) index, which is the designated item discrimination index for criterion-referenced assessment. A DI index tells us the degree to which a given item discriminates between examinees who have mastered a given test content from those who have not, or between those who have performed above a pre-determined performance level and those who have not. Pilot testing for a criterion-referenced test usually requires administering test items to these different groups of examinees. In the case of an achievement test, for instance, it is of primary interest to administer test items that best distinguish those who have learned the test content from those who have not. Thus, two pilot tests may be conducted with the same group of students twice, before and after instruction. Alternatively, if the purpose of a test is to identify examinees who satisfy a minimum acceptable level of performance in a certification test, a pilot test may be conducted once, but the participants may be selected carefully, so that the sample includes those who are known to be able to perform above the minimum acceptable level and those whose performance levels are known to be below the level.

Let us take the achievement test situation above as an example. In this case, the same items based on the instructional content can be administered as pilot tests to the same group of students twice, before and after instruction. Then, for each item, the IF values for the pretest and the posttest are calculated. Next, the DI value for a given item is obtained by subtracting the IF value for the pretest from that for the posttest. The DI value ranges from –1.0 to +1.0, where a large positive value indicates that the examinees' performance on the given item is better in the posttest than in the pretest. By contrast, negative DI values (indicating that the examinees have done worse on the posttest than on the pretest) and low positive DI values (indicating that there is little difference in examinee performance between the pretest and the posttest) are not preferable. Once the DI values are obtained for all items, those with relatively high positive DI values can be selected to construct a test that is sensitive to the effect of instruction on examinee performance.

3.3 Score reliability

3.3.1 Score reliability in norm-referenced assessment

A simple definition of test reliability is the consistency of information obtained from a test. Given that the purpose of norm-referenced tests is to rank-order examinees, the measurement consistency in this case concerns the degree to which a group of examinees are rank-ordered consistently across test forms, test occasions, and raters, among other sources. Reliability coefficients for norm-referenced tests were developed within the framework of classical test theory (CTT). In CTT, it is assumed that an observed test score (X) can be defined as a linear combination of two different parts: true score (T), which is defined as the average across scores obtained in an infinite number of repeated testing of an individual, and measurement error (E), which is always present to some extent in any measurement in real life:

$$X = T + E \qquad \text{(Equation 1)}$$

Likewise, CTT defines that the observed score variance (σ_X^2) is a linear combination of the true score variance (σ_T^2) and the error variance (σ_E^2):

$$\sigma_X^2 = \sigma_T^2 + \sigma_E^2 \qquad \text{(Equation 2)}$$

Then, building on Equation 2, CTT reliability ($r_{xx'}$) is formally defined as the proportion of the observed score variance that is explained by the true score variance:

$$r_{xx'} = \sigma_T^2 / \sigma_X^2 = \sigma_T^2 / (\sigma_T^2 + \sigma_E^2) \qquad \text{(Equation 3)}$$

Equation 3 is merely a theoretical definition because the true score variance (σ_T^2) cannot be obtained directly. For this reason, we need an operational definition of reliability. In CTT, reliability is defined as a correlation coefficient between observed scores on at least two sets of statistically parallel measures. When two measures are statistically parallel to each other, they have the same mean and standard deviation and have the same correlation to a third measure. It is worth noting that the measurement error in CTT does not distinguish random sources of error (e.g., candidate fatigue) from systematic sources of error (e.g., task difficulty, rater severity) and that only one type of error can be reflected in a given reliability coefficient. Thus, a variety of CTT reliability coefficients that focus on different aspects of measurement error have been developed. The first type is test-retest reliability, which is the correlation between scores on the same test administered to the same test takers twice. This coefficient focuses on the stability of test results between the different testing occasions. The second is parallel-forms reliability, which is the correlation between two parallel or alternative forms administered to the same examinees. This coefficient focuses on the equivalence of the test content between the alternative test forms. A third category comprises various types of internal consistency reliability coefficients that primarily concern the degree to which items included in a given test consistently assess the same ability. A major advantage of this category is that, unlike the case of the first two categories above, data from only one test administration are required for the calculation. This partly explains the frequent use of internal consistency reliability coefficients in practice. Split-half reliability coefficients in this category treat test halves as parallel to each other. The Spearman-Brown split-half reliability coefficient is based on the correlation between test halves, while the Guttman split-half reliability coefficient is based on the variances of test halves. Cronbach's alpha coefficient is another example of this type, which is based on the variances of individual items in a test, which are treated as parallel to one another. KR20 and KR21 are special cases of Cronbach's alpha coefficient that are applicable only to dichotomous items. The fourth category includes correlation-based reliability coefficients that are often employed in performance-based language assessments. For instance, the correlation between two sets of scores assigned by the same rater across different rating occasions is often used as an intra-rater reliability coefficient. Likewise, the correlation between scores assigned to the same set of test takers by two different raters is often reported as an inter-rater reliability coefficient. See Sawaki (2013) for further details about how to calculate these reliability indices as well as their assumptions and interpretations.

3.3.2 Score dependability in criterion-referenced assessment

It should be noted that the conceptualization of score reliability in criterion-referenced assessment is fundamentally different from the notion of score reliability as rank-ordering consistency in norm-referenced assessment. This is partly a reason why a different term, score dependability, is often preferred to refer to measurement consistency in criterion-referenced assessment. Score dependability in criterion-referenced assessment needs to be considered from two perspectives. One is the degree to which a test score serves as an accurate estimate of the domain score, which is analogous to the true score in CTT. Thus, in this sense, dependability of a criterion-referenced test can be defined as the proportion of the observed score variance that can be explained by the domain score variance. The index of dependability (Φ) developed within the G theory framework is an example that is often reported for criterion-referenced tests. There are a few different approaches to calculating Φ. For instance, Brown (1990) proposed a simple formula for dichotomous items that requires only basic test statistics and a KR20 reliability coefficient. Bachman (2004) provided an alternative formula employing Cronbach's alpha that can be used for both dichotomous and polytomous items. It is worth noting, however, that both formulas are appropriate only when a single systematic source of measurement error (e.g., test items) is taken into account. For other more complex measurement designs involving multiple sources of error, a G theory analysis (to be discussed in Section 3.5) should be conducted to calculate Φ.

The second approach to the dependability of criterion-referenced assessment concerns the degree to which candidates are classified consistently into different performance levels. Classifying candidates into different performance levels typically requires a cut score or multiple cut scores. Only one cut score is needed if examinees are classified into two levels (e.g., pass/fail), while two cut scores are needed to classify examinees into three levels (e.g., low, intermediate, and high). There are two types of indices that provide information about classification consistency using cut scores, depending on how the location of misclassification relative to the cut score is treated. The first category is called the threshold loss agreement indices. They are suitable if the investigator treats all classification errors as equally serious, regardless of their distances from the cut score. The simplest index is the agreement index ($\hat{p}_0$), which is the proportion of cases with consistent classification decisions. Suppose that two raters independently scored 30 examinees' speaking performance to make pass/fail decisions on a speaking test. If these two raters consistently classified 15 examinees as "pass" and nine examinees as "fail," then the agreement index in this case can be calculated as $\hat{p}_0 = (15 + 9) / 30 = 0.80$. One drawback of the agreement index is that it does not take account of agreement that might have occurred simply by chance. Thus, another index called kappa ($\hat{\kappa}$), which incorporates the chance agreement, is often used. The value of kappa can easily be obtained by hand from the data used to calculate the agreement index above. The agreement index and the kappa index are often used to examine rater agreement in language performance assessments. One note of caution, however, is that they are both based on the assumption of statistically parallel forms in CTT. They function differently relative to the cut score as well (see Brown and Hudson, 2002: 173–175, for more details).

The second category of classification agreement indices is called squared-error loss agreement indices. This category of indices is based on the assumption that classification errors made far from a given cut score are more serious than those made close to the cut score. Two indices often discussed in the language assessment literature are kappa squared ($\kappa^2_{(X, Tx)}$) and phi lambda (Φ_λ). Both can be interpreted as the proportion of correct decisions made at a given cut score. While calculation of kappa squared ($\kappa^2_{(X, Tx)}$) only requires basic test statistics and a KR20 reliability estimate, its use is generally not recommended because it is based on CTT assumptions (Brown and Hudson, 2002: 193–195). For this reason, the phi lambda index (Φ_λ), which was developed within the G theory framework and is free of the restrictive CTT assumptions, is often preferred. This index will be discussed briefly in relation to G theory in Section 3.5.

3.4 Limitations of classical approaches to item analysis and reliability analysis

The classical approaches to item analysis and reliability analysis for norm-referenced and criterion-referenced assessment above are widely used partly because the logic is transparent, and they are easy to implement. However, they are not free of criticisms. First, the statistics obtained above are sample-dependent. Consider how the IF, ID, and DI indices are calculated for test item analysis. All these values would vary greatly depending on the ability level of the study sample. Second, it is briefly noted above that CTT decomposes the observed score variance into the true score variance and the error variance, without distinguishing random sources of error from systematic sources of error or different types of systematic sources of error from each other. Since language assessment often involves multiple sources of systematic error (e.g., measurement error attributable to task difficulty and rater severity in speaking performance assessment), this can be a major drawback. Finally, standard error of measurement (SEM) is assumed to be equal across all ability levels in CTT. However, it is known that the amount of measurement error depends on the ability level. In general, measurement error is larger for scores farther away from the center of the distribution.

More recently developed measurement models address the limitations of the more traditional approach above to some extent. For instance, item response theory (IRT), which is a sophisticated scaling method, addresses the issue of the sample dependence of item statistics. Meanwhile, special types of IRT models (e.g., many-facet Rasch measurement) and G theory provide the machinery to explicitly model multiple systematic sources of error simultaneously. Estimates of SEM can be obtained for different ability levels or scores in both IRT and G theory as well. Hambleton, Swaminathan and Rogers (1991) provide helpful insights and guidance on IRT. The next section provides a brief overview of G theory primarily because it accommodates both norm-referenced and criterion-referenced test data and does not require large samples as IRT does.

3.5 Generalizability theory

Generalizability theory (G theory) developed by Cronbach and his associates (Cronbach et al. 1972) is a powerful measurement theory that builds on and extends CTT and analysis of variance (ANOVA). Nontechnical overviews of G theory are available in Bachman (2004), Brown and Hudson (2002), and Shavelson and Webb (1991), while a more advanced discussion is provided by Brennan (2001).

A key concept in G theory is the universe score. It is analogous to the true score in CTT and is defined as the mean score that a given candidate would earn across repeated testing under measurement conditions that the investigator is willing to accept as exchangeable to one another. The assumption of the use of these measures, called randomly parallel measures, is less restrictive than the assumption of statistically parallel measures in CTT. To facilitate the explanation of a typical G theory analysis procedure, consider an example where a 30-item vocabulary test is administered to 50 examinees. The items within the test were all in the same format, and the items were randomly sampled from a given domain. The G theory analysis design that describes this situation is called a one-faced crossed study design. Here, the 50 candidates (persons) are called the objects of measurement because the primary purpose of the test is to assess their vocabulary knowledge. This design is called a one-facet design because there is only one facet of measurement, or a systematic source of score variance, involved in the test design. Moreover, the test items represent a random facet because they have been randomly selected from a much larger number of randomly parallel items. Finally, this is a crossed design because all candidates complete all 50 items.

Typically, a G theory analysis of test data proceeds in two steps. The first step is called the generalizability study (G study), where the contribution of the objects of measurement and facets of measurement to the observed score variance is estimated for a hypothetical situation of a single observation, where only one item is administered to examinees. Then, in the second step, called the decision study (D study), the contribution of these different sources to the observed score variance is analyzed for a measurement design to which the investigator wants to generalize. The obtained results are then used for the calculation of various summary indices of score reliability and dependability.

Key pieces of information obtained in the G theory analysis are variance component estimates, which are parts of the observed score variance explained by different sources. The one-facet crossed study design in the hypothetical example above is associated with three variance components: 1. variance component for persons (σ_p^2), reflecting the candidates' ability differences; 2. variance component for the items (σ_i^2), reflecting the difficulty differences among the items; and 3. variance component for residuals ($\sigma_{pi,e}^2$), reflecting rank-ordering differences of persons across items and undifferentiated error. Undifferentiated error is a combination of other systematic sources of measurement error not taken into account and random sources of error (e.g., candidate fatigue). Then, a G study for these data is conducted by fitting a measurement model such as a random-effects ANOVA model to the data to obtain information required to calculate the variance component estimates for the G study. Variance component estimates for the D study with 30 items, which corresponds to the measurement design for this example, can then be calculated. Table 1 presents the results of the D study with 30 items:

Tab. 1: Variance component estimates for the one-facet crossed study design example.

Source	D study variance components (30 items)	
	Estimated VC	% of total variance
Persons (*p*)	0.022	75.9 %
Items (*i*)	0.001	3.4 %
pi, e	0.006	20.7 %
Total	0.029	100.0 %

Note. VC = variance component.

The middle column of Table 1 shows the variance component estimates for persons, items, and residuals, while they are converted to the percentages of the observed total score variance in the right-hand column. The results show that 75.9 % of the score variance in this test is explained by the candidates' ability differences. By contrast, the relative contributions of the difficulty difference among items and the residuals to the observed score variance are fairly small at 3.4 % and 20.7 %, respectively.

These D study variance components are then used to calculate summary indices of score reliability and dependability for the specific measurement condition as defined in the D study. For example, the generalizability coefficient (E_p^2) is a summary index of reliability for relative decisions (norm-referenced assessment), while the index of dependability (Φ) briefly discussed in Section 3.3.2 is for absolute decisions (criterion-referenced assessment). While both are defined as the proportion of the total score variance explained by the universe score variance, they use different error terms from each other. In this one-facet crossed study design example, the generalizability coefficient employs the relative error variance (σ_{Rel}^2), which equals the D study residual variance component ($\sigma_{Rel}^2 = \sigma_{pi,e}^2 = 0.006$). By contrast, the index of dependability (Φ) employs the absolute error variance (σ_{Abs}^2), which is a sum of the D study residual and item variance component estimates ($\sigma^2_{Abs} = \sigma^2_i + \sigma^2_{pi,e} = 0.001 + 0.006 = 0.007$). The difference in the definition of the error terms lies in the conceptualization that only the variance component involved in rank-ordering of persons (the residual variance component in this example) contributes to the measurement error for relative decisions, while not only variance components affecting rank-ordering but also those affecting performance levels (the item variance component in this example) contribute to the measurement error for absolute decisions. The generalizability coefficient and the index of dependability for this example are obtained as follows:

$$E^2_p = \sigma^2_p / (\sigma^2_p + \sigma^2_{Rel}) = 0.022 / (0.022 + 0.006) = 0.79$$

$$\Phi = \sigma^2_p / (\sigma^2_p + \sigma^2_{Abs}) = 0.022 / (0.022 + 0.007) = 0.76$$

In addition, the phi lambda coefficient (Φ_λ), the squared-error loss agreement index mentioned in Section 3.3.2, can be calculated based on the D study variance component estimates for different cut scores (λ).

It is worth noting that G theory and CTT are conceptually related to each other and that they yield the same results for one-facet crossed study designs for relative decisions. Thus, the generalizability coefficient (E^2_p) obtained for the 30-item case above is identical to the Cronbach's alpha coefficient. Despite this similarity between G theory and CTT, the true strength of G theory is revealed when it is applied to more complex measurement designs involving multiple facets as well as different types of facets.

4 Results of seminal/current research

As mentioned in Section 2.3, various previous empirical studies that analyzed language test data from norm-referenced and criterion-referenced perspectives have been published during the last three decades. Among them, two studies, Brown (1989) and Lee (2006), will be discussed below as illustrative examples of how analyses of test items and test reliability/dependability can inform test development and revision.

The first study by Brown (1989) demonstrated how a combined use of classical item analyses from norm-referenced and criterion-referenced perspectives led to the improvement in the validity of an institutional ESL reading placement test. The motivation for this study was a mismatch recognized by Brown and his colleagues between the test content and the instructional content of the ESL reading course. The 60-item reading test was administered to 194 students as a pretest at the beginning of an academic term. The same test was then administered again to a subsample of the students at the end of an academic term. As part of classical item analyses of the pretest and posttest data, the IF and ID indices for norm-referenced assessment and the DI index for criterion-referenced assessment were obtained. A total of 38 items that were high on all three values were then selected to construct a revised test, for which descriptive statistics were calculated as though it had been administered as the pretest and the posttest. Results showed that, despite the considerably smaller number of items involved in the revised test, the sufficiently normal score distribution showed the suitability of its use as a placement test for norm-referenced score interpretation. Furthermore, the posttest mean was significantly higher than the pretest mean, demonstrating that the revised test was sensitive to achievement in the ESL reading course.

The next example is Lee's (2006) application of G theory to the analysis of TOEFL iBT® speaking pretest data, which informed the decision about the measurement design for the new test section. Lee aimed to identify optimal measurement designs based on different numbers of tasks and raters that could yield acceptable values of the generalizability coefficient (E_p^2) and the index of dependability (Φ). In a series of G theory analyses, the objects of measurement (persons) and various systematic sources of error (tasks, raters, and ratings) were modeled in different ways. Results showed, first, that increasing the number of tasks, rather than the number of raters (or ratings), resulted in higher score reliability and dependability, given the relatively large contribution of tasks rather than raters to the observed score variance, although the effect leveled off for scenarios with more than five tasks. Moreover, results of a series of multivariate G theory analyses, which allowed an investigation of the different sources of measurement error on the relationship among three different speaking task types employed in the section, suggested the feasibility of reporting a single composite score due to high correlations among the universe scores for the different task types. The multivariate G theory analysis also showed that increasing the number of tasks of one task type (listen-to-speak tasks) would result in higher composite score reliability, although the reliability would not differ much among different combinations of the numbers of the three types of tasks when the section length was fixed.

Both studies above signify the importance of careful analyses of test items and score reliability/dependability that are appropriate for the test purpose in language test construction and revision. The successful complementary use of norm-referenced and criterion-referenced item analyses in Brown's (1989) study is noteworthy because it shows that the two frames of reference are not antithetical to each other. Lee's (2006) study demonstrates the strength and flexibility of G theory in accommodating various types of complex measurement designs with multiple facets of measurement for norm-referenced and criterion-referenced assessment purposes.

5 Future directions

As can be seen in the above discussion in this chapter, the notions of norm-referenced and criterion-referenced assessment are useful in understanding key characteristics of language tests that can be designed and used for different purposes. While the methodologies of test construction and analysis for these two frames of reference are now established, there are two possible future research directions that we could take to better integrate the discussion in this chapter into language assessment in practice. One is to discuss results of test item and reliability analysis within a broader context of test-score interpretation and use in decision making as well as their consequences. With the introduction of broad test validity frameworks that deal with language test validity and use such as argument-based approaches to test validation (e.g., Bachman and Palmer 2010; Chapelle, Enright and Jamieson 2008; Kane 2006), it is expected that such discussion will increase in the future. Another potential avenue is to better link the test design principles and statistical issues discussed in this chapter, particularly those concerning criterion-referenced assessment, to the discussion of classroom assessment. Current discussion on classroom and teacher-based assessment seems to focus on alternative assessment that is more closely related to day-to-day instructional activities in the classroom than traditional tests such as portfolio and self/peer assessment as well as dynamic assessment based on sociocultural theory (e.g., Lantolf and Poehner 2008; Poehner and Infante this volume). Some principles discussed in this chapter such as test specifications for criterion-referenced language assessment and some methods for analyzing test items and reliability/dependability can be better integrated into classroom practice (see Brown 2005). It is much hoped that discussion and training on these issues are promoted as part of the current attention to the importance of assessment literacy of various individuals involved in language assessment in the field.

6 References

Bachman, Lyle F. 2004. *Statistical analyses for language assessment.* Cambridge, UK: Cambridge University Press.

Bachman, Lyle F. and Adrian Palmer. 2010. *Language Assessment in Practice: Developing Language Assessments and Justifying their Use in the Real World.* Oxford, UK: Oxford University Press.

Bachman, Lyle F., Brian Lynch and Maureen Mason. 1995. Investigating variability in tasks and rater judgments in a performance test of foreign language speaking. *Language Testing* 12(2): 238–257.

Berk, Ronald A. (Ed.) 1980. *Criterion-referenced measurement: The state of the art.* Baltimore and London: Johns Hopkins University Press.

Brennan, Robert L. 2001. *Generalizability theory.* New York: Springer-Verlag.

Brown, James D. 1989. Improving ESL placement tests using two perspectives. *TESOL Quarterly* 23(1): 65–83.

Brown, James D. 1990. Short-cut estimates of criterion-referenced test consistency. *Language Testing* 7(1): 77–97.

Brown, James D. 1999. The relative importance of persons, items, subtests and languages to TOEFL test variance. *Language Testing* 16(2): 217–238.

Brown, James D. 2005. *Testing in language programs: A comprehensive guide to English language assessment*. New York: McGraw-Hill.

Brown, James D. and Thom Hudson. 2002. *Criterion-referenced language testing*. Cambridge, UK: Cambridge University Press.

Chapelle, Carol A., Mary K. Enright and Joan M. Jamieson. 2008. Test score interpretation and use. In: Carol A. Chapelle, Mary K. Enright and Joan M. Jamieson (eds.). *Building a validity argument for the Test of English as a Foreign Language™*, 1–26. Mahwah, NJ: Lawrence Erlbaum.

Cronbach, Lee J., Goldine C. Glaser, Harinder Nanda and Nageswari Rajaratnam. 1972. *The dependability of behavioral measurements: Theory of generalizability for scores and profiles*. New York: Wiley.

Cziko, G. A. 1981. Psychometric and edumetric approaches to language testing: Implications and applications. *Applied Linguistics* 2(1): 27–44.

Cziko, G. A. 1982. Improving the psychometric, criterion-referenced, and practice qualities of integrative language tests. *TESOL Quarterly* 16(3): 367–379.

Davidson, Fred and Brian K. Lynch. 2002. *Testcraft: A teacher's guide to writing and using language test specifications*. New Haven, CT: Yale University Press.

Ebel, Robert L. and David A. Frisbie. 1991. *Essentials of educational measurement*, 5th ed. Englewood Cliffs, NJ: Prentice-Hall.

Glaser, Robert 1963. Instructional technology and the measurement of learning outcomes: Some questions. *American Psychologist* 18. 519–521.

Hambleton, Ronald K., H. Swaminathan and H. Jane Rogers. 1991. *Fundamentals of item response theory*. Newbury Park, CA: Sage.

Hudson, Thom and Brian K. Lynch. 1984. A criterion-referenced measurement approach to ESL achievement testing. *Language Testing* 1(2): 171–201.

Kane, Michael T. 2006. Validation. In: R. L. Brennan (ed.). *Educational measurement*, 4th ed. 17–64. Westport, CT: American Council on Education and Praeger.

Kunnan, Antony J. 1992. An investigation of a criterion-referenced test using G theory, and factor and cluster analysis. *Language Testing* 9(1): 30–49.

Lantolf, James P. and Matthew E. Poehner (eds.). 2008. *Sociocultural theory and the teaching of second languages*. Oakville, CT: Equinox.

Lee, Yong-Won. 2006. Dependability of scores for a new ESL speaking assessment consisting of integrated and independent tasks. *Language Testing* 23(2): 131–166.

Lynch, Brian K. and Fred Davidson. 1994. Criterion-referenced language test development: Linking curricula, teachers, and tests. *TESOL Quarterly* 28(4): 727–743.

Poehner, E. Matthew and Paolo Infante. This volume. Dynamic assessment in the language classroom. In: Dina Tsagari and Jayanti Banerjee (eds.). *Handbook of Second Language Assessment*. Berlin: DeGruyter Mouton.

Popham, W. J. 1978. *Criterion-referenced measurement*. Englewood Cliffs, NJ: Prentice-Hall.

Popham, W. James. 1981. *Modern educational measurement: A practitioner's perspective*, 2nd ed. Englewood Cliffs, NJ: Prentice-Hall.

Sawaki, Yasuyo. 2007. Construct validation of analytic rating scales in a speaking assessment: Reporting a score profile and composite. *Language Testing* 24(3): 355–390.

Sawaki, Yasuyo. 2013. Classical test theory. In: Antony J. Kunnan (ed.). *Companion to language assessment*, Vol. 3, 1147–1164. New York: Wiley.

Shavelson, Richard J. and Noreen M. Webb. 1991. *Generalizability theory: A primer*. Newbury Park, CA: Sage.

Xi, Xiaoming. 2007. *Validating TOEFL® iBT Speaking and setting score requirements for ITA screening*. *Language Assessment Quarterly* 4(4): 318–351.

Xiaoming Xi and Larry Davis
5 Quality factors in language assessment

1 Introduction

The quality of language assessments has been examined under many different research paradigms and conceptualized in different terms including validity (Lado
1961; Bachman 1990), test usefulness (Bachman and Palmer 1996), fairness (Kunnan 2004), validity argument (Chapelle, Enright and Jamieson 2008) and assessment use argument (Bachman and Palmer 2010). These terms and the associated
concepts, structures and tools provide insights into the evolution of language testers' understanding of ways to characterize and evaluate the quality of a language
assessment. This chapter starts with a historical review of major concepts and
frameworks that have been used to guide investigations of the quality of language
tests. It then discusses a few major frameworks that are currently used in language
testing, and compares them on a number of dimensions. It concludes by charting
future directions and priorities.

2 History

The modern quest for ways to evaluate the quality of language assessments started
in the early 1960s with Lado's work (1961), and has continued vigorously through
the last few decades, drawing inspiration from major paradigm shifts in educational measurement (Cureton 1951; Cronbach 1971; Kane 2006; Messick 1989). While
conceptual developments in educational measurement have generally been the
main impetus for relevant developments in language testing, the field of language
testing has seldom adopted educational measurement approaches without extending, expanding or refining them to make them a closer fit for language assessment.
Another force that has driven developments in conceptual and empirical methods
for investigating the quality of language assessments has been the change in the
prevailing types of assessments, items and tasks, and scoring approaches at different times.

In the broader field of educational assessment, three major types of validity
were dominant from the 1950s to late 1980s: criterion-based (Cureton 1951), content-based (Anastasi 1988; Guion 1977), and construct-based (Cronbach and Meehl
1955). This tripartite approach became codified in the *Standards for Educational
and Psychological Tests and Manuals* (American Psychological Association 1966),
and the three types of validity were primarily used as alternatives to one another.

Early validation work in language testing was primarily concerned with using test scores to predict test takers' performance on other criterion measures through correlational analyses (criterion-related validity), and examining the correspondence between test items and real-world tasks through content analysis (content validity; Lado 1961). The dominance of discrete-point, multiple-choice items in language tests in the 1950s and 1960s led to a focus on criterion-related validity, content validity, test-retest reliability and internal consistency of multiple-choice test items.

The growing use of performance-based, constructed-response tasks in language tests in the 1970s and 1980s prompted applications of new methods for investigating the quality of assessments. Given the popularity during this time of semi-direct speaking tests that used tape-mediated speaking tasks, analyses of the relationship between direct tests such as face-to-face oral interviews and indirect tests (Clark and Swinton 1980) became a major piece of evidence toward validating semi-direct speaking tests. Inter-rater reliability also became a focus of reliability investigations (Clark 1975).

Although construct validity, as a theoretical concept, was proposed in the 1950s (Cronbach and Meehl 1955), it did not attract the attention of language testing researchers until almost three decades later (Bachman 2000). Rather than focusing on measures that are external to the test to aid score interpretation, initial attempts to evaluate construct validity zeroed in on factors that contribute to and account for test performance to explain the meaning of test scores (Palmer, Groot, and Trosper 1981).

Starting in the 1970s, a trend toward a unified view of validity was underway in professional standards and in the work of influential validity theorists including Anastasi (1982), Cronbach (1971, 1984) and Messick (1975, 1980). Messick's (1989) proposal of a unified concept of validity represented a watershed moment in that it not only consolidated earlier thinking and provided a mechanism to conceptualize and investigate validity as a unified phenomenon, but also formally expanded the concept of validity in a fundamental way. The primary contribution of Messick (1989) is that it brought different conceptualizations of validity into a coherent framework of construct validity in a formalized and systematic way. Another contribution is that value implications and test consequences were formally given a prominent role in validity rather than being viewed as a separate quality of a test. Messick emphasized that test constructs and score-based interpretations are not free of value implications and that the social consequences of test use, previously treated as policy issues, actually have important bearings on score interpretation and test use.

While gaining popularity in language testing through Bachman and others' work (Bachman 1990; Cumming and Berwick 1996; Kunnan 1998), the adoption of Messick's complex and highly abstract formulation presented challenges. Three major attempts, by Bachman and Palmer (1996), Kunnan (2000, 2004) and Kane

(Kane 1992; Kane, Crooks and Cohen 1999), responded to the need to simplify the model.

Bachman and Palmer (1996) proposed a notion of test usefulness in which six test qualities (reliability, construct validity, authenticity, interactiveness, impact and practicality) are discussed. They attempted to integrate some aspects of validity from Messick's unitary validity framework, but tried to unpack it in a way that would be accessible to language testing researchers and practitioners.

Kunnan (2000, 2004) developed a framework of test fairness as an overarching test quality to highlight the social, ethical, legal and philosophical aspects of test use. His framework consists of five fairness qualities: validity, absence of bias, access to the test, administration conditions and test consequence.

Kane (1992) started to develop an argument-based approach to test validation in the early 1990s, which later became the most dominant validation approach in both educational measurement and language testing. Kane has applied practical argumentation theories in the development and evaluation of validity arguments, and has continued to refine and expand his framework. In particular, he has increasingly emphasized test use and consequences (Kane 1992, 2006, 2013; Xi 2008).

Although the argument-based approach has established itself as the most prevalent conceptual framework, having been widely cited in both educational measurement and language testing, empirical language testing research has been slow to adopt this framework, and both Messick's unified validity approach and Bachman and Palmer's test usefulness approach still enjoy some degree of popularity (Chapelle and Voss 2013).

3 Comparison of major current frameworks

3.1 Argument-based approach to test validation

Kane's argument-based approach to validation specifies a two-step process (Kane 1992, 2006, 2013). The first step involves constructing an interpretation/use argument (IUA) that provides the claims and the reasoning behind them, through analyzing 1. the chain of inferences linking test performance to score-based interpretation and use, 2. the main warrants (a warrant legitimizes a claim by showing the backing to be relevant), and 3. the assumptions these claims rest on (Kane 2013). Kane shifted from the earlier terminology of interpretative argument to IUA to emphasize both score interpretation and use (Kane 2013). In the second step, the strength of the IUA is evaluated in the context of a validity argument. It starts with a logical evaluation of the IUA to examine whether the argument is complete, and whether the chain of reasoning is clear, coherent, and plausible. Then, the warrants and assumptions should be evaluated in light of different types of backing.

Kane (2013) does not see the network of inferences as a rigid set of rules that govern any possible test interpretation and use. Depending on the particular use of a test, the key inferences that require adequate backing may vary. The inferences that are the most vulnerable should be identified, and concentrated validation efforts should be committed to supporting them.

Kane also takes a pragmatic approach to test validation. He takes issue with Cronbach's view that validation needs to be "a lengthy, even endless process" (Cronbach 1989: 151), which makes validation a daunting exercise. He claims that a customized IUA defines boundaries for each validation effort, providing guidance for the concrete steps needed to evaluate the IUA. Once sufficient evidence has been gathered to provide reasonable support for the intended score interpretation and use specified in the IUA, he argues, the validation process can end (Kane 2013).

Chapelle and colleagues have adapted Kane's framework for language testing (Chapelle, Enright and Jamieson 2008). While the primary focus of Kane's work is to provide a generalized framework and mechanism for test validation rather than to explicate the exact chain of validity inferences, Chapelle et al. focus on expanding and formalizing the typical inferences that are highly relevant to language assessments. For example, in addition to the evaluation, generalization, extrapolation and utilization inferences that are discussed in Kane's earlier work, Chapelle et al. have added domain definition and explanation inferences (Chapelle, Enright and Jamieson 2008) and discussed extensively the types of evidence that can be gathered to support each inference given the intended test use. In more recent work, Chapelle and Voss (2013) attempt to articulate the key inferences, warrants and types of evidence required for tests used for high-stakes purposes vs. low-stakes purposes, offering even more structure and guidance for applying the argument-based approach.

The field of educational measurement has been split on the role of test consequences in validity, although it is generally accepted that test consequences should be addressed in evaluating testing programs (Cronbach 1971, 1988; Cureton 1951; Gulliksen 1950). There are continuing debates regarding whether test consequences should be evaluated as part of validity (Kane 2013; Messick 1989), or under other conceptions of test quality such as utility (Lissitz and Samuelsen 2007), evaluation (Shadish, Cook and Campbell 2002), justification (Cizek 2012), fairness (Kunnan 2004), and justification of assessment use (Bachman and Palmer 2010).

Both Kane and Chapelle maintain the position that major aspects of test consequences should be investigated as part of a validity argument (Chapelle, Enright and Jamieson 2008; Kane 2013). Kane argues that the validation of score interpretation and use should include investigations of test consequences. He further contends that to make the investigations more focused and manageable within the framework of validity, the focus should be on test consequences that are associated with groups of test takers rather than individuals and "widely accepted as legitimate public concerns" (Kane 2013: 61). The utilization inference in Chapelle's work pertains simultaneously to the usefulness of the scores for making the intended decisions, the consequences of score-based decisions, and the impact of assessment use on teaching and learning and the larger educational system or society.

Kane's theoretical work on the argument-based approach to test validation, coupled with its adaptation and application in language testing by Chapelle et al. (2008), provide both conceptual and practical guidance to language test validation researchers. Furthermore, this approach provides clear general guidance on how to determine emphases of validation efforts (Crooks, Kane and Cohen 1996; Kane 2013). It is argued that inferences in the IUA that are key to the proposed interpretation and use are given priority, and that the weakest among the key inferences require the most support. However, the question of how much evidence is sufficient to support a particular inference remains open.

Neither Kane nor Chapelle provides an elaborated and complete treatment of fairness issues in the argument-based approach to test validation. Kane (2013) argues that the differential impact that score-based decision rules have on groups is a major focus of investigations on test consequences. This differential impact of score-based decisions on groups is a critical and integral part of any fairness investigation (Xi 2010). However, it remains unclear what the major fairness issues are that pertain to other validity inferences such as domain definition, evaluation, generalization, explanation and extrapolation, and how these fairness issues may accumulate force through the chain of inferences to impact test use and score-based decisions.

The utility of this framework for classroom-based assessment (Moss 2003) and for local use of standardized assessments has also been questioned (Moss 2013). The argument-based approach to validation may be better suited for large-scale, standardized assessments, and new validity perspectives and paradigms are needed for classroom assessments (Moss 2003). In the argument-based approach, the primary focus is on the interpretation and use of an assessment rather than the local context of use and the problems and questions that are directly relevant to that particular context (Moss, Girard, and Haniford 2006; Moss 2013). Therefore, Moss and her colleagues argue for shifting the focus to the local context in validity inquiries.

3.2 The assessment use argument

Bachman (2005) and Bachman and Palmer (2010) have built on Kane's work and developed the concept of an assessment use argument (AUA) to guide both test development and test use. This approach guides test developers to start the design of a test from the intended outcomes or consequences, and then think about the decisions that need to be made to achieve these positive consequences. Next, test developers need to consider what inferences will need to be made regarding test takers' language ability to support these decisions. Finally, test developers need to develop assessments to elicit the intended language abilities and procedures to score test takers' performances. In evaluating an AUA, a validation researcher starts from claims about test takers' performance on assessment tasks, and works all the way up to claims about intended test outcomes and consequences, evaluating the robustness of the inferential link connecting each step to the next. This process of evaluating the actual interpretation, decision and consequences in relation to the intended interpretation and use is called justification of assessment use. In an AUA, four major claims are specified: intended consequences, decisions, interpretations and assessment records. For each claim, one or more essential qualities are specified. Consideration of these essential qualities prompts test developers to design assessments to optimize them, and guides validation researchers in collecting evidence in relation to each of these five qualities to evaluate the claims regarding intended interpretations.

Unlike the argument-based approach to test validation, which essentially focuses on guiding test validation, or the Evidence-Centered Design (ECD) approach (discussed below), which is primarily a framework guiding test development, the AUA approach attempts to maximize its utility by proposing a unified framework to guide the development as well as the use of assessments.

The AUA framework gives primary emphasis to assessment use and consequences. By labeling the framework as an assessment use argument rather than a validity argument, assessment use and consequences take center stage in test development and evaluation. Intended consequences, the first general claim that any test development effort is expected to begin with, are a central focus of this framework. This treatment has two implications: first, it implies that validity and validation are narrower concepts and may not be broad enough to accommodate discussions and evaluations of test consequences; second, the particular use of an assessment takes priority over score-based interpretations of test takers, teachers, schools or other objects of measurement (Kane 2013). Test fairness issues are also systematically integrated into an AUA by including specific warrants pertaining to fairness to support the four general claims, namely, beneficial consequences, equitable decisions, relevant and sufficient interpretations for the decisions to be made, and consistent assessment results.

Also, in a departure from earlier works characterized by a unified concept of test validity or quality but consisting essentially of a list of unrelated test characteristics, both the argument-based validation framework and the AUA approach offer mechanisms for guiding investigations of an interrelated set of test qualities (e.g., Bachman and Palmer 1996; Kunnan 2004). A particular strength of the AUA framework is that it provides a clear and logical grouping of validity inferences. For example, grouping all inferences relevant to score-based interpretations under the general claim of interpretations can potentially facilitate the synthesis of the evidence supporting this particular claim. Separating decisions and test consequences may also be seen as a positive step toward disentangling different sources of test consequences, not all of which are associated with score-based decisions.

Bachman and Palmer (2010) additionally stress the local nature of an AUA, arguing that evaluations of the qualities of language assessments associated with the four major claims have to be made in relation to particular intended test consequences, decisions, target language use domains and test-taker populations. While acknowledging that the expanded list of test qualities in an AUA framework may be seen as prescriptive, they stress the utility of the AUA in providing a structure and an associated set of tools for developing and justifying the use of assessments.

Bachman and Palmer's AUA framework attempts to provide a straightforward narrative for organizing key considerations and issues when developing and validating assessments. They have also attempted to use terminology that is more intuitive to non-specialists to help facilitate communication to a general audience regarding important concepts and considerations in test development and validation work. Despite this effort, this framework may still be too complex to be used by professional test developers and validation researchers without extensive training, not to mention by teachers. The claims and the kinds of validation approaches needed to support these different claims are still very sophisticated, and require advanced skills to understand and apply in practice. Moreover, the use of new terms for existing concepts may create confusion when trying to align Bachman and Palmer's framework with the work of others. Finally, although Bachman and Palmer discuss "trade-offs" in prioritizing the allocation of resources in a specific test development situation, no clear guidance is provided as to how to prioritize investigations of these four comprehensive claims. Teachers and practitioners may still be intimidated by the massive body of evidence that is required to support an AUA.

3.3 Evidence-centered design

Evidence-Centered Design (ECD) is a framework for implementing evidence-based arguments in assessment design and delivery (Mislevy and Risconcente 2005). Like other argument-based validity frameworks, a formal argument structure underlies the ECD approach, but the focus of this structure is to clarify the chain of reasoning in the design and delivery phases of assessment, rather than specifically to validate test uses.

Inspired by the domains of architecture and software design, the ECD framework conceptualizes assessment as a series of layers including Domain Analysis, Domain Modeling, Conceptual Assessment Framework, Assessment Implementation and Assessment Delivery (Mislevy and Risconcente 2005). Such layers allow a complex system to be organized as a collection of subsystems within which related components and their interactions can be more easily conceptualized. Each layer occupies a succeeding step in the design and implementation process, but it is recognized that development processes will usually occur iteratively, with repeated cycles of work occurring both across layers and concurrently within layers.

In the domain analysis layer information is developed regarding the construct to be measured, including both a definition of the language ability of interest and the target language use domain about which inferences will be made. In the domain modeling layer an assessment argument is developed that describes the linkage from evidence collected in the test to claims or inferences about test takers. The conceptual assessment framework (CAF) is where the technical elements of the test are described and organized including a) a student model, b) evidence models, c) a task model, and d) an assembly model (Mislevy and Yin 2012). In the assessment implementation layer the actual test materials and scoring procedures are finalized, and the design of the assessment is largely complete. Finally, the assessment delivery layer includes the operational processes of the test, including selection of test items, presentation of items to test takers, evaluation of test-taker responses, and reporting of scores.

As mentioned previously, the major focus of ECD is the design of assessments rather than the evaluation of specific test uses or consequences. Nonetheless, the ECD framework requires explicit and detailed descriptions of the type of evidence to be collected and how this evidence will lead to claims about test takers, which can then serve as a basis for prototyping, pilot and field studies, and subsequent validation efforts. The conceptual and empirical data gathered through the ECD-driven test design and development process also constitute validity evidence that can be integrated into a validity argument. Evidence-centered design employs a sophisticated argument structure, similar to the frameworks of Kane (2013) and Bachman and Palmer (2010), and provides highly practical guidance for organizing the assessment development process. Although more limited in focus than the other frameworks mentioned in this chapter, the targeted focus on test design means that ECD arguably provides the most specific and useful guidance for test developers.

3.4 Socio-cognitive framework

The socio-cognitive framework (Weir 2005) is so named because emphasis is placed on both the context in which language is used and the cognition of the test taker. Nonetheless, Weir's framework models the process of measurement generally, starting with the characteristics of the test taker and proceeding through test design, administration, scoring, and consequences. The socio-cognitive framework is organized both temporally in that it describes the sequential nature of test development and validation, and conceptually in that it identifies the major elements that influence validity and how these elements interact (Taylor 2011). In addition, the framework models the testing process itself, including the test taker, the response, and the resulting score; these aspects of the testing context serve to link the various aspects of validity.

The socio-cognitive framework essentially brings five traditional types of validity together, with a focus on the cognitive operations and processes involved in language use tasks. The first is theory-based validity, which pertains to the internal processes and resources that are of interest for measurement, and in traditional terms would correspond to construct validity. The second is context validity, which incorporates issues related to the design and administration of the test and the specific demands that assessment tasks make on the test taker, and includes elements often associated with content validity. The third is scoring validity, which entails issues of score reliability and the extent to which scores reflect the language abilities of interest, as captured in the quality of scoring rubrics. The fourth is criterion-related validity, which refers to the extent to which the test agrees with or predicts other measures of the same ability. The fifth and final element is consequential validity, which includes the impact of the assessment on individuals, classrooms, and the broader society.

The socio-cognitive framework is intended to guide a broad range of validation activities, and the focus on the interaction between test-taker cognition, task, and scoring makes the model suited for guiding test development activities as well. However, unlike the general frameworks of Kane (2013) and Bachman and Palmer (2010), the socio-cognitive framework does not explicitly include a formal argument structure for organizing validity claims and guiding research activities. Weir (2005) provides a number of case studies to exemplify his approach, but overall, there is relatively little guidance regarding how questions should be prioritized when collecting evidence to support score inferences.

Additionally, Weir (2005: 1) defines test validation as "the process of generating evidence to support the well-foundedness of inferences concerning [a] trait from test scores (...)." This definition of test validation seems to focus on score interpretation with little explicit consideration given to score use. This emphasis on score interpretation is also reflected in the omission of any discussion related to the quality of decisions made based on test scores, such as the appropriateness of decision rules and procedures and decision accuracy and consistency. Weir's definition of test validation also seems somewhat at odds with his framework as a whole, which explicitly includes consideration of test consequences. Finally, the temporal nature of Weir's model, while intended to provide "a map of *what* should be happening in terms of validation and just as importantly *when*" (Weir 2005: 43, italics in the original), may lead to the interpretation that validation is a linear process. Although some validity evidence can only be collected after the test goes operational (e.g., consequential validity), validation activities are typically much more dynamic and iterative.

3.5 Validity evaluation

While recent validity frameworks (e.g., Bachman and Palmer 2010) have stressed the importance of test use as an organizing concept in assessment validation, an even greater focus on the specific uses and contexts of assessment has been advocated by the proponents of validity evaluation (Moss 1998; Norris 2008; Shepard

1993). The organizing concept underlying this approach is that assessments are programs, and can be investigated using program evaluation techniques. Other characteristics of this approach include:
- A focus on the use or purposes of assessment within a specific context,
- A recognition that test users and other stakeholders play a key role in the evaluation process, and
- A commitment to the use of validation results.

Accordingly, validation activities must address questions of interest to those who are in a position to act on the findings, and must be understandable to these users. This approach has been informed by recent developments in program evaluation, particularly utilization-focused program evaluation (Patton 2008), and represents to some degree a reaction to the focus of most validity frameworks on the validation of standardized assessments. Moss (2013) notes that while argument-based validation frameworks have been useful for test developers, such frameworks do not necessarily capture the full range and complexity of assessment uses by teachers and others working in local contexts. In contrast, the validity evaluation approach prioritizes the local use of assessments, and Moss suggests that rather than organizing validation theory around a particular assessment, the needs or questions relevant to a specific context might be used as the organizing locus for validation work.

The application of the validity evaluation approach for language assessment has been most thoroughly explored in the work of Norris (e.g., Norris 2008). He outlines an evaluation process where an evaluator and test users work closely together to understand the characteristics of the educational program, identify the purpose(s) of the evaluation, select methods and gather the information needed to satisfy the evaluation purpose(s), and finally understand the results and take action.

Starting with use as the basis of validation efforts represents a way of looking at the world that is quite different from the frameworks discussed earlier. While it is mainstream to frame validation arguments in terms of uses, major validation frameworks have been motivated by the need to validate the uses (or inferences) of a particular assessment; one starts with the test and then validates various claims or uses. In contrast, the validity evaluation approach starts with the specific use, and then evaluates the extent to which different sources of information contribute to that use. An advantage of this approach is that it provides an explicit mechanism for prioritizing validation activities: the questions most central to the needs of the specific test users will be prioritized. In addition, the emphasis on how validity evidence is actually used by decision makers helps to ensure that the intended benefits of assessment are in fact realized. A related benefit is that involving test users in the validity evaluation process can build expertise among these users and may promote a more nuanced and sophisticated use of assessment.

On the other hand, the focus on local contexts makes this approach less useful for those concerned with the development and validation of large-scale assessments. Within language assessment, published work describing the use of the validity evaluation approach has typically been limited to local evaluation projects where the focus of evaluation was an educational program, and tests or other assessments were just one component of the program. Moreover, the existence of an "evaluator" to guide the validation process is implied in this approach, and in local situations such expertise may not be available. This validity evaluation approach also intensifies questions regarding who is responsible for ensuring the appropriate use of assessment instruments, especially when externally developed tools such as standardized tests are employed. To what degree are test developers versus local evaluators and decision makers ultimately responsible for the use (or misuse) of an assessment? Nonetheless, within local contexts, particularly where the motivation for assessment is instructional improvement or other local priorities, validity evaluation provides a model for making sure that assessment actually leads to the achievement of these priorities (Norris 2008).

4 Future directions

4.1 Articulating an elaborated argument for typical test uses

Most current test evaluation approaches (Bachman and Palmer 2010; Chapelle, Enright and Jamieson 2008; Kane 2013; Norris 2008) emphasize tailoring the construction and justification of a validity argument or an assessment use argument to a specific testing context. Test developers and researchers can make use of the general structures offered by these approaches, but they also have a fairly high level of latitude in developing the specific argument. However, the flexibility needed for specific testing contexts may introduce two challenges. First, constructing a high-quality IUA or AUA tailored to a specific language testing context requires technical skills and knowledge which may not be available to practitioners. Second, the local nature of arguments makes it harder to evaluate the completeness, coherence and plausibility of each argument as there is no common yardstick against which arguments can be judged.

We argue that to provide more specific guidance for test evaluation efforts, IUA or AUA templates could be developed for a variety of typical test uses, such as admission to academic institutions, immigration, or academic placement. Such templates would lay out the key claims, warrants, rebuttals and backing needed for the specific assessment use, and once reviewed and agreed upon, could potentially become part of language testing professional standards. In addition, guidelines could be provided for evaluating the strength of each piece of evidence and the combined body of evidence. A very straightforward example is the level of reliability that is acceptable for different assessment uses.

Chapelle and Voss (2013) have already moved in this direction by specifying the IUAs for assessments supporting high-stakes decisions versus low-stakes decisions, but more work is needed to develop more specific arguments for typical test uses, such as the one developed by Chapelle, Enright, and Jamieson (2008) for tests used for admissions purposes. The IUAs for different high-stakes uses such as admissions and teacher licensure may have important distinctions in terms of essential inferences, major warrants, and types of backing that may be needed.

4.2 Linking interpretations to decisions and assessment use

Some educational measurement researchers are in favor of confining validity to the "accuracy of score-based interpretations" (Popham 1997), which implies that score-based interpretation and use can be treated separately. However, we argue that test-score interpretations do not exist independently of score-based decisions and assessment use, which reflect value judgments and have consequences on different stakeholders in the assessment process. Kane acknowledges that interpretation and test use "tend to be entwined in practice" (2013: 2). Bachman and Palmer (2010) make it very explicit in their AUA approach that evaluations of the adequacy of score-based interpretations have to include their relevance to and sufficiency for the intended decision (Bachman and Palmer 2010).

Suppose we are developing an English proficiency test for certifying EFL teachers. We would need to sample the target language use domain appropriately to include test tasks that elicit evidence that is sensitive to the identification of minimally competent EFL teachers. We would need to include an appropriate range of difficulty levels to ensure we have sufficient items to maximize the measurement precision for certain ability ranges. We would need the test scores to be reliable for classifying candidates into qualified and unqualified teachers, and would also need to maximize the decision accuracy and consistency given the cut score (rather than the standard reliability estimates). We would need to establish that the test score can predict EFL teachers' English communication skills in the real-world teaching context. The score-based interpretation that an individual is qualified to teach must draw upon all evidence discussed so far and would be closely tied to the intended assessment use (certification). There is generally no such thing as an "abstract" score-interpretation that does not draw upon a defined test use.

Beyond score interpretation, we would also need to establish appropriate cut scores to prioritize one type of classification error over the other, after carefully weighing the potential consequences of making different types of classification errors. We would also need to investigate the impact of the decisions on test takers, the program, the educational system, and the broader society. The intended test use defines the score interpretation and builds on it. Therefore, we argue that future empirical research to support the score-based interpretation should systematically integrate considerations about the intended use of the assessment scores.

4.3 Test consequences and test providers' responsibilities

The quality of a test cannot be confined to technical qualities; whether the use of an assessment and its results for decision making brings about beneficial consequences is a key factor in evaluating the quality of a test (Bachman and Palmer 2010). Assessment use and consequences are integrated into all of the argument-based approaches, and also are a key element of Messick's framework (Messick 1989). However, a major challenge when considering test consequences is to identify the roles and responsibilities of different stakeholders, including test providers, test users/decision makers, and others.

There are several types of test consequences: those that can be traced back to the assessment or the assessment process, those associated with the score-based decision rule and/or procedure, those associated with effects on curriculum, teaching, or educational policies, and those incurred by the use of test scores for unintended purposes. Test consequences can have many different determinants, some of which, such as the design of the test, can be directly controlled by test providers. Some determinants, such as the choice of test preparation materials, curriculum and educational policies, are mostly beyond the control of the test providers, while others, such as the appropriate use of an assessment, or establishing an appropriate decision rule and procedure, can be jointly influenced by test providers and users. In many cases, multiple forces are at play to incur intended or negative consequences. While recognizing that test users play an important role in assessment use, language testers have the obligation to ensure that the positive consequences of a language assessment outweigh potential negative consequences. An important step toward that is to clearly define the roles and responsibilities of test providers.

The "social responsibility" view emphasizes the social mission of testing organizations, which entails assuming full responsibility for social consequences. In contrast, the "professional responsibility" view confines the responsibilities of test providers to "limited and predicted social responsibilities" that are manageable through codes of professional standards (Davies 1997). Kane holds a similar view that while the test user has the ultimate responsibility for appropriate test use, the test developer is obligated to facilitate appropriate test use to the extent possible (Kane 2013).

There is a general consensus that the test provider has a major responsibility for ensuring that negative consequences are not associated with the assessment or the assessment process (Messick 1989), but should we expand a test provider's responsibilities beyond this? It has become a more common practice for test providers to produce documentation describing their assessments (including test design principles, sample test tasks, scoring rubrics, etc.) to help score users understand their assessments and interpret scores. They are also moving in the direction of helping score users develop appropriate rules and procedures to ensure accurate and equitable decisions, as test providers have the knowledge and expertise to advise score users on how the assessment results may be best used to support decision-making in a particular context. The question of who bears responsibility for the broader consequences of an assessment is more difficult to answer. However, as Xi (2008) points out, this issue provides opportunities for researchers who focus on the washback of language tests to try to develop theories and guidelines that define the best practices for each responsible party involved.

Finally, using tests for unintended purposes may have severe adverse impacts on some stakeholders. And, it must be recognized that for many testing organizations there is a tension between a financial interest in promoting the maximum use of a test and an ethical duty to ensure that the test is used only where appropriate. Although it is not feasible for test providers to "police" the use of their own assessments, it is desirable for them to become more prescriptive about the types of uses that are supported by validity evidence, to communicate clearly what additional evidence may be collected by local users to support natural extensions of the intended test uses, and what uses are clearly discouraged. When a clear misuse of a particular test comes to the attention of the test provider, it is in the best interest of the provider to take action to help the user understand the potential adverse impact, and to encourage the user to select a more appropriate test for their specific purpose. While there is financial benefit to encouraging the widest possible use of a test, a proactive stance in encouraging appropriate use has benefits for both test stakeholders as well as the reputation of the test provider.

5 References

American Psychological Association (APA), American Educational Research Association (AERA) and National Council on Measurement in Education (NCME). 1966. *Standards for educational and psychological tests and manuals*. Washington, DC: American Educational Research Association.

Anastasi, Anne. 1982. *Psychological testing*, 5th ed. New York: Macmillan.

Anastasi, Anne. 1988. *Psychological testing*, 6th ed. New York: Macmillan.

Bachman, Lyle F. 1990. *Fundamental considerations in language testing*. Oxford, UK: Oxford University Press.

Bachman, Lyle F. 2000. Modern language testing at the turn of the century: Assuring that what we count counts. *Language Testing* 17(1): 1–42.

Bachman, Lyle F. 2005. Building and supporting a case for test use. *Language Assessment Quarterly* 2(1): 1–34.

Bachman, Lyle F. and Adrian Palmer. 1996. *Language testing in practice: Designing and developing useful language tests*. Oxford, UK: Oxford University Press.

Bachman, Lyle F. and Adrian Palmer. 2010. *Language assessment in practice: Developing language assessments and justifying their use in the real world*. Oxford, UK: Oxford University Press.

Chapelle, Carol and Erik Voss. 2013. Evaluation of language tests through validation research. In: Antony Kunnan (ed.). *The companion to language assessment*, 1081–1097. Boston: Wiley-Blackwell.

Chapelle, Carol A., Mary K. Enright and Joan M. Jamieson (eds.). 2008. *Building a validity argument for the test of English as a foreign language™*. Mahwah, NJ: Lawrence Erlbaum.

Cizek, Gregory. 2012. Defining and distinguishing validity: Interpretations of score meaning and justifications of test use. *Psychological Methods* 17(1): 31–43.

Clark, John L. D. 1975. Theoretical and technical considerations in oral proficiency testing. In: Randall Jones and Bernard Spolsky (eds.). *Language testing proficiency*, 10–24. Arlington, VA: Center for Applied Linguistics.

Clark, John L. D. and Spencer S. Swinton. 1980. *The test of spoken English as a measure of communicative ability in English-medium instructional settings*. TOEFL Research Report 7. Princeton, NJ: Educational Testing Service. http://www.ets.org/Media/Research/pdf/RR-80-33.pdf (accessed 19 June 2014).

Cronbach, Lee J. and Paul E. Meehl. 1955. Construct validity in psychological tests. *Psychological Bulletin* 52: 281–302.

Cronbach, Lee J. 1971. Test validation. In: Robert L. Thorndike (ed.). *Educational Measurement*, 2nd ed. 443–507. Washington, DC: American Council on Education.

Cronbach, Lee J. 1984. *Essentials of psychological testing*. New York: Harper and Row.

Cronbach, Lee J. 1988. Five perspectives on the validity argument. In: Howard Wainer and Henry I. Braun (eds.). *Test validity*, 3–17. Hillsdale, NJ: Erlbaum Associates.

Cronbach, Lee J. 1989. Construct validation after thirty years. In: Robert Linn (ed.). *Intelligence: Measurement, theory, and public policy*, 147–171. Urbana: University of Illinois Press.

Crooks, Terry J., Michael T. Kane and Allan S. Cohen. 1996. Threats to the valid use of assessments. *Assessment in Education: Principles, Policy & Practice* 3(3): 265–285.

Cumming, Alister and Richard Berwick (eds.). 1996. *Validation in language testing*. Clevedon, U.K.: Multilingual Matters.

Cureton, Edward. 1951. Validity. In: Everett F. Lindquist (ed.). *Educational Measurement*, 1st ed. 621–694.

Davies, Alan. 1997. Demands of being professional in language testing. *Language Testing* 14(3): 328–339.

Guion, Robert M. 1977. Content validity: The source of my discontent. *Applied Psychological Measurement* 1(1): 1–10.

Gulliksen, Harold. 1950. *Theory of mental tests*. New York: Wiley.

Kane, Michael. 1992. An argument-based approach to validity. *Psychological Bulletin* 112(3): 527–535.

Kane, Michael. 2006. Validation. In: Robert L. Brennan (ed.). *Educational measurement*, 4th ed. 18–64. Washington, DC: American Council on Education and Praeger.

Kane, Michael. 2013. Validating the interpretations and uses of test scores. *Journal of Educational Measurement* 50(1): 1–73.

Kane, Michael, Terence Crooks and Allan Cohen. 1999. Validating measures of performance. *Educational Measurement: Issues and Practice* 18(2): 5–17.

Kunnan, Antony J. (ed.). 1998. Validation in language assessment: Selected papers from the 17th Language Testing Research Colloquium (LTRC). Mahwah, NJ: Lawrence Erlbaum.

Kunnan, Antony J. 2000. Fairness and justice for all. In: Antony J. Kunnan (ed.). *Fairness and validation in language assessment*, 1–14. Cambridge, UK: Cambridge University Press.

Kunnan, Antony J. 2004. Test fairness. In: Michael Milanovic and Cyril Weir (eds.). *European language testing in a global context*, 27–48. Proceedings of the ALTE Barcelona Conference. Cambridge, UK: Cambridge University Press.

Lado, Robert. 1961. *Language testing*. New York: McGraw-Hill.

Lissitz, Robert and Karen Samuelsen. 2007. A suggested change in terminology and emphasis regarding validity and education. *Educational Researcher* 36(8): 437–448.

Messick, Samuel. 1975. The standard problem: Meaning and values in measurement and evaluation. *American Psychologist* 30(10): 955–966.

Messick, Samuel. 1980. Test validity and the ethics of assessment. *American Psychologist* 35(11): 1012–1027.

Messick, Samuel. 1989. Validity. In: Robert L. Linn (ed.). *Educational measurement*, 3rd ed. 13–103. New York: Macmillan.

Mislevy, Robert J. and Michelle Risconscente. 2005. Evidence-centered assessment design: Layers, concepts, and terminology. PADI Technical Report No. 9. Menlo Park, CA: SRI International and University of Maryland. http://padi.sri.com/downloads/TR9_ECD.pdf (accessed 27 November 2013).

Mislevy, Robert J. and Chengbin Yin. 2012. Evidence-centered design in language testing. In: Glenn Fulcher and Fred Davidson (eds.). *The Routledge handbook of language testing*, 208–222. London and New York: Routledge.

Moss, Pamela A. 1998. The role of consequences in validity theory. *Educational Measurement: Issues and Practices*, 17(2): 6–12.

Moss, Pamela A. 2003. Reconceptualizing validity for classroom assessment. *Educational Measurement: Issues and Practices* 22(4): 13–25.

Moss, Pamela A. 2013. Validity in action: Lessons from studies of data use. *Journal of Educational Measurement* 50(1): 91–98.

Moss, Pamela A., Brian J. Girard and Laura C. Haniford. 2006. Validity in educational assessment. *Review of Research in Education* 30: 109–162.

Norris, John M. 2008. *Validity evaluation in language assessment*. Frankfurt am Main: Peter Lang.

Palmer, Adrian S., Peter J. M. Groot and George A. Trosper (eds.). 1981. *The construct validation of tests of communicative competence*. Washington, DC: TESOL.

Patton, Michael Quinn. 2008. *Utilization-focused evaluation*, 4th ed. Thousand Oaks, CA: SAGE.

Popham, James W. 1997. Consequential validity: Right concern – wrong concept. *Educational Measurement: Issues and Practice* 16(2): 9–13.

Shadish, William R., Thomas D. Cook and Donald T. Campbell. 2002. *Experimental and quasi-experimental designs for generalized causal inference*. Boston: Houghton Mifflin.

Shepard, Lorrie A. 1993. Evaluating test validity. *Review of Research in Education* 19: 405–450.

Taylor, Lynda. 2011. *Examining speaking: Research and practice in assessing second language speaking*. Cambridge, UK: UCLES/Cambridge University Press.

Weir, Cyril J. 2005. *Language testing and validation: An evidence-based approach*. New York: Palgrave MacMillan.

Xi, Xiaoming. 2008. Methods of test validation. In: Elana Shohamy and Nancy H. Hornberger (eds.). *Encyclopedia of Language and Education*, Vol. 7, 177–196 (*Language Testing and Assessment*, 2nd ed.). New York: Springer.

Xi, Xiaoming. 2010. How do we go about investigating test fairness? *Language Testing* 27(2): 147–170.

Nick Saville and Hanan Khalifa
6 The impact of language assessment

1 Introduction

This chapter introduces the notion of impact in language assessment and illustrates the concept of impact by design in test development and validation. Impact appeared in the assessment literature as an extension of washback, the influence of assessment within educational contexts. Impact is now considered to be the superordinate concept covering the wider effects and consequences resulting from the development and use of language assessments in societal contexts.

In providing a historical perspective, we look first at effects and consequences within sociological research and then move on to cover washback, drawing on key works in the assessment literature from the 1990s (Alderson and Wall 1993), as well as models of washback and approaches to researching washback (Bailey 1996; Cheng 2004; Hughes 1993; Green 2003, 2007; Wall 2005; Watanabe 2004).

Moving beyond washback, we contextualize impact within validity theory, focusing on the seminal works of Messick (1989, 1996) and the influence of Bachman and Palmer (1996) in language testing, and we introduce the notion of a theory of action which incorporates the socio-political change processes that influence language teaching, learning and assessment (Saville 2009). It is argued that the investigation of impact needs to be integrated into routine validation procedures by test providers in order to anticipate and manage the effects and consequences of testing over time.

The methodology for investigating impact needs to take account of appropriate research paradigms for educational contexts. For example, "real world research" (Robson 2002) uses mixed methods designs collecting both qualitative and quantitative data to shed light on assessment use in context. The development of a suitable toolkit and standard operating procedures are central to the routine investigation of impact by examination providers.

Two research projects are used to illustrate how impact-related research can be situated within a real-world research paradigm and how researching impact is an integral feature of test validation programs. The concluding section briefly considers future challenges and ways in which this aspect of language assessment might develop.

2 A historical perspective

2.1 Effects and consequences

Since the early 20th century, sociologists have discussed the effects and consequences of social action, focusing on whether desirable and planned effects are achieved, or whether unplanned or undesirable effects occur as a result of social policies.

Famously, Robert K. Merton (1936) applied a systematic analysis to the problem of "unanticipated consequences of purposive social action", emphasising that planned ("purposive") action is always concerned with human behaviour and typically has unforeseen side effects. This became known as the law of unintended consequences.

Merton reminds us of the unpredictability of social action and the problem of causal imputation, i.e. of ascertaining "the extent to which 'consequences' may justifiably be attributed to certain actions" (1936: 897). He points out that it is difficult to attribute effects to specific causes and that unintended consequences typically fall into three categories: positive benefits which had not been planned, negative or perverse effects, and problems which arise as a result of mistakes or lack of knowledge. The interaction between policy, the incentives that are created, and the behaviour of the people involved, leads to both unintended and unanticipated consequences.

This analysis is central to our discussion of impact because assessment systems play a central role in educational policy-making and are expected to contribute to specific policy goals. However, as Fullan (1993) points out, educational systems are particularly prone to the unintended effects of government policies, noting that initiatives and reforms often do not work because the change process is "uncontrollably complex and in many cases unknowable." The causes of any unintended consequences are, therefore, not easily traceable to a single source, but are related to the inherent complexity of social systems and result from one part of a system responding to changes in another part of the same system or to changes in the wider environment.

The effects and consequences of high stakes examinations are wide ranging and significantly affect the life chances of individual test takers, e.g., by controlling access to education and employment. They also influence the social systems in which they play a part when results are used to make important decisions, e.g., about curriculum planning or funding in schools, or when commercial opportunities are created (e.g., in tutoring or publishing).

The unintended effects and consequences of assessment policies are particularly problematic when they create perverse incentives, a phenomenon sometimes known as Goodhart's Law (Goodhart 1975). Goodhart suggests that, when a social indicator is made a target for the purpose of conducting policy, it loses the information that enabled it to play such a role. This explains, for example, why high stakes tests can lead to negative effects when exam results are used to evaluate schools (e.g., using league tables). Teachers change their practices in order to improve test results, but in so doing impact negatively on learning (e.g., "too much teaching to the test").

In summary, these mechanisms need to be borne in mind when addressing the effects and consequences of language assessment and how they can be investigated. They operate on at least two levels: a macro level, within educational systems and society; and a micro level, focusing on the individuals directly involved in using tests in their own contexts. Understanding the interaction between the micro and macro contexts is central to the investigation of impact but first we need to consider washback hypotheses which are predominantly concerned with the micro context before moving to consider impact as a superordinate concept looking at both contexts.

2.2 Washback hypotheses and models

As noted, washback pre-dates the term impact and concerns the "backward flow" of effects from testing onto teaching and learning in schools and classrooms[1].

In 1993, Alderson and Wall asked whether washback is simply a "metaphor" that "encourages us to explore the role of tests in learning and the relationship between teaching and testing." They concluded that it is much more than that, and that we need to establish in what ways tests or other factors from the educational contexts influence language education. They also noted that many claims had been made about "washback effects", but were rarely backed up by evidence. A research agenda was needed, and so in posing the question "does washback exist?", they sought to problematise the concept and proposed 15 washback hypotheses as the basis for the necessary investigations (Alderson and Wall 1993: 120).

They suggested that appropriate research should be carried out to investigate these hypotheses and their call for an increase in empirical studies was taken up by a growing number of researchers in different parts of the world. The subsequent attention given to washback has shown that it is even more complex than originally envisaged. During the 1990s the various washback hypotheses were focused on and explored in more depth, and several researchers developed "washback models" in order to conceptualize and investigate washback effects more systematically. The publications of Bailey (1996, 1999), Cheng (1998, 2004, 2005), Hughes (1989), Milanovic and Saville (1996), Watanabe (1997, 2004), Wall (2005) and Green (2003, 2007) are particularly noteworthy.

Watanabe (1997) discusses *methodology* in washback studies and illustrates his points with examples taken from his research in Japan. He conceptualizes washback in terms of *five dimensions*: specificity, intensity, length, intentionality and value. He suggests the aspects of learning/teaching that may be influenced by an examination and three factors that facilitate the process of washback. They are: *test-related*; *status-related*; and *stakeholder-related*. He also sought to isolate the

---

1 Andrews (1994) notes that in the general educational literature backwash has been the preferred term, whereas in language education there is a preference for washback (see Alderson 2004).

features of a test which might be directly responsible for *observable behaviours* in classrooms.

Cheng (1998, 2005) reports on research into examination reforms in Hong Kong during the 1990s and the washback of these changes on *teaching materials* and *methodology*. In her conclusions she observed that the methodology employed by teachers tended to change more slowly than the content of teaching. In other words, the *what* changed as a consequence of the new examinations, but changes in the *how* were much more limited and slower to take effect.

In their jointly edited volume in 2004, Cheng and Watanabe brought together several other important papers based on work carried out in the 1990s. They classify the research into two major types: studies related to traditional high-stakes tests invoking *negative impacts* and studies related to examinations which had been modified to produce desirable, *positive change*. The volume also includes: a paper by Andrews on *washback and curriculum innovation* with reference to Hong Kong; two papers on *IELTS*, one by Saville and Hawkey dealing with *washback on teaching materials* and the other by Hayes and Read investigating IELTS test preparation classes in New Zealand; a paper by Watanabe on *teacher factors* mediating washback (discussed above); five papers dealing with *educational reforms* involving high-stakes language assessment in *different parts of the world* – in the USA (Stecher, et al.), Australia (Burrows), Hong Kong (Cheng), China (Qi), and Israel (Ferman).

This range of papers demonstrated how far the field had moved on in the decade since Alderson and Wall first asked the question "does washback exist?" In his foreword to the volume, Alderson claims that there is no doubt that "washback does indeed exist" and in light of the growing body of research, he notes that "the phenomenon is a hugely complex matter" and "very far from being a simple case of tests having negative impact on teaching." The question is no longer does washback exist but rather, *"what does washback look like?","what brings washback about?"* and *"why does washback exist?"*

Hughes (1989) was amongst the first to model the "backwash" concept and to provide testers with practical guidance for action. He focused on using tests to bring about positive effects in language learning contexts, seeing the relationship between teaching and testing as a key element, and suggested that test developers should "promote this beneficial effect." He suggested testers should:
– Test the abilities whose development you want to encourage.
– Sample widely and unpredictably.
– Use direct testing.
– Make testing criterion-referenced.
– Base achievement tests on objectives.
– Ensure the test is known and understood by students and teachers.
– Provide assistance to teachers.

Bailey (1996) was innovative in assembling a *basic model of washback*. Building on an unpublished paper of Hughes (1993), she proposed a three-pronged model fo-

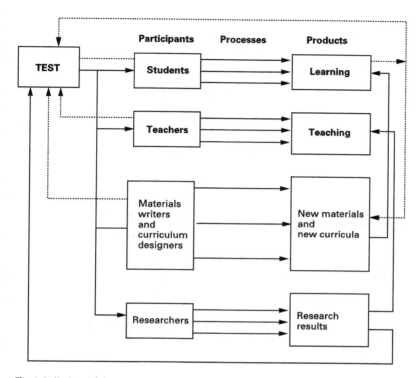

Fig. 1: Bailey's model.

cusing on *participants, processes and products* (see Figure 1). She concludes that a test will promote beneficial washback to the extent that it is based on sound theoretical principles, it uses authentic tasks and texts, and the test takers buy into the assessment process (Bailey 1996: 275–277).

Green's model (2007: 24) shifts the emphasis away from "a recipe" for achieving positive washback towards a descriptive and partially explanatory tool addressing what goes on in order to cause the various washback effects. He adds new features, particularly focusing on *process aspects* (washback direction, variability and intensity), and on how test design (the focal construct) influences the washback effects (see Messick (1996) on construct-irrelevant variance and construct under-representation). He concludes that washback has the most powerful effects on teaching and learning when the test is challenging and the results are important for the participants (see Figure 2).

At the same time as the washback models were being developed, other researchers were focusing on relevant *research methods* and the issues to be addressed in conducting washback research in educational contexts, e.g., the difficulty of establishing dependent variables (Green 2007); the importance of qualitative

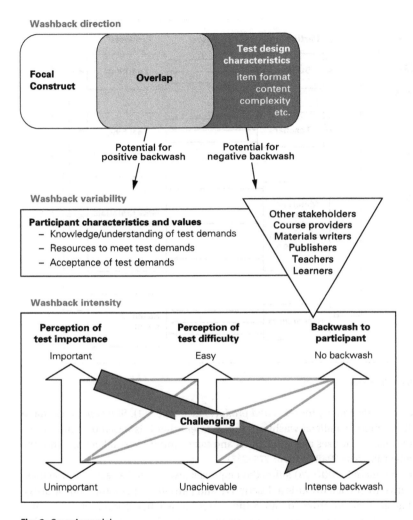

Fig. 2: Green's model.

methods, including use of case studies. The work of Wall (2005) was particularly influential in moving impact research beyond the washback models summarised above. She questioned how assessment policies reflect educational ideologies and how they operate overtly as a mechanism for change, leading to changes in teaching/learning practices. Using insights from innovation theory she demonstrates how the application of these ideas ("management of change" and "diffusion of innovation") increases our understanding of the *hows* and the *whys* of washback and the broader aspects of impact. From this body of work a more comprehensive understanding of impact emerged. The next section focuses on impact as a superordinate concept and addresses how impact is conceptualised within a validity theory.

2.3 Impact and validity

The adherence to theoretical principles and definition of focal constructs was highlighted in all washback models as necessary conditions in ensuring that a test is appropriate for its purpose and contexts of use. Appropriate uses of test scores depend on this, as set out for example, in a validity argument and in keeping with contemporary validity and validation theories. Messick (1996), in an influential paper on validity and washback, recommends seeking "validity by design" as a basis for washback and Bachman and Palmer (1996: 22) support this view in defining validation as "the on-going process of demonstrating that a particular interpretation of test scores is justified, and [validation] involves, essentially, building a logical case in support of a particular interpretation and providing evidence justifying that interpretation."

However, there has been growing concern for the *scope* of the validity argument. Messick (1989: 19) emphasises the importance of the consequential aspects of validity when he states that "the social values and the social consequences [of a test] cannot be ignored in considerations of validity", but some commentators think this does not go far enough. Moss (1998: 11), for example, in highlighting the importance of the social impact of assessment practices, suggests that "the scope of the argument goes well beyond … test specific evaluation practices; it entails on-going evaluation of the dialectical relationship between the products and practices of testing, writ large, and the social reality that is recursively represented and transformed."

McNamara and Roever also note that "integrating studies of washback and impact into a larger interpretive argument has the advantage of framing the significance of such studies more clearly in terms of investigating the policy assumptions involved in testing programs" (2006: 37). They argue that the wider social context in which language tests take place "is still not adequately theorised" (although the critical testing movement has provided a theoretical challenge by considering the role and function of tests in the broadest political light). The work of Shohamy (2001) in particular has drawn attention to the power of tests and how test uses can lead to injustice at the societal level. Even "good" tests based on sound constructs can have negative effects and consequences when used in political ways (cf. Spolsky's "use with care" warning in referring to language testing for migration purposes – 1981).

The main point here is that consideration of impact needs to be integrated within the processes and program of test validation, both in defining and operationalising the focal constructs and in collecting data and providing validity evidence. Impact research operates on a wider scale than washback and must entail the collection of adequate data to investigate how and to what extent an assessment system affects stakeholders, processes and systems in all the contexts in which it operates – both at macro and micro levels. Key considerations include:

- a view of educational systems as complex and dynamic;
- an understanding of how change can be anticipated and how change processes can be successfully managed;
- an understanding of the roles stakeholders play in the varied contexts where language learning and assessment operate;
- a capacity to take corrective action.

The superordinate concept of impact requires a broad discussion of the influence of policymaking and social action on assessment with references to the possible side effects and unintended (sometimes negative) consequences that can occur. However, anticipating impacts and finding out what happens in practice are not enough if improvements do not occur as a result; a theory of action is therefore required to guide practice. Similarly, the ability to develop realistic action plans, to engage in well-managed interaction with many stakeholder groups, to change systems to improve educational outcomes or mitigate negative consequences associated with tests are key to achieving the desired impact and are integral to the model of impact by design. The following part of this chapter elaborates on such a model.

3 Impact by design model – a theory of action

The "impact by design" model implements and manages assessment systems that inherently have the potential for positive impact (Saville 2009).

- It depends on well-defined focal constructs supported by appropriate theories (e.g., a socio-cognitive model of language).
- It takes an ex ante approach to anticipating the possible consequences of a given policy "before the event", the aim being to deliver assessments that include processes and procedures to enable the impact to be monitored and evaluated.
- Crucially it requires operational systems that include routine validation procedures to collect, store and access the necessary data and the capability to implement changes if/when necessary.

The following six features need to be factored into the model of impact by design:
1. **The assessment system and test features:** The role and nature of the language tests in education and in society – the purposes, uses, and intrinsic qualities, especially the nature of the focal constructs and how they are operationalized.

2. **The context(s):** The nature of social and educational contexts – the micro and macro levels – and how the language assessment processes fit within them.
3. **The participants:** A focus on the widest range of people who are involved in assessment practices, such as the participants or stakeholders, in order to understand what they think and how they behave.
4. **The timeline:** The importance of studying change and to understand how this happens over time and especially within complex dynamical systems.
5. **The research methods:** The procedures to conduct impact studies by extending what has been learnt in washback research, by developing real world research methods and tools and by finding practical ways of dealing with research outcomes for validation purposes.
6. **The outcomes:** How to anticipate possible effects and consequences more effectively and how to implement procedures to deal with unpredicted consequences when they occur, especially those which are detrimental.

In adopting this model, test providers need to re-conceptualize their research designs and data collection methods so that they are suitable for investigating socio-cultural and socio-political issues surrounding the use of their tests. They also need to develop an "impact toolkit" to provide methods and approaches to "finding out"; for example, to carry out macro-analyses of large-scale aggregated data, as well as micro-analyses of views, attitudes and behaviours in local settings. The quantitative analysis of macro level group data can capture the overall patterns, trends and growth, while the qualitative analysis of multiple cases enables researchers to monitor variability in local settings and to work with the ecological features of context. The toolkit should include standard operating procedures and use up-to-date technology; greater attention should also be given to the planning and resourcing of these activities. The next part of this chapter focuses on researching impact within the impact by design model.

4 Methodology for researching impact

Given the features of the impact-by-design model, we suggest that researching impact within that model is best contextualized within the domain of real-world research (Robson 2002) and research methodologies commonly used in the social sciences.

The abovementioned washback studies revealed the extent to which contextual variables confound the interpretation of research outcomes, and so an expanded view of impact is likely to encounter even greater challenges. The dual features of real world contexts and many complex variables mean that the research methodologies for investigating impact need to be robust and flexible. Robson (2002) contrasts two approaches to real world research: fixed vs. flexible designs. Because of the complex nature of real-world educational contexts, flexible research designs are likely to be of particular value in impact studies (as noted by Watanabe 2004). Most flexible designs have their origins in the social rather than the natural sciences and rely heavily on qualitative methods (see Robson 2002: 165 abridged from Creswell 1998).

Constructivist approaches to social research and case studies are especially useful for investigating impact at the micro level and for understanding the complexities of interaction between macro-level policies and implementation in local settings. Without such methods it can be difficult for examination providers to gain insights into the interaction of differing beliefs and attitudes which lead to consensus or divergence. Moreover given that assessment systems can collect both quantitative and qualitative data, mixed-methods research designs are particularly helpful in impact research. Creswell and Plano Clark (2007) define mixed-methods research as an approach to research design which guides the collection and integration of both qualitative and quantitative data in many phases of the research process. They list four types of mixed-methods studies which can occur concurrently or sequentially, as shown in Table 1. The timeline is considered to be important in mixed-methods designs and this is another reason why it is particularly relevant for impact-related research (noted above).

Tab. 1: Mixed-methods designs (based on Creswell and Plano Clark 2007).

Type	Triangulation	Embedded	Explanatory	Exploratory
Timeline	Concurrent	Concurrent/ Sequential	Sequential	Sequential
	Both used at the same time	Qualitative *within* a Quantitative design	Quantitative *followed by* Qualitative	Qualitative *followed by* Quantitative
Variants	Convergence; Data transformation; Validating quantitative data; Multilevel.	Experimental; Correlational.	Follow up explanations; Participant selection.	Instrument development; Taxonomy development.
Examples of purposes	Explain why/how data types converge. Gain insights from open ended questions to support survey data.	Use qualitative data to explain or expand on experimental outcomes	Gain insights from a large-scale survey by conducting experimental work and seeking to explain the observations by conducting more in-depth studies.	Gain insights into what might be happening on a small scale and then follow up with the collection of data from a wider population to provide confirmation.

Creswell and Plano Clark (2007: 111) discuss the sequencing of phases in research processes which combine qualitative and quantitative methods. Insights gained in one research phase can be followed up in a subsequent phase using techniques which were not used in the first, e.g., a quantitative survey followed up by interviews with participants. They describe how, in each phase, a number of considerations need to be addressed depending on which design is used and whether the weighting is predominantly qualitative or quantitative (e.g., sampling procedures, permissions needed, information to be collected, methods of recording data etc.). They also discuss longitudinal designs which have a number of anticipated phases over an extended period.

To illustrate the use of mixed-methods research design in investigating impact, to situate researching the impact-by-design model in a real-world research paradigm, and to show how researching impact is an integral element of any test validation program, we provide two examples below.

Example 1. Measuring the impact of Cambridge English TKT

Our first example is a study investigating the impact of the Teaching Knowledge Test (*TKT*) within a particular context[2]. For a detailed account of the research project, please refer to Khalifa, Papp, Valero and Howden (2013).

Before looking at the design and the findings of the study, we will consider the macro and micro contexts of the examination. The context is Mexico – a country witnessing an accelerated growth in students' enrolment in the formal education system (K-12) with enrolment in the tertiary sector growing by 46 % (Rolwing 2006). This expansion was met by several reform initiatives related to teacher education and professional development as well as institutional evaluation and accreditation. *TKT* is used in Mexico by different institutions as an indicator of teachers' pedagogic knowledge according to international standards. Among these institutions are the Centro Nacional de Evaluación para la Educación Superior (CENEVAL) and the Dirección General de Acreditación, Incorporación y Revalidación (DGAIR) of the Secretaría de Educación Pública y Cultura (SEP) who have recognised and approved the use of *TKT* (performance bands 3 and 4) in gaining a degree from the Técnico Superior Universitario en Enseñanza del Inglés. SEP has incorporated the *TKT* syllabus into its Programa Nacional del Inglés en la Educación Básica (PNIEB) where one of its aims is to retrain state primary and secondary teachers. SEP have also been using *TKT* as a recruitment tool for the teaching cadre in PNIEB schools – Sonora, Sinaloa, Coahuila, Nuevo Leon and Aguascalientes are a case in point. Similarly, some universities offering ELT undergraduate degrees incorporate *TKT* in their programmes, e.g., Universidad Autónoma de Baja California.

---

2 For exam details see http://www.cambridgeenglish.org/exams-and-qualifications/tkt/

Given the extensive usage of *TKT* in Mexico as a formal indicator of teachers' pedagogic knowledge, Cambridge English sought to understand the effects and consequences which result from this use within the Mexican educational context and society and to determine if any action is needed as a result of the study. An explanatory sequential mixed-methods design (Creswell and Plano Clark 2011) was used to conduct the study. Phase 1 of the research involved data collection from 10,000 teachers on their *TKT* performances and from 660 policy planners and implementers using a close-ended attitudinal survey. Results from phase 1 informed the qualitative phase in terms of the sampling procedures (i.e. types of participants purposefully selected for phase 2) and question formulation for focus groups and interviews.

Findings from quantitative data analysis showed that the standard of teachers has improved over time as indicated by a steady decrease in the numbers achieving Bands 1 and 2 (the lowest bands of *TKT*) with more teachers achieving Bands 3 and 4 (the highest bands of *TKT*). The analysis also revealed the positive effect of *TKT* as perceived by teachers. *TKT* has improved their knowledge in terms of a better understanding of theoretical and practical issues; their skills in terms of self-reflection and self-awareness; and their confidence and motivation. Teachers indicated that they can identify their students' needs better and can plan to meet those needs more effectively. This is especially true in state secondary schools, and in both private and state primary schools. Teachers in private language schools reported that they use more appropriate interaction patterns in the class and feel better equipped to evaluate available teaching materials as a result of gaining the *TKT* qualification. Quantitative data also showed that the key motivator for policy planners in adopting *TKT* is the need to raise the standards of pre-service and in-service English teacher training while the key motivator for policy implementers was compliance with regulatory bodies. Culminating the training of teachers with participants gaining an internationally recognised certificate like *TKT* was perceived as a way of improving the quality of teaching and the performance of the teaching staff. Policy implementers confirmed that the adoption of *TKT* has resulted in a diversity of teaching strategies, improved classroom practice, and a better understanding of the learning process.

Qualitative data analysis revealed the strategic thinking of policy planners in partnering with an internationally recognized assessment board – the desire to reach the intended goal of higher standards of teacher education and to satisfy the demand for qualified and certified teachers, as shown by this comment from the Sinaloa SEP Coordinator:

> The teachers who certified with *TKT* came to realize that there is much to learn about second language teaching and they continue to look for ways to improve their teaching skills. The results for the educational community (parents, administrators, permanent teaching staff, etc.) have been very positive. The fact that we have teachers certified by the University of Cambridge is a guarantee of the quality of these teachers' classes. (Claudia Rocío Valenzuela Ortiz, State Coordinator, SEP, Culiacan, Sinaloa State)

One of the major goals identified by higher education institutions is to equip university students with better skills for the job market in order to improve their job prospects. The beneficial effects among universities are seen in good *TKT* exam performance resulting in an increasing number of certified teachers, teachers becoming more motivated to develop professionally, and in improved classroom practice, better understanding of the learning process, higher proficiency levels, and better chances for teachers' employability:

> There has been an increase in confidence on the part of employers since we adopted *TKT* and our students show more confidence in their teaching abilities as well ... with Band 3 they have obtained employment in the institutes that are known as being the most demanding in their hiring practices in our state. (Blanca Margarita Tobias Delgado, Coordinator, Universidad Tangamanga, San Luis Potosi)

A positive unintended impact of *TKT* was that it encouraged teachers to attend professional development events, present at conferences and to undertake post-graduate studies in ELT and education. Another unintended impact of the use of *TKT* is institutional reputation and its ability to deliver reform initiatives:

> It is an honor to be able to say that our public school English teachers have the profile and the teaching skills that they need, and this is not only something that the state affirms but is certified by a formal exam applied by the University of Cambridge. We are finally on our way to achieving our goal of being able to state that the State of Aguascalientes has the highest quality English teachers (Valeria Alvarez Borrego, Academic Coordinator, Instituto de Educación de Aguascalientes)

The study reported here was a first step in measuring the impact of *TKT*'s use in Mexico. Given that the context within which *TKT* is used may change over time due to social, economic and political factors, it is the intention of Cambridge English to carry out a second iteration of the study. It is hoped that the next iteration of the study would be conducted with local experts who would provide valuable insight to data collection and interpretation.

Example 2. Researching the impact of the Cambridge English: Young Learners (YLE) examination

The context of the second research project is primary education where external assessment is used as an indicator of learner progression and as criteria for inclusion in state-funded intensive language programs. The external assessment used is the *Cambridge English: Young Learners (YLE)* examination[3]. The stakeholders in this project are: the Department of Education and Training (DOET) in Ho Chi Minh

---

3 For exam details see http://www.cambridgeenglish.org/exams/young-learners-english/

City (HCM), state-primary schools who are funded to run the intensive language program and the related school principals, English teachers, students who attend the program and their parents. The key research question was "What is the intended and unintended effect of HCM DOET's strategic decision to increase English Language provision through an Intensive English Program (IEP) and to ensure the quality of the provision through the use of external assessment, i.e. YLE examinations"? This study also exemplifies the benefits of collaborations between Cambridge English-based researchers and researchers with local knowledge who provided an understanding of and insights into the specific local context being studied. Such collaboration was extremely beneficial in qualitative data collection and interpretation.

Khalifa, Nguyen and Walker (2012) chose a convergent parallel mixed-methods design (Creswell and Plano Clark 2011) to conduct the study. In this approach, researchers simultaneously collect qualitative and quantitative data, analyse them separately and then compare results to see if the findings support or refute each other. Interviews ($n = 30$) with policy makers, district heads, and principals served as a basis for gathering contextual information, carrying out situational analysis, and investigating perceived potential effects. In focus groups ($n = 24$), children were encouraged to speak freely and spontaneously on five identified topics: a) why they have joined IEP, b) reasons behind their desire to learn English, c) incidences of using English in the classroom, d) their views on *Cambridge English: Starters*, and e) whether they feel their English has improved and why. Surveys completed by 113 teachers provided their views on external assessment; perceptions of the DOET intervention; and their expectations of learner progression as a result of the intervention. The survey also aimed to gain insights into IEP classroom practices. Similar views were also sought from parents who were asked to express their opinion on the influence of IEP and YLE exams on their child's motivation to learn English and their language learning progression. A total of 2,860 parents completed the survey. YLE test results in consecutive academic years 2010 and 2011 were investigated to see whether standards of English improved over time. To obtain comparative information, *Cambridge English: Starters* test data from other contexts within Vietnam and from the rest of the world were also examined.

The study revealed areas where positive effects have been achieved. For example, the notable change in terms of teaching practice with the adoption of certain Assessment for Learning principles (see Assessment Reform Group 2002, Black et al. 1990), the introduction of collaborative teaching, and the utilisation of best practices such as teacher reflection or adaptation of teaching methods to support students' learning goals and styles. Another example is the attention paid to teaching speaking skills because of the external assessment. Although test score data showed a notable language progression in terms of speaking, students also performed well on the other skills. DOET's intervention led to increased parental involvement in their child's learning in terms of encouraging them to learn English, taking them to the extra English classes provided by IEP and providing incentives for better performance as seen from a child's comment "Mom said if I do well, she'll take me to the ice cream shop." Parental involvement and teacher encouragement were a recurring theme in the findings of the study and seem to play a key role in learner motivation. On a different note, the study showed that when decentralization of decision-making is well executed, innovative approaches that suit the local context can lead to positive effects. Although the strategic objective for improving language standards came from central government in Hanoi, it was up to HCM DOET to determine how to achieve this and schools also decided whether to get involved in the initiative or not, which provided a sense of ownership in the intervention.

The study also revealed areas where improvements can be made such as DOET's need to have an effective plan to disseminate information on the intervention; the need for a school to be committed to providing consistent and adequate information to its stakeholders; further in-depth investigation as to why a large percentage of the sampled parents continue to send their children to private language institutes despite the introduction of IEP.

As was the case for the *TKT* impact research project, the interventions in this research study led to positive unintended consequences. For example, the better utilization of children's free time and the alleviation of working parents' anxiety as to how to engage their children's free time once the half day of schooling is over.

It is interesting to note that an unintended consequence of carrying out this research project is DOET's decision not to pursue their plans to use external assessment for gatekeeping purposes.

5 Future Directions

This chapter has argued for the integration of impact investigations into routine test development and validation via the use of an impact-by-design model and the deployment of a theory of action so that effects and consequences of tests can be anticipated and managed over time. The ability to change in order to improve educational outcomes or mitigate negative consequences associated with the examinations is ultimately the most important dimension of the impact-by-design model. In working closely with the stakeholders in their own contexts, this approach is now providing the necessary tools to determine what needs to be done and when/how to do it. The two illustrated examples imply the importance of the timing of an impact study in order to affect change and the benefits of collaboration with local researchers.

One of the major challenges which remain for the future will be the integration of digital technology into assessment systems, and the potential benefits that this might bring for studying test impact. At the centre of this challenge will be the achievement of an appropriate balance between the roles that machines and humans play in teaching and learning contexts.

An area which offers great promise, and of particular relevance to the investigation of impact, is the use of digital devices to capture and analyse large amounts of information obtained from micro contexts – in other words, data collected from traditional classrooms and digitally-mediated learning environments, such as blended learning programmes, in ways which hitherto have not been practicable.

By using automated systems of data collection and processing, the practical constraints of using humans to collect data in micro contexts can be reduced and activities which are carried out by teachers to support learning or to prepare learners for assessments can be opened up to greater scrutiny. If behavioural data, such as responses to learning or assessment tasks are automatically collected and made available for analysis, individual learner differences can be studied more effectively and teachers can use the information more effectively for diagnostic and formative purposes.

In this vision of the future, teaching and assessment systems become more closely related and are able to address the needs learners have in their own contexts. By breaking down the traditional dichotomy between formative and summative uses of assessment and focusing attention on learning and how feedback from assessment can be harnessed, we move in the direction of individualising learning and assessment processes, and potentially remove unhelpful or negative washback effects which currently persist in many classrooms.

6 References

Alderson, J. Charles. 2004. Foreword in Liying Cheng, Yoshinori Watanabe and Andy Curtis (eds.). *Washback in language testing: Research contexts and methods*, ix–xii. Mahwah: Lawrence Erlbaum.

Alderson, J. Charles and Dianne Wall. 1993. Does washback exist? *Applied Linguistics* 14(2): 115–129.

Andrews, Stephen 1994. The washback effect of examinations: Its impact upon curriculum innovation in English language teaching. *Curriculum Forum* 1: 44–58.

Assessment Reform Group. 2002. *Assessment for Learning: 10 principles*. http://cdn.aaia.org.uk/content/uploads/2010/06/Assessment-for-Learning-10-principles.pdf (accessed October 2015).

Bachman, Lyle F. and Adrian S. Palmer. 1996. *Language testing in practice: Designing and developing useful language tests*. Oxford, UK: Oxford University Press.

Bailey, Kathleen M. 1996. Working for washback: a review of the washback concept in language testing. *Language Testing* 13(3): 257–279.

Bailey, Kathleen M. 1999. *Washback in Language Testing*. RM-99-4. Princeton: ETS.

Black, Paul, Christine Harrison, Clare Lee, Bethan Marshall and Dylan Wiliam. 1990. *Working Inside the Black Box: Assessment for Learning in the Classroom*. London: King's College London.

Cheng, Liying. 1998. Impact of a Public English Examination Change on Students' Perceptions and Attitudes toward Their English Learning. *Studies in Educational Evaluation* 24(3): 279–301.

Cheng, Liying. 2004. The washback effect of an examination change on teachers' perception towards their classroom teaching. In: Liying Cheng, Yoshinori Watanabe and Andy Curtis (eds.). *Washback in language testing: Research contexts and methods*, 147–170. Mahwah: Lawrence Erlbaum.

Cheng, Liying. 2005. *Changing Language Teaching through Language Testing: A washback study*. Cambridge, UK: UCLES/Cambridge University Press.

Creswell, John W. 1998. *Qualitative enquiry and research design: choosing among five traditions*. Thousand Oaks: Sage.

Creswell, John W. and Vicki L. Plano Clark. 2007. *Designing and conducting mixed methods Research*. Thousand Oaks: Sage.

Creswell, John W. and Vicki L. Plano Clark. 2011. *Designing and conducting mixed methods research*. 2nd ed. Thousand Oaks: Sage.

Fullan, Michael. 1993. *Change Forces: Probing the Depths of Educational Reform*. London: The Falmer Press.

Goodhart, Charles. 1975. *Monetary relationships: a view from Threadneedle Street*. Paper presented at the Conference in Monetary Economics, Sydney, July 1975.

Green, Anthony. 2003. *Test Impact and EAP: a comparative study in backwash between IELTS preparation and university pre-sessional courses*. Roehampton: The University of Surrey at Roehampton dissertation.

Green, Anthony. 2007. *IELTS Washback in Context; Preparation for academic writing in higher education*. Cambridge, UK: UCLES/Cambridge University Press.

Hughes, Arthur. 1989. *Testing for language teachers*. Cambridge, UK: Cambridge University Press.

Hughes, Arthur. 1993. *Backwash and TOEFL 2000*. University of Reading: Unpublished manuscript.

Khalifa, Hanan, Szilvia Papp, Rosalia Valero and Debbie Howden. 2013. *Measuring the effectiveness of Teaching Knowledge Test (TKT): Mexico case study*. An internal report. Cambridge English Language Assessment.

Khalifa, Hanan, Thuyanh Nguyen and Christine Walker. 2012. An investigation into the effect of intensive language provision and external assessment in primary education in Ho Chi Minh City, Vietnam. *Research Notes* 50: 8–19.

McNamara, Tim and Carsten Roever. 2006. *Language testing: the social dimension*. Oxford: Wiley-Blackwell.

Merton, Robert K. 1936. The unanticipated consequences of purposive social action. *American Sociological Review* 1(6): 894–904.

Messick, Samuel. 1989. Validity. In: Robert L. Linn (ed.), *Educational measurement*, 3rd ed. 13–103. New York: Macmillan.

Messick, Samuel. 1996. Validity and washback in language testing. *Language Testing* 13(3): 241–256.

Milanovic, Michael and Nick Saville. 1996. *Considering the impact of Cambridge EFL Examinations, Manuscript Internal Report*. Cambridge: Cambridge ESOL.

Moss, Pamela A. 1998. The role of consequences in validity theory. *Educational Measurement: Issues and Practice* 17(2): 6–12.

Robson, Colin. 2002. *Real World Research*, 2nd ed. Oxford: Blackwell.

Rolwing, Kevin. 2006. Education in Mexico. *World Education News and Reviews* 19(3). http: www.wes.org/ewenr/06jun/practical.htm (accessed October 2015).

Saville, Nick. 2009. *Developing a Model for Investigating the Impact of Language Assessments within Educational Contexts by a Public Examination Provider*. Bedfordshire: University of Bedfordshire dissertation.

Shohamy, Elaine. 2001. *The power of tests: A critical perspective on the uses of language tests*. London: Longman.

Spolsky, Bernard. 1981. Some ethical questions about language testing. In: Chiristine Klein-Braley and Douglas K. Stevenson (eds.). *Practice and problems in language testing*. 5–21. Frankfurt am Main: Peter Lang.

Wall, Dianne. 2005. *The Impact of High-Stakes Testing on Classroom Teaching: A Case Study Using Insights from Testing and Innovation Theory*. Cambridge, UK: UCLES/Cambridge University Press.

Watanabe, Yoshinori. 1997. *The Washback Effects of the Japanese University Entrance Examinations of English-Classroom-based Research*. Lancaster: University of Lancaster dissertation.

Watanabe, Yoshinori. 2004. Methodology in washback studies. In: Liying Cheng and Yoshinori Watanabe with Andy Curtis (eds.). *Washback in language testing: Research contexts and method*. 19–36. Mahwah: Lawrence Erlbaum Associates.

II. Assessing second language skills/areas

II. Assessing second language skilfulness

Tineke Brunfaut

7 Assessing listening

1 Introduction

In their editors' preface to the seminal volume *Assessing listening* (Buck 2001), Alderson and Bachman (2001: x) stated that "[t]he assessment of listening is one of the least understood, least developed and yet one of the most important areas of language testing and assessment." Fortunately, listening has received increasing research interest over the past decade, as will become clear from this review, but there is still a long way to go before we will have full insight (if that is even possible) into this skill and its assessment.

One of the reasons for our limited understanding is the methodological challenges researchers face when looking into listening. Due to its receptive and covert nature, we cannot directly observe listening comprehension. We need to make inferences about what goes on when someone is processing and interpreting verbal input, and we need tasks that elicit listening performances to base our inferences on. Another reason for our incomplete insights is the complex and interactive nature of listening processes. In fact, the word 'complex' has been adopted in nearly all literature defining listening. Examples of other adjectives used to describe this skill include 'active', 'automatic', 'implicit', 'temporal' (e.g., Vandergrift 2011), 'dynamic' (e.g., Vandergrift and Goh 2009), and 'invisible' (e.g., Lynch 2009). However, if our aim is to assess someone's listening ability, getting a better grasp of this skill is a challenge we have to face. It is crucial that we have a good understanding of the skill we are interested in measuring, i.e. the construct underlying our assessment instrument. In other words, insights into the nature of listening are key to the construct validity of a test and need to form the basis of any listening assessment.

This chapter is laid out in two main sections. The first part will provide potential answers to the question 'What is listening?' The second part will focus on the assessment of listening ability. More specifically, ways in which listening ability can be evaluated, and task- and listener-related factors that have an impact on listening task difficulty will be discussed. In addition, challenges for listening assessment practice and research will be considered.

2 What is listening?

Listening has been described as a complex cognitive process that involves the interaction of four types of processes: neurological, linguistic, semantic, and pragmatic processing (Rost 2011). *Neurological processing* concerns the physical and neurological processes involved in hearing and listening. This includes the perception of external sound waves by our ears, their transferral to our brain, and their transformation into auditory perceptions – all involving complex neural activity. As explained by Rost (2011), the difference between hearing and listening is one of intention and involvement; listening means acknowledging a particular oral source (amongst many other possible stimuli) and displaying openness and preparedness to deal with this source. A crucial role is thereby played by attention mechanisms, which encompass the quasi simultaneous, interrelated activities of neural reactions to stimuli (arousal), neurotransmitter spread to processing areas in the brain (orientation), and registration of the stimuli in these parts of the brain (focus).

Linguistic decoding includes a perception phase, which is often referred to as bottom-up processing, whereby the incoming speech sounds and intonation units are encoded, and initial word segmentation is conducted. During a lexical parsing or word recognition phase, words and lexical phrases are identified and lexical knowledge related to these words and phrases is activated. This process is led by meaning searching and involves potential word candidate selection (Vandergrift 2011). In addition, linguistic decoding involves syntactic parsing whereby the incoming speech is plotted against the listeners' grammatical model of language and translated into syntactic representations of the textual input at the sentence and discourse level. It is thought that these forms of linguistic processing are enhanced by pragmatic knowledge of common discourse functions and types (e.g., greeting patterns or topic shift moves), by intertextual knowledge of potential speaker experiences (e.g., speaker preferences for certain figures of speech), and by knowledge of common formulaic sequences or phrases (Rost 2011). Also, these decoding processes do not necessarily operate in a neat sequential manner, but the various 'levels of analysis' (Field, 2013: 94) may work in simultaneous, overlapping, and dynamic manners.

Semantic processing requires listeners to connect the input with their conceptual, long-term memory knowledge base, and make use of information not included in the linguistic input in order to develop a textual representation in memory. This type of processing constitutes a search for coherence and relevance in what the speaker says through separating new from prior information, integrating textual information into known or real world information, and the activating and targeted selecting of schemata relevant to the input. This happens whilst also interpreting against a background of social frameworks and a common ground between speaker and listener. The memory access processes activated during listening, which on the one hand require existing knowledge activation and on the other hand often involve formation of new knowledge networks or amendment of existing ones, mean that semantic processing is considered a problem-solving, reasoning process. Importantly, semantic processing can be characterised as relying on inference processes in order to form interpretations of and establish connections between different elements of what is said and in order to unveil the speaker's intended meaning. However, due to our brain's limited memory capacities (Baddeley 2003), semantic processing is associated with the use of compensatory strategies. This type of processing is often referred to as top-down processing (Rost 2011) and reflects what Anderson (1995) called 'the utilization phase'.

Making use of linguistic information or background knowledge, however, is not something that happens in isolation; listeners do this within a particular social context. Contextualised meaning is established as part of the *pragmatic processing* that takes place when listening. It involves understanding the speaker's intended meaning within a particular context and considering what is said in relation to one's expectations as a listener, whilst also taking into account the speaker and listener's interpersonal relationship (e.g., their role and status in the interaction). From the perspective of this sort of processing, Rost (2011: 98) coined listening as a co-constructed meaning building process, and it is mainly through this type of processing that he recognised the social dimension of what is otherwise presented as a highly demanding cognitive activity. To highlight the social side of listening, Vandergrift and Goh (2009) have additionally emphasised the role of gestures, of non-verbal and cultural cues in interpreting listening input, and of psychological traits such as anxiety and motivation.

It should be pointed out that the four different kinds of processing outlined above are complementary and happen in a parallel manner. Vandergrift (2011) has described the overall listening process as a dynamic and interactive interplay between the bottom-up decoding processes and the top-down processes of context and prior knowledge applications. He has added to this that the exact nature of the interaction between the different processes and the degree of reliance on each of these will depend on the purpose for listening (e.g., to confirm from a lecturer announcement the time of a rescheduled lecture versus to gain an idea of the overall purpose and focus of the rescheduled lecture), on the characteristics of the listener (e.g., level of language proficiency), and on the context in which the listening takes place (e.g., an informal lecturer-student corridor conversation versus an official lecturer-student attendance evaluation meeting). Together with Goh, he has furthermore emphasized that the ability to (self-)regulate the various processes and their interactions, that is, a listener's metacognitive knowledge and skills, are decisive for successful listening comprehension (Vandergrift and Goh 2012). Also, as indicated above, as part of the processing, listeners make use of resources such as linguistic knowledge, world knowledge, and knowledge about the specific communicative context in which an utterance is made (Buck 2001; Hulstijn 2003; Vandergrift 2007). Therefore, the ability to assimilate the various sources in real time is vital (Rost 2005). In addition, listeners need to be able to simultaneously process speech and attend to further incoming speech. As a consequence, listening may be a particularly intensive and demanding process for less proficient listeners (e.g., second language learners), since, unlike proficient listeners whose processing can largely be characterised as automatic, less able listeners' processing is likely to require more conscious control (Segalowitz 2003) and draw more heavily on their working memory resources. Due to the limitations of our working memory capacity, less proficient listeners may experience more problems in processing aural input with partial or miscomprehension as the outcome (Buck 2001; Vandergrift 2007; Vandergrift and Goh 2009). Given the complexity of the overall listening process, it is thus not without reason that Vandergrift (2011: 455) has described what a listener has to do as "no small feat." By extension, therefore, assessing this skill is not either.

3 Assessing listening

3.1 Ways of testing listening

The main approach to assessing listening comprehension in the last couple of decades has been independent skills testing whereby listening is isolated as a target skill. However, since listening is not directly observable as such, listening test tasks always involve some reading, writing and/or speaking to demonstrate one's level of comprehension. The aim of independent forms of testing, however, is to keep the extent to which these other skills need to be employed to a minimum in order to avoid construct-irrelevant variance, and consequently these other skills do not form the focus of the assessment (and thus also not the scoring). Frequently used test techniques in independent listening tasks include selected-response item types such as multiple-choice questions or matching tasks whereby the options may be presented in writing or as visuals (see e.g., IELTS and the Oxford Young Learners online placement test, respectively). Constructed-response item types such as note-taking, gap-filling, sentence-completion tasks, or short-answer questions are also often used. The responses to items of this nature may need to be given in written or oral format (see e.g., TestDaF and the Trinity College London GESE Advanced, respectively). These test formats, however, may be restrictive in what is being tested. Field (2012), for example, found that test takers who completed a set of IELTS multiple-choice and gap-fill questions primarily engaged in lexical processing and not in so-called higher-level processing such as inferring logical connections between propositions or building a structural representation of the listening input.

Communicative approaches to language assessment have pleaded for more integrated ways of testing listening, driven by a concern over authenticity and the extent to which independent task types tap into the ability to use language beyond the test situation, i.e. in "real-world" communication. Although it has been acknowledged that tests may be inherently different from more authentic settings and thus unable to fully capture abilities that represent the demands of language use in the real world (Norris, Bygate, and Van den Branden 2009), it has been argued that integrated test tasks more closely correspond with language use beyond the test context since, as in many acts of "real-life" communication, they involve two or more skills (see e.g., Brown, Iwashita, and McNamara 2005; Lewkowicz 1997). Integrated tasks involving listening have particularly been introduced in large-scale tests for academic purposes such as the PTE Academic (see e.g., the Summarize Spoken Text and the Retell Lecture tasks) and the TOEFL iBT (e.g., writing tasks which require the test takers to first read a text and listen to a lecture before integrating the content input into a written performance). These task types are thought to engage test takers not only in lexical processing, but also semantic and discourse level processing, since they need to comprehend the input and then produce a summary of the input materials without any pre-determined questions (Field 2013; Rost 2011). Comprehension of the listening input is typically evaluated through the content reproduced in the written or oral performance, although determining whether content inaccuracies are listening or speaking/writing proficiency problems (or both) have proven to be difficult (Brown, Iwashita, and McNamara 2005).

3.2 Factors affecting listening test task difficulty

A wide range of factors have been suggested to influence listening task difficulty, however, a more limited, but still substantial number have been empirically shown to relate to or impact on listening task difficulty. In line with Bachman and Palmer's (1996) conceptualisation of language test performance as resulting from and interacting with test task and situation characteristics and with test-taker characteristics, two broad groups of factors are typically distinguished in listening task difficulty research, namely characteristics of the listening task (see 3.2.1) and characteristics of the listener (see 3.2.2).

3.2.1 Task-related factors
There are different elements to any listening test. The critical one is some form of listening input, for example an audio or video recording or live-delivered speech. In addition, in order to be able to observe whether the input is understood, a task is needed which instructs the test taker to do something that will demonstrate his or her level of comprehension. As a consequence, different types of task-related factors have been explored, namely factors associated with a) the listening task input, b) the task procedures, c) the task output, and d) interactions between the task input and output characteristics.

3.2.1.1 Factors associated with the listening task input
A large array of linguistic as well as non-linguistic information presented in the listening task input has been shown to play a role in listening comprehension.

Linguistic complexity. Listening task difficulty has been found to be associated with a wide range of linguistic characteristics of the listening passage. These include phonological, lexical, syntactic and discourse features (see Révész and Brunfaut 2013, for a more extensive review). Of these, in particular, lexical complexity aspects of the listening texts appear to be related to listening task difficulty. For example, Révész and Brunfaut (2013) found that greater listening task difficulty was associated with higher lexical density of listening texts. More lexically diverse passages and texts containing more academic vocabulary were also found to be more challenging. Furthermore, in a different study, Brunfaut and Révész (2015) observed that easier listening tasks contained higher occurrences of multiword expressions in the passages. These researchers also discovered relationships between listening task difficulty and discourse features of the listening texts, i.e. passages with more causal content were more difficult (Révész and Brunfaut 2013) and passages with more overlap between sentences were less demanding (Brunfaut and Révész 2015).

Speed. Since faster speech gives listeners less time for real-time processing, it has been proposed that it results in more comprehension difficulties, particularly for less proficient second language listeners. A number of experimental as well as non-experimental studies have confirmed this hypothesis. For example, by means of an experiment on the effect of speech rate and noise with Hebrew second language listeners who had Arabic as their first language, Rosenhouse, Haik, and Kishon-Rabin (2006) found that rate of delivery was associated with weaker listening performances in both first and second language, with the strongest effect in the second language. In a non-experimental study, Buck and Tatsuoka (1998) were unable to identify speech rate as a predictor of task difficulty on its own. However, in combination with the factors textual redundancy and whether the information necessary to respond correctly was part of longer idea units, increased speech rate appeared to influence listening difficulty.

Explicitness. More implicit textual meaning is thought to require more engagement in pragmatic processing (e.g., inferencing) and therefore carry a higher "risk" of listening difficulties. Although few studies have focused on this topic, their results were as anticipated; Kostin (2004), Nissan, DeVincenzi, and Tang (1996), and Ying-hui (2006) all observed that texts requiring higher levels of inferencing were associated with greater listening difficulty.

Text type. When exploring the effect of text type on listening test scores, Shohamy and Inbar (1991) discovered that, on an oral-literate continuum, passages which were more oral in nature were better understood by a group of secondary school English foreign language listeners. It should be noted, however, that the passages not only differed in genre, but also showed many differences in other characteristics such as linguistic complexity and explicitness.

Visuals. Listening test tasks are not necessarily restricted to audio input with accompanying questions, but may, for example, consist of video-recorded input or include visual images. Potentially, visuals have an effect on listening comprehension. Improved listening test performance, due to the presence of visuals has, for instance, been corroborated by Wagner (2013). However, the body of research on visuals contains very mixed findings, with other studies showing no impact (Coniam 2001) or even suggesting a negative effect (Gruba 1993). Ginther's (2002) work, for example, indicates that it is not simply a matter of the presence or absence of visuals, but that the type of visual (providing contextual or content information in relation to the audio input) may play a role in the nature of the effect, and that this effect may also depend on the audio input's discourse type.

Similar to the contradicting conclusions on the impact of visuals, it should be noted that for other task input characteristics there has also been variation in the detection of effects of the factors and their strength (see Révész and Brunfaut 2013 for a discussion). Potentially, diverging findings can be attributed to factors such as differences in task types, task conditions, the overall context, test-taker background characteristics, and the analytical tools employed in different studies.

3.2.1.2 Factors associated with the listening test task procedures

The specific manner in which the task is implemented may also have an effect on the difficulty of the listening task.

Number of times listening. For example, when looking into the potential effect of repeated hearings of oral input, Berne (1995) and Elkhafaifi (2005a) found that listeners performed significantly better after the second listening. Thus, whether test takers are allowed to listen to a passage once or twice requires a careful decision by test developers.

Pre-listening activities. Elkhafaifi's (2005a) study also suggested a performance effect of the use of pre-listening activities, that is, students who previewed the questions or vocabulary occurring in the listening input performed better than those who were given a distractor activity, with those with question access prior to the task scoring the highest. Similar positive performance effects of question preview have been found by Berne (1995), and of combined question preview and vocabulary pre-teaching by Chung (2002).

Note-taking. Carrell, Dunkel and Mollaun (2004) explored the potential benefits of another task procedural variable, namely, allowing note-taking when completing lecture comprehension test tasks. They found a positive effect of note-taking in interaction with the topic of the lecture (i.e. better performance when note-taking on arts and humanities topics) and the length of the lecture (i.e. better performance if note-taking was allowed on short lectures). In a related study, Carrell (2007) also found a moderate association between note-taking and listening test performance with consistent positive correlations between task performance and the number of content words in the notes and the number of task answers occurring in the notes.

3.2.1.3 Factors associated with the listening test task output

In addition to listening task input factors, a number of characteristics of the listening task response have also been found to relate to listening task difficulty. One such feature is the format of the response.

Response format. For example, on the basis of a meta-analysis of research on the effects of multiple-choice and open-ended item types on second language listening test performance, In'nami and Koizumi (2009) concluded that multiple-choice formats are easier than open-ended formats in second language listening, with the strength of the format effect varying between medium and large. Similarly, when comparing the effect of the item types multiple-choice, multiple-choice cloze, and open-ended questions, Cheng (2004) found that second language listeners did least well on the constructed-response tasks and performed best on the multiple-choice cloze tasks.

Response length. Another response characteristic that has been found to relate to task difficulty is the length of the required response. For example, Buck and Tatsuoka (1998) identified an impact on listening task difficulty of short-answer questions that required more than one word for a correct response (but note that they also found interactions between different variables looked into). Similarly, Jensen et al. (1997) found that long, multiple-word answers to listening comprehension questions in a test for academic purposes were associated with more difficult items.

However, when looking into the relationship between listening task difficulty and the linguistic complexity of the options in multiple-choice items, Brunfaut and Révész (2015) did not observe an association between a series of individual lexical complexity aspects of the response options and item difficulty.

3.2.1.4 Factors associated with the interactions between the listening test task input and output

Relationships with listening difficulty have not only been shown for isolated characteristics of the listening task input or of the output, but particular combinations of task input and response characteristics also seem to contribute to listening task difficulty. For example, Révész and Brunfaut (2013) found a relationship between listening difficulty and linguistic complexity characteristics of that information in the listening passage which is necessary to be able to respond correctly to an item. More specifically, they found that the necessary information in less difficult listening items contained more function words or phrasal expressions, or had higher lexical density. In a study on a different type of listening test task, Brunfaut and Révész (2015) came to a similar conclusion on the association of listening task difficulty with the presence of multiword expressions in the textual information that is key to the correct answer (namely, less difficult listening tasks were those with more phrasal expressions in the necessary information). Jensen et al. (1997) furthermore reported that tasks were more difficult when there was no direct lexical overlap between parts of the listening input and the words in the expected response.

Other combinations of task input and response characteristics that appear to contribute to the difficulty of listening tasks include the speech rate and the location in the passage of the necessary information (see e.g., Buck and Tatsuoka 1998, and Freedle and Kostin 1996, respectively), the length of time of the listening input foregoing the necessary information (Jensen et al. 1997), the linguistic characteristics of the text surrounding the necessary information (Buck and Tatsuoka 1998), and whether the necessary information is repeated in the oral input (Buck and Tatsuoka 1998; Freedle and Kostin 1996; Jensen et al. 1997).

In addition, Rupp, Garcia, and Jamieson (2001) have shown that individual characteristics also interact with one another. For example, they reported that on the one hand increased sentence length, higher numbers of words and higher type-token ratios in the input was associated with more difficult items, but that on the other hand this could be influenced by the text-item interaction characteristics of information density, of the lexical overlap between the text and multiple-choice distractors, and of the type, and the number and complexity of the cognitive processes needed to solve the item. They also found that the number of plausible multiple-choice distractors (as related to propositions in the input) and the lexical overlap between distractors and the key had particularly strong effects on item difficulty.

3.2.2 Listener-related factors

An assessment context is not limited to the provision of a task with its own demands; there is also a person involved who completes the test task and interacts with it. Not surprisingly, therefore, in addition to several task-related factors, a range of cognitive, affective and linguistic characteristics of the listener have been found to relate to listening difficulty.

3.2.2.1 Factors associated with cognitive characteristics of the test taker

Working memory. Given the complex, real-time processing that is required when listening for comprehension (see Section 2), limitations to our working memory capacity have been hypothesized and shown to be associated with listening difficulty. For example, Kormos and Sáfár (2008) reported a significant positive relationship between complex working memory capacity and performance on the listening section of the Cambridge English: First (FCE) exam. Brunfaut and Révész (2015) found that listeners who had higher listening scores on the PTE Academic were also those with higher phonological short-term memory and higher complex working memory capacity. However, when looking into one specific item type (the

PTE Academic Select Missing Word task) Brunfaut and Révész did not observe a significant relationship between listening task performance and working memory measures. They suggested that factors such as task type, nature of the listening text and response characteristics, and type of listening assessed by the task may play a role in the impact of working memory on listening.

Metacognition. Listening scholars Vandergrift and Goh have dedicated an important part of their research to exploring listeners' self-reflection and self-awareness of their listening strategy use and management. They have also shown the impact of test takers' metacognitive awareness on listening test performance. Namely, the study reported in Vandergrift et al. (2006) discovered that second language listeners' scores on the University of Ottawa's Placement Test could partially be explained by the listeners' metacognitive awareness, as measured by the Metacognitive Awareness Listening Questionnaire developed and validated by the researchers. Test takers with higher self-reported metacognitive listening awareness were those who performed better on the listening placement test items. In particular, better listeners indicated that they make more use of problem-solving strategies, planning and evaluation strategies, attention direction strategies, self-knowledge strategies, and avoid mental translations of the listening input. Similar conclusions on skilled listeners' more extensive use of metacognitive and comprehension monitoring strategies were drawn from verbal protocol research during listening task completion (see e.g., Goh 2002; Vandergrift 2003).

Background knowledge. Contextualised listening is thought to enhance top-down processing and reduce the demands placed on listeners' working memory (Vandergrift 2011), and knowledge pre-activation activities have indeed been shown to be beneficial (see 3.2.1.2). In addition, better listening performance when possessing background knowledge on the listening topic has, for example, been shown by Long (1990) who compared comprehension of a passage on the listener-unfamiliar topic of the Ecuadorian gold rush with a listener-familiar topic of the rock band U2. Similar research was done by Markham and Latham (1987), who compared comprehension of a range of religious topics with which listeners were more or less familiar, and by Schmidt-Rinehardt (1994). However, on the basis of a comprehensive literature review on the role of background knowledge in listening, Macaro, Vanderplank, and Graham (2005) cautioned that prior knowledge can also be over relied on and can distract from the actual content of the textual input if not listening with an open mind.

3.2.2.2 Factors associated with the linguistic characteristics of the test taker

Second language proficiency and first language listening ability. The much investigated question whether foreign language reading problems result from reading problems or foreign language knowledge problems (or both) (Alderson 1984) has also been posed with reference to second language listening. In a study with English-speaking secondary school learners of French as a second language, Vandergrift (2006) found that both second language proficiency and first language listening ability accounted for part of the variance in French second language listening (for 25 % and 14 %, respectively). The variance explained by second language proficiency was about the same for items tapping into literal text comprehension versus inferencing. However, first language listening ability contributed only to literal listening comprehension (explaining 13 % of the variance). Second language proficiency thus seems to be an important factor for second language listening. Testtakers' listening ability in their first language also plays a role, but the impact may differ depending on the type of listening targeted.

Lexical knowledge. Vandergrift's (2006) study used information on immersion programme enrolment and interaction with a French-speaking parent to define learners' second language proficiency. More precise measures to look into the impact of second language knowledge have been adopted in other research. Meccarty (2000) looked into the predictive power of Spanish learners' syntactic and lexical knowledge. Of these two variables, she found that second language lexical knowledge explained 14 % of the variance in second language listening. Staehr (2009) was similarly able to explain a significant amount of the variance of Danish-speaking learners' English listening test comprehension (i.e. 51 %) by means of these learners' breadth and depth of English vocabulary knowledge. Vocabulary size appeared to be the main predictor of the two variables, explaining 49 % of the variance in second language listening.

Andringa et al. (2012) simultaneously explored the impact of four variables on first and on second language listening in Dutch. The factor language knowledge (using vocabulary, grammar, and processing and segmentation accuracy measures) was found to be a strong predictor for both first and second language listening.

Linguistic processing speed. In the same study (Andringa et al. 2012) first language listeners' performance also appeared to be a function of the efficiency with which they process linguistic information. Using five different measures (including indicators of semantic and syntactic processing speed), faster processing was shown to be characteristic of better first language listeners.

IQ. Processing speed, however, did not impact on second language listening comprehension in Andringa et al.'s investigation, but reasoning ability did. Higher non-verbal IQ was found to be an explanatory factor for better second language listening performance. Contrary to expectations (see 3.2.2.1), however, memory did not explain listening variance in Andringa et al.'s four-predictor model.

Phonological knowledge. Although research on the impact of this listener attribute in relation to testing listening is relatively scarce, studies investigating the variable 'accent' have revealed its complex role. For example, Harding (2012) studied potential shared-first-language advantages on a listening test with speakers with second language accents. He found that some listener groups who shared their first language with the speaker had an advantage on many second language listening items with that speaker (and not a speaker from a different first language and second language accent). However, this was not an entirely consistent finding for different shared-first-language speaker-listener combinations.

Pragmatic knowledge. Although pragmatic processing has been theorised to constitute a crucial aspect of proficient listening, limited research has looked into the effect of listeners' pragmatic knowledge on their comprehension. Those exploring this topic have found an interaction effect with language proficiency, namely listeners' level of knowledge of the task input language seems to determine the degree to which they have the capacity to activate and make use of their pragmatic knowledge whilst listening (see e.g., Garcia 2004; Taguchi 2005).

3.2.2.3 Factors associated with the affective characteristics of the test taker

Anxiety. One listener trait that has been looked into in only a limited number of studies, but has nevertheless consistently been shown to correlate with second language listening test difficulty is listening anxiety. It is thought to be situation-specific (MacIntyre and Gardner 1991); learners may only experience it when engaged in second language listening. Empirical studies that have explored whether listening anxiety and listening test performance are related include Brunfaut and Révész (2015), Elkhafaifi (2005b), and Kim (2000). They found moderate to strong negative associations between anxiety and performance, or, put differently, less anxious listeners achieved higher listening scores. This was found for a range of listening item types with a variety of task demands, for different target languages, and test takers from a variety of first language backgrounds.

Motivation. Motivation has been considered to play a key role in language learning success (see e.g., Dörnyei 2012), and has been hypothesised to play a similar role in relation to listening. Vandergrift (2005) empirically explored this by correlating the answers of adolescent French second language learners on the validated Language Learning Orientations Scale with their scores on a French listening proficiency test. Whilst he found a negative association between lack of motivation and listening test performance – confirming the existence of some kind of relationship between motivation and listening, surprisingly no significant correlation was found between listening test performance and high degrees of extrinsic motivation (e.g., driven by reasons such as getting a job) or intrinsic motivation (e.g., personal enjoyment motives).

4 Future directions

An important caveat which has been hinted at in the above review and which is specifically discussed in research aiming to explain variability in listening (see e.g., Andringa et al. 2012; Tafaghodtari and Vandergrift 2008) is that the answer may not always be found in individual task or listener characteristics. Often, more powerful explanations are observed in clusters of interrelated variables. Therefore, there is a need for more research looking into the effect of interactions between variables on listening test performance. Exploring research from the fields of second language acquisition and cognitive psychology in greater depth may prove beneficial to inform variable selection. From a methodological perspective, such investigations also require more complex analytic procedures than, for example, correlational studies (see Aryadoust and Goh 2014 for promising statistical innovations). In addition, more extensive use of techniques such as stimulated recalls (see e.g., Révész and Brunfaut 2013) or eye-tracking could shed more light on the impact of variables on the listening process and on listening itself.

An additional area for careful evaluation is the type of measures used to observe test-task and test-taker characteristics. As discussed in Révész and Brunfaut (2013), to date the characteristic indicators adopted in many studies have not always been comprehensive or the most suitable ones. Thus, when designing research looking into listening difficulty, considerable thought should go into the selection of research instruments and measures. This, however, may need to be preceded by a larger body of research specifically looking into the development and validation of instruments and measures suitable for listening (assessment) research.

From the point of view of listening assessment practice, a promising research strand may be found in more elaborate listening task manipulation studies whereby one or more task characteristics are purposefully adapted and the impact on difficulty and on processing is explored against a number of listener characteristics. The findings on factors that have been empirically shown to be associated with listening test performances and difficulty (see Section 3) could help determine the selection of variables for manipulation.

Finally, it is worth noting that research on listening task and test-taker characteristics, and on listening assessment in general, has primarily involved independent-approach listening tests. However, due to the increasing use of integrated test tasks with listening input (for example in tests for specific purposes – some of which are high-stakes), more research on such tasks and task performances is desirable.

5 References

Alderson, J. Charles and Lyle F. Bachman. 2001. Series editor's preface. In: Gary Buck, *Assessing listening*, x–xi. Cambridge, UK: Cambridge University Press.

Alderson, J. Charles. 1984. Reading in a foreign language: A reading problem or a language problem? In: J. Charles Alderson and Alexander H. Urquhart (eds.). *Reading in a foreign language*, 122–135. New York: Longman.

Anderson, John R. 1995. *Cognitive psychology and its implications*. 4th ed. New York: Freeman.

Andringa, Sible, Nomi Olsthoorn, Catherine van Beuningen, Rob Schoonen and Jan Hulstijn. 2012. Determinants of success in native and non-native listening comprehension: An individual differences approach. *Language Learning* 62 (Supplement s2): 49–78.

Aryadoust, Vahid and Christine C. M. Goh. 2014. Predicting Listening Item Difficulty with Language Complexity Measures: A Comparative Data Mining Study. *CaMLA Working Papers* 2014-02. Michigan: Cambridge Michigan.

Bachman, Lyle F. and Adrian S. Palmer. 1996. *Language testing in practice: Designing and developing useful language tests.* Oxford, UK: Oxford University Press.

Baddeley, Alan. 2003. Working memory: Looking back and looking forward. *Nature Reviews Neuroscience* 4: 829–839.

Berne, Jane E. 1995. How does varying pre-listening activities affect second language listening comprehension? *Hispania* 78(2): 316–329.

Brown, Annie, Noriko Iwashita and Tim McNamara. 2005. An examination of rater orientations and test-taker performance on English-for-academic-purposes speaking tasks. *TOEFL Monograph Series* MS-29. Princeton, NJ: Educational Testing Service.

Brunfaut, Tineke and Andrea Révész. 2015. The role of listener- and task-characteristics in second language listening. *TESOL Quarterly.* 49(1): 141–168.

Buck, Gary and Kikumi Tatsuoka. 1998. Application of the rule-space procedure to language testing: Examining attributes of a free response listening test. *Language Testing* 15(2): 119–157.

Buck, Gary. 2001. *Assessing listening.* Cambridge, UK: Cambridge University Press.

Carrell, Patricia L. 2007. Notetaking strategies and their relationship to performance on listening comprehension and communicative assessment tasks. *TOEFL Monograph Series* RR-07-01. Princeton, NJ: Educational Testing Service.

Carrell, Patricia L., Patricia A. Dunkel and Pamela Mollaun. 2004. The effects of note taking, lecture length, and topic on a computer-based test of EFL listening comprehension. *Applied Language Learning* 14(1): 83–105.

Cheng, Hsiao-fang. 2004. A comparison of multiple-choice and open-ended response formats for the assessment of listening proficiency in English. *Foreign Language Annals* 37(4): 544–553.

Chung, Jing-mei. 2002. The effects of using two advance organizers with video texts for the teaching of listening in English. *Foreign Language Annals* 35(2): 231–241.

Coniam, David. 2001. The use of audio or video comprehension as an assessment instrument in the certification of English language teachers: A case study. *System* 29(1): 1–14.

Dörnyei, Zoltan. 2012. *Motivation in language learning.* Shanghai: Shanghai Foreign Language Education Press.

Elkhafaifi, Hussein. 2005a. The effects of prelistening activities on listening comprehension in Arabic learners. *Foreign Language Annals* 38(4): 505–513.

Elkhafaifi, Hussein. 2005b. Listening comprehension and anxiety in the Arabic language classroom. *The Modern Language Journal* 89(2): 206–219.

Field, John. 2012. The cognitive validity of the lecture-based question in the IELTS Listening paper. In: Lynda Taylor and Cyril Weir (eds.). *IELTS Collected Papers 2: Research in reading and listening assessment*, 391–453. Cambridge, UK: Cambridge University Press.

Field, John. 2013. Cognitive validity. In: Ardeshir Geranpayeh and Lynda Taylor (eds.). *Examining listening*, 77–151. Cambridge, UK: Cambridge University Press.

Freedle, Roy O. and Irene W. Kostin. 1996. The prediction of TOEFL listening comprehension item difficulty for minitalk passages: Implications for construct validity. *TOEFL Research Report* RR-96-29. Princeton, NJ: Educational Testing Service.

Garcia, Paula. 2004. Pragmatic comprehension of high and low level language learners. *TESL-EJ* 8(2). http://www.tesl-ej.org/wordpress/issues/volume8/ej30/ej30a1/ (accessed 31 August 2013).

Ginther, April. 2002. Context and content visuals and performance on listening comprehension stimuli. *Language Testing* 19(2): 133–167.

Goh, Christine C. M. 2002. Exploring listening comprehension tactics and their interaction patterns. *System* 30(2): 185–206.

Gruba, Paul. 1993. A comparison study of audio and video in language testing. *JALT Journal* 15(1): 85–88.

Harding, Luke. 2012. Accent, listening assessment and the potential for a shared-L1 advantage: A DIF perspective. *Language Testing* 29(2): 163–180.

Hulstijn, Jan. 2003. Connectionist models of language processing and the training of listening skills with the aid of multimedia software. *Computer Assisted Language Learning* 16(5): 413–425.

In'nami, Yo and Rie Koizumi. 2009. A meta-analysis of test format effects on reading and listening test performance: Focus on multiple-choice and open-ended formats. *Language Testing* 26(2): 219–244.

Jensen, Christine, Christa Hansen, Samuel B. Green and Terri Akey. 1997. An investigation of item difficulty incorporating the structure of listening tests: a hierarchical linear modeling analysis. In: Ari Huhta, Viljo Kohonen, Liisa Kurki-Suonio and Sari Luoma (eds.). *Current developments and alternatives in language assessment: Proceedings of LTRC 96:* 151–164. Tampere: University of Jyvaskyla.

Kim, Joo-Hae. 2000. *Foreign language listening anxiety: A study of Korean students learning English.* Austin: University of Texas dissertation.

Kormos, Judit and Anna Sáfár. 2008. Phonological short term-memory, working memory and foreign language performance in intensive language learning. *Bilingualism: Language and Cognition* 11(2): 261–271.

Kostin, Irene. 2004. Exploring item characteristics that are related to the difficulty of TOEFL dialogue items. *TOEFL Research Report* RR-79. Princeton, NJ: Educational Testing Service.

Lewkowicz, Jo. 1997. The integrated testing of a second language. In: Caroline Clapham and David Corson (eds.). *Encyclopedia of language and education* (Vol. 7: Language testing and assessment), 121–130. The Netherlands: Kluwer Academic Publishers.

Long, Donna Reseigh. 1990. What you don't know can't help you: An exploratory study of background knowledge and second language listening comprehension. *Studies in Second Language Acquisition* 12(1): 65–80.

Lynch, Tony. 2009. *Teaching Second Language Listening: A guide to evaluating, adapting, and creating tasks for listening in the language classroom.* Oxford, UK: Oxford University Press.

Macaro, Ernesto, Robert Vanderplank and Suzanne Graham. 2005. *A systematic review of the role of prior knowledge in unidirectional listening comprehension.* London: EPPI-centre. http://www.eppi.ioe.ac.uk/cms/LinkClick.aspx?fileticket=0YJczAHkdBg%3Dandtabid=299andmid=1149 (accessed 31 August 2013).

MacIntyre, Peter D. and Robert C. Gardner. 1991. Methods and results in the study of anxiety and language learning: A review of the literature. *Language Learning* 41(1): 85–117.

Markham, Paul and Michael Latham. 1987. The influence of religion-specific background knowledge on listening comprehension of adult second language students. *Language Learning* 37(2): 157–170.

Mecartty, Frances H. 2000. Lexical and grammatical knowledge in reading and listening comprehension by foreign language learners of Spanish. *Applied Language Learning* 11(2): 323–348.

Nissan, Susan, Felicia DeVincenzi and K. Linda Tang. 1996. An analysis of factors affecting the difficulty of dialogue items in TOEFL listening comprehension. *TOEFL Research Report* RR-51. Princeton, NJ: Educational Testing Service.

Norris, John, Martin Bygate and Kris Van den Branden. 2009. Task-based language assessment. In: Kris Van den Branden, Martin Bygate and John M. Norris (eds.). *Task-based language teaching: A reader*, 431–434. Amsterdam: John Benjamins.

Révész, Andrea and Tineke Brunfaut. 2013. Text characteristics of task input and difficulty in second language listening comprehension. *Studies in Second Language Acquisition* 35(1): 31–65.

Rosenhouse, Judith, Lubna Haik and Liat Kishon-Rabin. 2006. Speech perception in adverse listening conditions in Arabic-Hebrew bilinguals. *International Journal of Bilingualism* 10(2): 119–135.

Rost, Michael. 2005. L2 Listening. In: Eli Hinkel (ed.). *Handbook of research on second language teaching and learning*, 503–528. Mahwah, NJ: Lawrence Erlbaum.

Rost, Michael. 2011. *Teaching and researching listening*. 2nd ed. Harlow: Longman.

Rupp, Andre A., Paula Garcia and Joan Jamieson. 2001. Combining multiple regression and CART to understand difficulty in second language reading and listening comprehension test items. *International Journal of Testing* 1(3–4): 185–216.

Schmidt-Rinehart, Barbara C. 1994. The effect of topic familiarity on second language listening comprehension. *Modern Language Journal* 78(2): 179–189.

Segalowitz, Norman. 2003. Automaticity and second languages. In: Catherine J. Doughty and Michael H. Long (eds.). *The handbook of second language acquisition*, 382–408. Oxford: Blackwell.

Shohamy, Elana and Ofra Inbar. 1991. Construct validation of listening comprehension tests: The effect of text and question type. *Language Testing* 8(1): 23–40.

Staehr, Lars Stenius. 2009. Vocabulary knowledge and advanced listening comprehension in English as a Foreign Language. *Studies in Second Language Acquisition* 31(4): 577–607.

Tafaghodtari, Marzieh H. and Larry Vandergrift. 2008. Second/foreign language listening: Unraveling the construct. *Perceptual and Motor Skills* 107(1): 99–113.

Taguchi, Naoko. 2005. Comprehending implied meaning in English as a foreign language. *The Modern Language Journal* 89(4): 543–562.

Vandergrift, Larry and Christine C. M. Goh. 2009. Teaching and testing listening comprehension. In: Michael H. Long and Catherine Doughty (eds.). *Handbook of language teaching*, 395–411. Malden, MA: Blackwell.

Vandergrift, Larry and Christine C. M. Goh. 2012. *Teaching and learning second language listening: Metacognition in action*. New York: Routledge.

Vandergrift, Larry, Christine C. M. Goh, Catherine J. Mareschal and Marzieh H. Tafaghodtari. 2006. The Metacognitive Awareness Listening Questionnaire (MALQ): Development and validation. *Language Learning* 56(3): 431–462.

Vandergrift, Larry. 2003. Orchestrating strategy use: Toward a model of the skilled second language listener. *Language Learning* 53(3): 463–496.

Vandergrift, Larry. 2005. Relationships among motivation orientations, metacognitive awareness and proficiency in L2 listening. *Applied Linguistics* 26(1): 70–89.

Vandergrift, Larry. 2006. Second language listening: Listening ability or language proficiency? *The Modern Language Journal* 90(1): 6–18.

Vandergrift, Larry. 2007. Recent developments in second and foreign language listening comprehension research. *Language Teaching* 40(3): 191–210.

Vandergrift, Larry. 2011. L2 listening: Presage, process, product and pedagogy. In: Eli Hinkel (ed.). *Handbook of research in second language teaching and learning* (Vol. 2), 455–471. New York: Routledge.

Wagner, Elvis. 2013. An investigation of how the channel of input and access to test questions affect L2 listening test performance. *Language Assessment Quarterly* 10(2): 178–195.

Ying-hui, Hu. 2006. An investigation into the task features affecting EFL listening comprehension test performance. *The Asian EFL Journal Quarterly* 8(2): 33–54.

Fabiana M. MacMillan

8 Assessing reading

1 Introduction

A number of approaches have been taken to assess second language reading comprehension, and in all cases, attempts have been made to establish some concept of what reading comprehension entails. Nevertheless, as suggested by decades of reading research, defining the construct of reading is not an easy task. Opposing views on what reading is, how it works, and how to best elicit evidence that comprehension has or has not occurred have emerged, and consensus has yet to be reached. Two of these views are the product and process approaches to reading, of which the first has had a stronger impact on the field of reading assessment. The focus on the product of reading (what readers understand from text) has led to the development of models of reading describing different "levels of understanding" and identifying specific reading abilities believed to be required to reach each level of comprehension. In reading assessment this has often translated into efforts to develop reading tasks that target specific reading skills and determine what variables make these tasks more or less challenging.

This chapter will begin by providing a brief overview of different models of reading and developments in reading assessment research, including a review of the *assessment use argument* (Bachman and Palmer 2010) framework for creating evidence-based assessments. It will then draw on studies in written discourse analysis and describe a framework for the analysis of reading assessment items in terms of what reading skills are essential to successfully complete such tasks. Specifically, it will discuss how Hoey's (1991) model, based on the text-forming function of lexical cohesion, has been modified to investigate bases for backing warrants about reading assessment tasks and the skills they elicit (MacMillan 2006b, 2007, 2008, 2010). The penultimate section will discuss the methodology and results of research, applying Hoey's model to the analysis of large-scale standardized reading assessments. It will be suggested that examining the number and type of lexical connections between reading comprehension questions and their keys (as well as elements disambiguating keys from distractors in multiple-choice items) is a helpful tool in evaluating the effectiveness of reading assessments and, by extension, better understanding some key elements involved in second language reading comprehension. Finally, the chapter will close with a brief discussion of possible next steps in research exploring the interface between reading assessment and written discourse analysis.

2 Models of reading and their limitations

2.1 Focusing on the product of reading

Earlier research into reading used a product approach, which focused on what understanding was reached, rather than on how that understanding was reached (e.g., Carrell 1991; Perkins, Brutten and Pohlmann 1989). Studies of this nature often involved the use of some measure of text understanding (e.g., test questions), and the subsequent drawing of a parallel between the results reached and specific variables of interest. One frequent goal was to distinguish levels of understanding. To that end, different theories proposed to describe components of reading ability, or distinct reading skills (e.g., Davis 1968, Kintch and van Dijk 1978). Discussions about separable reading skills, sometimes referred to as sub-skills or micro-skills (Munby 1978), have often included a distinction between "higher-order" and "lower-order" skills. For example, understanding ideas explicitly stated in the text, may be classified as a lower-order skill, whereas using background knowledge to make an inference might be considered a higher-order reading skill. In reading assessment research, the proposed distinction between higher- and lower-order skills has prompted investigations of levels of difficulty associated with reading tasks targeting these skills.

Despite its popularity, the product model of reading is not without its limitations. Alderson (2000: 5) mentions that one problem with this approach is the variation in the product. Different readers may reach different understandings of the same text, and this diversity in comprehension may be due, in part, to the fact that texts do not necessarily "contain" meaning that needs to be unveiled by capable readers. Rather, it might be argued that "texts gain their meaning from a reader's interaction with them" (Hoey 2001: 5). It can be challenging to objectively decide which interpretations are acceptable and which are not. This has serious implications for the design of reading assessment tasks, as objectivity is an essential component to fairness.

Another limitation associated with a product approach to reading is the fact that the methods used to assess comprehension are less than perfect. Alderson (2000: 7) points out that certain test methods, including cloze techniques and gap-filling, may be said to induce certain readers to read in a particular way (e.g., reading the text preceding the gap, and ignoring other portions of the text), thus affecting the reading product. In addition, certain methods are restricted in terms of the levels of understanding they are capable of assessing. While cloze and gap-filling tasks may be used to assess a reader's ability to read "the lines," or the literal meaning of text, these methods seem to be of limited use with regards to assessing a reader's ability to read "between the lines" or "beyond the lines," i.e. inferred meanings and critical evaluations of text, respectively (Gray 1960, cited in Alderson 2000: 7–8).

One final limitation of the product model of reading is the lack of consensus in terms of what and how many components of reading ability can be identified. Different studies have introduced reading skill taxonomies varying in number of sub-skills from as few as two or three (e.g., Bernhardt 1991, Hoover and Tunmer 1993) to as many as thirty-six (e.g., Lunzer and Gardner 1979). Additionally, the true separability of the components identified in these studies has been called into question. Some taxonomies have been criticized for overlap between skills purported to be distinct (e.g., Davies 1981). Similar problems have been reported in reading assessment studies analyzing reading tasks intended to elicit and measure specific skills, an issue that I will return to in section 3 of this chapter.

2.2 Focusing on the process of reading

In more recent years, research on both first and second language reading has used a process approach (e.g., Anderson 1999; Millis, Magliano, and Todaro 2006). In this model, reading is viewed as an interactive process whereby information within the text is combined with information the reader brings to the text. The reader samples the text to confirm or reject hypotheses and to form new hypotheses in a process that has been described as a "psycholinguistic guessing game" (Goodman 1976).

Studies have attempted to tap the mental, or cognitive, processes through which readers interact with text by means of miscue analysis (Goodman 1969), where participants are asked to read a text aloud and mistakes made are analyzed, as well as through eye tracking (Rayner 1998), where the eye movements of readers are examined. Introspective methodologies have also been used to investigate the reading process, including think-aloud protocols, also termed verbal protocols (Hosenfeld 1984). As with most methods for data collection in reading studies, the aforementioned techniques have their limitations. Miscue analysis has been criticized because reading aloud is not the way people typically read, meaning that results obtained may not be representative of the processes involved in silent reading. While eye tracking provides useful insights into what portions of a text the reader deems relevant or irrelevant (with eye fixations being longer for relevant sentences at first-pass reading) (Kaakinen and Hyönä 2005), it cannot reveal with certainty in each case whether a) backward eye movements (or rereading) result from comprehension difficulty or other reasons, such as faulty focal point positioning (or "losing" one's place) (Samuels, Rasinski and Hiebert 2011), and b) whether rereads stemming from text complexity lead to a comprehension failure or success (Hyönä 2011). Finally, data collected through introspective methods may be misleading because "subjects' reports on their mental processes are not complete, and may be influenced by their perception of what the researcher 'wants' them to do" (Rankin 1988: 121).

3 Reading assessment research: Some challenges

In spite of the shortcomings associated with clearly defining the construct of reading ability, the use of reading assessments is a common – and necessary – practice. Although admittedly imperfect, reading assessments are an essential tool to infer learners' stage of development and help make decisions about, for example, their preparedness for educational and professional opportunities. Moreover, and perhaps more importantly, it has been found that the study of reading assessments and the abilities that appear to be measured can contribute to a better understanding of the nature of L2 reading itself (Alderson 2000; Grabe 2009).

As previously mentioned, the product model of reading has had a strong influence on reading assessment. Its contribution to assessment research may be seen in investigations aimed at measuring theory-based reading skills by means of reading tests (Lennon 1962, cited in Alderson 2000: 7–8). Attempts have also been made to identify a possible connection between reading task difficulty and the class of the sub-skill being targeted, with an expectation that items focusing on higher-order skills might be more challenging than those testing lower-order skills (Alderson and Lukmani 1989: 259). However, studies have shown that expert judges often have difficulty agreeing on which skills test developers intended to target in reading tasks (Alderson 1990a), bringing into question the separability of these skills and the merits of the classification of some of them as superior to others. Additional studies analyzing the performance of reading tasks have found no evidence to support a hierarchy of difficulty stemming from reading skill class (Alderson 1990b).

Fewer studies in reading assessment have focused on the process of reading. Predominantly, these studies have sought to investigate how readers interact with texts when answering reading comprehension tasks using introspective techniques (e.g, Allan 1992, Cohen and Upton 2006). Often times readers' reports centered on their use of test-wiseness strategies rather than the processes by which they engaged with text. This may be partly due to an inherent limitation of think-aloud protocols whereby participants have a tendency to allow their assumptions of what the researcher wants to influence their performance. Allan (1992) has suggested that readers' reports are also in part influenced by task format, with multiple-choice items eliciting more test-taking strategies than free-response ones.

Irrespective of what reading model assessment studies may be classified as representing, a frequent point of interest has been to determine what factors make reading more or less challenging to different students and whether such factors can help provide evidence of a learner's level of reading proficiency. In many instances, this interest has been operationalized as studies investigating the features affecting the difficulty of reading test items.

3.1 Investigating factors affecting reading test item difficulty

A number of studies have looked into variables affecting item difficulty in reading comprehension tests (e.g., Freddle and Kostin 1993; Kirsch 2001). Kirsch (2001) identified three groups of features that were found to contribute to an item's level of difficulty, namely type of information requested, type of match, and plausibility of distracting information. Two types of information requested were compared, concrete and abstract, with the second yielding more difficult items. Under type of match, items were classified in a rising scale of difficulty as requiring readers to a) locate a single piece of information explicitly stated in the text, b) cycle through the text to locate multiple pieces of information, c) integrate information by making an inference about the relationship between two or more pieces of information in the text (e.g., cause and effect), or d) generate, or infer, categories under which to group different pieces of information in the text. The type of match feature also categorized items according to how the item stem matched with the key in the text, with literal or synonymous matches being the easiest and matches involving inference being more challenging. Finally, as regards plausibility of distractors, items were classified in an ascending order of difficulty according to a) the amount of distracting information, or the extent to which information in the text shares one or more features with the information requested without fully satisfying the conditions specified in the question, and b) the location of the distracting information relative to the correct response within the text. Kirsch (2001: 17) found that items "tend to become more difficult as the number of distractors increases, as the distractors share more features with the correct response, and as the distractors appear in closer proximity to the correct response."

Freddle and Kostin (1993) analyzed different variables that contribute to item difficulty in the reading comprehension section of the Test of English as a Foreign Language (TOEFL®), including, among others, use of negative forms, location of main idea statements, and percentage of word overlap between text and test item. Concerning this last variable, they found that items with a higher percentage of lexical overlap with the key in the text tend to be easier. This finding is in line with results in Kirsch (2001), where items with a literal or synonymous type of match with the text were found to be easier. The following two sections will further explore the contribution of lexical overlap to reading task difficulty by reference to studies in written discourse analysis, and how results from these studies have been used to support a recent approach to reading test development and use.

4 The assessment use argument and Hoey's (1991) model of written discourse analysis

In the past two decades, an influential line of research, particularly in standardized language testing, has been to ground reading assessments in evidence-based constructs of reading ability by reference to target populations (Grabe 2009). Bachman and Palmer (2010: 99) proposed a conceptual framework – the assessment use argument – for "guiding the development and use of a particular language assessment, including the interpretations and uses made on the basis of the assessment." Following this framework, claims about specific components of reading ability at given levels of language proficiency are built from gathered evidence in the form of learners' performance on reading tasks (e.g., Jamieson et al. 2000; Clapham 1996; Weir and Milanovic 2003). This evidence-based approach to building reading constructs represents a step forward in relation to previous approaches based exclusively on theoretical models of reading.

The assessment use argument structure follows Toulmin's (2003) strategy for practical reasoning and includes six elements: data, claims, warrants, backing, rebuttals, and rebuttal backing. These elements can be applied to different stages of test development and use. To illustrate, the data in question could be test takers' performance on a reading comprehension test, the claim would then be the scores achieved and their interpretation, i.e. the statements made about test takers' reading proficiency based on their test scores, a warrant could be that such interpretation is meaningful, i.e. that we can be confident that test takers' performance on the reading assessment indeed provides an indication of their reading ability in the criterion environment (e.g., educational setting), and, in this case, an example of backing could be research results showing that the assessment tasks engage the same reading skills typically accessed in a target language use situation (e.g., academic reading). A rebuttal, if present, would aim to challenge a given claim made about the test, and rebuttal backing would include evidence that the claim is unsubstantiated or untrue.

When applying the assessment use argument to the design and evaluation of reading assessment tasks, an important question is how to substantiate warrants that these tasks indeed elicit target reading skills. This is quite challenging as studies have shown that the characteristics of assessment tasks (e.g., item format) are always likely to affect test results to a certain extent (e.g., Alderson and Urquhart 1985; Shohamy 1984) so that, as Bachman and Palmer (2010: 64) point out, "there is no assessment that yields only information about the ability we want to assess." That said, it is possible to investigate the degree of correspondence between target language use and assessment tasks. One avenue that has been explored in recent years to achieve this goal is to apply written discourse analysis models to reading assessment tasks (e.g., Batista 2002; Jones 2009; MacMillan 2006a, 2007, 2008, 2010). A particularly influential model is Hoey's (1991) system of text analysis focusing on lexical cohesion.

Hoey's (1991) approach is unlike that of previous works on lexical cohesion in that the attention is not primarily on itemizing and classifying different types of cohesive features (e.g., synonym, ellipsis) but on observing how they combine to organize text. Another factor that distinguishes Hoey's model from previous efforts in written discourse description is how he attempts to represent the concept of text. He uses an analogy, which he dubbed "the collection of texts metaphor" (Hoey 1991: 31), and compares sentences in a text to a group of academic papers. The same way academic papers signal intertextual relations by means of bibliographical references, different sentences in a text may be said to "cite" one another through lexical repetition.

In order to demonstrate the validity of the collection of texts metaphor, Hoey (1991) describes an analytical model focusing on the lexical devices in non-narrative texts. In his system, Hoey (1991) identifies as *links* the kinds of lexical relation that permit repetition across sentences. In addition to lexical relations, he also considers a small set of cohesive devices which are not lexical in nature but which make it possible for repetition to take place. The model includes several types of links, namely lexical repetition (simple and complex), paraphrase (simple, complex antonymous and complex link triangle), superordinate/hyponymic repetition, co-reference, and substitution.

Hoey establishes three as the minimal number of links for two sentences to be considered significantly connected, or *bonded*, as in example (1) showing the first two sentences of an article about literary criticism (Wagner 2011: 29):

(1) *If **literary criticism** is to survive in this **digital age**, it must **adapt** to become something **new**, different, and more intimately personal.*

*The **old** academic paradigm of **literary criticism** is based upon a print model and makes certain assumptions about its readers, assumptions that need to **be reworked** in the **digital age**.*

Here, the two sentences are bonded by means of four links: literary criticism – literary criticism (simple lexical repetition), digital age – digital age (simple lexical repetition), adapt – be reworked (simple paraphrase), and new – old (complex antonymous paraphrase). It should be noted that in some cases three links may not be sufficient to form a bond between two sentences. Hoey (1991: 92) explains that given that bonds are established by means of an above average number of links, the cut-off point determining the minimal number of links required to form a bond between sentences is "related indirectly and uncertainly to the relative length and lexical density of the sentences of the text in question."

According to Hoey (1991), sentences that have an unusually high level of bonding with other sentences may be regarded as central to the development of the theme of the text. Moreover, he claims that sentences forming the majority of their bonds with later sentences may be considered topic-opening sentences, and sentences forming the majority of their bonds with earlier sentences may be considered topic-closing. Batista (2002) proposed applying the principles in Hoey's (1991) model to the analysis of the reading section of university entrance examinations in Brazil. MacMillan (2007) modified and expanded on a few aspects of Hoey's

(1991) original model and used this revised analytical system to check reading items in the TOEFL® test for the presence of bonds connecting item keys with target portions in the reading passages in question. MacMillan's (2007) version of Hoey's (1991) model was subsequently used to investigate the role of lexical cohesion in reading item difficulty in the TOEFL® (MacMillan 2007, 2010), the International English Language Testing System (IELTS) (MacMillan 2008), and the academic Pearson Test of English (PTE) (Jones 2009). The section that follows will outline MacMillan's (2007) modified version of Hoey's (1991) model and provide a summary of the methodology and results of research using this analytical system to investigate characteristics of reading assessment tasks.

5 Research on the role of lexical cohesion in reading assessment tasks

Following a study in which MacMillan (2006a) used Hoey's (1991) lexical cohesion model to analyze a small sample of TOEFL® reading items, MacMillan (2007) introduced a few modifications to the original analytical system intended to make differences between certain types of lexical links more clear-cut and to include an additional link category stemming from results of her earlier study. The resulting revised taxonomy is shown in Table 1.

MacMillan (2006a, 2007) sought to investigate whether bonds, marked by a large number of links, could be observed connecting the correct option in multiple-choice reading comprehension items and target sentences in the related passage.

Tab. 1: Link Taxonomy.

Link Taxonomy	
Lexical Relations	
Lexical Repetition	Simple
	Complex
Synonymy	Simple
	Complex
Antonymy	Simple
	Complex
Superordinate Repetition	
Hyponymic Repetition	
Co-Reference	
Labeling	
Non-lexical Relations	
Substitution	By pro-forms
	By Ø (Ellipsis)

(MacMillan 2007: 78)

The hypothesis was that, as sentences that are central to the development of a theme are significantly bonded (Hoey 1991), in like manner the correct options (or statements formed by combining the question stem and the correct option) and key sentences in the passage would feature an above average number of links with one another.

I will now examine how each of the link types in Table 1 contributes to the identification of semantic bonds between test items and passages with examples drawn from *Writing About Literature in the Digital Age* (Burton 2011a). Sentences are numbered and multiple link categories labeled with letters in superscript for ease of reference. Numbers in bold refer to the position of the sentences within the page on which they appear in the original text.

The first type of link considered in MacMillan (2007), *lexical repetition*, may be classified as either simple or complex. Simple lexical repetition involves items which Hoey (1991: 55) defines as "formally identical," i.e. items sharing the exact same form or the same morpheme with minimum alterations, such as those marking the 3rd person singular, simple past, past participle or gerund forms of a verb. Complex lexical repetition, on the other hand, occurs when a) two lexical items share a lexical morpheme but are not formally identical, or b) when they have the same form, but represent different parts of speech. Example (2) shows instances of a) simple repetition and b) complex repetition:

(2) **8** *Students take ownership of **personal**[b] **blogs**[a] in ways impossible within more traditional academic genres.*
9 *They do not conceptualize **blogs**[a] as instruments of thought; they experience them as expressions of **personality**[b].*
(Burton 2011b: 22)

Hoey's (1991) simple, complex antonymous, and complex link triangle paraphrase have been replaced in MacMillan (2007) with two more simply defined categories: *synonymy* and *antonymy*. While the original model categorized antonyms sharing a morpheme (e.g., happy – unhappy) as instances of complex repetition and notional gradable and non-gradable antonyms (e.g., hot – cold, dead – alive, respectively) as complex antonymous paraphrase, the revised model treats both cases simply as synonymy. MacMillan (2007) categorizes as simple synonymy those instances where two words or phrases share both the same meaning and part of speech. Complex synonymy encompasses those cases where terms have similar meanings but do not belong to the same word class. Example (3) features instances of a) simple and b) complex synonymy:

(3) **1** *The informality of blogging is its genius.* **2** *When writing isn't precious, rare, and elevated, it has a better chance of being frequent, authentic, and (in the **aggregate**[b]), **copious**[a].*

9 *More immediately, a student's **accumulated**[b] blog posts create an **ample**[a] supply of less developed ideas that can readily become more developed* (...)
(Burton 2011b: 21)

The adjective *copious* in sentence 1 is repeated by means of another adjective of similar meaning, *ample* in sentence 9, thus forming a simple synonymy link. On the other hand, the noun *aggregate* in sentence 1 is repeated in sentence 9 by means of a word of similar meaning but different part of speech, the adjective *accumulated*, thus forming a complex synonymy link.

The third type of lexical relation considered in MacMillan (2007), antonymy, is also classified as either simple or complex. Simple antonymy involves the repetition of the concept of a given lexical item by means of an antonymous term which is part of the same word class. Conversely, complex antonymy involves antonymous terms that do not share the same part of speech. Example (4) demonstrates instances of a) simple and b) complex antonymy:

(4) **17** *The principal benefit I have observed in asking students to blog has been removing the stigma of meaning making from the activity of writing – or at least, unshackling students from the feeling that if they are not making some **formal**[a], reasoned, **well-supported**[b], logically sound argument, then they have nothing to say.*
12 *The many **tentative**[b], **informal**[a], largely uncoordinated posts that make up a student literary blog end up documenting a process that proves as valuable as a more formal academic product.*
(Burton 2011b: 20–21)

Superordinate and *hyponymic repetition* account for cases when two items are interpreted as having identical referents. These links occur when the terms sharing the same referent are connected by a lexical relation of class membership. Superordinate repetition involves a general term that may be said to designate a class of which the earlier term is a member. When, on the other hand, a specific term is used to refer back to a more general term in an earlier sentence, the resulting link is categorized as hyponymic repetition, as in (5):

(5) **16** *Within such a persona-creative context, writing about **literature** can become a far more living thing.*
17 *It is connected not just to an assignment, nor to a period of academic schooling, nor to a particular semester, nor to a particular **book**.*
(Burton 2011b: 22)

In a similar way to superordinate and hyponymic repetition, *co-reference* links involve items that share the same referent. Unlike those, however, co-reference items do not hold a lexical relation in the language system and, thus, the link between them is context-dependent. Example (6) shows a co-reference link:

(6) **7** *I love great **works of literature** because of their ability to read us, to make a map of the present and renew their relevance for each generation, including our digital age.*
   8 Moby Dick *has been working that way for me.*
   (Burton 2011b: 17)

The *labeling* category was not present in Hoey's (1991) original model. It is based on Francis' (1994) description of *retrospective labels*. The term retrospective label refers to a nominal group which encapsulates a stretch of discourse and indicates to the reader how it should be interpreted. Francis (1994: 89) points out that these labels are more often than not formed by deictics, such as *this*, *that* or *such*, followed by a head noun, which is unspecific in nature, as in (7):

(7) **12** *When the high point of engaging the **online world** is merely judging the quality of internet sites or citing them properly, then literary studies are at a low point in the digital culture that is now dominant.*
   1 *I will go so far as to say that teachers of writing who persist in training students to write in ways that ignore **this context** are endangering the literacy of their students.*
   (Burton 2011b: 27–28)

Finally, *substitution* is the only category in the link taxonomy which incorporates grammatical members of closed systems whose function is to stand in, or substitute, for lexical items. Substitution may occur by means of pro-forms (e.g., demonstrative pronouns, clausal *so*), or zero in instances of ellipsis. An example of substitution with a pronoun is shown in (8):

(8) **13** *It is okay **to explore, to be tentative**.*
   15 This *is part of a valuable process, a process you must document.*
   (Burton 2011b: 20)

MacMillan (2007) used this link taxonomy to analyze a corpus of 608 TOEFL® reading test items from past administrations for the presence of bonds between test items and relevant sentences in the passages in question, as well as bonds connecting those sentences to correct options. Example (9) shows a TOEFL® item from the corpus in MacMillan (2010):

(9) *According to the passage, what made it almost impossible for other groups to conquer the Anasazi?*

a) *The political and social organization of the Anasazi*
b) *The military tactics employed by the Anasazi*
c) *The Anasazi's agricultural technology*
d) *The natural barriers surrounding Anasazi villages*
(ETS 2002: 213)

Each of the options in the item can be joined to the question to form a statement. The validity of that statement can be confirmed by the presence of a considerable number of links forming a bond with one or more sentences in the excerpt indicated in the question (paragraph 4). The statement formed by the correct option c) bonds with last sentence in the passage (sentence 18) by means of as many as ten links, grouped in three chunks as demonstrated in the following analysis (10).

(10) **(A)** *What <u>made it almost impossible for other groups to conquer</u>[1] <u>the Anasazi</u>[2] was the <u>political and social organization of the Anasazi</u>[3].*
   18 *The cohesive <u>political and social organization of the Anasazi</u>[3] <u>made it almost impossible for other groups to conquer</u>[1] <u>them</u>[2].*
   1. *made it almost impossible for other groups to conquer – made it almost impossible for other groups to conquer* (Simple Repetition, 5 links)
   2. *the Anasazi – them* (Substitution, 1 link)
   3. *political and social organization of the Anasazi – political and social organization of the Anasazi* (Simple Repetition, 4 links)

MacMillan (2007) found instances of links connecting the key to target sentences in the related passages in all of the 608 TOEFL® reading comprehension questions in her corpus. In 380 of the items (62.5%), correct options bonded with the passage by means of multiple lexical links. In the remaining 228 items (37.5%), the connection between correct options and the passage was marked by a single lexical link, rather than a bond involving several links. Cases involving bonds between test items and passages account for most of the question types in her corpus, with the exception of vocabulary and reference questions, which almost invariably required the identification of a single simple synonymy link (in vocabulary items), or substitution (in reference items). Finally, one specific question type, negative factual information, was unique in that it called for the identification of the one option that was untrue according to the passage. For this reason, bonds were observed connecting each of the three distractors, rather than the correct option, with the passage.

MacMillan (2008) applied this same analytical system to a small corpus of IELTS reading items to investigate whether assessments featuring a different test method than multiple-choice (including, for example, matching, sentence completion and short answer items) would also display lexical bonds or links connecting items, correct options and passage. In this study, MacMillan (2008) obtained very similar results to those she had previously reached with TOEFL® items. As had occurred in her previous study, in most cases, keys connected with target portions of the passage by means of an above average number of lexical links. Additionally, she found that the types of lexical links observed had a bearing on item difficulty according to the type of match variable (Jamieson et al. 2000; Kirsch 2001) and the requirements to identify the key. Less challenging tasks in terms of type of match seemed to mainly involve the identification of simple and complex repetition links, as well as simple synonymy within a single sentence or a small number of adjacent sentences in the passage. More challenging tasks as regards type of match more frequently required the identification of complex synonymy and antonymy links in non-adjacent sentences in the passage. In terms of the requirements to identify the key, MacMillan (2008) reported that some less challenging items, which involved the "identification of a paradigmatic relationship" (Kirsch 2001: 53), were often marked by the presence of strings of simple synonymy, as well as simple and complex repetition links. Finally, more challenging items, requiring "high-level text-based inference" (Kirsch 2001: 53) were more likely to include instances of complex synonymy and antonymy.

Jones (2009) investigated the role of lexical cohesion as a predictor of item difficulty by using MacMillan's (2007) model to analyze 52 multiple-choice reading items in the PTE Academic. One hypothesis that Jones (2009) investigated was that items with many cohesive links between question and passage are easier than items with few cohesive links. Based on his analyses he concluded that "simply counting cohesive links does not offer a reliable way of predicting item difficulty" and that "lexical cohesion may be a moderate predictor of item difficulty when links are assigned differential values and considered in combination with other factors." These results are in line with previous studies (Kirsch 2001; MacMillan 2008) showing that different factors combine to affect item difficulty, including the distance between occurrences of lexical links (i.e. whether links occur within adjacent or non-adjacent sentences) and additional variables, such as *plausibility of distractors* (Kirsch 2001).

In a subsequent study considering the type of match and plausibility of distractors variables in 59 TOEFL® items broadly categorized by the test designers as easy and difficult (ETS 2002), MacMillan (2010) found that, in the vast majority of items, the key established a stronger bond with the target sentence(s), (i.e. had a higher number of links) than did the distractors. In more challenging items, one or more distractors also featured some links with the target sentence itself or sentences adjacent to it in the passage. This matches Kirsch's (2001: 17) finding that "tasks are judged to be most difficult when two or more distractors share most of the features with the correct response and appear in the same paragraph or node of information as the correct response." Finally, MacMillan (2010) reported a high level of agreement between obtained difficulty and the complexity of what she termed *dominant links* in correct options. Dominant links were defined as those link categories carrying the most weight in the establishment of bonds with target sentences in the passage. Link weight was determined by frequency (i.e. when most of the links forming a bond were of a specific type) or by uniqueness, when a given link was present in the key but in none of the distractors.

The pervasiveness of lexical bonds in reading assessments of different formats as evidenced in this brief survey suggests that this property of reading assessment tasks may be a reflection of textual organization and processing observed in target language use. In other words, the act of identifying significant lexical connections between items and passage may be likened to the skill readers access when locating portions in a text that are central to the development of a theme of interest, or determining where a new topic begins and ends, thus providing a suitable backing to warrant that such assessment tasks indeed elicit target components of reading ability.

6 Future directions

This chapter has presented different models of reading and approaches to reading assessment, and highlighted connections between principles of evidence-based reading assessment design and written discourse analysis. It has suggested that the analysis of the text-forming properties of lexical cohesion is a valuable tool in evaluating reading assessment tasks and that provides backing for warrants made about the correspondence between the skills these tasks elicit and target language use.

In terms of future research, it would be of interest to explore the processes by which test takers use lexical cues to find connections between test items and text. Cohen and Upton's (2006) research on strategies used by candidates responding to reading tasks on the TOEFL® test provide some indication that lexis plays an important role in test takers' decision-making process. Two of the most frequent test-management strategies used by the participants in their study include "select[ing] options through vocabulary, sentence, paragraph, or passage overall meaning (depending on item type)," and "[d]iscarding option(s) based on vocabulary, sentence, paragraph, or passage overall meaning as well as discourse structure" (Cohen and Upton 2006: 36, 43). Cohen and Upton's (2006) study involved highly proficient learners, and the strategies described there were intended to reflect the practices of successful EFL readers. Additional insights into the possible influence of the identification of lexical links on how test takers arrive at the correct answer may be reached by using eye-tracking technology in combination with other methods. For example, following the eye-tracking session, participants may be shown their eye-movement records and asked to comment on them (Jarodzka, Scheiter, Gerjets, and van Gog 2010), particularly on instances where peaks are observed in first-pass eye-fixation time and look-back time. Additionally, it would be beneficial to investigate whether the medium in which the test items and texts are presented, paper-based or computer-based, has an impact on patterns of identification of lexical links.

Finally, further research is needed to investigate possible differences in how learners at different levels of proficiency utilize lexical cues when interacting with reading assessment tasks, which might ultimately refine our understanding of how these same cues contribute to reading comprehension outside the testing environment.

7 References

Alderson, J. Charles. 1990b. Testing reading comprehension skills (Part One). *Reading in a Foreign Language* 6(2): 425–438.

Alderson, J. Charles. 1990b. Testing reading comprehension skills (Part Two). *Reading in a Foreign Language* 7(1): 465–503.

Alderson, J. Charles and Alexander H. Urquhart. 1985. The effect of students' academic discipline on their performance on ESP reading tests. *Language Testing* 2(2): 192–204.

Alderson, J. Charles and Yasmeen Lukmani. 1989. Cognition and reading: cognitive levels as embodied in test questions. *Reading in a Foreign Language* 5(2): 253–270.

Alderson, J. Charles. 2000. *Assessing reading*. Cambridge, UK: Cambridge University Press.

Anderson, Neil. 1999. *Exploring Second Language Reading: Issues and Strategies*. Boston: Heinle and Heinle.

Allan. 1992. *EFL reading comprehension test validation: investigating aspects of process approaches*. Lancaster: Lancaster University dissertation.

Bachman, Lyle F. and Adrian S. Palmer. 2010. *Language testing in practice: Designing and developing useful language tests*. Oxford, UK: Oxford University Press.

Batista, Fabiana M. 2002. *Investigating reading strategies using think aloud protocols*. Rio de Janeiro: Universidade Federal Fluminense MA thesis.

Bernhardt, Elizabeth B. 1991. A psycholinguistic perspective on second language literacy. In: J. H. Hulstijn and J. F. Matter (eds.). Reading in two languages: *AILA Review* 8: 31–44. Amsterdam.

Burton, Gideon O. (ed.). 2011a. *Writing about literature in the digital age*. Paris: Feedbooks. http://www.feedbooks.com/book/6681/writing-about-literature-in-the-digital-age (accessed 6 October 2013).

Burton, Gideon O. 2011b. Chasing the White Whale of Literary Blogging. In: Gideon O. Burton (ed.). *Writing about literature in the digital age*, 15–28. Paris: Feedbooks. http://www.feedbooks.com/book/6681/writing-about-literature-in-the-digital-age (accessed 6 October 2013).

Carrell, Patricia L. 1991. Second language reading: Reading ability or language proficiency? *Applied Linguistics* 12(2): 159–179.

Clapham, Caroline. 1996. *The development of IELTS: a study of the effect of background knowledge on reading comprehension*. Cambridge, UK: Cambridge University Press.

Cohen, Andrew D. and Thomas A. Upton. 2006. *Strategies in responding to the new TOEFL reading tasks*. TOEFL-MS-33. Princeton, NJ: Educational Testing Service.

Davis, Frederick B. 1968. Research in comprehension in reading. *Reading Research Quarterly* 3(4): 499–545.

Davies, Alan. 1981. Review of Munby, J., "Communicative syllabus design." *TESOL Quarterly* 15(3): 332–344.

Educational Testing Service. 2002. *TOEFL® Test preparation kit workbook*. Princeton, NJ: Educational Testing Service.

Francis, Gill. 1994. Labelling discourse: an aspect of nominal-group lexical cohesion. In: Malcolm Coulthard (ed.). *Advances in Written Text Analysis*, 83–101. New York: Routledge.

Freedle, Roy O. and Irene Kostin. 1993. *The prediction of TOEFL reading comprehension item difficulty for expository prose passages for three item types: Main idea, inference, and supporting idea items*. TOEFL-RR-44. Princeton, NJ: Educational Testing Service.

Goodman, Kenneth S. 1969. Analysis of oral reading miscues: Applied psycholinguistics. *Reading Research Quarterly* 5(1): 9–30.

Goodman, Kenneth S. 1976. Reading: A psycholinguistic guessing game. In: Harry Singer and Robert B. Ruddell (eds.). *Theoretical Models and Processes of Reading*, 497–508. Newark, DE: International Reading Association.

Grabe, William. 2009. Teaching and Testing Reading. In: Michael L. Long and Catherine J. Doughty (eds.). *The Handbook of Language Teaching*, 441–462. Oxford: Wiley-Blackwell.

Gray, William S. 1960. The major aspects of reading. In: Helen Mansfield Robinson (ed.). *Sequential development of reading abilities* (Supplementary Educational Monographs 90): 8–24. Chicago: Chicago University Press.

Hoey, Michael. 1991. *Patterns of lexis in text*. Oxford, UK: Oxford University Press.

Hoey, Michael. 2001. *Textual interaction: An introduction to written discourse analysis*. London: Routledge.

Hoover, Wesley A. and William E. Tunmer. 1993. The components of reading. In: G. Brian Thompson, William E. Tunmer and Tom Nicholson (eds.). *Reading acquisition processes*. 1–19. Clevedon: Multilingual Matters.

Hosenfeld, Carol. 1984. Case studies of ninth grade readers. In: J. Charles Alderson and Alexander H. Urquhart (eds.). *Reading in a Foreign Language*, 231–249. Harlow: Longman.

Hyönä, Jukka. 2011. The usefulness and limitations of eye-tracking in the study of reading (and writing). Paper presented at the Summer school Writing Process Research 2011: Keystroke logging and Eyetracking, University of Antwerp, 7–9 September.

Jamieson, Joan, Stan Jones, Irwin Kirsch, Peter Mosenthal and Carol Taylor. 2000. *TOEFL 2000 framework: A working paper*. TOEFL-MS-16. Princeton, NJ: Educational Testing Service.

Jarodzka, Halszca, Katharina Scheiter, Peter Gerjets and Tamara van Gog. 2010. In: the eyes of the beholder: how experts and novices interpret dynamic stimuli. *Learning and Instruction* 20(2): 146–154.

Jones, Glyn. 2009. Lexical cohesion as a predictor of item difficulty. Paper presented at the European Association for Language Testing and Assessment, University of Turku, 4–7 June.

Kaakinen, Johanna and Jukka Hyönä. 2005. Perspective effects on expository text comprehension: evidence from think-aloud protocols, eyetracking, and recalls. *Discourse Processes* 40(3): 239–257.

Kintch, Walter and Teun van Dijk. 1978. Toward a model of text comprehension and production. *Psychological Review* 85(5): 363–394.

Kirsch, Irwin. 2001. *The international adult literacy survey: Understanding what was measured*. RR-01-25. Princeton, NJ: Educational Testing Service.

Lennon, Roger T. 1962. What can be measured? *Reading Teacher* 15(5): 326–337.

Lunzer, Eric and Keith Gardner (eds.). 1979. *The effective use of reading*. London: Heinemann Educational Books.

MacMillan, Fabiana M. 2006a. Lexical Patterns in the Reading Comprehension Section of the TOEFL® Test. *Revista do GEL* 3: 143–172.

MacMillan, Fabiana M. 2006b. *Lexical Patterns in the Reading Comprehension Section of the TOEFL® Test*. Rio de Janeiro: Universidade Federal Fluminense dissertation.

MacMillan, Fabiana M. 2007. The role of lexical cohesion in the assessment of EFL reading proficiency. *Arizona Working Papers in Second Language Acquisition and Teaching* 14: 75–93.

MacMillan, Fabiana M. 2008. Lexical cohesion in the TOEFL® and IELTS: what can standardized tests tell us about academic reading? Paper presented at the East Coast Organization of Language Testers Conference, George Washington University, 7–8 November.

MacMillan, Fabiana M. 2010. The role of lexical cohesion in multiple-choice reading item difficulty. Paper presented at the Midwest association of Language Testers Conference, Wright State University, 25 September.

Millis, Keith, Joseph Magliano and Stacey Todaro. 2006. Measuring discourse-Level processes with verbal protocols and latent semantic analysis. *Scientific Studies of Reading* 10(3): 225–240.

Munby. 1978. *Communicative syllabus design.* Cambridge, UK: Cambridge University Press.

Perkins, Kyle, Sheila R. Brutten and John T. Pohlmann. 1989. First and second language reading comprehension. *Regional Language Center Journal* 20: 1–9.

Rankin, J. Mark. 1988. Designing Thinking-Aloud Studies in ESL Reading. Reading in a Foreign Language 4(2): 119–132. http://nflrc.hawaii.edu/rfl/PastIssues/rfl42rankin.pdf (accessed 8 October 2013).

Rayner, Keith. 1998. Eye movements in reading and information processing: 20 years of research. *Psychological Bulletin* 124(3): 373–422.

Samuels, S. Jay, Tim Rasinski and Elfrieda H. Hiebert. 2011. Eye movements and reading: What teachers need to know. In: Alan E. Farstrup and S. Jay Samuels (eds.). *What reasearch has to say about reading instruction*, 25–50. Newark, DE: IRA.

Shohamy, Elana. 1984. Does the testing method make a difference? The case of reading comprehension. *Language Testing* 1(2): 147–170.

Toulmin, Stephen E. 2003 [1958]. *The uses of argument*, updated ed. Cambridge, UK: Cambridge University Press.

Wagner, Ben. 2011. Not the Same Old Sport: The Need for an Evolutionary Step in Literary Criticism in the Digital Age. In: Gideon O. Burton (ed.). *Writing about literature in the digital age*, 29–35. Paris: Feedbooks. http://www.feedbooks.com/book/6681/writing-about-literature-in-the-digital-age (accessed 6 October 2013).

Weir, Cyril J. and Mike Milanovic. 2003. *Continuity and innovation: Revising the Cambridge Proficiency in English examination 1913–2002.* Cambridge, UK: Cambridge University Press.

Talia Isaacs

9 Assessing speaking

1 Introduction

Economic globalization and technological advances are bringing together people from different linguistic and cultural backgrounds who were once oceans apart (Gatbonton and Trofimovich 2008). On a global scale, speaking ability is increasingly, albeit sometimes tacitly acknowledged as a highly coveted skill and a source of cultural capital in many educational and workplace settings today. In the case of learning a second language (L2) in a host country, achieving effective oral communication in the target language is often emphasized as essential for achieving successful integration, removing barriers to academic performance, adequately performing on the job, accessing vital social services, and, on a more macro level, mitigating social isolation and reducing language barriers in linguistically heterogeneous societies (e.g., Derwing and Munro 2009; Isaacs 2013). In addition to L2 interactions occurring with native or native-like members of the target language community, oral communication is also increasingly common in learners from different linguistic communities who use the target language as the lingua franca to carry out business transactions or to promote cultural exchange, particularly in prestigious or widely spoken languages with international currency (Jenkins 2000). Thus, it would seem that, to buttress and compliment nonverbal communication strategies, the ability to respond to an interlocutor in an appropriate and effective way during the time pressures of real-world face-to-face communication, be it in a dominant language or an L2, are of great human importance.

   In light of the current global context, the notion that speaking ability has always been a source of instructional focus in the development of L2 proficiency and in classroom-based and high-stakes assessment instruments might seem intuitive. In fact, this has not always been the case, with speaking ability proving susceptible to paradigmatic swings in approaches to L2 teaching and, in turn, assessment over time (e.g., Weir, Vidaković and Galaczi 2013). While some standardized tests have included spoken production as a mandatory component of L2 proficiency testing for decades (e.g., the *Certificate of Proficiency in English* in 1913), others have incorporated compulsory speaking tasks only relatively recently (e.g., the *Test of English as a Foreign Language* in 2005). Existing commercial tests with an oral proficiency component underscore vastly different approaches to providing large-scale speaking tests that are practical to administer, that simulate test takers' real world oral communication demands, and that yield reliable (sometimes defined as objective) assessments, and there are inevitable trade-offs (Bachman and Palmer 1996).

   Situated in the context of a global L2 testing culture where technological innovations have resulted in novel approaches and possibilities for capturing speech, which is an essentially ephemeral and intangible medium, and where incorporating a speaking component in L2 proficiency testing is increasingly prevalent, the goal of this chapter is to elucidate contemporary challenges in the assessment of L2 speaking through a description of emergent notions and practices. The focus is broadly on the ways in which the construct of L2 speaking ability has been defined and operationalized in assessment instruments, on sources of variability in speaking performances, and on the validity of human judgments and technology-mediated assessments. A historical overview is used as a launching pad for highlighting matters that have currency in teaching, researching, and assessing speaking and as a springboard for discussing future trends.

2 Historical perspective and link to current conceptualizations and practice

In a 1929 *Modern Language Journal* article, Lundeberg (1929: 193) contends that "oral-aural skills are today recognized as desirable and attainable objectives. A great many teachers and administrators ... rank the attainment of ear and tongue skills very high among their objectives. The layman, especially the parent, would often have this practical phase of language study placed first in the list."

Notably, Lundeberg's reference to "ear and tongue skills" groups aural/oral skills together. Although the relationship between human speech perception and production has been the object of considerable scientific debate and inquiry (Baker and Trofimovich, 2005), with some L2 communication models particular to speech perception (e.g., Flege 1995), and others to L2 speech production (e.g., de Bot 1992), Lundeberg's reference to aural/oral skills in tandem reflects the notion that "listening and speaking are theoretically and practically very difficult to separate" (Douglas 1997: 25). From a macro-level perspective of real-world interactional demands (as opposed to a technical perspective involving input processing and/or output mechanisms), verbal communication between human interlocutors is often a two-way process, involving, to use the transmission (broadcasting) metaphor, both a sender and a receiver of a speech signal (i.e. sound wave) that needs to be encoded and, in turn, decoded by the relevant parties, to achieve successful communication in real-time (De Bot, Lowie and Verspoor 2007). Thus, in settings involving the exchange of verbal information, conversational partners often switch seamlessly between the role of speaker and listener to keep the flow of the conversation going under time pressure, sometimes modifying or adapting their speech to promote informational exchange (Jenkins 2000). In light of such conversational contexts, it is sometimes conceptually difficult or artificial to separate speaking and listening. This may be an important consideration in more contemporary notions of construct definition within the field of language testing, in view of conceptualizing and concretizing the real-world context(s) that test scores need to extrapolate to, which could have bearing on task design in a language test (Bachman and Palmer 1996).

Grouping "ear and tongue skills" together is also at the exclusion of the written medium, which raises crucial challenges inherent to speech perception and production. In contrast to written language, speech is both ephemeral and intangible, with technology needed to both render it visually, and to generate and digitally store a record of a performance (Hewlett and Beck 2006). Audio recording devices afford speech some permanency so that an utterance can be captured in time then played, replayed, sped up, slowed down, edited to optimize the recording quality, or digitally altered to experimentally manipulate a particular linguistic feature that might be the subject of an empirical investigation (e.g., establishing even versus uneven syllable length conditions to examine temporal duration effects on test performance). Presuming that a reasonable sound quality is obtained in the original recording, capturing a speaking performance using a digital recorder offers possibilities for scoring or transcribing a spoken L2 performance after its live rendering, or for administering standardized prerecorded speech elicitation prompts or audio-mediated instructions for completing a task. Technology has also allowed invisible sound waves, which humans perceive auditorily, to be represented visually (e.g., via waveforms or spectrographs). The ability to visually inspect speech, coupled with the use of recording devices to render sounds permanent, has made the study of speech more conducive to precise scientific measurement. Thus, advancements in technology have made it possible to turn the auditory, dynamic, and ephemeral phenomenon of speech into a visual, static medium that can be stored indefinitely or transcribed at leisure. That is, technology has transformed speech, which "consists of inherently difficult patterns for humans to attend to" (Port 2007: 362) into a tangible entity that can be quantified instrumentally (e.g., using speech editing software such as *PRAAT*), and that also opens up possibilities of obtaining ratings after the fact from any number of human raters who may not have been present at the L2 performance.

The possibilities afforded by the use of technology give rise to crucial distinctions between different modes of speaking assessment. A *direct* speaking test denotes assessing speaking through face-to-face oral communication with an interlocutor, interviewer, or examiner. This contrasts with a *semi-direct* speaking test, which denotes a machine-mediated assessment involving the test takers uttering responses into a recording device without a human interlocutor being present to elicit the output (Qian 2009). Finally, an *indirect* test involves assessing speaking without having the test taker actually produce spoken language (e.g., using written multiple choice item as indicators or predictors of speaking ability; O'Loughlin 2001). Examples of speaking tests that incorporate these modes and a discussion of the use of technology on scoring are expanded upon in subsequent sections of this chapter.

Reverting to the substance of Lundeberg's (1929) quote cited above, it is evident that he champions the importance of aural/oral communication in classroom settings and emphasizes its importance to stakeholders. Echoing this, Lado's seminal book, *Language Testing*, which is widely regarded as constituting the birthplace of language assessment as a discipline in its own right (Spolsky 1995), heralds speaking as "the most highly prized language skill" (1961: 239). Lado buttresses this claim with the logic that being able to speak an L2 implies an ability to understand it. He further argues that in the case of most world languages, L2 speaking ability facilitates and accelerates learning how to write it.

Despite these historical views endorsing an emphasis on L2 speaking ability, which seem consonant with speaking needs in the 21st century, a focus on speaking ability in instruction and, by implication, assessment in modern history has not been a given, with speaking ability and the linguistic skills focused on within that broad construct proving unrobust to instructional pendulum swings over the course of modern pedagogical history. Lundeberg (1929: 193) decries the lack of instructional emphasis on aural/oral skills as "one of the heaviest broadsides delivered against our teaching." The Grammar Translation Method, which was introduced in the late 18th century and which dominated L2 instruction until the 1940s (Richards and Rodgers 2001) centered on "grammatical exactness and translating ability" as a means of intellectual development, effectively sidelining speaking (Kelly 1969: 382). With respect to assessment, the *Certificate of Proficiency in English (CPE)*, introduced in 1913 and produced within the British assessment tradition (Spolsky 1995), is an early and pioneering exception. Theoretically inspired by the Reform Movement's emphasis on speaking ability, which centred on the instruction of phonetics (e.g., Sweet 1899), the mandatory speaking component of the *CPE* included a conversation task – spearheading a tradition of oral interaction in Cambridge exams – to complement more traditional read-aloud and oral dictation tasks (Weir, Vidaković and Galaczi 2013). The Cambridge English Centenary Symposium on Speaking Assessment, held in 2013 in Cambridge, UK, celebrated this major development in the evolution of the speaking construct and inclusion of speaking as an integral component in L2 proficiency testing.

However, it was not until the Second World War that a concerted focus on the assessment of L2 speaking emerged (Fulcher 2003), with the American role in international affairs catalyzing the "demand for ability to actually speak the foreign tongue" (Kaulfers 1944: 136). In a *Modern Language Journal* article on wartime developments in American testing, Kaulfers emphasizes the need of ordinary citizens travelling abroad, as military personnel, to "communicate information in an intelligible way" in their spoken interactions. For assessments for military purposes in particular, he emphasizes the high-stakes consequences of miscommunications, commenting that the role of the task from a test development perspective is to generate "recognizable evidence of the examinee's readiness to perform in a life-situation where lack of ability to understand and speak the language extemporaneously might be a serious handicap to safety and comfort, or to the effective execution of military responsibilities" (1944: 137).

Kaulfers' "oral fluency" test, which assesses L2 readiness for military deployment, requires test takers to translate key phrases from the first language (L1) into the L2 under the broad categories of asking for or responding to information requests and giving directions or polite commands. Speaking performances are then scored by human raters on a rating instrument comprised of two 4-level subscales, with a procedure for deriving median scores across language functions. The first subscale, which assesses "quality of language," describes the functions that the test taker demonstrates being able to execute, ranging from "can make known only a few essential wants in set phrases or sentences" to "can converse extemporaneously on any topic within the range of his knowledge or experience" (1944: 144). This scale is arguably a precursor to performance descriptors or "can do statements" in contemporary rating scales that outline the functions that learners are able to accomplish when carrying out selected communicative tasks, such as the *Canadian Language Benchmarks* (Pawlikowska-Smith 2002) or the *English Profile* linked to the *Common European Framework of Reference* (Salamoura and Saville 2010). This represents a source of continuity between past and present for gauging raters' judgments of the extent to which communicative goals on envisioned tasks have successfully been achieved, with an emphasis on extrapolating score results to tasks that test takers are likely to perform in real-world settings.

Kaulfers' second subscale, which assesses the "quality of oral performance," appears as a scale with the bolded headings "unintelligible or no response," "partially intelligible," "intelligible but labored," and "readily intelligible," underpinned by more elaborate descriptors designating the extent to which a "literate native" (possibly the rater him- or herself) is able to understand the speech at each level of the scale (1944: 144). At the lowest band, the test taker's speech results in the "literate native" (listener) being "confused or mislead [sic]" whereas "poor pronunciation or usage" or the presence of pronunciation errors designates the mid-levels of the scale. Finally, the highest band descriptor refers to the listener's inability "to identify the speaker's particular foreign nationality," which implies the absence of a detectable, or at least readily identifiable, L2 accent.

Of great historical importance in Kaulfer's scale is the very early reference to the notion of intelligibility – a construct that has currency in the teaching and assessment of L2 speech. Although intelligibility has been defined and measured in different ways for research and assessment purposes, paralleling the multiple interpretations that abound for a term such as "fluency," for example (Koponen and Riggenbach 2000), intelligibility, in the broad sense of the word, denotes the ease or difficulty with which a listener understands L2 speech (Isaacs and Trofimovich 2012). Widely regarded as the goal of L2 pronunciation instruction, and by implication, assessment (Levis 2006), intelligibility is featured as an assessment criterion in the speaking scales of standardized tests, including the *Test of English as a Foreign Language* (*TOEFL*) and the *International English Language Testing System* (*IELTS*). However, there is a need to pinpoint, with greater precision and empirical substantiation, the linguistic factors most important for achieving intelligible speech at different scale bands to guide raters' judgments and to crystalize the linguistic factors associated with this construct that are most important for making level distinctions (Isaacs and Trofimovich 2012). Although intelligibility has traditionally been associated with pronunciation, recent research has revealed that a listener's ability to understand L2 speech is not confined to pronunciation, but also extends to other linguistic domains, including discourse measures, lexical richness, lexicogrammatical, and fluency (temporal) variables (Trofimovich and Isaacs 2012). That is, many linguistic features in addition to pronunciation can have bearing on a listener's understanding of L2 speech. By contrast, L2 accent appears to be a much narrower construct that is most strongly related to the linguistic factors commonly referred to under the umbrella term "pronunciation," including word stress, rhythm, and segmental (vowel and consonant) production accuracy.

Although the notion of the native speaker is not without controversy in language testing circles and among applied linguists more generally (Davies 2011; Kubota 2009), in operational assessment and research settings, native or native-like speakers still routinely conduct ratings of L2 speech (Levis 2006). Reference to the absence of a recognizable nonnative accent in Kaulfers's (1944) scale is reminiscent of L2 speaking scales in use today that explicitly refer to achieving the native speaker standard (i.e. L2 accent-free speech) at the highest level of the scale (e.g., *Cambridge ESOL Common Scale for Speaking*; see Taylor 2011). However, it is possible to be highly intelligible but to still have a lingering L2 accent. The consensus view among applied linguists today is that, although accents are perceptually salient, accent reduction is not an appropriate instructional goal (Derwing and Munro 2009). This is in part because L2 learners are able to integrate into a new society and to perform well in workplace or academic settings without needing to sound like native speakers. This argument can be extrapolated to assessment contexts (Isaacs 2014). Notwithstanding the extremely rare situations in which the L2 learner needs to sound like a native speaker to conceal his/her identity in the real-world domain to which speaking scores are being generalized (e.g., employment as a secret service agent), it is only when the accent interferes with a learner's ability to be understood by the listener that it should be alluded to in speaking scale descriptors (Alderson 1991). In sum, referring to intelligible speech at the high end of the scale without resorting to a native-like accent is an assessment challenge now as then.

In terms of the logistics of his proposed speaking assessment, Kaulfers (1944: 150) suggests that test takers' responses be audio recorded, with an examiner administering the test and independent raters scoring the recorded responses. Although he concedes that this "pioneering" speaking test development effort is not without its limitations, he suggests that the proposed test may expose the shortcomings of "silent pen-and-ink exercices" (i.e. indirect speaking test items). After inviting classroom teachers to trial the proposed assessment, he emphasizes that examining the reliability, validity, and norming procedures in speaking assessments in general would comprise a good dissertation topic, since "the need is real."

3 Key issues and challenges in assessing L2 speech

Issues associated with assessing L2 speech articulated in historical texts decades ago shed light on the nature of the challenges inherent in the medium that still resonate today. Arguments that aural/oral skills "are less measurable because they are less tangible, more subject to variation, and probably will involve the cumbersome and time-consuming expedient of the individual oral examination" (Ludenberg 1929: 195) have served as a historical deterrent for developing and implementing direct or semi-direct speaking tests as part of L2 proficiency testing, particularly in the American testing tradition (Spolsky 1995). Wood's (1927) concern that some teachers base their scoring decisions on the content or substance of the test taker's message while other teachers' decisions are informed by properties of the test-taker's oral production could at least partially be redressed through clearly defining the focal construct and explicitly addressing sources of construct-irrelevant variance in rater training (i.e. factors that should have no bearing on raters' scoring decisions; Bachman and Palmer 1996; Winke, Gass and Myford 2013). Alternatively, a more controlled task-type that constrains test takers' expected output, such as a read-aloud task, would remove content as a source of variation across test takers to enable a sole focus on the linguistic properties of their speech, if this was desired. However, as Lado (1961) clarifies, even in the case of decontextualized, discrete-point items measuring goodness of articulation (e.g., individual words or sounds), listeners may not achieve consensus in making simple binary judgments about whether a test taker's oral production is "right" or "wrong" (e.g., an accurate or inaccurate production of a target sound), as this is, to an extent, contingent upon listeners' subjective perceptions. Indeed, recent research has shown that listeners' familiarity with the L2 accent of the test taker may facilitate their understanding of L2 speech (Harding 2012) and bias their assessments (Winke, Gass and Myford 2013). The implication is that ideally, this rater effect should be controlled for in high-stakes speaking assessments so as not to unduly influence raters' scoring decisions on a factor extraneous to the L2 speaking ability being measured.

Even if listeners do arrive at a numerically identical scores based on a given speaking performance, they may assign scores for qualitatively different reasons (Douglas 1994). To elaborate, when it comes to dichotomously scored items which are objectively verifiable and are not dependent on human judgment, the measurement model is relatively simple: the test taker interacts with the test task to produce a score (Upshur and Turner 1999). When the assessment is listener-mediated and the resulting scores are not objectively verifiable, additional sources of systematic variance are introduced into the measurement model and reflected in the score that is generated. One such factor, listener or rater characteristics, has the potential to influence both the quantitative scores that raters assign, including the criteria that raters attend to when making their scoring decisions (Brown, Iwashita and McNamara, 2005), and the strategies they use to condense their possibly complex impressions of an L2 performance into a single numerical score (Lumley 2005). Further, the assessment framework, most often a rating scale, is yet another source of variance. The need to balance the practical consideration of providing raters with a user-friendly assessment instrument which features a manageable number of criteria in scale descriptors appears to be at odds with representing the construct comprehensively in rating scales, particularly when the construct of interest is global or multifaceted. Thus, rating descriptors necessarily oversimplify the complex and possibly nonlinear processes involved in L2 acquisition or task performance that they aim to represent (Isaacs and Thomson 2013). In addition, they are likely to fall short of reflecting the myriad factors that listeners attend to when arriving at their scoring decisions or the possible interactions among these factors, especially when the speaking task is complex (e.g., an extemporaneous speech sample or an interaction between a test taker and an interlocutor, the latter of which would introduce yet another source of variance). In sum, the intangible nature of speech makes it arguably more challenging to assess than the written medium. This notwithstanding, eliciting raters' evaluative judgments of speech opens up a series of complexities and possible threats to the validity of the assessment that is also common to the scoring of L2 writing production.

Lundeberg's quote that aural-oral tests "probably will involve the cumbersome and time-consuming expedient of the individual oral examination" (1929: 195) underscores the practical problems associated with human-mediated assessments of speech. They are neither cost effective nor time efficient. For example, examiners' salaries for individually administering and scoring the test task(s), and, in the case of test performances that need to be recorded, mechanisms for securely storing test performance data (sound or video files) may make it too expensive or time consuming to engage in the direct testing of L2 speech en masse, and this consideration may ultimately outweigh the use of more authentic task types. Such practical considerations led Lado (1961) to advocate the use of indirect testing as an alternative to oral production tests, although his hypothesis that written responses and actual oral productions of the tested word would strongly correlate was not borne out in empirical studies which tested his hypothesis. In fact, indirect test items modelled on Lado's prototype indirect items yielded "catastrophically low reliabilities" and concomitant validity issues (Buck 1989: 54). Thus, despite the practical challenges involved in assessing speaking, direct or semi-direct tests are considered the only valid formats for assessing L2 speech today (O'Loughlin 2001).

The reliance on listeners' impressionistic judgments of speech is arguably at odds with the strongly psychometrically-influenced American assessment tradition. Some of the hallmarks of this tradition are the superordinate focus on the technical (statistical) reliability of test items, heralding of multiple choice as the gold standard of measurement, and tendency to opt for the most administratively feasible test formats and item types in the context of large-scale, high-stakes tests (Bachman et al. 1995; Spolsky 1995). The *TOEFL*, a product of this tradition, was launched in 1964 as an English proficiency test for academic purposes (ETS 2011). In the initial paper-based version (*pBT*) of the test, only the reading and listening sections were compulsory. In the subsequent computer-based version (*cBT*), separate speaking and writing tests were developed as optional supplementary tests, with the speaking test (*Test of Spoken English*) becoming operational in the early 1980s (Spolsky 1995). It was only with the introduction of the internet-based version (*iBT*) of the test in 2005 – the most recent revision to date – that the speaking component became compulsory and was included as part of the mainstream *TOEFL*. Due to its widespread use as a language screening instrument at many English-medium universities internationally, students who took earlier versions of the test (*pBT* or *cBT*) were admitted to postsecondary institutions without any assessment of their speaking ability, with no separate speaking component generally mandated for university entrance purposes (Isaacs, 2008). In addition, some higher education institutions did not screen international teaching assistants for spoken proficiency, although speaking is clearly of importance in the academic domain, particularly in the case of individuals bearing instructional responsibilities (Isaacs, 2013; Saif 2002). To complement research on the validity of the *TOEFL iBT* (e.g., Farnsworth 2013), there is a growing body of work examining washback effects, particularly as English teachers have sought to adapt to the addition of the speaking section, which constituted a major change. In a multiphase washback study that included a baseline study to describe pedagogical practice prior to the introduction of the *TOEFL iBT*, Wall and Horák (2006; 2008; 2011) found overall positive teacher attitudes toward testing speaking, with the effect of more class time reportedly being allocated to speaking at the Central and Eastern European TOEFL test centers examined, suggesting a positive influence of the *TOEFL iBT* speaking test on instruction from the teachers' perspective.

The *TOEFL iBT* speaking tasks are semi-direct (computer-mediated) with standardized recorded prompts. The scoring is conducted by trained *TOEFL* raters using separate scales for the two different speaking task types – independent (involving speaking only) and integrated (involving speaking after listening to either a spoken prompt, or to both a spoken and written prompt, with the task directive of summarizing and synthesizing information from these sources in the spoken response; ETS 2008). These factors are major innovations of the *TOEFL iBT*. The first, related to constructing and using rating scales specific to the task type, arguably draws, at least implicitly, on the sociointeractional view that L2 ability and the assessment context are inseparable, since assessments are locally-situated, with the task embedded in the way that the construct is operationalized in the scale (Chalhoub-

Deville 2003). This contrasts with the traditional psychometric view that the L2 ability being measured can be completely disentangled from the task or task type and, more broadly, from the context of the assessment (i.e. what is being assessed is the individual's cognitive ability, as opposed to his/her interaction with a particular task or task type to yield the performance; Bachman 2007). This locus of debate has implications for the specificity of rating scales and for the generalizability of the speaking performance beyond the local context of the assessment. The second innovation is challenging the Ladoesque (1961) notion of partitioning the assessment of language ability into separate component skills. Because speaking, listening, and writing skills often occur in tandem in the real-world tasks that test-takers are likely to undertake, grouping such skills together arguably enhances the authenticity of the test task to a greater extent than does simply assessing isolated skills and abilities (Plakans 2013).

In contrast to the American assessment tradition, the British tradition has not been driven by forefronting technical reliability, nor by using practically expedient task types in terms of test administration and scoring, with a speaking assessment tradition involving the use of direct, face-to-face test tasks (Weir, Vidaković and Galaczi 2013). Less driven by psychometric concerns about the need to replicate exact testing conditions across test takers, the British tradition has tended to emphasize interactional tasks involving human interlocutors, with little experimentation with semi-direct or indirect task types and with reliance on expert judgments in scoring as an integral part of the tradition (Taylor 2011). In comparison with semi-direct tasks, face-to-face interactions tend to be more appealing to test takers and may result in more authentic assessments, which is a trade-off for a more efficient and possibly cheaper assessment involving the use of technology for test administration and scoring (Qian 2009).

Drawing on the oral proficiency interview tradition, which can be traced back to the American Council on the Teaching of Foreign Languages in the 1950s (Fulcher 2003), the *IELTS* is a face-to-face oral interview with a trained *IELTS* examiner. The interviewer variable opens up an additional source of systematic variance in the measurement model, with individual differences in the interviewer's behavior while administering the *IELTS* having been shown to exert an influence on both test takers' performance, and on raters' perceptions of the test taker's speaking ability (Brown 2005). The scripting of test prompts is the primary mechanism that the exam provider has implemented to minimize interviewer variation and ensure a degree of standardization in test administration procedures (Taylor 2011).

Although oral interviews have been the preferred and most commonly used method of speaking assessment since the Communicative era (Luoma 2004), there has been a growing trend toward the assessment of peer performance on interactional tasks. This has been buttressed by findings from Second Language Acquisition (SLA) research on the facilitative effects of peer interactions on L2 learning (e.g., Mackey and Goo 2007) and on the value placed on pair and group work in the L2 classroom – which is generally regarded as good pedagogical practice – in promoting positive washback. In addition, peer interactions have the advantage of bypassing the power imbalance that is inherent in oral proficiency interviews (Ducasse and Brown 2009).

The Cambridge main suite of exams first adopted the paired speaking test format in 1996. Following a brief monologue task and response to interviewer questions, the test culminates in a peer collaborative task, thereby eliciting different interactional patterns within the scope of the speaking test and sampling from a broader range of dimensions within the L2 oral proficiency construct than would be possible on a single monologic task (Saville and Hargreaves 1999). However, the caveat is that interlocutor variables (i.e. test-taker characteristics) on the paired interaction task could affect the quality of the interaction that is generated and, consequently, test takers' individual and collective performance and scoring outcomes. Such peer interlocutor variables (e.g., L2 proficiency, L1 background, gender, personality characteristics, attitudinal variables, etc.) are extraneous to the construct being measured and could threaten the validity of the assessment (Isaacs 2013). The different interactional patterns elicited in the Cambridge main suite of exams arguably serve as a buffer against this concern, since test scores are based on examiner cumulative judgments of test-taker performance on all three tasks (monologue and interactions with both the examiner, and the test-taker partner; Saville and Hargreaves 1999). An issue of current debate associated with paired speaking test tasks is whether they should be individually scored or subject to joint scoring to reflect the co-constructed nature of the resulting discourse, with implications for rating scale design (May 2009). This topical debate often revolves around issues regarding the appropriate definition and operationalization of the speaking construct (which could include interactional competence) and on concerns about fairness to test takers. Notably, a difficulty with research in this area is in isolating the effects of interlocutor variables on test-taker performance, since they may interact in complex ways and are difficult to control for, sometimes resulting in contradictory findings about interlocutor effects across studies (Davis 2009).

Taken together, the British assessment tradition offers a striking contrast to the American tradition, with advantages and disadvantages to both.

4 From current trends to future directions

A central theme that has permeated this discussion has been issues and challenges associated with the assessment of L2 speech, with reference to the role of technology in rendering this fleeting and intangible medium more amenable to measurement. In addition to enabling time-delayed human subjective judgments of L2 performances, technological innovations have made it possible to instrumentally analyze speech using measures such as grammatical accuracy, lexical frequency, acoustic variables (e.g., pitch range), and temporal variables (e.g., mean length of run; Isaacs and Trofimovich 2012; Zechner et al. 2009). Such machine-derived measures can then be weighted and combined to derive machine-scored assessments of L2 speaking proficiency. In this way, it is possible to address the age-old concern about the reliability of subjectively scored oral test data without resorting to the indirect testing of objectively scored items (e.g., written multiple choice questions).

The debate about the removal of the human element in language testing has been catapulted by the launch of fully automated (i.e. machine-mediated) L2 speaking tests, including the *Versant* test (formerly *Phonepass*), available in various languages and used for high-stakes purposes (Downey et al. 2008) and *Speech-Rater*, which is, as yet, intended for low-stakes *TOEFL iBT* test preparation purposes (Zechner et al. 2009). To train the speech recognizer or machine scoring system, L2 speech samples are scored by a large cross-section of human raters. Averaging scores across the resulting large volume of ratings effectively neutralizes individual rater idiosyncrasies, thereby removing concerns about rater effects that are present in nonautomatically-scored tests that normally involve the scalar judgments of just two or three trained raters (Van Moere & Downey, this volume).

Validation studies on the *Versant* have demonstrated strong statistical associations between the automated scores generated by the speech recognition algorithm and human ratings. In addition, strong correlations with scores on traditional L2 speaking subtests (e.g., *TOEFL iBT*; *IELTS*) suggest that the *Versant* is measuring a related speaking construct to these more traditional tests (Downey et al. 2008), although this is only part of the validity argument. This notwithstanding, *qualitatively* speaking, automated measures of speech do not replicate the factors that human listeners attend to or that feed into their scoring decisions (Isaacs 2014). Furthermore, because automated scoring involves pattern matching, controlled tasks that generate highly predictable L2 productions (e.g., constructed response or utterance repetition tasks) are much more amenable to automated scoring than communicatively-oriented extemporaneous speech tasks that elicit relatively unpredictable test-taker output (Zechner et al. 2009). It follows that the use of "constrained" tasks on the *Versant* has led to concerns within the language testing community about the narrowing of the speaking construct, especially in comparison with speaking tests that elicit different interactional patterns and are deemed more authentic (Chun 2006). However, as the *Versant* test developers have argued, there is a strong psycholinguistic basis for the use of such tasks, although this is not likely to be embraced by language testers coming from a more sociocultural tradition (Downey et al. 2008). Such debates about the value of automated speaking assessments are ongoing and serve to counterbalance and occasionally interface with contemporary debates on the use of paired or group oral tests.

With continued improvements in technology, speech recognition will become increasingly prominent in operational speaking tests and, thus, a growing subject of research and debate in the field. However, in the same way that the world is not, as yet, run by robots, machine scoring systems are not likely to completely supplant assessments of L2 speech. In our increasingly globalized world, it is ultimately human interlocutors who, in informal evaluative contexts, are the ultimate arbitrators of the extent to which the intended message has been transmitted and whether or not the communicative transaction has successfully been achieved. Thus, human judgments are likely to remain the standard against which automated speaking assessment systems will continue to need to be trained and, ultimately, benchmarked. Finally, as technology (e.g., social media) continues to revolutionize the nature of human communication and to open up new interactional possibilities on a global scale (Kramsch 2012), the need to perform and assess complex speaking tasks in reliable and valid ways will continue to persist.

5 References

Alderson, J. Charles. 1991. Bands and scores. In: J. Charles Alderson and Brian North (eds.). *Language testing in the 1990s: The communicative legacy*, 71–86. London: Macmillan.

Bachman, Lyle F. 2007. What is the construct? The dialectic of abilities and contexts in defining constructs in language assessment. In: Janna Fox, Mari Wesche, Doreen Bayliss, Liying Cheng, Carolyn E. Turner and Christine Doe (eds.). *Language testing reconsidered*, 41–70. Ottawa, ON: University of Ottawa Press.

Bachman, Lyle F. and Adrian S. Palmer. 1996. *Language testing in practice: Designing and developing useful language tests*. Oxford, UK: Oxford University Press.

Bachman, Lyle F., Fred Davidson, Katherine Ryan and Inn-Chull Choi. 1995. *An investigation into the comparability of two tests of English as a foreign language*. Cambridge, UK: Cambridge University Press.

Baker, Wendy and Pavel Trofimovich. 2005. Perceptual paths to accurate production of L2 vowels: The role of individual differences. *International Review of Applied Linguistics in Language Teaching* 44(3): 231–250.

Brown, Annie. 2005. *Interviewer variability in oral proficiency interviews*. Frankfurt am Main: Peter Lang.

Brown, Annie, Noriko Iwashita and Tim F. McNamara. 2005. *An examination of rater orientations and test-taker performance on English for academic purposes speaking tasks*. Monograph Series MS-29. Princeton, NJ: Educational Testing Service. http://www.ets.org/Media/Research/pdf/RR-05-05.pdf (accessed 12 April 2014).

Buck, Gary. 1989. Written tests of pronunciation: Do they work? *ELT Journal* 43(1): 50–56.

Chalhoub-Deville, Micheline. 2003. Second language interaction: Current perspectives and future trends. *Language Testing* 20(4): 369–383.

Chun, Christian W. 2006. An analysis of a language test for employment: The authenticity of the PhonePass test. *Language Assessment Quarterly* 3(3): 295–306.

Davies, Alan. 2011. Does language testing need the native speaker? *Language Assessment Quarterly* 8(3): 291–308.

Davis, Larry. 2009. The influence of interlocutor proficiency in a paired oral assessment. *Language Testing* 26(3): 367–396.

De Bot, Kees. 1992. A bilingual production model: Levelt's "speaking" model adapted. *Applied Linguistics* 13(1): 1–24.

De Bot, Kees, Wander Lowie and Marjolijn Verspoor. 2007. A dynamic systems theory approach to second language acquisition. *Bilingualism: Language and Cognition* 10(1): 7–21.

Derwing, Tracey M. and Murray J. Munro. 2009. Comprehensibility as a factor in listener interaction preferences: Implications for the workplace. *Canadian Modern Language Review* 66(2): 181–202.

Douglas, Dan. 1994. Quantity and quality in speaking test performance. *Language Testing* 11(2): 125–144.

Douglas, Dan. 1997. *Testing speaking ability in academic contexts: Theoretical considerations.* TOEFL-MS-08. Princeton, NJ: Educational Testing Service.

Downey, Ryan, Hossein Farhady, Rebecca Present-Thomas, Masahiro Suzuki and Alistair Van Moere. 2008. Evaluation of the usefulness of the Versant for English test: A response. *Language Assessment Quarterly* 5(2): 160–167.

Ducasse, Ana Maria and Annie Brown. 2009. Assessing paired orals: Raters' orientation to interaction. *Language Testing* 26(3): 423–443.

ETS. 2008. *TOEFL® iBT Tips: How to prepare for the TOEFL iBT.* Princeton, NJ: Educational Testing Service.

ETS. 2011. TOEFL® program history. *TOEFL iBT® Research* 1. Princeton, NJ: Educational Testing Service.

Farnsworth, Timothy L. 2013. An investigation into the validity of the TOEFL iBT speaking test for international teaching assistant certification. *Language Assessment Quarterly* 10(3): 274–291.

Flege, James E. 1995. Second language speech learning: Theory, findings, and problems. In: Winifred Strange (ed.). *Speech perception and linguistic experience: Issues in cross-language research*, 233–277. Timonium, MD: York Press.

Fulcher, Glenn. 2003. *Testing second language speaking.* London: Pearson.

Gatbonton, Elizabeth and Pavel Trofimovich. 2008. The ethnic group affiliation and L2 proficiency link: Empirical evidence. *Language Awareness* 17(3): 229–248.

Harding, Luke. 2012. Accent, listening assessment and the potential for a shared-L1 advantage: A DIF perspective. *Language Testing* 29(2): 163–180.

Hewlett, Nigel and Janet Mackenzie Beck. 2006. *An introduction to the science of phonetics.* Mahwah, NJ: Lawrence Erlbaum.

Isaacs, Talia. 2008. Towards defining a valid assessment criterion of pronunciation proficiency in non-native English speaking graduate students. *Canadian Modern Language Review* 64(4): 555–580.

Isaacs, Talia. 2013. International engineering graduate students' interactional patterns on a paired speaking test: Interlocutors' perspectives. In: Kim McDonough and Alison Mackey (eds.). *Second language interaction in diverse educational settings*, 227–246. Amsterdam: John Benjamins.

Isaacs, Talia. 2014. Assessing pronunciation. In: Antony J. Kunnan (ed.). *The companion to language assessment*, 140–155. Hoboken, NJ: Wiley-Blackwell.

Isaacs, Talia and Ron I. Thomson. 2013. Rater experience, rating scale length, and judgments of L2 pronunciation: Revisiting research conventions. *Language Assessment Quarterly* 10(2): 135–159.

Isaacs, Talia and Pavel Trofimovich. 2012. "Deconstructing" comprehensibility: Identifying the linguistic influences on listeners' L2 comprehensibility ratings. *Studies in Second Language Acquisition* 34(3): 475–505.

Jenkins, Jennifer. 2000. *The phonology of English as an international language.* Oxford, UK: Oxford University Press.

Kaulfers, Walter V. 1944. Wartime development in modern-language achievement testing. *Modern Language Journal* 28(2): 136–150.

Kelly, Louis G. 1969. *25 centuries of language teaching: An inquiry into the science, art, and development of language teaching methodology, 500 B.C.–1969*. Rowley, MA: Newbury House.

Koponen, Matti and Heidi Riggenbach. 2000. Overview: Varying perspectives on fluency. In: Heidi Riggenbach (ed.). *Perspectives on fluency*, 5–24. Ann Arbor, MI: University of Michigan Press.

Kramsch, Claire. 2012. Why foreign language teachers need to have a multilingual outlook and what that means for their teaching practice. *Muitas Vozes* 1(1–2): 181–188.

Kubota, Ryuko. 2009. Rethinking the superiority of the native speaker: Toward a relational understanding of power. In: Neriko Musha Doerr (ed.). *The native speaker concept: Ethnographic investigations of native speaker*, 233–247. Berlin: Mouton de Gruyter.

Lado, Robert. 1961. *Language testing: The construction and use of foreign language tests*. London: Longman.

Levis, John. 2006. Pronunciation and the assessment of spoken language. In: Rebecca Hughes (ed.). *Spoken English, TESOL and applied linguistics: Challenges for theory and practice*, 245–270. New York: Palgrave Macmillan.

Lumley, Tom. 2005. *Assessing second language writing: The rater's perspective*. Frankfurt am Main: Peter Lang.

Luoma, Sari. 2004. *Assessing speaking*. Cambridge, UK: Cambridge University Press.

Lundeberg, Olav K. 1929. Recent developments in audition-speech tests. *The Modern Language Journal* 14(3): 193–202.

Mackey, Alison and Jaemyung Goo. 2007. Interaction research in SLA: A meta-analysis and research synthesis. In: Alison Mackey (ed.). *Conversational interaction in second language acquisition: A collection of empirical studies*, 407–453. Oxford, UK: Oxford University Press.

May, Lyn. 2009. Co-constructed interaction in a paired speaking test: The rater's perspective. *Language Testing* 26(3): 397–421.

O'Loughlin, Kieran J. 2001. *The equivalence of direct and semi-direct speaking tests*. Cambridge, UK: Cambridge University Press.

Pawlikowska-Smith, Grazyna. 2002. *Canadian Language Benchmarks 2000: Additional sample task ideas*. Ottawa, ON: Centre for Canadian Language Benchmarks.

Plakans, Lia. 2013. Assessment of integrated skills. In: Carol A. Chapelle (ed.). *The encyclopedia of applied linguistics*. Vol. 1: 204–212. Hoboken, NJ: Wiley-Blackwell.

Port, Robert F. 2007. The graphical basis of phones and phonemes. In: Ocke-Schwen Bohn and Murray Munro (eds.). *Language experience in second language speech learning: In honor of James Emil Flege*, 349–365. Amsterdam: John Benjamins.

Qian, David D. 2009. Comparing direct and semi-direct modes for speaking assessment: Affective effects on test takers. *Language Assessment Quarterly* 6(2): 113–125.

Richards, Jack C. and Theodore S. Rodgers. 2001. *Approaches and methods in language teaching*. 2nd ed. Cambridge, UK: Cambridge University Press.

Saif, Shahrzad. 2002. A needs-based approach to the evaluation of the spoken language ability of international teaching assistants. *Canadian Journal of Applied Linguistics* 5(1–2): 145–167.

Salamoura, Angeliki and Nick Saville. 2010. Exemplifying the CEFR: Criterial features of written learner English from the English Profile Programme. In: Inge Bartning, Maisa Martin and Ineke Vedder (eds.). *Communicative proficiency and linguistic development: Intersections between SLA and language testing research*, 101–132. http://eurosla.org/monographs/EM01/101-132Salamoura_Saville.pdf (accessed 12 April 2014).

Saville, Nick and Peter Hargreaves. 1999. Assessing speaking in the revised FCE. *ELT Journal* 53(1): 42–51.

Spolsky, Bernard. 1995. *Measured words: The development of objective language testing*. Oxford, UK: Oxford University Press.

Sweet, Henry. 1899. *The practical study of languages: A guide for teachers and learners*. London: Dent.

Taylor, Lynda. 2011. (ed.). *Examining speaking: Research and practice in assessing second language speaking*. Cambridge, UK: Cambridge University Press.

Trofimovich, Pavel and Talia Isaacs. 2012. Disentangling accent from comprehensibility. *Bilingualism: Language and Cognition* 15(4): 905–916.

Upshur, John A. and Carolyn E. Turner. 1999. Systematic effects in the rating of second-language speaking ability: Test method and learner discourse. *Language Testing* 16(1): 82–111.

Van Moere, Alistair and Ryan Downey. This volume. Technology and artificial intelligence in language assessment. In: Dina Tsagari and Jayanti Banerjee (eds.). *Handbook of second language assessment*. Berlin: DeGruyter Mouton.

Wall, Dianne and Tania Horák. 2006. *The impact of changes in the TOEFL examination on teaching and learning in Central and Eastern Europe: Phase 1, the baseline study*. TOEFL Monograph MS-34. Princeton, NJ: Educational Testing Service.

Wall, Dianne and Tania Horák. 2008. *The Impact of changes in the TOEFL examination on teaching and learning in Central and Eastern Europe: Phase 2, coping with change*. Research Report RR-08-37. Princeton, NJ: Educational Testing Service.

Wall, Dianne and Tania Horák. 2011. *The impact of changes in the TOEFL examination on teaching in a sample of countries in Europe: Phase 3, the role of the coursebook and phase 4, describing change*. TOEFL iBT Research Report TOEFL iBT-17. Princeton, NJ: Educational Testing Service.

Weir, Cyril J., Ivana Vidaković and Evelina Galaczi. 2013. *Measured constructs: A history of Cambridge English language examinations 1913–2012*. Cambridge, UK: Cambridge University Press.

Winke, Paula, Susan Gass and Carol Myford. 2013. Raters' L2 background as a potential source of bias in rating oral performance. *Language Testing* 30(2): 231–252.

Wood, Ben D. 1927. *New York experiments with new-type modern language tests*. New York: MacMillan.

Zechner, Klaus, Derrick Higgins, Xiaoming Xi and David M. Williamson. 2009. Automatic scoring of non-native spontaneous speech in tests of spoken English. *Speech Communication* 51(10): 883–895.

Thomas Eckes, Anika Müller-Karabil and Sonja Zimmermann
10 Assessing writing

1 Introduction

Writing is a multifaceted and complex skill, both in first language (L1) and in second or foreign language (L2) contexts. The ability to write is commonly regarded as essential to personal and social advancement, as well as to a nation's economic success. Against this background, it is hardly surprising that research into, and professional concern about, writing instruction and assessment have increased tremendously in recent years (e.g., Hinkel 2011; MacArthur, Graham and Fitzgerald 2008; Weigle 2013a).

This chapter first provides a brief historical review of the field of writing assessment. It then introduces the notion of language frameworks and discusses the construction and use of writing tasks and rating scales. Subsequently, the focus shifts to evaluating the quality of writing assessments, highlighting the critical role of raters. After a brief glance at current controversies, the chapter concludes with possible future directions.

2 The development of writing assessment: historical reflections

2.1 The dual nature of writing assessment

Much like language testing more generally, writing assessment is characterized by a mix of theories, concepts, and approaches drawn from two major fields of inquiry: applied linguistics and psychometrics (Bachman 1990, 2000; McNamara 2011). These fields are inextricably linked with one another when it comes to developing, analyzing, and evaluating writing assessment procedures on a scientifically sound basis. When the first textbooks on language testing appeared (Lado 1961; Valette 1967), this inherent duality was already visible. Yet, only in more recent years the great potential of taking advantage of both field's expertise has begun to be fully recognized.

The growing recognition of mutual dependencies between linguistic and psychometric approaches to writing has led to the emergence of what some authors have called the "new discipline" of writing assessment (Behizadeh and Engelhard 2011; Huot 2002; Yancey 1999). Indeed, this discipline as it presents itself today has brought together lines of development in research and theorizing on the nature of writing ability on the one hand and advances in measurement methodology and statistical analysis on the other. No wonder, therefore, that writing assessment looks back on a varied and sometimes controversial history (Elliot 2005; Spolsky 1995).

2.2 Developing factors for writing assessment

Focusing on the uptake of a particular psychometric approach (i.e. Rasch measurement) within the broader context of language testing, McNamara and Knoch (2012) discussed two main factors that have been critical in shaping the field: a) regional traditions, and b) professional background and training. These factors also apply to the discipline of writing assessment.

Regarding the first factor, McNamara and Knoch (2012) pinpointed significant differences between the American and British traditions. In the United States, early on there was a strong emphasis on psychometric approaches to language testing. At the same time, there was less of a concern for the changing demands from language teaching and curriculum development – changes that were gaining extra momentum with the communicative turn in language testing, emerging around the late 1970s (Bachman 2000; McNamara 1996; Morrow 1979). By comparison, the British tradition put more weight on issues of language test content and its relationship to language teaching, and was less concerned with rigorous measurement and statistical analysis (Hamp-Lyons 2002; Spolsky 1995).

The second factor is partly associated with regional differences in language testing traditions. As McNamara and Knoch (2012) noted, upon entering the field most language testing researchers have extensive training in the humanities, linguistics, or language teaching rather than in psychometrics or quantitative methods. If at all, requisite psychometric knowledge and expertise typically have been acquired in graduate university courses or in specialized workshops. Reflecting the divergence in regional research traditions, training programs in language testing that cover relevant psychometric and statistical issues have a longer tradition in the United States than in European countries. As a result, the much lamented gap between applied linguistics and psychometrics has become less of a problem in the States.

The joint impact of these developing factors is exemplified by perennial debates addressing two themes that are closely intertwined – the reliability and the validity of assessment outcomes.

2.3 The quest for assessment reliability

In Europe and the United States, written exams were administered to increasing numbers of candidates during the second half of the 19th century, mainly for university admission and placement, as well as for certification of professional qualification. This was about the time when dissatisfaction with low internal consistency or reliability of essay marking was growing. Edgeworth (1890) was among the first to level heavy criticism at the "element of chance" and the "unavoidable uncertainty" of essay examinations.

Illustrating the different regional traditions in language testing mentioned earlier, the critical stance taken by Edgeworth (1890) and others had only weak impact on writing assessment practices in Britain, where subjective essay marking, "uncontaminated by psychometric notions" (Spolsky 1995: 63), remained the predominant method for decades to come. Quite in contrast, the focus in the U.S. quickly shifted towards studying the reliability of writing assessments. To ensure sufficiently high reliability, "objective" tests were constructed, usually multiple-choice tests measuring discrete skills deemed relevant for the ability to write. These tests were also called "new-type" or "indirect" assessments, as opposed to "direct", essay-based tests.

A study by Huddleston (1954) provided a typical example of this approach. Huddleston showed that a multiple-choice test of composition skill, consisting of items on punctuation, idiomatic expression, grammar, and sentence structure, correlated substantially higher with teacher ratings of student writing ability than scores on a 20-minute essay (.58 vs. .40). Moreover, the verbal section of the College Board's Scholastic Aptitude Test (SAT), including items on analogies, antonyms, sentence completion, and reading comprehension, correlated even higher with teacher ratings (.76). Huddleston concluded that "measurable 'ability to write' is no more than verbal ability" (1954: 204). Clearly, this conclusion, if correct, would have serious implications for the very construct of writing ability, particularly in second and foreign language contexts.

2.4 Concerns about assessment validity

By the middle of the 20th century, indirect writing assessment had gained much ground in U.S. assessment programs, and direct writing assessment had fallen into disfavor (Hamp-Lyons 1991a). However, it did not take too long before the pendulum swung back again: Beginning in the 1970s, more and more voices were raised again in favor of direct writing assessment (Brown 1978; Diederich 1974).

At least three inter-related concerns fostered the re-emergence of essay testing. First, the tradition of indirect writing assessment was almost exclusively focused on writing as form, or as a set of isolated skills, rather than on writing as the expression of ideas or writing as a creative, communicative process embedded in a socio-cultural context (Behizadeh and Engelhard 2011). In other words, indirect tests suffered from construct underrepresentation (Messick 1989, 1994). Second, restricting writing assessment to the use of multiple-choice tests often had a negative effect on writing instruction (i.e. negative washback), particularly in schools and at the college-entry level (Hamp-Lyons 2001). Third, within more recent assessment validation frameworks (Kane 1992, 2011; Messick 1989), the empirical evidence needed to support the interpretation and use of writing assessment outcomes has been extended beyond simply computing correlations with some external criterion, including the study of washback effects and raters' judgmental and decision processes (Bejar 2012; Lumley 2005; Wall 2012).

In view of the essay-based tests administered in ancient China more than 2,000 years ago (Hamp-Lyons 2001), it is tempting to conclude that writing assessment has a long past but a short history, paraphrasing a famous quote by Ebbinghaus (1908), who thus characterized the discipline of psychology at the time. Indeed, as a formally defined field writing assessment has existed for a relatively short period of time, approximately 100 years. Over the years, the field has made significant progress in theoretical analysis, empirical research, and methodology, finally realizing the "psychometric-communicative trend" that Bachman (1990: 299) once considered necessary for advancing language testing in general.

3 Frameworks for writing assessment

3.1 The notion of frameworks

Within the present context, frameworks, in particular foreign language frameworks, are classification systems that provide definitions of key concepts and practices of language curriculum design, development, and implementation. Frameworks also provide guidelines and standards for developing, analyzing, and evaluating language assessments (Saville 2014). "Currently the most exciting of all of these frameworks in terms of recent research, the flurry of development activities, and its increasing spread worldwide" (Chalhoub-Deville 2009: 248) is the Common European Framework of Reference for Languages (CEFR; Council of Europe 2001). The CEFR comprises definitions and descriptions of what language learners should be able to do at a number of proficiency levels. Writing performance is described using illustrative scales for Overall Written Production, Creative Writing, and Reports and Essays. Moreover, the CEFR gives examples of writing activities and discusses production strategies, such as planning, compensating, and monitoring.

3.2 Limitations and extensions

From the perspective of language assessment, however, the CEFR suffers from severe limitations (Fulcher this volume). In particular, the CEFR levels and descriptors have been considered as much too broad for direct applications in a local assessment context (Harsch and Martin 2012). On a more theoretical note, the CEFR proficiency scale has been criticized as being confounded with intellectual functioning such that higher CEFR levels can only be achieved by learners with higher intellectual or educational level (Hulstijn 2011).

In addition, the CEFR gives only little attention to factors that are relevant for the development of practical writing tasks, such as linguistic demands or cognitive processing. For instance, Harsch and Rupp (2011) examined how, and to what extent, the theoretical model of writing discussed in the CEFR can be operationalized in terms of test specifications and rating criteria to produce level-specific writing assessments for use in a large-scale standards-based assessment project. Their findings suggested that the CEFR should solely be regarded as a basis for task design and assessment since its writing model does not sufficiently take into account facets like task environment and the social context of the writing activity. Therefore, they additionally drew on key results from research on writing, as well as on a systematic classification of writing tasks according to relevant criteria from the CEFR Grid for Writing Tasks, including task demands, time allotted to solve a task, or linguistic features of the expected response.

Frameworks can function as an instrument for validation, allowing writing test developers to justify the use of a particular assessment through a set of scientifically sound procedures. Validation frameworks like Bachman and Palmer's (2010) assessment use argument (AUA) or Weir's (2005) socio-cognitive approach included an analysis of assessment tasks focusing on target language use (Xi and Davis this volume). Both Bachman and Palmer and Weir stressed the importance of cognitive and contextual parameters of assessment tasks to make inferences from test performance to language ability as manifested in contexts different from the test itself. Shaw and Weir (2007) provided a comprehensive analysis of writing tasks based on Weir's socio-cognitive approach that is also relevant for the issue of task difficulty across proficiency levels.

4 Operationalizing the construct: writing tasks and rating scales

In writing assessment, the construct of interest is typically reflected in two components: The first component is the test task, which is designed to represent the construct and aims at eliciting a corresponding written performance; the second component is the rating scale, which explicitly represents the construct through its descriptors, guides the scoring procedure and, thus, impacts greatly on the assessment outcomes.

4.1 Task formats

Writing task formats cover the entire spectrum of a general item-format continuum, ranging from selected-response tasks at one end (e.g., multiple-choice tests) to performance assessment tasks at the other (e.g., essay testing, portfolio-based assessment; Johnson, Penny and Gordon 2009). These formats vary greatly in terms of authenticity, cognitive complexity, response structure, and efficiency of assessment. Moreover, the task format has strong implications for the rating process.

Often-used formats in writing assessment are selected-response (SR) tasks, constructed-response (CR) tasks, and portfolio-based assessment. SR tasks assess writing ability indirectly, usually by means of multiple-choice items. Because of validity concerns, negative washback on writing instruction, and lack of authenticity, SR tasks are often used in combination with CR formats, such as essays (Hamp-Lyons 2003). Carr (2011) further distinguished between extended production tasks, which correspond to prompt-based CR tasks, and limited production tasks, which most commonly refer to short-answer questions.

Over the last two decades performance-based assessment has played an increasingly dominant role. In fact, CR tasks have come to be the most widely accepted format to assess students L2 writing ability (Cumming 1997; Weigle 2002). Despite its frequent usage, the CR prototype task, that is, the timed impromptu essay, has often been subject to serious critique. It has been argued that general conclusions about the writing ability of examinees are difficult to draw based on just one writing product, in one genre, on a new topic, and in a low-authentic, timed context (Bouwer et al. 2015; Weigle 2007).

Furthermore, timed impromptu essay tests have been criticized for falling short of capturing the nature of academic writing, which has led to a growing popularity of *integrated* writing tasks, especially in the academic context. Since transforming knowledge gained from various sources plays an important role in academic writing, integrated writing tasks are credited with mirroring academic literacy activities in a valid and authentic way (Gebril 2009). Further advantages refer to reducing the impact of individual background knowledge by providing sources and achieving positive washback effects (Weigle 2004).

Integrated writing tasks are already common practice in large-scale assessment and have been researched from many perspectives (Cumming 2014; Plakans 2012). However, the underlying construct is still an open issue due to the complex nature of such tasks and the lack of a sufficiently detailed theoretical analysis of the ability to write from sources (Hirvela 2004). Promising approaches to capture this ability have recently been made (e.g., Asención Delaney 2008; Plakans 2008). According to an assessment-focused definition given by Knoch and Sitajalabhorn (2013), integrated writing tasks provide examinees with one or more language-rich source texts to write a composition by operations such as mining the source text(s) for ideas, selecting and synthesizing these ideas, transforming the input language, and organizing ideas by using stylistic conventions.

The well-known weaknesses of timed writing tests have also fostered the development of portfolio-based writing assessment (Hamp-Lyons and Condon 2000; Yancey and Weiser 1997). In fact, portfolio assessment reflects a shift from a product-oriented approach to a more process-oriented writing pedagogy, focusing on the steps involved in creating a written product (Romova and Andrew 2011). Use of portfolios has been suggested for reasons of high authenticity and validity, as well as for its relevance for writing instruction, curriculum design and low-stakes assessment. However, problems may come about when portfolios are to be used in large-scale contexts, mainly because of practical restrictions and lack of standardized scoring procedures (Weigle 2002; Williams 2000).

4.2 Task dimensions and design issues

Tasks direct the writing process by providing context and purpose. Designing clear, interesting, and authentic writing tasks that elicit the specific ability of interest presents a major challenge to test developers. Task specifications are an important tool to meet this challenge (Carr 2011). For writing tasks, specifications should include the construct to be measured, the task dimensions (e.g., audience, genre/rhetorical function, topics, linguistic characteristics of the prompt, source material, sample prompt), the response mode, and the scoring methods (Weigle 2002). Specifications help to make the purpose and the requirements of a task transparent and serve as a blueprint for further task and prompt development (Bachman and Palmer 1996).

The prompt, or instruction, is the core of a performance-based writing task. Prompts have been studied from many perspectives, for example by looking at their comparability in terms of difficulty. Prompt difficulty has been addressed regarding various aspects of prompts, such as topic domain, rhetorical task, or prompt length. Lim (2010) investigated the influence of these and other prompt dimensions on writing scores. He found that the only dimension yielding significant differences was topic domain: prompts on social topics appeared to be more difficult than prompts on education topics.

Research on prompt difficulty clearly points to the need to write "good" prompts. Yet, what constitutes a good prompt is a fairly complex issue. In practice, prompt writing is monitored through rigorous item writing, expert judgments, and careful pretesting. Guidelines aim to support this by suggesting ways to design prompts as comparable as possible in terms of difficulty and accessibility (Kroll and Reid 1994). However, research has shown that prompt-specific effects, or more general task characteristics, cannot be separated from other factors, such as the writer, the reader/rater, and the scoring methods (McNamara 1996; Weigle 2002). Hence, tasks cannot simply be labeled "easy" or "difficult" since they interact with other variables. One of these is the scale used to rate written performances.

4.3 Rating scales

In order to evaluate written performances, raters are usually provided with a detailed set of criteria. These criteria are presented to raters in the form of rating scales along with various scale descriptors which operationalize and verbalize the construct to be assessed. To ensure valid scoring, the descriptors should be distinct and describe writing performances that examinees are likely to show on the assessment tasks (van Moere 2014).

Three types of rating scales are commonly employed: holistic scales, analytic scales, and primary trait scales. The advantages and disadvantages of each type have been widely discussed (McNamara 1996; Weigle 2002; Shaw and Weir 2007). With holistic scales, one single overall score is assigned to a given performance. In analytic scoring, different features of the performance are rated separately (e.g., task fulfillment, organization, vocabulary). Whereas both holistic and analytic scales are usually generalizable to a larger class of tasks, primary trait scales focus on how well the candidate's performance meets the requirements on a particular task (Weigle 2002). While primary trait scoring may offer deep insight into students' abilities, it is only rarely used, mainly because it is time-consuming to develop (Hamp-Lyons 1991b). Holistic scales are relatively easy and fast to develop; they require less intense rater training, and are considered more authentic, since holistic reading reflects the natural reading process better than the analytic approach. By comparison, analytic scales can provide more detailed diagnostic information on distinct features of writing performances (Montee and Malone 2014).

The choice of a rating format should be made in accordance with the aims, needs, and resources of the assessment. If, for example, responses to an integrated reading-to-write task are to be evaluated, it might be more beneficial to employ an analytic scale that has been developed especially for this task, and which might even include references to the specific content and language of the reading sources. Developing appropriate rating scales for integrated tasks poses a challenge, however, because the underlying construct is difficult to define in many instances, and little is yet known about the manner in which raters deal with reading-to-write tasks (Gebril and Plakans 2014). Furthermore, the problem of task dependency is a central issue in evaluating performances elicited by integrated tasks. Task dependency leads to "muddied measurement" (Weir 1990), and hence complicates the interpretation of results, since it is unclear whether writing ability, reading skills, or other variables account for the performance. Even though research has indicated that scores achieved on integrated writing tasks correlated more strongly with writing than with reading ability (Asención Delaney 2008), further research on this topic is required. More generally, what is needed is a consistent research agenda for integrated writing tasks, accounting for construct and task development issues, rating procedures, and score interpretations (Cumming 2013).

5 Evaluating the quality of writing assessments

As discussed previously, CR tasks have become the predominant format for writing assessments. In most instances, specifically trained and experienced human raters evaluate the quality of the written responses provided by examinees. Though often referred to as a kind of direct assessment (e.g., Huot 1990), the process of assessing examinee performance actually is an indirect one, involving a complex reading–evaluation–scoring process that is more aptly captured by the term *rater-mediated assessment* (Engelhard 2002; McNamara 2000).

5.1 Rater variability

Generally speaking, rater variability is a component of unwanted variability contributing to construct-irrelevant variance (CIV) in assessment outcomes (Messick 1989, 1994). When CIV is present, the assessment is too broad, covering processes, factors, or dimensions not relevant to the construct being measured. Traditionally, rater variability has been studied in terms of rater effects, rater errors, or rater bias.

Rater effects most commonly studied are a) *severity/leniency*: raters provide scores that are consistently too low or too high compared to other raters or to established benchmark ratings; b) *central tendency*: raters provide scores primarily around the scale midpoint; c) *halo*: raters provide similar ratings on conceptually distinct criteria; and d) *rater bias*: raters fluctuate between harsh and lenient ratings depending on some aspect of the assessment situation (e.g., groups of examinees, scoring criteria, or tasks).

5.2 Quality control procedures

The usual approach to dealing with rater variability, especially in standardized large-scale assessments, consists of three parts: rater training, independent ratings of the same performance by two or more raters (repeated ratings), and demonstration of interrater reliability. Rater training typically aims at familiarizing raters with the overall aim and format of the assessment, the tasks, and the rating procedure (Baldwin, Fowles and Livingston 2005).

Ideally, differences between raters that may still exist after training should be so small as to be practically unimportant; that is, raters should not contribute to CIV. However, most often rater training procedures have failed to achieve this aim. Research has shown that within-rater consistency may be increased, but important rater effects, notably between-rater differences in severity, remain largely unaffected (Knoch 2011; Lumley and McNamara 1995; Weigle 1998, 1999).

To quantify the extent to which raters disagree with one another and to provide evidence on the overall quality of an assessment program, some index of interrater reliability is usually computed. But there are many different indices (Stemler and Tsai 2008), some of which can lead to incongruent, sometimes even contradictory results and conclusions. For example, one rater may award scores to examinees that are consistently one or two scale points lower than the scores that another rater awards to the same examinees. The relative ordering of the examinees will be much the same for both raters, yielding high correlations between ratings; that is, interrater *consistency* will be high. Yet, the raters have not reached exact agreement in any one case; that is, interrater *consensus* will be low. Even if raters exhibit both high consistency and high consensus, the evidence for high accuracy can be on shaky ground. Thus, two raters may be in fine agreement with each other simply because they are subject to the same systematic errors or biases to much the same degree (Eckes 2015; Wind and Engelhard 2013).

Therefore, any study that reports on interrater reliability should meet the following minimum requirements: a) specifying the design used for collecting the rating data (e.g., number of raters, examinees, and criteria, plan for assigning raters to examinees, kind of rating scale or scales etc.); b) defining the index or indices that were computed; c) computing at least two different indices, one consensus index (e.g., percentage agreement) and one consistency index (e.g., Pearson correlation). More sophisticated quality control procedures rest on the use of measurement models.

5.3 Measurement models

Two broad classes of measurement models have been employed with increasing frequency: *generalizability theory* (G-theory; Brennan 2001) and *many-facet Rasch measurement* (MFRM; Linacre 1989).

G-theory extends classical test theory by recognizing multiple sources of measurement error, estimating the magnitude of each source separately, and providing a strategy for optimizing the reliability of the assessment. One source of measurement error is random error; other sources refer to factors that may be contributing to CIV, such as raters, assessment occasions, or writing tasks (Gebril 2009; Huang 2012).

Much the same factors and their interactions are considered in the MFRM approach, albeit in a different way. The factors, or facets, specified in a MFRM model are analyzed simultaneously and calibrated onto a single linear scale (i.e. the logit scale). The joint calibration of facets makes it possible to measure rater severity on the same scale as examinee proficiency or task difficulty. This approach also allows exam boards to correct assessment outcomes for between-rater severity differences (Eckes 2005, 2015; Engelhard 2013).

6 Controversial issues in writing assessment

6.1 Automated essay scoring

Automated essay scoring (AES) has been increasingly employed in the L2 writing context, both for teaching (evaluation) and assessment (scoring). The discussion on AES, however, has remained controversial and the systems that have been proposed are often subject to serious critique (Carr 2014; Van Moere and Downey this volume).

Arguments for the use of AES often refer to their effectiveness and reliability. Once installed, computer systems for essay scoring work fast and at low prices, and many studies found that their scores correlated highly with holistic human ratings (Attali and Burstein 2006). Most state-of-the-art AES engines rate a text by measuring indicators of text production skills and language proficiency (i.e. fluency, grammar and word usage, organization), but prove to be less sensitive towards more elaborate writing skills such as strength of argumentation, rhetorical effectiveness, or content appropriateness (Dean 2013b; Shermis 2014).

Accordingly, AES systems seem to be more suitable for assessing language proficiency through writing rather than writing ability *per se* – an assumption that may explain the harsh critique of AES from writing/composition practitioners, as compared to the views in L2 testing (Weigle 2013b). In the latter, many acknowledge the potential of AES, provided that the systems are employed in a sensitive and transparent manner and are complemented by human raters in large-scale assessments (Xi 2010).

AES will certainly influence L2 writing assessment and evaluation in the near future. Current approaches to building a validity argument for AES are therefore an important step towards a responsible usage (Elliot and Williamson 2013; Xi 2010). Regardless of one's position towards AES, its increasing use has informed the discussion on what characterizes good writing and has led to the development of general models to assess this ability, like the socio-cognitive, process-oriented approach suggested by Deane (2013a, 2013b).

6.2 Standardized versus site-based, locally controlled writing assessment

Another contentious issue is concerned with paradigms or theoretical positions in writing assessment. Hamp-Lyons (2013) referred to "the proverbial 'elephant in the room'" and noted, especially for the U. S. context, "a divide, almost a chasm, between the psychometricians working in writing assessment and the rhetoric/compositionists working in writing assessment" (2013: A2). AES, as mentioned before, is just one topic where different positions become apparent.

The tension between psychometric and composition approaches is also reflected in the discussion of the extent to which a multifaceted, context-based ability like writing can or should be tested in a standardized way. Some writing scholars have voiced concerns about privileging reliability at the expense of validity. Taking up Moss' (1994) hermeneutical approach to assessment that highlights the situated, unique, and varying contexts of writing, Huot (1996, 2002) criticized the negative impact of standardized writing assessment and suggested alternative practices that are site-based, locally controlled, and accessible for all stakeholders involved.

These practices would take into account varied facets of writing assessment, such as the socio-cultural nature of writing, the strong interplay between assessment and instruction, and contextualized, purpose-specific assessment procedures. In principle, local procedures, if implemented on a sound, fair, and transparent basis, may be beneficial for both L1 and L2 performance assessment (Hamp-Lyons 2003).

However, transferring the appealing features of locally controlled L2 writing assessment to international, large-scale contexts is highly problematic, if not infeasible. Testing the writing ability of people across diverse geographical regions and cultural backgrounds requires standardized assessment procedures to produce reliable, valid, and fair outcomes.

Discussions on re-conceptualizing reliability will continue. According to Parkes (2007) one way to provide reliability evidence in local assessment contexts is to consider reliability, like validity, within an argument-based approach and, thus, to provide evidence appropriate for particular assessment purposes.

7 Future directions

Looking ahead, there are a number of recent developments that will further advance the discipline of writing assessment. Foremost among these are inquiries into the suitability of integrated writing tasks and the extension of models and procedures for automated essay scoring. Human raters will, in our view, not be replaced completely by AES systems in most instruments for direct writing assessments. Therefore, a key issue that needs to be addressed refers to ubiquitous rater effects as a source of CIV. Today, measurement models are available to closely study or even control for many of these effects and thus meet the challenge of the communicative movement that led to the re-emergence of essay tests. McNamara (2011: 436) euphorically welcomed one particular model, the many-facet Rasch model, as a "quantum leap in our capacity to investigate and to a considerable extent to deal with this psychometric challenge." However, this and related models will bear fruit only if they become standard part of the training of those involved in overseeing the assessment of writing; that is, there is a clear need to develop writing assessment literacy (Taylor 2009; Weigle 2007).

A related issue concerns the study of rater cognition, that is, the study of the attentional, perceptual, and judgmental processes involved when raters award scores to examinees. Research into these cognitive processes is directly relevant for validating the use and interpretation of essay scores. Thus, as Bejar (2012: 2) pointed out, "it is important to document that the readers' cognitive processes are consistent with the construct being measured." Though not labeled as such, early research on this issue was conducted by Diederich, French and Carlton (1961), who showed that readers (raters) could be classified into five *schools of thought*. These schools of thought were reliably distinguished by the weight they attached to different aspects of the written performances. More recently, the term *rater types* has been used to describe groups of raters manifesting systematic patterns of similarities and dissimilarities in perceived criterion importance that also relate to criterion-specific biases in operational scoring contexts (Eckes 2008, 2012; He et al. 2013).

Taken together, much progress has been made since Edgeworth's (1890) critique of the "element of chance" in essay examinations, echoing the emergence of an integrative science of writing assessment. Yet, much more needs to be done to establish assessment procedures that come close to the goal of providing valid and fair measures of writing ability in highly varied writing contexts.

8 Acknowledgements

We would like to thank our colleagues at the TestDaF Institute for many stimulating discussions on issues of foreign-language writing assessment. Special thanks go to Claudia Harsch (University of Warwick, UK) for thoughtful comments on an earlier version of this chapter.

9 References

Asención Delaney, Yuly. 2008. Investigating the reading-to-write construct. *Journal of English for Academic Purposes* 7(3): 140–150.

Attali, Yigal and Jill Burstein. 2006. Automated essay scoring with e-rater® V.2. *Journal of Technology, Learning, and Assessment* 4(3): 1–30.

Bachman, Lyle F. 1990. *Fundamental considerations in language testing*. Oxford, UK: Oxford University Press.

Bachman, Lyle F. 2000. Modern language testing at the turn of the century: Assuring that what we count counts. *Language Testing* 17(1): 1–42.

Bachman, Lyle F. and Adrian S. Palmer. 1996. *Language testing in practice: Designing and developing useful language tests*. Oxford, UK: Oxford University Press.

Bachman, Lyle F. and Adrian S. Palmer. 2010. *Language assessment in practice: Developing language assessments and justifying their use in the real world*. Oxford, UK: Oxford University Press.

Baldwin, Doug, Mary Fowles and Skip Livingston. 2005. *Guidelines for constructed-response and other performance assessments*. Princeton, NJ: Educational Testing Service.

Behizadeh, Nadia and George Engelhard Jr. 2011. Historical view of the influences of measurement and writing theories on the practice of writing assessment in the United States. *Assessing Writing* 16(3): 189–211.

Bejar, Issac I. 2012. Rater cognition: Implications for validity. *Educational Measurement: Issues and Practice* 31(3): 2–9.

Bouwer, Renske, Anton Béguin, Ted Sanders and Huub van den Bergh. 2015. Effect of genre on the generalizability of writing scores. *Language Testing* 32(1): 83–100.

Brennan, Robert L. 2001. *Generalizability theory*. New York: Springer.

Brown, Rexford. 1978. What we know now and how we could know more about writing ability in America. *Journal of Basic Writing* 4: 1–6.

Carr, Nathan T. 2011. *Designing and analyzing language tests*. Oxford, UK: Oxford University Press.

Carr, Nathan T. 2014. Computer-automated scoring of written responses. In: Anthony J. Kunnan (ed.). *The companion to language assessment*. Vol. 2, 1063–1078. Chichester, UK: Wiley.

Chalhoub-Deville, Micheline. 2009. Content validity considerations in language testing contexts. In: Robert W. Lissitz (ed.). *The concept of validity: Revisions, new directions, and applications*, 241–263. Charlotte, NC: Information Age.

Council of Europe. 2001. *Common European framework of reference for languages: Learning, teaching, assessment*. Cambridge, UK: Cambridge University Press.

Cumming, Alister. 1997. The testing of writing in a second language. In: Caroline Clapham and David Corson (eds.). *Encyclopedia of language and education: Language testing and assessment*, 51–63. Dordrecht, The Netherlands: Kluwer.

Cumming, Alister. 2013. Assessing integrated writing tasks for academic purposes: Promises and perils. *Language Assessment Quarterly* 10(1): 1–8.

Cumming, Alister. 2014. Assessing integrated skills. In: Anthony J. Kunnan (ed.). *The companion to language assessment*. Vol. 1, 216–229. Chichester, UK: Wiley.

Deane, Paul. 2013a. Covering the construct: An approach to automated essay scoring motivated by a socio-cognitive framework for defining literacy skills. In: Mark D. Shermis and Jill Burstein (eds.). *Handbook on automated essay evaluation: Current application and new directions*, 298–312. New York: Routledge.

Deane, Paul. 2013b. On the relation between automated essay scoring and modern views of the writing construct. *Assessing Writing* 18(1): 7–24.

Diederich, Paul B. 1974. *Measuring growth in English*. Urbana, IL: National Council of Teachers of English.

Diederich, Paul B., John W. French and Sydell T. Carlton. 1961. *Factors in judgments of writing ability*. RB-61-15. Princeton, NJ: Educational Testing Service.

Ebbinghaus, Hermann. 1908. *Psychology: An elementary text-book*. Boston, MA: Heath.

Eckes, Thomas. 2005. Examining rater effects in TestDaF writing and speaking performance assessments: A many facet Rasch analysis. *Language Assessment Quarterly* 2(3): 197–221.

Eckes, Thomas. 2008. Rater types in writing performance assessments: A classification approach to rater variability. *Language Testing* 25(2): 155–185.

Eckes, Thomas. 2012. Operational rater types in writing assessment: Linking rater cognition to rater behavior. *Language Assessment Quarterly* 9(3): 270–292.

Eckes, Thomas. 2015. *Introduction to many-facet Rasch measurement: Analyzing and evaluating rater-mediated assessments*, 2nd ed. Frankfurt am Main: Lang.

Edgeworth, Francis Y. 1890. The element of chance in competitive examinations. *Journal of the Royal Statistical Society* 53(4): 644–663.

Elliot, Norbert. 2005. *On a scale: A social history of writing assessment in America*. New York: Lang.

Elliot, Norbert and David M. Williamson. 2013. *Assessing Writing* special issue: Assessing writing with automated scoring systems. *Assessing Writing* 18(1): 1–6.

Engelhard, George Jr. 2002. Monitoring raters in performance assessments. In: Gerald Tindal and Thomas M. Haladyna (eds.). *Large-scale assessment programs for all students: Validity, technical adequacy, and implementation*, 261–287. Mahwah, NJ: Erlbaum.

Engelhard, George Jr. 2013. *Invariant measurement: Using Rasch models in the social, behavioral, and health sciences*. New York: Routledge.

Fulcher, Glenn. This volume. Standards and frameworks. In: Dina Tsagari and Jayanti Banerjee (eds.). *Handbook of second language assessment*. Berlin: DeGruyter Mouton.

Gebril, Atta. 2009. Score generalizability of academic writing tasks: Does one test method fit it all? *Language Testing* 26(4): 507–531.

Gebril, Atta and Lia Plakans. 2014. Assembling validity evidence for assessing academic writing: Rater reactions to integrated tasks. *Assessing Writing* 21(1): 56–73.

Hamp-Lyons, Liz. 1991a. Basic concepts. In: Liz Hamp-Lyons (ed.). *Assessing second language writing in academic contexts*, 5–15. Westport, CT: Ablex.

Hamp-Lyons, Liz. 1991b. Scoring procedures for ESL contexts. In: Liz Hamp-Lyons (ed.). *Assessing second language writing in academic contexts*, 241–276. Westport, CT: Ablex.

Hamp-Lyons, Liz. 2001. Fourth generation writing assessment. In: Tony Silva and Paul K. Matsuda (eds.). *On second language writing*, 117–127. Mahwah, NJ: Erlbaum.

Hamp-Lyons, Liz. 2002. The scope of writing assessment. *Assessing Writing* 8(1): 5–16.

Hamp-Lyons, Liz. 2003. Writing teachers as assessors of writing. In: Barbara Kroll (ed.). *Exploring the dynamics of second language writing*, 162–189. Cambridge, UK: Cambridge University Press.

Hamp-Lyons, Liz. 2013. What is the role of an international journal of *writing assessment*? *Assessing Writing* 18(4): A1–A4.

Hamp-Lyons, Liz and William Condon. 2000. *Assessing the portfolio: Principles for practice, theory, and research*. Cresskill: Hampton Press.

Harsch, Claudia and Guido Martin. 2012. Adapting CEF-descriptors for rating purposes: Validation by a combined rater training and scale revision approach. *Assessing Writing* 17(4): 228–250.

Harsch, Claudia and André A. Rupp. 2011. Designing and scaling level-specific writing tasks in alignment with the CEFR: A test-centered approach. *Language Assessment Quarterly* 8(1): 1–33.

He, Tung-Hsien, Wen J. Gou, Ya-Chen Chien, I-Shan J. Chen and Shan-Mao Chang. 2013. Multi-faceted Rasch measurement and bias patterns in EFL writing performance assessment. *Psychological Reports: Measures and Statistics* 112(2): 469–485.

Hinkel, Eli. 2011. What research on second language writing tells us and what it doesn't. In: Eli Hinkel (ed.). *Handbook of research in second language teaching and learning*. Vol. 2, 523–538. New York: Routledge.

Hirvela, Alan. 2004. *Connecting reading and writing in second language writing instruction*. Ann Arbor, MI: University of Michigan Press.

Huang, Jinyan. 2012. Using generalizability theory to examine the accuracy and validity of large-scale ESL writing assessment. *Assessing Writing* 17(3): 123–139.

Huddleston, Edith M. 1954. Measurement of writing ability at the college-entrance level: Objective vs. subjective testing techniques. *Journal of Experimental Education* 22(3): 165–213.

Hulstijn, Jan H. 2011. Language proficiency in native and nonnative speakers: An agenda for research and suggestions for second-language assessment. *Language Assessment Quarterly* 8(3): 229–249.

Huot, Brian A. 1990. The literature of direct writing assessment: Major concerns and prevailing trends. *Review of Educational Research* 60(2): 237–263.

Huot, Brian A. 1996. Toward a new theory of writing assessment. *College Composition and Communication* 47(4): 549–566.

Huot, Brian A. 2002. *(Re)articulating writing assessment for teaching and learning*. Logan, UT: Utah State University Press.

Johnson, Robert L., James A. Penny and Belita Gordon. 2009. *Assessing performance: Designing, scoring, and validating performance tasks*. New York: Guilford Press.

Kane, Michael T. 1992. An argument-based approach to validation. *Psychological Bulletin* 112(3): 527–535.

Kane, Michael. 2011. Validating score interpretations and uses: Messick Lecture, Language Testing Research Colloquium, Cambridge, April 2010. *Language Testing* 29(1): 3–17.

Knoch, Ute. 2011. Investigating the effectiveness of individualized feedback to rating behavior: A longitudinal study. *Language Testing* 28(2): 179–200.

Knoch, Ute and Woranon Sitajalabhorn. 2013. A closer look at integrated writing tasks: Towards a more focussed definition for assessment purposes. *Assessing Writing* 18(4): 300–308.

Kroll, Barbara and Joy Reid. 1994. Guidelines for designing writing prompts: Clarifications, caveats, and cautions. *Journal of Second Language Writing* 3(3): 231–255.

Lado, Robert. 1961. *Language testing: The construction and use of foreign language tests*. New York: McGraw-Hill.

Lim, Gad S. 2010. Investigating prompt effects in writing performance assessment. *Spaan Fellow Working Papers in Second or Foreign Language Assessment* 8: 95–116. Ann Arbor, MI: University of Michigan.

Linacre, John M. 1989. *Many-facet Rasch measurement*. Chicago, IL: MESA Press.

Lumley, Tom. 2005. *Assessing second language writing: The rater's perspective*. Frankfurt am Main: Lang.

Lumley, Tom and Tim F. McNamara. 1995. Rater characteristics and rater bias: Implications for training. *Language Testing* 12(1): 54–71.

MacArthur, Charles A., Steve Graham and Jill Fitzgerald (eds.). 2008. *Handbook of writing research*. New York: Guilford Press.

McNamara, Tim F. 1996. *Measuring second language performance*. London: Longman.

McNamara, Tim F. 2000. *Language testing*. Oxford, UK: Oxford University Press.

McNamara, Tim F. 2011. Applied linguistics and measurement: A dialogue. *Language Testing* 28(4): 435–440.

McNamara, Tim and Ute Knoch. 2012. The Rasch wars: The emergence of Rasch measurement in language testing. *Language Testing* 29(4): 555–576.

Messick, Samuel. 1989. Validity. In: Robert L. Linn (ed.). *Educational measurement*, 3rd ed. 13–103. New York: Macmillan.

Messick, Samuel. 1994. The interplay of evidence and consequences in the validation of performance assessments. *Educational Researcher* 23(2): 13–23.

Montee, Megan and Margaret Malone. 2014. Writing scoring criteria and score reports. In: Anthony J. Kunnan (ed.). *The companion to language assessment*. Vol. 2, 847–859. Chichester, UK: Wiley.

Morrow, Keith. 1979. Communicative language testing: Revolution or evolution? In: Christopher J. Brumfit and K. Johnson (eds.). *The communicative approach to language teaching*, 143–157. Oxford, UK: Oxford University Press.

Moss, Pamela A. 1994. Can there be validity without reliability? *Educational Researcher* 23(2): 5–12.

Parkes, Jay. 2007. Reliability as an argument. *Educational Measurement: Issues and Practice* 26(4): 2–10.

Plakans, Lia. 2008. Comparing composing processes in writing-only and reading-to-write test tasks. *Assessing Writing* 13(2): 111–129.

Plakans, Lia. 2012. Writing integrated items. In: Glenn Fulcher and Fred Davidson (eds.), *The Routledge handbook of language testing*, 249–261. New York: Routledge.

Romova, Zina and Martin Andrew. 2011. Teaching and assessing academic writing via the portfolio: Benefits for learners of English as an additional language. *Assessing Writing* 16(2): 111–122.

Saville, Nick. 2014. Using standards and guidelines. In: Anthony J. Kunnan (ed.). *The companion to language assessment*. Vol. 2, 906–924. Chichester, UK: Wiley.

Shaw, Stuart D. and Cyril J. Weir. 2007. *Examining writing: Research and practice in assessing second language writing*. Cambridge, UK: Cambridge University Press.

Shermis, Mark D. 2014. State-of-the-art automated essay scoring: Competition, results, and future directions from a United States demonstration. *Assessing Writing* 20: 53–76.

Spolsky, Bernard. 1995. *Measured words: The development of objective language testing*. Oxford, UK: Oxford University Press.

Stemler, Steven E. and Jessica Tsai. 2008. Best practices in interrater reliability: Three common approaches. In: Jason W. Osborne (ed.). *Best practices in quantitative methods*, 29–49. Los Angeles, CA: Sage.

Taylor, Lynda. 2009. Developing assessment literacy. *Annual Review of Applied Linguistics* 29: 21–36.

Valette, Rebecca M. 1967. *Modern language testing*. New York: Harcourt, Brace and World.

Van Moere, Alistair. 2014. Raters and ratings. In: Anthony J. Kunnan (ed.). *The companion to language assessment*. Vol. 3, 1358–1374. Chichester, UK: Wiley.

Van Moere, Alistair and Ryan Downey. This volume. Technology and artificial intelligence in language assessment. In: Dina Tsagari and Jayanti Banerjee (eds.). *Handbook of second language assessment*. Berlin: DeGruyter Mouton.

Wall, Dianne. 2012. Washback. In: Glenn Fulcher and Fred Davidson (eds.). *The Routledge handbook of language testing*, 79–92. New York: Routledge.

Weigle, Sara C. 1998. Using FACETS to model rater training effects. *Language Testing* 15(2): 263–287.

Weigle, Sara C. 1999. Investigating rater/prompt interactions in writing assessment: Quantitative and qualitative approaches. *Assessing Writing* 6(2): 145–178.

Weigle, Sara C. 2002. *Assessing writing*. Cambridge, UK: Cambridge University Press.

Weigle, Sara C. 2004. Integrating reading and writing in a competency test for non-native speakers of English. *Assessing Writing* 9(1): 27–55.

Weigle, Sara C. 2007. Teaching writing teachers about assessment. *Journal of Second Language Writing* 16(3): 194–209.

Weigle, Sara C. 2013a. Assessment of writing. In: Carol A. Chapelle (ed.). *The encyclopedia of applied linguistics*, 257–264. New York: Blackwell.

Weigle, Sara C. 2013b. English language learners and automated scoring of essays: Critical considerations. *Assessing Writing* 18(1): 85–99.

Weir, Cyril J. 1990. *Communicative language testing*, 2nd ed. New York: Prentice Hall.

Weir, Cyril J. 2005. *Language testing and validation: An evidence-based approach*. Basingstoke, UK: Palgrave Macmillan.

Williams, James D. 2000. Identity and reliability in portfolio assessment. In: Bonnie S. Sunstein and Jonathan H. Lovell (eds.). *The portfolio standard: How students can show us what they know and are able to do*, 135–148. Portsmouth: Heinemann.

Wind, Stefanie A. and George Engelhard. 2013. How invariant and accurate are domain ratings in writing assessment? *Assessing Writing* 18(4): 278–299.

Xi, Xiaoming. 2010. Automated scoring and feedback systems: Where are we and where are we heading? *Language Testing* 27(3): 291–300.

Xi, Xiaoming and Larry Davis. This volume. Quality factors in language assessment. In: Dina Tsagari and Jayanti Banerjee (eds.). *Handbook of second language assessment*. Berlin: DeGruyter Mouton.

Yancey, Kathleen B. 1999. Looking back as we look forward: Historicizing writing assessment. *College Composition and Communication* 50(3): 483–503.

Yancey, Kathleen B. and Irwin Weiser (eds.). 1997. *Situating portfolios: Four perspectives*. Logan, UT: Utah State University Press.

Kirby C. Grabowski
11 Assessing pragmatic competence

1 Introduction

There is little doubt in the second language (L2) literature that language includes a layer of meaning that goes beyond syntax and literal meaning – one that is critical in understanding language. Even in many early theoretical language testing papers (Carroll 1968; Oller 1979; Spolsky 1973), the importance of trying to measure this aspect of language was evident, even if it was clear that assessing it might be unwieldy and potentially problematic. The components of this meaning dimension of language have often been subsumed in the L2 literature as part of a learner's *pragmatic competence*, and researchers have been trying to find ways to systematically assess it for more than thirty years. Pragmatics has been eloquently defined as "the study of language from the point of view of users, especially the choices they make, the constraints they encounter in using language in social interaction and the effects their use of language has on other participants in the act of communication" (Crystal 1997: 301). Yule (1996: 3) further asserts that pragmatics has "more to do with the analysis of what people mean by their utterances than what the words or phrases in those utterances might mean by themselves." In this way, pragmatics necessarily involves the ways in which context contributes to meaning in interaction. As such, pragmatics encompasses a broad range of core concepts that nearly always integrate the linguistic and situational context in the interpretation of meaning.

While language theorists have produced exhaustive volumes on what constitutes pragmatics, and this body of research contains much of the history of the hypothesized elements under the domain of pragmatics, there still seems to be no ultimate consensus as to a hierarchical or organizational structure of these elements in language, even though many of these core concepts have also been integrated into models of second language ability. Rather, they are more or less thrown together in a sort of "pragmatics wastebasket" (Yule 1996: 6). This lack of delineation and articulation in the pragmatics literature further complicates language testing, especially since most current influential models of language ability hypothesize some sort of a relationship between grammatical and pragmatic competence (Bachman and Palmer 1996; Canale and Swain 1980; Purpura 2004). Although these models provide structure and much needed guidance for pragmatics assessment researchers, much of the pragmatics testing research to date has focused on piece-meal attributes of pragmatic competence and relatively decontextualized instances of pragmatic use. In fact, the various taxonomies that have been employed in the lion's share of pragmatics assessment research have essentially been lists of disconnected features in language whose relationship to grammatical knowledge, and to language proficiency more generally, has been largely atheoretical. Thus, it is difficult to generalize test takers' knowledge beyond single instances of performance. Further complicating matters is that operationalizing the construct of pragmatic competence in high-context, interactive language use situations, which is a necessity for the interpretation of contextually-situated meanings, magnifies the complexities associated with assessing it. Consequently, empirical research in pragmatics assessment has often faced a number of limitations, including construct underrepresentation and the resulting lack of generalizability, as well as inauthentic tasks, in which a narrow, static operationalization of context has been the norm.

Models of language ability are critical for assessment researchers in the development of tests since the hypothesized constructs underlying them provide a basis for the interpretation of test performance. It is therefore crucial that a broad definition of communicative language ability (CLA), including an explicit pragmatic component, be articulated before attempts at operationalizing and measuring pragmatic competence can be made. Without a comprehensive underlying construct, the validity of test scores as a representation of test-taker ability cannot be adequately investigated and confirmed. Only when a theoretically based definition of its constituent components and its relationship to CLA are put forth can score-based inferences actually be generalized to ability beyond the test performance itself. The first step in the process of operationalizing a comprehensive model of pragmatic competence is articulating what the constituent components of pragmatics are.

2 Pragmatic dimensions of language

2.1 Speech acts

One major concept central to pragmatics, is the notion of speech acts, and Speech Act Theory (Austin 1962; Searle 1969) took root in the early 1960s. Austin (1962) was the first to discuss the functional capacity of language. He maintained that interpersonal communication incorporates a dimension distinct from and extending beyond literal interpretation. He argued that many utterances are the equivalent of actions. He distinguished between speech act types in a tertiary paradigm, including *locutionary act* (i.e. the literal conveyance of information or meaning), *illocutionary act* (e.g., the underlying meaning, or force, of an utterance), and *perlocutionary act* (i.e. the effect or consequence of the speaker's utterance on the interlocutor). Influenced by Austin's (1962) work, Searle (1969) further delineated different groups of illocutionary acts that can be performed through language. In addition, he introduced a now widely recognized distinction between direct and indirect speech acts. Although his typology has been influential in pragmatics, it does not capture important relationships between certain language functions and social variables. Specifically, his theory only applies to the most stereotypical and decontextualized examples in discourse, while meaning can be much more multi-dimensional in actual communication (Thomas 1995). For instance, his model does not account for social variables (e.g., power and social distance) among interlocutors (Brown and Levinson 1987), nor is the component of listener interpretation fully developed. As a result, several subsequent theoretical papers on pragmatics have attempted to fill this and other gaps by addressing contextually-based interpretations of meaning.

2.2 Implicature

Using a different paradigm, Grice (1975, 1978), a language philosopher, introduced his theory of implicature, which has had an extremely influential impact on the field of pragmatics. As part of his Cooperative Principle, he stipulated four maxims, or conditions, that are assumed to be followed in typical conversational contexts. A deviation from any of these maxims would result in an implicature, and thus generate a meaning beyond the actual words used in an utterance. He defined implicature in terms of how a hearer is able to decipher the implied meanings of an utterance as different from its literal meaning in conversation. In his theory, he distinguished between conventional and conversational implicature. Whereas conventional implicatures (e.g., *Is the Pope Catholic?* to mean *Unequivocally yes*) do not usually change according to the context of the situation, the conversational implicature of an utterance (e.g., *It's hot in here* to mean *Please open the window*) is entirely dependent on the context. Although Grice's (1975) theory does not account for intentional disregard of the maxims, his work was especially important to pragmatics in expanding speech act theory to include an additional dimension to interpretation on the part of the listener, as well as context-dependent communication. In this way, meaning rather than structure is brought to the forefront of pragmatics.

2.3 Politeness

Another theme – politeness – has evolved to become one of the most prominent research areas in pragmatics. Leech (1983) saw politeness as contributing to the (in)directness of utterances. In his view, interlocutors' disregard of the Cooperative Principle may be a direct result of their politeness strategies. For instance, in a face-threatening situation, a given speaker may choose to convey a relatively polite, and perhaps indirect, utterance that may flout convention rather than threaten the hearer's face (i.e. a person's public self-image; Yule 1996). In Leech's Politeness Principle, politeness strategies may contribute to the generation of implicatures that are more (or less) socially agreeable, and therefore support (or break down) amiable social relationships. In basic terms, his theory relates to a speaker's desire to be appropriate in a certain situation while still conveying his intended meaning. Leech also outlined guidelines for polite speech in the guise of maxims meant to account for the divergence of the meaning and pragmatic force of an utterance.

Brown and Levinson (1987) further extended the idea of linguistic politeness hypothesizing that an interlocutor's linguistic choices will vary depending on three sociolinguistic variables: power, distance, and absolute ranking of imposition. According to their theory, a speaker must assess the context based on these three variables, and then choose a strategy for optimizing a match between the appropriate degree of politeness expected in that context with the linguistic features used to express the intended meaning. They also asserted that these dimensions have the potential to shift since talk in interaction is locally managed. This theory has had a profound effect on empirical research in testing pragmatic competence dimensions, which will be discussed later in this chapter.

2.4 The pragmalinguistics and sociopragmatics dichotomy

Interlanguage pragmatics researchers generally divide pragmatic competence into two components: *pragmalinguistics* and *sociopragmatics*. According to Leech (1983) and Thomas (1983), pragmalinguistics can be defined as the ability to use appropriate linguistic devices to perform a particular speech act, whereas sociopragmatics relates to the ability to perform a speech act appropriate to a particular situation or context. Thomas further argues that pragmatic failure can occur in either (or both) of these domains. In short, pragmalinguistic failure relates to a linguistic deficiency whereas sociopragmatic failure results from a lack of sociocultural knowledge.

While this paradigm offers a seemingly useful distinction between the linguistic and social dimensions of language use that have been extensively researched in the L2 literature, in practice, it may be impossible to determine to which domain pragmatic failure can be attributed when looking at learner performance. A still greater issue with this distinction may be that pragmalinguistic knowledge, as it is conventionally defined, is not necessarily limited to the pragmatic domain. More specifically, by definition, pragmalinguistic knowledge also subsumes grammatical knowledge, since it encompasses the linguistic devices necessary to perform speech acts. In fact, it is difficult to think of a situation in which grammatical knowledge is not used to perform a speech act.[1] Therefore, it is nearly impossible to disentangle whether or not pragmalinguistic failure is due to a deficit in gram-

---

[1] Rare exceptions could include exaggerated and limited vocalizations and/or gestures, but these strategies are not *linguistic* in the traditional sense.

matical and/or pragmatic competence (Beebe and Waring 2005). Sociopragmatics, on the other hand, is a more viable pragmatic domain since it specifically relates to high-context, situational language use. However, within this paradigm, socio-pragmatic competence is limited to the appropriate use of speech acts, which, in a decontextualized situation, may simply require grammatical knowledge alone. Reducing pragmatics to speech acts, or equating the two, which is all too often the case in pragmatics assessment research, and trying to completely separate prag-matics from grammatical knowledge in high-context situations artificially limits a domain of language ability that is much more comprehensive and dynamic than is represented in the pragmalinguistic and sociopragmatic paradigm. In other words, what is most important in pragmatic use are the *meanings* that are generated in relation to the social and linguistic context in which the utterance or discourse occurs, independent of what speech act may be expected. This generalizable view of language knowledge is consistent with beliefs about how pragmatic competence should be represented in models of communicative language ability – the impor-tance of which is well-documented in the L2 testing literature.

3 Explicit pragmatic components in models of CLA

Although most current researchers in pragmatics recognize the heart of pragmatics to be meaning in interaction, the most influential representations of pragmatic as-pects in multicomponential models of language ability have emerged slowly and somewhat differentially through the years. Bachman and Palmer (1996) were the first to introduce a model of communicative language ability (CLA), perhaps the most dominant in second language testing theory to date, which includes an ex-plicit pragmatic component, which they further subdivide into functional and so-ciolinguistic knowledge. They define functional knowledge in terms of "how utter-ances or sentences and texts are related to the communicative goals of language users" (1996: 68), and link this to sociolinguistic knowledge, defined in terms of the features of the language use setting and their effect on language use. Although their model accounts for some of the metacognitive processes involved in pragmat-ic use through a strategic competence component, their model minimizes the role of meaning in utterances, and does not emphasize the importance of the grammati-cal resources necessary to realize pragmatic meanings in performance (Purpura 2004). Furthermore, although Bachman and Palmer's (1996) model of CLA repre-sents language as contextually situated, the focus is on the underlying ability of the individual learner without taking into account how contextual features (e.g., the presence of another interlocutor) might affect performance, a key consideration in the conveyance and interpretation of pragmatic meanings.

From a different theoretical perspective, Chapelle (1998) argues that there ex-ists an interaction between underlying L2 ability and the context in which the language use occurs. She contends that the trait perspective, which Bachman and Palmer's (1996) model represents, is inadequate for construct definition and that "the knowledge and fundamental processes that are required within a particular context as well as the metacognitive strategies controlling performance in that context" (1998: 48) should both be specified in the test construct. From the interactionalist perspective, Chapelle's idea is that a language test must attempt to capture both language knowledge and the metacognitive processes used in a particular context, and how language performance may, in turn, be affected by it. In Young's words (2000: 3–4, italics in original): "The interactionalist definition is ... a way to have your cake and eat it too: to infer from test performance something about *both* a practice-specific behavior *and* a practice-independent, person-specific trait." Under this definition, a test that measures language ability through a variety of tasks, for instance, would theoretically tap into generalizable knowledge through a variety of contexts.

In an attempt to address the shortcomings of prior models through an emphasis on meaning, Purpura's (2004) multicomponential model of language ability proposes that language knowledge consists of two reciprocal (i.e. mutual) but distinguishable components – grammatical knowledge and pragmatic competence. More specifically, Purpura (2004: 74) distinguishes the literal and intended meanings of an utterance encoded in grammar from the pragmatic, or *implied*, layers of meaning that are contextually driven, and often not derived solely from "the meanings of the words arranged in syntax." Therefore, pragmatic meanings (and their level of appropriateness) can only be determined in high-context situations. The strength of this model lies in the representation of the evolution of meaning across grammatical forms, grammatical meanings, and pragmatic meanings in actual contextual use. In this way, meaning can be literal, figurative, and contextual, paralleling form, meaning, and pragmatic use in context. He argues that these three components are separable, in that a learner can make an error (or be more or less appropriate in conveying and/or interpreting a range of pragmatic meanings) in any or all of these three dimensions; therefore, the assessment of these individual components may be possible. Without a level of specification in the relationship between components of language ability comparable to Purpura's, it is hard to generalize performance beyond a test itself. Therefore, if test users are interested in making inferences about a broad notion of test takers' pragmatic competence instead of, say, pragmatic routines or speech acts alone, employing a comprehensive model like Purpura's (2004) is advisable.

4 The measurement of pragmatic competence in second language assessments

Although pragmatic competence may be difficult to operationalize in testing contexts, many researchers have attempted to assess it, and increasing numbers are following suit given the realization of its importance in CLA. Most of the research thus far has focused on individual aspects of pragmatic competence, including speech acts, implicature, and pragmatic routines elicited through indirect and semi-direct tasks, though there is a growing interest in interactive, discursively-oriented tests given the optimization of authenticity and generalizability associated with these approaches.

4.1 Hudson, Detmer, and Brown's framework for assessing pragmatic competence

In their ground-breaking work on the assessment of cross-cultural pragmatics, Hudson, Detmer, and Brown (1992, 1995), used Brown and Levinson's (1987) politeness theory to create a battery of six tests, including a multiple-choice discourse completion task (MC DCT), a written DCT, a semi-direct (oral) DCT, a role-play, and two self-assessment measures, one for the DCT sections and one for the role-play. They operationalized cross-cultural pragmatic competence in terms of three sociolinguistic variables: relative power (P), social distance (D), and absolute ranking of imposition (R). They argued that these components could be fixed as the independent variable in a test task, resulting in a way to systematically specify causes of pragmatic failure, control for contextual features, and limit error to the pragmalinguistic domain. The focus of their evaluation (i.e. their construct) was on the ability to use the correct speech act, appropriateness of formulaic expressions, amount of speech used, and degrees of formality, directness, and politeness. Astutely, they hoped to minimize threats to reliability and validity with a systematic approach (i.e. by controlling what they deemed to be fixed contextual features, namely, P, D, and R). However, they found that some of their tests did not elicit the expected speech act strategy from either native or nonnative speakers; instead, the test takers produced a range of different responses, many of which could be considered equally appropriate. This unexpected variability is evidence that in tasks such as these, test takers can find a variety of ways to be appropriate, whether or not they use the anticipated or pre-determined speech act. Thus, tying pragmatic success to test takers' production of a particular speech act can be seen as limiting at best and misrepresentative at worst.

This issue was particularly evident in Liu's (2006) study, which employed three of Hudson, Detmer, and Brown's (1992, 1995) tests. He found that when performance on requests versus apologies was compared in the absence of a general proficiency measure, the factor loadings indicated that there was no relationship between the form and use of the two. In other words, pragmatic competence was not generalizable beyond the particular speech act tested. In response to this, McNamara and Roever (2006: 63) argued that it is "difficult to think of a case in which a learner's knowledge of requests is in no way predictive of their knowledge of apologies; this makes for a very complicated construct, and it is nearly impossible to explain in acquisitional terms." These findings further indicate that reducing the construct of pragmatic competence to knowledge of speech acts (or other fragmented and decontexualized aspects of language, like routines, for instance, which are often more closely tied to semantic propositions rather than pragmatic meanings) may be overly simplistic as an operational definition for testing purposes. A broader more comprehensive definition of pragmatic competence rooted in a model of CLA may serve as the most viable operational model given the inference test-users are likely to want to make.

4.2 Using speech acts to test pragmatic competence

As outlined above, arguably, the most influential work on testing L2 pragmatics thus far has been based on Hudson et al.'s (1995) framework. Researchers who have subsequently adopted this framework (Enochs and Yoshitake-Strain 1996, 1999; Liu, 2006; Yamashita, 1996; and others) have focused almost exclusively on a limited number of speech acts (i.e. requests, refusals, apologies). Although the importance of speech acts in pragmatics is evident given the fact that most speech acts are realized indirectly (Leech 1983), pragmatic competence involves more than speech acts, and conversely, speech act use employs abilities other than pragmatic competence. Ultimately, the meanings encoded in speech acts, both intended and implied, are contextually driven (Purpura 2004). In other words, identical linguistic forms can be used to convey very different meanings depending on the context. For example, it is possible to use the surface structures of a directive to be sarcastic (e.g., the imperative in *Get outta here!* to mean *I don't believe you*), just as it is conceivable to have a person trying to get loud music turned down use a request, a demand, or a threat. In the latter example, these are all different speech acts, but the *intended* meaning is arguably the same (i.e. I want you to turn down your music). What changes are the *implied* meanings associated with them (i.e. a request would signify a different sociolinguistic relationship and/or psychological stance than, say, a threat). However, both pragmatic strategies may be equally appropriate depending on the context and how the interaction unfolds. Therefore, it may be possible to go about achieving a communicative goal in pragmatically different ways, while still being pragmatically appropriate to the context. Unfortunately, the primary emphasis on a finite set of speech acts in many assessments of pragmatic competence has undermined and diminished the overarching focus of pragmatics, which is on implied meaning in context, irrespective of the use of a particular speech act. In other words, what is ultimately most important in communication are the meanings that are generated – not the particular speech act that is used.

In light of the issues outlined above, it is arguable that tests aimed at measuring a broad notion of pragmatic competence could alternatively *not* require test-takers to use specific speech acts to realize a communicative goal (unless, of course, the purpose of the test is to make inferences about test takers' knowledge of specific speech acts). In practical terms, test takers would be allowed to use any pragmatic strategy they wished in achieving the communicative goal as long as the meanings conveyed were appropriate to that context. This approach would also reconcile the dilemma of trying to operationalize and/or restrict affective and volitional factors, which are also involved in test performance (McNamara 1997). Within this alternative paradigm, a learner's score would not necessarily be contingent upon the use of a specific speech act; rather, the test takers' understanding and use of forms to convey appropriate meanings could be used as evidence of pragmatic competence. Ideally, this would also involve rooting pragmatic competence in an overarching model of CLA, where pragmatic meanings were specified as being fluid, but contextually-bound, as they are in Purpura's (2004) approach. Failing to operationalize context in an assessment of pragmatic competence renders the interpretations of meanings generated in these assessments, for lack of a better term, meaningless and ungeneralizable.

4.3 Limitations of context as static in tests designed to measure pragmatic competence

The fact that power (P), social distance (D), and absolute ranking of imposition (R) were seen as fixed characteristics of the social context in tests based on Hudson et al.'s (1995) framework may be a cause for concern given that these features, according to Jefferson (1989) and Schegloff (1987), may actually be subject to locally situated interpretive activity. In other words, the interpretation of these contextual features can shift and evolve during a conversation. In support of this argument, Tarone (1998) also asserts that social variables, which may appear static, are often co-constructed as an interaction unfolds. Likewise, McNamara (1997: 451) warns against tests that operationalize context in terms of fixed characteristics in which "social interaction is incorporated in a largely static way [...] In non-testing contexts, this approach has been the subject of a powerful critique by Widdowson (1983: 25), who questions the assumption "that language behaviour is rule governed, determined by a knowledge system which only has to be invoked and applied on particular occasions for communication to take place."

This is not to say that there are no systematic commonalities in the language system; rather, this is meant to illustrate how, in reality, a test taker is required to do more than simply interpret a fixed context in order to be pragmatically appropriate. In fact, s/he must continually reinterpret the context as it is renewed with each subsequent turn in the conversation. This view is consistent with Johnson's (2001) assertion that language and context have the potential to shape each other in a reciprocal way in communicative tests.

It has also been argued that social identity is often not easily boiled down to a single label. As Schegloff (1987: 219) points out:

> The fact that [social interactants] are "in fact" respectively a doctor and a patient does not make those characterizations *ipso facto* relevant ... Their respective ages, sex, religions, and so on, or altogether idiosyncratic and ephemeral attributes (for example, "the one who just tipped over the glass of water on the table") may be what is relevant at any point in the talk ... That is, there should be some tie between the context-as-characterized and its bearing on "the doing of the talk" or "doing the interaction."

In other words, interactional meanings are locally managed, on a turn-by-turn basis. For example, while it may be true that labels such as "boss" and "employee", or "co-workers", activate a series of assumptions about a power relationship between two people, in reality, power may be more a state of mind and a matter negotiated through discourse rather than a fixed social role. In other words, it is the difference between externally assigned power and interactionally negotiated power. Discursively-oriented tasks, and reciprocal tasks in particular, explicitly allow for interactional meanings to be locally managed and systematically interpreted according to pragmatic norms, preferences, and expectations, as long as enough contextual information is given.

4.4 Assessing implicature

Given the obvious complications with trying to measure meaning interpretation that happens in the mind of each test taker, one of the limitations of the empirical research in the assessment of pragmatic competence has been the lack of an interpretational component (see Taguchi 2005, for a discussion). In an attempt to assess pragmatic competence including both productive and interpretive aspects, Roever (2005, 2006) examined learners' pragmalinguistic knowledge by measuring knowledge of situational routines and comprehension of implicature using a multiple-choice task. He measured the use of speech act strategies with a productive, short answer DCT, all through a web-based test. He argued that *sufficient* (but not an overabundance of) context must be provided in order for learners to meet a "good enough" norm for appropriateness. Although he found that test takers' knowledge of speech acts and implicatures increased with proficiency, their knowledge of situational routines (defined as, "situationally bound utterances ... which conventionally occur in specific contexts and whose meaning is disambiguated by the situational context," (Roever 2005: 232) did not. Thus, his findings show that sociocultural knowledge may be more difficult to acquire than other aspects of pragmatic competence, and the appropriate interpretation of these types of meanings is made even more difficult when they are not embedded in a high-context situation. Therefore, L2 testing researchers must be aware of these factors when attempting to assess pragmatic competence, since it may be difficult to see how meanings are co-constructed by participants in indirect and semi-direct tasks. A potential way to address this limitation is with reciprocal, discourse-oriented tasks (e.g., role-plays and simulations) that show the progression and negotiation of meaning in context as conveyed *and* interpreted by the test takers. Communicative tasks that elicit a range of possible responses could provide complementary support to information from more controlled tasks, which have the benefit of practicality.

5 A way forward: discursively-oriented tasks

As language testing has moved from a discrete-point approach to more integrated practices over the last fifty years, the perspective behind the underlying language ability being measured has also shifted from a cognitive one, referring to various kinds of mental traits within a single individual, to a more social/behavioral one in which performance and co-construction of meaning are the main focus (McNamara 1997). Although any testing situation can carry a certain degree of contrivance, and a test, no matter its format, is still a test, language assessments designed to measure interpersonal communication should be as interactive as possible, in order to simulate authentic language use situations. Only then are test-users able to make valid inferences about a test taker's communicative ability. These concepts have had a profound effect on performance testing, and have undoubtedly had an effect on attempts to systematically test contextually bound elements of pragmatic competence, particularly in the context of speaking.

   With particular attention on pragmatics testing, one of the most popular methods for collecting samples of spoken data has been the discourse completion task (DCT). While DCTs can be a reliable way of efficiently collecting large samples of data, there is limited validity evidence for the use of non-reciprocal tasks, such as multiple-choice (MC) DCTs (Kasper and Rose 2003), for measuring pragmatic competence. Artificially reducing an interactive speaking context to a single-turn may be especially problematic for eliciting pragmatic meanings, which are often negotiated and co-constructed throughout an entire conversation. For instance, researchers are aware that many speech acts generally occur over several turns (Korsko 2004; Levinson 1983), and "their exact shape takes into account interlocutor reactions" (McNamara and Roever 2006: 63). Although it is clear that DCTs have an advantage over interactive tasks with respect to practicality, response patterns in DCTs have been shown not to resemble real life communication in some ways (Beebe and Cummings 1985, 1996; Golato 2003; Wolfson, Marmor, and Jones 1989). In other words, though the purpose of DCTs is often to measure some aspect of language ability in the context of speaking, they may not fully represent the interactive process between interlocutors, especially where pragmatic meanings are concerned.

This limitation might be addressed by incorporating reciprocal tasks, such as role-plays, into assessments of pragmatic competence. Although role-plays tend to be less practical than DCTs, researchers (Edmondson, House, Kasper, and Stemmer 1984; Gass and Houck 1999; Sasaki 1998) have shown that role-plays have the potential to elicit performance data more closely resembling naturally occurring conversation, and allow for the additional analysis of paralinguistic features, which may carry additional pragmatic meanings (Grabowski 2014). Reciprocal tasks have a degree of reactivity (Bachman and Palmer 1996) not represented in MC or limited production DCTs. Unlike an MC DCT or limited production DCT in which the test-taker does not interact with an interlocutor, reciprocal tasks allow the test taker to, "receive feedback on the relevance and correctness of the response, and the response in turn affects the input that is subsequently provided by the interlocutor," (Bachman and Palmer 1996: 55). As a result, reciprocal tasks are considered interactive, since they represent the intersection of receptive and productive skills in language use. This notion of linguistic reciprocity supports the assertion that social context is also negotiated, dynamic, and co-constructed in interaction.

In an attempt to address issues associated with prior pragmatics assessment research, such as construct underrepresentation, lack of generalizability, and non-reciprocal tasks, Grabowski (2009, 2013) created a highly contextualized, role-play test rooted in Purpura's (2004) comprehensive model of language ability. The test measured the test takers' grammatical knowledge (defined in terms of accuracy and meaningfulness) and pragmatic knowledge (defined in terms of sociolinguistic, sociocultural, and psychological appropriateness) in the context of speaking. The test was given to test takers at three levels of ability (Intermediate, Advanced, and Expert), who completed four open role-play tasks, all paired with the same native-speaker partner. The study used a mixed methods design in two phases. Findings from the quantitative phase of the mixed-methods study, employing both multivariate generalizability theory and many-facet Rasch measurement, presented empirical evidence in support of the validity of the underlying construct operationalized in the test, both within and across levels of ability. The findings also suggested that pragmatic knowledge was highly context-dependent, particularly with respect to sociocultural knowledge, reflecting an interactionalist approach to construct definition. Grabowski also found psychological stance (i.e. tone) to be primarily expressed through paralinguistic features and hedging, which may be difficult to accurately and reliably elicit in a systematic way on a written test. Perhaps most importantly, however, the results suggested that pragmatic knowledge should be explicitly tested at all levels of ability, and at the expert level, in particular, since it was the most salient differentiating factor among the test takers. Findings from the qualitative phase of the study, involving an interactional sociolinguistics-informed discourse analysis of the pragmatic meanings present in the responses at different ability levels leant support to the efficacy of the test tasks in eliciting selected dimensions of pragmatic knowledge that were scalable across different levels of language ability, something that had not been previously demonstrated. The findings from the study ultimately demonstrated that highly contextualized, reciprocal tasks can be used to reliably assess pragmatic competence.

6 Future directions

Although pragmatics assessment researchers are continuing to successfully address some of the limitations associated with prior pragmatics assessment research, there is a clear need for innovative and interdisciplinary approaches in this area. For instance, since test takers' performance has been shown to be heavily influenced by task (i.e. context) in reciprocal tasks (Grabowski 2009), the specific rhetorical structure of different task responses, as well as the grammatical and pragmatic features used, could be analyzed in order to understand how the test-takers used specific forms to convey a range of meanings in different contexts. These factors could also be investigated at a range of proficiency levels, since there is a dearth of research looking into developmental patterns. In a similar vein, there is somewhat conflicting information in the current assessment literature about what contextual features (e.g., exposure to the target culture, instruction, L1 typology) influence pragmatic competence. Research of this type would have implications for both teaching and testing.

With respect to task type, unscripted role-plays have an obvious advantage over other elicitation methods in terms of showing the progression of meaning through an entire conversational exchange and eliciting large samples of discourse. Nonetheless, the fact remains that they can be impractical to administer and score, especially in large-scale contexts. Prior pragmatics testing research has also shown that selected-response and DCTs are often limited in terms of what is tested, and/or are unreliable when it comes to pragmatics assessment. In order to reconcile the two methods, and maximize both authenticity and practicality, the way forward could involve an item development process that first uses authentic samples of discourse to derive DCTs, which are then transformed into selected-response items based on data collected from both native and non-native speakers. While this approach to item development is not new to second language testing, using it to craft item responses with varying degrees of appropriateness, deviating on one or more dimensions of pragmatic knowledge would be a novel application. Though this process would still undoubtedly involve the subjective judgments of the item developers to a certain extent, the keys and distractors would actually be empirically derived in the hope of reflecting more authentic discourse.

Lastly, a very useful tool, verbal protocols, explicitly called for in Messick's (1996) validation framework, would also be revealing in pragmatics assessment research in terms of providing further evidence of construct validity. Although Liu (2006) and Roever (2005) used verbal protocols in their testing studies, their research did not involve communicative tasks. Verbal protocols could potentially provide insight into the underlying processes learners use in their conveyance and interpretation of pragmatic meanings. In other words: What did the learners really intend to say in choosing to use the words they used? And, how were they able to make the interpretations they did based on their interlocutor's discourse and the task context? Verbal protocols could also potentially provide insight into how raters interpret the appropriateness of dimensions of pragmatic knowledge, as they are often thought to be highly subjective. These suggestions are by no means exhaustive; the field is too new for a finite list of recommendations. What is clear is that this area of language testing research needs more attention and advocacy. Without clearer answers about the measurement of pragmatic competence, any measure of L2 proficiency is necessarily incomplete.

7 References

Austin, John Langshaw. 1962. How to do things with words. Oxford, UK: Clarendon Press.

Bachman, Lyle F. and Adrian S. Palmer. 1996. *Language testing in practice: Designing and developing useful language tests*. Oxford, UK: Oxford University Press.

Beebe, Leslie and Martha Cummings. 1985. *Speech act performance: A function of the data collection procedure?* Paper presented at the TESOL Convention, New York (5–14 April).

Beebe, Leslie and Martha Cummings. 1996. Natural speech act data versus written questionnaire data: How data collection method affects speech act performance. In: Susan M. Gass and Joyce Neu (eds.). *Speech acts across cultures: Challenges to communication in a second language*, 65–86. Berlin: Walter de Gruyter.

Beebe, Leslie and Hansun Zhang Waring. 2005. Pragmatic development in responding to rudeness. In: Jan Frodesen and Christine Holten (eds.). *The power of context in language teaching and learning*, 67–80. Boston, MA: Heinle and Heinle.

Brown, Penelope and Stephen Levinson. 1987. *Politeness: Some universals in language usage*. Cambridge, UK: Cambridge University Press.

Canale, Michael and Merrill Swain. 1980. Theoretical bases of communicative approaches to second language teaching and testing. *Applied Linguistics* 1(1): 1–47.

Carroll, John Bissell. 1968. The psychology of language testing. In: Alan Davies (ed.). *Language testing symposium: A psycholinguistic approach*, 46–69. London: Oxford University Press.

Chapelle, Carol. 1998. Construct definition and validity inquiry in SLA research. In: Lyle Bachman and Andrew Cohen (eds.). *Interfaces between second language acquisition and language testing research*, 32–70. Cambridge, UK: Cambridge University Press.

Crystal, David (ed.). 1997. *The Cambridge encyclopedia of language*. New York: Cambridge University Press.

Edmondson, Willis, Juliane House, Gabriele Kasper and Brigitte Stemmer. 1984. Learning the pragmatics of discourse: A project report. *Applied Linguistics* 5(2): 113–127.

Enochs, Kenneth and Sonia Yoshitake-Strain. 1996. Self-assessment and role plays for evaluating appropriateness in speech act realizations. *ICU Language Research Bulletin* 11: 57–76.

Enochs, Kenneth and Sonia Yoshitake-Strain. 1999. Evaluating six measures of EFL learners' pragmatic competence. *JALT Journal* 21(1): 29–50.

Gass, Susan and Noel Houck. 1999. *Interlanguage refusals: A cross-cultural study of Japanese-English*. New York: Mouton de Gruyter.

Golato, Andrea. 2003. Studying compliment responses: A comparison of DCTs and naturally occurring talk. *Applied Linguistics* 24(1): 90–121.

Grabowski, Kirby. 2009. *Investigating the construct validity of a test designed to measure grammatical and pragmatic knowledge in the context of speaking*. New York, NY: Teachers College, Columbia University dissertation.

Grabowski, Kirby. 2013. Investigating the construct validity of a role-play test designed to measure grammatical and pragmatic knowledge at multiple proficiency levels. In: Steven Ross and Gabriele Kasper (eds.). *Assessing second language pragmatics*, 149–171. New York: Palgrave MacMillan.

Grabowski, Kirby. 2014. Describing pragmatic performance at a range of ability levels on a role-play speaking test. Paper presented at the Language Testing Research Colloquium. Amsterdam, The Netherlands, 4–6 June.

Grice, H. Paul. 1975. Logic and conversation. In: Peter Cole and Jerry Morgan (eds.). *Syntax and semantics*, 41–58. New York: Academic Press.

Grice, H. Paul. 1978. Further notes on logic and conversation. In: Peter Cole and Jerry Morgan (eds.). *Syntax and semantics*, 113–127. New York: Academic Press.

Hudson, Thom, Emily Detmer and James Dean Brown. 1992. *A framework for testing cross-cultural pragmatics*. Honolulu, HI: Second Language Teaching and Curriculum Center, University of Hawai'i at Manoa.

Hudson, Thom, Emily Detmer and James Dean Brown. 1995. *Developing prototypic measures of cross-cultural pragmatics*. Honolulu, HI: Second Language Teaching and Curriculum Center, University of Hawai'i at Manoa.

Jefferson, Gail. 1989. Preliminary notes on a possible metric which provides for a "standard maximum" silence of approximately one second in conversation. In: Derek Roger and Peter Bull (eds.). *Conversation: An interdisciplinary perspective*, 166–196. Clevedon, UK: Multilingual Matters.

Johnson, Marysia. 2001. *The art of non-conversation*. New Haven, CT: Yale University Press.

Kasper, Gabriele and Kenneth Rose. 2003. *Pragmatic development in a second language*. Malden, MA: Blackwell.

Korsko, Paula. 2004. *The narrative shape of two-party complaints in Portuguese: A discourse analytic study*. New York, NY: Teachers College, Columbia University dissertation.

Leech, Geoffrey. 1983. *Principles of pragmatics*. London: Longman.

Levinson, Stephen C. 1983. *Pragmatics*. Cambridge, UK: Cambridge University Press.

Liu, Jianda. 2006. *Measuring Interlanguage Pragmatic Knowledge of EFL Learners*. Frankfurt am Main: Peter Lang.

McNamara, Tim. 1997. "Interaction" in second language performance assessment: Whose performance? *Applied Linguistics* 18(4): 446–466.

McNamara, Tim and Carsten Roever. 2006. *Language testing: The social dimension*. Malden, MA: Blackwell.

Messick, Samuel. 1996. Validity and washback in language testing. *Language Testing* 13(3): 241–256.

Oller, John. 1979. *Language Tests at School: a pragmatic approach*. London: Longman.

Purpura, James. 2004. *Assessing grammar*. Cambridge, UK: Cambridge University Press.

Roever, Carsten. 2004. Difficulty and practicality in tests of interlanguage pragmatics. In: D. Boxer and A. Cohen (eds.). *Studying speaking to inform language learning*, 283–301. Clevedon, UK: Multilingual Matters.

Roever, Carsten. 2005. *Testing ESL pragmatics: Development and validation of a web-based assessment battery*. Frankfurt am Main: Peter Lang.

Roever, Carsten. 2006. Validation of a web-based test of ESL pragmalinguistics. *Language Testing* 23(2): 229–256.

Sasaki, Miyuki. 1998. Investigating EFL students' production of speech acts: A comparison of production questionnaires and role plays. *Journal of Pragmatics* 30(4): 457–484.

Schegloff, Emanuel. 1987. Between micro and macro: Contexts and other connections. In: Jeffrey Alexander, Bernhard Giesen, Richard Munch and Neil Smelser (eds.). *The micro-macro link*, 207–234. Berkeley, CA: University of California Press.

Searle, John. 1969. *Speech acts: An essay in the philosophy of language*. Cambridge, UK: Cambridge University Press.

Spolsky, Bernard. 1973. What does it mean to know a language? Or, how do you get someone to perform his competence? In: John Oller and Jack Richards (eds.). *Focus on the learner: Pragmatic perspectives for the language teacher*, 164–176. Rowley, MA: Newbury House.

Taguchi, Naoko. 2005. Comprehending implied meaning in English as a foreign language. *The Modern Language Journal* 89(4): 543–562.

Tarone, Elaine. 1998. Research on interlanguage variation: Implications for language testing. In: Lyle Bachman and Andrew Cohen (eds.). *Interfaces between second language acquisition and language testing research*, 71–89. Cambridge, UK: Cambridge University Press.

Thomas, Jenny. 1983. Cross-cultural pragmatic failure. *Applied Linguistics* 4(2): 91–112.

Thomas, Jenny. 1995. *Meaning in interaction: An introduction to pragmatics*. London: Longman.

Wolfson, Nessa, Thomas Marmor and Steve Jones. 1989. Problems in the comparison of speech acts across cultures. In: Shoshana Blum-Kulka, Juliane House and Gabriele Kasper (eds.). *Cross-cultural pragmatics: Requests and apologies*, 174–196. Norwood, NJ: Ablex.

Yamashita, Sayoko. 1996. *Six measures of JSL Pragmatics*. Honolulu, HI: Second Language Teaching and Curriculum Center, University of Hawai'i at Manoa.

Yoshitake-Strain, Sonia. 1997. *Measuring interlanguage pragmatic competence of Japanese students of English as a foreign language: A mutli-test framework evaluation*. Novata, CA: Columbia Pacific University dissertation.

Young, Richard. 2000. *Interactional competence: Challenges for validity*. Paper presented at the Annual Meeting of the Language Testing Research Colloquium, Vancouver, Canada.

Yule, George. 1996. *Pragmatics*. Oxford, UK: Oxford University Press.

Gila Schauer
12 Assessing intercultural competence

1 Introduction

Intercultural competence is considered to be an important skill in many different disciplines, such as business and management studies (e.g., Trompenaars and Hampden-Turner 1997; Moran, Youngdahl and Moran 2009), communication studies (e.g., Gudykunst and Kim 2003; Ting-Toomey and Kurogi 1998), linguistics (e.g., Fantini 1995; Byram 1997; Spencer-Oatey and Franklin 2009), pedagogy and teacher training (e.g., Cushner and Mahon 2009), and psychology (e.g., Thomas 2011).

This interest in intercultural competence across academic disciplines has resulted in a large number of definitions and models, but, perhaps rather surprisingly, has not led to an interdisciplinary discussion of the concept (cf. Dreyer 2011, but see Spencer-Oatey and Franklin 2009 as an exception). This means that although a wealth of models and conceptualizations can be found in the literature, components of intercultural competence that are considered to be of great importance by some disciplines, may be absent in the models developed by others and thus the number of models that are useful for any individual discipline is considerably smaller. It also needs to be noted that some models of intercultural competence that are well known across disciplinary borders, such as Hofstede and Hofstede (2005), have, rightly or wrongly, become so popular that other models that may be more appropriate and suitable to an individual discipline's needs may be overlooked.

This chapter will provide an overview of key terms, concepts and models that are relevant for the study of intercultural competence from a second language perspective. I will first discuss the concepts of culture and communicative competence as they are necessary prerequisites for understanding intercultural competence and intercultural competence models suitable for second language assessment research. I will then provide definitions for intercultural competence and review four models of intercultural competence. Subsequent to this, I will review assessment methods used in intercultural competence studies that are relevant for second language acquisition and will then discuss the research challenges and future directions in this field.

2 Culture

Similar to intercultural competence, researchers are also faced with an embarrassment of riches with respect to definitions of the term culture. To illustrate similarities and differences in the conceptualization of culture that are relevant from a second language perspective, three definitions are provided below that include components that are particularly important for the later discussion of intercultural competence:

> The development of human culture is made possible through communication and it is through communication that culture is transmitted from one generation to another. Culture and communication are intertwined so closely that Hall (1959) maintains that 'culture is communication' and 'communication is culture'. In other words, we communicate the way we do, because we are raised in a particular culture and learn its language, rules and norms. Because we learn the language, rules and norms of our cultures by a very early age (between 5 and 10 years old), however, we generally are unaware of how culture influences our behavior in general and our communication in particular. (Gudykunst and Kim 2003: 4)

> Culture is a universal orientation system for a nation, a society, an organization, a group, i.e. all kinds of social units or communities, that people may be members of, which is very specific and has the function of providing [its members with] an identity. This orientation system manifests itself in specific symbols (e.g., language, non-verbal symbols, gestures, facial expressions, etiquette, customs, values, norms, codes of conduct, behavioral scripts) and is conveyed in each social community by the socialization process (...). The culture specific orientation system influences the perception, thinking, values, judgments, emotional and motivational processes, and the actions of all members of the community and thus defines their membership (identity forming function) of the individual community. (...) (Thomas 2011: 100, English translation[1] of the German original by the author of this chapter)

> Culture is not simply a body of knowledge, but a framework in which people live their lives, communicate and interpret shared meanings, and select possible actions to achieve goals. Seen in this way, it becomes fundamentally necessary to engage with the variability inherent in any culture. This involves a movement away from the idea of a national culture to recognize that culture varies with time, place, and social category, and for age, gender, religion, ethnicity and sexuality (Norton 2000). (...) People can resist, subvert or challenge the cultural practices to which they are exposed in their first culture and in additional cultures they acquire. (...) Culture in this sense is dynamic, evolving and not easily summarized for teaching; it is the complexity of culture with which the learner must engage. (Liddicoat and Scarino 2013: 32)

All three definitions emphasize the relationship between language and culture. However, they also highlight other important issues, such as the fact that culture is a complex and dynamic phenomenon that should not automatically be equated

---

1 The following is original German text: Kultur ist ein universell verbreitetes, für eine Nation, eine Gesellschaft, eine Organisation, eine Gruppe, also für jedes soziale Gebilde, zu denen Menschen sich zugehörig fühlen, sehr spezifisches, typisches und identitätsstiftendes Orientierungssystem. Dieses Orientierungssystem manifestiert sich in spezifischen Symbolen (z. B. Sprache, nichtsprachlichen Symbolen, Gestik, Mimik, Etiketten, Sitten, Gebräuchen, Werten, Normen, Verhaltensregeln, Verhaltensskripts) und wird in der jeweiligen sozialen Gemeinschaft über den Prozess der Sozialisation und der Enkulturation tradiert. Das kulturspezifische Orientierungssystem beeinflusst die Wahrnehmung, das Denken, Werten, Urteilen, die emotionalen und motivationalen Prozesse und das Handeln aller Mitglieder der Gemeinschaft und definiert somit deren Zugehörigkeit (identitätsstiftende Funktion) zur jeweiligen sozialen Gemeinschaft. (Thomas 2011: 100)

with national culture. Especially with regard to intercultural communication the notion that individuals are often not aware to what extent culture affects and influences their communication styles, thinking and perceptions because socialization into an individual's culture(s) occurs very early in life, is of considerable significance.

For successful intercultural communication then, interlocutors need to be aware that their communication styles, values, norms and rules are not universal but rather represent the complex orientation system of their culture, which may or may not match those of their interlocutors' orientation system. As a consequence, an individual's communicative competence is of key importance for intercultural competence. The next section provides an overview of communicative competence models.

3 Communicative competence

Several models[2] of communicative competence (e.g., Canale and Swain 1980; Bachman and Palmer 1982; Canale 1983; Bachman 1990; Celce-Murcia, Dörnyei and Thurrell 1995; Bachman and Palmer 1996; Knapp and Lehmann 2006; Celce-Murcia, 2007; Bachman and Palmer 2010) have been developed since the 1970s when researchers became interested in defining and testing the skills learners of a second or foreign language (L2) need when communicating. It is beyond the scope of this chapter to discuss all of the communicative competence models mentioned above, so I will concentrate on Bachman (1990), whose framework has been particularly influential in second language assessment research.

Bachman's (1990) model is the result of empirical research on an earlier communicative competence model by Bachman and Palmer (1982), which included the three main components grammatical, pragmatic and sociolinguistic competence, and was therefore rather similar to the well-known model suggested by Canale and Swain (1980) that also included three main components: grammatical, sociolinguistic and strategic[3] competence. The findings from the empirical study of the

---

2 While Bachman and Palmer's paper published in 1982 focuses on communicative competence, the models in their joint or single authored publications that followed after that were given different names, such as 'language competence model' (Bachman 1990) or 'areas of language knowledge' (Bachman and Palmer 2010). Although the names of the later models do not directly refer to communicative competence, the decision was taken to include them, since these later conceptualisations are of interest to the field of language testing and are related to the scholars' earlier research on communicative competence.

3 Strategic competence refers to "verbal and non-verbal communication strategies that may be called into action to compensate for breakdown in communication" (Canale and Swain 1980: 30), such as paraphrasing in the case of grammatical problems.

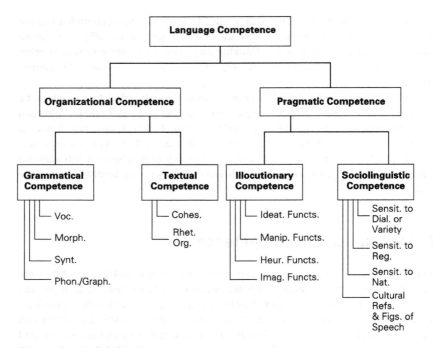

Fig. 1: Bachman's (1990) model.

earlier model by Bachman and Palmer (1982) led to a revised model of language competence that consists of two main components, organizational competence and pragmatic competence. The model is schematically illustrated in Figure 1.

Although Canale and Swain's (1980) and Bachman's (1990) models differ in several aspects (e.g., number of main components, terminology, grouping of sub-components), there are also some fundamental similarities in both frameworks, e.g., the conceptualization of grammatical competence and components of socio-linguistic competence. This is encouraging as it suggests that there is broad agreement about the essential abilities or skills an individual needs to have to be considered a competent communicator in their L2.

4 Intercultural competence

As mentioned above, there is no definition of intercultural competence that is generally referred to. Instead, different definitions have been proposed that reflect the research foci of the scholars working in this area. What makes defining intercultural competence even more difficult is the terminological inconsistency in this field, as intercultural competence, cross-cultural competence, intercultural communicative competence, intercultural interaction competence, intercultural effectiveness, intercultural facework competence are sometimes used interchangeably. Spencer-Oatey and Franklin (2009: 51) point out that "sometimes one term is used to refer to different conceptualizations, and sometimes a different term is chosen for the same conceptualization. This is confusing and makes discussions of the concept and research into it difficult to handle." In this chapter the term intercultural competence will mainly be used and other terms will be referred to only where relevant, such as when the term reflects the name of a model.

Coming back to defining intercultural competence, it is perhaps not surprising that scholars in linguistics see a very close relationship between intercultural competence and language. Fantini (1995: 143) argues that "the goal of intercultural competence concerns both language and intercultural areas", while Sercu (2010: 20) notes that "[w]hen discussing intercultural competence in foreign language education, it is important to underline that 'intercultural competence' always implied 'communicative competence'."

A very detailed definition of intercultural competence is the following one by Fantini (2009: 458, original emphasis):

> Intercultural competence may be defined as complex abilities that are required to perform *effectively* and *appropriately* when interacting with others who are linguistically and culturally different from oneself. Whereas effective reflects the view of one's own performance in the target language-culture (LC2; i.e. an outsider's or "etic" view), appropriate reflects how natives perceive such performance (i.e. an insider's or "emic" view).

The discussion of intercultural competence models in the following section will concentrate on models[4] that include language and communicative competence components and are therefore relevant for researchers interested in language assessment.

---

4 For an overview of intercultural competence models relevant for communication studies and social psychology, see Spitzberg and Chagnon (2009), for models relevant for anthropology, business studies and psychology see Spencer-Oatey and Franklin (2009). A model that is frequently referred to is the result of the IBM employee study by Geert Hofstede (e.g., Hofstede and Hofstede 2005). The model distinguishes five dimensions of cultural difference (individualism versus collectivism, high power distance versus low power distance, masculinity versus femininity, high uncertainty avoidance versus low uncertainty avoidance, long term versus short term orientation). However, while this model has been used in a large number of studies, in recent years, it has been criticized severely for "doubts about the viability of the [short term versus long term] dimension" (Fang 2003: 362), and for "identification claims [that] are fundamentally flawed" (McSweeney 2002: 112).

5 Intercultural competence models

This section reviews intercultural competence models that are relevant for researchers interested in language assessment. The models will be discussed in chronological sequence. The following models will be reviewed: Fantini (1995), Byram (1997), Ting-Toomey and Kurogi (1998), and Deardorff (2006).

Fantini (1995) made an important contribution to the discussion of what intercultural competence is and what it should include by addressing a number of key issues. His own conceptualizations are a reaction against the research literature[5] on intercultural competence that at that time mostly disregarded communicative competence or language as a component of intercultural competence. He argues that: "with rare exceptions (Ting-Toomey and Korzenny 1989), interculturalists often overlook (or leave to language teachers) the task of developing language competence, just as language teachers overlook (or leave to interculturalists) the task of developing intercultural abilities, despite wide acknowledgement that language and culture are dimensions of each other, interrelated and inseparable" (1995: 143–144).

He considers the lack of proficiency in another language to be one of the reasons why many scholars disregard communicative competence and language in their intercultural models and criticizes this harshly:

> Surprisingly, too few interculturalists have linguistics as part of their formation; more surprising still is to find interculturalists without proficiency in a second language. More than the actual attainment of language proficiency is the fact that without a second language experience, they have not grappled with the most fundamental paradigm of all – language, and the benefits that derive from this process. For all of the research and concepts *about* other cultures and world views, the monolingual interculturalist engages mostly in intellectualized endeavors when concepts are not also accompanied by *direct experiences* of other cultures and languages *on their own terms*. (1995: 144, original emphasis)

To emphasize the inseparable relationship of language and culture, he introduces the new superordinate term *linguaculture* and argues that "components of each linguacultura form a cohesive world view" (Fantini 1995: 150). The notion that this world view is linked to an individiual's linguaculture is at the centre of his model and is illustrated in Figure 2 below. The model shows the importance of communicative competence components, many of which we already encountered in Bachman's (1990) communicative competence model, and suggests that while there may be an overlap in worldviews (the shaded sections of the triangles), linguacultures may also have areas in which they do not overlap.

---

5 See Spitzberg and Chignon (2009) for a detailed chronological discussion of intercultural competence in the English speaking world.

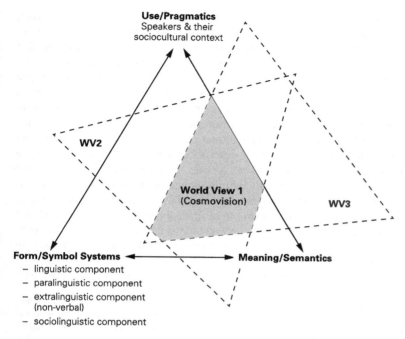

Fig. 2: Fantini's (1995) model of world views and intercultural competence.

House's (2010) research on polite and impolite language use in English and German can help to illustrate Fantini's (1995) model. She argues that there are certain overlaps in the German and English linguacultures (such as the notions of tact, truthfulness, clarity, and saving an interlocutor's face), but that perceptions of what constitutes appropriate and effective language use can also differ considerably. Her research has shown that German speakers tend to be "more direct, explicit and verbose, more self-referenced and content oriented" (2010: 570) than English native speakers and that this is the result of differing world views that are then encoded in language. Thus, directness may be more prevalent in German because it reflects the world view that being truthful, open and clear is considered essential, while in English being tactful and saving an interlocutor's face by using indirect language may generally be considered more important.

Fantini's (1995) article helped progress ideas on intercultural competence and also clearly called for more engagement with this concept from linguists, as the inseparable nature of language and culture, the linguaculture, means that a foreign language cannot be taught and another individual's culture cannot be understood, if interlocutors are not aware of potential differences in each other's linguacultures.

The close link between culture and language is also emphasized by Byram (1997). His model of intercultural communicative competence proposes that intercultural competence consists of five factors (savoirs) that interact with three further communicative competence components. Before describing his model in more detail, it is necessary to first of all address a terminological issue. One problem with the conceptualization of intercultural competence (mentioned above) that is that a variety of terms are used to refer to the same concept and that the use of terminology is often inconsistent and confusing. Byram, however, provides a detailed discussion on the differences between intercultural competence and intercultural communicative competence. Although his views about how these two terms should be differentiated are not shared by all researchers, it is nevertheless helpful to see his definitions of the two terms. He defines intercultural competence as follows: "Individuals have the ability to interact *in their own language* with people from another country and culture, drawing upon their knowledge about intercultural communication, their attitudes of interest in otherness, and their skills in interpreting, relating and discovering, i.e. of overcoming and enjoying intercultural contact" (Byram 1997: 70, emphasis mine).

An individual's intercultural communicative competence is then defined as:

> [the] abil[ity] to interact with people from another country and culture *in a foreign language*. [Individuals who have this competence] are able to negotiate a mode of communication and interaction which is satisfactory to themselves and the other and they are able to act as mediator between people of different cultural origins. Their knowledge of another culture is linked to their language competence through their ability to use language appropriately – sociolinguistic and discourse competence – and their awareness of the specific meanings, values and connotations of the language. (Byram 1997: 71, emphasis mine)

Byram's (1997) main distinction between intercultural competence and intercultural communicative competence then refers to whether an individual uses their first or foreign language. His definition of the latter concept is also very similar to Fantini's (1995) thoughts on key issues in intercultural communication, as both emphasize appropriate language use, and also refer to components of communicative competence.

Coming back to Byram's (1997) model of intercultural communicative competence, Figure 3 below illustrates the interplay between the communicative competence components[6] and intercultural competence.

The model (Byram 1997: 34, 50–53) shows the five factors (savoirs) that influence or result in an individual's intercultural competence, which are defined as follows:

---

6 Byram's (1997) conceptualization of communicative competence includes components suggested by Canale and Swain (1980) and others. His linguistic competence is similar to Canale and Swain's grammatical competence.

Intercultural Communicative Competence

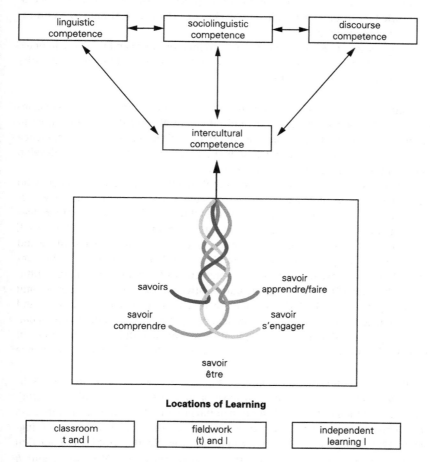

Fig. 3: Byram's (1997) model of intercultural communicative competence.

- Savoir être (Attitudes): Curiosity and openness, readiness to suspend disbelief about other cultures and belief about one's own
- Savoir comprendre (Skills of interpreting and relating): Ability to interpret a document or event from another culture, to explain it and relate it to document's from one's own
- Savoir s'engager (Critical cultural awarenss / political education): An ability to evaluate critically and on the basis of explicit criteria perspectives, practices and products in one's own and other cultures and countries

- Savoir apprendre / faire (Skills of discovery and interaction): Ability to acquire new knowledge of a culture and cultural practices and the ability to operate knowledge, attitudes and skills under the constraints of real-time communication and interaction
- Savoirs (Knowledge): of social groups and their products and practices in one's own and in one's interlocutor's country, and of the general processes of societal and individual interaction

Like Fantini (1995), Byram's (1997) model also suggests a strong link between communicative competence components and intercultural competence. In contrast to Fantini, however, the five factors (savoirs) that result in intercultural competence are defined in greater detail and thus make it easier for researchers to develop assessment instruments that test the savoirs.

The next model, Ting-Toomey and Kurogi (1998), shows that researchers who include language in their intercultural competence models share some views regarding the centrality of certain key concepts, but that there are also differences in the way in which these models are conceptualized and in the terminology used. While Fantini (1995) talks about world views and the concept of linguaculture and mainly refers to linguistic components in his model, Byram (1997) takes a broader approach that includes linguistic components but also five other factors that influence an individual's intercultural communicative competence. Ting-Toomey and Kurogi's approach is similar to Byram's in that it is broader than Fantini's and shares some terminology, but it also offers a new perspective on intercultural competence by emphasizing the concepts of face[7] and mindfulness, the former of which is also included in the name of their intercultural facework competence model.

Ting-Toomey and Kurogi define face as "... a claimed sense of favorable self-worth that a person wants others to have of him or her" (1998: 187). Facework competence is then defined as "an optimal integration of knowledge, mindfulness and communication skills in managing self and other face-related concerns (Ting-Toomey 1994, 1997)" (1998: 200) that can be assessed "by the criteria of interaction appropriateness, effectiveness, adaptability and satisfaction" (1998: 201). Figure 4 below illustrates how the different components of the model interact.

Although some of the components, knowledge and interaction skills, are somewhat similar to Byram's (1997) conceptualization of intercultural communicative

---

7 In linguistics, face is generally regarded to be a key concept of politeness theories. Goffman's definition of face as "the positive social value a person effectively claims for [them]self by the line others assume he [or she] has taken during a particular contact" (1967: 5) is often quoted. Other well-known conceptualizations of face are for example, Brown and Levinson's (1987) distinction of positive and negative face and Spencer-Oatey's rapport (2008) management framework that includes different types of face.

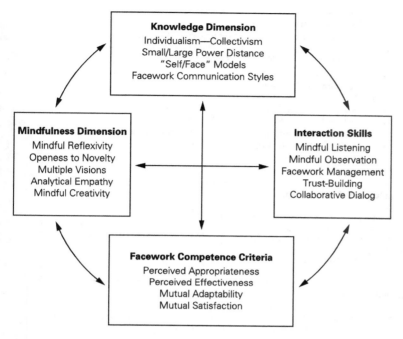

Fig. 4: Ting-Toomey and Kurogi's (1998) intercultural facework competence model.

competence and the key terms, effectiveness and appropriateness, that Fantini (1995) also referred to are also mentioned in this model, Ting-Toomey and Kurogi's (1998) conceptualization of facework competence also shows a markedly different approach, as the components of communicative competence that are clearly referred to in the other two models are not mentioned here. (Since the lead author is not a linguist, but a communication studies scholar, this is perhaps not surprising.) Instead, competence that relates to language is included under knowledge and interaction skills, and the emphasis here is very much on knowledge and skills that relate to sociolinguistic and pragmatic competence. What distinguishes this model from many others is the central role of mindfulness, a concept that is both used as the name of one of the main dimensions, but also as a subcategory in the mindfulness and interaction skills dimension.

Ting-Toomey and Kurogi (1998: 203) define mindfulness for the purpose of their model as "attending to one's internal assumptions, cognitions and emotions while focusing the five senses. Mindfulness reflexivity requires us to tune into our own cultural and habitual assumptions." The concept of mindfulness has its origins in Buddhist philosophy and psychology (Kornfield 2008). The use of this term in the model is interesting, as it indicates that the model offers a perspective that includes both western and eastern thought. The informed inclusion of concepts

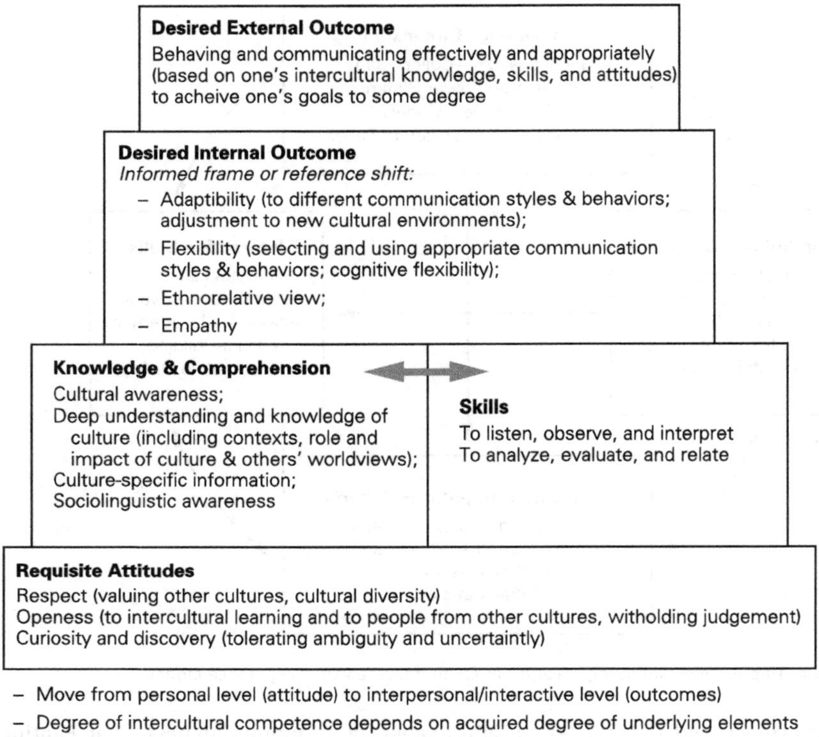

Desired External Outcome
Behaving and communicating effectively and appropriately
(based on one's intercultural knowledge, skills, and attitudes)
to acheive one's goals to some degree

Desired Internal Outcome
Informed frame or reference shift:
  – Adaptibility (to different communication styles & behaviors;
    adjustment to new cultural environments);
  – Flexibility (selecting and using appropriate communication
    styles & behaviors; cognitive flexibility);
  – Ethnorelative view;
  – Empathy

Knowledge & Comprehension
Cultural awareness;
Deep understanding and knowledge of
  culture (including contexts, role and
  impact of culture & others' worldviews);
Culture-specific information;
Sociolinguistic awareness

Skills
To listen, observe, and interpret
To analyze, evaluate, and relate

Requisite Attitudes
Respect (valuing other cultures, cultural diversity)
Openness (to intercultural learning and to people from other cultures, witholding judgement)
Curiosity and discovery (tolerating ambiguity and uncertaintly)

  – Move from personal level (attitude) to interpersonal/interactive level (outcomes)
  – Degree of intercultural competence depends on acquired degree of underlying elements

Fig. 5: Deardorff's (2006) Pyramid Model of Intercultural Competence.

that reflect thinking that is not only influenced by Western traditions is very important in intercultural models, as this helps to make them more generally applicable and also acknowledges the contribution of different cultures and philosophies.

The final model of intercultural competence discussed is one of the most recent conceptualizations of intercultural competence. Deardorff (2004, 2006) developed two models of intercultural competence, a pyramid and a process model. These models are the result of her empirical study in which 24 administrators of internationalization strategies at US American institutions and a panel of 23 intercultural scholars (22 from the United States, 1 from Canada, 1 from the United Kingdom) were asked for their definitions and views on intercultural competence. The data were collected with questionnaires and the Delphi technique, a process method that "allows all members to contribute equally without dominance by a few" (Deardoff 2006: 244). Figure 5 above illustrates Deardorff's pyramid model, while Figure 6 presents her process model.

Figure 5 and 6 include the components of intercultural competence that 80 percent of administrators and scholars agreed on. The findings illustrated in these

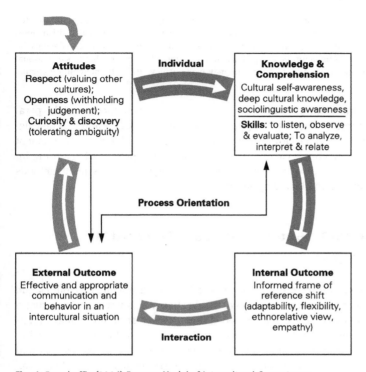

Fig. 6: Deardorff's (2006) Process Model of Intercultural Competence.

models show an agreement with key concepts of Fantini's (1995) and Ting-Toomey and Kurogi's (1998) models and Fantini's (2009) emphasis on effective and appropriate communication. The models also show that central components of Byram's (1997), e.g., curiosity, openness, knowledge and skills, and Ting-Toomey and Kurogi's models, e.g., empathy and observation, are also included. While the two models proposed by Deardorff (2004, 2006) include the same components, their schematic illustration represent different perspectives on intercultural competence.

Deardorff (2006: 255) argues that her pyramid model:

> allows for degrees of competence (the more components acquired and developed increases probability of greater degree of intercultural competence as an external outcome) [...]. This model enables the development of specific assessment indicators within a context or situation while also providing a basis for general assessment of intercultural competence, [...] [it] moves from the individual level of attitudes and interpersonal attributes to the interactive cultural level in regard to the outcomes. [...] A unique element of this pyramid model [...] is its emphasis on internal as well as external outcomes of intercultural competence.

The perspective of the process model is somewhat different and is described by Deardorff (2006: 257) as follows:

[It] depicts the complexity in acquiring intercultural competence in outlining more of the movement and process orientation that occurs between the various elements. [It] denotes movement from the personal to the interpersonal level.[...] The process model also denotes the ongoing process of intercultural competence development, which means that it is a continual process of improvement and, as such, one may never achieve ultimate intercultural competence.

Assessment of intercultural competence is thus an important concern of the pyramid model. Deardorff does not emphasize assessment considerations when describing her process model. However, her subsequent discussion of the assessment of intercultural competence clearly demonstrates that the process of acquiring intercultural competence also has implications for what types of assessment methods may be considered suitable and appropriate.

6 Instruments used to assess intercultural competence

Given the interest in intercultural competence in many academic disciplines and the use of the term in many government publications, it is not surprising that a variety of instruments have been developed that aim to test an individual's intercultural competence or some aspect of it. In their review of instruments used to assess a range of aspects of intercultural competence, Fantini (2009) lists 44 and Spencer-Oatey and Franklin (2009) list 77 different instruments, some of them commercial, others developed by researchers and government agencies, that are targeted at a range of different individuals (e.g., business people, international teams, missionaries, students, counselors, etc.). Many of these instruments are web-based and involve some kind of questionnaire format and self-assessment.

Very few of the listed tests seem to consider language or communicative competence to be a core component of intercultural competence. One questionnaire instrument, the International Profiler, developed by World Works Ltd., which targets individuals and companies that operate in a multi-national context, refers to some of the competencies that were suggested by communication scholars. The 80-item instrument assesses a set of 10 main competencies[8] (openness, flexibility,

---

8 The 10 competencies each consist of at least one factor: openness (being open to new ideas & thinking, welcoming strangers, accepting people that differ from oneself and display different behavior), flexibility (showing flexible behavior, keeping an open mind, making an effort to learn and use foreign languages), personal autonomy (being guided by values and having a sense of direction, focusing on goals), emotional strength (being resilient, having strategies to effectively deal with stress and pressure, being open to and interested in new experiences), perceptiveness (being sensitive to non-verbal communication, being aware of how one portrays oneself and the impression this may give to other people), listening orientation (actively listening to others), transparency (communicating clearly, making one's intentions clear), cultural knowledge (gathering information

personal autonomy, emotional strength, perceptiveness, listening orientation, transparency, cultural knowledge, influence, synergy) that are then further subdivided into 22 skills, attitudes and knowledge areas (also called factors by World Works). The main competencies, perceptiveness and listening orientation are partly based on the concept of mindfulness that is included in Ting-Toomey and Kurogi's (1998) framework and the documentation for the test specifically refers to Ting-Toomey. While not being referred to explicitly, the main categories cultural knowledge and openness shares some similarities with Byram's (1997) savoir être and savoir apprendre.

Each test question of the International Profiler is followed by three possible answers that are scored on a scale based on the test taker's agreement with the answers. Test takers receive detailed feedback in the form of a document showing their scores for the 10 competencies on a 0–100 point scale and an interpretative report that provides them with more detailed information on their scoring behavior. According to the test documentation, however, full validity tests have not been completed for this instrument.

Another instrument that is frequently referred to in the literature and which was, in contrast to the International Profiler, not developed commercially but funded by the EU's Leonardo da Vinci II programme, is the Intercultural Competence and Assessment (INCA) Project. The INCA Project was developed in the early 2000s mainly as a result of demands from British companies employing and working with multinational individuals who were looking for an assessment instrument that would provide them with insights into an individual's intercultural awareness. The INCA team developed two test types: a questionnaire available online or in paper format that focused on cognitive/affective aspects and group exercises that intended to provide insights into an individual's actual behavior in intercultural contact situations. The test suite assesses six main components (tolerance for ambiguity, behavioral flexibility, communicative awareness, knowledge discovery, respect for otherness and empathy) which are then further subdivided into motivations, skills/knowledge and behaviors. The theoretical framework is partly based on Byram (1997). Participants complete the questionnaire and are then observed and assessed in group situations with interlocutors from different countries. Their results are then scored on a three point range corresponding to basic, intermediate and full competence. However, similar to the International Profiler above, Prechtl and Davidson Lund (2009: 486) state that "the present INCA model, the grid and the assessment exercises, require more extensive testing, in particular to check their validity and to investigate their wider applicability and usefulness."

---

about other cultures, valuing and expressing appreciation for cultural differences), influencing (establishing rapport with others, using a style that fits the audience, being sensitive to context), synergy (synthesizing and creating new alternatives originating from cultural differences).

Unfortunately, this ties in with Spencer-Oatey and Franklin's (2009) assessment of intercultural competence tests that they reviewed. They come to the rather depressing conclusion that "it is only rarely that [these instruments] have been shown to have the degree of validity and reliability, which, for example, applied linguists require of language tests used in research contexts" (2009: 197). The next section will discuss the challenges of assessing intercultural competence that may explain the difficulties test developers and assessment specialists face and point to future directions for this field.

7 Future directions

The fact that intercultural competence is included in a recent edited volume entitled "Testing the Untestable in Language Education" (Paran and Secru 2010) is not very encouraging, but is in agreement with Spencer-Oatey and Franklin's findings above and Deardorff's (2009: 481) view that "since assessing the whole of intercultural competence can be a daunting task, it is recommended to prioritize specific aspects of [it]." The following quotes from the contributors to the volume on testing the untestable highlight the challenges that test developers interested in intercultural competence face:

> Intercultural competence in the context of language education imposes a number of challenges for assessment. In part, the difficulty lies in the diverse understandings of the construct to be assessed [...] , but even then eliciting the performances of interculturality has proved to be problematic and assessment approaches may elicit only part of the overall construct, considering this to reflect the whole. Byram et al. (2002) argue that while assessing facts or knowledge and understanding about facts is relatively straightforward, any assessment of knowledge will not capture what it means to be intercultural (Liddicoat 2002, 2005, Liddicoat et al. 2003). (Liddicoat and Scarino 2010: 52)

> [There is] the as yet unresolved issue of how to assess language development and intercultural development simultaneously, for poor foreign language skills can prevent learners from demonstrating high intercultural competence. (Secru 2010: 19)

> The question arises whether it is possible to score learners' answers objectively. [...] Assessors must ask themselves what score learners will be assigned when they put forward a personal interpretation of a particular cultural phenomenon that differs from the interpretation put forward in class, but which is perfectly feasible when accepting other cultural points of view. Will they still pass or will they fail? Will they be assigned a point for their answer or not? (Secru 2010: 27)

To summarize, the main challenges in assessing intercultural competence are considered to be:
1. Disagreement about the components of intercultural competence
2. Developing or using holistic assessment methods that capture all aspects of intercultural competence

3. Moving beyond the assessment of mere knowledge
4. Considering the impact of second language proficiency when assessing intercultural competence
5. Developing a scoring and evaluation system that is as fair and objective as possible

Some of the challenges above can be addressed more easily than others. The first, now frequently reiterated issue of disagreement about the components of intercultural competence can be addressed by an informed selection of a model of intercultural competence that fits the assessment needs of the institution and the individuals that will be tested. While a large number of intercultural competence models have been proposed, a considerably smaller number is suitable for the assessment of intercultural competence that regard language or communicative competence as a key component. This then limits the number of models that can be chosen. Further factors that may influence the selection of a particular model is whether a broader or narrower approach is more suitable, or whether the model should be the result of an empirical study (e.g., Deardorff 2006) or not.

The second and third challenge, using an appropriate and suitable assessment method that assesses all aspects of the intercultural competence model selected and does not only test knowledge, can be addressed by using an assessment suite that ensures that these issues are taken into consideration. Fantini (2009: 464) suggests the following assessment strategies and techniques:
– Closed and open questions
– Objective strategies that involve scoring (e.g., matching items, true/false questions, multiple choice questions, cloze or gap filling items)
– Oral and written activities (e.g., paraphrasing, translation, essay)
– Active and passive activities
– Individual and interactive activities in pairs and groups
– Dialogue, interview, debate, and discussion
– Demonstrations, poster sessions, role-plays and simulations
– Structured and unstructured field tasks and experiences
– Questionnaires that require self-evaluation, peer evaluation, group evaluation, and/or teacher evaluation

He also notes that

> [r]ecent developments both in the field of assessment in general and in assessing intercultural competence in particular facilitate the use of multiple combinations of assessment types, formats, and strategies. These developments, coupled with processes that now include the learner in the evaluative process (through self-evaluation, reflection, and feedback), result in better and more varied indicators of progress and of attainment of learning objectives. (Fantini 2009: 464)

Thus, one of the key strategies to make the untestable testable involves a combination of assessment methods that ideally should also take place over a period of time. Consequently, single moment tests are generally not suitable for the assessment of intercultural competence. This view is also shared by Liddicoat and Scarino (2013) who argue for a combination of formative and summative assessment over a period of time that is in line with Deardorff's (2006) process model of intercultural competence.

To what extent a learners' language proficiency level impacts on their ability to show their intercultural competence, which is the fourth challenge in the list, may depend on a variety of issues, such as the combination of assessment methods and the model of intercultural competence chosen. If the assessment measures are varied and allow learners to show their intercultural competence in relation to all four skills (e.g., mindful and supportive listening accompanied by appropriate body language in a group discussion, writing an email, selecting culture specific interpretations in a multiple choice test, interviewing representatives of another culture for a task) then it is less likely that, for example, poor speaking skills will have a disproportionate effect on learners' ability to demonstrate their intercultural competence. The choice of the intercultural model can also help show the link between foreign language proficiency and intercultural competence. If a model is selected that includes communicative competence components and assigns them a high status, then the comparison of the scores learners achieve in these components with scores achieved in the components that test other aspects of intercultural competence can help provide insights into the relationship between the two.

The fifth challenge, developing a scoring and evaluation system that is as fair and objective as possible, is perhaps that most difficult of all to address. Bachman quoting Pilliner (1968) argues that "language tests are subjective in nearly all aspects" (1990: 38). However, while the selection of the test by the assessor and the interpretation of the test are certainly subjective to a certain degree, there are at least some areas where a test can objectively be scored as either right or wrong, such as in a grammar cloze test eliciting regular or irregular verbs. As the definitions of culture at the beginning of this chapter have shown, culture is a very complex phenomenon that influences the views of all individuals. When it comes to assessing cultural knowledge and skills, testers need to be very aware that they themselves may be influenced by their own culture and that this can have an effect on how they evaluate and score the tasks of their test takers. For example, testers need to know if certain behaviors or utterances in a target culture are associated with or considered only appropriate for individuals of a particular gender, age, religion, region, sexual orientation or social class, and they need to know this even if they themselves do not belong to this group to enable test takers to receive an evaluation or score that reflects their intercultural skills if they demonstrate this behavior or use this utterance.

Considering the list of challenges, assessing intercultural competence with language or communicative competence as a core component, may seem like an insurmountable problem. However assessment suites that address a number of these challenges may already exist, but may only rarely be included in publications about intercultural competence for a number of reasons, such as the name of the study and the use of different keywords. An example of such an assessment suite is Roberts et al's (2001) language learners as ethnographers project also known as the Ealing Project. This innovative and ambitious three year-project combines the teaching of foreign language and ethnographic skills. Undergraduate students of a foreign language are taught ethnographic skills alongside their language classes, then spend one year abroad in which they conduct an ethnographic research project in the target language, and then write up the project in their final year. The continuous assessment of language and ethnographic skills includes many of the assessment techniques suggested by Fantini (2009) above. And by having to engage with members of their target cultures, language learners are also likely to receive feedback from a variety of individuals that can help them improve their intercultural competence.

The discussion has shown that assessing intercultural competence is not an easy task and is still rather in its infancy, at least if viewed from a linguist's perspective. The holistic assessment of intercultural competence involves a process approach and is likely to be rather time-consuming. The good news is, however, that it is not necessary to start from scratch. The Ealing Project shows that assessment suites may already exist that can be used by linguists to assess intercultural competence and that it may just be a labeling issue that has resulted in them not being referred to more frequently in the general literature. The Ealing project is an encouraging example that indicates that the untestable can be tested and the insurmountable surmounted.

8 References

Bachman, Lyle F. 1990. *Fundamental considerations in language testing*. Oxford, UK: Oxford University Press.

Bachman, Lyle F. and Adrian S. Palmer. 1982. The construct validation of some components of communicative proficiency. *TESOL Quarterly* 16(4): 449–465.

Bachman, Lyle F. and Adrian Palmer. 1996. *Language testing in practice: Designing and developing useful language tests*. Oxford, UK: Oxford University Press.

Bachman, Lyle F. and Adrian S. Palmer. 2010. *Language Assessment in Practice: Developing language assessments and justifying their use in the real world*. Oxford, UK: Oxford University Press.

Brown, Penelope and Stephen Levinson. 1987. *Politeness: some universals in language usage*. Cambridge, UK: Cambridge University Press.

Byram, Michael. 1997. *Teaching and assessing intercultural communicative competence*. Clevedon: Multilingual Matters.

Canale, Michael. 1983. From communicative competence to communicative language pedagogy. In: Jack C. Richards and Richard W. Schmidt (eds.). *Language and communication*, 2–27. New York: Longman.

Canale, Michael and Merril Swain. 1980. Theoretical bases of communicative approaches to second language teaching and testing. *Applied Linguistics* 1(1): 1–47.

Celce-Murcia, Marianne. 2007. Rethinking the role of communicative competence in language teaching. In: Eva Alcón Soler and Maria Pilar Safont Jordà (eds.). *Intercultural Language Use and Language Learning*, 41–57. Dordrecht: Springer.

Celce-Murcia, Marianne, Zoltan Dörnyei and Sarah Thurrell. 1995. Communicative competence: a pedagogically motivated model with content specifications. *Issues in Applied Linguistics* 6(2): 5–35.

Cushner, Kenneth and Jennifer Mahon. 2009. Developing the intercultural competence of educators and their students. In: Darla K. Deardorff (ed.). *The Sage Handbook of Intercultural Competence*, 304–320. Thousand Oaks: Sage.

Deardorff, Darla K. 2004. *The identification and assessment of intercultural competence as a student outcome of international education at institutions of higher education in the United States*. Raleigh: North Carolina State University dissertation.

Deardorff, Darla K. 2006. Identification and assessment of intercultural competence as a student outcome of internationalization. *Journal of Studies in International Education* 10(3): 241–266.

Deardorff, Darla K. 2009. Implementing Intercultural Competence Assessment. In: Darla K. Deardorff (ed.). *The Sage Handbook of Intercultural Competence*, 477–491. Thousand Oaks: Sage.

Dreyer, Wilfried. 2011. Hofstedes Humbug und die Wissenschaftslogik der Idealtypen. In: Wilfried Dreyer and Ulrich Hößler (eds.). *Perspektiven interkultureller Kompetenz*, 82–96. Göttingen: Vandenhoek und Rupprecht.

Fantini, Alvino E. 1995. Introduction – language, culture and world view: exploring the nexus. *International Journal of Intercultural Relations* 19(2): 143–153.

Fantini, Alvino E. 2009. Assessing intercultural competence: issues and tools. In: Darla K. Deardorff (ed.). *The Sage Handbook of Intercultural Competence*, 456–476. Thousand Oaks: Sage.

Fang, Tony. 2003. A critique of Hofstede's fifth national cultural dimension. *International Journal of Crosscultural Management* 3(3): 347–368.

Goffman, Erving. 1967. Interaction ritual: Essays on face-to-face behavior. New York: Pantheon.

Gudykunst, William B. and Young Yun Kim. 2003. *Communicating with strangers: an approach to intercultural communication*. New York: McGraw-Hill.

Hofstede, Geert and Gert J. Hofstede. 2005. *Cultures and organizations: software of the mind*. New York: McGraw-Hill.

House, Juliane. 2010. Impoliteness in Germany: intercultural encounters in everyday and institutional talk. *Intercultural Pragmatics* 7(4): 561–595.

Knapp, Karlfried and Christian Lehmann. 2006. Sprachliche Kompetenz. *Neurolinguistic* 20(1–2): 81–98.

Kornfield, Jack. 2008. *The wise heart- Buddhist psychology for the West*. London: Rider.

Liddicoat, Anthony J. and Angela Scarino. 2010. Eliciting the intercultural in foreign language education at school. In: Amos Paran and Lies Sercu (eds.) *Testing the untestable in language education*, 52–76. Bristol: Multilingual Matters.

Liddicoat, Anthony J. and Angela Scarino. 2013. *Intercultural language teaching and learning*. Oxford: Wiley-Blackwell.

McSweeney, Brendan. 2002. Hofstede's model of national cultural differences and their consequences: a triumph of faith – a failure of analysis. *Human Relations* 55(1): 89–118.

Moran, Robert T., William E. Youngdahl and Sarah V. Moran. 2009. Leading global projects: bridging the cultural and functional divide. In: Darla K. Deardorff (ed.). *The Sage Handbook of Intercultural Competence*, 287–303. Thousand Oaks: Sage.

Paran, Amos and Lies Secru (eds.). 2010. *Testing the Untestable in Language Education*. Bristol: Multilingual Matters.

Prechtl, Elisabeth and Anne Davidson Lund. 2009. Intercultural Competence and Assessment: perspectives from the INCA project. In: Helga Kotthoff and Helen Spencer-Oatey (eds.). *Handbook of Intercultural Communication*, 467–490. Berlin: Mouton de Gruyter.

Roberts, Celia, Michael Byram, Ana Barro, Shirley Jordan and Brian Street. 2001. *Language learners as ethnographers*. Clevedon: Multilingual Matters.

Secru, Lies. 2010. Assessing intercultural competence: more questions than answers. In: Amos Paran and Lies Secru (eds.). *Testing the Untestable in Language Education*, 17–34. Bristol: Multilingual Matters.

Spencer-Oatey, Helen. 2008. Face, (im)politeness and rapport. In: Helen Spencer-Oatey (ed.). *Culturally speaking: Culture, communication and politeness theory*, 11–47. London: Continuum.

Spencer-Oatey, Helen and Peter Franklin. 2009. *Intercultural interaction. A multidisciplinary approach to intercultural communication*. Basingstoke: Palgrave.

Spitzberg, Brian H. and Gabrielle Chagnon. 2009. Conceptualizing intercultural competence. In: Darla K. Deardorff (ed.). *The Sage Handbook of Intercultural Competence*, 2–52. Thousand Oaks: Sage.

Thomas, Alexander. 2011. Das Kulturstandardkonzept. In: Wilfried Dreyer and Ulrich Hößler (eds.). *Perspektiven interkultureller Kompetenz*, 97–124. Göttingen: Vandenhoek and Rupprecht.

Ting-Toomey, Stella and Atsuko Kurogi. 1998. Facework competence in intercultural conflict: an updated face-negotiation theory. *International Journal of Intercultural Relations* 22(2): 187–225.

Trompenaars, Fons and Charles Hampden-Turner. 1997. *Riding the waves of culture: Understanding cultural diversity in business*. London: Nicholas Brealey.

Nivja H. de Jong

13 Fluency in second language assessment

1 Introduction

While speaking, a speaker needs to translate his thoughts into intelligible sounds fast. This rapid translation of thoughts to speech transpires in roughly three stages: by conceptualizing what to say, then by formulating how to say it, and finally by articulating the appropriate sounds (Dell et al. 1997; Levelt, Roelofs, and Meyer 1999). The processes run incrementally which means that speakers conceptualize and formulate the next (part of the) message while articulating the current (e.g., Roelofs 1998). If at any stage of the speech production process the speaker cannot keep up with his own articulation, the speaker will become disfluent. Perhaps he stops speaking (and is temporarily silent), perhaps he will use a filled pause (e.g., "uh", "uhm"), slow down the current articulation, or use a repetition (e.g., "the the"). In addition to lagging behind his own articulation, a speaker also becomes disfluent when, while monitoring his own speech, he notices some kind of error that needs a repair.

In everyday speech, the processes needed to articulate intelligible sounds that reflect the intended message run at an astonishing speed, as evidenced by a normal articulation rate of around 6 syllables per second (Janse 2003). At the same time, everyday speech is strewn with disfluencies such as silent pauses, filled pauses, lengthenings, repetitions, and repairs. As many as six to ten per hundred spoken words in speech are, in fact, disfluencies (Bortfeld et al. 2001; Fox Tree 1995). The filled pause "uh" is the most frequent 'word' in Dutch, according to the Corpus of Spoken Dutch (CGN). In other words, disfluencies in native everyday speech are normal.

To communicate effectively in everyday conversation, a speaker of a second language (L2) needs to translate intended messages into comprehensible speech rapidly as well. Becoming fluent in the L2, together with attaining a native-like accent, may be the hardest skill for an L2 speaker. Speaking is a skill that is challenging in particular because of the strict time constraints under which the speaker needs to operate. A fluent speaker of a language is a speaker who is able to handle these time constraints such that he can deliver his intended message in time.

In this chapter, I will introduce two views on fluency: fluency as a phenomenon that is revealing of underlying processes in first language (L1) speaking (a psycholinguistic/cognitive view) and fluency as an aspect of L2 acquisition and proficiency (an applied linguistic/evaluative view).[1] The third section describes objective measures that may be used to globally assess L1 or L2 fluency.

---

[1] In both views, I will confine this chapter to describing non-pathological speakers only (thereby ignoring, for example, stutterers).

2 Psycholinguistic views on fluency

In psycholinguistic research since the 1950's, aspects of fluency and speech errors by typical L1 speakers have been investigated to shed light on the underlying cognitive processes of speech production. The research methods that have been employed to investigate causes for disfluencies are corpus research and (controlled) speaking experiments. Both research methods struggle with the extremely time-consuming data analysis that is needed to answer research questions.

More recently, researchers have also started to investigate the possible effect of disfluencies on the listener's comprehension processes. For this purpose, tightly-controlled listening experiments are set up, in which participants listen to sentences or short passages and need to respond by mouse-clicking or are otherwise simply instructed to listen, while eye-movements or event-related-potentials (ERP's) are recorded. In what follows, I will briefly describe psycholinguistic research investigating where disfluencies come from (speech production processes) and what their effect may be (comprehension processes).

2.1 Production

As briefly described in the introduction to this chapter, speaking involves a number of processes that run incrementally. If, at any of these stages of processing, a speaker encounters a problem, the articulation of the previously planned speech may "run out", causing a speaker to be disfluent. In general, whenever conceptualizing and/or linguistic formulation is relatively difficult, speakers are more likely to be disfluent. For instance, when speakers plan what to say, before (major) constituents or at syntactic boundaries, disfluencies are more likely to occur (e.g., Swerts 1998). Within clauses, pauses are more likely to occur before open-class words (Maclay and Osgood 1959), unpredictable lexical items (Beattie and Butterworth 1979), low-frequent words (Kircher et al. 2004), and when more word choices are available (Hartsuiker and Notebaert 2010; Schachter et al. 1991). In addition, speakers are more likely to be disfluent before naming discourse-new referents as compared to referents that are mentioned recently and are therefore more accessible (Arnold et al. 2000).

In addition to such local indicators of disfluencies, global aspects also play a role. Disfluencies are more likely to occur when talking about an unfamiliar topic as compared to a familiar topic (Bortfeld et al. 2001; Merlo and Mansur 2004). Finally, inter-individual differences can also be predicted to some extent: older speakers tend to be more disfluent than younger (Bortfeld et al. 2001), male speakers more than female (Branigan, Lickley, and McKelvie 1999), and extraverts more so than introverts (Dewaele and Furnham 1999; Ramsay 1968).

2.2 Perception

Traditionally, in (psycho)linguistic views of speech comprehension, disfluencies are seen as aspects of speech without added value for the listener (Fox Tree 1995), which listeners therefore need to "edit out" to understand the actual message of the speaker (Levelt 1989). More recently, however, the communicative meaning of disfluencies has been acknowledged. Clark and Fox Tree (2002) argue that the filled pauses "uh" and "uhm" are conventional English words (interjections) that speakers use to indicate that they are searching for a word or deciding what to say next. Although they do not add to the propositional content of the speaker (the *primary* message), they are part of the *collateral* message, in which the speaker is informing the listener about his performance (Clark 2002).

Research using response times, eye-tracking, as well as ERP recordings in controlled listening experiments, has indeed found that listeners use information carried by disfluencies and predict speech following disfluencies to be relatively complex (e.g., Arnold et al. 2007; Bosker et al. 2014; Brennan and Schober 2001; Fox Tree 2001; MacGregor, Corley, and Donaldson 2010). Listeners apparently suppose that the speaker is having difficulty whilst planning the linguistic message when the speaker is disfluent. It has been suggested that upon hearing a disfluency, the listener will heighten his attention to be able to integrate the upcoming (likely complex) speech more easily into the ongoing discourse (Collard et al. 2008).

3 Applied linguistic views on fluency

In the applied linguistics approach, aspects of L2 fluency are seen as indicators of L2 proficiency. However, from the psycholinguistic research described above, it is now clear that being a proficient speaker does not entail speaking without disfluencies. Indices of L2 fluency will therefore reflect L2 proficiency only partially because disfluencies are also elements of communicative successful (native) speech.

3.1 Production

Applied researchers have investigated the effect of task complexity on linguistic output, namely on linguistic complexity, accuracy, and fluency showing that increasing task complexity in any way leads to decreases in speaking fluency. For instance, less planning time (Mehnert 1998; Yuan and Ellis 2003), talking about there and then versus here and now (Gilabert 2007), and tasks that require talking about more elements as opposed to fewer elements (Michel, Kuiken, and Vedder 2007) lead to decreases in fluency.

In addition to effects of tasks on linguistic output, applied research has investigated the relation between L2 proficiency and fluency. For language assessment purposes, this research is crucial as it may indicate which measures of fluency are indicative of L2 proficiency.

3.1.1 L2 Proficiency and skills

In general, L2 speech for most speakers is less fluent than their L1 speech (Derwing et al. 2009) and fluency is at least partly dependent on L2 proficiency (De Jong et al. 2013; De Jong et al. 2015; Riazantseva 2001), which is also evidenced by progress in fluency aspects of L2 speakers over time (Towell, Hawkins, and Bazergui 1996; Segalowitz and Freed 2004). Summarizing these results, researchers have found that speed of speech (usually speech rate) and pausing (usually mean length of run) are related to proficiency, except for the measure mean duration of silent pauses (Towell, Hawkins, and Bazergui 1996; De Jong et al. 2013; De Jong et al. 2015). From these results one could conclude that some aspects of pausing and speed of speech can be used to indicate levels of proficiency or to discriminate L1 from L2 speech. However, because L1 speakers also show individual differences with respect to amount and types of disfluencies, and because there is considerable overlap in measures of fluency when comparing a group of L1 speakers with a group of L2 speakers, it is impossible to give a quantitative definition of "fluent speech."

Davies (2003) claims that it is not the total number of disfluencies that distinguishes L1 from L2 speech, but that the difference is to be found in the distribution of the disfluencies: L2 speakers will pause more often within clauses than L1 speakers do. The claim has also been tested empirically and indeed, L2 speakers pause more often within Analysis of Speech (AS) units[2] (Skehan and Foster 2007), clauses (Tavakoli 2011) or constituents (Riazantseva 2001) than L1 speakers do.

But even when we consider pauses that fall within AS-units only, there is still considerable overlap between pausing behavior in the L1 and pausing behavior in the L2, as shown by De Jong et al. (2015). This means that when we measure aspects of L2 fluency, we partly measure personal speaking style, in addition to L2-specific fluency that is related to proficiency. Segalowitz (2010: 40) proposes that to measure aspects of L2-specific fluency, one should gather both L1 data and L2 data to take speakers' L1 fluency into account and "partial out sources of variability that are not related specifically to the disfluencies in L2 but that characterize a person's general performance in the given testing conditions." In this way, disfluencies that are specifically related to the use of an L2 are distinguished from disfluencies as they appear in L1 speech. De Jong et al. (2015) followed this suggestion, collected both L1 and L2 data, and related measures of fluency to a measure of proficiency and indeed found that, at least for (inverse) articulation rate, the relation with proficiency significantly improved after partialling out L1 fluency behavior.

---

2 An AS-unit is "a single speaker's utterance consisting of an independent clause, or a subclausal unit, together with any subordinate clause(s) associated with either" (Foster et al. 2000).

3.2 Perception

Whereas L1 psycholinguistic research has found that disfluencies are beneficial for the listener, and therefore are part of successful communication, L2 applied research on perception of fluency is mainly about evaluation of speech, as fluency is seen as a component of overall speaking proficiency. This research thus investigates how disfluencies negatively impact the impression on the listener of a speaker's proficiency.

3.2.1 Evaluating oral proficiency

The goal of the evaluative approach to research on fluency is to develop valid language tests that measure L2 oral ability. Such language tests, as well as current research in this approach, is influenced by leading models of L2 ability (see Fulcher 2000). Canale and Swain (1980) posit that communicative competence consists of grammatical, sociolinguistic, and strategic competence. Bachman and Palmer (1996) extended this model, regarding language ability as consisting of linguistic knowledge, pragmatic language knowledge (both functional and sociolinguistic), and strategic competence (metacognitive components and strategies).

Within the realm of L2 oral ability, research has investigated this theorized componential structure of speaking proficiency in different ways. Some studies have used global holistic ratings on the one hand, and then compared these to analytic ratings of potential subcomponents (e.g., Higgs and Clifford 1982) to gauge how raters weigh the different subcomponents to arrive at global scores. Others have used global ratings and related these to measurable linguistic aspects in the speech performances. In this line of research, Iwashita et al. (2008) found that the most important predictor of their ratings on overall performance was speech rate. A related measure (the token and type counts of the number of words that were produced in the time-limited responses which was labeled "vocabulary") was the other major predictor of the holistic ratings.

In summary, a componential view of speaking proficiency can be supported and fluency, or the skill to efficiently use L2 linguistic knowledge (De Jong et al. 2012), is among the most important aspects of speech that makes an L2 speaking performance successful. It is therefore no wonder that in rubrics of language tests, fluency is a recurring aspect of the speaking performance that is to be judged.

3.2.2 Evaluating L2 fluency

Research on the evaluation of L2 fluency has investigated how ratings (mostly by teachers, but also by novice raters) on fluency can be explained by objective measures of fluency (e.g., Bosker et al. 2013; Derwing et al. 2004; Lennon 1990; Riggenbach 1991; Kormos and Dénes 2004; Cucchiarini, Strik, and Boves 2002). All researchers report that (pruned) speech rate and some aspect of (silent) pausing are good predictors of ratings on fluency. In addition, articulation rate (Bosker et al. 2013); measures of mean length of run (Lennon 1990; Kormos and Dénes 2004; Cucchiarini, Strik, and Boves 2002), repetitions (Lennon 1990; Bosker et al. 2013), and repairs (Bosker et al. 2013) are mentioned as predictors of fluency ratings. These studies have all asked raters to give judgments on fluency. In Ginther, Dimova, and Yang (2010), however, raters were asked to judge overall proficiency and they also report strong correlations between judged overall proficiency and objective measures of fluency, such as speech rate, articulation rate, and mean length of run. Similarly, Kang, Rubin, and Pickering (2010) related ratings on comprehensibility and oral proficiency to a range of measures of both fluency and intonation and they found that the suprasegmental measures collectively accounted for 50 % of the variance in both types of ratings.

In sum, strong associations between the objective measures of fluency and subjective ratings on proficiency or fluency have been found. Bosker et al. (2013) report that as much as 84 % of the variance on ratings on fluency can be explained by objective measures of fluency. For all studies that relate subjective scores to objective measures, however, one should be cautious in drawing conclusions about the construct of fluency. The main determinant of the construct of fluency in these studies is the conception of fluency by the human raters. If raters are instructed to pay attention to aspects of fluency (as in Bosker et al. 2013; Derwing et al. 2004; Rossiter 2009), it is likely that the resulting ratings will be related to objective measures of fluency. When no instructions are given prior to the rating, raters will use their own definition of what constitutes fluency to judge the speaking samples (Kormos and Dénes 2004; Cucchiarini, Strik, and Boves 2002).

In other words, it may simply be the case that raters will do as they are told. If their instructions or speaking rubrics concentrate on the use of silent pauses, fluency scores will reflect use of silent pauses. However, some aspects of speaking fluency may be more salient than others. Therefore, when judges are rating on fluency or global oral performance, the aspects that are perceptually most salient will have the strongest influence on their ratings. To investigate this, Bosker et al. (2013) instructed three groups of raters to focus on sub-components of fluency (either breakdown fluency, speed fluency, or repair fluency). The results revealed that the ratings of the group of judges listening for breakdowns in speech were most highly related to the objective measures. So if, time and time again, breakdown fluency measures are found to be good (the best) predictors of perceived fluency, this may partly be a reflection of the fact that perceptually, pauses stand out more than speed of speech and repairs in speech do.

3.2.3 The role of fluency in language assessment
In what follows, I describe the role of fluency in four current tests of English: International English Language Testing System Academic (henceforth IELTS), Test of

English as a Foreign Language internet Based Test (henceforth TOEFL), American Council on the Teaching of Foreign Languages (henceforth ACTFL), and Pearson Test of English Academic (henceforth PTEA). The largest difference between these tests is between IELTS, TOEFL, and ACTFL on the one hand, and PTEA, on the other. In the first three tests, interlocutors speak with the examinees, either live or over the phone, but in PTEA, no live interviews take place, and there are no interlocutors. In PTEA, scores are calculated automatically, and in the other tests human judges are used to arrive at scores.

Upon inspection of the speaking rubrics of these tests, it can be seen that the way in which raters are instructed to rate fluency differs. In IELTS (IELTS, n.d.), there are four categories that judges use to distinguish between learners: "fluency and coherence", "lexical resource", "grammatical range and accuracy", and "pronunciation." In the first category, aspects of fluency and coherence are mentioned together or combined into one description, implying that a speaking performance loses coherence if it lacks in fluency. The descriptors mention length of the performance, pauses, hesitations, repetitions, and self-correction but there is hardly any mention of "speed", except for band 5 ("uses repetition, self-correction and/or slow speech"). The term "pausing" is mentioned at the lower levels exclusively; at the higher levels, "hesitations", in combination with repetitions and self-repairs, are mentioned.

Judges evaluating the overall performance on the independent speaking performances of the TOEFL (Educational Testing Service 2004) consider the combined impact of delivery, language use, and topic development. Fluency is not a separate category but can be found both in the descriptors of "Delivery", which combines aspects of fluency with pronunciation, and in the descriptors of "Language Use", which is a combination of aspects of accuracy, complexity, and fluency. For instance, under "Language Use" at score 4, it is stated, "The response demonstrates effective use of grammar and vocabulary. It exhibits a fairly high degree of automaticity." Under the category "Delivery", most of the descriptions mention "pace" but not disfluencies such as pauses or other hesitations. At the lowest level, however, there is mention of "frequent pauses and hesitations."

The speaking rubrics of the ACTFL (American Council on the Teaching of Foreign Languages 2013) are not divided into categories. Five main levels describe speaking proficiency from Distinguished to Novice. The descriptors differentiate levels by functional can-do statements, but there is also mention of aspects of coherence, grammar, vocabulary, pronunciation, and fluency. In a separate glossary, fluency itself is defined thus: "the flow in spoken or written language as perceived by the listener or reader. Flow is made possible by clarity of expression, the acceptable ordering of ideas, use of vocabulary and syntax appropriate to the context." In other words, for raters of ACTFL, fluency is in the ear of the beholder and encompasses all aspects of (speaking) proficiency, with the exception of accuracy. At most levels, there is specific mention of fluency, referring to unnaturally lengthy hesitations, pauses, reformulations, and self-corrections.

In the PTEA (Pearson Education Ltd 2012), speaking is assessed in about 40 items. Fluency is scored in the sections: reading aloud a passage, repeating a sentence, describing an image, and retelling a lecture. Bernstein, Van Moere and Cheng (2010) describe the scoring procedure (for the Versant Spanish Test, but the main procedures for the PTEA are the same). The fluency score is derived by comparing the candidate's responses to those from a native speaker database. The aspects of speech that are considered in this comparison are all from duration of speech events: response latency (i.e. duration of silent pauses before beginning the response), words per time, segments per articulation time, pauses between words, and a combination of these. A training set was used to construct a formula for the fluency score that reflects human judgments on fluency. The human raters used rubrics that are specific for fluency, discriminating between six levels (Pearson Education Ltd 2012: 21). Compared to the references to fluency in the ratings scales just described, they are precise, including information about pauses, repetitions, repairs, and rhythm. For instance, at level 2, it reads "Speech may be uneven or staccato. Speech (if >= 6 words) has at least one smooth three-word run, and no more than two or three hesitations, repetitions or false starts. There may be one long pause, but not two or more."

Summing up, the role of fluency within these four language tests of English differs widely. Fluency is seen as a separate construct (PTEA); as a construct that goes hand in hand with pronunciation, on the one hand, and with complexity and accuracy, on the other (TOEFL); as a construct that cannot be seen separately from coherence (IELTS); or as a construct that is part of the integral construct of language ability (ACTFL). In the speaking scales used by judges, there is no mention of pauses at the higher levels (IELTS, TOEFL, and ACTFL). With the exception of PTEA, the descriptions in the scales that relate to fluency leave room for subjective interpretation of fluency, because they are more or less circular. For instance in TOEFL level 4, Delivery is described as "fluid." In addition, the notions of "well-paced" (TOEFL) and "unnaturally lengthy" hesitations (ACTFL) can be interpreted in different ways and there is no indication on how the rater should know whether production occurred automatically (TOEFL), or whether hesitations are either language- or content-related (IELTS). In the PTEA, on the other hand, the descriptions of fluency are more precise. Note, however, that these speaking rubrics are only used to investigate to what extent the automatically extracted scores are related to human judgments.

The current speaking rubrics for judges and the algorithm for automatic assessment may be improved by incorporating recent research on the relation between disfluencies and L2 proficiency. For instance, as described above, it has become clear that (inverse) articulation rate is an aspect of fluency that is strongly related to L2 proficiency, and only weakly (if at all) to personal speaking style (De Jong et al. 2015). Mean duration of silent pauses, on the other hand, seems to be a much weaker indicator of proficiency (e.g., Towell, Hawkins, and Bazergui 1996). Because raters are quite capable of following instructions (at least naïve raters that are carefully instructed, see Bosker et al. 2013), it seems worthwhile to incorporate such weighing in the current language testing practice.

4 Measures of fluency

Most research asking questions from a psycholinguistic point of view, investigates disfluencies on a local level because disfluencies are seen as manifestations of problems in underlying cognitive processes. For this reason, there has been little discussion about global measures of fluency. In research on L2 fluency, in contrast, most research questions have revolved around the issue of relating global aspects of fluency to proficiency. Essentially all studies in this line of research investigate fluency on a global level. To quantify fluency at such a global level, a multitude of measures have been introduced. Tavakoli and Skehan (2005) have proposed a distinction between several aspects of fluency: breakdown fluency, speed fluency, and repair fluency[3]. Breakdown fluency has to do with "breakdowns" in speech such as pauses and filled pauses. Speed fluency is the speed with which speech is delivered in between such breakdowns. Repair fluency has to do with the frequency with which the speaker uses corrections or repairs. In Table 1, eleven measures most commonly used in research on fluency are presented, together with the ways in which they can be calculated.[4]

For research that aims to unravel which aspects of speech are related to ratings on fluency or to speakers' L2 abilities, it is wise to use measures that are not confounded. For instance, speech rate is mathematically related to number and duration of silent pauses because the more or longer a speaker tends to pause, the slower the speech rate will be. Another example is phonation time ratio, which measures both number and duration of silent pauses at the same time. The king of confounded measures must be pruned speech rate, which is a measure that includes speed of speech (number of syllables or words per minute), silent pausing information (in the same way as speech rate does), and information about other disfluencies that are subtracted from the number of syllables in the numerator.

---

3 This division in breakdown, speed, and repair fluency leaves out one major aspect of fluency: turn-taking fluency. In dialogues, speakers need to manage their turns. Speaking fluently therefore also entails being able to keep the floor when needed and knowing how (not) to overlap with the interlocutor's speech. Because research on this topic in L2 speech is relatively scarce (but see Riggenbach 1991), this chapter leaves out a discussion on turn-taking fluency.
4 This table presents almost the same variables as Kormos (2006: 163) had in her Table 8.2. I have added the measure pruned speech rate, and subdivided her measure "number of disfluencies per minute" into "number of repetitions" and "number of repairs." Finally, her measure "Space" has been omitted here.

Tab. 1: Global measures of fluency.

Measure	Formula
Speech rate	Number of syllables / total time
Pruned speech rate	(Number of syllables – number of disfluent syllables) / total time
Articulation rate	Number of syllables / speaking time*
Pace	Number of stressed syllables / total time
Mean length of utterance	Speaking time / number of utterances# *or*
	Number of syllables / number of utterances#
Number of silent pauses	Number of silent pauses / total time or speaking time*
Duration of silent pauses	Pausing time / number of silent pauses
Phonation time ratio	Speaking time / Total time
Number of filled pauses	Number of filled pauses / total time or speaking time*
Number of repetitions	Number of repetitions / total time or speaking time*
Number of repairs	Number of repairs and restarts / total time or speaking time*

* Speaking time is equal to total time minus silent pausing time.
\# Number of utterances is equal to the number of silent pauses *plus* 1.

For speed of delivery, articulation rate is the one measure that is mathematically unrelated to other measures of fluency and thus can be considered as a pure measure of speed. Its inverse measure, mean syllable duration, has an advantage over articulation rate because its distribution is more normal than the skewed distribution that articulation rates tend to show. A problem with any measure of speed is that counting syllables is by no means a straightforward task. If the researcher decides to make transcripts, counting the number of canonical syllables (as can be looked up in dictionaries for instance) is feasible. However, in running speech, native speakers tend to reduce pronunciation of frequent words, such that three-syllable sequences may be compressed into one single syllable (Johnson 2004; Ernestus and Warner 2011). The number of actually pronounced syllables can be counted by inspecting the spectogram and waveform of the speech signal or, if the speech is recorded with relatively little noise, it can be measured automatically (De Jong and Wempe 2009). The number of actually pronounced syllables may be significantly lower than the number of canonical syllables, and therefore, counting actually pronounced syllables will lead to lower measures of speech rate and articulation rate. It is as yet unknown, however, how raters judge reduced speech as opposed to unreduced speech, and to what extent reducing speech is related to L2 proficiency.

Turning to the aspect of breakdown fluency, a number of measures that are conceptually and mathematically not confounded can be calculated. For instance, there is a difference between the number of breakdowns in speech and their duration. Therefore, number of silent pauses can be measured separately from mean duration of silent pauses. Another measure within the category breakdown fluency that has been popular in fluency research is mean length of utterance. If mean length of utterance is calculated as mean duration of speech between silent pauses, it is almost the exact inverse of number of pauses per second, as can be seen in Table 1. Consequently, calculating mean length of utterance as well as number of silent pauses per second amounts to measuring the same aspect twice. A researcher should choose, therefore, between using number of breakdowns (such as silent and filled pauses) per second or mean length of utterance between breakdowns. An additional decision one needs to make when dealing with silent pauses has to do with their lower threshold. Short silent pauses are actually part of speech, because stop consonants such as "p", "t", and "k" are always preceded by short silences. Goldman-Eisler (1968) proposed that a threshold of 250 milliseconds should filter out such articulatory pauses, but other cut-off times (100 ms: Rossiter 2009; 400 ms: Derwing et al. 2004; 1000 ms: Iwashita et al. 2008) have been used. De Jong and Bosker (2013) showed that choosing a threshold of around 250–300 ms leads to the highest correlations between a measure of L2 proficiency on the one hand, and number of silent pauses in L2 speech, on the other. Furthermore, choosing thresholds higher than 300 ms leads to confounding the number of pauses and their duration as choosing a high threshold effectively implies counting long pauses only.

For repair fluency, researchers usually measure both number of repetitions and number of repairs. However, repetitions need not be corrections or repairs. They may be, but that holds for other disfluencies as well. Even filled pauses and silent pauses may be the result of errors that are repaired by the speaker before the error has been uttered (Levelt 1983).

Finally, for all measures that count frequencies of disfluencies (number of silent pauses, filled pauses, repetitions, or repairs), researchers usually correct these for length of the speaking performance. Most researchers divide the count per total time, others per speaking time, and yet others per number of words or syllables. However, correcting for total time (including silent pausing time), leads to a measure that confounds the frequency of disfluency with silent pauses (see also De Jong and Bosker 2013). Because more proficient speakers use lower frequency and hence longer words (containing more syllables), and because there are cross-linguistic differences in length of words and also in length of syllables, there is an advantage in choosing the frequency measures corrected for speaking time.

This short review of measures has thus far ignored possible cross-linguistic differences. If cross-linguistic comparisons with respect to fluency are made, such differences need to be taken into account. For measures of speed fluency especially, this may prove to be problematic. Firstly, languages differ in how they are paced. Some languages, such as Japanese, are mora-timed; others, like Spanish, are syllable-timed; and yet others, such as English, are stress-timed. Secondly, languages differ in syllable lengths. In Turkish, for example, CCVC and CVCC are extremely rare syllable structures, whereas in English two or more consecutive consonants within a syllable are more frequent. This makes comparisons with respect to speed of speech measured as number of syllables per time (or mean duration of syllables) across these languages meaningless.

Pausing in speech is also language-specific. Riazantseva (2001) suggested that cultural differences between English and Russian could explain the differences in mean pause duration found in her data (where Russian speakers tended to pause longer than English speakers). With respect to filled pauses, the cross-linguistic differences are remarkable. For instance, the realization of filled pauses differs across languages: English and Dutch speakers most frequently use very similar (two) forms "uh" and "uhm", but Japanese speakers, for instance, use multiple different forms, and choose the correct form depending on context.

In summary, if measures are used to compare speakers within a language, and if a researcher needs measures that are theoretically unrelated, a reasonable subset of measures would be: mean syllable duration, mean duration of silent pauses, and frequency measures of number of silent pauses, filled pauses, repetitions, and repairs. These frequency measures need to be corrected for the length of the speaking performance (by dividing by speaking time). If a researcher needs one single measure that encompasses all aspects of fluency at the same time, the measure of pruned speech rate is the best choice, although by doing so, the researcher no longer has insight into the possible weights that the subcomponents within this measure may have.

5 Future directions

When comparing the psycholinguistic/cognitive approach to fluency with the applied linguistic/evaluative approach, a couple of observations can be made. Firstly, psycholinguistic studies have investigated the cause and effect of *local* disfluencies with their main research questions "how is a disfluency revealing of underlying cognitive processes" and "how does a disfluency affect a listener's comprehension"? Applied linguists, in contrast, have been mainly interested in cause and effect of *global* measures of fluency, by answering the research questions "which measures of fluency are revealing of a speakers' L2 proficiency" and "how do measures of fluency affect raters' impression of the speaker"? Secondly, from spelling out these research questions, it becomes clear that psycholinguists are interested in the positive role of disfluencies in communication, and have focused on beneficial effects for the listener. Applied linguists, on the other hand, have focused on negative effects of disfluencies in evaluation and on showing which aspects of fluency may be indicative of L2 proficiency.

Researchers in both fields should learn from each other and adopt each other's research questions. For research on L1 fluency, psycholinguists need to ask the question why individuals differ with respect to speaking style (which includes fluency), and what effects these speaking styles may have on evaluations about the speaker. For research in the applied field, in addition to furthering our understanding about measures of fluency that are telling of proficiency, researchers should investigate local effects of disfluencies: will the beneficial effects of L1 disfluencies also exist when L2 speakers are disfluent? By expanding the research from negative global effects on ratings to beneficial local effects on listeners, we will get a better understanding of which disfluencies help, and which disfluencies hinder communication.

In the end, language testing scores are valid when the scores reflect communicative language ability. A component of this ability is to be able to get the intended message across within strict time constraints. This component entails that a speaker needs to be able to efficiently access his linguistic knowledge, effectively anticipate potential problems and come up with strategies to circumvent these, and to inform his interlocutor when he is experiencing problems in the speech production processes. In other words, being fluent also means using disfluencies in a communicatively meaningful manner.

Rubrics of speaking tests already partly reflect this (e.g., "hesitations are language- rather than content-related") but as yet it is unclear whether raters are capable of distinguishing between such different types of hesitations, and how automated tests would be able to differentiate between different types of hesitations. To get a clearer picture of how aspects of fluency are indicative of L2 proficiency, we need more research disentangling L2 disfluencies that are caused by L2-specific problems in speech production from those that are related to personal speaking style and from those that are part of a communicatively successful performance. Subsequently, the language testing practice may change speaking rubrics and algorithms to exclusively penalize disfluencies that are L2-specific, and that hinder communication.

6 References

American Council on the Teaching of Foreign Languages (ACTFL). 2013. *The ACTFL proficiency guidelines 2012 – Speaking*. http://actflproficiencyguidelines2012.org/speaking (accessed 23 September 2013).

Arnold, Jennifer E., Carla L. Hudson Kam and Michael K. Tanenhaus. 2007. If you say -thee uh- you're describing something hard: The on-line attribution of disfluency during reference comprehension. *Journal of Experimental Psychology: Learning, Memory, and Cognition* 33(5): 914–930.

Arnold, Jennifer E., Tom Wasow, Anthony Losongco and Ryan Ginstrom. 2000. Heaviness vs. newness: The effects of structural complexity and discourse status on constituent ordering. *Language* 76(1): 28–55.

Bachman, Lyle F. and Adrian Palmer. 1996. *Language testing in practice: Designing and developing useful language tests*. Oxford, UK: Oxford University Press.

Beattie, Geoff W. and Brian L. Butterworth. 1979. Contextual probability and word frequency as determinants of pauses and errors in spontaneous speech. *Language and Speech* 22(3): 201–211.

Bernstein, Jared, Alistair Van Moere and Jian Cheng. 2010. Validating automated speaking tests. *Language Testing* 27(3): 355–377.

Bortfeld, Heather, Silvia D. Leon, Jonathan E. Bloom, Michael F. Schober and Susan E. Brennan. 2001. Disfluency rates in conversation: Effects of age, relationship, topic, role, and gender. *Language and Speech* 44(2): 123–147.

Bosker, Hans Rutger, Hugo Quené, Ted J. M. Sanders and Nivja H. De Jong. 2014. Native 'um's elicit prediction of low-frequent referents, but non-native 'um's do not. *Journal of Memory and Language* 75: 104–116.

Bosker, Hans Rutger, Anne-France Pinget, Hugo Quené, Ted J. M. Sanders and Nivja H. De Jong. 2013. What makes speech sound fluent? The contributions of pauses, speed and repairs. *Language Testing* 30: 159–175.

Branigan, Holly, Robin Lickley and David McKelvie. 1999. Non-linguistic influences on rates of disfluency in spontaneous speech. In: John J. Ohala, Yoko Hasegawa, Manjari Ohala, Daniel Granville and Ashlee C. Bailey (eds.). *Proceedings of the 14th International Conference of Phonetic Sciences*, 387–390. Berkely, CA.

Brennan, Susan E. and Michael F. Schober. 2001. How listeners compensate for disfluencies in spontaneous speech. *Journal of Memory and Language* 44(2): 274–296.

Canale, Michael and Merrill Swain. 1980. Theoretical bases of communicative approaches to second language teaching and testing. *Applied Linguistics* 1(1): 1–47.

Clark, Herbert H. 2002. Speaking in time. *Speech Communication* 36(1): 5–13.

Clark, Herbert H. and Jean E. Fox Tree. 2002. Using uh and um in spontaneous speaking. *Cognition* 84(1): 73–111.

Collard, Philip, Martin Corley, Lucy J. MacGregor and David I. Donaldson. 2008. Attention orienting effects of hesitations in speech: Evidence from ERPs. *Journal of Experimental Psychology: Learning, Memory, and Cognition* 34(3): 696–702.

Cucchiarini, Catia, Helmer Strik and Lou Boves. 2002. Quantitative assessment of second language learners' fluency: Comparisons between read and spontaneous speech. *The Journal of the Acoustical Society of America* 111(6): 2862–2873.

Davies, Alan. 2003. *The native speaker: Myth and reality.* Clevedon: Multilingual Matters Ltd.

De Jong, Nivja H. and Hans Rutger Bosker. 2013. Choosing a threshold for silent pauses to measure second language fluency. In: Robert Eklund (ed.). *Proceedings of Disfluency in Spontaneous Speech*, DiSS 2013, 17–20.

De Jong, Nivja H., Rachel Groenhout, Rob Schoonen and Jan H. Hulstijn. 2015. Second language fluency: speaking style or proficiency? Correcting measures of second language fluency for first language behavior. *Applied Psycholinguistics.* 36(2): 223–243.

De Jong, Nivja H., Margarita P. Steinel, Arjen F. Florijn, Rob Schoonen and Jan H. Hulstijn. 2012. Facets of speaking proficiency. *Studies in Second Language Acquisition* 34(1): 5–34.

De Jong, Nivja H., Margarita P. Steinel, Arjen F. Florijn, Rob Schoonen and Jan H. Hulstijn. 2013. Linguistic skills and speaking fluency in a second language. *Applied Psycholinguistics* 34(5): 893–916.

De Jong, Nivja H. and Ton Wempe. 2009. Praat script to detect syllable nuclei and measure speech rate automatically. *Behavior Research Methods* 41(2): 385–390.

Dell, Gary S., Myrna F. Schwartz, Nadine Martin, Eleanor M. Saffran and Deborah A. Gagnon. 1997. Lexical access in aphasic and nonaphasic speakers. *Psychological Review* 104(4): 801–838.

Derwing, Tracy M., Murray J. Munro, Ron I. Thomson and Marian J. Rossiter. 2009. The relationship between L1 fluency and L2 fluency development. *Studies in Second Language Acquisition* 31(4): 533–557.

Derwing, Tracy M., Marian J. Rossiter, Murray J. Munro and Ron I. Thomson. 2004. L2 fluency: Judgments on different tasks. *Language Learning* 54(4): 655–679.

Dewaele, Jean Marc and Adrian Furnham. 1999. Extraversion: The unloved variable in applied linguistic research. *Language Learning* 49(3): 509–544.

Educational Testing Service. 2004. *iBT/Next Generation TOEFL Test. Speaking Rubrics.* http://
www.ets.org/Media/Tests/TOEFL/pdf/Speaking_Rubrics.pdf (accessed 23 September 2013).
Ernestus, Mirjam and Natasha Warner. 2011. An introduction to reduced pronunciation variants.
Journal of Phonetics 39: 253–260.
Foster, Pauline, Alan Tonkyn and Gillian Wigglesworth. 2000. Measuring spoken language: A unit
for all reasons. *Applied Linguistics* 21(3): 354–375.
Fox Tree, Jean E. 1995. Effects of false starts and repetitions on the processing of subsequent
words in spontaneous speech. *Journal of Memory and Language* 34(6): 709–738.
Fox Tree, Jean E. 2001. Listeners' uses of um and uh in speech comprehension. *Memory and
Cognition* 29(2): 320–326.
Fulcher, Glenn. 2000. The 'communicative' legacy in language testing. *System* 28(4): 483–497.
Gilabert, Roger. 2007. The simultaneous manipulation of task complexity along planning time and
[+/−Here-and-Now]: Effects on L2 oral production. In: Maria del Pilar Garcia Mayo (ed.).
Investigating tasks in formal language learning, 44–68. Clevedon: Multilingual Matters.
Goldman-Eisler, Frieda. 1968. *Psycholinguistics: Experiments in spontaneous speech.* New York:
Academic Press.
Ginther, April, Slobodanka Dimova and Rui Yang. 2010. Conceptual and empirical relationships
between temporal measures of fluency and oral English proficiency with implications for
automated scoring. *Language Testing* 27(3): 379–99.
Hartsuiker, Robert J. and Lies Notebaert. 2010. Lexical access problems lead to disfluencies in
speech. *Experimental Psychology* 57(3): 169–177.
Higgs, Theodore V. and Ray Clifford. 1982. The push toward communication. In: T. V. Higgs (ed.).
Curriculum, competence and the foreign language teacher, 243–265. Skokie, Illinois, USA:
National Textbook Company.
IELTS. n.d. *IELTS Speaking band descriptors.* http://www.ielts.org/PDF/UOBDs_SpeakingFinal.pdf
(accessed 23 September 2013).
Iwashita, Noriko, Annie Brown, Tim McNamara and Sally O'Hagan. 2008. Assessed levels of
second language speaking proficiency: How distinct? *Applied linguistics* 29(1): 24–49.
Janse, Esther. 2003. *Production and perception of fast speech.* Utrecht, the Netherlands: Utrecht
University dissertation.
Johnson, Keith. 2004. Massive reduction in conversational American English. In: Kiyoko Yoneyama
and Kikuo Maekawa (eds.). *Spontaneous Speech: Data and Analysis. Proceedings of the 1st
Session of the 10th International Symposium*, 29–54. Tokyo, Japan: The National International
Institute for Japanese Language.
Kang, Okim, Don Rubin and Lucy Pickering. 2010. Suprasegmental measures of accentedness and
judgments of language learner proficiency in oral English. *The Modern Language Journal*
94(4): 554–566.
Kircher, Tilo T. J., Michael J. Brammer, Willem J. M. Levelt, Mathias Bartels and Philip K. McGuire.
2004. Pausing for thought: engagement of left temporal cortex during pauses in speech.
NeuroImage 21(1): 84–90.
Kormos, Judit. 2006. *Speech production and second language acquisition.* Mahwah, NJ: Erlbaum.
Kormos, Judit and Mariann Dénes. 2004. Exploring measures and perceptions of fluency in the
speech of second language learners. *System* 32(2): 145–164.
Lennon, Paul. 1990. Investigating fluency in EFL: A quantitative approach. *Language Learning*
40(3): 387–417.
Levelt, Willem J. M. 1983. Monitoring and self-repair in speech. *Cognition* 14(1): 41–104.
Levelt, Willem J. M. 1989. *Speaking: From intention to articulation.* Cambridge, MA: MIT Press.
Levelt, Willem J. M., Ardi Roelofs and Antje S. Meyer. 1999. A theory of lexical access in speech
production. *Behavioral and Brain Sciences* 22: 1–37.

MacGregor, Lucy J., Martin Corley and David I. Donaldson. 2010. Listening to the sound of silence: Investigating the consequences of disfluent silent pauses in speech for listeners. *Neuropsychologia* 48(14): 3982–3992.

Maclay, Howard and Charles E. Osgood. 1959. Hesitation phenomena in spontaneous English speech. *Word* 15: 19–44.

Mehnert, Uta. 1998. The effects of different lengths of time for planning on second language performance. *Studies in Second Language Acquisition* 20(1): 83–108.

Merlo, Sandra and Leticia Mansur. 2004. Descriptive discourse: topic familiarity and disfluencies. *Journal of Communication Disorders* 37(6): 489–503.

Michel, Marije C., Folkert Kuiken and Ineke Vedder. 2007. The influence of complexity in monologic versus dialogic tasks in Dutch L2. *IRAL-International Review of Applied Linguistics in Language Teaching* 45(3): 241–259.

Pearson Education Ltd. 2012. *PTE Academic score guide*. http://www.pearsonpte.com/ PTEAcademic/scores/Documents/PTEA_Score_Guide.pdf (accessed 23 September 2013).

Ramsay, Ronald W. 1968. Speech patterns and personality. *Language and Speech* 11(1): 54–63.

Riazantseva, Anastasia. 2001. Second language proficiency and pausing: A study of Russian speakers of English. *Studies in Second Language Acquisition* 23(4): 497–526.

Riggenbach, Heidi. 1991. Towards an understanding of fluency: A microanalysis of nonnative speaker conversation. *Discourse Processes* 14(4): 423–441.

Roelofs, Ardi. 1998. Rightward incrementality in encoding simple phrasal forms in speech production: Verb-participle combinations. *Journal of Experimental Psychology: Learning, Memory, and Cognition* 24(4): 904–921.

Rossiter, Marian J. 2009. Perceptions of L2 fluency by native and non-native speakers of English. *Canadian Modern Language Review* 65(3): 395–412.

Schachter, Stanley, Nicholas Christenfeld, Bernard Ravina and Frances Bilous. 1991. Speech disfluency and the structure of knowledge. *Journal of Personality and Social Psychology* 60(3): 362–367.

Segalowitz, Norman. 2010. *Cognitive bases of second language fluency*. New York: Routledge.

Segalowitz, Norman and Barbara F. Freed. 2004. Context, contact and cognition in oral fluency acquisition: Learning Spanish in at home and study abroad contexts. *Studies in Second Language Acquisition* 26(2): 173–99.

Skehan, Peter and Pauline Foster. 2007. Complexity, accuracy, fluency and lexis in task-based performance: A meta-analysis of the Ealing research. In: Siska Van Daele, Alex Housen, Folkert Kuiken, Michel Pierrard and Ineke Vedder, I. (eds.). *Complexity, accuracy, and fluency in second language use, learning, and teaching*, 207–226. Brussels: University of Brussels Press.

Swerts, Marc. 1998. Filled pauses as markers of discourse structure. *Journal of Pragmatics* 30: 485–496.

Tavakoli, Parvaneh and Peter Skehan. 2005. Strategic planning, task structure and performance testing. In: Rod Ellis (ed.). *Planning and task performance in a second language*, 239–276. Amsterdam: John Benjamins.

Tavakoli, Parvaneh. 2011. Pausing patterns: differences between L2 learners and native speakers. *ELT Journal* 65(1): 71–79.

Towell, Richard, Roger Hawkins and Nives Bazergui. 1996. The development of fluency in advanced learners of French. *Applied Linguistics* 17(1): 84–119.

Yuan, Fangyuan and Rod Ellis. 2003. The effects of pre-task planning and on-line planning on fluency, complexity and accuracy in L2 monologic oral production. *Applied linguistics* 24(1): 1–27.

June Eyckmans, Philippe Anckaert and Winibert Segers

14 Translation and interpretation skills

1 Introduction

In this chapter on the assessment of translation and interpreting skills we will
briefly outline the origins of translation and interpretation testing and we will review current assessment practices in the educational as well as the professional
domain along reliability and validity criteria. In view of the scope of this volume,
we will focus on the relationship between language testing and the assessment of
translation and interpreting skills. Both translation assessment and interpreting
assessment have an obvious link with the measurement of foreign language competence since knowledge of the target language (understanding the source language and mastering the target language) is prerequisite for delivering a successful
translation or interpreting performance. However, both translation competence
and interpreting competence encompass more than foreign language competence
as is evidenced by the definitions of translation and interpreting competence in the
literature and the test constructs that have been proposed in reported assessment
practices. A sound assessment practice within this domain should therefore take
the different dimensions of translation and interpreting competence into account.

Because Interpreting Studies is a much more recent research domain than
Translation Studies and because the act of interpreting brings with it an entirely
different set of assessment concerns, a separate section in this chapter will be devoted to interpreting assessment. The spoken mode that is characteristic of interpreting but not of translation implies a test construct and test reality that is quite
separate from that in translation assessment. The differences in sample size between interpreting and translation performances and the extraordinary cognitive
load of examining an interpreting performance have repercussions for the discussion of the reliability and validity of translation and interpreting assessment, which
is why they warrant a separate discussion.

What is common to both disciplines however, is the fact that researchers from
both translation and interpreting research have voiced the need for more empirical
research on assessment in order to provide a sound methodological basis to the
assessment practices, which would consequently contribute to the justification of
test scores in educational as well as professional contexts (Waddington 2004;
Anckaert et al. 2008; Eyckmans et al. 2012; Kockaert and Segers 2012; Skaaden
2013; Wu 2013). The fact that the teaching and testing of both translation and interpreting skills has generally been more in the hands of practitioners than of researchers has led to a situation in which assessment has been informed by practice
rather than by empirical research. Hence, questions regarding the reliability of the

assessment methods have remained largely unanswered (Anckaert et al. 2008; Eyckmans et al. 2009; Eyckmans et al. 2013). In language assessment the introduction of psychometrics has led to the development of numerous studies on the reliability and validity of language tests, but these issues have only been addressed sparingly in the domain of Translation and Interpreting Studies. In fact, a screening of 25 much cited articles on translation assessment between 1966 and 2012 shows that the terms reliability and/or validity are used in only 16 of them. A similar investigation of 22 much cited articles on interpreting assessment shows that reliability and validity as assessment terms are treated in only 6 of them. Moreover, authors who demonstrate the intent to objectify assessment practices, often lack the knowledge or appropriate use of assessment methodology. A few exceptions aside, the field clearly suffers a lack of psychometric literacy.

In this chapter we hope to illustrate the importance of the recent shift to empirically-driven interpreter and translator testing and point to the many interesting avenues which open up if the gap between Language Testing theory and the specific epistemological characteristics of Translation and Interpreting Studies is bridged.

2 The assessment framework in Translation and Interpreting Studies

In the domain of Translation and Interpreting Studies the term assessment is used in four different contexts. Firstly, it can concern the evaluation of a product in which case the product is a written or spoken text that is the result of a translation or interpreting process. Secondly, it can refer to the evaluation of the translation or interpreting process, namely the different steps that were taken by the translator or interpreter to transform the original source text into a target text. Thirdly, it can refer to the evaluation of translation or interpreting competence, i.e. the underlying set of knowledge and skills that is put into operation when translating or interpreting. Fourthly, it is used to denote the translation or interpreting service that was delivered to the client. This includes tendering the offer, following up on agreements, interacting with the client, billing and handling complaints.

Although the constructs that are being assessed in these four different contexts are linked – one would hope that someone whose translation competence has been deemed good would be able to deliver good translation products – they imply different assessment methods.

Translation or interpreting products are usually assessed according to a holistic or an analytical assessment method. When applying a holistic approach the assessor listens or reads the product and awards it a score on the basis of a global impression of the product rather than of a detailed analysis of its characteristics.

Because of the highly subjective nature of this approach, personal tastes or individual views on the essence of translation of interpreting quality may cause an identical product to receive diverging scores from different assessors (Garant 2009; Waddington 2004).

Evaluation by means of an analytical method means that a system is developed in which errors and the importance to be attributed to these errors is decided on. Such a categorization of errors is called a matrix or analytical grid and it enables the assessment to become more detailed than is the case in the holistic approach. Examples of such matrices in the professional field are:

- the ATA Certification Exam that lists addition, ambiguity, literalness, omission and misunderstanding amidst its 23 error categories;
- the ITR BlackJack with 21 error categories such as non-application of glossary term, wrong treatment of acronym/of proper noun, syntactic/grammatical error, spelling error, punctuation error, local formatting error/inconsistency, wrong register, flawed style or inconsistent style;
- and the SAE J2450 Translation Quality Metric that counts 7 kinds of errors namely wrong term, syntactic error, omission, word structure or agreement error, misspelling, punctuation error and miscellaneous error.

Although the analytical method is more time-consuming than the holistic method, it provides a more detailed diagnosis of the weak and strong points of the translation or interpreting product. A disadvantage is the fact that the attention that is paid to the different text segments may obscure the appreciation of the target text as a whole. Also, relatively recent research (Anckaert et al. 2008; Eyckmans et al. 2009) has shown that applying an analytical approach to assessment is no guarantee for an objective or reliable assessment since different assessors do not always agree on the typology or weight of a mistake.

In recent translation process research, authors have directed their attention to the evaluation and study of the translation and interpreting process (Tirkkonen-Condit and Jääskeläinen 2000; Alvstad et al. 2011). In order to investigate the cognitive processes that influence translation and interpreting behaviour new methodologies are being applied that range from using think-aloud protocols and retrospective interviews to eye tracking and key logging.

Translation and interpreting service assessment requires the establishment of a service norm. A certification agency (or a client) can make use of the service criteria that are exemplified in the norm to attest whether the delivered service complies with it. Examples of such service norms are the European Standard Translation services – Service requirements EN 15038 and the ASTM F2089-01 (2007) Standard Guide for Language Interpretation Services.

Last but not least there is the assessment of translation and interpreting competence that is at the heart of the matter in educational settings where students have to be trained and certified. Within educational methodology it is widely accepted that the assessment of competence in any field requires five steps: 1. defining the competence, 2. defining its subcomponents (sub-competences), 3. formulating competence descriptors for each of the sub-competences, 4. linking the competence descriptors to observable behaviour, and 5. developing instruments to elicit and score this behaviour. In the case of the certification of translation or interpreting competence, five sub-competences have been put forward in the literature: interpreting or translation competence, language competence (source language as well as target language), cultural competence (in both source and target culture), heuristic competence and technical competence (PACTE 2005; Göpferich and Jääskelainen 2009; Kalina 2000; Malmkjær 2009; Schäffner and Adab 2000). For each of these subcompetences reliable and valid tests should be developed. A review of the different codes of practice in translation and interpreting colleges around the world shows that sub-competences such as cultural competence, heuristic and technical competences are almost never measured separately.

Different types of evaluation require different methodologies and because of the subjective nature of assessment and the high-stakes decisions that are at the core of certification, care must be taken in developing assessment procedures. An assessor's subjectivity can be reduced by using a multitude of tests that include multiple-choice questions, Yes/No statements, gap fill exercises, etc. Use of many different tests will enhance the reliability of the assessment but one should be aware that this can be at the detriment of the validity of the measure of translation or interpreting competence. Developing valid and reliable tests is a time-consuming and costly affair and it should involve both education and professional stakeholders.

3 Language Testing and assessment in Translation Studies: an epistemological gap

In order to understand how assessment in Translation Studies is related to language testing it seems useful to discuss how the views about language skills on the one hand and translation and interpreting skills on the other hand have evolved throughout the years. When we use the term translation in the subsequent section, we mean to encompass both translation and interpreting.

3.1 Language and translation competence

The relationship between language competence assessment and translation competence assessment has a long history since languages, both mother and foreign, have been learned and taught for centuries through the use of translation, more particularly by means of the Grammar Translation method. Even after the decline of this method, translation was considered the preferential way of checking reading comprehension. (For a detailed and well documented account of the historical love and hate relationship between translation and language teaching, see Kelly 1976).

Translation as a language teaching tool was already used in the third century AC in Alexandria and in Gaul. During the Renaissance the first ideas of what was to become the Grammar Translation method at the end of the eighteenth century took shape. The underlying postulate was that there is one underlying grammatical system for all languages, a notion much abhorred by the Direct Methodists. During the nineteenth century the grip of the Grammar Translation method was tightened since the need for language analysis had become paramount in language pedagogy, whereas (oral) communicative competences were deemed of secondary importance.

The first reactions against this 'traditional' method came at the beginning of the twentieth century, when the need was felt to distinguish between the ability to "feel at home in a language" and "skill in translation" (Jespersen 1904: 50). Criticism about the limits of the Grammar Translation method became so acute that the usefulness of using translation in the foreign language learning classroom was denied (Laudenbach et al. 1899: 10). By the 1940's the method was irretrievably discredited and replaced by a behavioural emphasis in foreign language pedagogy which viewed language learning as the acquisition of certain behavior instead of perceiving language as a collection of abstractions.

While the literature suggests that the communicative approach to language teaching (Widdowson 1978) marks the end of the use of translation in the foreign language classroom – with Klein-Braley's (1987) famous reference to the use of translation for developing foreign language tests as a "fossil at large" – many educational institutions that were not so receptive to methodological innovation continued to give translation a central role in language teaching and language assessment (Richards and Rodgers 1986; Sewell and Higgins 1996). With the return of the contrastive hypothesis (Beheydt 2001; Hiligsman and Wenzel 2001; Kuiken 2001), the use of translation regained new justification within the scholarly domain. Colina (2002) regrets that language teachers have banished translation from their classrooms and perceive of it as an 'evil' of the past because it reminds them of the inadequate Grammar Translation method. She argues that the associations with the Grammar Translation method are unfounded because using translation as a language learning device in the classroom is a very different activity from that performed by professional translators (2002: 4). She blames this misconception on the fact that Second Language Acquisition (SLA) and Translation Studies are disconnected fields of study.

From this short historical review we can conclude that despite the fact that the Grammar Translation method was considered out of vogue, the practice of using translation in the foreign language classroom continued. This situation has undoubtedly caused misunderstandings about the definition of translation competence in the professional domain. In the foreign language classroom translation products were judged by their textual faithfulness to the original. In the professional domain, translators' skills encompass the comprehension of the meaning and intention of a source text, the ability to recreate the text in the target language, the ability to take cultural differences into account, and the competence to effectively use Computer-Assisted Translation tools. This duality has influenced the ways in which translation competence has been assessed until recently.

3.2 Translation as a test of language competence

For centuries translation exercises have been used as a means to teach foreign languages throughout the world. In the same vein translation has been used as a testing technique in order to verify knowledge of the target language. In the early sixties of the previous century, Robert Lado, who is considered one of the founders of the language testing discipline, stated that translation tests do not constitute valid measures of foreign language knowledge because the ability to translate is an altogether different skill from the ability to use a foreign language. It is possible to speak a foreign language well without being able to translate properly and the reverse is also true: people with defective foreign language control can nevertheless be able to translate written material reasonably well.

Although the use of translation was by no means championed by the language testing experts in the seventies, John Oller considered it as a viable pragmatic procedure that deserved more research. With a pragmatic test – as opposed to a discrete point test – he referred to "any procedure or task that causes the learner to process sequences of elements in a language that conform to the normal contextual constraints of that language and which requires the learner to relate sequences of linguistic elements via pragmatic mappings to extralinguistic context" (1979: 38).

Swain, Dumas and Naiman (1974) similarly found that if translation was used in ways that approximate its normal application in real life contexts, it could provide valuable information about language proficiency. For instance, if the language sequences that need to be translated are sufficiently long to challenge the short term memory of examinees, the technique could be considered a particular kind of pragmatic task. When translating from the native language to the target language, translation can be construed as a test of productive ability in the target language. When translating from the target language to the native language, translation can function as a measure of comprehension ability in the target language.

According to Simon Kemp (2011), testing linguistic competence is one of the goals of the translation exams since the student's vocabulary range as well as his comprehension of linguistic structures and register awareness can be verified. On the basis of speculation rather than empirical evidence, he concludes that translation is a practical, fair and efficient way of evaluating competence in the aforementioned areas.

At the other end of the spectrum, Christine Klein-Braley's efforts in comparing translation tests with a number of traditional tests of linguistic competence resulted in her conclusion that translation 'appears to be the least satisfactory and least economical of the tests examined in determining L2 proficiency' (Klein-Braley 1987: 128–129). According to her translation assessment is 'two-dimensional', contaminating the measure of linguistic competence by simultaneously testing other factors.

In conclusion, using translation as a technique to evaluate the command of a foreign or second language has been deemed attractive by scholars because the translation task has the required features of a pragmatic test. It allows information to be gathered about aspects of communicative competence that would be difficult to access otherwise (e.g., cultural awareness, register). Nevertheless, issues about reliability and validity have been raised from the start. The assessor's subjectivity when scoring translations undermines the format's reliability and the interference of factors that belong to the construct of translation competence rather than language competence may cast a shadow on the validity of the use of translation as a language test.

3.3 Translation as a test of translation ability

When authors broach the subject of translation ability assessment, they usually refer to the work of Juliane House that is seen as seminal within the field of translation assessment (Gile 2005: 254; Lee-Jahnke 2001). She was the first to propose a scientific approach to the assessment of translation competence. However, two decades earlier, Robert Lado already devoted a chapter to the assessment of translation ability in his influential book mentioned above. This historical omission says a lot about the epistemological gap between SLA and Translation Studies (Eyckmans et al. 2012: 172; Colina 2002) and is all the more surprising given that Lado starts his chapter on translation assessment with a paradox that should have captivated translation teachers and scholars, namely: "ironically, translation tests that are so common in testing other skills are not available as tests of the ability to translate" (1961: 261).

In order to illustrate the scale of the missed opportunity that was caused by the epistemological gap between SLA and Translation Studies we will list Lado's proposals for a reliable and valid measurement of translation ability.

The first thing to notice with respect to reliability is that Lado proposes to work with a battery of tests whereas most later scholars in the field of Translation Studies base their assessment on the translation of one single text. By including a test that is based on the dichotomous scoring of many items the direct calculation of test reliability is made feasible. This reliability index can be used to estimate the concurrent validity of the other parts of the test battery by means of correlations. With respect to validity one could argue that translating words or phrases (even contextualized) is not the same as being able to translate whole texts. However, being a competent translator implies being able to translate isolated words or phrases. Mastering sentence structure, pattern selection, vocabulary, punctuation and spelling can therefore be considered as important subcomponents of the construct of translation competence as defined in the European norm (EN 15038) or by PACTE (2005). Although Lado does not mention on which empirical basis the translation problems should be selected for the creation of test items, it seems evident that the literature on comparative stylistics – for which Malblanc (1960), Vinay & Darbelnet (1968) and Zajicek (1973) paved the way – could furnish the item writer with more than enough inspiration. It is exactly the combination of research knowledge from the field of Translation Studies with the methodological tools of language testing that will lead to more reliable and valid translation assessment. Regrettably, only a few researchers have taken up the challenge to use dichotomous items to assess (components of) translation competence in order to maximize the reliability of translation testing (Eyckmans et al. 2009).

Another pioneering proposal by Lado was to test the ability to translate by instructing the students to deliver two versions of the same text, namely an accurate and a free translation. This practice corresponds to the classical opposition *verbum e verbo* vs *sensum de sensu* that has been recognized since St. Jerome and has been reformulated many times since then. When Translation Studies came into being as a new discipline in the second part of the 20th century, Nida (1964) reframed this century-old concept as formal and dynamic equivalence. House (1977) called the two types of translation covert and overt translations, Newmark (1982) saw an opposition between semantic and communicative translation, Ladmiral (1986) dichotomized between "sourciers" vs. "ciblistes", Toury (1995) built a framework using the terms adequacy and acceptability, and Venuti (1995) wrote about the polarity between foreignization vs domestication. From a dialectical point of view, one could argue that the Skopos Theory (Reiß and Vermeer 1984), incorporates the oppositions by stating that the purpose or function of the translation is the measuring stick by which translation quality should be assessed. Lado's task to create two different kinds of translation on the basis of one source text seems to fit the bill because it allows for the testing of the ability to produce a translation that fits the expectations of the reader in the target culture. It becomes possible to test the flexibility and situational expertise of the candidate translator, which reinforces the validity of the testing procedure.

Concerning the question of validity, Lado takes into account the speed with which one translates as an important dimension of translation competence. Moreover, his remarks on the effective use of works of reference while translating and the study of cultural aspects for the sake of quality translation can be considered as the germs of what is now called research sub-competence on the one hand and cultural sub-competence on the other hand (see 2.4).

In conclusion, from the first reflections on translation as a mean to assess translation ability till nowadays, translation tests have always been considered to have self-evident validity. However, one of the fundamental principles of measurement theory is that no test can be considered valid if it is not proven reliable (Bachman 1990: 238). Where language testers systematically measure the reliability of their tests, to be sure of the exactness of their measurement, only very few scholars in the field of Translation Studies have taken this dimension into account (Waddington 2001). In view of the fact that the few studies on the reliability of translation tests (Anckaert et al. 2013) show that most translation test procedures are rather unreliable, the basic assumption of self-evident validity should be reconsidered.

4 Interpreting Assessment

In the Interpreting domain the necessity for reliable and valid assessments of interpreting skills has been recognized since the 1990s with a number of authors investigating aspects of interpreting quality (Lee-Jahnke 2001; Pöchhacker 2001; Kalina 2005; Grbic 2008) and others directing their attention to a meaningful assessment of interpreting skills, what is commonly referred to within the Interpreting Studies literature as interpreter aptitude (Sawyer 2004; Wu 2013; Campbell and Hale 2003). Not only is this recent surge of interest in the evaluation of interpreting performance vital for the stakeholders of interpreting in the professional domain, the link between reliable assessment of interpreting skills and the quality of an interpreting training programme is self-evident. As Sawyer has pointed out in his book on the fundamental aspects of interpreting education, the decisions that are made on the basis of interpreting assessment go beyond decisions about programme entry or certification as these decisions also inform the process of curriculum design. He provides a thorough discussion of the ethical and political importance of test validation in interpreter education programmes in which he describes the personal, institutional and professional consequences that arise when the validity of the assessment is unattested. In the last decade of the previous century concerns about the consistency in examination procedures have been voiced by authors such as Hatim and Mason who reported their unease with "the unsystematic, hit-and-miss methods of performance evaluation which, it is assumed, are still in operation in many institutions" (Hatim and Mason 1997: 198). The challenge to improve assessment practices has slowly been taken up by researchers who have gradually introduced measurement concepts from the field of Language Testing to the field of Interpreting Studies in a bid to arrive at more valid and reliable assessment of interpreting processes as well as products (Wu 2010, 2013).

Within interpreting assessment a distinction can be made between the evaluation of the interpreting product, which is assessed in studies focusing on interpreting quality, and the evaluation of interpreting skills which is the subject of studies investigating the performance of professional interpreters and interpreter trainees during their training or on an examination. There is an obvious link between the assessment of interpreting skills and the assessment of the interpreting product in the sense that the ability to interpret is assumed to lead to the delivery of acceptable interpreting products. That is also why interpreting trainees are given realistic tasks within their training programme and as tests in examination procedures such as interpreting actual speeches from a conference. Hence, the trainees' ability to produce an acceptable interpreting product is put to the test. This means that the interpreting product is seen as indicative of the competence that is required in order to interpret. The emphasis on such performance assessment is in line with the plea for authenticity in language testing where a congruence is sought between tasks completed in the test situation and in the real world. At the same time performance assessment is related to the concept of construct validity since a construct is defined as an attribute or a skill that is assumed to be reflected in performance.

Since it has been established that a good interpreting test should be one in which the elicited performance is an adequate measure of the underlying skill that is required to live up to the interpreting task, a detailed definition of the interpreting construct appears quintessential in any assessment procedure. Although several researchers have discussed the criteria that are used for assessing interpreting skills (Altman 1994; Riccardi 2002), definitions of the test construct remain rare and this leaves the field with a dubious reputation in establishing reliability and validity standards.

It can be remarked that the congruence between the task in the test situation and in the real world is also the reason why the juries in examination procedures quite often count professional interpreters among their members. Although the selection of examiners on the basis of their professional experience is an attempt to enhance the validity of the assessment procedure, Kalina has pointed out that "they are unable to express their subjective judgments by objectively measurable standards" (2005: 768). The consistency of scoring across raters, also known as inter-rater reliability, has been the subject of recent studies (Sawyer et al. 2002; Wu 2013). Indeed, most discussions revolve around the inter-subjective assessment of interpreting quality and the procedures that can be followed in order to hold it up for methodological scrutiny. In these few empirical investigations of the psychometric qualities of interpreting assessment procedures, inter-rater reliability was often found wanting (Sawyer 2004; Wu 2010, 2013). Since inter-rater reliability seems to be the most relevant type of reliability in the case of the subjective judgement of spoken performances such as interpreting tests, it would be wise for interpreting colleges to invest time and effort in rater training in an attempt to reduce the measurement error that finds its source in the examiner. Rater-training and the use of testing instruments such as rating scales can also combat primacy or recency effects, stereotyping or biased response patterns from raters. Such rater-training can clarify the intended scoring criteria for raters and may modify the expectations that the raters have of the interpreter-trainees. Rater-training combined with the use of proper test procedures will lead to a sound and reliable judgement of interpreting examinations.

Similarly as in translation assessment, the use of matrices might enhance the objectivity of the assessment, at least within one organization. Riccardi (2002) developed an assessment scheme with four macro-criteria (equivalence, precision, adequacy, functionality) and a set of micro-criteria ranging from pronunciation to omissions and interpreting technique. Kutz (2005) developed an extensive evaluation scheme with four main sets of criteria in which he differentiates between trainers and customers. For information on the many quality parameters that have been proposed within interpreting studies, see Garzone (2002).

There are quite a lot of publications dealing with the notion of quality in Interpreting Studies and the terminology that is used in these contributions that focus on quality control and quality assurance is derived from management studies. This is the result of the fact that interpreting is most often viewed as a professional skill, not an educational skill. Kurz, who published an overview of user surveys in conference interpreting in 2001 and 2003 puts it like this: "Quality must begin with customer needs and end with customer perception. There is no reason why this generally accepted marketing principle should not apply to conference interpreting as well" (Kurz 2001: 394).

Although most researchers will agree with a general definition of interpreting quality as the accurate rendition of the intended meaning, correct target language use, appropriate booth manners and good voice quality, interpreting assessment practices are notorious for their variability as a result of the different perspectives of the stakeholders in question (be it client, peer, trainer, professional organisation). Research has demonstrated that the subjective judgements of clients are strongly influenced by first impressions, stereotypes and personal feelings rather than norms (Edwards et al. 2005). Also, analysis of customer evaluations has shown that the target audience in conference settings for example is very heterogeneous (Diriker 2004). This is even more profound in court and community interpreting settings (Pöchhacker 2000). As Nadja Grbic has so aptly pointed out: "the quality yardsticks defined by these agents and systems are not intrinsic to the interpreted interaction but are constructed in order to satisfy the everyday needs of the respective system (...)" (Grbic 2008: 240–241). If quality is acknowledged as being relative to its situational context, the benchmark against which quality can be measured becomes all the more important. Dutiful exemplification of the test construct is therefore of the utmost importance in every interpreting assessment setting.

5 Concluding remarks

In higher education as well as in the professional domain there is a marked interest in an accurate assessment of translation and interpreting skills. In this chapter we have highlighted that this concern did not arise simultaneously in the professional, educational and scholarly domain, nor has it witnessed the same evolution. Depending on the need and the maturation of the translation and interpreting domain the focus has been placed on the assessment of a product, a process, a service or a skill.

In the first half of our contribution we have addressed the epistemological gap between SLA and Translation Studies, as a result of which the opportunity was missed to firmly ground the assessment of translation ability in the language testing methodology that was developed in the 1960s (Lado 1961; Carroll 1966). It has taken the scholars in the field of Translation Studies two more decades before the issue was raised of making translation assessment less subjective or the need to distinguish translation assessment from language assessment was felt (House 1977).

We went on to illustrate how the emergence of Translation and Interpreting Studies as specific domains within applied linguistics went hand in hand with an evolution towards a definition of the construct of translation and interpreting competence as separate from the construct of foreign language competence. This has been a long and painstaking process as a result of the Lado-paradox that we have described. While translation has been used as a test of foreign language competence for ages, its use to assess translation competence has lacked a sound psychometric basis. Gradually the advancement of the discipline has led to the now widely established notion that translation ability encompasses more than foreign language mastery. This has led to the realisation that translation tests are not the most suitable measure to assess language competence and that language competence constitutes only one of the dimensions that make up the constructs of translation and interpreting competence.

In this chapter we have distinguished four different assessment contexts within Translation and Interpreting Studies (product, process, competence and service) and we have touched on the research trends in each of these. We have reported that the assessment of translation competence and translation products in the educational domain are characterized by practices that mainly use a holistic or an analytical approach. In most cases the analytical approach is to assess the quality of a product, which is then inferred onto the translator's competence. Discussions about the assessment of translation competence have been adressed on many levels – practical as well as theoretical – and have led to the establishment of models of translation competence (PACTE 2005) but the number of studies that have dealt with issues of reliability and validity have been scarce hitherto.

Where the evaluation of translation services is concerned, we have observed how the issuance of benchmarks such as the EN 15038 has shifted the assessment focus to service quality in the professional domain. From 2006 on this European norm enables the translation agencies to certify the quality of their services by independent control authorities. Businesses make increasing use of a wide assortment of software to quantify the quality of their translation products in the belief that an assessment performed by a computer programme ensures objectivity. However, it has to be noted that – just like the analytical grids that are used in the educational domain – the matrices on which these software programmes are based are themselves grounded in subjective criteria.

As far as the assessment of translation processes goes, we have remarked that the evaluation and study of translation or interpreting processes is solely a scholarly endeavour that centers on the cognitive processes underlying translation and interpreting. It aims to identify expert patterns of processing by making use of self-reports and expert interviews or of technologies such as eye tracking devices or key logging. The results of this research have didactic implications because it generates knowledge to improve translation and interpreting training.

In the second half of our contribution we have put forward Interpreting Studies as an independent and relatively young discipline in which a surge of interest into the reliable and valid assessment of interpreting performances is felt. Quite a lot of the research in this field centers on interpreting quality and is thus focused on the interpreting product which is seen as an emanation of interpreter skill or competence. Most of these studies gather information about interpreting quality in the professional field by means of survey research. Similar to Translation Studies, the assessment of service quality is on the rise in this field since more and more interpreting providers wish to obtain a quality certification. We have mentioned the emphasis on professional skills in this domain that is highly influenced by quality control and quality assurance procedures from the world of management. It seems fair to state that in Interpreting Studies the primary focus has not been on the development of instruments to measure interpreting competence – aside from a few exceptions – and consequently definitions of the test construct are scarce.

Finally, we have broached the issue of the presumed validity of the translation and interpretation performance format. This presumption of self-evident validity has caused scholars, teachers and practitioners to take the reliability of their examination procedures for granted and can be explained by the historical epistemological gap between Language Testing and Translation Studies.

In future research due attention should be paid to the detailed definition of the test constructs as this will improve the validity of the testing practices. Next to that, a better understanding of the multidimensional nature of translation competence will instill a more complete assessment practice in the professional and educational domain. Cultural, technical or heuristic competence that are hardly ever tested in examination procedures today merit further scrutiny and so do the psycho-physiological components that are deemed important components of strategic competence by translation scholars. Last but not least, application of well-established methodologies from Language Testing will make it possible to establish the reliability of translation and interpreting tests. A meeting of the minds from both disciplines seems the way forward.

6 References

Altman, Janet. 1994. Error analysis in the teaching of simultaneous interpreting: A pilot study. In: Sylvia Lambert and Barbara Moser-Mercer (eds.). *Bridging the gap: empirical research in simultaneous interpretation*, 25–38. Amsterdam and Philadelphia: John Benjamins.

Alvstad, Cecilia, Adelina Hild and Elisabet Tiselius (eds.). 2011. *Methods and strategies of process research: integrative approaches in translation studies*. Amsterdam and Philadelphia: John Benjamins.

Anckaert, Philippe, June Eyckmans and Winibert Segers. 2008. Pour une évaluation normative de la compétence de traduction. *International Journal of Applied Linguistics* 155: 53–76.

Anckaert, Philippe, June Eyckmans, Daniel Justens and Winibert Segers. 2013. Bon sens, faux-sens, contresens et non-sens sens dessus dessous. Pour une évaluation fidèle et valide de la compétence de traduction. In: Jean-Yves Le Disez and Winibert Segers (eds.). *Le bon sens en traduction*, 79–94. Rennes: Presses universitaires de Rennes.

Bachman, Lyle F. 1990. *Fundamental considerations in language testing*. Oxford, UK: Oxford University Press.

Beheydt, Ludo. 2001. Contrastiviteit in taal- en cultuuronderwijs. In: Gerard Elshout, Carel ter Haar, Guy Janssens, Marja Kristel, Anneke Prins and Roel Vismans (eds.). *Perspectieven voor de internationale neerlandistiek in de 21ste eeuw: handelingen Veertiende Colloquium Neerlandicum*, 337–352. Münster: Nodus-Publ.

Campbell, Stuart and Sandra Hale. 2003. Translation and interpreting assessment in the context of educational measurement. In: Gunilla Anderman and Margaret Rogers (eds.). *Translation today: trends and perspectives*, 205–224. Clevedon: Multilingual Matters.

Carroll, John B. 1966. An experiment in evaluating the quality of translations. *Mechanical Translations and Computational Linguistics* 9(3–4): 55–66.

CEN (ed.). 2006. EN 15038 Translation services – Service requirements. www.cen.eu (accessed 23 September 2013).

Colina, Sonia. 2002. Second language acquisition, language teaching and translation studies. *The Translator* 8(1): 1–24.

Diriker, Ebru. 2004. *De-/Re-contextualizing conference interpreting: Interpreters in the ivory tower?* Amsterdam and Philadelphia: John Benjamins.

Edwards, Rosalind, Bogusia Temple and Claire Alexander. 2005. Users' experiences of interpreters: The critical role of trust. *Interpreting* 7(1): 77–95.

Eyckmans, June, Philippe Anckaert and Winibert Segers. 2009. The perks of norm-referenced translation evaluation. In: Claudia Angelelli and Holly Jacobson (eds.). *Testing and assessment in translation and interpreting*, 73–93. Amsterdam and Philadelphia: John Benjamins.

Eyckmans, June, Winibert Segers and Philippe Anckaert. 2012. Translation assessment methodology and the prospects of European collaboration. In: Dina Tsagari and Ildikó Csépes (eds.). *Collaboration in language testing and assessment*, 171–184. Frankfurt am Main: Peter Lang.

Eyckmans, June, Philippe Anckaert and Winibert Segers. 2013. Assessing translation competence. In: Leonel Ruiz Miyares, Maria Rosa Alvarez, Silva and Alex Muñoz Alvarado (eds.).

Actualizaciones en communicacion social, Vol. 2, 513–515. Santiago de Cuba: Ediciones Centro de Linguistica Applicada.

Garant, Mikel. 2009. A case for holistic translation assessment. *AFinLA-e Soveltavan kielitieteen tutkimuksia* 1: 5–17.

Garzone, Giulana. 2002. Quality and norms in interpretation. In: Giulana Garzone and Maurizio Viezzi (eds.). Interpreting in the 21st Century: Challenges and Opportunities. *Selected Papers from the First Forlì Conference on Interpreting Studies, 9–11* November 2000, 107–119. Amsterdam: John Benjamins.

Gile, Daniel. 2005. *La traduction. La comprendre, l'apprendre.* Paris: PUF.

Göpferich, Susanne and Riitta Jääskelainen. 2009. Process Research into the Development of Translation Competence: Where are we, and where do we need to go? *Across Languages and Cultures* 10(2): 169–191.

Grbic, Nadia. 2008. Constructing interpreting quality. *Interpreting* 10(2): 232–257.

Hatim, Basil and Ian Mason. 1997. *The translator as communicator.* London and New York: Routledge.

Hiligsmann, Philippe and Veronika Wenzel. 2001. Contrastief taalonderzoek: nuttig, nodig of overbodig? In: Gerard Elshout, Carel ter Haar, Guy Janssens, Marja Kristel, Anneke Prins and Roel Vismans (eds.), *Perspectieven voor de internationale neerlandistiek in de 21ste eeuw: handelingen Veertiende Colloquium Neerlandicum*, 317–336. Münster: Nodus-Publ.

House, Juliane. 1977. *A model for translation quality assessment.* Tübingen: Narr.

Jespersen, Otto. 1901/1904. *How to teach a foreign language.* London: Swan Sonnenschein. [Translation by S. Yhlen-Olsen Bertelsen of *Sprogundervisning*, Copenhagen: Schuboteske Forlag.]

Kalina, Sylvia. 2000. Interpreting competences as a basis and a goal for teaching. *The Interpreters' Newsletter* 10: 3–32.

Kalina, Sylvia. 2005. Quality assurance for interpreting processes. *Meta: journal des traducteurs / Meta: Translators' Journal* 50(2): 768–784.

Kelly, Louis G. [1969] 1976. *25 Centuries of language teaching. An inquiry into the science, art, and development of language teaching methodology.* Massachusetts: Newbury House Publishers.

Kemp, Simon. 2011. Translation studies and the integrated modern languages degree. *Journal of Second Language Teaching and Research* 2(1): 121–134.

Klein-Braley, Christine. 1987. Fossil at large: Translation as a language testing procedure. In: Rüdiger Grotjahn, Christine Klein-Braley and Douglas K. Stevenson (eds.). *Taking Their Measure: The Validity and Validation of Language Tests*, 111–132. Bochum: Brockmeyer.

Kockaert, Hendrik J. and Winibert Segers. 2012. L'assurance qualité des traductions: items sélectionnés et évaluation assistée par ordinateur. *Meta: journal des traducteurs / Meta: Translators' Journal* 57(1): 159–176.

Kuiken, Folkert. 2001. Contrastief en taakgericht: een contrast? In: Gerard Elshout, Carel ter Haar, Guy Janssens, Marja Kristel, Anneke Prins and Roel Vismans (eds.). *Perspectieven voor de internationale neerlandistiek in de 21ste eeuw: handelingen Veertiende Colloquium Neerlandicum*, 353–362. Münster: Nodus-Publ.

Kurz, Ingrid. 2001. Conference interpreting: Quality in the ears of the user. *Meta: journal des traducteurs / Meta: Translators' Journal* 46(2): 394–409.

Kutz, Wladimir. 2005. Zur Bewertung der Dolmetschqualität in der Ausbildung von Konferenzdometschern. *Lebende Sprachen* 50(1): 14–34.

Ladmiral, Jean-René. 1986. Sourciers et ciblistes. *Revue d'esthétique* 12 : 33–42.

Lado, Robert. 1961. *Language testing. The construction and use of foreign language tests. A Teacher's Book.* London: Longman.

Laudenbach, Henri, Paul Edouard Passy and Georges Delobel. 1899. *De la méthode directe dans l'enseignement des langues vivantes.* Paris: Colin.

Lee-Jahnke, Hannelore (ed.). 2001. Évaluation: paramètres, méthodes, aspects pédagogiques / Evaluation: Parameters, Methods, Pedagogical Aspects. *Meta: journal des traducteurs / Meta: Translators' Journal* 46(2).

Malblanc, Alfred. 1960. *Stylistique comparée du français et de l'allemand*. Paris: Didier.

Malmkjær, Kirsten. 2009. What is translation competence? *Revue française de linguistique appliquée* 1(XIV): 121–134.

Newmark, Peter. 1982. *Approaches to Translation*. Oxford: Pergamon.

Nida, Eugene. 1964. *Toward a Science of Translation*. Leiden: Brill.

Oller, John W. Jr. 1979. Language Tests at School. A Pragmatic Approach. London: Longman.

PACTE group. 2005. Investigating Translation Competence: Conceptual and Methodological Issues. *Meta: journal des traducteurs / Meta: Translators' Journal* 50(2): 609–619.

Pöchhacker, Franz. 2000. *Dolmetschen: Konzeptuelle Grundlagen und descriptive Untersuchungen*. Tübingen: Stauffenburg.

Pöchhacker, Franz. 2001. Quality assessment in conference and community interpreting. *Meta: journal des traducteurs / Meta: Translators' Journal* 46(2): 410–425.

Reiß, Katharina and Hans J. Vermeer. [1984] 1991. *Grundlegung einer allgemeinen Translationstheorie*. Tübingen: Niemeyer. [Linguistische Arbeiten 147].

Richards, Jack C. and Theodore S. Rodgers. 1986. *Approaches and methods in language teaching: A description and analysis*. Cambridge, UK: Cambridge University Press.

Riccardi, Alessandra. 2002. Evaluation in interpretation: macrocriteria and microciteria. In: Eva Hung (ed.). *Teaching Translation and Interpreting* 4: Building Bridges, 115–126. Amsterdam and Philadelphia: John Benjamins.

Sawyer, David. 2004. *Fundamental aspects of interpreter education*. Amsterdam and Philadelphia: John Benjamins.

Sawyer, David, Frances Butler, Jean Turner and Irene Stone. 2002. Empirically-based test design and development for telephone interpreting. *Language Testing Update* 31: 18–19.

Schäffner, Christina and Beverly Joan Adab (eds.). 2000. *Developing translation competence*. Amsterdam and Philadelphia: John Benjamins.

Sewell, Penelope and Ian Higgins. 1996. *Teaching translation in universities: present and future perspectives*. London: AFLS/CILT.

Skaaden, Hanna. 2013. Assessing interpreter aptitude in a variety of languages. In: Dina Tsagari and Roelof van Deemter (eds.). *Assessment issues in language translation and interpreting*, 35–50. Frankfurt am Main: Peter Lang.

Swain, Merrill, Guy Dumas and Neil Naiman. 1974. Alternatives to spontaneous speech: elicited translation and imitation as indicators of second language competence. *Working Papers on bilingualism: Special Issue on Language Acquisition Studies* 3: 33–44.

Tirkkonen-Condit, Sonja and Riitta Jääskeläinen (eds.). 2000. *Tapping and mapping the processes of translation and interpreting: Outlooks on empirical research*. Amsterdam and Philadelphia: John Benjamins.

Toury, Gideon. 1995. *Descriptive translation studies and beyond*. Amsterdam: John Benjamins.

Venuti, Lawrence. 1995. *The translator's invisibility: A history of translation*. London: Routledge.

Vinay, Jean-Paul and Jean Darbelnet. 1968. *Stylistique comparée du français et de l'anglais*. Paris: Didier.

Waddington, Christopher. 2001. Different methods of evaluating student translations: The question of validity. *Meta: journal des traducteurs / Meta: Translators' Journal* 46(2): 311–325.

Waddington, Christopher. 2004. Should student translations be assessed holistically or through error analysis? *Lebende Sprachen* 49(1): 28–35.

Widdowson, Henry G. 1978. *Teaching language as communication*. Oxford, UK: Oxford University Press.

Wu, Shao-Chuan. 2010. Some reliability issues of simultaneous interpreting assessment within the educational context. In: Valerie Pellatt, Kate Griffiths and Shao-Chuan Wu (eds.). *Teaching and testing interpreting and translating*, 301–325. Frankfurt am Main: Peter Lang.

Wu, Fred S. 2013. How do we assess students in the interpreting examinations? In: Dina Tsagari and Roelof van Deemter (eds.). *Assessment issues in language translation and interpreting*, 15–33. Frankfurt am Main: Peter Lang.

Zajicek, Jacques. 1973. Études stylistiques comparatives. Néerlandais-français. Den Haag and Paris: Mouton.

III. Second language asessment contexts

Karmen Pižorn and Ari Huhta
15 Assessment in educational settings

1 Introduction

In this chapter we focus on large-scale national foreign language assessments (LS-NFLAs) that are related in some way to a country's educational system. In the first part of the chapter we define what we mean by LS-NFLAs and discuss features that characterize them. We then give an account of the changes in these assessments in the past few decades and discuss some current trends in them. In the second part, we focus on their uses and purposes, their development phases and administration issues, their common structure, the sustainability of good testing practice, the influence of politics, and the washback effect of the assessments on teaching and learning. Finally, in the third part, we discuss how national assessments are likely to evolve in the future.

We begin by defining what kind of large-scale assessments are covered in this chapter. We focus on assessments that are related to the educational system of a fairly large entity such as an entire country or a major part of a country, for example, a state or a region. Because of the wide geographical coverage of these assessments and also because they usually have an official status, they are often called national assessments. National assessments are typically centralized, standardized and based on a national or regional curriculum, that is, they are designed outside the school by an assessment organization or an examination board, although some locally designed assessment instruments may also be used as part of the national assessment. These assessments are almost always carried out by using tests, although information from other types of assessments such as the portfolio or assessments by the teachers may complement the test scores (therefore, we often refer to national assessments also as national tests or national examinations below). National assessments often take place at the end of a major educational level such as the end of primary, lower secondary, or upper secondary education, although in some countries they may be administered more often.

It is important to consider the purposes of national assessments, as they can differ considerably and also their role and impact on the educational system can differ depending on the use of the assessment results. The uses of national assessments fall into two main categories: assessment of the learners and assessment of the educational programmes (see Brown 2013). The use of national assessments as a way to measure how much of the curriculum the students have achieved by the end of some important unit of studies such as compulsory education is probably the most common use of national assessment/examination results. That is, the students' learning is evaluated and they are given grades that indicate how well they have achieved the goals of whatever education they have just completed. These tests are typically quite high-stakes for the students, since the results are often used for gaining entry into the next level of education. For example, the final primary school examination may determine the kind of secondary education the student can enter (e.g., vocational or academic). It should be added that the results of school-leaving examinations can also be used by educational authorities for the other major purpose of assessment, which is discussed below: to evaluate the quality of an educational programme (e.g., a national curriculum).

There is, however, another type of national assessment that is not concerned with awarding individual students grades. The sole purpose of these assessments is to investigate the quality of an educational programme or system so that its current state could be determined and also to find out how much variation there is in the performance of different schools, regions or genders, and whether certain aspects of the curriculum are mastered better than others. International examples of this type of assessment are the PISA studies (however, unlike national assessments with a similar purpose, the PISA studies are not based on any national curricula). Based on the findings, the authorities may decide to introduce changes in the educational system, for example, a revision of the curriculum or allocation of more resources to schools with lower results. It is important to understand that this type of national assessment is closer to a research study than to a national school-leaving examination. Therefore, the administration of a national assessment intended purely for programme evaluation purposes can differ radically from a national achievement test. Because one (perhaps the main) purpose of a national *achievement test* is to award grades to individual students, it is imperative that the test is administered to all eligible students. To do otherwise would be unfair to the students, especially if the test results are important for their further education or entry into labour market. The fact that the results from such national achievement tests are in some countries also used for informing the educational authorities (and possibly also the schools) can be seen as only a secondary use of the test results.

When a national test is not used for grade-giving and other such high-stakes purposes for individual students but merely to gather data to assess the quality of an educational programme, it is not necessary to administer it to all students. It is enough to take a statistically representative sample of schools and students, which is less expensive and which yields basically the same information about the educational system as testing all schools and all students would. Unlike the achievement tests, these assessments are not high-stakes for the students, although the results can be very important for politicians, educational decision makers and curriculum planners.

In our review, we focus on large-scale national foreign language (FL) assessments whose principal purpose is to measure students' achievement in primary and secondary education, and to give them grades based on their test results. These tests are often school-leaving examinations and may also be used for assessing the quality of a country's educational system. This review predominantly focuses on the national FL assessments in Europe but the examples, though contextualised in Europe, reveal themes that are relevant globally. We also refer to selected examples from other regions of the world.

2 Historical development of national foreign language assessments

Next we briefly discuss selected major trends discernible in the development of large-scale national FL assessments in the past few decades: communicativeness, the CEFR, standardization, and professionalization.

It is obvious that national language assessments have become more communicative in the past forty years, as have language tests more generally (see, e.g., Kunnan 2008; Davies 2014). Most tests regardless of their purpose tended to measure knowledge about language till the 1970s because of the focus on errors and discrete elements of language, especially grammatical structures and vocabulary. The widespread use of multiple-choice and translation as test methods contributed to this emphasis. The testing of the productive skills was not common in national assessments, partly for practical reasons and partly because of concerns about their reliability.

Largely because of changes in how language proficiency was conceptualized, language testing started to change. Since the 1970s, language proficiency has no longer been viewed as knowledge about distinct aspects of language but rather as an ability to use language for various communicative purposes, in different contexts and with different interlocutors or recipients. Language tests nowadays attempt to incorporate features of real-life communication as much as is feasible.

The Common European Framework of Reference for languages (Council of Europe 2001) started as a purely European initiative, as its name suggests, but in the past decade it has become influential in other regions of the world, too, particularly in Asia, the Middle East, and South America. This document defines in quite some detail what it means to communicate in a FL and how ability to use language can be defined as levels of ascending skill and sophistication. In this way, the CEFR has supported and further contributed to the prominence of communicative language teaching and testing.

The CEFR has become increasingly important in high-stakes language testing. This is particularly evident in international language testing as even tests not based in Europe have considered it important to align themselves with the CEFR, presumably to ensure their relevance not only for their European users but also for other contexts in which the CEFR has become popular. For example, the US-based TOEFL iBT has carried out such alignment procedures (Tannenbaum and Wylie 2008). The impact of the CEFR on language education and on language testing in Europe has been significant (Martyniuk 2011; Figueras 2012). Martyniuk and Noijons summarise their survey on the use of the CEFR across Europe: "The overall impression is that the majority of countries have already been trying to implement the CEFR for some time in the development of tests and examinations either for primary and secondary schools or for adult education" (2007: 7).

Language testing has become more professional in many countries during the past few decades. Interestingly, Figueras (2007, 2012) argues that the CEFR has played a part in this, for example because of the need to link various examinations and assessments with its levels. The increasing standardization of national high-stakes examinations that will be described later in this chapter is one indication of that professionalization. Another sign is the creation of international organisations for professional language testers as well as for researchers, teachers and other people interested in language assessment. These include ILTA (International Language Testing Association), ALTE (Association for Language Testers in Europe) and EALTA (European Association for Language Testing and Assessment). These associations organize conferences and workshops that serve as arenas for disseminating research results and for exchanging information about good practice in language assessment. They also promote and sometimes even fund local activities such as training events that aim at increasing different stakeholders' awareness of language testing issues and principles of good practice. An important aspect of the associations' work is the design of codes of ethics and guidelines for practice that guide good professional conduct in language testing.

3 The key issues of large-scale foreign language national assessments

3.1 Test use and purposes of large-scale foreign language national assessments

According to Davies (1990) defining the test purpose is the first step in the test design process and must be asked and answered before we can decide upon the test content and test methods. This is because the purpose for which the test will be used influences what is tested and how it will be tested, i.e. which language skills, which topics and test methods, more or less specific language use etc. So, for example, a school-leaving examination in English as a FL will be indicating progress according to the objectives set by the national curricula, but may also be used for certification or form part of a process of program evaluation. It can even have a diagnostic function, which in turn may assist in selection decisions, for example, functioning as a university entrance examination. This is exactly the case with many European secondary-school leaving examinations (Eckes et al. 2005) where national examinations have different purposes. This can also be observed from the Eurydice[1] report (2009) where test purposes of national assessments are often varied and rarely one-dimensional.

In Europe, national assessment of students is becoming increasingly important as a means of measuring and monitoring the quality of education, and structuring European education systems (Eurydice 2009). According to Eurydice (2009), the national FL assessments are developed and influenced by national policy frameworks and contexts, and are usually part of the assessment of other school subjects or areas of study. They should contribute to a more comprehensive picture of student knowledge and skills by providing additional information to parents, teachers, schools and the entire educational system. The national assessment systems within compulsory education levels have been introduced in almost all European countries over the last three decades, and have become an important instrument in the organisation of educational systems (Eurydice 2009). In fact, more than one third of European countries administer national assessments in foreign languages starting at primary level, and 60 % of countries assess FL proficiency of their students at the end of compulsory education (Eurydice 2009).

The analysis of the objectives and uses of national assessments including assessing foreign languages in the 35 countries/country communities at ISCED levels 1 and 2[2] reveals that the main objectives of such assessments are monitoring and evaluating educational systems (17 countries or over 40 %) and examining whether the objectives set by the national curricula have been achieved (17 countries). These are followed by providing schools with the information on their students' achievements and offering a tool for their self-evaluation (seven countries), and informing all stakeholders about students' attainments (six countries). Surprisingly, providing teachers, one of the main educational stakeholder groups, with extra information on their students' achievements is explicitly stated as an objective of national assessments only in five countries/country communities. Another interesting finding is that even though the *assessment for learning* movement (Black and Wiliam 1998) has had quite a long history now, only four countries/country communities clearly listed providing learning opportunities for schools as a main objective of the national assessment in their educational context. There are also only four countries where the main objectives of the national assessment incorporate

---

1 The Eurydice Network provides information on and analyses of European education systems and policies. As of 2014 it consists of 40 national units based in 36 countries participating in the EU's Erasmus+ programme.
2 Standard Classification of Education (ISCED) to facilitate comparisons of education statistics and indicators across countries on the basis of uniform and internationally agreed definitions. Primary education (ISCED 1) usually begins at ages five, six or seven and lasts for four to six years. Lower secondary education (ISCED 2) generally continues the basic programmes of the primary level, although teaching is typically more subject-focused, often employing more specialised teachers.

providing certification of attainment or making necessary policy changes. Only two countries reported utilizing national assessment to guide the streaming of pupils, to provide diagnostic information on students' achievement, or to inform parents of the pupil's summative achievement. It is interesting to observe that, with the exception of Finland, national assessments do not focus on monitoring the implementation of equality and equity in education.

Whether and to what extent the LS-NFLAs mentioned above actually measure the stated purposes should be carefully investigated by taking into account the effect the test is intended to have in the real world. In other words, do tests test what they claim to test? To answer this we need to do a validation analysis of a particular test. Validation is concerned with the gathering of as much evidence as possible, which would support or refute the inferences that are made about test takers based on their performance on the test, and the decisions that are made about learners based on their test scores. According to Fulcher and Davidson (2009) the intended score meaning should be explicitly and carefully linked to test design, as otherwise it is not possible to relate the users' interpretation of the score to the decisions that they take on the basis of the score. Another issue that may undermine the appropriateness of tests is the lack of need for justifying the validity of a test among decision makers who are predominantly not language assessment experts. They are usually also not aware that it is not only high-stakes tests which require rigorous validation but also the low-stakes ones, if they are used nationally. Further, the difference between low- and high-stakes national FL tests cannot be universally and simply defined and national assessments may have unintended consequences from the original objectives. Pižorn and Moe (2012: 81) report that the national FL assessments for young learners in two European countries are not supposed to directly influence the students' final grades or have implications for their future career. That said, the language teachers in these countries have expressed considerable concern about the pressure they are under from the head teachers and parents. This is especially so because, despite opposition from the Ministry of Education, the test results are published in national newspapers along with the ranking of schools. It is, therefore, vital that more validation studies of national FL tests are performed and that these studies are open to scrutiny by the international language testing community. Chapelle, Jamieson and Hegelheimer (2003: 413) propose doing regular analyses, which would make explicit the links between the components of test purpose (the inferred test use and its intended impact) and the design and validation decisions.

Not many LS-NFLAs have been openly validated in peer-reviewed academic journals, so there is not much evidence of whether these instruments test what they claim to test. When investigating different types of validity (content, face, construct etc.), it is the content validity of the test that may have a strong influence on what is being taught in the classroom and may narrow the curriculum goals and objectives. Content validity includes any validity strategies that focus on the content of the test. To demonstrate content validity, test designers should investigate the degree to which a test is a representative sample of the content of whatever objectives or specifications the test is originally designed to measure (Anderson 1975: 460; Hughes 2003).

3.2 Test development and test implementation

LS-NFLAs are gradually adopting standardization procedures including the use of quantitative and qualitative methodologies for item and test analysis, the detailed description of exam organization and testing conditions, as well as rater training and monitoring.

The whole process of test development consists of designing, planning, item-writing, pre-testing, editing and printing, distribution to schools, marking, setting pass marks if applicable, analyzing and reporting the results and the overall evaluation. Test development is a standardized procedure, which consists of various independent stages, which come at a specific time and place in the development process, yet each stage functions only in relation to the others. Tests should be developed according to clearly defined specifications. Language assessment requires measuring instruments constructed on the basis of sound psychometric criteria and appropriately chosen test methods. Reforming language assessment practices needs to be embedded in continuing efforts of establishing the highest quality, encompassing a number of aspects ranging from the objective measurement of examinee proficiency and item difficulty to precise definitions of test administration conditions and scoring systems (Alderson 2004; Weir 2004). So, for example, Alderson and Pižorn (2004) point out that designing papers and detailed marking schemes should not be developed successively but simultaneously. If the stages of the test development, which are inextricably interwoven and dependent on the idiosyncrasies of an educational system, are not interrelated, the system will not enable alterations and improvements and cannot be transparent from the point of view of test developers, administrators and test users. Constraints that test developers may encounter at national levels are numerous, and range from time, human and financial resources, to political interference.

In the remainder of this section, we will discuss challenges that testing teams are faced with. It is not uncommon for testing team members, who frequently consist of ordinary language teachers and/or a few (university) language specialists, to have very little or no expertise in constructing FL assessments on a national level. This can only lead to inappropriately designed tests, if not to a total disaster. In the 90s many countries of East-European block started to set up national large-scale examinations and assessments and some test designers received a proper training in language assessment while others did not. In some cases language teachers had been trained as items writers for years, but were ultimately not selected to design the 'real' examination tasks and were replaced by total novices (Eckes et al. 2005). Test developers not only need the professional skills to produce good measurement instruments, but also to be able to apply these skills in creative ways, and to novel situations.

Another burning issue is the time one has to set up the assessment system. It takes time to build a national assessment system and if the tests are not well prepared and/or stakeholders are not informed properly and far enough in advance, the consequences may be damaging. The decision-makers in two East-European countries were forced to postpone the introduction of a new examination due to the students' and/or teachers' protests (Eckes et al. 2005; Pižorn and Nagy 2009). As Buck (2009: 174) observes there is often considerable pressure for test developers to complete a test as quickly as possible, simply to make the project go ahead and/or make it cheaper but with more or less unpredictable and fatal consequences.

Piloting is another issue that in the context of national assessments is treated in different ways. There are very few countries where all test items are piloted on a sufficient number of test takers who have similar characteristics to the target test population. Cost is often cited as a barrier to piloting; it is an expensive activity. Yet a lack of funding is not the only barrier to piloting but also the assessment culture. Eckes et al. (2005) report on the experience of one country where no central piloting of examination items was planned, as some stakeholders feared that pretesting could jeopardize security. The result was that the items for the centrally designed papers at both levels were written behind desks, based upon the expertise of the individual item writers. Though Buck (2009: 174) is right in saying that there is no alternative to piloting tests as otherwise we have no idea whether the items are working properly, if the test providers on national level do not understand the need for piloting, language test designers have a very difficult job in persuading decision makers to offer support. Thus, many testing teams have to live with small-scale piloting or pilot test items in their free time, without the decision makers' support.

3.3 The structure of large-scale national foreign language assessments

Currently, most national FL assessments show a number of advances in language assessment and have moved away from traditional knowledge-based tasks measuring rote learning. These can be seen through their considerations of a) the theoretical view of language ability being multi-componential, b) the correlation and the impact of test tasks and test-taker characteristics on the test scores, c) the application of sophisticated measurement instruments including more and more advanced statistical tools, and d) the development of communicative language tests that incorporate principles of communicative language teaching (Bachman 1990; Bachman and Palmer 1996). Hence, students are assessed through more authentic tasks,

Tab. 1: The Structure of the Slovene Matura secondary-school leaving exam in English.

Paper No.	Skill/knowledge	Time	Weighting	Marking
1A	Reading comprehension	35 min	20 %	Centralised
1B	Knowledge and Use of language	25 min	15 %	Centralised
2	Listening comprehension	Up to 20 min	15 %	Centralised
3A	Writing (short, guided) (150–180 words)	30 min	10 %	Centralised; double marking;
3B	Writing (essay) (220–250 words)	60 min	20 %	Centralised; double marking;
4A	Speaking, picture discussion; the tasks prepared centrally;	Up to 20 min	20 %	Internal by the teachers using centrally designed criteria
4B	Speaking Teacher-prepared guided task			
4C	Speaking; interpretation of a literary text and a follow-up discussion on the text topic; the tasks prepared centrally			

which measure their reading and listening comprehension skills, writing and speaking interactional and transactional skills, and the use of vocabulary and grammar in context. While decades ago test takers tested on a national level were supposed to translate sentences, recite grammatical rules and dialogues by heart, they are now expected to be able to skim, scan and infer information from an authentic newspaper article, talk about their views and attitudes to the topics of their interests and relevance and write a letter of application or complaint, as well as compose a narrative or a discursive essay. How far these tasks are authentic and appropriate for the targeted audience of test takers has to be investigated in each individual educational context as each has its own idiosyncrasies. For example, Table 1 shows the structure of a secondary-school leaving examination in English at the basic level in Slovenia.

The exam may be characterized as performance assessment reflecting the cognitive-constructivist view of learning. In performance assessment, real life or simulated assessment exercises are used to elicit original responses, which are directly observed and rated by a qualified judge. As such, performance-based tests could serve as the driving-force for a thinking-oriented curriculum geared towards developing higher-order thinking skills (Resnick and Resnick 1992). However, investigations into the impact of tests upon teaching and learning (e.g., Alderson and Wall 1993 and Wall 2005) show that this is too simplistic a view.

3.4 Sustainability of good testing practice

From the 90s up to the middle of the 21st century, many countries of Central and Eastern Europe went through dramatic changes in language learning, teaching and assessment. In most instances (e.g., the Baltic states, Hungary, Slovenia), assessment reforms started as projects and were supported financially, and what is more important professionally (Eckes et al. 2005). The aims of these projects were similar: to develop a model for a transparent and coherent system of evaluation of FL performance. Foreign agencies, such as the British Council, helped with leading experts as advisors and provided training for item writers, examiners, teachers and other personnel who would be involved in the new examination process. The outcomes involved detailed requirements and test specifications, training materials and courses for examiners, item-writer guidelines, calibrated test items, test preparation books, etc. Unfortunately, when projects end, some good testing practices are not sustained due to a lack of financial support, appropriate infrastructure, and assessment expertise in the educational context and the wider society (Wall, 2013).

The most worrying issues may be summarized as follows:
- Absence of validation of the language tests
- Absence of piloting of test items
- Oral parts remain internal (i.e. they are delivered and rated by the students' own teacher)
- No double-marking or monitoring of rating standards in the writing and speaking tests
- Inadequate or no quality control of the test development process
- No training for novice item writers

3.5 The influence of politics

Heyneman (1987) claims that testing is a profession but may be dramatically affected by politics. He warns that the quality of tests relies on how much the test designer is willing and able to pursue professionalism in language assessment. This is even more so in the case of national FL assessments, which are usually part of a larger national educational and assessment scheme with many different agendas expressed by different stakeholders. Negotiation, compromise and concession are a major part of every test development process at this level. Furthermore, this often takes place in a complex organizational structure, with some people operating under their own particular agendas, which may be legitimate but also personal and even egoistic. They may have a completely inaccurate and/or simplistic view of what it takes to make a good test (Buck 2009: 177).

At the macro-political level, national educational policy may involve innovations in assessment in order to influence the curriculum and/or teaching practice. For example, the Slovene secondary-school leaving examination was introduced as a lever for change, to promote communicative language teaching and assessment but the new language curriculum was developed and implemented only several years after the introduction of examination. Politics, however, can also operate at lower levels, and can be a very important influence on test development and its implementation. Alderson and Banerjee (2001) point out that in most testing institutions, test development is a complex process where individual and institutional motives interact and are interwoven. Alderson (2009) further argues that politics with a small 'p' does not only include institutional politics, but also personal politics. Different stakeholders (ministers, ministry bureaucrats, university teachers, chairs of educational bodies etc.) have their own agendas and may impact the test development process and test use. Eckes et al. (2005) report that in Hungary in 2002 a few top decision-makers decided to create a unified examination model for all foreign languages despite differences of opinion between the various language teams. Classroom teachers became responsible for developing their own speaking tests, as well as marking them, with no quality control. This led the English team to resign.

3.6 Washback effect of the national foreign language assessments

Large-scale national FL assessments may have an intended and unintended impact on learning and teaching. In the research literature, this impact is referred to as the "washback effect." Most researchers define it as a complex phenomenon which influences language teachers and students to do things they would not necessarily otherwise do (Alderson and Wall 1993: 117; Bailey 1996: 259). It also indicates an intended direction and function of curriculum change on aspects of teaching and learning by means of a change of an examination (Cheng 2005: 28–29).

Such impact may be seen as negative; tests may be assumed to force teachers, students and other stakeholders to do things they would not otherwise do. For example, the General English Proficiency Test (GEPT) in Taiwan is targeted at high school students and adults. However, due to parents' influence, primary school students started to take the GEPT. To meet parents' expectations, language schools provided young learners with test preparation programmes. In 2006, learners at the primary school level were barred from registering for the GEPT (Wu 2012).

On the other hand, some researchers claim that tests may also be 'levers for change' in language education: the argument being that if a bad test has a negative impact, a good test should or could have positive washback (Pearson 1998). However, washback effect is far too complex a process; any test, good or bad, may have beneficial or detrimental effects on learning and teaching. Research findings on the washback effects of the university entrance examinations on teaching and learning show that washback is inextricably linked to the context and that tests changed teachers' teaching methods in some but not all studies and that washback works on teachers at different levels (Hassan and Shih 2013; Cheng 2005; Qi 2005). This implies that each examination needs a tailor-made research project to investigate its washback.

4 Future directions

As we described earlier, national assessments have become more standardized in many countries and their design more professional. This is an indication of an increasing awareness among educational decision makers and assessment organizations that language testing needs to be taken seriously if test results are to be trusted. It is to be hoped that this trend continues and the issues with certain national assessment systems reported in, e.g., Eckes et al. (2005) will be exceptions rather than the rule in the future. Improved assessment literacy is obviously also important for language teachers for whom assessment is in fact part of their profession (see also Inbar-Lourie 2013). Indeed, ordinary classroom teachers are one of the target groups of international language assessment associations such as EALTA in their efforts to promote a better understanding of the principles of good language testing.

A very clear trend in both national and international large-scale assessments is the increasing use of computers and other types of ICT in all phases of the assessment process, from item writing to test delivery and scoring of responses. International high-stakes language examinations from the Educational Testing Service (responsible for the TOEFL) and the Pearson publishing company are the most prominent examples of very advanced utilizations of computer technology and the Internet (Chapelle, Enright and Jamieson 2008; Owen 2012). Interestingly, there are also computerized large-scale low-stakes language tests such as DIALANG, which is a multilingual diagnostic language assessment system available through the Internet that provides its users with feedback on the strengths and weaknesses in their proficiency (Alderson 2005). Large-scale programme evaluations are also becoming computerized; for example, the European Commission's recent survey of FL proficiency (European Commission 2012) was delivered on a computer in some of the participating countries. Computerization has also become the delivery mode in some national examinations (e.g., in Norway; Moe 2012) and this trend is likely to gain speed in the future.

Computerization is just not an alternative way to administer test content: it can in fact expand and change the constructs measured (see Van Moere and Downey, this volume; Sawaki 2012; Kunnan 2014). An obvious expansion is the use of multimedia in speaking and listening tests, another is the possibility of allowing test takers to use on-line dictionaries or other such tools that are used in real-life language tasks (Chapelle et al. 2008).

Increasing computerization of national assessments relates to the final trend we single out in this review, namely an increase in the amount and detail of information obtainable from such assessments. The primary purpose of most national assessments is to provide summary information for educational authorities (information about large groups of learners) or for individual learners (overall grades based on achievement). However, it is, in principle, possible to extract and report much more than just overall test scores from major tests, if this is considered useful for the stakeholders and if it is practical to do so. Recent interest in forms of assessment that support learning, such as formative (e.g., Black and Wiliam 1998), diagnostic (e.g., Alderson 2005; Alderson and Huhta 2011) and dynamic (e.g., Poehner and Lantolf 2013; Poehner and Infante, this volume) assessment has generated more interest in the value of detailed information and feedback from language assessments. Advances in the utilization of computers in testing have provided the tools to address this need in practice. The automatic calculation of sub-test and item level scores in computer based tests makes the provision of profile scores and detailed feedback a viable option for assessment organizations. Related advances in the automated analysis and evaluation of language learners' speech and writing offer truly amazing possibilities for detailed and individualized feedback to learners and their teachers (Chapelle 2008; Bernstein, Van Moere and Cheng 2010). Large-scale national assessments that provide detailed feedback to teachers and learners do not seem to exist yet. However, recent developments indicate that this may become more common in the future, such as the current plans in the Netherlands to introduce nationwide diagnostic tests in several subjects, including Dutch as L1 and English as a FL (see CITO 2014). It is likely that many other countries will introduce similar assessment systems in the future.

5 References

Alderson, J. Charles. 2004. The shape of things to come: Will it be the normal distribution? In: Michael Milanovic and Cyril J. Weir (eds.). *Studies in language testing 18: European language testing in a global context: Proceedings of the ALTE Barcelona Conference July 2001*, 1–26. Cambridge, UK: Cambridge University Press.

Alderson, J. Charles. 2005. *Diagnosing foreign language proficiency: The interface between learning and assessment*. London, UK: Continuum International Publishing.

Alderson, J. Charles. 2009. *The politics of language education: individuals and institutions*. Bristol: Multilingual Matters.

Alderson, J. Charles and Jayanti Banerjee. 2001. State of the Art Review: Language Testing and Assessment Part 1. *Language Teaching* 34: 213–236.

Alderson, J. Charles and Ari Huhta. 2011. Diagnosing strengths and weaknesses in second and foreign language reading: What do second language acquisition and language testing have to offer? *EUROSLA Yearbook* 11(1): 30–52.

Alderson, J. Charles and Karmen Pižorn (eds.). 2004. *Constructing school-leaving examinations at a national level – Meeting European standards*. Ljubljana, Slovenia: British Council and Državni izpitni center.

Alderson, J. Charles and Dianne Wall. 1993. Does washback exist? *Applied Linguistics* 14(2): 115–129.

Anderson, Scarvia B. 1975. *Encyclopedia of educational objectives*. San Francisco, CA: Jossey-Bass Publisher.

Bachman, Lyle F. 1990. *Fundamental considerations in language testing*. Oxford, UK: Oxford University Press.

Bachman, Lyle F. and Adrian Palmer. 1996. *Language testing in practice: Designing and developing useful language tests*. Oxford, UK: Oxford University Press.

Bailey, Kathleen M. 1996. Working for washback: A review of the washback concept in language testing. *Language Testing* 13(3): 257–279.

Bernstein, Jared, Alistair Van Moere and Jian Cheng. 2010. Validating automated speaking tests. *Language Testing* 27(3): 355–377.

Black, Paul and Dylan Wiliam. 1998. Inside the black box: raising standards through classroom assessment. *Phi Delta Kappan* 80(2): 139–48.

Brown, Annie. 2013. Uses of language assessments. In: Carol A. Chapelle (ed.). *The encyclopedia of applied linguistics*. Oxford, UK: Wiley-Blackwell. DOI: 10.1002/9781405198431.wbeal1237

Buck, Gary. 2009. Challenges and constraints in language test development. In: J. Charles Alderson (ed.). *The politics of language education: individuals and institutions*, 166–184. Bristol: Multilingual Matters.

Chapelle, Carol A., Mary K. Enright and Joan M. Jamieson (eds.). 2008. *Building a validity argument for the Test of English as a Foreign Language*. New York, NY: Routledge.

Chapelle, Carol A., Joan M. Jamieson and Volker Hegelheimer. 2003. Validation of a Web-based ESL Test. *Language Testing* 20(4): 409–439.

Cheng, Liying. 2005. *Changing Language Teaching Through Language Testing: A Washback Study*. Cambridge, UK: UCLES/Cambridge University Press.

CITO. 2014. De diagnostische tussentijdse toets. Tussenstand in http://www.cito.nl/onderwijs/voortgezet%20onderwijs/diagnostische_tussentijdse_toets (accessed 1 October 2014).

Council of Europe. 2001. *Common European Framework of Reference for Languages: Learning, Teaching, Assessment*. Cambridge, UK: Cambridge University Press.

Davies, Alan. 1990. *Principles of language testing*. Oxford: Blackwell.

Davies, Alan. 2014. Fifty years of language assessment. In: Antony Kunnan (ed.). *The Companion to Language Assessment I* 1(1): 1–21. John Wiley and Sons, Inc. DOI: 10.1002/9781118411360.wbcla127

Eckes, Thomas, M. Ellis, Vita Kalnberzina, Karmen Pižorn, Claude Springer, K. Krisztina Szollás and Constantia Tsagari. 2005. Progress and problems in reforming public language examinations in Europe: Cameos from the Baltic States, Greece, Hungary, Poland, Slovenia, France and Germany. *Language Testing* 22(3): 355–377.

European Commission. 2012. First European survey on language competences. Final report. http://ec.europa.eu/languages/policy/strategic-framework/documents/language-survey-final-report_en.pdf (accessed 22 June 2014).

EURYDICE. 2009. *National testing of pupils in Europe: objectives, organisation and use of results*. Brussels: Eurydice EACEA. http://eacea.ec.europa.eu/education/eurydice/documents/thematic_reports/109EN.pdf (accessed 1 October 2014).

Figueras, Neus. 2007. The CEFR, a lever for the improvement of language professionals in Europe. *The Modern Language Journal* 91(4): 673–675.

Figueras, Neus. 2012. The impact of the CEFR. *ELT Journal* 66(4): 477–485.

Fulcher, Glenn and Fred Davidson. 2009. Test architecture, test retrofit. *Language Testing* 26(1): 123–144.

Hassan, Nurul Huda and Shih Chih-Min. 2013. The Singapore-Cambridge General Certificate of Education Advanced-Level General Paper Examination. *Language Assessment Quarterly* 10(4): 444–451.

Heyneman, Stephen P. 1987. Uses of examinations in developing countries: selection, research, and education sector management. *International Journal of Educational Development* 7(4): 251–263.

Hughes, Arthur. 2003. *Testing for language teachers.* 2nd ed. Cambridge, UK: Cambridge University Press.

Inbar-Lourie, Ofra. 2013. Language assessment literacy. In: Carol A. Chapelle (ed.). *The encyclopedia of applied linguistics.* Oxford, UK: Wiley-Blackwell. DOI: 10.1002/9781405198431.wbeal0605.

Kunnan, Anthony J. 2008. Large scale language assessments. In: Elana Shohamy and Nancy Hornberger (eds.). *Language and Education* 7: 135–155. New York, NY: Springer.

Kunnan, Antony J. (ed.). 2014. *The Companion to Language Assessment.* Hoboken, NJ: Wiley-Blackwell.

Martyniuk, Waldemar and Jose Noijons. 2007. Executive summary of results of a survey on the use of CEFR at national level in Council of Europe member states. Intergovernmental Forum: The Common European Framework of Reference for Languages CEFR) and the development of language policies: Challenges and responsibilities. Strasbourg: Council of Europe, 6–8 February 2007, Report of the Forum. www.coe.int/t/dg4/linguistic/source/survey_cefr_2007_en.doc (accessed 1 October 2014).

Martyniuk, Waldemar (ed.). 2011. *Aligning tests with the CEFR: Reflections on using the Council of Europe's Draft Manual.* Cambridge, UK: Cambridge University Press.

Moe, Eli. 2012. Valid testing of young learners – an achievable endeavour? Presentation at the ALTE Conference, Munich, 23 November, 2012. http://www.alte.org/attachments/pdfs/files/valid_testing_of_young_learners_an_achievable_eneavour_eli_moe_166ml.pdf (accessed 1 October 2014).

Owen, Nathaniel. 2012. Can PTE Academic be used as an exit test for a course of academic English? Pearson Research Notes. http://pearsonpte.com/wp-content/uploads/2014/07/Owen_Executive_Summary.pdf (accessed 1 October 2014).

Pearson, Ian. 1988. Tests as levers for change. In: Dick Chamberlain and Robert J. Baumgardner (eds.). *ESP in the classroom: Practice and evaluation*, 98–107. Great Britain: Modern English Publications.

Pižorn, Karmen and Eli Moe. 2012. A validation study of the national assessment instruments for young English language learners in Norway and Slovenia. *CEPS journal* 2(3): 75–96. http://www.cepsj.si/pdfs/cepsj_2_3/cepsj_2_3_pp75_pizorn%20etal.pdf (accessed 9 February 2014).

Pižorn, Karmen and Edit Nagy. 2009. The politics of examination reform in Central Europe. In: J. Charles Alderson (ed.). *The politics of language education: individuals and institutions*, 185–202. Bristol: Multilingual Matters.

Poehner, Matthew and James Lantolf. 2013. Bringing the ZPD into the equation: Capturing L2 development during Computerized Dynamic Assessment (C-DA). *Language Teaching Research* 17(3): 323–342.

Poehner, E. Matthew and Paolo Infante. This volume. Dynamic assessment in the language classroom. In: Dina Tsagari and Jayanti Banerjee (eds.). *Handbook of Second Language Assessment.* Berlin: DeGruyter Mouton.

Qi, Luxia 2005. Stakeholders' conflicting aims undermine the washback function of a high-stakes test. *Language Testing* 22(2): 142–173.

Resnick, Lauren B. and Daniel P. Resnick. 1992. Assessing the thinking curriculum: New tools for educational reform. In: Bernard R. Gifford and Mary C. O'Connor (eds.). *Changing assessment: Alternative views of aptitude, achievement and instruction*, 37–76. London: Kluwer Academic Publishers.

Sawaki, Yasuo. 2012. Technology and language testing. In: Glenn Fulcher and Fred Davidson (eds.). 2012. *The Routledge handbook of language testing*, 426–437. New York, NY: Routledge.

Tannenbaum, Richard and Elaine C. Wylie. 2008. Linking English-language test scores onto the Common European Framework of Reference: An application of standard-setting methodology. RR-08-34. Princeton, NJ: Educational Testing Service.

Van Moere, Alistair and Ryan Downey. This volume. Technology and artificial intelligence in language assessment. In: Dina Tsagari and Jayanti Banerjee (eds.). *Handbook of second language assessment*. Berlin: DeGruyter Mouton.

Wall, Dianne. 2005. *The impact of high-stakes examinations on classroom teaching*. Cambridge, UK: UCLES/Cambridge University Press.

Wall, Dianne. 2013. Factors affecting long-term examination impact, and the fate of the examinations. Paper presented at the Tenth Annual Conference of EALTA, Istanbul, Turkey 23–26 May. http://www.ealta.eu.org/conference/2013/programme.html (accessed 29 July 2014).

Weir, Cyril J. 2004. *Language testing and validation. An evidence-based approach*. Basingstoke: Palgrave Macmillan.

Wu, Jessica R. W. 2012. GEPT and English Language Teaching and Testing in Taiwan. *Language Assessment Quarterly* 9(1): 11–25.

Carolyn E. Turner and James E. Purpura

16 Learning-oriented assessment in second and foreign language classrooms

1 Introduction

What comes to mind when the word *assessment* is mentioned for language class-rooms? How is it to be interpreted? For many years, it has mainly been viewed as a tool to record student achievement through the types of items and tasks employed in traditional large-scale testing. In reality, however, much more happens in classrooms in terms of using assessment to support learning and inform teaching. With the growing awareness of assessment activities internal to the classroom and managed by teachers, classroom assessment has become an emerging paradigm of its own with a focus on learning and an evolving research agenda (Turner 2012). This chapter underscores this paradigm and concentrates on the local context of classrooms, where assessment has the potential to serve the learning process. Specifically, the focus is on second and foreign language (henceforth, L2) classrooms, where it has been claimed that assessment can serve as the "bridge" between teaching and learning (Colby-Kelly and Turner 2007). This culture in L2 classrooms, where assessment is central, has been referred to as *learning-oriented assessment (LOA)* (Purpura 2004, 2009; and more recently Purpura and Turner, forthcoming). The LOA approach is not to be confused with nor is it in competition with other current L2 classroom assessment techniques (e.g., diagnostic, Alderson 2005; dynamic, Lantolf and Poehner 2011), but certainly shares common characteristics with them. Its premise is to begin with learning, that is, to prioritize learning when considering the interrelationships across instruction, assessment and learning. Although research has moved in the direction of exploring these relationships, no study to date has "proposed that the discussion begin with an examination of the learning process" followed by considerations of how assessment can serve to enhance this process (Purpura 2004, 2009). This is the central theme on which LOA is based. A related challenge is to identify and determine the ways in which teachers and learners can make use of assessments and capitalize on the generated information to guide and support the learning process.

In this chapter we propose an initial framework in which to provide a way forward to explore the following questions: What are the characteristics of assessment instances in the classroom (planned and unplanned) that appear to provide a context for learning, and how is this supported by a theory of learning? What is the evidence that indicates that these interventions bring about change in learning as viewed through changes in proficiency? What is the nature of teacher/student and student/student feedback and interaction that influences the effort towards an outcome of further learning? We do this by first situating the emergence of LOA in an interdisciplinary, historical setting, which focuses on context, learning theory, and proficiency. We then discuss current research within this context. Next, we build on the research to date and present a working framework, which serves to explain as well as deconstruct LOA. Finally, we examine key issues that affect LOA and provide our view of future directions, both in practice and research.

2 Historical lens and current research

Over the years assessment researchers have increasingly highlighted the central role that assessment plays in classrooms. Alongside these developments has been evolving research across several disciplines that has contributed to the nature of how assessment can be learning oriented. LOA draws on this literature as it moves towards refining its own definition.

2.1 General education

LOA has been motivated by formative assessment (FA) research on "content" learning in mainstream classrooms (specifically in math and science). Black and Wiliam (1998a) brought this research together in their review of 250 studies, where they found that "effective" use of classroom assessment produced student achievement outcomes (Wiliam 2011b: 13). Despite the challenges in such a review (e.g., variability in effect sizes due to classroom context, population and operationalization of the concept of FA), their review significantly furthered the discussion on the effectiveness of FA, which the Assessment Reform Group (ARG) began refining and labeled "assessment for learning (AFL)" (Black et al. 2004). Black and Wiliam's review also demonstrated that pedagogy has begun to view assessment as the collection of information to support and enhance learning, and that this change was driven by the nature of teachers' instructional activities, the students' active engagement in the assessment process (self/other), and the responsibility of the stakeholders to provide and respond to quality feedback. Four types of activities emerged as central to implementing FA: classroom dialogue (including discussion), comment-only marking, peer- and self-assessment, and formative use of summative tests. Expanding on these and wanting to situate FA more in a theoretical grounding, Wiliam and Thompson (2008) drawing on Ramaprasad (1983) and Sadler (1989), identified three processes prevalent in the current literature:

- Establishing where the learners are in their learning (assessment: teacher/self/ peer);
- Establishing where they are going (shared curriculum and intermediary goals);
- Establishing what needs to be done to get them there (instruction, self/peer-study).

They then related these to the three main stakeholders (i.e. agents): teacher, learner, and peer.

Simultaneously, as FA was being explored, research developments in specific areas of educational practice were gaining influence, and contributing to the idea and practice of assessment as being learning oriented. Some examples include: descriptive versus evaluative feedback (Tunstall and Gipps 1996), motivation (Harlen 2012), self-regulation and self-assessment (Andrade 2012a), peer assessment (Topping 2010), socio-cognition (Vygotsky 1978), and instructional design through formative assessment/assessment for learning (Black and Wiliam 2012).

Despite encouraging results from FA research, room for improvement still remains as this research also revealed an overemphasis on grades (less on learning); promotion of superficial/rote learning; inappropriate use of self-/peer-assessment; confusion and lack of consensus over traditional distinctions between summative and formative assessment; and a failure to highlight the importance of using quality feedback to close learning gaps (Black and Wiliam 1998b; Carless 2011; Fuchs and Fuchs 1986; Pellegrino, Chudowsky, and Glaser 2001; White and Frederickson 1998; Way, Dolan, and Nichols 2010). These accumulated findings have led to a reconsideration of the following features in classroom assessment: choice of tasks; content and strategies involved in classroom discourse; use and timing of feedback, questions, and grades; and teacher and student roles in the assessment process (Andrade 2012b; Brookhart 2003; Gardner 2012; Moss 2003; Wiliam 2011a, b). As a result, the following three areas of research have emerged with implications for practice: quality feedback; the roles of the stakeholders (teacher, learners, peers) in the assessment process; and the characteristics that distinguish summative from formative assessment. While these aspects all interface in classroom contexts, for the sake of explanation, each will be briefly discussed separately. Quality feedback is viewed as a salient component of learning, but research demonstrates that it serves no purpose unless it is used and acted upon by the learners to alter learning gaps (Sadler 1989). In other words, "what matters is the mindfulness with which students engage in the feedback" (Wiliam 2011a: 111). In addition, feedback does not serve learning if it consists only of a teacher grade. Pellegrino et al. (2001: 234) label FA as "assessment to assist learning" and in a section devoted to "classroom assessment" reiterate that in all cases of learning, feedback is "essential to guide, test, challenge, or redirect the learner's thinking." Wiliam (2011a) provides a discussion on "quality feedback" designed to move learning forward, where, through examples of scaffolding, he shows that effective feedback primarily concerns particular qualities of students' work, concluding that feedback is actually a very complex action to carry out successfully.

The second prevalent discussion in the literature highlights the salience of stakeholder roles in the FA process. In order to move learning forward, researchers increasingly conceptualize the classroom context as a "community of practice" (Wenger 1998), where cognitive, sociocognitive, and sociocultural factors all contribute to learning. In this view, teachers are clearly responsible for creating opportunities for FA in an effective learning environment. To accomplish this, however, they need to develop an understanding of how students learn (i.e. an understanding of cognition and learning in the area they teach) (Pellegrino et al. 2001) in order to develop appropriate assessments, recognize spontaneous moments for assessment, understand how to interpret the results, and make informed decisions concerning next steps. Teachers also need to help students understand the success criteria. This discussion highlights the ongoing need for pre- and in-service teacher education in these areas (Stiggins 2010). On the other hand, it also insists that students are responsible for their learning, and need to familiarize themselves with the success criteria and use the assessment information to guide their own learning by asking questions, reflecting, and revising their own work. These activities serve to motivate students to share in the responsibility, which, in turn, is likely to enhance learning (Deci and Ryan 1994). Also highlighted in the general education literature is the usefulness of self-assessment, self-regulation, and peer assessment in promoting learning (Andrade 2010a; Thompson, Pilgrim, and Lover 2005). Of note in this discussion is that self-assessment, when used to enhance the learning process, is not related to grades; it is comment based. Also, it is integrated into FA with the goal of guiding students to reflect on the quality of their own and their peers' work by referring to pre-set goals/criteria, and revising their work accordingly. Furthermore, in this context, student roles include peer-assessment.

The third prevalent discussion in the general education literature revolves around definitions of formative and summative assessment. Traditionally, these terms were labeled as distinctive (Harlen, 2012). Formative was viewed as "helping learning" and answering the question: *What are the next steps in learning?* Summative was viewed as "reporting on learning" and answering the question: *What has been achieved to date?* Harlen (2012) questions the usefulness of this dichotomy, preferring to describe them as a dimension of assessment purposes and practices. Harlen argues that different kinds of inferences are made depending on the purpose of the data. Brookhart (2010) views any kind of FA/SA distinction as blurred in classroom practice, and proposes a research agenda to explore "teacher mixing practices." Wiliam and Black (1996) observed problems with these distinctions early on. They maintained that it is not the actual instrument that dictates formative or summative assessment; rather, it is the function that the data generated serves. In other words, it is how the information is used that defines whether assessment is formative or summative. This situation remains confusing for teachers, because different sources take different views.

2.2 Second language education and LOA

We now turn to research on LOA in L2 classrooms. Although much of the theoretical and practical underpinnings of L2 LOA are informed by the educational psychology and general education research, LOA in L2 educational contexts has its own distinct focus, drawing primarily on research insights from L2 assessment, acquisition, classroom-based discourse, pedagogy, and L2 teacher education. As Colby-Kelly (2010) reiterates, it is important to recognize that most of the research in general education has been done in the science and math content areas. These subjects lend themselves well to anticipated linear learning progressions. Caution needs to be taken, however, when considering the implications for L2 contexts due to the often non-linear nature of L2 acquisition.

L2 assessment researchers have recognized the central role that assessment plays in L2 classrooms and specifically how it can contribute to L2 learning. The literature has been scattered, however, and only recently have there been efforts to synthesize L2 classroom assessment studies with the goal of pursuing a coherent research agenda (e.g., Davison and Leung 2009; Hill and McNamara 2011; Turner 2012). Even though L2 studies may appear segmented, the combination of their findings demonstrates considerable interest in classroom assessment. LOA draws on this research as it pertains to an assessment to enhance learning.

An examination of the L2 classroom assessment studies shows that research efforts have focused primarily on teachers and the teacher perspective. Some of the principal areas of interest include:

1. assessment as central to teaching and learning (Genesee and Upshur 1996; Leung 2004; McNamara 2001; Purpura 2004; Rea-Dickens 2008; Shohamy 1998; Turner 2012);
2. teacher processes in L2 assessment (Colby-Kelly and Turner 2007; Davison 2004; Leung and Teasdale 1997; Rea-Dickins 2001);
3. specific assessment methods employed by teachers (Brown and Hudson 1998; Cheng, Rogers, and Hu 2004);
4. teacher decision-making and rating scales (Brindley 2001; Chalhoub-Deville 1997; Turner and Upshur 2002);
5. the role of teacher knowledge, experience, beliefs in assessment (Rea-Dickins 2004; Yin 2010);
6. the role of diagnostic and dynamic assessment in promoting teaching and learning (Alderson 2005; Lantolf and Poehner 2011);
7. the value of self- and peer-assessment for promoting self-regulation, autonomy, motivation, and learner outcomes (Oscarson 1997; Patri 2002; Saito 2008); and
8. the role of technology in learning and assessment (Chapelle and Douglas 2006; Sawaki 2012).

In sum, theoretical and empirical research in both L2 and academic content assessment has provided many important insights. Findings suggest that the critical factors in the use of assessments to create and support an environment for learning involve: the context of the specific classroom, the classroom participants (learners, teachers, peers), and the relationships across these agents. Within these settings, LOA emphasizes the centrality of cognition, sociocognition, and processing as a basis for sustained development. It remains unclear, however, how the agents and dimensions of classroom assessment work together within a theory of LOA. It is also uncertain how empirical findings might contribute to a coherent set of localized best practices for conceptualizing and implementing classroom assessment within a learning framework. Due to the variability in and unpredictability of context and the diverse characteristics of classroom agents in classrooms, it appears unrealistic to propose a model of LOA. Some researchers have employed the word "messy" to describe such classroom-based explorations. We prefer to use the words "complex" or "multifaceted" due to the various combinations of interacting factors in each individual classroom. One message emerging from the literature is that "there appear to be no universal progressions/trajectories" in learning (e.g., one size does not fit all), whether in math or science (Daro, Mosher and Corcoran, 2011) or in languages (Colby-Kelly and Turner 2007). Identifying ongoing "learning" patterns can be complex in that development may transpire with no overt manifestation in performance (Pellegrino et al. 2001; Turner and Upshur 1995).

There is work to be done to further understand LOA due to the multiplicity of factors involved in L2 assessment from a learning orientation (Purpura and Turner forthcoming). Rather than a model, it seems a description of the dimensions underlying LOA might be helpful. In the next section we propose a working framework in an attempt to deconstruct the components of LOA. It acknowledges the close interrelationships among instruction, assessment, and learning, as experienced by teachers and learners working individually and collaboratively to advance learning.

3 What is a learning-oriented approach to language assessment?

A *learning-oriented assessment* (LOA) approach (Purpura 2004) maintains a clear and unambiguous focus on assessment in the service of learning through evidence elicited in a variety of L2 contexts. The inferences drawn from these assessments concern what L2 knowledge, skills and abilities (KSAs) learners have and how they develop competence within a specific domain. Unlike other assessment approaches, however, LOA prioritizes the interpretation of L2 performance evidence on both learning outcomes and L2 processes, so that goal-referenced decisions can be made by individual classroom agents to further L2 processing and achieve target-like performance. Thus, an LOA approach highlights learning goals, performance evaluation and feedback, and the role they play in developing individual learning progressions. In fact, an assessment cannot really be considered "learning-oriented" until evidence is available to demonstrate that feedback or other assistance related to a learning goal has led in some way to L2 system change. An LOA approach also assumes that learning an L2 is a highly individual cognitive process, and when situated within collaborative settings that depend on the participatory practices of interaction to exchange meanings or to jointly develop competencies, it is also a highly intricate socio-cognitive and sociocultural process. Finally, an LOA approach to assessment assumes that while curriculum, instruction, and assessment impact L2 processing and learning success, other factors (e.g., learner engagement) also play an important role in the assessment process of L2 learning.

4 A working framework of LOA

The goal of this chapter is to focus on the role of assessment as a vehicle for furthering learning. As a result, learners, and how they use information from assessment to close learning gaps and improve performance, are the central component of a learning-oriented approach to assessment. After all, learning from assessment cannot transpire without the learners' full engagement (Andrade 2010a; Hall and Goetz 2013; William 2010). Learning in classrooms, however, does not occur in a vacuum. Teachers, along with the curriculum and other elements of the learning context, play a critical role in facilitating (or inhibiting) processing and the achievement of learning outcomes, since it is curriculum and instruction that often guide what is assessed and how. Finally, while assessment is often perceived as only testing, in actuality, assessment occurs continuously, on a moment-to-moment basis, throughout instruction as learners, interacting with others, are made aware of their communicative successes and failures, and are given assistance when

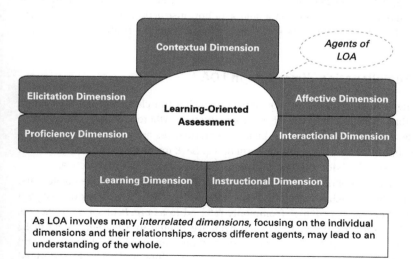

As LOA involves many *interrelated dimensions*, focusing on the individual dimensions and their relationships, across different agents, may lead to an understanding of the whole.

Fig. 1: Working framework of LOA.

needed. In sum, LOA is a very complex and multifaceted undertaking. This section highlights this complexity by discussing the various dimensions of LOA. In order to gain a more complete understanding of LOA and how it unfolds in the classroom, we propose a working framework with interrelated dimensions (see Figure 1). By studying these dimensions individually, we seek a more complete understanding of the whole.

4.1 The contextual dimension

On the macro-level, curriculum, instruction, and assessment in the service of learning are influenced by several contextual factors (Carless 2011; McMillan 2010). These include, among others, the socio-political forces that influence educational cultures and the sociocultural norms, assumptions, and expectations of classrooms (e.g., values associated with feedback). On the micro-level, curriculum, instruction, and assessment are driven by numerous contextual factors. Some relate to the personal attributes of teachers (e.g., experience); others relate to teacher choices such as the creation of a classroom culture conducive to the co-construction of meaning and knowledge, the sharing of feedback, and the importance of self-regulation. Teachers also make choices about what is taught, when, and how, and what role assessment will play in instructional processes. For example, one teacher may elect to assess through periodic planned, but ungraded, assessments embedded into the lesson, while another may assess only at the lesson's end in the form of an essay. Finally, micro-contextual factors involve a wide range of students' personal attributes (e.g., level of engagement). In sum, the contextual dimension is a critical dimension of LOA in that it sets parameters for how instruction, learning, and assessment will transpire within the social, cultural, and political context of learning.

4.2 The elicitation dimension in LOA

Eliciting language for assessment purposes inside the classroom involves much more than standardized tests. It involves situations where language is elicited in diverse ways by different agents. Learner performances are noticed, discussed, reflected upon, and reacted to in the form of feedback for further action. This section describes such activity internal to the classroom from an LOA perspective.

Inside classrooms, teachers use a wide range of *planned* language elicitations, the majority of which involve practice activities taken from a textbook or designed by a teacher. These activities (commonly referred to as *practice*) serve, in fact, as LOA, since they are designed to elicit evidence related to a learner's state of L2 KSAs, and to generate inferences about student performance through feedback and assistance. These elicitations are linked to the curriculum, and are fully embedded in instruction, with no grades assigned.

Planned elicitations come in many forms depending on the learning goal(s). They can be designed to ask learners to select or construct responses. For example, if the learning goal in beginning French is to distinguish between present and past tense verb forms, the teacher might ask students to underline the present and circle the past tense forms in a passage. She could then ask learners to compare answers with those of a peer, negotiate discrepancies, compare answers with a key, and resolve misunderstandings. In a different context, if the goal is to learn about dinosaur extinction, the teacher might ask students to use available resources (e.g., the internet) to create a poster to present to the class. Learners are given the criteria for success (e.g., precise language, meaningful content), and periodically, are asked to assess their own or a peer's work – to promote self-regulated learning. They are also given success criteria for the poster presentation. Presenters might have to evaluate their own posters according to specific criteria and compare their ratings with the teacher's. Learners then receive feedback and are asked to focus on improving their performance in a later activity.

While planned language elicitations embedded in instruction are important components of LOA, they represent a mere fraction of the elicitations that occur spontaneously in classrooms through observation or through mutually-constructed talk-in-interaction, as participants are working collaboratively to communicate and learn. Most *unplanned* or *spontaneous* elicitations are teacher-initiated, and engineered to evaluate a student's and group of students' state of KSA, with the goal of helping them notice, understand, remember, analyze, internalize, and use learning targets. Spontaneous elicitations also occur regularly when students are engaged in peer assessment. Teachers and students alike need to understand the importance of these discourse-based assessments in learning.

A final type of *planned* language elicitation in classrooms is the achievement test (e.g., quizzes, unit or midterm tests, finals), typically designed to evaluate performance and assign grades. In the best of circumstances, these will be learning-oriented in that teachers will use the information to infer both where students are in their development and the kind of scaffolded assistance they need to further processing and to close learning gaps. Unfortunately, many teachers downplay the importance of "going over the test."

In other instances, however, a brief quiz can be an effective means of having students and teachers check for understanding or application of a new learning point. For example, a quiz can be used to see if students know the meaning differences between the past and past progressive in English, or if they know past tense verb forms of regular Italian verbs. These elicitations are often not graded, serving only as a formal check.

In sum, classroom language elicitation comes with many purposes and in many forms and can serve LOA. The fundamental questions are: To what extent do these elicitations promote L2 processing and facilitate learning? Are they treated and capitalized on in a way that serves LOA? Figure 2 schematizes language elicitation in the form of assessments inside and outside the classroom.

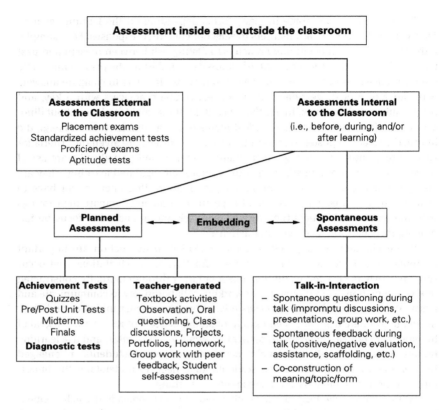

Fig. 2: Ways to elicit language for assessment inside and outside the classroom. How can they serve LOA?

4.3 The L2 proficiency dimension

The cornerstone of LOA is an explicit or implicit model of L2 proficiency, which underlies curriculum, instruction, and assessment. This model is used to characterize 1. what learners of different proficiency levels are taught in the aspirational curriculum (often mandated externally by standards or a school curriculum), 2. what they actually *are* taught in the enacted curriculum (the curriculum interpreted by teachers and students), 3. what students are ultimately expected to know and be able to do, and 4. how learners generally develop KSAs. The same model is used to inform 1. what should be assessed, 2. how evidence from performance is interpreted and tracked, and 3. what should be targeted by feedback and assistance. In LOA, learners should have a clear understanding of what it is that they are expected to learn and what the criteria for success are. Teachers and learners need to maintain a steady focus on the learning purpose and on L2 target(s) of instruction and assessment. This is especially important in L2 classrooms, where the opportunities for assessment and instruction are many, but where a focus on *too many* learning targets or targets beyond the learner's readiness will only lead to cognitive overload and confusion.

Given the importance of a model of L2 proficiency in L2 classrooms, teachers need to have a deep understanding of the language elements (e.g., forms, meanings and uses) and the skills (e.g., writing) they expect students to learn (referred to as *L2 content knowledge*). They also need to understand how L2 knowledge is conceptualized and developed over time (*knowledge of SLA*), how best to present this information to learners (*L2 pedagogical content knowledge*), and knowledge of the theme (e.g., cooperation and competition), topic (e.g., exotic marriages), or subject matter content (e.g., desalination) in which as L2 assessment is contextualized (*topical content knowledge*). Unfortunately, a research base in applied linguistics for making such complex learning decisions is not yet available. Consequently, L2 teachers, for better or worse, often base these decisions on intuition and practical experience. In sum, the proficiency dimension is a critical lens to consider in determining the effectiveness of LOA in furthering L2 processing or ultimate learning success.

4.4 The learning dimension

4.4.1 LOA and theories of learning and cognition

Another cornerstone of LOA is the learning dimension of L2 classrooms. Broadly speaking, this involves an understanding of how L2 learners process information and eventually learn, and the effect this has on how instruction and assessment are conceptualized and implemented, how performance evidence is interpreted, and how inferences from evidence are used to provide feedback and, if needed, learning assistance. Although L2 educators have their own opinions about how L2 learning is achieved, numerous theoretical conceptualizations of L2 learning and cognition exist in the literature, each having merit and offering insights. But given that no one theory of learning and cognition can accommodate all purposes of L2 learning, we believe that all theories have resonance, depending on what is being learned and in what context, and can contribute to our own understanding of L2 learning. Furthermore, in practice, we believe that teachers intuitively invoke several theories of learning and cognition in the implementation of LOA during instruction.

For example, in teaching intermediate learners to distinguish between the past and past progressive tenses to discuss "close calls" (*What were you doing when the storm hit?*), a teacher might provide students with an activity requiring them to discuss a recent "close call." They are encouraged to refer to their textbook for language support. The interaction contains several spontaneous elicitations, as students work together to construct meanings and understanding about the tenses through a discussion of close calls. This activity reflects a conceptualization of learning and LOA rooted to the assumption that learning transpires as interlocutors engage in the participatory practices of meaning making (i.e. clarifying, verifying, giving/responding to feedback) in social interaction.

4.4.2 Learning, LOA, the role of feedback and assistance

Another critical feature of LOA is the role of feedback in helping to close learning gaps. Feedback has many purposes. It can help learners develop an awareness of some aspect of the target learning point, sort out differences between new information and prior knowledge, remember new information, understand learning goals, and compare current performance with expected criteria for success. Feedback can also be given on learning processes, and on a range of other non-linguistic aspects of learning (e.g., effort).

Much has been written on feedback and its effectiveness in achieving learning success. One insight is that feedback is more effective when delivered prospectively – telling learners how to improve, rather than retrospectively – telling them what they did wrong (Wiliam 2010). Less research is available on how feedback, defined in terms of positive or negative evaluation moves accompanied by targeted assistance if needed, might promote L2 processing on the way to achieving learning success. In LOA, the role between the nature and quality of feedback in planned and unplanned language elicitation activities on the one hand and L2 processing and learning outcomes on the other are critical areas for further research and practice.

4.4.3 Learning, LOA and the role of self-regulation

Another important feature of LOA is the role that self-regulation plays in getting learners to be responsible for their own learning (Andrade 2010a; Wiliam 2010; Hall and Goetz 2013), and the extent to which self-regulation is successful in promoting L2 processing and ultimate learning success (Oxford 2011; Purpura 2013, 2014). Andrade (2010a: 91) defines self-regulated learning as "the process whereby learners set goals for their learning and then attempt to monitor, regulate, and control their cognition, motivation and behavior in order to reach their goals." The ability to self-regulate one's L2 learning or performance allows learners to step back and take stock, and is closely tied to the development of expertise (Bransford et al. 2000). Self-regulation typically refers to the use of *metacognitive strategies* (thinking) to set goals, plan, organize, self-monitor, and evaluate one's learning or performance (e.g., evaluating an essay) (Hall and Goetz 2013). However, for metacognitive strategies to be effective, they must translate into action, commonly referred to as *cognitive strategies (doing)*, such as reorganizing the essay or correcting grammar errors. In LOA contexts, learners also need to self-regulate their interaction (e.g., ask for clarification), and their affective dispositions (e.g., overcoming nervousness).

4.5 The instructional dimension

Fundamental aspects of classroom instruction are teachers' L2 content knowledge (i.e. knowledge of the language), their topical content knowledge (i.e. knowledge of the subject matter such as science), and their pedagogical content knowledge (i.e. knowledge of how to teach the language and topical content). These are included in the instructional dimension of LOA. Important questions are: How do these types of knowledge in relation to the theme/subject (e.g., science) being taught impact teachers' processing of content and their ability to use it when developing, adapting or adopting tasks for learning? Also, to what degree and in what ways does teachers' L2 content knowledge, their topical content knowledge, and their pedagogical content knowledge of the L2 impact learners' L2 processing and ultimate success? Or in the case of content based assessment, how does this impact the learners' processing of the new topical content and ultimate learning?

One clear finding in teacher education is that these types of knowledge are strong predictors of learning success (Lange et al. 2012). Most L2 teachers are usually familiar with the grammatical forms of the language and their metalinguistic labels (e.g., noun or verb), but are less familiar with the semantic meanings of the forms or how they are used in pragmatically appropriate ways in context. Teachers also often do not think about how language resources (the object of L2 instruction) relate naturally to topical content domains (e.g., science) or task domains (e.g., writing up a lab report). Fortunately, most teachers acquire this knowledge over time by teaching, seeing others teach, and through reflection. In the meantime, however, or if they do not acquire this knowledge, this could have a negative impact on LOA, because they would not know how to identify, categorize and resolve language performance errors (forms, meanings, uses). This would ultimately affect the quality of the assistance teachers could provide, which in turn could impact student learning.

4.6 The interactional dimension

Another important aspect of LOA is the interactional dimension. As all spontaneous language elicitation activities are embedded in talk-in-interaction, it is important to understand how LOAs are organized interactionally. In classroom contexts, interaction is typically organized as a sequence of two-or three-turn exchanges. These exchanges represent a number of patterns, including some that involve multiple turns over long stretches of talk. LOA is particularly interested in exchange patterns that provide a positive evaluation of a learner's learning or performance

(*Good!*) related to a learning goal, or a negative evaluation (*well* ...) followed by scaffolded assistance from teachers or peers in repairing some aspect of communication or learning with hints (*did that happen today or yesterday?*) or by a more elaborated learning intervention. These interventions will hopefully translate into student awareness of the problem with respect to a learning goal, and decisions on next steps, resulting in processing and ultimate learning success. These repair sequences can be seen as *unplanned* language elicitation activities that are fully embedded in classroom discourse and that focus on the co-construction of meaning or knowledge, followed by targeted action (an attempt to improve). As evaluation and assistance are organized interactionally as repair sequences, the nature and structure of these sequences are important as they may contribute to the effectiveness of feedback (i.e. evaluation and assistance) on learning success. Unfortunately, we know of little research on the structure of assessment-type repair sequences, and their effect on L2 processes and outcomes (see Tsagari and Michaeloudes 2012, 2013).

4.7 The affective dimension

As in the case of the sociocognitive dimension, nobody would question the fact that affective factors (e.g., engagement level) affect success in learning and play an important role in assessment. Thus, the affective dimension is another key lens through which to examine LOA (Hall and Goetz 2013). The affective dimension describes learners' socio-psychological predispositions to how learners experience and engage in the assessment process. The affective dimension is then concerned with characteristics such as the learners' emotions, their beliefs about learning and competence, their personality characteristics (e.g., extroversion), their attitudes towards learning and performance (e.g., persistence), and their motivation. Considerable research on these factors and language learning is available (Dörnyei 2005), but there is little research that examines the affective dimension of learning and assessment.

5 Future directions

This chapter examined several questions pertinent to LOA, laid out the research in which LOA is situated, defined LOA, and then presented a working framework to help deconstruct LOA to start understanding its complex nature. The working framework presented in the previous section is informed by empirical research as well as our own observations of classroom practice in educational settings (Purpura and Turner forthcoming). In our view, the work to date when pulled together in this framework has the potential to inform a robust research agenda.

This brings us to LOA and validity research. In discussing Black and Wiliam's (1998a) work, Moss (2003: 20–21) discusses the need to reconceptualize validity for classroom assessment since all learning events are situated in complex, social situations, which co-determine the results. She highlights the importance of case studies in classroom assessment and how validity needs to be conceptualized in "the contexts of the classrooms in which the assessment occurs" (Moss 2003: 20). Her comments help explain the complex nature of LOA, and why years of classroom assessment research ended by saying the setting was fraught with challenges when trying to determine any kind of model. These realizations in our own work have led us to develop a working framework as an alternative approach. It identifies several dimensions, as we have come to view them, when learning unfolds. In doing so, we conclude this chapter with persistent questions related to LOA that, in fact, address a way forward.

– What are the characteristics of language elicitation assessment instances in classrooms (planned and unplanned) that appear to provide a context for learning?
– What evidence indicates that sustained development has taken place as viewed through enhanced proficiency?
– What are the critical contextual, cognitive, socio-cognitive, and affective determinants of LOA?
– What is the nature of teacher and peer feedback and interaction that influences the effort towards an outcome of further learning in a sociocultural setting?
– How can teacher education best prepare teachers to understand how students learn, how they experience learning, and how to assess the development of student proficiency?
– How can teachers guide students to raise awareness of and effectively use information in both self- and peer assessment with the goal of self-regulation?
– To help address all of the above, how can we collect evidence from case studies that clearly display evidence of learning or learning impediments?

As we learn more about the potential of LOA through our work, we are encouraged. At the same time, we acknowledge that much work remains. For more information on some of the current research on LOA in L2 assessment and mainstream education, we recommend visiting the website for the first Roundtable on LOA in Classroom and Large-Scale Assessment Contexts held in October 2014 at Teachers College, Columbia University (http://www.tc.columbia.edu/tccrisls/).

6 References

Alderson, J. Charles. 2005. Diagnosing foreign language proficiency: The interface between learning and assessment. London: Continuum.

Andrade, Heidi L. 2010a. Students as the definitive source of formative assessment: Academic self-assessment and the self-regulation of learning. In: Heidi L. Andrade and Gregory J. Cizek (eds.). *Handbook of formative assessment*, 90–105. New York: Routledge, Taylor and Francis Group.

Andrade, Heidi L. 2010b. Summing up and moving forward: Key challenges and future directions for research and development in formative assessment. In: Heidi L. Andrade and Gregory J. Cizek (eds.). *Handbook of formative assessment*, 344–351. New York: Routledge, Taylor and Francis Group.

Black, Paul, Christine Harrison, Clare Lee, Bethan Marshall and Dylan Wiliam. 2004. Working Inside the Black Box: Assessment for Learning in the Classroom. *Phi Delta Kappan* 86(1): 8–21.

Black, Paul and Dylan Wiliam. 1998a. Assessment and classroom learning. *Assessment in Education: Principles, policy & practice* 5(1): 7–74.

Black, Paul and Dylan Wiliam. 1998b. Inside the black box: Raising standards through classroom assessment. *Phi Delta Kappan* 80(2): 139–148.

Black, Paul and Dylan Wiliam. 2012. Developing a theory of formative assessment. In: John Gardner (ed.). *Assessment and learning*, 2nd ed., 206–229. Los Angeles: Sage.

Bransford, John D., Ann L. Brown and Rodney R. Cocking (eds.). 2000. *How people learn: Brain, mind, experience and school*, expanded ed, Washington, DC: National Academy Press.

Brindley, Geoff. 2001. Outcomes-based assessment in practice: Some examples and emerging insights. *Language Testing* 18(4): 393–407.

Brookhart, Susan. 2003. Developing measurement theory for classroom assessment purposes and uses. *Educational Measurement: Issues and Practices* 22(4): 5–12.

Brookhart, Susan. 2010. Mixing it up: Combining sources of classroom achievement information for formative and summative purposes. In: Heidi L. Andrade and Gregory J. Cizek (eds.). *Handbook of formative assessment*, 279–296. New York: Routledge, Taylor and Francis Group.

Brown, James D. and Tom Hudson. 1998. The alternatives in language assessment. *TESOL Quarterly* 32(4): 653–675.

Carless, David. 2011. *From testing to productive student learning*. New York, NY: Routledge, Taylor and Francis Group.

Chapelle, Carol A. and Dan Douglas. 2006. *Assessing language through computer technology*. Cambridge, UK: Cambridge University Press.

Cheng, Liying, Todd Rogers and Huiqin Hu, 2004. ESL/EFL instructors' classroom assessment practices: Purposes, methods, and procedures. *Language Testing* 21(3): 360–389.

Chalhoub-Deville, Micheline. 1997. Theoretical models, assessment frameworks and test construction. *Language Testing* 14(1): 3–22.

Colby-Kelly, Christian. 2010. *Using "assessment for learning" practices with pre-university level ESL students: A mixed methods study of teacher and student performance and beliefs*. Montreal, QC: McGill University dissertation.

Colby-Kelly, C. and Carolyn E. Turner. 2007. AFL research in the L2 classroom and evidence of usefulness: Taking formative assessment to the next level. *Canadian Modern Language Review* 64(1): 9–37.

Daro, Phil, Frederic A. Mosher and Tom Corcoran. 2011. *Learning trajectories in mathematics (CPRE Research Report # RR-68)*. Consortium for Policy Research in Education. Retrieved from http://www.cpre.org/sites/default/files/researchreport/1220_learningtrajectoriesinmathcciireport.pdf (accessed January 2014).

Davison, Chris. 2004. The contradictory culture of teacher-based assessment: ESL teacher assessment practices in Australian and Hong Kong secondary schools. *Language Testing* 21(3): 305–334.

Davison, Chris and Constant Leung. 2009. Current issues in English language teacher-based assessment. *TESOL Quarterly* 43(3): 393–415.

Deci, Edward L. and Richard M. Ryan. 1994. Promoting self-determined education. *Scandinavian Journal of Educational Research* 38(1): 3–14.

Dörnyei, Zoltan. 2005. *The psychology of the language learner: Individual differences in second language acquisition*. Mahwah, NJ: Lawrence Erlbaum.

Fuchs, Lynn and Douglas Fuchs. 1986. Effects of systematic formative evaluation – A meta-analysis. *Exceptional Children* 53(3): 199–208.

Gardner, John. 2012. Quality assessment practice. In: John Gardner (ed.). *Assessment and learning*, 2nd ed. 103–121. Los Angeles, CA: Sage.

Genesee, Fred and John A. Upshur. 1996. *Classroom-based evaluation in second language education*. Cambridge, UK: Cambridge University Press.

Hall, Nathan C. and Thomas Goetz. 2013. *Emotion, motivation, and self-regulation: A handbook for teachers*. Bingley, UK: Emerald Group Publishing Limited.

Harlen, Wynne. 2012. The role of assessment in developing motivation for learning. In: John Gardner (ed.). *Assessment and Learning*, 2nd ed., 171–183. Los Angeles, CA: Sage.

Hill, Kathryn and Tim McNamara. 2011. Developing a comprehensive, empirically based research framework for classroom-based assessment. *Language Testing* 29(3): 395–420.

Lange, Kim, Thilo Kleickmann and Kornelia Möller. 2012. Elementary teachers' pedagogical content knowledge and student achievement in science education. In: Catherine Bruguiere, Andrée Tiberghien and Pierre Clément (eds.). E-Book Proceedings of the ESERA 2011 Conference: Science learning and Citizenship. Strand 13. Lyon, France: European Science Education Research Association.

Lantolf, James and Matthew Poehner. 2011. Dynamic assessment in the classroom: Vygotskyan praxis for second language development. *Language Teaching Research* 15(1): 11–33.

Leung, Constant. 2004. Developing formative teacher assessment: Knowledge, practice and change. *Language Assessment Quarterly* 1(1): 19–41.

Leung, Constant and Alex Teasdale. 1997. Expanding horizons and unresolved conundrums: Language testing and assessment. *TESOL Quarterly* 40(1): 211–234.

McMillan, James H. 2010. The practical implications of educational aims and contexts for formative assessment. In: Heidi L. Andrade and Gregory J. Cizek (eds.). *Handbook of formative assessment*, 41–58. New York, NY: Routledge.

McNamara, Tim. 2001. Language assessment as social practice: Challenges for research. *Language Testing* 18(4): 333–349.

McNamara, Tim and Carsten Roever. 2006. *Language testing: The social dimension*, Malden, MA: Blackwell Publishing.

Moss, Patricia. 2003. Reconceptualizing validity for classroom assessment. *Educational Measurement: Issues and Practices* 22(4): 13–25.

Oscarson, Matthew. 1997. Self-assessment of foreign and second language proficiency. In: Caroline Clapham and David Corson (eds.). *Encyclopedia of language and education*. Vol 7: *Language testing and assessment*, 175–187. Dordrecht, Germany: Kluwer Academic.

Oxford, Rebecca L. 2011. *Teaching and researching language learning strategies*. New York, NY: Pearson.

Patri, Mrubula. 2002. The influence of peer feedback on self- and peer-assessment of oral skills. *Language Testing* 19(2): 109–131.

Pellegrino, James W., Naomi Chudowsky and Robert Glaser (eds.). 2001. *Knowing what students know: The science and design of educational assessment*. Washington, DC: National Academy Press.

Purpura, James E. 2004. *Assessing grammar*. Cambridge, UK: Cambridge University Press.

Purpura, James E. 2009. The impact of large-scale and classroom-based language assessments on the individual. In: Lynda Taylor and Cyril J. Weir (eds.). *Language testing matters:*

Investigating the wider social and educational impact of assessment – Proceedings of the ALTE Cambridge Conference, April 2008, 301–325. Cambridge, UK: Cambridge University Press.

Purpura, James E. 2013. Cognition and language assessment. In: A. Kunnan (ed.). *Companion to Language Assessment III*, 12(86): 1452–1476. Oxford, UK: Wiley-Blackwell.

Purpura, James E. 2014. Language learner styles and strategies. In: Marianne Celce-Murcia, Donna Brinton and Ann Snow (eds.). *Teaching English as a Second or Foreign Language*, 4th ed., 532–549. Boston, MA: National Geographic Learning/Cengage Learning.

Purpura, James E. and Carolyn E. Turner. Forthcoming. *Learning-oriented assessment in language classrooms: Using assessment to gauge and promote language learning*. New York, NY: Routledge, Taylor and Francis.

Ramaprasad, Arkalgud. 1983. On the definition of feedback. *Behavioral Science* 28(1): 4–13.

Rea-Dickins, Pauline. 2001. Mirror, mirror on the wall: Identifying processes of classroom assessment. *Language Testing* 18(4): 429–462.

Rea-Dickins, Pauline. 2004. Understanding teachers as agents of assessment. *Language Testing* 21(3): 249–258.

Rea-Dickens, Pauline. 2008. Classroom-based language assessment. In: Elana Shohamy and Nancy H. Hornberger (eds.). *Encyclopedia of language and education*. Vol. 7: *Language testing and assessment*, 2nd ed., 257–271. New York, NY: Springer Science + Business.

Sadler, Royce. 1989. Formative assessment and the design of instructional systems. *Instructional Science* 18: 119–144.

Saito, Hidetoshi. 2008. EFL classroom peer assessment: Training effects on rating and commenting. *Language Testing* 25(4): 553–581.

Sawaki, Yasuyo. 2012. Technology in language testing. In: Glenn Fulcher and Fred Davidson (eds.). *The Routledge Handbook of Language Testing*, 426–437. New York: Routledge, Taylor and Francis Group.

Shohamy, Elana. 1998. Critical language testing and beyond. *Studies in Educational Evaluation* 24(4): 331–345.

Stiggins, Rick. 2010. Essential formative assessment competencies for teachers and school leaders. In: Heidi L. Andrade and Gregory J. Cizek (eds.). *Handbook of formative assessment*, 233–250. New York: Routledge, Taylor and Francis Group.

Thompson, Graham, Alan Pilgrim and Kristy Oliver. 2005. Self-assessment and reflective learning for first-year university geography students: A simple guide or simply misguided? *Journal of Geography in Higher Education* 29(3): 403–420.

Topping, Keith J. 2010. Peers as a source of formative feedback. In: Heidi L. Andrade and Gregory J. Cizek (eds.). *Handbook of formative assessment*, 61–74. New York, NY: Routledge.

Tsagari, Dina and George Michaeloudes. 2012. Formative assessment practices in private language schools in Cyprus. In: Dina Tsagari (ed.). *Research on English as a Foreign Language in Cyprus*. Vol. 2: 246–265. Nicosia: University of Nicosia Press.

Tsagari, Dina and George Michaeloudes. 2013. Formative assessment patterns in CLIL primary schools in Cyprus. In: Dina Tsagari, Salomi Papadima-Sophocleous and Sophie Ioannou-Georgiou (eds.). *International Experiences in Language Testing and Assessment*, 75–93. Frankfurt am Main: Peter Lang GmbH.

Tunstall, Pat and Caroline Gipps. 1996. Teacher feedback to young children in formative assessment: A typology. *British Educational Research Journal* 22(4): 389–404.

Turner, Carolyn E. 2012. Classroom assessment. In: Glenn Fulcher and Fred Davidson (eds.). *The Routledge Handbook of Language Testing*, 65–78. New York: Routledge, Taylor and Francis Group.

Turner, Carolyn E. and John A. Upshur. 2002. Rating scales derived from student samples: Effects of the scale maker and the student sample on scale content and student scores. *TESOL Quarterly* 36(1): 49–70.

Upshur, John A. and Carolyn E. Turner. 1995. Constructing rating scales for second language tests. *English Language Teaching Journal* 49(1): 3–12.

Vygotsky, Lev. 1978. *Mind in society: The development of higher psychological processes.* Cambridge, MA: Harvard University Press.

Way, Walter D., Robert P. Dolan and Paul Nichols. 2010. Psychometric challenges and opportunities in implementing formative assessment. In: Heidi L. Andrade and Gregory J. Cizek (eds.). *Handbook of formative assessment*, 297–315. New York, NY: Routledge, Taylor and Francis Group.

Wenger, Etienne. 1998. *Communities of practice.* Cambridge, UK: Cambridge University Press.

White, Barbara and John R. Frederickson. 1998. Inquiry, modeling, and metacognition: Making science accessible to all students. *Cognition and Instruction* 16(1): 3–118.

Wiliam, Dylan. 2010. An integrative summary of the research literature and implications for a new theory of formative assessment. In: Heidi L. Andrade and Gregory J. Cizek (eds.). *Handbook of formative assessment*, 18–40. New York, NY: Routledge.

Wiliam, Dylan. 2011a. *Embedded formative assessment.* Bloomington, IN: Solution Tree Press.

Wiliam, Dylan. 2011b. What is assessment for learning? *Studies in Educational Evaluation* 37(1): 3–14.

Wiliam, Dylan and Paul Black. 1996. Meanings and consequences: A basis for distinguishing formative and summative functions of assessment. *British Educational Research Journal* 22(5): 537–548.

Wiliam, Dylan and Marnie Thompson. 2008. Interpreting assessment with instruction: What will it take to make it work. In: Carol A. Dwyer (ed.). *The future of assessment: Shaping teaching and learning*, 53–82. Mahwah, NF: Lawrence Erlbaum Associates.

Yin, Muchun. 2010. Understanding classroom language assessment through teacher thinking research. *Language Assessment Quarterly* 7(2): 175–194.

Matthew E. Poehner and Paolo Infante
17 Dynamic Assessment in the language classroom

1 Introduction

A commonly held perspective, and one that resonates with initiatives such as formative assessment and assessment-for-learning, views classroom-based assessment as not merely providing evidence of previous learning or mastery of material but also as a means of guiding teachers' subsequent instructional decisions by helping to identify areas in which additional effort is needed for learners to reach an established criterion (for examples, see Tsagari and Csépes 2011). Our understanding of the writings of Russian psychologist, L. S. Vygotsky (1978, 1987), originator of the Sociocultural Theory of Mind (SCT), compels us to take a somewhat different perspective, wherein teaching and assessment are understood as dialectically related features of a single educational activity intended to promote learner development. It is this view that defines our understanding of and approach to Dynamic Assessment (henceforth, DA). The defining feature of DA, and what distinguishes it from other conceptualizations of assessment, is that it intentionally aims to provoke change in the abilities being assessed. DA advocates the provision of feedback or other forms of support (e.g., prompts, models, leading questions) during the procedure for the purpose of observing learner responsiveness. In most conventional assessments, such a move would likely be regarded as compromising the information obtained about learner abilities. DA, in contrast, maintains that how learners respond during this interaction reveals how close they are to more independent functioning; the more support learners require, the greater the investment will be before they will perform the relevant tasks on their own. At the same time, the quality of this interaction aims to further promote learner development. Thus, the term 'assessment' from this perspective entails both the activity of obtaining insights into learner abilities as well as the beginning of a process to stimulate continued development.

In this chapter, we provide an overview of L2 DA work as well as the relevant principles of SCT that inform DA practice. Especially important is the tenet that *mediation* is the primary driver of the development of human psychological abilities. After discussing mediation in relation to Vygotsky's general explanation of psychological development, we consider how the concept has been interpreted and realized in DA. We then provide examples from a recent L2 DA project that showcase the process through which learner development is diagnosed and promoted. We also highlight the fact that this work represents an important step forward from much previous DA research as it broadens the analytical focus beyond interaction between assessor/teacher (or mediator) and learner to also include the introduction of other resources into the procedure. Specifically, this project examines mediator and learner use of pedagogical materials representing abstract conceptual knowledge relevant to the immediate language tasks employed in the activity. We conclude with commentary concerning questions of the feasibility of implementing DA in L2 educational contexts.

2 Vygotsky's Sociocultural Theory of mind

Perhaps the clearest articulation of Vygotsky's scientific enterprise and its relation to other trends in psychology occurs in his influential paper *The historical meaning of the crisis in psychology: A methodological investigation* (Vygotsky 1997). Here Vygotsky outlines a framework to unify the various branches of psychology by proposing concepts and principles that allow for the systematic explanation of phenomena in each of the specialized fields and sub-fields of the discipline. In its broadest sense, then, the aim of SCT is to provide a coherent account of the human mind, including the processes of its formation. Understanding this as Vygotsky's aim helps to clarify why his proposals have been taken up in fields ranging from special education to child development to second language acquisition.

2.1 Development through mediation

Full discussion of Vygotsky's theory is beyond the scope of this chapter. Interested readers are referred to Lantolf and Poehner (2014) for a detailed examination of SCT and its implications for L2 education. For purposes of the present discussion, we wish to stress that the hallmark of the theory is that the human mind emerges as a process wherein biologically endowed psychological abilities (e.g., memory, attention, perception) are transformed through social and cultural means. More specifically, Vygotsky held that just as human beings create and employ physical tools to mediate our physical activity in the world, we also create and employ semiotic tools to mediate our psychological activity. Essential to this process is social interaction, which relies upon our greatest semiotic tool, language, and allows us access to the knowledge and experiences of others. Through interaction we encounter other culturally available semiotic tools (e.g., counting systems, art, conceptual knowledge). As we gain greater facility with these tools, we come to control, or regulate, our psychological functioning, and this allows us to think, plan, reflect, and create in intentional ways rather than merely reacting to stimuli in our immediate field of sensory perception, as occurs in the world of other animals. For this reason, mediation is considered in SCT to be the primary driver of human psychological abilities.

An important corollary of this view of human abilities is that psychological development is a process that can continue across the lifespan as individuals continue to encounter and appropriate semiotic tools. These tools are initially encountered in an external form, as for example, when learners in school are introduced to models, charts, and images that they may use to mediate their engagement in problem-solving or other instructional tasks. However, unlike physical tools, the meaning these semiotic tools carry can be internalized such that they lead to new understandings and new ways of acting in the world, regardless of whether they are present in their external form. In fact, Vygotsky (1987) argued that the major contribution of formal schooling to psychological development is that it creates opportunities for learners to internalize abstract conceptual knowledge from various subject areas that represent the cumulative accomplishment of human societies.[1]

2.2 The Zone of Proximal Development

While Vygotsky was committed to the idea that development may continue across the lifespan, much of his own research examined processes of development as they occurred during very short periods of time, often during the course of an experiment. Wertsch (1985) coined the term *microgenesis* to capture this phenomenon, and the concept has subsequently received a good deal of attention in educational research framed by SCT. Such studies have generally followed the approach Vygotsky established in his own research of introducing forms of mediation while individuals work through difficult tasks in order to understand their responsiveness. External mediation might include symbolic tools, dialogic interaction, or both. Experiments of this sort led Vygotsky to his most well known proposal, the *Zone of Proximal Development (ZPD)*. Vygotsky (1978: 86) explained the ZPD in terms of the contrast between the level of functioning individuals reach independently (i.e. relying on internalized forms of mediation to self-regulate) and the level they reach when external forms of mediation are provided. From the perspective of a diagnosis, this range is indicative of abilities that have not yet fully formed but are in the process of developing. Judged in relation to a set criterion, the greater an individual's reliance on external forms of mediation, the further s/he is from self-regulating.

---

1 It is worth noting that while Vygotsky (1978) conceived of schooling as a leading activity of development during later childhood and adolescence, he also famously advocated the developmental importance of play. In fact, he described socio-dramatic play as the leading activity of development during early childhood. In his analysis, children come to a sophisticated understanding of how signs function during play, as objects and individuals can be assigned various meanings within the context of play activity and individuals are free to try on different social roles. This development provides the necessary background for the more complex use of sign systems as children enter school and develop literacy and numeracy (see Karpov 2005).

In contrast, individuals who require relatively little external mediation are much closer to being able to function fully independently.

An additional insight that becomes available when engaging with learners as they encounter difficulties concerns the psychological processes underlying development. Through questioning and prompting, mediators endeavor to externalize learner thinking, rendering what Vygotsky (1978) called *intramental functioning* visible on the external plane of dialogic interaction. This allows mediators to identify sources of difficulty and to jointly engage in *intermental functioning* with learners by collaboratively working through tasks. It is in this regard that the ZPD is of importance not only to diagnosing learner abilities but also to intervening to guide developmental processes (Poehner 2008). As Vygotsky (1998) explained, the significance of the ZPD for education is that it allows instructional decisions to optimally align with learners' emerging abilities. In particular, instruction should not be too far beyond what individuals are capable of nor should it wait for development to happen; rather, abilities that have not fully developed but are in the process of forming are the ones that can most easily be guided by instructional intervention. This insight is the basis for the view of DA as an activity in which teaching and assessment are dialectically related (see Lantolf and Poehner 2004; Poehner 2008, 2009a).

Before concluding this section, we wish to briefly describe an illustration of the ZPD that Vygotsky frequently used and that points to its relevance for assessment. Vygotsky (e.g., 1978) refers to two children who are able to successfully complete tasks at a given age level but who respond differently when offered mediation in the form of prompts and leading questions. Specifically, this process brings into the one child's reach tasks that are a full two years beyond his independent level of functioning. The other child, in contrast, progresses to tasks that are only a half-year over what he accomplished independently. For Vygotsky, this raises two important points. The first is that while the children appear to be the same with regard to their independent functioning, they differ in terms of their ZPD. Thus, for assessment to capture the full range of an individual's abilities it must be organized to target not only independent performance but responsiveness to mediation as well. The other, related, point is that one cannot simply infer the ZPD on the basis of independent performance. Indeed, if this were the case then the two children in Vygotsky's example would have exhibited very similar responses when offered mediation and the ZPD would not have added anything to the diagnosis of their development. Both of these points have been further substantiated by research since Vygotsky's time that has employed the ZPD as a guiding concept in the design, administration, and interpretation of assessments. Collectively, these approaches are referred to as DA.

3 Dynamic Assessment

While L2 DA research has underscored ZPD activity as a teaching-assessment dialectic that both diagnoses and promotes learner development, this has not been the majority view among DA proponents in the fields of cognitive education and psychology. Elsewhere, Poehner (2008, 2009a) has suggested that the commitment among DA practitioners in those fields to viewing assessment as an activity separated from teaching may be due to the strong tradition in those fields of emphasizing standardized administration procedures and reliance on statistical analysis of test scores. As should be clear, from the point of view of the ZPD, the search for ways to connect assessment with teaching makes little sense as their separation in the first place is erroneous; one may wish to foreground assessment or teaching at particular times and for particular purposes and audiences, but they remain two features of developmental education (Lantolf and Poehner 2014).

3.1 Approaches to DA

Much of the research in DA has been concerned with identifying latent capacities among individuals believed to underperform on conventional assessments that simply describe their performance as correct or incorrect (Sternberg and Grigorenko 2002). Within this tradition of DA, the procedures are seen as sampling individuals' propensity for change rather than trying to provoke or stimulate learner development during the procedure itself. Perhaps reflecting this orientation to sampling responsiveness rather than guiding development, the most widely used DA format in psychological research consists of test, intervention, and post-test stages reminiscent of the classic pre-test – treatment – post-test experimental design (Haywood and Lidz 2007). According to Haywood and Lidz, it is the three stages taken together that render the assessment dynamic, with the original test administration providing a baseline of learner actual development and the retest seeking to capture any change in learner development brought about by the intervention. The intervention stage itself is typically aimed at helping learners understand principles and concepts relevant to the tests.

Another common format for administering DA embeds mediation in the test itself, so that some form of support is available for each item or task in the assessment. As with the test-intervene-retest format, specific approaches to DA differ with regard to how they conceptualize mediation. In some, mediation is scripted in advance of the procedure and offered in a standardized form. For example, the *Graduated Prompt Approach* to DA developed by Anne Brown and colleagues (e.g., Campione et al. 1984) relies upon prompts or hints that are arranged from most implicit (e.g., suggesting that a learner check his/her answer) to most explicit (revealing the solution and providing an explanation). The most implicit prompt is offered when a learner's first (independent) attempt is unsuccessful, and the process of offering an additional prompt following each subsequent attempt is continued until either the learner succeeds or the mediator reveals the solution. The level of prompting required is interpreted as an indication of the learner's relative distance from independent functioning. Lantolf and Poehner (2004) have proposed the term *interventionist DA* to refer to approaches that orient to mediation as a kind of treatment administered to learners in a standardized manner to evaluate their responsiveness. They contrast this tradition of DA with *interactionist DA* approaches, which favor dialogic interaction between mediators and learners.

In interactionist DA, mediators are able to anticipate problems learners might encounter during the procedure because they understand the task specifications and dimensions employed in the assessment as well as the underlying constructs to be evaluated. However, they do not script mediation in advance, opting instead to continually calibrate their support to learner needs and responsiveness during the assessment. As a result, interactionist DA typically yields qualitative profiles of learner development instead of precise counts of the number of prompts used. Following Lantolf and Poehner (2004), the preference in interactionist DA for open-ended dialoguing and qualitative profiling of development means that comparisons across learners become more challenging, and thus such approaches may be better suited to classroom contexts than to large-scale testing situations, where an interventionist DA approach would likely be more efficient. To date, L2 DA has primarily been pursued in instructional contexts and has followed an interactionist approach, encouraging mediators and learners to collaboratively examine problems, propose and implement solutions, and reflect on outcomes.

3.2 DA and L2 development

As in cognitive education and psychology, mediation in L2 DA has principally been conceived in terms of what mediators *say* to learners during the activity. This is true regardless of whether mediator utterances are following a scripted inventory or reflect the mediator's interpretation of learner needs at a particular moment during interaction. For example, Poehner (2009b) describes an approach to mediation developed by a primary grades teacher of L2 Spanish. During her instructional planning each day, the teacher designed a menu of six to eight prompts that she used to mediate learners as they encountered difficulties completing tasks. The first prompt was to simply pause when a learner produced an error in order to determine if this was sufficient for the learner to recognize the problem and self-correct. Aside from this initial prompt, the remaining were all verbal in nature, with the teacher indicating that an error was made, drawing learner attention to the location of the error, employing metalinguistic terminology to help the learner identify the nature of the error, offering learners a choice between two forms, and revealing and explaining the necessary linguistic form. The teacher's approach to mediation was itself inspired by the work of Aljaafreh and Lantolf (1994), who reported on tutor-learner efforts to engage in ZPD activity in the context of ESL writing instruction. Although Aljaafreh and Lantolf's study was not framed as DA, the 'regulatory scale' of mediator behaviors that they described influenced considerably the subsequent work of L2 DA researchers. As with the classroom teacher in

Poehner's (2009b) study, the fourteen points on Aljaafreh and Lantolf's scale primarily concern verbal behaviors directed to help learners identify and overcome difficulties.[2]

3.3 Broadening the scope of mediation in L2 DA beyond interaction

As explained, Vygotsky understood schooling to offer a unique opportunity for the provision of academic content knowledge, presented as abstract concepts that learners might appropriate as tools for solving problems within particular domains. The research of Gal'perin (1992) and Davydov (2008) offered robust models of instructional systems organized around sets of abstract concepts that included specific recommendations for how concepts can be represented and explained to learners as well as activities that support learners' use of the concepts as tools for thinking. A growing body of research reports efforts to develop concept-based approaches to L2 education (for examples, see Lantolf and Poehner 2014). These studies have been carried out with learners of a range of languages and have focused on topics including locative prepositions, phrasal verbs, and interpreting and using sarcasm. While the precise methods employed in concept-based teaching vary, they generally include a visual depiction of the concept through images or models, verbal explanations of the concept, activities in which learners refer to the images and models while making choices about language use, and elicited verbalizations from learners of how they are thinking about the ways they can use the L2 to construct and express particular meanings. According to Negueruela (2003), the aim of concept-based instruction is to help learners move beyond simple rules that characterize patterns of L2 use and to enable them to more expertly control the language for their own purposes. In the next section, we discuss an ongoing L2 DA project in which dialogic interaction and a conceptual tool function in tandem to help a mediator diagnose and promote an L2 English learner's understanding of the English tense and aspect system during a writing activity.

4 Illustrating social and cultural mediation in L2 DA

The teaching and learning of the English tense and aspect system has been noted as a source of difficulty for L2 learners of English (Bardov-Harlig and Reynolds

---

2 More recent L2 DA work has broadened beyond reporting mediator verbal utterances to include nonverbal features of interaction and has drawn on various traditions within discourse analysis, including Conversation Analysis, for documenting these behaviors and interpreting how they function in DA interactions (e.g., Poehner and van Compernolle 2011).

1995; Celce-Murcia and Larsen-Freeman 1999; Ganem-Gutierrez and Harun 2011). For this study, learners were recruited from an ESL composition course at a large American research university during the 2013 spring semester. The aim of the project is to investigate the use of DA principles along with a concept-based approach to help L2 learners better control the English tense and aspect system as they construct meaning in everyday and academic writing. As our interest in this chapter is to highlight how dialogic mediation and symbolic tools can together create opportunities for diagnosing learner abilities and promoting development, we limit our discussion to a single DA session where this process is particularly salient.

Before turning to the DA interaction, some preliminary information about the approach to tense and aspect followed in this project will help readers to follow how mediator and learner oriented to the writing task. Briefly, tense refers to a speaker/writer's perspective on time when viewing an action or event, and as such it represents a set of choices regarding how to convey the action or event to a perceived audience (Fauconnier 2007). Aspect, on the other hand, represents a perspective that is "internal" to an event or action (Comrie 1976). In particular, the inner properties of an event or action are delineated by the presence or absence of clearly demarcated beginning and end boundaries. In this way, one may opt to use the simple aspect to signal an event or action with definite boundaries while progressive aspect portrays the same action or event as continuous rather than completed or as having no definite boundaries. Perfect aspect denotes events or actions that occurred during a preceding point in time but that have an indefinite end boundary and thus may still be relevant in the present. To be sure, tense and aspect work together to create particular perspectives on actions and events, and the responsibility of a writer is to ascertain which perspective s/he wishes to create and then to make the appropriate tense and aspect selections.

The concept-based approach followed in this project sought to make these choices – and their consequences for the meanings expressed to readers – explicit through a symbolic tool that in included verbal definitions of the concepts of tense and aspect as well as visual representations of events and how they might be viewed in relation to the present and the presence or absence of beginning and end boundaries. These materials were introduced to participants in the program and contrasting example sentences were discussed to highlight the different meanings expressed through one tense-aspect selection or another.

The three data excerpts that follow were taken from a DA session involving one learner, Nadia (a pseudonym). Like other learners in the program, Nadia had been asked to produce an initial written composition that was reviewed by the mediator, a veteran ESL teacher who was also well acquainted with Vygotskian theory, including DA and concept-based pedagogies. Nadia's composition, like those of other participants, revealed numerous errors and inconsistencies in her use of tense and aspect. Weekly sessions were organized over approximately eight weeks during which learners met one-on-one with the mediator. For each session, learners were asked to prepare a composition that would be the focus of interaction. The excerpt below is from the second session in the program, at which point Nadia had been introduced to the pedagogical materials and was attempting to understand how to use them while writing and revising her compositions. As will become clear, Nadia's responses to the mediator's questions and prompts over the course of the three data excerpts below provide insights into her understanding of tense and aspect. At the same time, the relevance she assigns to the pedagogical materials and her attempts to make use of them during the session are also revealing of both her understanding of the concepts but also her ability to use this understanding to orient to the writing task and employ the L2 to appropriately convey her intended meanings.

For this particular session, Nadia prepared an essay on the topic of her experiences as an English language learner. Prior to reviewing the narrative, Nadia with the assistance of the mediator was asked to verbalize her understanding of the pedagogical materials, a move that in itself featured in the diagnosis of her abilities. According to the mediator, Nadia articulated a detailed understanding of tense and aspect, as explained and illustrated in the pedagogical materials. The dyad then turned to reviewing the narrator. We enter the exchange at a point when the mediator (M) identified a specific portion of the text they could jointly analyze: *One important reason to go to college is for an opportunity to receive a higher education. However, I worried about my English. Because I am as a non-native speaker can study material or I can understand them.* Nadia (N) struggled to determine which language feature she would like to examine, and she elected instead to rearrange the elements of the sentence.[3]

(1)

1. N: *However, I worried about my English.* ++ *Because I am as a non-native speaker* (7) mhm (4) because uhh (7) like uhh (11) however I uhh (4) I thought

---

3 Transcription conventions are as follows:

**	quieter in volume than surrounding talk
+	short pause
++	long pause
+++	very long pause
.	full stop marks falling intonation
?	question mark indicates raised intonation (not necessarily a question)
(word)	single parentheses indicate uncertain hearing
((comment))	double parentheses contain transcriber's comments or descriptions
-	abrupt cutoff with level pitch
underline	underlining indicates stress through pitch or amplitude
italics	words from participant's composition
=	latched utterances

like I thought <u>how</u> + I can study material for under<u>standing</u> them as a non-native speaker ((N looks up at M))

2. M: <u>sure</u> + so we can change the order + or maybe change a few things with that + I am just wondering what time frame + uhm + are we currently in with this sentence + what time frame + =

3. N: = uhm =

4. M: = are you creating here?

5. N: (12) Uh + because on that time (2) uhm I really don't know uhm I'm in college + like I was in college or not ++ so it would be + uhm ((N looking down at the pedagogical instrument)) event 2

6. M: *okay*

7. N: (2) event 2 I think <u>uhm</u> because we don't know when the action start and we don't <u>know</u> + the end of the boundary I think

We see beginning in turn 2 that M attempts to prompt N to consider how she wishes to portray being a college student and being concerned about her English abilities as the selection of a perspective on time (or "time frame") is an important first step for determining which tense and aspect choices best suit the meaning she wishes to convey. After a long pause of twelve seconds (turn 5), N expresses her confusion stating that she wanted to express two time perspectives: her current reality as a college student and a past reality in which her concern about her English abilities began. Based on these semantic requirements for her choice of verb tense and aspect, she consulted the pedagogical tool and selected event 2, the past progressive, as a candidate response.

N went on to supply a justification for her choice, indicating that the action has a starting boundary but not one that clearly marks an ending. N's explanation was therefore revealing of the source of her difficulty. At issue was not merely the use of particular verb forms but rather N was attempting to think of events as temporally bounded, but doing so explicitly was new to her and was resulting in challenges in determining the precise meaning she wished to express and the tense-aspect options that would convey it. In response to N's attempt to invoke the concepts of tense and aspect to explain her choices, M physically placed the pedagogical materials in a central position in front of them and requested that they make greater use of them to guide their thinking. This move is important because while N had clearly taken up something from the explanations and introduction of the pedagogical materials, as evidenced by her references to boundaries, she had not yet internalized the conceptual meanings they represented and was therefore unable to use the tools on her own to mediate her tense and aspect choices. The materials therefore continued to be required in their external form, and in fact M's presence was also necessary to guide N's use of them.

At M's prompting, N consulted the materials once again, but this resulted in her oscillating between whether the event had any boundaries at all. M then intervened to mediate the meaning of the visual representations and their relevance to the task at hand. We resume the interaction at this point:

(2)
8. M: okay so you're saying we don't have any boundaries + ((M points to image of event 2 on instrument)) do you see the action <u>being</u> + firmly placed in the past?
9. N: (3) past and continue
10. M: to when? =
11. N: = to now + I am worried now too about my English ++ and how understanding you know the material of the class like + uh I don't know the end of the boundary too
12. M: okay
13. N: *that is my feeling I think*
14. M: and so you said that we don't know the end of the boundary
15. N: no
16. M: so uhm ++ but does the + action continue to today?
17. N: yes
18. M: okay so let's look at our- our didactic tool for a moment + what + tense aspect combination would fit your description?
19. N: (3) it's would be uhhh (5) like uh not the past perfect + the past progressive?

In turn 8, M inquired whether N wished to convey a meaning that resided solely in the past, to which N reiterated that the tense and aspect combination must both reflect her past experiences but "continue" to her present reality, although she was still unable to connect this information to the present perfect (event 3) (turn 11). Furthermore, this exchange prompted N to identify the verb phrase (i.e. copula and past participle) "be worried" as the linguistic feature she would eventually correct based on her choice of tense and aspect.

At this point, M echoed N's remarks about the state of her worries beginning but continuing to the present time, thereby confirming how N wished to portray this in the context of her narrative. M then directed their attention back to the pedagogical materials in order to help N connect the abstract representations (verbal and imagistic) of the materials to her desired message (turn 20):

(3)
20. M: no no + it's firmly placed in the past. +++ and it's- if we look back to our descriptions ((pointing to slide 1)) uhm it's an action that yes it does not have any definite boundaries + the past progressive + but if we look at here ((pointing to slide 2)) all three tense aspect combinations of the recalled point we see that the past progressive is only in the past ((pointing to event 2 on slide 2)) it's firmly placed back there

> N: (3) so if I want to say- it would be past perfect
> M: past perfect?
> 23. N: uhm present perfect sorry
> 24. M: okay ( ) and because- why the present perfect
> 25. N: because it continues to now ((N slides pencil along the timeline from the beginning boundary to the end of the event 3 aspect frame on slide 2)) it's much uh uh + closer view to this action + I think it would be present perfect ((N looks up at M))
> 26. M: yeah great ((head nodding))

M's explicit metalinguistic explanation (turn 20) directly referenced the pedagogical materials, serving not only to underscore why N's suggestion of the past progressive did not correspond to her intended meaning but also modeling how the materials may be called upon to mediate selection of linguistic forms. After a short pause, N provided another tense and aspect combination, the past perfect, to resolve the dilemma (turn 21). What is important to note here is that the past perfect was not mentioned in the pedagogical instrument, and in fact N had mistakenly referred to the present perfect as the past perfect prior to this particular exchange. M therefore did not accept her response but instead posed a clarification question, to which N responded by switching to the present perfect.

In order to determine whether N actually understood why this was the appropriate choice, M prompted her to explain her reasoning. N's response (turn 25) demonstrated her conceptual understanding of the present perfect and its relation to the particular emotional state (being worried) that she wished to express. To be sure, this could not be taken as a sign that N now fully understands the English tense and aspect system and will make appropriate choices in future writing. Rather, it is our contention that her understanding is in a state of developing, or ripening. Importantly, this determination was not arrived at through observation of N's independent written performance but was achieved through collaborative activity in which N was asked to verbalize reasons behind her choices and prompted to revisit and revise those choices, and this was mediated through dialogic interaction with M and through use of the pedagogical materials.

5 Future directions

Intentionally introducing external mediation as learners encounter difficulties completing tasks is sure to be regarded by some as beyond the purview of assessment and perhaps more in line with teaching and learning. Following Vygotsky, our position is that it is only when we expand the scope of assessment beyond learner independent performance to include their responsiveness to mediation that we can hope to diagnose the full range of their abilities, including those that are still developing. We wish to be clear, however, that the goal of DA is not merely to help learners do better on a test. While one can reasonably expect most learners to perform challenging tasks more successfully when they can turn to external forms of social and cultural mediation, as in the examples we have considered in this chapter, this enhanced performance is not in itself the aim of the activity. Rather, DA seeks to reveal and promote psychological processes.

It is this orientation toward diagnosis and intervention that restrains mediators from simply providing an explicit correction at the first occurrence of an error. Doing so might allow mediators and learners to move quickly to the next item or task in the assessment, but it would also entail sacrificing the opportunity to uncover the source of learner difficulty and to begin the process of guiding them toward a more appropriate understanding of the relevant features of language. For this reason the provision of mediation during DA must be approached quite carefully and in a manner guided by SCT. In particular, cultural mediation such as the symbolic tool described here is designed to offer a systematic and theoretical account of complex phenomena (in this case, the English tense and aspect system) in order to inform learners' linguistic choices as they use the language to interpret and construct meanings. The dialogic interaction that is a hallmark of DA is similarly shaped by SCT as mediators begin by offering implicit mediation and become more explicit only as learner responsiveness suggests this is needed.

As we conclude this chapter, we would like to make two additional observations that arise from the examples we have discussed as both point to areas within DA practice that are the focus of ongoing research. In the project we described, the DA sessions led to qualitative profiles of learner development that included difficulties individuals experienced as well as particular moves on the part of the mediator that elicited correct responses from learners. Such an approach to capturing learner development is likely to be more relevant to classroom contexts and the need to systematically trace learner development over time than to formal testing situations. Owing to the large number of individuals who may be involved, the latter context is more apt to favor the use of standardized procedures and to represent learner performance through scores or sets of scores.

Poehner and Lantolf (2013) report efforts to migrate mediation from person-to-person DA interactions into an online format whereby a computer program offers learners mediating prompts arranged from most implicit to most explicit when they fail to correctly respond to questions on multiple-choice tests of reading and listening comprehension. The authors point out that scripted prompts cannot respond to learner needs in the way that is possible through dialogic mediation, and therefore the procedure is limited with regard to the creation of opportunities to intervene in and guide learner development. That said, this particular computerized approach to DA offers learners the option to view an explanation of relevant principles even after they have correctly answered a test item. In this way, even students who reached the correct answer through guessing, a test-taking strategy, or as the result of partial comprehension of the text still have the opportunity to learn an appropriate process for answering the question based on the text's meaning. Moreover, Poehner and Lantolf explain that the mediation they designed for the tests was the result of an analysis of the various mediating moves that had proved useful to learners during a piloting phase in which the tests were administered in a dialogic DA format. For these reasons, the authors argue that while their approach to computerized DA clearly foregrounds an assessment function, there is still potential for teaching to guide development during the tests.

We also recognize that even classroom settings may not allow DA to be implemented in a one-to-one format. Poehner (2009b) proposed group DA (G-DA) as a framework in which tasks are introduced that no learner in a group can complete independently but that are within reach of all learners when mediation is offered. He argued that this creates the conditions for operating simultaneously in the ZPD of individuals but also that of the group as a whole. Drawing on classroom data involving primary school learners of L2 Spanish, Poehner documents how a teacher shifts her attention from one class member to the next, providing mediation to each one until a task solution is reached before moving on to another learner. Through this process, children in the class were able to benefit from mediation offered to their classmates before it was their turn to attempt the instructional tasks. In a project that is currently underway, we are endeavoring to elaborate this model through the use of DA in individual, small group, and whole class formats. This project, carried out with advanced university learners of L2 Japanese, focuses on writing and follows a procedure in which a one-to-one DA session between teacher and learner allows the teacher to identify difficulties in learner writing but also to determine learner responsiveness when mediation is offered. Learners are then placed in groups to discuss and identify the types of errors they had committed in their narratives from a sentence packet the instructor had compiled while the teacher circulates among the groups and dialogues with them to support their understanding of relevant issues in their writing. This is followed by a whole class discussion in which the teacher leads the class through analysis of recurring problems in their writing and mediates their efforts to correct them.

As with computerized DA, much more work is needed to better understand the challenges associated with G-DA as well as its potential to inform assessment decisions and teaching. In our view, classroom-based DA and the use of DA for formal testing purposes can together offer a powerful framework for L2 education concerned with learner development.

6 References

Bardov-Harlig, Kathleen and Dudley W. Reynolds. 1995. The role of lexical aspect in the acquisition of tense and aspect. *TESOL Quarterly* 29(1): 107–131.

Campione, Joseph C., Ann L. Brown, Roberta A. Ferrera and Nancy R. Bryant. 1984. The zone of proximal development: Implications for individual differences and learning. In: Barbara Rogoff and James V. Wertsch (eds.). *Children's Learning in the 'Zone of Proximal Development'*, 77–91. San Francisco: Jossy-Bass.

Celce-Murcia, Marianne and Diane Larsen-Freeman. 1999. *The grammar book: ESL/EFL teacher's course.* 2nd ed. Boston: Heinle and Heinle.

Comrie, Bernard. 1976. *Aspect.* Cambridge, UK: Cambridge University Press.

Davydov, Vasily V. 2008. *Problems of developmental instruction. A theoretical and experimental psychological study.* New York: Nova Science.

Fauconnier, Gilles A. 2007. Mental spaces. In: Dirk Geeraerts and Hubert Cuyckens (eds.). *The Oxford handbook of cognitive linguistics*, 351–376. Oxford, UK: Oxford University Press.

Feuerstein, Reuven, Louis Falik, Yaacov and Refael S. Feuerstein. 2003. *Dynamic assessment of cognitive modifiability.* Jerusalem: ICELP Press.

Gal'perin, Piotr Y. 1992. Stage-by-stage formation as a method of psychological investigation. *Journal of Russian and East European Psychology* 30(4): 60–80.

Gánem-Gutiérrez, Gabriela A. and Haliza Harun. 2011. Verbalisation as a mediational tool for understanding tense-aspect marking in English: an application of Concept-Based Instruction. *Language Awareness* 20(2): 99–119.

Haywood, H. Carl and Carol S. Lidz. 2007. *Dynamic Assessment in practice.* Cambridge, UK: Cambridge University Press.

Karpov, Youri V. 2005. *The neo-Vygotskian approach to child development.* Cambridge, UK: Cambridge University Press.

Lantolf, James P. and Matthew E. Poehner. 2004. Dynamic Assessment: Bringing the past into the future. *Journal of Applied Linguistics* 1(1): 49–74.

Lantolf, James P. and Matthew E. Poehner. 2014. *Sociocultural theory and the pedagogical imperative in L2 education: Vygotskian praxis and the research/practice divide.* London: Routledge.

Negueruela, Eduardo. 2003. *A sociocultural approach to the teaching and learning of second languages: Systemic-theoretical instruction and L2 development.* Unpublished doctoral dissertation. University Park, PA: The Pennsylvania State University.

Poehner, Matthew E. 2008. *Dynamic assessment: A Vygotskian approach to understanding and promoting second language development.* Berlin: Springer.

Poehner, Matthew E. 2009a. Dynamic Assessment as a dialectic framework for classroom activity: Evidence from second language (L2) learners. *Journal of Cognitive Education and Psychology* 8(3): 252–268.

Poehner, Matthew E. 2009b. Group dynamic assessment: Mediation for the L2 classroom. *TESOL Quarterly* 43(3): 471–491.

Poehner, Matthew E. and James P. Lantolf. 2013. Bringing the ZPD into the equation: Capturing L2 development during computerized dynamic assessment. *Language Teaching Research* 17(3): 323–342.

Poehner, Matthew E. and Rémi A. van Compernolle. 2011. Frames of interaction in dynamic assessment: Developmental diagnoses of second language learning. *Assessment in Education: Principles, Policy & Practice* 18(2): 183–198.

Sternberg, Robert J. and Elena L. Grigorenko. 2002. *Dynamic testing. The nature and measurement of learning potential.* Cambridge, UK: Cambridge University Press.

Tsagari, Dina and Ildikó Csépes (eds.). 2011. *Classroom-based language assessment.* Frankfurt am Main: Peter Lang.

Vygotsky, Lev S. 1978. *Mind in society. The development of higher psychological processes.* Cambridge, MA: Harvard University Press.

Vygotsky, Lev S. 1987. *The collected works of L. S. Vygotsky*. Vol. 1: *Problems of general psychology, including the volume thinking and speech*. Robert W. Rieber and Aaron S. Carton (eds.). New York: Plenum.

Vygotsky, Lev S. 1997. *The collected works of L. S. Vygotsky*. Vol. 3: *Problems of the theory and history of psychology*. Robert W. Rieber and Jeffrey Wollock (eds.). New York: Plenum.

Vygotsky, Lev S. 1998. *The collected works of L. S. Vygotsky*. Vol. 5: *Child psychology*. Robert W. Rieber (ed.). New York: Plenum.

Wertsch, James V. 1985. *Vygotsky and the Social Formation of Mind*. Cambridge, MA: Harvard University Press.

Ute Knoch and Susy Macqueen
18 Language assessment for the workplace

1 Introduction

With an increasingly mobile global workforce, English language proficiency has become a sought-after commodity in workplaces across the world. This has given rise to the need for English-language assessments in both English as a lingua franca contexts as well as in traditionally English-speaking countries, which are increasingly relying on an overseas migrant workforce. There have been two main reasons for the increased use of such assessments: firstly, there are several professions in which insufficient English language proficiency is seen as a safety risk (e.g., medicine and aviation) necessitating policies such as minimum language requirements. Secondly, there is the widespread view held by employers that graduates are entering the workplace without the English language competence required to transition into the labour market. In this chapter, we will begin with a historical overview of languages for specific purposes (LSP) testing. We then provide a definition and classification scheme of tests falling under this umbrella, and we examine the construct of LSP tests and detail key examples. Finally, we discuss issues in assessing languages for professional purposes and suggest avenues for future research.

2 Historical overview

The beginnings of LSP testing can be traced to the emergence of the notion of communicative competence (Hymes 1972) and the concomitant concept of authenticity as the key to creating successful contexts for learning and assessment (Douglas 1997; O'Loughlin 2008; Lewkowicz 2000). Three examples of English tests from the late seventies can be considered prototypes of the kinds of approaches which have come to dominate current LSP assessment for occupational purposes.

One of the first occupation-specific tests, introduced in 1975, was the Temporary Registration Assessment Board test for medical practitioners wishing to practice in Britain. Based on analyses of the language used in British hospitals (Rea-Dickens 1987), the test is an example of a high level of interaction between professional knowledge and language ability as it was designed to assess both (Douglas 1997). Around the same time, the predecessor to the International English Language Testing Service (IELTS) was introduced for non-native speaking students wishing to enter British universities. The test was based on a needs analysis of target test takers (Carroll 1980) and contained reading and listening subtests which were taken by all candidates and speaking, writing and study skills modules which were specific to five subject areas. Although much more specific than the current IELTS test, it advanced the now widely accepted notion that there is a general academic language proficiency threshold for university admission (i.e. across diverse subject areas). Designed by Educational Testing Service (ETS), the Test of English for International Communication (TOEIC) originated in 1979 through a partnership between the Japanese Ministry of Economy, Trade, and Industry and ETS to assess the business-related language skills of Japanese workers (McCrostie 2009). Research undertaken at the time by ETS in Japan identified several features which were to guide the test design including the use of a less embellished variety of English between non-native speakers, short texts and less idiomatic, rare and technical vocabulary. These aspects remain part of the test construct in the modern version of the test (ETS, 2007).

These early examples of English language assessments for specific purposes illustrate issues in the development of LSP testing which have remained key concerns. These are the notion of a "readiness threshold" for context-specific language use, the interaction between field-specific knowledge and language knowledge and the link between target language use (TLU) domain and test construct demonstrated by methods of enquiry such as needs and domain analyses.

3 Defining and classifying LSP assessments

The area of languages for specific purposes can be divided into two sub-branches: languages for academic purposes and languages for occupational purposes. Language assessments for occupational purposes are usually designed based on an analysis of the TLU domain, so that the tasks and the content of the assessment mirror those in the target context. The tests are therefore generally performance-oriented. The assessments commonly evaluate a range of linguistic and communicative knowledge and this allows inferences to be drawn about the test takers' abilities to perform in specific vocational or professional domains (Basturkmen and Elder 2004; Douglas 2000).

One way to classify such assessments is based on their level of specificity, i.e. how closely the test tasks relate to tasks in the TLU domain. Thus, the notion of specificity encompasses both authenticity and purpose. It can be conceptualized as a continuum of specificity, with tests falling at points on the continuum between very general and very specific (Douglas 1997). This is depicted in Figure 1 below.

On the left end of the continuum are tests that are designed to relate to a broad range of domains, disciplines or registers. Such tests are used to indicate language readiness for a cross-section of contexts and claim not to require any "specialist" background knowledge. A distinction can be drawn at this more general end between "occupational" tests which are designed to encompass the common lan-

Fig. 1: LSP Assessment Specificity Continuum.

guage of a range of (frequently business-oriented) workplaces, e.g., TOEIC (Test of English for International Communication) or GSLPA (Graduating Students' Language Proficiency Assessment), and "academic" tests which are designed to encompass the common language of a range of disciplines in academic settings, e.g., IELTS Academic (International English Language Testing System), TOEFL (Test of English as a Foreign Language). There is some variability and overlap at the more general end of the continuum, for example an academic test used as a language requirement for professionals seeking registration for a specific profession.

On the right side of the continuum in Figure 1 are language assessments which are designed to closely simulate the real world tasks of specific professions. Often-cited examples here are the OET (Occupational English Test), a language test for health professionals, and language assessments designed for the aviation context, e.g., RMIT English Language Test for Aviation (RELTA) for pilots and air traffic controllers. These assessments are usually designed as screening tests for professionals who have trained in a country where English is not used as the medium of communication and are required to use English for their work either because of migration or international requirements to speak English. The tests are generally designed for smaller, more homogenous groups of professionals. The level of specificity of such assessments is a much-discussed issue, for example, should an assessment of English for health professionals have separate sub-tests for doctors, nurses, and dentists or even focus on specialisations within a profession (with, for example, different tests for general practitioners and neurologists)? Specificity increases as the context of assessment gets closer to direct observation in the TLU domain, for example, a highly specific language assessment could take place during the simulator training of operational pilots.

Performance-based assessments for specific purposes have further been categorized into strong or weak performance tests (McNamara 1996). Weak performance tests are those in which the test materials are designed to reflect the TLU domain, but the assessors are language experts who use linguistic criteria. Strong performance tests, on the other hand, will include real-world tasks and the performance will be judged against real-world criteria in terms of fulfilment of the task. It is therefore possible that language-based criteria are not included or not the main focus of the assessment as adequate language proficiency is necessary but

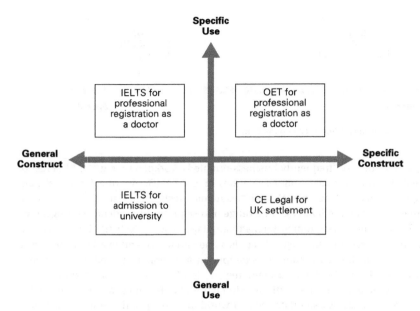

Fig. 2: Specificity of assessment construct and assessment use.

not the only condition of success (McNamara 1996: 49). Again, rather than seeing this as a dichotomy, it can also be conceived as a continuum. For example, in some assessments, the criteria used are a mixture of linguistic criteria and professionally relevant, indigenous criteria (the term "indigenous criteria" will be further discussed below).

A second possible classification of profession-relevant language assessments is based on the purpose of the assessments, illustrated in Figure 2 above. Assessments for professional or occupational purposes have been used to provide information for professional registration, for promotion or professional development, as low-stakes, non-hiring diagnostic assessments (see e.g., Greenberg 2012) or as exit tests from higher education institutions (e.g., Berry and Lewkowicz 2000; Lumley and Qian 2003). It is important to note however that assessments are often used for purposes for which they have not been developed and that validation work for the new purposes is often not undertaken. For example, tests like IELTS and TOEFL are often used as university exit tests or tests to make high-stakes employment decisions even though they were developed as university entry tests. It could therefore be argued that these tests are only suitable to make predictions about university study but not beyond to possible performance in the workplace. Any use of tests beyond the purpose they were designed for casts serious doubt on the validity of the score-based interpretations made based on the assessment.

In determining the "adequacy and appropriateness of inferences and actions based on test scores" (Messick 1989: 33), LSP tests must be conceptualised, not just in terms of specificity of their constructs aligned with their theoretical or intended purposes, but also the specificity of their *actual* uses. This can be represented as two intersecting continua depicted in Figure 2.

The horizontal continuum represents the degree of specificity of the assessment construct, including the assessment design and the language it elicits (as in Figure 1). The degree of specificity is largely a question of how many domains the assessment applies to. As discussed above, a more general test will comprise topics, tasks and texts which present and elicit discourse that is common across a broader range of domains whereas a more specific test will be linguistically related to fewer domains. The horizontal 'construct' continuum is related to the TLU domain/s through the degree of authenticity and context-sensitivity of the test tasks and the language elicited as well as the TLU-context-relevance of rating scales and rater behaviour, amongst other things (see further discussion below). The vertical continuum represents the actual interpretation and use of test scores, which may or may not be the same as the designed purpose of the test. Test uses also range from very general to very specific, i.e. inferring linguistic expertise in many or few domains. An example of a well-known English test and one of its actual current uses is shown in each quadrant, representing the relative interactions between test construct and test use.

In all these instances, the main question is the justifiability of the fit between the test construct and the test interpretation/use: the diagram brings together the tensions inherent in the validity argument whereby the test design is connected by a series of inferences to the interpretation/use of the test scores (e.g., Kane, Crooks and Cohen, 1999; Bachman and Palmer, 2010). One test might have uses at different levels of specificity in the case of IELTS (both general university admission and specific professional registration). Uses of a more general test construct to serve a specific purpose (top left quadrant) are more common than the reverse (bottom right quadrant), exemplified by the use of the Cambridge English: Legal test (designed to indicate proficiency appropriate for practising international law) and listed until 2015 as an appropriate proficiency indicator for settlement in the UK. The degree to which a test fits within a quadrant is a question for on-going validation research since a test construct is the result of a dynamic cluster of variables. A test with a relatively specific construct, for example, may be broadened covertly through the use of raters who are language experts rather than profession experts and who are therefore not privy to the same level of interaction between content knowledge and language knowledge as the test takers themselves might be (e.g., Elder et al. 2012; see also further discussion on this below). Justifying a position for an assessment in any quadrant necessitates a thorough consideration of the degree to which field-related knowledge and language ability must interact in order for the assessment to be fair as well as the test's effects on stakeholders (see Macqueen, Pill and Knoch, in press).

4 Defining the construct of languages for specific purposes tests

The issue of test use discussed above makes it necessary to consider in some depth the construct of LSP assessments. While the construct of assessments designed, for example, for university entry (such as IELTS and TOEFL) is fairly well understood and researched, defining the construct of more specific LSP tests is far more complex. This is due to the range of disciplines and (cultural) contexts found in the TLU domain of different professions as well as the range of tasks these professionals engage with. Using a language within a certain professional context requires a more specialised and nuanced set of skills than is captured by general or academic proficiency tests, for example, whether a doctor is able to communicate complicated medical facts to a patient in 'plain language' in an empathetic way or whether he or she uses appropriate questioning techniques during the collection of the medical history. Another example is whether a pilot is able to communicate effectively with an air traffic controller by using standard aviation phraseology and switching to plain language when standard phraseology does not suffice (see Section 5.3 below). Elder (2001), for example, proposed that teacher language proficiency be viewed broadly as including specialist skills such as a command of subject-specific terminology and language competence to complete a range of classroom management skills, including giving clear, succinct instructions and managing students from a range of age groups or backgrounds.

Whether these profession-specific skills are inseparable from language knowledge has been a subject of some discussion in the literature on specific-purpose testing. Douglas (2001b), for example, has argued that these two aspects of the performance on specific-purpose tests cannot be separated as they are "inextricably intertwined" (Jacoby and McNamara 1999: 50). While the impact of background knowledge is an aspect that test designers in general proficiency tests usually try to minimize as much as possible as it is not directly related to language knowledge, Douglas (2000, 2001b) and others have called for recognising it as a part of the construct of LSP testing. He has therefore argued that the assessment criteria should reflect the perspectives of key stakeholders knowledgeable of the professional context. However, how much content knowledge or profession-specific skills can or should be part of the test construct and how these skills can be successfully measured is in need of further research.

The discussion above shows that it is important to consider whether a general or academic proficiency test can really adequately measure what is required of professionals in their TLU domain. It is equally important to reflect on whether it is fair to test candidates with no or very limited professional experience on skills they might only acquire through professional training or placement in the workplace (see also Clapham, 2000).

5 Current practice in assessing languages for professional and occupational purposes

5.1 Test of English for International Communication (TOEIC)

TOEIC is an example of a test construct on the more general end of the specificity continuum: TOEIC test scores indicate 'how well people can communicate in English with others in the global workplace' (ETS 2007: 2). The test measures reading, listening and speaking and writing components and task topics are mostly related to corporate workplaces and business (e.g., corporate development, human resources). The construct, as it was originally conceived, bears some similarity to the features of Business English as a Lingua Franca (BELF). A redesign of the listening component in 2006 led to the incorporation of different native-speaker accents in the test to improve authenticity (Schedl 2010), although most communication by BELF users occurs between non-native speakers. Despite the business focus of the test, the actual interpretations/uses of TOEIC vary widely in terms of specificity (the vertical continuum in Figure 2), particularly as TOEIC is used for both academic and occupational purposes. Examples of its current uses are as a precondition requirement for registration with US nursing boards and as a means of monitoring employee English language progress over time in major international companies. Some companies also use particular TOEIC score levels as requirements for different jobs (see http://www.ets.org/toeic/successes).

5.2 The Occupational English Test (OET)

The OET was designed to evaluate the English language competence of health professionals wishing practice in Australia (but is now being used in many more countries) and therefore falls on the more specific end of the construct and use continua. The test is designed for twelve health professions – medicine, nursing, dentistry, physiotherapy, veterinary science, pharmacy, occupational therapy, dietetics, radiography, speech pathology, podiatry and optometry. All professions complete the same reading and listening tasks, while the speaking and writing tasks are designed to be profession-specific. The test tasks are designed to simulate performance tasks required in the workplace. For example, the writing task requires most professions to write a letter of referral, while the speaking task involves two consultations with patients based on role-play prompts. A comprehensive account of the development of the OET can be found in McNamara (1996). The OET has been fairly well researched and is often cited as a typical example of an LSP performance-based test.

5.3 Language proficiency requirements for pilots and air traffic controllers

Another example at the more specific end of the continuum is testing for the aviation domain, which uses English as a lingua franca. Following a number of incidents and accidents in international aviation which were deemed to have been caused by communication breakdowns, the International Civil Aviation Authority (ICAO) introduced a set of language proficiency requirements in 2003 which stipulated that all pilots and air traffic controllers engaged in international operations must have their English proficiency certified by their national civil aviation authority. To guide any test activities, ICAO published a manual (ICAO 2004) outlining the Language Proficiency Requirements (LPR) which at its core includes a rating scale. The scale outlines six levels of proficiency and comprises six rating criteria: structure, vocabulary, pronunciation, fluency, comprehension and interaction. ICAO stipulated the minimum level required for certification (Level 4 on all criteria). No information was provided on how the scale was created and how the standard on the scale was set. Crucially, however, the policy did not mandate the use of any particular test and also did not stipulate the format the test should take (beyond some basic requirements). The implementation was left up to the aviation authorities in the 190 member states of ICAO. Following the release of the policy, there was large variation in the activities to implement the policy. A flurry of test development activities ensued, as many of the developers of these tests were hoping to cash in on the new lucrative market of testing pilots and air traffic controllers. Unfortunately, many of these tests were developed without sufficient input from experts in language testing, in particular, as the LPRs did not provide sufficient guidance on test development and the nature of the test construct at stake. A review conducted by Alderson (2010) showed that many of these tests were lacking in quality. A further issue was that rather than requiring all pilots and air traffic controllers to be tested, ICAO allowed the exemption of native speakers of English on the assumption that they would automatically meet the proficiency set at Level 6 (the highest levels of the LPR rating scale) (see ICAO 2009).

A closer examination of the construct of aviation English proficiency is necessary to understand some of the issues relating to aviation English testing. Air traffic control and pilots communicate using radiotelephony. To be able to conduct these conversations as efficiently as possible, both professions learn a simplified code referred to as standard phraseology as part of their training. Standard phraseology is designed to be not only efficient in transmitting key messages but also has inbuilt routine checks which ensure that the messages have been passed on and understood correctly. Most conversations between air traffic control and pilots are conducted using standard phraseology but this code at times does not suffice to take care of all possible emergency situations or incidents that can occur. At this point, the interlocutors need to switch to plain English if they do not share the same language. Once plain English is used, it is important that this is kept as simple as possible without the use of redundancies or idiomatic language. Kim (2012), for example, was able to show that the communication breakdown is often caused by native speakers not sticking to the conventions described above, rather than a non-native speaker's lack of language proficiency. Directly exempting native speakers from the policy, as was the case with Circular 318 (ICAO 2009) is clearly problematic and an issue of fairness. For many of the reasons described above, the ICAO policy, while clearly important, has been criticized. In fact, some national civil aviation authorities quite openly disagreed with the policy and either did not comply (see e.g., Alderson and Horák 2008, 2010) or complied only on the surface by making all their test materials available to potential test candidates. The experience of aviation testing shows the ethical importance of informed test design in linking policy and purpose to TLU domain.

6 Issues in assessing languages for professional and occupational purposes

The examples discussed above illustrate the complexity of the interaction between the goals of the various stakeholders. Policy makers, for instance, may wish to improve accountability, safety or control access. Test providers may wish to deliver a reliable service at a profit. Institutional test users may wish to monitor employees' language expertise in an efficient and economical manner, whereas individual users may wish to improve their life chances through professional recognition or promotion. In achieving the balance of the needs of these various groups, several key issues concerning the degree of construct specificity arise: authenticity, context-sensitivity, background knowledge and performance rating.

6.1 Authenticity

Douglas (2000, 2001b) argues that authenticity is one of the key defining features of LSP assessment. Assessment tasks closely simulating the TLU domain enable an interaction between test takers' language ability, their specific-purpose content knowledge and the test tasks. Simulating tasks and profession-specific content to provide the context for the assessment has the further positive effect of making candidates feel comfortable when taking the test. Authentic assessment tasks are also more likely to result in positive washback as they influence the development of preparation materials and courses and as they help set appropriate expectations of test takers of their future role in the workplace.

Achieving authenticity during test development involves a close examination of the TLU domain as well as the involvement of key stakeholder informants. Test designers and researchers have drawn on a variety of approaches to achieve this, including the use of questionnaires (e.g., Estival and Molesworth 2009), focus groups (e.g., Kim 2012), target-language analyses or the use of corpora (e.g., Moder and Halleck 2010; van Moere et al. 2009) and the close examination of published manuals and documentation (e.g., Moder and Halleck 2012). Furthermore, communication in the workplace is changing rapidly and it is therefore important to continually review, for instance, the types of tasks included in an LSP test to ensure that they remain current in terms of the TLU domain. Technology is transforming the way professionals communicate and this might affect the construct tested and approaches used to testing, including the test task. Examples of such studies have been conducted by Elder, Harding and Knoch (2009) and Macqueen et al. (2012) in the continued validation of the OET.

6.2 Context-sensitivity

A further concern in LSP assessment related to the issue of specificity discussed above, is the correspondence of test tasks to the context of use. Many occupation-specific LSP assessments are initially developed for a very specific context of use. For example, the OET was first developed for health professionals planning on immigrating to Australia. However, once a test is applied more broadly and transferred to different contexts, test developers are often required to change the test content to be linguistically and culturally appropriate for all contexts. Lockwood (2013), for example, reports on an occasion in one well-known English test for business purposes in Hong Kong where test candidates did not understand the term 'conference centre' in the UK sense. Similarly, in a test for health professionals, the same medications might have different names in different countries, conversations with patients might be less patient-centred in certain countries or the treatment of certain conditions might differ substantially (see also Elder and Kim 2014, on the discussion of a similar issue relating to a test designed to assess teacher language proficiency). Certain topics might be culturally inappropriate in some countries but deemed absolutely acceptable in others. Language test developers need to ensure that the tests remain context-sensitive and profession-relevant even if they are more broadly administered. However, certain aspects of language might remain difficult to test. For example, health professionals working in Australia have been criticized for not understanding common slang terms used by patients; however Taylor and Pill (2014) suggest that this type of language knowledge is probably best acquired in situ.

6.3 The role of background knowledge in LSP testing

Douglas (2000, 2001a) has repeatedly argued that language knowledge and content (technical) knowledge are integral to the construct of LSP testing and cannot be separated. Building on this, others have argued that more research is needed to gain a deeper understanding of how background knowledge and language knowledge interact with and influence each other (e.g., O'Loughlin 2008). In a small-scale study in the context of investigating the validity of the ICAO language proficiency descriptors, Knoch (2014) found an interaction between the two aspects of knowledge. She compared the ratings of language-trained raters and pilots on the communicative effectiveness of trainee and qualified pilots who had taken an aviation English test. She also asked the pilot judges to complete questionnaires and discuss the performance of each pilot in a focus group interview. She focused on performances around the crucial cut-off in the ICAO policy (between Levels 3 and 4). Based on the results of the study, she was able to show that industry specialists used their judgment of a speaker's technical knowledge to override their estimate of the speaker's language proficiency when making their judgment of the speaker's overall communicative effectiveness and therefore, job readiness. Because of this complicated interaction of the industry-specialists' judgment, she recommended their inclusion in not only the test development and validation process, but also in the rating process (see further discussion below). The extent of incorporation of background knowledge, whether the test merely focuses on linguistic skills or whether aspects of professional knowledge are included, is often ultimately a matter of policy and depends on how different jurisdictions or industries and registration bodies approach the testing of their professionals.

6.4 Rating scale criteria and raters

The rating scale criteria used to rate performances on workplace assessments should represent the test construct as envisaged by the test developers. In the stronger sense of performance assessment, these criteria should reflect what is valued by professionals in the workplace rather than solely focusing on linguistic criteria. However, including non-linguistic criteria in the rating criteria is one of the issues in LSP assessment that has received substantial attention from researchers. As Basturkmen and Elder (2004: 677) point out, "the problem of reconciling the different perspectives of language and non-language professionals is a perennial concern for LSP practitioners."

Jacoby (1998) coined the term "indigenous assessment criteria" for criteria applied to a performance by insiders who share a common perspective. Language assessment specialists have studied the indigenous assessment criteria of a variety of speech communities. Brown (1993), for example, engaged members of the tourism industry in her development of criteria for a test of second language Japanese tour guides. Other studies compared the criteria applied by domain experts with those used by language-trained raters. Douglas and Myers (2000), for example, used this methodology in the assessment of communication skills of veterinary students revealing that while applied linguists focused on language, the trained vets were more concerned with the students' professional relationship with their clients and their content knowledge. Elder (1993, 2001), in the context of the language assessment of teachers in a classroom setting, found that domain specialists not only lacked the metalinguistic knowledge to identify and describe language features, they also had a different orientation to the assessment process and applied different criteria to language experts. In a recent study in the context of the OET, Pill (2013) elicited the indigenous assessment criteria of doctors through their commentaries on trainee doctors' interactions with patients. He used his data to develop a model of what is valued by doctors in the doctor-patient consultation. Pill gives a detailed account of how he distilled two new proposed test criteria from the rich discourse data collected from the practitioners.

Regardless of whether indigenous assessment criteria are used in an assessment or not, there is also the question of who is the best placed to judge a performance – domain experts or language-trained raters. As described above, these two groups of raters have been shown to disagree on their judgments and to employ different criteria in their rating processes. Because of this, a number of authors (Douglas 2000, 2001a; Elder and Kim 2014; Knoch 2014) have argued for using both rater groups in the judgment process. While this solution is clearly in line with bringing specific-purpose assessment practice closer to the construct the tests are designed to measure, more research is necessary in understanding how the ratings of these two groups of raters can be consolidated and which group would be given the final decision if judgments result in different categorizations of candidates.

7 Future directions

There are several future directions for research on LSP assessments. Firstly, we recommend that more work is undertaken in the area of test consequences of LSP tests. In particular, it is important to investigate how candidates who have passed an LSP test cope in the professional setting. This work is important to understand more fully why certain test takers may pass an LSP test but fail to communicate adequately in the workplace, a problem reported for some successful IELTS and OET test takers who later entered a health profession in New Zealand or Australia (see Wette 2011). Pill and Woodward-Kron (2012) were able to show that many of the aspects of communication listed by Wette (2011: 201) which include aspects of the "mastery of relevant professional discourses in healthcare settings" are indeed beyond the scope of a test such as the OET and that these aspects are assessed in the clinical examination designed to evaluate health professionals' clinical skills. However, we do feel that more detailed research into this issue is warranted to establish what aspects of communication in the workplace are challenging for overseas-trained professionals and to gain a deeper understanding of the magnitude of any such problems. A small-scale study currently undertaken in this area

(Macqueen et al. 2013; Macqueen et al. in press) has shown that the specificity of the OET test construct is generally valued by successful past candidates, with test preparation perceived as contributing beneficially to actual workplace communication. Further research could explore the types of washback effects generated by the use of a more generic test such as IELTS for these more specific purposes.

A further area of research should focus on standard-setting for specific purpose tests as very little has been published on this topic. A body of research is available on standard-setting activities on generic tests for occupational purposes (such as the TOEFL, IELTS or Pearson Test of English). Studies setting passing standards for the US National Council of State Boards of Nursing have been undertaken on the previous version of the TOEFL (O'Neill, Tannenbaum, and Tiffen 2005), on the TOEFL internet-based test (TOEFL iBT) (Wendt, Woo, and Kenny 2009), the IELTS (O'Neill et al. 2007) and the Pearson Test of English (Woo, Dickison, and de Jong 2010). Studies documenting the standard-setting activities for health professionals are also available for the Test of Spoken English (e.g., Powers and Stansfield 1983, 1985, 1989). Commenting on the use of generic English tests for specific purpose decisions, Elder and Kim (2014) report the common practice of setting cut-scores on generic tests high to ensure professional standards, but they argue that this is "to no avail if tests are under-representing the test construct or measuring construct-irrelevant language abilities and may result in inaccurate decisions". Studies detailing the standard-setting procedures undertaken for specific-purpose tests are far more rare. One exception is a very recent study which involved a standard-setting exercise for the speaking sub-test of the OET (Elder et al. 2013a; Elder et al. 2013b) using three groups of informants – doctors, nurses and physiotherapists. The results showed that the different professions applied slightly different standards although this only resulted in a small rate of different classification of candidates around the crucial pass/fail cut-score. Overall, the project shows just how complex the standards applied by health professionals are and that more detailed research, including the collection of concurrent think-aloud protocols are necessary.

The discussion of the aviation language testing policy described above shows the ramifications that a well-meant policy decision can have on language testing in general and on the quality of language tests being developed. While the aviation language testing policy is relatively unique, matters of policy will always influence language tests and their implementation on various levels. This is particularly true of workplace assessments. Berry and Lewkowicz (2000), for example, describe how discussions about introducing university English-language exit tests to ensure graduates enter professions with acceptable minimum levels of language proficiency led to the fear that the universal use of these tests could lead to them being used as instruments of accountability of the institutions themselves with direct implications for funding of institutions whose graduates are not achieving so well. Professional bodies are clearly key stakeholders when it comes to workplace assessments. As Taylor and Pill (2014) point out, whether a language test is recognized by a professional body does not only depend on the content or quality of the test, but is often related to much more practical considerations, such as the costs to test takers, the frequency of test administrations, availability of test centres, the turnaround of results and test security. Policies are also not only made by professional bodies but by governments who need to control the migration of professionals within and between borders. In the future, it is important that language testers become more involved and visible in policy debates and advice to try and guide decisions before they are written into policy. This will inevitably also involve gaining a better understanding of all the different LSP stakeholder groups who are involved and affected by policy decisions.

8 References

Alderson, J. Charles. 2010. A survey of aviation English tests. *Language Testing* 27(1): 51–72.

Alderson, J. Charles and Tania Horák. 2008. Report on a survey of national civil aviation authorities' plans for implementation of ICAO language proficiency requirements. Unpublished manuscript. Lancaster, UK: Lancaster University.

Alderson, J. Charles and Tania Horák. 2010. *A second report on National Civil Aviation Authorities' implementation of ICAO LPRs*. Unpublished manuscript. Lancaster, UK: Lancaster University.

Bachman, Lyle F. and Adrian S. Palmer. 2010. *Language assessment in practice: Developing language assessments and justifying their use in the real world*. Oxford, UK: Oxford University Press.

Basturkmen, Helen and Cathie Elder. 2004. The practice of LSP. In: Alan Davies and Cathie Elder (eds.). *Handbook of Applied Linguistics*, 672–694. Oxford, England: Blackwell.

Berry, Vivien and Jo Lewkowicz. 2000. Exit-tests: Is there an alternative? *Hong Kong Journal of Applied Linguistics* 5(1): 19–49.

Brown, Annie. 1993. LSP testing: The role of linguistic and real-world criteria. *Melbourne Papers in Language and Testing* 2(2): 35–54.

Carroll, Brendan J. 1980. *Testing communicative performance: An interim study*. Oxford: Pergamon Press.

Clapham, Caroline. 2000. Assessment for academic purposes: where next? *System* 28(4): 511–521.

Douglas, Dan. 1997. Language for specific purposes testing. In: Caroline Clapham and David Corson (eds.). *Encyclopedia of Language and Education* (Vol. 7: *Language Testing and Education*), 111–119. Dordrecht: Kluwer Academic Publishers.

Douglas, Dan. 2000. *Assessing languages for specific purposes*. Cambridge, UK: Cambridge University Press.

Douglas, Dan. 2001a. Language for Specific Purposes assessment criteria: Where do they come from? *Language Testing* 18(2): 171–185.

Douglas, Dan. 2001b. Three problems in testing language for specific purposes: Authenticity, specificity and inseparability. In: Cathie Elder, Annie Brown, Elizabeth Grove, Kathryn Hill, Noriko Iwashita, Tom Lumley, Tim McNamara and Kieran O'Loughlin (eds.). *Experimenting with uncertainty: Essays in honour of Alan Davies*, 45–52. Cambridge, UK: UCLES/Cambridge University Press.

Douglas, Dan and Ron Myers. 2000. Assessing the communication skills of veterinary students: Whose criteria? In: A. Kunnan (ed.). *Fairness and validation in language assessment*.

Selected papers from the 19th Language Testing Research Colloquium. 60–81. Cambridge, UK: UCLES/Cambridge University Press.

Elder, Cathie. 1993. How do subject specialists construe classroom language proficiency? *Language Testing* 10(3): 235–254.

Elder, Cathie. 2001. Assessing the language proficiency of teachers: Are there any border controls? *Language Testing* 18(2): 149–170.

Elder, Cathie, Luke Harding and Ute Knoch. 2009. *OET Reading Revision Study.* Final report to the OET Centre. Melbourne: University of Melbourne, Language Testing Research Centre.

Elder, Cathie and Sun Hee Kim. 2014. Assessing teachers' language proficiency. In: Antony Kunnan (ed.). *The Companion to Language Assessment.* John Wiley and Sons, Inc. DOI: 10.1002/9781118411360.wbcla138

Elder, Cathie, Tim McNamara, Robyn Woodward-Kron, Elizabeth Manias, Geoff McColl and Gillian Webb. 2013a. *Towards improved healthcare communication. Development and validation of language proficiency standards for non-native English speaking health professionals.* Final report for The Occupational English Test Centre. Melbourne: University of Melbourne.

Elder, Cathie, Tim McNamara, Robyn Woodward-Kron, Elizabeth Manias, Geoff McColl, Gillian Webb, John Pill and Sally O'Hagan. 2013b. Developing and validating language proficiency standards for non-native English speaking health professionals. *Papers in Language Testing and Assessment* 2(1): 66–70.

Elder, Cathie, John Pill, Robyn Woodward-Kron, Tim McNamara, Elizabeth Manias, Gillian Webb and Geoff McColl. 2012. Health professionals' views of communication: Implications for assessing performance on a health-specific English language test. *TESOL Quarterly* 46(2): 409–419.

Estival, Dominique and Brett Molesworth. 2009. A study of EL2 pilots' radio communication in the general aviation environment. *Australian Review of Applied Linguistics* 32(3): 24.1–24.16.

ETS. 2007. User guide. http://www.ets.org/Media/Tests/Test_of_English_for_International_Communication/TOEIC_User_Gd.pdf (accessed 10 October 2013).

Greenberg, Ingrid. 2012. ESL needs analysis and assessment in the workplace. In: Christine Coombe, Peter Davidson, Barry O'Sullivan and Stephen Stoynoff (eds.). *The Cambridge Guide to Second Language Assessment*, 178–186. Cambridge, UK: Cambridge University Press.

Hymes, Dell. 1972. On Communicative Competence. In: John Pride and Janet Holmes (eds.). *Sociolinguistics. Selected Readings.* 269–293. Harmondsworth: Penguin.

ICAO. 2004. *Manual on the implementation of the language proficiency requirements (Doc 9835).* Montreal: International Civil Aviation Organization. retrieved from http://caa.gateway.bg/upload/docs/9835_1_ed.pdf (accessed 10 October 2013).

ICAO. 2009. *Language testing criteria for global harmonization (Circular 318).* Montreal, Canada: International Civil Aviation Organisation. retrieved from http://www.jarfcl.at/fileadmin/user_upload/icao_cir318.pdf (accessed 10 October 2013).

Jacoby, Sally. 1998. *Science as performance: Socializing scientific discourse through conference talk rehearsals.* Los Angeles, CA: University of California, Los Angeles dissertation.

Jacoby, Sally and Tim McNamara. 1999. Locating competence. *English for Specific Purposes* 18(3): 213–241.

Kane, Michael, Terence Crooks and Allan Cohen. 1999. Validating measures of performance. *Educational Measurement: Issues and Practice* 18(2): 5–17.

Kim, Hyejeong. 2012. *Exploring the construct of aviation communication: A critique of the ICAO language proficiency policy.* Melbourne: University of Melbourne dissertation.

Knoch, Ute. 2014. Using subject specialists to validate and ESP rating scale: The case of the International Civil Aviation Organization (ICAO) rating scale. *English for Specific Purposes* 33(1): 77–86.

Lewkowicz, Jo A. 2000. Authenticity in language testing: some outstanding questions. *Language Testing* 17(1): 43–64.

Lockwood, Jane. 2013. Assessment of business and professional language for specific purposes. In: Chapelle (ed.). *The Encyclopedia of Applied Linguistics*, 155–161. Blackwell Publishing.

Lumley, Tom and David Qian. 2003. Assessing English for employment in Hong Kong. In: Christine Coombe and Nancy Hubley (eds.). *Assessment practices*, 135–147. Alexandria, Virginia, USA: Teachers of English to Speakers of Other Languages, Inc. (TESOL).

McCrostie, James. 2009. *TOEIC no turkey at 30*. http://www.japantimes.co.jp/community/2009/08/11/issues/toeic-no-turkey-at-30/#.Uk4FGBbJBSU (accessed 4 October 2013).

McNamara, Tim. 1996. *Measuring second language performance*. London and New York: Longman.

Macqueen, Susy, John Pill, Cathie Elder and Ute Knoch. 2013. *A qualitative investigation of the impact of OET*. Unpublished report to the OET Centre. Melbourne: University of Melbourne.

Macqueen, Susy, Sharon Yahalom, Hyejeong Kim and Ute Knoch. 2012. *Exploring writing demands in healthcare settings*. Unpublished report to the OET Centre. Melbourne: University of Melbourne.

Macqueen, Susy, John Pill and Ute Knoch. in press. Test as boundary object: the case of healthcare communication. *Language Testing* 33(3).

Messick, Samuel. 1989. Validity. In: Robert L. Linn (ed.). *Educational measurement*, 3rd ed., 13–103. New York: Macmillan.

Moder, Carol and Gene Halleck. 2010. *Can we get a little higher? Proficiency levels in Aviation English*. Paper presented at the Language Testing Research Colloquium, Cambridge. April 14–16.

Moder, Carol and Gene Halleck. 2012. Designing language tests for specific social uses. In: Glenn Fulcher and Fred Davidson (eds.). *The Routledge Handbook of Language Testing*, 137–149. Abingdon, Oxon, United Kingdom: Routledge.

O'Loughlin, Kieran. 2008. Assessment at the workplace. In: Elana Shohamy and Nancy H. Hornberger (eds.). *Encyclopedia of Language and Education* (Language Testing and Assessment 7), 69–80. Springer Science + Business Media LLC.

O'Neill, Thomas R., Chad W. Buckendahl, Barbara S. Plake and Lynda Taylor. 2007. Recommending a nursing-specific passing standard for the IELTS examination. *Language Assessment Quarterly* 4(4): 295–317.

O'Neill, Thomas R., Richard J. Tannenbaum and Jennifer Tiffen. 2005. Recommending a minimum English proficiency standard for entry-level nursing. *Journal of Nursing Measurement* 13(2): 129–146.

Pill, John. 2013. *What doctors value in consultations and the implications for specific-purpose language testing*. Melbourne: The University of Melbourne dissertation.

Pill, John and Robyn Woodward-Kron. 2012. How professionally relevant can language tests be?: A response to Wette (2011). *Language Assessment Quarterly* 9(1): 105–108.

Powers, Donald and Charles W. Stansfield. 1983. *The Test of Spoken English as a measure of communicative ability in the health professions: Validation and standard setting*. RR-83-01. Princeton, NJ: Educational Testing Service.

Powers, Donald and Charles W. Stansfield. 1985. Testing the oral English proficiency of foreign nursing graduates. *The ESP Journal* 4(1): 21–36.

Powers, Donald and Charles W. Stansfield. 1989. An approach to the measurement of communicative ability in three health professions. In: Hywel Coleman (ed.). *Working with language: A multidisciplinary consideration of language use in work contexts*, 341–366. Berlin: Mouton de Gruyter.

Rea-Dickens, Pauline. 1987. Testing doctors' written communicative competence: an experimental technique in English for specialist purposes. *Quantitative Linguistics* 34: 185–218.

Schedl, Mary. 2010. Background and goals of the TOEIC listening and reading test redesign project. TC-10-02. Princeton, US: Educational Testing Service. http://www.ets.org/Media/Research/pdf/TC-10-02.pdf (accessed 4 October 2013).

Taylor, Lynda and John Pill. 2014. Assessing health professionals. In: Antony Kunnan (ed.). *The Companion to Language Assessment*, 497–512. John Wiley and Sons, Inc.

van Moere, Alistair, Masanori Suzuki, Ryan Downey and Jian Cheng. 2009. Implementing ICAO language proficiency requirements in the Versant Aviation English test. *Australian Review of Applied Linguistics* 32(3): 27.1–27.17.

Wendt, Anne, Ada Woo and Lorraine Kenny. 2009. Setting a passing standard for English proficiency on the Internet-based Test of English as a Foreign Language. *JONA's Healthcare Law, Ethics, and Regulation* 11(3): 85–90.

Wette, Rosemary. 2011. English proficiency tests and communication skills training for overseas – qualified health professionals in Australia and New Zealand. *Language Assessment Quarterly* 8(2): 200–210.

Woo, Ada, Philip Dickison and John de Jong. 2010. *Setting an English language proficiency passing standard for entry-level nursing practice using the Pearson Test of English Academic.* Chicago, IL: NCLEX Technical Brief. National Council of State Boards of Nursing.

Kerry Ryan

19 Language assessment and analysis for immigration, citizenship and asylum

1 Introduction

In 2009, Elana Shohamy and Tim McNamara co-edited a special issue of *Language Assessment Quarterly* dedicated to the theme of language tests for citizenship, immigration and asylum. Their goal in presenting the issue was to lay bare the complexities of language testing in such contexts. They wrote that language testers, typically "detached from policy agendas", are increasingly aware of the need to engage not only in the day-to-day activities and research agendas surrounding test development and design but in the broader questions of test use and impact, particularly in jurisdictions where governments are intent on using language tests as instruments of power and control (Shohamy and McNamara 2009: 1).

The range of questions identified as pertinent by Shohamy and McNamara is in essence a context-specific embodiment of Shohamy's (2001) Critical Language Testing (CLT) agenda in which she advocates the development of "critical strategies to examine the uses and consequences of tests, to monitor their power, minimize their detrimental force, reveal the misuses, and empower the test-takers" (Shohamy 2001: 131). The contexts of citizenship, immigration and asylum are, consequently, an apt fit for the exploration of the issues of social justice foregrounded in CLT. Shohamy's questions include: Who are the testers? What is their agenda? Who are the test takers? What is their context? Who is going to benefit from the test? Why is the test being given? What will its results be used for? What is being tested and why? What is not being tested and why? What ideology is delivered through the test? (2001: 134). These questions are important for those attempting to make sense of the theoretical, technical and ethical issues of testing regimes for their profession. When implementing language tests and analyses in citizenship, immigration and asylum contexts, however, governments worldwide, and/or the agencies they employ, have typically shown scant regard for such concerns.

McNamara and Shohamy call on language testers to reflect on their profession's involvement in such testing regimes. For example, should language testers involve themselves in test development, design and delivery in an attempt to ensure that the government agencies that implement them observe sound language

Note: Research for this chapter was conducted with support from the Australian Research Council (Discovery Project Grant DP120100472).

testing practices and principles as determined by their profession? Unsurprisingly, agreement on the involvement of language testers in government-run testing regimes remains elusive. McNamara and Ryan (2011) write that language testing theorists who have written about the use of language tests for immigration and/or citizenship have tended to focus on the quality of the tests as instruments (what they see as a *fairness* focus on the internal properties of tests) or on the social and political contexts in which the tests are used (a focus on the external aspects that they term the *justice* of the test).

With the aim of broadening the debate, this chapter focuses particularly on contributions from researchers outside the discipline of applied linguistics. It also examines the conditions under which citizenship testing has flourished. In the context of language analysis for asylum, the chapter examines the process of Language Analysis for the Determination of Origin (LADO) and its role in refugee status determination.

2 Terms and contexts

While the three contexts – immigration, citizenship and asylum – are related, and often *conflated*, there are differences within and between each that have ramifications for any discussion on the role of language assessment and analysis. In general, the term *immigration* refers to the movement of people to a country with the intention of settling there. While the reasons people do so vary, the underlying motivation is usually to improve one's circumstances, be they economic (work/career prospects, financial investments, higher wages), political (positive and negative freedoms), or personal (lifestyle, education, standard of living, family reunification and marriage).

Countries that *receive* immigrants typically seek to control the influx through immigration laws and procedures, which cover rights of entry as well as access and rights to services and benefits within the country. Some of these laws and procedures involve language assessment, and immigrants across the world are increasingly being required to pass language tests in order to gain entry to, and/or remain domiciled in, their host countries. In some cases, language tests are taken in the country of origin and must be passed *before* entry is granted in the first instance. If admitted, and after a period of lawful residence, immigrants are often required to then pass a language and/or knowledge test in order to gain permanent residency status. As a *permanent resident* they may then be eligible to apply for citizenship, which often requires more testing, and which typically confers the greatest access to security, rights and privileges in the host country including a passport, and the right to vote, and if applicable, public education and or healthcare.

The more typical examples of language assessment as immigration policy instruments are well-known in language testing literature. Language testers know that employers and universities worldwide, for example, commonly require evidence of language proficiency from overseas applicants before offering work or study opportunities. Testers also know that governments with selective migration programs frequently prioritise local language ability along with other designated skills among prospective applicants. In situations such as these, the roles of language and language assessment as gatekeeping devices, while never absolutely agreed upon, are familiar to language assessment professionals, and the broader academy. That is, language tests have been used in such contexts for many years and debates about their suitability and efficacy for such purposes are established and on-going.

Less established however, are debates about the role of language and language assessment in "uncontrolled" or unforeseen circumstances, such as in periods of rapid growth in migration patterns or in the numbers of people fleeing persecution. United Nations (UN) statistics[1] at the time of writing show that in 2013 there were 232 million international migrants worldwide, an increase of 57 million people living abroad since 2000, and of 78 million since 1990. In terms of regions, the UN states that the proportion of migrants (per total population) has "grown rapidly" in Europe, Northern America and Oceania. Oceania, for example, saw increases in the number of migrants from 17 per cent of population in 1990 to 21 per cent in 2013, while Northern America went from 10 per cent in 1990 to 15 per cent in 2013, and Europe increased from 7 per cent in 1990 to 10 per cent in 2013. With regard to those fleeing persecution, the United Nations High Commissioner for Refugees (UNHCR), reported that at the end of 2012, there were 45.2 million forcibly displaced persons worldwide, a figure which includes around fifteen million refugees and almost one million asylum seekers.[2]

It is significant that the regions that the UN identifies as having experienced rapid growth in immigrant numbers since 1990 are also the regions that have been most active in the use of language assessment and analysis for citizenship and immigration purposes. Much of the activity has taken place in the EU but Australia, Canada and the US have also introduced or revised (read "strengthened") language guidelines in relation to citizenship and immigration. Commenting on the "rapid and constant changes" in citizenship policies in the European Union (EU), van Avermaet (2009) notes that while in 2002, the Association of Language Testers in Europe (ALTE) reported that four out of fourteen countries surveyed had language requirements for citizenship, a second ALTE survey in 2007 found that eleven out of eighteen countries surveyed had them (van Avermaet, 2009: 32). In a 2010 report for the European University Institute, Wallace Goodman compared naturalisation

1 http://esa.un.org/unmigration/wallchart2013.htm
2 http://unhcr.org/globaltrendsjune2013/UNHCR%20GLOBAL%20TRENDS%202012_V08_web.pdf

policies in thirty-three European countries, comprising the EU-27 countries as well as Croatia, Iceland, Moldova, Norway, Switzerland, and Turkey, and found that twenty-seven had explicit language requirements for naturalisation, ranging from extensive purpose-built tests designed in the country of use to off-the-shelf external tests and certificates (Wallace Goodman 2010: 25). Guild, Groenendijk and Carrera (2009) observe that while most EU states have stipulated language or integration requirements for more than fifty years, the formalisation of the regimes since 2000 has seen the required levels of language and knowledge increase considerably.

Knowledge of host country language(s) is usually just a part of a regime. Among security and character stipulations for individuals, governments also employ so-called "Knowledge of Society" (KOS) tests where prospective citizens are tested for their civic knowledge. Such tests are typically based upon the customs, values, history, systems of government, and the rights and responsibilities of citizens in the host country. Formal KOS tests are also a relatively new phenomenon. In Wallace Goodman's European citizenship report mentioned above, seventeen out of the thirty-three countries had either formal or informal KOS tests in 2010. Of those tests in Western European countries, *all* had come into operation in the previous decade (Wallace Goodman 2010: 17). One of the main features of citizenship testing regimes is that a single test commonly serves the dual purpose of determining an individual's knowledge of the local language *and* their knowledge of the host society. That is, citizenship tests are administered in the language of the host nation from materials based on the customs, values, history and systems of government from that nation. KOS tests then become *de facto* language tests, often pitched at a level that outstrips legislation. That is, despite laws stipulating that newcomers possess not much more than rudimentary language skills for citizenship, the tests themselves often require high levels of language ability in order to pass them.

3 Citizenship testing

The emergence of widespread citizenship testing was preceded by a rise in interest in citizenship itself. An area of academic enquiry not known for its dynamism, citizenship has enjoyed renewed activity since the early 1990s. In 1994, Kymlicka and Norman wrote that there had been "an explosion of interest in the concept of citizenship among political theorists" and that citizenship had "become the 'buzz word' among thinkers on all points of the political spectrum" (Kymlicka and Norman 1994: 352). One of the reasons they gave was that political philosophers in the 1970s and 1980s had been concerned primarily with issues of justice and community membership, and that citizenship, being concerned with both, was a natural progression in the discussions. They also cited a number of other factors that contributed to citizenship's resurgence during that time including "the resurgence of nationalist movements in Eastern Europe, the stresses created by an increasingly multicultural and multiracial population in Western Europe, the backlash against the welfare state in Thatcher's England, the failure of environmental policies that rely on voluntary citizen participation, and so forth" (Kymlicka and Norman 1994: 352).

While three decades on these factors remain relevant to the debate on citizenship, much has occurred since. In 1994, the authors could not properly account for the mid-to-longer-term effects of the collapse of the Berlin Wall in 1989 and the subsequent recalibration of national identities that occurred throughout Europe in its aftermath; nor could they foresee the fallout from the Bosnian War from 1992 to 1995; the race riots of northern England in the summer of 2001; the events of September 11, 2001, or the turbulent decade that followed – a decade which, as well as major terrorist bombings in Bali, Madrid and London, saw the assassination murders of outspoken Dutch politician Pim Fortuyn in 2002 and the similarly forthright film-maker Theo van Gogh in 2004, both of whom had spoken out strongly against immigration in the Netherlands.

It is in this climate that formal citizenship testing regimes have proliferated, to the point where, as noted above, language and/or civic knowledge requirements for citizenship are currently the rule in Europe, *not* the exception. While to assume convergence across countries and contexts is inherently fraught, many of the arguments for or against citizenship tests, regardless of the country in which they are administered, have been conducted within the political and public arenas along similar lines. Generally, testing proponents reason that shared civic knowledge, and/or a shared language, are necessary prerequisites for social cohesion and a more participatory, active form of citizenship. They also argue that citizenship is a prize and that if it is to mean anything at all, such a prize – which confers certain "privileges" upon recipients – should not be simply given away, but should be earned.

The arguments in favour of a language component in testing regimes usually rest on language as necessary for meaningful political and/or social engagement, or as a necessary precursor for employment in the host country. Employment, it is claimed, leads to independence and reduces the welfare load (in states where this is applicable); it simultaneously increases social opportunities, which lead to improvements in language ability, which in turn lead to a better, more integrated life for the individual immigrants, their families and to the greater societal good in general. *Not* knowing the language, on the other hand, is often promoted as a disaster-in-waiting, reflective of a lack of respect for, and/or a failure or unwillingness to embrace, the local population, its customs, language and ways of life.

Many of those opposed to testing for citizenship consider that knowledge of the dominant language in a society is optimal. Indeed, immigrants themselves often acknowledge the importance of the local language for increased opportunities in the host society. There is less agreement, however, on whether language should be a stipulation upon which the allocation of citizenship hinges. Many of the tests themselves provide ample ammunition for arguments raised against them, as they often prove to be discriminatory against more vulnerable groups. Tests that split the body politic into haves and have-nots provide ready-made arguments for supporters of the notion that social cohesion is a more likely by-product of *inclusion* rather than *exclusion*. Other arguments centre around the types of materials upon which the tests are based. For example, the "official" statements of nationhood and accounts of history that governments tend to present in test materials (usually in the form of a study booklet) represent fertile ground for conflict among politicians, academics, social commentators and members of the public.

As formal citizenship testing is a relatively recent phenomenon, academic deliberations on the full range of issues involved are essentially undeveloped. Most of the research to date has been descriptive, focusing on the practices of citizenship testing in particular national contexts (cf. edited volumes by Guild, Groenendijk and Carrera, 2009; Extra, Spotti and Van Avermaet, 2009; and Hogan-Brun, Mar-Molinero and Stevenson, 2009) as opposed to broader studies of their actual effects and likely attainment of the almost universally stated aims of improved social cohesion and successful integration of migrant populations, both of which are largely unquantifiable, particularly without the passage of time.

There has been widespread debate about citizenship testing by thinkers outside of applied linguistics. Some of their concerns are familiar to those of language testers: the types of questions asked, the ease of access to materials (and their cost) for test preparation, the overall difficulty of the test, and/or the ramifications and effects that failing the tests have on particular groups, for example. Such questions influence judgements about the acceptability, or reasonableness, of testing regimes. For example, many of those who (often grudgingly) acquiesce to the existence of citizenship tests question what types of tests might be acceptable within a liberal-democratic framework. Discussions here may focus on the nature and content of the tests themselves. A EUDO-Citizenship forum debate in 2010 (Bauböck and Joppke 2010) – sparked by Christian Joppke with a contribution entitled "How liberal are citizenship tests?" – is a useful summary of many such issues relating to citizenship testing in Europe.

Joppke (2010) advances the notion that any tests that are not particularly onerous ought to be acceptable from a liberal standpoint. That is, a government should be able to ask a prospective citizen to clear a hurdle or two to gain citizenship, provided that the hurdle is not particularly high. With test difficulty the benchmark of acceptability, he expresses no particular objection to the content of test materials. For Joppke, cultural, political and historical knowledge is fair game, provided that questions do not encroach upon an individual's beliefs. He cites the interview guidelines designed for use by naturalisation officers in the German state of Baden-Württemberg as an example of the extreme end of illiberal practices (cf. Michalowski 2010: 5; von Koppenfels 2010: 12; Orgad 2010: 21–22; Hansen 2010: 26). The infamous Baden-Württemberg test (superseded by the introduction of Germany's national citizenship test in 2008) was a series of questions about applicants' attitudes and beliefs regarding contentious topics such as race, gender roles and homosexuality (Hawley 2006).

The basis of Joppke's argument against testing individuals' beliefs is that it is fundamentally illiberal to insist that all who live in a country be liberal. Citizenship testing regimes, therefore, have no business in matters of the heart, and governments should go no further than the expectation that regardless of what individuals may believe privately, they do not act illegally against the established order. On this point, Joppke (2010) quotes Miller: "Liberal states do not require their citizens to *believe* liberal principles, since they tolerate communists, anarchists, fascists and so forth. What they require is that citizens should conform to liberal principles in practice and accept as legitimate policies that are pursued in the name of such principles, while they are left free to advocate alternative arrangements" (Miller 2004: 14).

For Joppke, provided that they are not too difficult and do not ask for individuals to concede or modify their inner dispositions, citizenship tests should be free to test knowledge of language, culture and history because they are external topics and the required knowledge can be learned, regurgitated and then discarded without any cost to the individual in terms of identity or true beliefs.

Groenendijk and van Oers (2010) argue that the *effects* of the tests are an apt measure of whether they are liberal or not. Where certain nationalities and/or visa categories in particular countries are affected more than others, tests, regardless of content, represent barriers to immigration that are more difficult for some to overcome than others. Such differential treatment is illiberal because, according to Kostakopoulou, liberalism does not abide "domination, discrimination and unequal treatment, the stigmatisation of certain individuals and the consistent devaluation of their contributions" (2010: 16). On this basis, i.e. of differential effects on certain groups, it is difficult to see any language-based citizenship test qualifying as liberal. In the context of the Australian citizenship test, which Joppke (2007: 7) lauds for its "phenomenally high pass rate of 96.7% between October 2007 and March 2009", Ryan (2012) found that four years of test data had shown that there were large disparities in test outcomes for skilled migrants and for those who had arrived in Australia via the country's humanitarian aid program. In short, the Australian citizenship test, promoted as a tool for improved social cohesion and integration, was withholding security (citizenship status) and political participation (voting rights), from the most vulnerable group of test takers.

For Kostakopoulou, a disjunct exists between the expectations that states have of newcomers in terms of burden-sharing (e.g., paying taxes and national insurances) and the newcomers' rights to share in the benefits that they bring to a society through such contributions. For many liberals then, the ease or difficulty of a testing regime is perhaps not the issue; rather, that there is a regime at all and that migrants have no choice other than to comply. This stance aligns somewhat with McNamara and Ryan's (2011) proposed distinction between fairness and justice in language tests. On the subject of whether people should be excluded from the democratic process by a test, Carens (2010: 19) states "as a matter of fundamental democratic principle, people who have been settled in a country for several years are members of society and should be able to participate in the political process governing their society. Their opportunity to do so should not depend upon their capacity to pass a test, however it is designed."

While he advocates a personal view that all citizenship tests are objectionable in principle, Carens (2010: 20) notes that "they are not all equally objectionable in practice" and suggests that instead of arguments about *thresholds* of liberality, it would be more pertinent to approach the issue from the point of view of *degrees* of liberality. To do so, he says, would require closer examination of the particular local contexts within which such tests operate. Pertinent issues for Carens include not only what the effects of the tests in any given country are, but more sociological questions such as who defends them and why; who opposes them and why; what advocates say the tests are for; and whether the stated purposes are genuine or whether they mask other intentions. Carens, it seems, advocates a CLT agenda (Shohamy 2001).

Hansen (2010) defends citizenship tests on the grounds that the state, as well as other citizens, can reasonably expect fellow participants in the democratic process to "have a basic knowledge of the country's history, institutions and culture." Also, citizenship tests are not unfair simply because immigrants are required to take tests that native-born citizens are not. Citing Barry's notion that "all general laws have differential effects" (2010: 25) Hansen notes that tax laws have differential effects according to income, that anti-smoking laws affect smokers more than non-smokers, and that anti-noise laws affect noisy people more than quiet ones. Such effects do not make the laws unfair.

While his contention on laws is a point of difference for political theorists, from an applied linguistics perspective, Hansen's point in support of his reasonableness argument for tests is a curious one. He states that "citizenship tests are in a fundamental sense a substitute for education", and that locally born and educated individuals should have acquired the necessary civic knowledge through the school system (Hansen 2010: 25). If they did not, it is the system's failure. Complaining against tests imposed upon newcomers about knowledge that locals are unlikely to possess amounts to a tribute to "shoddy schools", he concludes (Hansen 2010: 25). While Hansen does concede that tests are not necessarily a *good* substitute for education, they are, in his opinion, still an education and that "making tests a requirement rather than an expectation is no different from making education a requirement rather than an expectation" (Hansen 2010: 25).

While his argument may have surface appeal for some, like many commentators on the topic Hansen takes no account of the fact that such tests are de facto language tests that require high levels of language ability in order to pass them. Instead, he argues that those who fail tests because of their language skills have an obligation to improve them because "there can be no meaningful political participation without knowledge of the national language." Notwithstanding the fact that in most liberal democracies where citizenship tests operate political participation (in the form of voting) is not compulsory, this is a common position taken by citizenship testing proponents. Citizenship rights and political participation, however, are not the same thing. While there can certainly be no meaningful political participation without citizenship rights, the idea that a person is unable to participate in politics because of an arbitrary threshold of language proficiency is dismissive of the way that individuals or groups seek out information and organise and represent themselves and their constituents – many of whom do not speak the language of their host societies – in the political arena.

4 Language analysis for asylum

Article 1 (A.2) of the 1951 UN Convention relating to the Status of Refugees, in part, defines a refugee as a person who is outside the country of their nationality or habitual residence, and who, because of a "well-founded fear of being persecuted for reasons of race, religion, nationality, membership of a particular social group or political opinion" is either unable or unwilling to return to that country. The status of "refugee", and the extended rights that come with it, apply to an individual only if and when their claim has been recognised as legitimate by the relevant authorities within the country in which the claim is made. The term "asylum seeker" on the other hand applies to the individual *before* his or her claim is fully assessed; it is a period spent in limbo, during which the status of refugee is uncertain.

The process of evaluating the claims of asylum seekers, Refugee Status Determination (RSD), includes an initial "credibility assessment", which, put simply, is a judgement made as to the plausibility of the claim (UNHCR 2013). In short, is the claimant's statement believable and does it fit the definition of a refugee? That is, are they *actually* from where they *claim* to be from and would they face persecution if returned to their country of nationality or habitual residence? Confounding the process is the fact that many asylum seekers present with no documentation – it is often safer to travel without it – and, as Patrick (2012) describes, with nothing more than their body and their story as evidence of their claims. In situations where immigration officials have reason to doubt the credibility of claims for asylum, language analysis is often used to assist the determination process. This process, known as Language Analysis for the Determination of Origin (LADO), is underpinned by the assumption that the way a person speaks holds clues as to their origins (Eades 2005). While this is relatively uncontroversial, national boundaries rarely coincide neatly with linguistic ones and the assumption therefore does not necessarily hold for nationality or citizenship, the bases upon which asylum claims are often assessed.

Muysken, Verrips and Zwaan (2010: 2) write that use of language analysis in the asylum claims process began in "various immigration departments, notably in Sweden and Switzerland," in the 1990s. Writing in 2004, Reath traces the use of language analysis in asylum cases to the Swedish Migration Board in 1993, and notes its subsequent growth as a private enterprise utilised by governments and their agencies throughout various countries in Europe and the world into the early 2000s. Reath also notes the dearth of publicly available information and independent research at that time on the practices, procedures and consequences of language analyses in the asylum context, calling for urgent academic scrutiny of the field. She knew, however, that such scrutiny was underway, citing a report from Eades et al. (2003) in which Eades and her colleagues studied 58 asylum seeker case appeal decisions from Australia's Refugee Review Tribunal from October 2000 to July 2002. The 58 case decisions were based on language analyses provided by agencies outside of Australia. On reviewing the cases, Eades and her colleagues concluded that the type of language analysis being used to determine the nationality of asylum seekers was "not valid or reliable" and that the Australian government was in all likelihood, flouting its obligations under the Refugee Convention (Eades et al 2003: 179).

Perhaps the main area of contention surrounding the practice of LADO is who performs the analysis and what level of expertise they have. Early papers (Eades et al 2003; Reath 2004; Eades 2005) convey a sense of alarm about the practices employed in LADO and the "'folk views' about the relationship between language and nationality and ethnicity" upon which decisions are often based (Eades et al 2003: 179).

In 2004, the Language and National Origin Group, comprised of nineteen linguistic experts from around the world, formulated and countersigned the *Guidelines for the Use of Language Analysis in Relation to Questions of National Origin in Refugee Cases*. The Guidelines (reproduced in Eades 2005) were intended as a set of minimum standards to assist governments and agencies involved in LADO "in assessing the general validity of language analysis in the determination of national origin, nationality or citizenship" (Eades 2005: 520). According to Patrick (2012) "the Guidelines have been endorsed worldwide by professional associations of linguists, both theoretical and applied" (2012: 535). It is true to say however that while the Guidelines have been endorsed by professional associations there is no obligation for governments or their agencies to apply them and the practice of LADO is carried out with varying adherence to the Guidelines set out by the Language and National Origin Group (cf. Patrick 2012 for a discussion of organisations that perform LADO).

McNamara, Verrips and van den Hazelkamp (2010) outline the processes by which speech samples are elicited for analysis by agencies that perform LADO.

They note that there is "considerable variation" in practices among different agencies (2010: 63). Speech samples may be elicited via structured or unstructured interviews; they may also be a monologue, or a (seemingly) informal dialogue with a trained or untrained interviewer. Participants may be quizzed on topics related to their claim and the country or culture from which they come. Fellow interlocutors may be there simply to gather speech samples or they may be the analysts themselves, in which case they may be "either a native speaker or non-native speaker, and with or without formal academic training in linguistic analysis" (2010: 63). Interviews vary in length anywhere from five minutes to an hour; they may also be conducted via telephone, in the asylum seeker's first language or a variety related to it, in a lingua franca, or a combination of these. The authors cite such variations, individually or in combination, as likely to have an impact upon the validity of the assessment.

For Patrick (2012) the folk conception of the term "linguist" is problematic. He notes that there is a tendency for people to assume that a linguist is simply a person who speaks two or more languages, as opposed to one who is trained in the structure of language and is equipped to perform considered and reliable language analysis. LADO reports, for example, incorporate knowledge of "phonetics, phonology, the lexicon, syntax, and morphology" (Patrick 2012: 540), the knowledge of which is typically beyond the untrained. Another "folk-view" of concern expressed by Eades et al (2003: 180) and Fraser (2009) is the notion that native speakers of a particular language are able to recognise their language as spoken by another. On this, Fraser (2009: 114) writes "people without extended training in academic linguistics are often ignorant not just about many aspects of language, but about their own ignorance, and so tend to put unjustified faith in their own 'folk knowledge'."

Other significant problems that face LADO practitioners are inherent in the nature of asylum itself. Many of the world's trouble-spots from which people flee are linguistically, ethnically and culturally diverse. War and upheaval often makes them more so, or at the very least, means that up-to-date knowledge of predominant language varieties is difficult to attain, particularly the type of structural language knowledge required for detailed and reliable analysis such as that required in the LADO process (Eades et al. 2003). Also, as Blommaert (2009) has shown in his account of the troubled life of "Joseph", a refugee from Rwanda, flight from one's homeland can take years; it can involve all manner of horrors and degradations in and out of refugee camps and/or detention camps, and exposure to a multiplicity of languages and dialects. Such life histories such are not unusual among asylum seekers and raise questions about the ability of language analysis, whatever form it takes, to determine accurately a person's origins.

While it is generally accepted among linguistic professionals that the greatest likelihood of performing LADO to the highest possible standards comes with the use of sociolinguistic experts as analysts, this has also been controversial. Writing about the "two schools of thought" in the practice of LADO – one being the use of trained native speakers supervised by linguists and the other being the use of a linguist specialised in the target language – Cambier-Langeveld (2010a) defends the former. As a practitioner in the Dutch context she notes that the "crucial point" in determining the suitability of the analyst for the task set is that the "analyst's knowledge of the relevant varieties is tested, developed and determined by the supervising linguist" (2010a: 23). In a study of eight asylum seeker cases with known outcomes, Cambier-Langeveld (2010b) compares the Dutch Immigration and Naturalization Service (INS) reports for each case – as performed by non-expert native speakers (NENS) in the Office for Country Information and Language Analysis (OCILA) – with counter expert reports as prepared by academic experts. In her study of the eight cases, all of which were false claims from asylum seekers, counter experts did not perform as well as NENS, leading Cambier-Langeveld to conclude that the necessity for a "strictly analytical approach" was "untenable" (2010b: 84).

Patrick (2012) acknowledges that NENS have a role to play in LADO but suggests that the type of training they receive is unclear as organisations do not readily divulge information about the level of training and supervision of the NENS they employ. His main contention is that NENS lack the type of rigorous training necessary to perform LADO free of the "folk beliefs, prejudices, and assumptions about language that we are all socialized into in our communities" (2012: 544). For him, the issue is not whether NENS have a place in LADO analysis but how they should be used. Given that they are being used and that cases of asylum are only likely to increase into the future, there is an urgent need to clarify the nature of native speaker competence and its role in LADO.

5 Future directions

This chapter has attempted to outline the thoughts of researchers outside of applied linguistics in order to broaden the debates surrounding language assessment and analysis in the immigration, citizenship and asylum contexts. It includes discussions about the *reasonableness* of testing regimes and, in the case of citizenship tests at least, how reasonableness should be conceptualised. As much of the activity across all contexts discussed here has been relatively recent much remains unresolved and further exploration of the concept of reasonableness is justified. What is reasonableness in these contexts, for example? Should it be framed as a liberal argument, and conceptualised as it is above in terms of test difficulty, test content, or the effects that language assessment and/or analysis have on both individuals and on societies? Systematic comparative studies of testing regimes across these categories and across the world – not just in the EU where much of the research to date has been focused – is necessary to lend weight to such discussions.

The chapter also noted that applied linguists have a tendency to focus primarily on improving test instruments in order to observe best practice when making determinations that may affect the lives of the vulnerable. This, of course, is what they are trained to do. Such approaches are necessary, particularly in high-stakes testing and analysis – in cases of asylum seeker claims the stakes could get no higher – where procedures need to be transparent, reliable and legally defensible. It is vital however that such a focus does not distract from the urgent need for studies of the *actual* effects that language assessment and analysis in these contexts are having on individuals as well as groups of test takers. There is little research available to date on the lived experiences of test takers with regard to their engagement and experiences as subjects of testing regimes.

Also, little to date is known about the effects that language testing regimes have on democracy at both the individual and societal levels. An individual who fails a citizenship test is in most cases denied a vote, as well as the security and stability that a passport offers. A large and growing group of individuals living in a society under such conditions is an obvious impediment to a fully functioning democracy and the security and stability upon which democracy itself relies. Again, systematic comparative studies of local and international test data relating to the individuals and groups of test takers excluded through testing regimes presents as an urgent need.

Finally, in commenting on the US media's reportage of the Vietnam War, Chomsky (Chomsky, Mitchell and Schoeffel 2002) lamented that what was perceived to be anti-war criticism at the time was less about the folly of being in a war in Vietnam at all and more about the fact that the US was not winning it. Chomsky called this a "fight it better" kind of criticism (2002: 64). In the study of language assessment and analysis for immigration, citizenship and asylum, endeavouring to "fight it better" by focusing on refining the tools by which population economies are shaped risks an underdeveloped critique of the underlying policies and ideologies that drive their existence. It is these underlying policies and ideologies that present the greatest challenge to researchers, not necessarily because they are particularly difficult to expose, more because they are particularly difficult to shift.

6 References

Blommaert, Jan. 2009. Language, asylum, and the national order. *Current Anthropology* 50(4): 415–425.

Cambier-Langeveld, Tina. 2010a. The validity of language analysis in the Netherlands. In: Karin Zwaan, Maaike Verrips and Pieter Muysken (eds). *Language and Origin: The Role of Language in European Asylum Procedures: A Linguistic and Legal Survey*, 21–33. Nijmegen: Wolf Legal Publishers.

Cambier-Langeveld, Tina. 2010b. The role of linguists and native speakers in language analysis for the determination of speaker origin. *The International Journal of Speech, Language and the Law* 17(1): 67–93.

Carens, Joseph. 2010. The most liberal citizenship test is none at all. In: Rainer Bauböck and Christian Joppke (eds). How liberal are citizenship tests? European University Institute Working Papers EUI Working Paper RSCAS 2010/41. Robert Schuman Centre for Advanced Studies. European University Institute.

Chomsky, Noam, Peter R. Mitchell and John Schoeffel (eds). 2002. *Understanding power: the indispensible Noam Chomsky.* New York: New Press.

Eades, Diana. 2005. Applied linguistics and language analysis in asylum seeker cases. *Applied Linguistics* 26: 503–526.

Eades, Diana, Helen Fraser, Jeff Siegel, Tim McNamara and Brett Baker. 2003. Linguistic identification in the determination of nationality: A preliminary report. *Language Policy* 2: 179–199.

Extra, Guus, Massimiliano Spotti and Piet Van Avermaet (eds). 2009. *Language Testing, Migration and Citizenship: Cross-National Perspectives on Integration Regimes.* London: Continuum.

Fraser, Helen. 2009. The role of "educated native speakers" in providing language analysis for the determination of the origin of asylum seekers. *International Journal of Speech Language and the Law* 16: 113–138.

Groenendijk, Kees and Ricky van Oers. 2010. How liberal tests are does not merely depend on their content, but also their effects. In: Rainer Bauböck and Christian Joppke (eds.). How liberal are citizenship tests? European University Institute Working Papers EUI Working Paper RSCAS 2010/41. Robert Schuman Centre for Advanced Studies. European University Institute.

Guild, Elspeth, Kees Groenendijk and Sergio Carrera. 2009. Understanding the contest of community: Illiberal practices in the EU. In: Elspeth Guild, Kees Groenendijk and Sergio Carrera (eds.). *Illiberal Liberal States: Immigration, Citizenship and Integration in the EU*, 1–25. Farnham, UK: Ashgate.

Hansen, Randall. 2010. Citizenship tests: An unapologetic defense. In: Rainer Bauböck and Christian Joppke (eds.). How liberal are citizenship tests? European University Institute Working Papers EUI Working Paper RSCAS 2010/41. Robert Schuman Centre for Advanced Studies. European University Institute.

Hawley, Charles. 2006. Muslim profiling: A German state quizes (sic) Muslim immigrants on Jews, gays and swim lessons. *Der Spiegel*, 31 Jan. http://www.spiegel.de/international/muslim-profiling-a-german-state-quizes-muslim-immigrants-on-jews-gays-and-swim-lessons-a-397482.html (accessed 31 Oct 2014).

Hogan-Brun, Gabrielle, Clare Mar-Molinero and Patrick Stevenson (eds). 2009. Discourses on Language and Integration: Critical Perspectives on Language Testing Regimes in Europe. Amsterdam: John Benjamins.

Joppke, Christian. 2007. Beyond national models: Civic integration policies for immigrants in Western Europe, West European Politics. 30(1): 1–22.

Joppke, Christian. 2010. How Liberal Are Citizenship Tests? In: Rainer Bauböck and Christian Joppke (eds.). How liberal are citizenship tests? European University Institute Working Papers EUI Working Paper RSCAS 2010/41. Robert Schuman Centre for Advanced Studies. European University Institute.

Kostakopoulou, Dora. 2010. What liberalism is committed to and why current citizenship policies fail this test. In: Rainer Bauböck and Christian Joppke (eds) How liberal are citizenship tests? European University Institute Working Papers EUI Working Paper RSCAS 2010/41. Robert Schuman Centre for Advanced Studies. European University Institute.

Kymlicka, Will and Wayne Norman. 1994. Return of the citizen: A survey of recent work on citizenship theory. *Ethics* 104(2): 352–381.

Language and National Origin Group. 2004. Guidelines for the use of language analysis in relation to questions of national origin in refugee cases. *International Journal of Speech Language and the Law* 11: 261–266.

McNamara, Tim. 2009. Language tests and social policy: A commentary. In: Gabrielle Hogan-Brun, Clare Mar-Molinero and Patrick Stevenson (eds.). *Discourses on Language and Integration: Critical Perspectives on Language Testing Regimes in Europe.* 153–163.

McNamara, Tim and Kerry Ryan. 2011. Fairness vs justice in language testing: The place of English literacy in the Australian citizenship test. *Language Assessment Quarterly* 8(2): 161–178.

McNamara, Tim, Maaike Verrips and Carolien van den Hazelkamp. 2010. LADO, validity and language testing. In: Karin Zwaan, Maaike Verrips and Pieter Muysken (eds.). *Language and Origin: The Role of Language in European Asylum Procedures: A Linguistic and Legal Survey.* 61–71. Nijmegen: Wolf Legal Publishers.

Michalowski, Ines. 2010. Citizenship tests and traditions of state interference with cultural diversity. In: Rainer Bauböck and Christian Joppke (eds.). How liberal are citizenship tests? European University Institute Working Papers EUI Working Paper RSCAS 2010/41. Robert Schuman Centre for Advanced Studies. European University Institute.

Miller, David. 2004. Immigrants, nations and citizenship. Paper presented at conference on Migrants, Nations, and Citizenship, University of Cambridge, 5–6 July.

Muysken, Pieter, Maaike Verrips and Karin Zwaan. 2010. Introduction. In: Karin Zwaan, Maaike Verrips and Pieter Muysken (eds.). *Language and Origin: The Role of Language in European Asylum Procedures: A Linguistic and Legal Survey.* 1–6. Nijmegen: Wolf Legal Publishers.

Orgad, Liav. 2010. Illiberal liberalism: Cultural restrictions on migration and access to citizenship in Europe. *American Journal of Comparative Law* 58(1): 53–106.

Patrick, Peter L. 2012. Language analysis for determination of origin: Objective evidence for refugee status determination. In: Peter M. Tiersma and Lawrence M. Solan (eds.). *The Oxford Handbook of Language and Law,* 533–546. Oxford, UK: Oxford University Press.

Reath, Anne. 2004. Language analysis in the context of the asylum process: Procedures, validity and consequences. *Language Assessment Quarterly* 1: 209–233.

Ryan, Kerry. 2012. Citizenship for Beginners. Inside Story, 16 Apr. http://inside.org.au/citizenship-for-beginners/ (accessed 31 October 2014).

Shohamy, Elana. 2001. *The Power of Tests: A Critical Perspective of the Use of Language Tests.* Singapore: Longman.

Shohamy, Elana and Tim McNamara (eds.). 2009. *Language assessment for immigration, citizenship, and asylum* [Special Issue]. *Language Assessment Quarterly* 6(1).

Shohamy, Elana and Tim McNamara. 2009. Language tests for citizenship, immigration, and asylum. *Language Assessment Quarterly* 6(1): 1–5.

van Avermaet, Piet. 2009. Fortress Europe? Language policy regimes for immigration and citizenship. In: Gabrielle Hogan-Brun, Clare Mar-Molinero and Patrick Stevenson (eds.). Discourses on Language and Integration: Critical Perspectives on Language Testing Regimes in Europe. 15–43.

von Koppenfels, Amanda K. 2010. Citizenship tests could signal that European states perceive themselves as immigration countries. In: Rainer Bauböck and Christian Joppke (eds.). How liberal are citizenship tests? European University Institute Working Papers EUI Working Paper RSCAS 2010/41. Robert Schuman Centre for Advanced Studies. European University Institute.

Wallace Goodman, Sara. 2010. *Naturalisation Policies in Europe: Exploring Patterns of Inclusion and Exclusion.* Robert Schuman Centre for Advanced Studies, European University Institute.

UN High Commissioner for Refugees (UNHCR). 2013. Beyond Proof, Credibility Assessment in EU Asylum Systems: Summary, May 2013. http://www.refworld.org/docid/51a704244.html (accessed 21 March 2014).

IV. Issues in second language assessment

Spiros Papageorgiou
20 Aligning language assessments to standards and frameworks

1 Introduction

In recent years, educational reforms around the world have resulted in increased interest in aligning curricula, textbooks and, in particular, assessments to external standards. In the field of second language assessment, the alignment of tests to the Common European Framework of Reference (CEFR; Council of Europe 2001) has dominated relevant research for more than a decade. Aligning test content and scores to the six main levels of the CEFR has been advocated as a way to facilitate score interpretations across different educational contexts (Council of Europe, 2009). However, researchers have noted issues with the use of the CEFR for 1. designing test specifications (Alderson et al. 2006), 2. setting minimum score requirements for its levels (Papageorgiou 2010a) and 3. comparing scores across tests designed for different purposes (Fulcher 2004; Weir 2005). This chapter discusses issues of alignment related to the CEFR and other educational standards and frameworks. The chapter concludes by arguing that although alignment to an external framework or standard should not be seen as a substitute for test validation (Fulcher, this volume), it should, however, be part of validation efforts because it might offer more concrete meaning to assessment results (Kane 2012: 8).

2 History of aligning language assessments

2.1 Definitions and descriptions of standards and frameworks

The terms *frameworks* and *standards* are often used interchangeably in the language testing literature. A standard might refer to a set of guidelines on which tests are constructed and evaluated (Alderson et al. 1995: 236) for example the *Standards for Educational and Psychological Testing* (AERA, APA, and NCME 1999). Standards might also describe learning outcomes used to assess and report learner progress and achievement, typically in the form of behavioral scales of language proficiency (Brindley 1998) and they are found not only in educational contexts, but also professional ones where language proficiency is a requirement for performing in the workplace. In the context of aviation English, for example, the International Civil Aviation Organization (ICAO) has set English language requirements for air traffic controllers and pilots (Alderson 2009, 2010).

In the educational measurement literature descriptions of what learners must do in order to demonstrate performance at a given level are called *performance standards* whereas descriptions of what should be taught in the curriculum are called *content standards* (Hambleton 2001). When training raters or familiarizing test takers with test content, language testers often use the term *benchmarks* to refer to speaking and writing performance standards (Kantarcioglu and Papageorgiou 2011). In this chapter, the term standard is used to refer to documents such as the ACTFL Guidelines (American Council on the Teaching of Foreign Languages 2012) and the CEFR to which testing agencies attempt to align their assessments.

The ACTFL Proficiency Guidelines (American Council on the Teaching of Foreign Languages 2012) were published in 1986 as the academic version of the U.S. Government's Interagency Language Roundtable (ILR) Skill Level Descriptions (see Lowe, 1983). The Guidelines describe what individuals can do with language in speaking, writing, listening, and reading in real-world situations on "a continuum of proficiency from that of the highly articulate, well-educated language user to a level of little or no functional ability" (American Council on the Teaching of Foreign Languages 2012: 3). For each skill there are five major levels of proficiency: Distinguished, Superior, Advanced, Intermediate, and Novice. Advanced, Intermediate, and Novice are subdivided into High, Mid, and Low sublevels. The Guidelines are not based on any particular theory, pedagogical method, or educational curriculum. They neither describe how an individual learns a language nor prescribe how an individual should learn a language, and they should not be used for such purposes. They are an instrument for the evaluation of functional language ability. Revisions to the 2012 edition of the Guidelines include:

- the addition of the major level of Distinguished for Speaking and Writing
- the division of the Advanced level into the three sublevels of High, Mid, and Low for the Listening and Reading
- the addition of a general level description at the Advanced, Intermediate, and Novice levels for all language skills

The 2012 version of the Guidelines contains a glossary of terms, and annotated, multimedia samples of performance at each level for Speaking and Writing, and examples of oral and written texts and tasks associated with each level for Reading and Listening (see www.actfl.org).

The CEFR proficiency scales and performance descriptors were developed based on both quantitative and qualitative methodologies during a large-scale research project reported in North and Schneider (1998) and in more detail in North (2000). An initial pool of forty-one proficiency scales with their constituent descriptors was created based on existing ones, such as the ACTFL Proficiency Guidelines discussed above (for a detailed list, see Council of Europe 2001: 224–225). In the next qualitative phase, the scales were refined though consultations with teachers representing all educational sectors in Switzerland. The refined scales and descriptors underwent quantitative analysis by asking teachers to use them to rate the performance of their students as well as selected student performance provided by the project team in video format. Using the many-facet Rasch model (Linacre 1994), the descriptors were then calibrated and placed at different proficiency levels that subsequently formed the CEFR levels. Although the CEFR is mostly known for these proficiency scales, it also contains rich information on language learning and assessment. For example, Chapter 5 discusses general competences and communicative language competences. Chapter 7 analyzes the role of tasks, both real-life and classroom ones, in language learning and teaching. Chapter 9 is concerned with topics related to assessment, in particular the various assessment purposes and types of assessments. The CEFR document also contains a number of appendices which provide supplementary material, including a discussion of technical issues specific to the development of language proficiency scales and performance descriptors.

Milanovic and Weir (2010: viii) point out that the CEFR levels do not constitute standards in the strictest sense, but instead provide a useful frame of reference and a source of meta-discourse. However, the CEFR is increasingly used as an external standard by governments and international agencies in order to set policy (see Fulcher, this volume). Another reason for referring to the CEFR as a standard is the potentially misleading use of the word *framework*. According to Davidson and Fulcher (2007: 232) and Fulcher and Davidson (2009: 4), documents such as the CEFR are in fact models, because they constitute a general description of language competence and demonstrate a theoretical understanding of language knowledge and use.

Alignment of language tests to the Common European Framework of Reference has dominated the relevant language assessment literature for more than a decade. One of the aims of the Council of Europe is to promote plurilingualism and pluriculturalism among European citizens. To this end, the Council of Europe published a number of documents in the 1970s that have been influential in second language teaching. Such documents include the notional-functional syllabus by Wilkins (1976) that describes what a learner communicates through language and three ascending levels describing language achievement: Waystage (Van Ek and Trim 1991), Threshold (Van Ek and Trim 1998) and Vantage (Van Ek and Trim 2001). The CEFR emerged from this ongoing work of the Council of Europe, as well as North's research (North 2000), as a publication in 2001 (Council of Europe 2001). It contains dozens of language proficiency scales, describing language activities and competences at six main levels: A1 (the lowest) through A2, B1, B2, C1 and C2 (the highest). These six "criterion" levels (Council of Europe 2001: 32) are complimented in some scales by intermediate "plus" levels, e.g., A2+, B1+, and B2+. The CEFR scales comprise statements called "descriptors", which were designed following an action-oriented approach where language users are seen as members of a society who have tasks to accomplish, including those that are not language-related (Council of Europe 2001: 9).

2.2 The process of aligning tests to standards

The publication of the CEFR has been recognized as the "most significant recent event on the language education scene in Europe" (Alderson 2005: 275), and its impact has been felt beyond the continent's borders, as language examination providers inside and outside Europe follow various methodologies to align their tests to the CEFR levels, as reported in several case studies in Figueras and Noijons (2009) and Martyniuk (2010). The most common approach to aligning tests to the CEFR is the one recommended in the *Manual* published by the Council of Europe (2009). The approach consists of two main stages: content alignment and setting of cut scores. For content alignment, the *Manual* provides forms to be completed for each language skill (Council of Europe 2009: 25–34). The forms require the developer of an exam to describe various aspects of the test content for each language skill in relation to the CEFR, for example communicative language activities, tasks, communication themes and text types. The intended CEFR level for each language skill should also be specified. The completed forms constitute a claim of how an exam covers the above content aspects of language ability described in the CEFR. The second stage involves the setting of minimum scores on the test. This would indicate that a test taker has demonstrated performance expected at that CEFR level (Council of Europe 2009: 35–88). These minimum scores (cut scores) are established following a well-researched process in the educational measurement literature called "standard setting" (Cizek and Bunch 2007). During standard setting, a panel of expert judges (often called "panelists") is required under the guidance of one or more meeting facilitators to make judgments on which examination providers will base their final cut-score decisions. Statistical information about test items and the distribution of scores are also used to help panelists with their judgment task. A fairly common practice in standard-setting meetings is that more than one round of judgments takes place (see Hambleton 2001; Plake 2008). Between rounds, the panel discusses individual judgments, receives the statistical information about items and scores and repeats the judgments. Even though the panel will offer a recommended cut score, the decision whether to accept this score rests with the examination provider. In this sense, standard setting is in fact a procedure for recommending cut scores to the provider of the test (Cizek and Bunch 2007: 13; Tannenbaum and Katz 2013: 455–456). Procedures for validating the recommended cut scores are also presented in the *Manual* (Council of Europe 2009: 89–118).

In the educational measurement literature, alignment typically refers to the extent to which the content of an assessment covers the types of skills and abilities described in K-12 content standards. As Webb (2007) points out, the No Child Left Behind Act (2001) in the United States has resulted in increased demand for assessments to demonstrate alignment with content standards in terms of comprehensiveness, emphasis, depth, and clarity for users. More recently the Common Core State Standards (http://www.corestandards.org/resources), an initiative supported by most states in the United States to describe the skills and abilities expected by students at each grade level, has further raised demand for aligning assessments to content standards. The demand for alignment of assessment to various content standards has also increased worldwide, because of education reforms which push for accountability, including close monitoring of students' progress and use of standardized tests (Deville and Chalhoub-Deville 2011).

3 Key issues in research approaches investigating alignment

A major issue with alignment, according to Webb (2007: 7–8), is determining and evaluating the extent to which alignment has been completed in an acceptable way. Webb proposes four criteria to evaluate the alignment of assessments to content standards, which addressed the following questions:
- Categorical occurrence: does the test cover the content discussed in the standard?
- Depth-of-Knowledge (DOK) consistency: given the description of what learners are expected to know and to be able to do in the standard, is the assessment as cognitively challenging for the test takers as might be expected?
- Range of Knowledge Correspondence – how does the breadth of knowledge in the assessment correspond to the knowledge expected by the standard?
- Balance of Representation: how is specific knowledge emphasized in comparison to the standard?

The *Manual* (Council of Europe 2009) does not provide criteria like Webb's (2007) for evaluating alignment of test content to the CEFR. However, the various forms that should be completed during the Specification stage cover to some extent the aspects of content alignment described above.

It is important to note that content alignment as described in both the *Manual* and Webb (2007) involves the use of human judgment. Likewise, researchers in educational measurement point out that a central issue throughout the process of setting cut scores is the need to apply human judgment (Zieky and Perie 2006: 7). Kantarcioglu and Papageorgiou (2011) note that judgments are not only involved during the planning of a standard setting meeting, for example when a standard setting method is chosen, but in every step of the decision-making process of setting cut scores: deciding on the number of levels to classify test takers, selecting and training panelists, and scheduling the activities in the standard setting meeting. Despite this reliance on judgments, the standard setting meeting and its outcomes can be evaluated based on several criteria (Hambleton 2001; Tannenbaum and Cho 2014) typically grouped into three categories (Council of Europe 2009; Hambleton and Pitoniak 2006; Kane 1994):

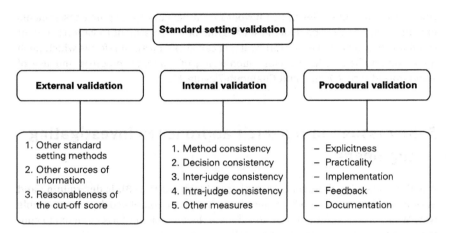

Fig. 1: Validation of cut scores (Papageorgiou 2010b, reproduced with permission).

– Procedural validation, e.g., examining whether the procedures followed were practical, implemented properly, that feedback given to the judges was effective and that documentation has been sufficiently compiled.
– Internal validation, e.g., addressing issues of accuracy and consistency of the standard setting results.
– External validation, e.g., collecting evidence from independent sources which support the outcome of the standard setting meeting.

The *Manual* presents in detail how (mostly) quantitative data under these three categories should be collected and analyzed to support the proposed cut scores in relation to the CEFR levels. These data are summarized in Figure 1 above.

Research studies in language testing have offered some alternatives to the use of expert judges to set minimum score requirements for placement purposes (Xi 2007; Papageorgiou and Cho 2014). Xi (2007) investigated the use of the speaking section of TOEFL iBT for the initial screening of international teaching assistants (ITAs) in universities in the United States. Potential ITAs took the TOEFL iBT Speaking section, while their performance on local ITA tests formed the criterion measure. Cut scores on the TOEFL iBT Speaking section were determined based on how well scores grouped ITAs into categories based on their performance on the ITA tests (e.g., no teaching restrictions, teach only after taking a course, and not qualified to teach). This last step was conducted statistically by employing logistic regression. Papageorgiou and Cho (2014) examined the relationship between 92 secondary school students' language test scores from a standardized English-language test and the placement of these students into ESL classes by their language teachers. Teachers' judgments regarding the ESL classes the students should attend formed the criterion measure. The test scores and the teacher-assigned ESL levels correlated strongly and, following logistic regression, the majority of the students were placed in the same ESL class when comparing the observed ESL placement (suggested by the teachers) and the predicted placement results based on the test scores. Although these studies are not situated in the alignment context discussed in this chapter, they are, nevertheless, relevant because they demonstrate how cut scores can be derived without the participation of panelists. Both studies followed a criterion-related validity paradigm, whereby data from an external measure (criterion), such as local test scores or teachers' ratings, and scores from the test for which validity evidence was sought were collected at the same time. Logistic regression was applied to derive cut scores to separate subjects into a number of categories based on the external criterion (see also Council of Europe, 2009: 72–73). It should be pointed out, however, that despite the absence of panelists in these studies, the setting of cut scores still involved judgments regarding the selection of a criterion measure and the scores produced by it. Therefore, standard setting is not unique when it comes to employing human judgment to make decisions and investigating and validating cut-score results, as discussed in this section, remains critical.

4 Research in aligning assessments to standards

In the field of language assessment, the CEFR has been the driving force behind the increased interest in aligning assessments to standards; for this reason, this section focuses specifically on research in this particular alignment context. Alignment in such studies is typically associated with two procedures that are to some extent interrelated as described in the *Manual*: alignment of test content to provide adequate coverage of the language activities described in the CEFR descriptors (see earlier discussion of Webb 2007) and alignment of scores to the CEFR levels, to support classification decisions in relation to the CEFR levels through the setting of cut scores.

Two collections of case studies (Figueras and Noijons 2009; Martyniuk 2010) report on the experience of various test providers and researchers in aligning tests to the CEFR. The case studies vary in several ways. For example, some case studies in Martyniuk (2010) report on the alignment of a single assessment to the CEFR, whereas others deal with suites of examinations or multinational, large-scale research projects. Despite the differences found in terms of test content, score use and methodology, common threads can found in these papers. One thread is that alignment to an external standard, such as the CEFR, might not be straightforward because, by design, its description of what learners are expected to do is underspecified to allow for a wider application. However, this intended under-specification might mean that when a standard is too generic, alignment for specific groups of test takers might be particularly challenging. For example, alignment of young learner assessments to the CEFR might be particularly problematic (see also Hasselgreen 2005). Despite several issues faced during the process of alignment to the CEFR, a reportedly positive effect of this process is raising awareness of important assessment design issues, in particular in contexts where local tests are developed. For example, following the alignment project of the COPE test (Kantarcioglu et al. 2010), revisions were made to the writing prompts, and features that differentiated passages and items across levels of language ability were included in the test specifications.

Studies reporting on the alignment of assessments to the CEFR routinely employ quantitative techniques to provide validity evidence for the setting of cut scores in relation to the CEFR levels (see also discussion of the validation of cut scores in the previous section). For example, the alignment of the reading and listening scores of the Michigan English Test to the CEFR levels (Papageorgiou, 2010b) involved examination of both intrajudge and interjudge consistency, such as standard error of judgment, agreement coefficient, and Kappa indices as part of the internal validation of the cut score. In another study, Kantarcioglu et al. (2010) applied the many-facet Rasch model (Linacre 1994) to explore the judges' agreement in setting cut scores for the Certificate of Proficiency in English of Bilkent University to the CEFR levels.

The panelists' decision making process when setting cut scores to the CEFR has also been investigated by Papageorgiou (2010a) following a qualitative approach. Specifically, the study investigated the factors reported by the panelists to affect their decision to set a cut score and the problems these panelists faced when setting cut scores in relation to the CEFR. The panelists' group discussions were analyzed based on a coding scheme built both inductively, i.e. drawing codes from the actual data, and deductively, i.e. drawing codes from existing theory, such as qualitative research into standard-setting participants' experiences (Buckendahl 2005). The findings of the study suggest that decision-making might be affected by factors irrelevant to the description of expected performance in the standard, such as panelists' personal expectations and experiences, which might threaten the validity of the cut score. For example, the panelists were found to have their own preconception of the CEFR levels based on their experience with students they had taught; this was contrary to the purpose of the study, which was to set cut scores based on a substantive judgment of the students' performance in relation to the descriptors in the CEFR proficiency scales, not the panelists' prior knowledge of the level of their students. The study also found that the CEFR might be useful for defining learning objectives, but not sufficiently specified for the purpose of setting cut scores because of the tendency of the CEFR scales to describe language use in real-life contexts, as opposed to classroom contexts. By describing real-life tasks, the CEFR descriptors ignore the notion of "artificiality of assessment" (Hambleton 2001: 100); thus, the panelists faced lack of congruence between descriptions of real-life language use in the CEFR descriptors and the inevitable limitations of the tasks performed in the context of an assessment.

5 Future directions

Although content coverage is an important part of any attempt to align assessments to a standard such as the CEFR, standard setting is required at some point during the alignment process, as can be seen in the relevant documentation of the Council of Europe (Council of Europe 2009; Kaftandjieva 2004). In fact, as the authors of the *Manual* point out, allocating students to a specific level based on their test scores is the most crucial point of the CEFR alignment process (Figueras et al. 2005: 269–270). Although standard setting has been criticized as a one-off procedure (Milanovic and Weir 2010: xiv), it actually remains a critical component of any alignment process if test scores are to be used to classify test takers into different proficiency levels described in a standard. This is because even if an assessment provides adequate content coverage in relation to a standard, for example by satisfying criteria such as those discussed earlier (Webb 2007), setting a cut score too low or too high will have important unintended consequences. If the cut score is set too high, many examinees will be incorrectly classified as not achieving a specific level of performance (false negative classification). If a cut score is set too low, many examinees will be classified as achieving a specific level of performance when they actually are not at that higher level, resulting in false positive classifications. Given that no assessment is perfectly reliable and also that moving "the cut score up or down to reduce one type of error will necessarily increase the chances of making the other type of error" (Zieky and Perie 2006: 8), providers of these assessments need to set cut scores following acceptable procedures and also collect and present sufficient validity evidence to support a specific cut score, including an explanation as to which type of classification error is more important to minimize.

A challenge for those aligning test scores to an external standard is deciding whether a score demonstrating sufficient performance on the test also indicates sufficient performance in relation to the standard. This is particularly the case for assessments reporting results in the form of a pass/fail result, typically accompanied by a certificate which documents that a test taker performed satisfactorily on the assessment. If the content of this assessment has been aligned to a specific performance level on a standard such as the CEFR, then the implication is that all test takers passing the exam should be at the intended level. Therefore, two decisions need to be made regarding the use of the scores from such an assessment: first, whether a score indicates that a test taker has passed the assessment and second, whether a score indicates that the targeted CEFR level has been achieved (Council of Europe 2009: 58). The relationship between these two score decisions remains unclear and more research is needed to guide future attempts to align assessments to external standards.

The consequences of aligning assessments to frameworks and standards constitute another challenge that should be explored in future studies. There has been considerable criticism of the use of the CEFR as a policy document (McNamara 2006; McNamara and Roever 2006). Fulcher (2004) argues that the CEFR serves a political mandate for harmonization of educational systems through the (perceived) comparability of assessments that can be achieved by aligning them to the CEFR. According to Alderson (2007: 662), an unintended consequence of the adoption of the CEFR as a policy tool is that policy makers who have no understanding of language learning impose requirements for language proficiency without any consideration as to whether such levels are achievable. For example, proficiency at B1 level is required for settlement or naturalization in the United Kingdom (Blackledge, 2009). The Ministry of Justice in the Netherlands mandated that the reporting scale of the test of spoken Dutch (TGN), taken by individuals who want to permanently migrate to country, be aligned to the CEFR levels, with more measurement precision around the A1 and A2 levels (De Jong et al. 2009). Therefore, more research is needed in local contexts to identify reasonable standards for specific purposes of language use, in order to inform policy making.

Another possible unintended consequence of aligning tests to the same standard is that learners and score users might view these assessments as equivalent in terms of difficulty or content coverage when this should not be the case (Council of Europe 2009: 90). For example, achieving CEFR Level B1 on a general proficiency test intended for young learners and a test intended for professional purposes does not mean that the scores on these two tests have the same meaning because the intended test purpose, test content and test taking population are notably different. For this reason, empirically-derived, test specific performance levels and descriptors might need to be designed for a given test, for example by following a scale anchoring methodology (e.g., Garcia Gomez et al. 2007). Such levels and descriptors can be provided in addition to information regarding alignment to an external standard, in order to help learners and score users better understand the meaning of test scores.

Concerns have also been expressed regarding the perception of alignment as a substitute to procedures for validation (Fulcher, this volume). This is particularly problematic when the intention behind the alignment of an assessment to a standard, such as the CEFR, is mostly driven by commercial interests to gain wider recognition for the assessment, (Fulcher 2004). The *Manual* strongly emphasizes that a prerequisite for any alignment effort to the CEFR is that an examination be of high quality, otherwise alignment is "a wasted enterprise" (Council of Europe 2009: 90). For example, it is pointless to set a cut score in relation to a specific CEFR level for a test with low internal consistency, as the measurement error associated with this cut score will be large. However, it should be pointed out that for score users familiar with a specific standard, alignment might offer more concrete meaning to assessment results (Kane 2012: 8). Therefore, the position of alignment within validation procedures remains an important topic for researchers and practitioners in the field of second language assessment.

A final point to be made in this chapter relates to the quality of the standards themselves. Taking the context of aviation English, Alderson (2009) reports concerns about the development and validation of the descriptors introduced by the International Civil Aviation Organization (ICAO) to set English language requirements for air traffic controllers and pilots. For example, aviation language testing experts and pilots and pilot trainers who participated in a study by Knoch (2009) questioned ICAO's decision to set Level 4 as the minimum requirement for certifying air traffic controllers and found the terminology in the descriptors too technical for aviation experts who lack expertise in language learning. Alderson (2010) further raises the issue of whether the ICAO scale represents a solid foundation for identifying the appropriate language levels required for aviation communication. In such a high-stakes context, such issues are critical, especially because of potential false positive classification errors occurring when aviation English examinations are used to certify pilots and air traffic controllers. Additionally, despite evidence supporting the hierarchy of the CEFR descriptors (Kaftandjieva and Takala 2002, North 2000, 2002, North and Schneider 1998) and the detailed methodology for creating them based on a combination of qualitative and qualitative approaches (Council of Europe 2001: 207–209), the theoretical underpinnings of the CEFR remain weak (Alderson 2007). For example, there is no theory of comprehension behind the "mental operations" (Alderson et al. 2006: 12) that a reader or listener would need to engage at the different levels of the CEFR or what constitutes an appropriate task for a given proficiency level. In fact, as North (2007) points out, the descriptors that appear in the CEFR language proficiency scales are not based on second language acquisition (SLA) research because SLA research could not provide such descriptors at the time of the development of the CEFR. Therefore, the CEFR language proficiency scales, which in reality are based on Swiss teachers' perceptions of language proficiency, are primarily a taxonomy that makes sense to practitioners, rather than empirically validated descriptors of the language learning process (North and Schneider 1998: 242–243). Such issues suggest that alignment of both content coverage and cut scores to an external standard remains an important area of inquiry in the field of second language assessment, because of potentially critical role of alignment in drawing valid inferences from assessment results.

6 References

AERA, APA, NCME, (American Educational Research Association, American Psychological Association, and National Council on Measurement in Education). 1999. *Standards for educational and psychological testing.* Washington, DC: American Educational Research Association.

Alderson, J. Charles. 2005. Editorial. *Language Testing*, 22(3): 257–260.

Alderson, J. Charles. 2007. The CEFR and the need for more research. *The Modern Language Journal* 91(4): 659–663.

Alderson, J. Charles. 2009. Air safety, language assessment policy, and policy implementation: the case of aviation English. *Annual Review of Applied Linguistics* 29(1): 168–187.

Alderson, J. Charles. 2010. A survey of aviation English tests. *Language Testing* 27(1): 51–72.

Alderson, J. Charles, Caroline Clapham and Dianne Wall. 1995. *Language test construction and evaluation*. Cambridge, UK: Cambridge University Press.

Alderson, J. Charles, Neus Figueras, Henk Kuijper, Gunter Nold, Sauli Takala and Claire Tardieu. 2006. Analysing tests of reading and listening in relation to the Common European Framework of Reference: The experience of the Dutch CEFR Construct Project. *Language Assessment Quarterly* 3(1): 3–30.

American Council on the Teaching of Foreign Languages. 2012. ACTFL proficiency guidelines. http://www.actfl.org/sites/default/files/pdfs/public/ACTFLProficiencyGuidelines2012_FINAL.pdf (accessed 7 July 2012).

Blackledge, Adrian. 2009. "As a Country We Do Expect": The further extension of language testing regimes in the United Kingdom. *Language Assessment Quarterly* 6(1): 6–16.

Brindley, Geoff. 1998. Describing language development? Rating scales and second language acquisition. In: Lyle F. Bachman and Andrew D. Cohen (eds.). *Interfaces between second language acquisition and language testing research*, 112–140. Cambridge, UK: Cambridge University Press.

Buckendahl, Chad W. 2005. Guest editor's introduction: Qualitative inquiries of participants' experiences with standard setting. *Applied Measurement in Education* 18(3): 219–221.

Cizek, Gregory J. and Michael Bunch. 2007. *Standard setting: A guide to establishing and evaluating performance standards on tests*. London: Sage Publications.

Council of Europe. 2001. *Common European Framework of Reference for Languages: Learning, teaching, assessment*. Cambridge, UK: Cambridge University Press.

Council of Europe. 2009. Relating language examinations to the Common European Framework of Reference for Languages: Learning, teaching, assessment. A Manual. https://www.coe.int/t/dg4/linguistic/Source/ManualRevision-proofread-FINAL_en.pdf (accessed 5 April 2010).

Davidson, Fred and Glenn Fulcher. 2007. The Common European Framework of Reference (CEFR) and the design of language tests: A matter of effect. *Language Teaching* 40(3): 231–241.

De Jong, John H. A. L., Matthew Lennig, Anne Kerkhoff and Petra Poelmans. 2009. Development of a test of spoken Dutch for prospective immigrants. *Language Assessment Quarterly* 6(1): 41–60.

Deville, Craig and Micheline Chalhoub-Deville. 2011. Accountability-assessment under No Child Left Behind: Agenda, practice, and future. *Language Testing* 28(3): 307–321.

Figueras, Neus and Jose Noijons (eds.). 2009. *Linking to the CEFR levels: Research perspectives*. Arnhem: CITO.

Figueras, Neus, Brian North, Sauli Takala, Norman Verhelst and Piet Van Avermaet. 2005. Relating examinations to the Common European Framework: a manual. *Language Testing* 22(3): 261–279.

Fulcher, Glenn. 2004. Deluded by artifices? The Common European Framework and harmonization. *Language Assessment Quarterly* 1(4): 253–266.

Fulcher, Glenn and Fred Davidson. 2009. Test architecture, test retrofit. *Language Testing* 26(1): 123–144.

Fulcher, Glenn. This volume. Standards and Frameworks. In: Dina Tsagari and Jayanti Banerjee (eds.). *Handbook of second language assessment*. Berlin: DeGruyter Mouton.

Garcia Gomez, Pablo, Aris Noah, Mary Schedl, Christine Wright and Aline Yolkut. 2007. Proficiency descriptors based on a scale-anchoring study of the new TOEFL iBT reading test. *Language Testing* 24(3): 417–444.

Hambleton, Ron K. 2001. Setting performance standards on educational assessments and criteria for evaluating the process. In: Gregory J. Cizek (ed.). *Setting performance standards: Concepts, methods, and perspectives*, 89–116. Mahwah, NJ: Lawrence Erlbaum Associates.

Hambleton, Ron K. and Mary J. Pitoniak. 2006. Setting performance standards. In: Robert L. Brennan (ed.). *Educational Measurement*, 433–470. Westport, CT: Praeger Publishers.

Hasselgreen, Angela. 2005. Assessing the language of young learners. *Language Testing* 22(3): 337–354.

Kaftandjieva, Felianka. 2004. *Standard setting. Section B of the Reference Supplement to the preliminary version of the Manual for relating language examinations to the Common European Framework of Reference for Languages: Learning, teaching, assessment*. Strasbourg: Council of Europe.

Kaftandjieva, Felianka and Sauli Takala. 2002. Council of Europe scales of language proficiency: A validation study. In: J. Charles Alderson (ed.). *Common European Framework of Reference for Languages: Learning, teaching, assessment. Case studies*, 106–129. Strasbourg: Council of Europe.

Kane, Michael. 1994. Validating the performance standards associated with passing scores. *Review of Educational Research* 64(3): 425–461.

Kane, Michael. 2012. Validating score interpretations and uses. *Language Testing* 29(1): 3–17.

Kantarcioglu, Elif and Spiros Papageorgiou. 2011. Benchmarking and standards in language tests. In: Barry O'Sullivan (ed.). *Language Testing: Theories and Practices*, 94–110. Basingstoke: Palgrave.

Kantarcioglu, Elif, Carole Thomas, John O'Dwyer and Barry O'Sullivan. 2010. Benchmarking a high-stakes proficiency exam: the COPE linking project. In: Waldemar Martyniuk (ed.). *Relating language examinations to the Common European Framework of Reference for Languages: Case studies and reflections on the use of the Council of Europe's draft manual*, 102–116. Cambridge, UK: Cambridge University Press.

Knoch, Ute. 2009. Collaborating with ESP stakeholders in rating scale validation: The case of the ICAO rating scale. *Spaan Fellow Working Papers*, Vol. 7. Ann Arbor: University of Michigan.

Linacre, John M. 1994. *Many-facet Rasch measurement*. 2nd ed. Chicago: MESA Press.

Lowe, P. 1983. The ILR Oral Interview: Origins, applications, pitfalls and implications. *Die Unterrichtspraxis / Teaching German* 16(2): 230–244.

Martyniuk, Waldemar (ed.). 2010. *Relating language examinations to the Common European Framework of Reference for Languages: Case studies and reflections on the use of the Council of Europe's Draft Manual*. Cambridge, UK: Cambridge University Press.

McNamara, Tim. 2006. Validity in language testing: the challenge of Sam Messick's legacy. *Language Assessment Quarterly* 3(1): 31–51.

McNamara, Tim and Carsten Roever. 2006. *Language testing: the social dimension*. Oxford: Blackwell.

Milanovic, Michael and Cyril J. Weir. 2010. Series Editors' note. In: Waldemar Martyniuk (ed.). *Relating language examinations to the Common European Framework of Reference for Languages: Case studies and reflections on the use of the Council of Europe's Draft Manual*, viii–xx. Cambridge, UK: Cambridge University Press.

No Child Left Behind Act. 2001. Public Law No. 107–110, § 115 Stat. 1425.

North, Brian. 2000. *The development of a common framework scale of language proficiency*. New York: Peter Lang.

North, Brian. 2002. A CEF-based self-assessment tool for university entrance. In: J. Charles Alderson (ed.). *Common European Framework of Reference for Languages: Learning, teaching, assessment. Case studies*, 146–166. Strasbourg: Council of Europe.

North, Brian. 2007. The CEFR Illustrative Descriptor Scales. *The Modern Language Journal* 91(4): 656–659.

North, Brian and Gunther Schneider. 1998. Scaling descriptors for language proficiency scales. *Language Testing* 15(2): 217–262.

Papageorgiou, Spiros. 2010a. Investigating the decision-making process of standard setting participants. *Language Testing* 27(2): 261–282.

Papageorgiou, Spiros. 2010b. *Setting cut scores on the Common European Framework of Reference for the Michigan English Test*. (Technical Report). Ann Arbor: University of Michigan. http://www.lsa.umich.edu/UMICH/eli/Home/Test%20Programs/MET/Researchers/METStandardSetting.pdf (accessed 9 September 2011).

Papageorgiou, Spiros and Yeonsuk Cho. 2014. An investigation of the use of TOEFL® Junior™ Standard scores for ESL placement decisions in secondary education. *Language Testing* 31(2): 223–239.

Plake, Barbara S. 2008. Standard setters: Stand up and take a stand. *Educational Measurement: Issues and Practice* 27(1): 3–9.

Tannenbaum, Richard J. and Yeonsuk Cho. 2014. Criteria for evaluating standard-setting approaches to map English language test scores to frameworks of English language proficiency. *Language Assessment Quarterly* 11(3): 233–249.

Tannenbaum, Richard J. and Irvin R. Katz. 2013. Standard setting. In: K. F. Geisinger (ed.). *APA handbook of testing and assessment in psychology*: Vol. 3. *Testing and assessment in school psychology and education*, 455–477. Washington, DC: American Psychological Association.

Van Ek, Jan A. and John L. M. Trim. 1991. Waystage 1990. Cambridge, UK: Cambridge University Press.

Van Ek, Jan A. and John L. M. Trim. 1998. Threshold 1990. Cambridge, UK: Cambridge University Press.

Van Ek, Jan A. and John L. M. Trim. 2001. Vantage. Cambridge, UK: Cambridge University Press.

Webb, Norman L. 2007. Issues related to judging the alignment of curriculum standards and assessments. *Applied Measurement in Education* 20(1): 7–25.

Weir, Cyril J. 2005. Limitations of the Common European Framework of Reference for Languages (CEFR) for developing comparable examinations and tests. *Language Testing* 22(3): 281–300.

Wilkins, David A. 1976. Notional syllabuses. Oxford, UK: Oxford University Press.

Xi, Xiaoming. 2007. Validating TOEFL® iBT Speaking and setting score requirements for ITA screening. *Language Assessment Quarterly* 4(4): 318–351.

Zieky, Michael and Marianne Perie. 2006. A primer on setting cutscores on tests of educational achievement. http://www.ets.org/Media/Research/pdf/Cut_Scores_Primer.pdf (accessed 7 July 2012).

Alistair Van Moere and Ryan Downey
21 Technology and artificial intelligence in language assessment

1 Introduction

The use of automated scoring technology to evaluate speech and writing has, arguably, reached a global, tentative acceptance. Paraphrasing Whithaus, to pretend that automated technology is *not* here to stay would be "simply naïve" (2013: ix). Fewer are asking, "Does it actually *work*?" Now, the question to be answered is, "Okay, *how* does it work for our purposes?" This chapter aims to provide readers with information necessary to answer both questions.

One common (mis)perception about automated scoring is the expectation that a computer has been trained to "do what humans do" (e.g., Ericsson and Haswell 2006). Automated scoring technology does not make computers behave like humans. Rather, it takes advantage of the fact that computers can be programmed to identify and quantify features in speaking and writing, combine them and weight them in a multidimensional space, and identify which specific features and their weightings best *predict* the score a human would provide. For example, there is no need to support the claim that a computer can "understand" a spoken utterance, which computers cannot do, any more than there is a need to claim that a human judge can accurately count millisecond-level subphonemic timing events in natural speech (which computers can do better than humans). Both kinds of evaluation can produce proficiency scores for spoken utterances with consistency. Correlations between human and machine scores in high quality applications like those described in this chapter are comparable to – or better than – correlations between trained human judges (Shermis 2014; Van Moere 2012).

The goal of this chapter, then, is to provide an accessible explanation of how current state-of-the-art assessments use automated scoring technology, and to review research that has demonstrated that the technologies are appropriate in the assessment context.

1.1 History

One compelling motivation for automated scoring is the increasing need to evaluate large numbers of language learners and return results in a timely fashion. Widespread availability of computers and the Internet have already produced shifts in the way language proficiency is assessed (Alderson 2000). But it is also clear that this need will continue to grow. Consider the standardization of educational initiatives such as the Common Core State Standards in the United States, which requires, among other things, evaluation of speaking and writing skills on a very large scale; immigration and civic integration testing around the world, where concerns about bias and prejudice must be weighed with consideration of the impartial nature of automated scoring; and the increasingly global workforce, which requires rapid language-based testing for screening, hiring, and advancement decisions in international business contexts (TIRF 2009). All these scenarios demand assessments with efficient administration, scoring, and reporting.

In language testing, technological innovations have taken many forms and have influenced all areas of the test development cycle, including task design, delivery, scoring, reporting, and even validation. For example, the traditional oral proficiency interview (OPI) involves one candidate and two examiners, where one examiner acts as interlocutor and one examiner listens and rates the performance. By delivering the test over the telephone, the examiners and candidate could be thousands of miles apart. Similarly, the widespread availability of audio-cassette tapes starting in the 1960's and VHS tapes in the 1970's enabled both a standardized delivery of listening and speaking test items and the capability to record test performances, allowing learner speech to be graded at a different time or place, and by multiple raters.

Many researchers point to the introduction of optical mark recognition in the 1960's, and the bubble-card reader popularized by ScanTron in the early 1970's, as a very important technological influence on scoring which caused a dramatic shift in the ease with which certain language skills were tested. Since multiple choice answer-sheets could be scored rapidly by machine, this technology shifted the focus of how language was tested, and testing of "passive" reading and listening skills was popularised through the multi-choice item-type. The widespread emphasis on polytomous scoring in skill testing – as well as language testing – occurred almost synchronously with advances in Rasch modeling and Item Response Theory (IRT). The influence of these technologies, combined with increased availability of smaller, more cost-effective computers, drove the capabilities that make computer adaptive testing (CAT) possible (e.g., Reckase 1974). With proper design, computer-based testing of language skills can be more efficient and accurate than traditional kinds of testing (Chalhoub-Deville and Deville 1999; Chapelle 2001).

With this context, it should be no surprise that research in recent years has focused on using automated scoring technology to score productive language skills like speaking and writing. Improved technology enhances access to testing resources; reduces practical constraints surrounding test administration and scoring; imposes standardization of delivery, objectiveness and reliability of scoring; all leading to scalability of use. Support for arguments about the usefulness of automated scoring are found in the literature (e.g., Balogh et al. 2012; Downey et al. 2010).

The sections that follow avoid description of statistical models used to predict scores (e.g., regression analysis; random forest) and their associated formulas.

Rather, they explain concepts in machine learning and natural language processing to help familiarize the reader with how the technology works.

2 Automated scoring of writing

The terms *automated essay scoring* (AES) and *automated essay grading* (AEG) typically refer to computer scoring of writing in high-stakes tests. *Automated writing evaluation* (AWE), on the other hand, describes a more formative, feedback-rich use of the technology for purposes of language learning. Although there is considerable overlap in the artificial intelligence (AI) methodologies for AES and AWE, this chapter focuses on the scoring of language assessment and so refers to AES. However, many of these intelligent scoring systems are also leveraged in AWE-related feedback systems (e.g., *Criterion* by ETS, *WriteToLearn* by Pearson, *My Access!* by Vantage Learning, etc.).

The automated scoring of writing requires test takers to type at a computer. We know of no operational high-stakes exams where handwritten essays are scanned and converted to digital type, primarily due to the error rates in optical character recognition software (OCR). Depending on the purpose of the test, an AES system might pre-process the test taker's writing before scoring it. For example, if a young test taker writes entirely in block capitals, this could be converted to lower case so that the scoring algorithms do not perceive every word as an acronym. Moreover, spelling dictionaries can ensure that "summarise" and "summarize", for example, are both scored as correct in a test of "international English."

We can divide AES models into two types: prompt-specific and generic. In *prompt-specific* models, each prompt or essay topic must first be administered to test takers from the target population in order to collect a sample of responses representing the entire range of ability/performance. These responses are used to develop the scoring model (or "train the engine"). It may take anywhere between one hundred and many thousands of responses to develop a scoring model, depending on the complexity of the writing task, the rating scales, and the type of modeling techniques applied – Intelligent Essay Assessor, for example, typically requires 300–400 responses per model. Expert judges assign rubric-based scores to each response in the training set, and the model is optimized to predict these scores. Thus, in prompt-specific models a unique combination of features is developed to optimally predict human scores for each prompt. In contrast, *generic* models are trained once and applied to all essay prompts; they apply the same set of features and feature-weighting to score every prompt on some pre-determined scale. Generic models tend to rely more on surface features such as frequency of grammar errors, punctuation errors, number and location of discourse markers, metrics of sentence complexity, word frequency, etc. Prompt-specific models can more accurately evaluate "deeper" concepts involving the content of the essay, completion of the task, organization and coherence of thoughts, and appropriacy of register and authorial voice.

The process of building scoring models involves several steps. First, a set of variables is identified that have relevance to the construct to be assessed. For example, variables such as lexical density or word frequencies could be applied to score a trait called "Vocabulary range and accuracy." Second, a large number of training essays are analysed and "decomposed" into a set of statistics; for example, the number of words in the top 1,000 frequency level, at the 2,000 level, and so on. Third, these statistics are used in models to find how well they predict the expert human scores, and the best combination of variables and their weightings are identified. Model curators could simply select the combination of features and weights that result in the best prediction. However, if the writing is judged on analytical rating criteria consisting of several different traits, a more responsible approach involves selecting only the variables that are relevant to the criteria on a theoretical basis. Essay length is often the single strongest predictor of writing proficiency, but it would not be valid to use this variable to predict, say, organizational competence. Moreover, knowing that essay length featured in the scoring algorithm would cause test takers to write longer essays simply to gain extra points. Thus, model curators must be wary of identifying variables of global competence and attaching them to specific analytic traits. Often, modelers and content experts may collaborate to come up with the best model based on both scoring accuracy and scoring validity. In the following section we explain modeling techniques used in AES, along with one commercial product that takes advantage of each technique. Most AES systems use a combination of methods.

2.1 Surface features and grammar checkers

Project Essay Grade (PEG) was the earliest AES system, produced by Ellis Page in the late 1960's. At the time, hand-written essays had to be entered manually into a mainframe computer for scoring. Page believed that writing skills could be measured indirectly through proxy traits (Page 1994), so the computer scoring algorithm focused on quantifying surface linguistic features of a block of text (e.g., essay length, average word length, part of speech, count of punctuation, counts of grammatical function words such as prepositions and pronouns, lexical variation, etc.), without reference to semantic content of the essay. Using multiple regression, PEG produced a holistic score correlation with human scores as high as $r = 0.87$ (Page 2003).

In 2002, the PEG system was acquired by Measurement, Inc. and developed into a web-based writing practice program. Between 300 and 500 intrinsic characteristics of writing are now linked to proxy traits like content, word variety, grammar, text complexity, sentence variety, fluency, diction, etc. Though recent developments of PEG have included incorporating new parsers and improving classification schemes, a continuing criticism of this style of analysis is its immunity to the semantics, or meaning, of the passage.

2.2 Latent Semantic Analysis

Pearson's scoring engine, Intelligent Essay Assessor (IEA), evaluates meaning using a natural language processing technique called Latent Semantic Analysis (LSA; see Foltz, Streeter, Lochbaum and Landauer, 2013). With LSA, each word, sentence, and passage becomes a vector in relation to a multidimensional semantic space. Foltz et al (2013: 78) provide the following example:

> *Surgery is often performed by a team of doctors.*
> *On many occasions, several physicians are involved in an operation.*

Although the two sentences contain no words in common, their meanings are approximately the same based on the contexts of the words that comprise them. For example, the words "physicians" and "doctors" appear in similar contexts in English. In an LSA vector space, these two sentences would describe effectively the same "vector" because their underlying meaning is the same.

Content-based scoring is enabled by a "background" model using an enormous corpus to evaluate a newly submitted essay or summary. When scoring prompt-specific traits, IEA compares the incoming essay with all known scored essays from the training set, and determines the new essay's vector proximity (cosine) to other known pre-scored essay vectors in the semantic space.

LSA variables are not only used to predict content, word choice and task completion, but also organizational traits such as sentence fluency and essay coherence. If sentences follow one another logically, the sentence vectors will be in close proximity. The same is true at the paragraph level. Thus, proximity of sentence vectors in a paragraph can be used to predict expert human judgments of, for example, writing coherence.

IEA supports numerous assessments, including the Pearson Test of English – Academic (Pearson 2009b) and the English for Professionals Exam (E^Pro; Pearson 2013), as well as writing practice tools such as WriteToLearn and Summary Street. In addition to LSA, IEA uses a range of measures including n-grams, syntactic complexity, and surface features to achieve correlations with human judgments between 0.80 and 0.86 (Landauer, Laham and Foltz, 1998; Pearson 2013) which is comparable to the reliability of human scorers.

2.3 Part of speech categorizing

The Educational Testing Service (ETS) e-rater system draws on part of speech categorizing, among other techniques, for scoring capabilities (Attali and Burstein

2006; Burstein 2003; Leacock and Chodorow 2003). This approach assigns part of speech (POS) tags to each word in the text, e.g., noun, verb, etc. In e-rater, three modules operate on each submitted essay: a syntactic parser, a discourse analyzer, and a topical analysis module that operates in a conventional vector space (Burstein 2003). From the output of these modules, e-rater identifies a set of microfeatures including the presence (and counts) of errors of various types. These microfeatures are aggregated into a set of features that fall into 8 broad categories: grammar, usage, mechanics (GUM), style, organization, development, lexical complexity, and topic-specific vocabulary usage (i.e. content) (Enright and Quinlan 2010).

E-rater uses multiple regression, weighted by quantitative evaluation of features (e.g., proportion of grammar errors, proportion of usage errors, etc.) found in a set of human-scored training essays, to predict a final holistic score representing the average score produced by two human judges. Scoring models may be prompt-specific or generic, and both model types strongly predict scores assigned by human judges (Attali and Burstein 2006). Even with a generic scoring model, the correlation between human and e-rater scores ($r = 0.76$) is comparable or slightly higher than between paired human raters ($r = 0.70$) (Attali 2011).

E-rater provides scoring of the Graduate Management Achievement Test (GMAT) and one of two scores on the writing portion of the Test of English as a Foreign Language (TOEFL) iBT; the second score is assigned by a human expert. Scores are produced from 0 to 6. If there is a discrepancy between the scores of more than 1.5 point, the passage is sent to a second human for arbitration (Enright and Quinlan 2010).

2.4 N-grams

An n-gram is a contiguous sequence of items (syllables, letters, or words); in the context of automated writing scoring, it typically refers to words. N-gram generically includes the set unigram (e.g., "beautiful"), bigram (e.g., "beautiful day"), trigram ("a beautiful day"), etc. When analyzing a large corpus, a parser can break the text into a series of overlapping n-grams, and the frequency of all n-grams in the corpus can be obtained.

The presence or distribution of n-grams in the sample can be used in scoring writing. Often, lower frequency n-grams are associated with higher quality. For example, an essay about "a beautiful day", a frequent trigram, is fine albeit average, but an essay about "a gorgeous day", a less frequent trigram, is probably written by a more skilled student. However, probabilistic models looking only n-grams are insufficient: "a day beautiful" is also infrequent but should not be associated with a higher score. N-gram analyses are often combined with meaning-based or POS approaches to help determine the accuracy or appropriacy of word sequences in the student's writing.

3 Automated scoring of speaking

While automated systems for evaluation and remediation of pronunciation have been available for some time (e.g., EduSpeak, Franco et al. 2010), systems which evaluate the wider set of competencies required for spoken communication are now becoming more common. These systems must evaluate *what* was said as well as *how* it was said.

Automated scoring of spoken language requires three important models to be developed: acoustic model; language model; and scoring model. The construction of these three models, together with test and task design, makes accurate automated scoring possible. Therefore, before describing test providers and the differences in their scoring models, this section first elaborates on the three kinds of models employed in automated scoring of speech.

3.1 Acoustic model

The acoustic model is the main component of the speech recognizer. Speech recognition software often applies hidden Markov models (HMMs) to represent each phone, or sound (Young 2001). Recognition can be thought of as a series of probabilities; the model estimates the likeliest phoneme or word from among a number of possibilities. Spectral features are extracted for each 10-millisecond frame of the speech, and a model associates probabilities for each possible phone. The output is the best statistical estimate of which words were spoken, in the form of a transcript.

Acoustic models must be "trained" or optimized on a set of speech data. The training process involves pairing the audio speech with transcriptions of that speech, so that the model associates sounds with orthographic representations. Any speech data can be used for training, including radio broadcasts or audio from Youtube (Hinton et al. 2012). However, the acoustic model should be trained on speech that matches the speech to be recognized. Background noise, microphone type, and resolution of the speech signal will all impact the quality of the training data. Speakers' accents are also a crucial factor, as each potential test taker demographic may have a distinct pronunciation repertoire. Thus, it is best to gather speech data and train the acoustic model on a sample that matches the target population of the test.

3.2 Language model

Next, the language model comprises words that are likely to be spoken in the response. The model is made of frequencies for n-grams. Thus, if the language task is to describe a picture of a girl eating an apple, the bigram "an apple" and the trigram "eating an apple" are likely to appear frequently in test-taker responses.

To ensure a representative sample of responses, test items are typically trialed on the target population. For example, for PTE Academic, each item was presented to over 300 learners in field-testing and their responses were recorded (Pearson 2009b). Using this prior information, the language model assists in the assigning of probabilities in the word recognition process.

Speech is easier to recognize if the model can anticipate what the speaker may say. Thus, tasks such as reading aloud or repeating sentences can result in word recognition accuracy well above 90%, even in accented speech (Balogh et al. 2012). On the other hand, recognizing spontaneous speech can be very difficult. Ivanov et al. (2016) report a word error rate of 23% (or, roughly three in four words recognized accurately) on spontaneous speech from non-native speakers. Similarly, the gold standard for recognition of spontaneous native-speaker speech under optimal conditions and with ample computing power is above 80%, depending on the speech to be recognized (Hinton et al. 2012).

3.3 Scoring model

The scoring model refers to the method for selecting features from the speech recognition process and applying them to predict human ratings. In language assessment, the test developer should consider not only features of the output which are the best predictors of the human score, but also which predictors are *relevant* to the human score. For example, imagine that a duration measure such as speech rate were a strong statistical predictor of human judgments of grammar ability. If neither the rating scales nor the human raters paid attention to speech rate in evaluation of grammar ability, then it would not be responsible to use this measure in the scoring model.

The Versant tests exemplify several kinds of scoring models (Bernstein, Van Moere and Cheng 2010). Pronunciation models are developed from spectral properties that are extracted during the recognition process. First, the rhythmic and segmental aspects of a performance are defined as likelihoods with reference to a set of native speaker utterances, and then these measures are used in non-linear models to predict human judgments of pronunciation. Fluency models are similarly developed from durations of events, such as response latency, words per time, segments per articulation time, and inter-word times. Sentence mastery is mainly derived from the number of word errors given in a response and scaled using a partial credit Rasch model. Vocabulary items which elicit single words or phrases simply use the recognized output to ascertain whether the response was correct or incorrect, and the result is entered into dichotomous Rasch models. In constructed responses, such as retelling a story, the recognized output is used in a Latent Semantic Analysis approach to predict human judgments of vocabulary coverage. Thus, the Versant tests attempt to preserve construct validity by using distinct, relevant features in models to predict each trait separately, and then combine the subscores to create an overall score.

Xi et al. (2008) describe a very different approach to scoring models using TOEFL iBT's SpeechRater 1.0. Numerous features associated with pronunciation, fluency, and vocabulary were entered into a regression model to predict holistic scores on the speaking tasks, rather than individual traits. Then, a committee evaluated and selected the final features, taking into account the construct representation of each feature (i.e. its linkage to the rating scale) and the strength of its relationship with human scores. Based on the data, the committee advised on over-weighting fluency variables which were the strongest predictors, and under-weighting grammar and vocabulary which were weakest for predicting human ratings. Interestingly, durational variables associated with fluency are the best-understood and measurable aspects of spoken proficiency (see, for example, Cucchiarini, Strik and Boves 2002). In Xi et al.'s model (2008), words-per-second is the best predictor of all, and correlated with human holistic scores at 0.49.

3.4 Machine performance

Having developed these three models, how well can machine scores be expected to predict human scores for unseen (or new) spoken responses? Any evaluation of machine-to-human correspondence must be interpreted with reference to human rater reliability as this is the standard against which the machine is measured.

The Versant tests report machine-to-human correlation of 0.97 for overall scores and 0.88–0.97 at the trait level (Pearson 2009a). Human split-half reliability is 0.99 for overall scores and 0.93–0.99 at the trait level. This is based on validation data consisting of a flat (rather than normal) score distribution that spans the entire score scale. Operationally, performance is somewhat lower; Van Moere (2012) reports overall machine-to-human correlation of 0.94, and split-half reliability 0.84–0.88 at the trait level, based on a class of English major undergraduates at a Hong Kong university.

Xi et al.'s (2008) study using SpeechRater 1.0 reports machine-to-human correlation of 0.57 for the spoken section of the TOEFL iBT test, where human agreement was 0.74. This is with a dataset with restricted score distribution. Using test-taker responses from the TOEFL iBT field study which had a wider score distribution more representative of operational testing, the correlation was 0.68, where human agreement was 0.94. Trait level scores were not computed separately, as the scoring model combined them into one holistic model, as described above.

Differences in reliability and machine-to-human correlation among tests can be partly explained by the different modeling employed, and partly explained by the test and task design. The Versant test and the PTE Academic were both designed with automated scoring, as well as construct representativeness in mind. They present approximately 62 and 36 items respectively, where the item-types elicit a mix of constrained speech (read aloud and sentence repeats) and constructed speech which is controlled in terms of output (describing a picture, retelling a lecture or story). The mix of item-types plays to strengths of the automated system: pronunciation can be measured more accurately from constrained speech than from unconstrained speech (Chen, Zechner and Xi 2009); vocabulary, language use and communication effectiveness can be measured more appropriately from constructed or communicative speech tasks. In contrast, the TOEFL iBT presents six items that elicit long turns. The speech exhibits degrees of spontaneity – some items elicit opinions on a given topic, some items are in response to stimulus. Because the speech is unpredictable and has high perplexity the recognition performance is low, and so the scoring relies heavily on fluency measures irrespective of the content (vocabulary and language use) in the speech.

When enquiring about automated scoring of spoken language, the question is often asked, "What kind of speech recognition software do you use?" However, it should be clear after reading the preceding sections that the actual speech recognition software is of secondary importance. Rather, the important variables are: the type of speech data used in the optimization of the acoustic models; the predictability and perplexity of the speech elicited and the resulting usefulness of language models; the quality and reliability of the human ratings which the models are developed to predict; and the features which are extracted from the recognition process, and how the features are combined and formulated to predict human ratings.

4 Validity and automated scoring technology

Used appropriately and responsibly, technology can make language assessments considerably richer and more practical in terms of delivery, task types, and scoring. At the same time, care must be taken to justify each element of the technology utilized within the assessment's validity argument. Kane (2012) defines an argument-based framework as having two steps: "First, specify the proposed interpretations and uses of the scores in some detail. Second, evaluate the overall plausibility of the proposed interpretations and uses" (2012: 4). The validity argument for a test should define inferences intended to underlie test-score interpretation and use, and empirical evidence is collected to support each inference or claim. This means that, in evaluating the technology used in an assessment, the test developer should gather studies which show that the technology facilitates score interpretations (or at least does not have an adverse impact upon them).

Many computer-assisted language assessments also have paper-and-pencil versions, or parallel methods of delivery. To ensure that the score interpretations are the same regardless of whether the test is computer-based or paper-based, questions such as the following may need to be investigated:

Do examinees score the same on essay tasks when they hand-write them versus when they type at computers? Are some examinees disadvantaged due to typing ability?
Are different strategic skills activated when students read passages onscreen versus on paper?

Test developers must gather evidence on their own assessment instrument; supplementary evidence can be gained by drawing upon the existing literature. For example, the ACTFL OPI is an oral test administered by examiners face-to-face or over the telephone. When tape-mediated (SOPI) and computer-mediated (COPI) versions of the test were released, the practical benefits were obvious: there was no longer a need for a test proctor or interviewer to monitor test activities or capture examinee performances; and moreover the COPI allows examinees to self-select easier or harder questions (see Norris 2001). Substantial research began to show that while test scores could be comparable across different delivery modes, the speech elicited was actually substantively different (see O'Loughlin 2001), implying that the speaking construct assessed is altered to some degree. This research is invaluable for test developers designing and validating direct or indirect oral proficiency tests.

Even when no comparable paper-based test is required, the test developer must establish that the computer-based design features of the test are consistent with score interpretations. For example, imagine we are designing a computer-based test which assesses students' academic writing ability and readiness for undergraduate study:

Should the automatic spell-checker be enabled, as this functionality is available to all students when writing reports or essays for their course credit?
Should an Internet browser be enabled during the test, as all students will have access to the Internet when composing critical, evaluative, or research essays?

These questions are matters of construct definition, practicality and authenticity, and the test developer must demonstrate that test performance is predictive of performance in real-word tasks (see Chapelle and Douglas 2006).

Concerning the use of automated scoring, Xi (2010) lists numerous fundamental questions that should be asked. The following are drawn and adapted from Xi (2010: 5):

Does the use of assessment tasks which are constrained by automated scoring technologies lead to construct under- or misrepresentation?
Would examinees' knowledge of the scoring algorithms impact the way they interact with test tasks, thus negatively impacting the accuracy of scores?
Does the use of automated scoring have a positive impact on examinees' test preparation practices?

These questions reflect the general opinion that automated scores must go beyond demonstration of close correspondence with human ratings. Rather, the development and implementation of the models is integral to the test, and should be tied to the types of inferences that we want to draw from test scores. One opinion is that, since human judgments are fallible and vary over time between raters, then expert human judgments are themselves problematic as a criterion on which to compare the validity of machine scores (Chapelle 2003). Yang et al. (2002) suggest that, in addition to verifying machine scores against human judgments, machine scores should also be verified against external criteria or measures of the same ability. Weigle (2010), for example, compares machine-scored TOEFL iBT writing tests with several non-test indicators of writing ability, including instructors' assessments and independent ratings of non-test writing samples.

Interestingly, in some ways machine scores are more transparent than human judgments. Human raters evaluate language samples, refer to scale descriptors, and apply judgment and experience to assign a final score, but we have no quantifiable way of measuring how they weight and combine the various pieces of information in an essay. In contrast, it is possible to achieve something replicable with machine scoring: every piece of data analyzed, and its precise weighting in the scoring model, is verifiable in the machine algorithms. Thus, in automated models it is possible to empirically exclude extraneous information (e.g., sentence length), and explicitly weight relevant information (e.g., the use of discourse markers) in the desired way, in a way not replicable with human raters. As Bernstein, Van Moere and Cheng (2010) point out, scoring models are data-driven, verifiable and falsifiable.

5 Future directions

A theme suffusing this chapter is that thoughtful application of artificial intelligence to scoring language performances can provide reliable approximations of human scoring to enable valid use of test scores. These relatively recent advances in technology have had an impact on the field of language assessment, but more advances are needed.

Although automated scoring is very rapid once the sample arrives at the scoring service – usually only a few seconds or less per essay or speech file – publishers of language assessments must balance the need for rapid scoring with robust data transmission to the scoring service. A speech file sent for scoring typically must travel hundreds or thousands of miles from the testing location to the scoring service. Breakdowns in Internet connection can result in a delay in scoring, or, worse, a loss of data. Users of voice or video conferencing programs such as Skype may be familiar with packet loss and speech or silence compression, which may contribute to loss of integrity in the recorded signal. These challenges may be overcome through the use of more local scoring capabilities, such as browser-based speech recognition engines, or scoring componentry placed on the learner's computer.

Video capture of learner performance opens doors to many new possibilities. Gesture recognition technology is already in widespread use in games (e.g., Nintendo's Wii, Microsoft's Kinect) and applications running such technology (e.g., Flutter) may soon make possible robust automated assessment of sign language (e.g., Nayak, Sarkar and Loeding 2009). Gestural components of pragmatics also may be evaluated. The ubiquity and availability of webcams and other portable, mobile video devices makes remote proctoring more tenable; video tracking of a learner taking a language test contributes significantly to test security by deterring fraud.

Advances in automated scoring of a broader range of traits could result in more accurate estimates of learner abilities. For example, software exists to evaluate the use of tone in languages such as Mandarin (Cheng 2012). Research on the use of automated measures of spoken prosody (Cheng 2011), rhythm (Tepperman and Nava 2011; Chen and Zechner 2011) and intonation (Tepperman, Kazemzadeh, and Narayanan 2007) in speech, shows promise to increase the reliability of nativeness estimates. Comparable advances yielding insight into written language competencies are also in the pipeline.

Technological advances are also expanding the repertoire of tasks possible for use in language assessment. For example, relatively more "authentic" tasks can be constructed and automatically scored that emulate real-life tasks that a learner might engage in in their target language domain. Academic language can be evaluated while a learner is giving a recorded presentation; or workplace language can be evaluated while the learner writes an email, engages in a chat-like dialogue with a customer, or multi-tasks during a performance-based proficiency task. The widespread availability of touch-pad devices such as iPads and tablet computers allows test publishers to develop tasks whose only response modality involves pointing or touching, broadening the possibilities for fairly assessing very young learners or populations with challenges dealing with keyboards or the computer mouse.

So-called chat bot (or chatterbot) applications take advantage of artificial intelligence and machine learning algorithms to conduct seemingly authentic, back-and-forth real-time exchanges with learners[1]. With enough training data and sufficiently robust machine learning support, such applications are beginning to produce authentic-feeling interactional exchanges. Even communication breakdowns can be "created" to probe a learner's conversational repair strategies. Such technology could allow for performance-based testing of second language pragmatics in an efficient way that is currently not possible on a large-scale basis (see Roever 2013).

Finally, technology offers additional, converging (albeit inferential) evidence about a learner's proficiency in a second language. Evidence from the fields of psycholinguistics and neurolinguistics has long shown that, while engaging in cer-

---

1 For an entertaining example of this kind of technology, the reader is directed to Cleverbot (2014), created by British AI scientist Rollo Carpenter.

tain linguistic tasks, differences exist at a neural level in the processing of a second language between learners at different levels of ability (Ardal et al. 1990; Weber-Fox and Neville 1996). This evidence converges from numerous research methodologies including behavioral measures, functional brain imaging (e.g., functional magnetic resonance imaging, magnetoencephalography, and event-related potentials), and eye-tracking (see Just, Carpenter and Miyake 2003 for a summary). Even the pupillary response – in which the pupil dilates measurably as the learner encounters an event imposing increased cognitive processing demands – can be leveraged to provide proficiency estimates (e.g., Schmidtke 2014).

For the discipline of language assessment, advances in technology have improved speed, accuracy, availability, objectivity, and reliability of measuring aspects of learner language. Continuing technological advances will allow for expansion of our constructs to capture – and automatically score or infer – more nuanced aspects of language competence. Many of the technologies described in this chapter are already being used in large-scale assessments and show great promise, though more development and innovation is needed. At the heart of assessment lies an imperative for fairness and equitability, which points to the need for methodologies that offer a level of transparency and impartiality that few humans can achieve. Expanding demand for global access to language assessments of the highest quality makes it clear that judicious use of technology must form the core of any solution. This logical marriage represents an obligation for us to continue to engage with automated scoring technology and understand how further advancements can help us accomplish our goals as a field.

"O brave new world, that has such technology in't!"

6 References

Alderson, J. Charles. 2000. Technology in testing: The present and the future. *System* 28(4): 593–603.

Ardal, Sten, Merlin W. Donald, Renata Meuter, Shannon Muldrew and Moira Luce. 1990. Brain responses to semantic incongruity in bilinguals. *Brain and Language* 39(2): 187–205.

Attali, Yigal and Jill Burstein. 2006. Automated essay scoring with e-rater® V.2. *Journal of Technology, Learning, and Assessment*, 4(3). Available from http://www.jtla.org (accessed 22 October 2013).

Attali, Yigal. 2011. Automated subscores for TOEFL iBT® independent essays. *ETS Research Report*. RR–11–39. Princeton, NJ: Educational Testing Service.

Balogh, Jennifer, Jared Bernstein, Jian Cheng, Alistair Van Moere and Masanori Suzuki. 2012. Validation of automated scoring of oral reading. *Educational and Psychological Measurement* 72(3): 435–452.

Bernstein, Jared, Alistair Van Moere and Jian Cheng. 2010. Validating automated speaking tests. *Language Testing* 27(3): 355–377.

Burstein, Jill. 2003. The E-rater® scoring engine: Automated essay scoring with natural language processing. In: Mark D. Shermis and Jill Burstein (eds.). *Automated essay scoring: A cross-disciplinary perspective*, 113–121. Mahwah: Lawrence Erlbaum Associates.

Chalhoub-Deville, Micheline and Craig Deville. 1999. Computer adaptive testing in second language contexts. *Annual Review of Applied Linguistics* 19: 273–299.

Chapelle, Carol. 2001. *Computer applications in second language acquisition: Foundations for teaching, testing, and research*. Cambridge, UK: Cambridge University Press.

Chapelle, Carol. 2003. *English language learning and technology: Lectures on applied linguistics in the age of information and communication technology*. Amsterdam: John Benjamins.

Chapelle, Carol and Dan Douglas. 2006. *Assessing language through computer technology*. Cambridge, UK: Cambridge University Press.

Chen, Lei and Klaus Zechner. 2011. Applying rhythm features to automatically assess non-native speech. *INTERSPEECH* 2011: 1861–1864.

Chen, Lei, Klaus Zechner and Xiaoming Xi. 2009. Improved pronunciation features for construct-driven assessment of non-native spontaneous speech. *Proceedings of Human Language Technologies: The 2009 Annual Conference of the North American Chapter of the Association for Computational Linguistics*, 442–449. Stroudsburg: Association for Computational Linguistics.

Cheng, Jian. 2011. Automatic assessment of prosody in high-stakes English tests. *INTERSPEECH* 2011: 1589–1592.

Cheng, Jian. 2012. Automatic tone assessment of non-native Mandarin speakers. *INTERSPEECH* 2012: 1299–1302.

Cleverbot. 2014. www.cleverbot.com (accessed 22 September 2014).

Cucchiarini, Catia, Helmer Strik and Lou Boves. 2002. Quantitative assessment of second language learners' fluency: comparisons between read and spontaneous speech. *Journal of the Acoustical Society of America* 111(6): 2862–2873.

Downey, Ryan, Hossein Farhady, Rebecca Present-Thomas, Masanori Suzuki and Alistair Van Moere. 2010. Evaluation of the Usefulness of the "Versant for English" Test: A Response. *Language Assessment Quarterly* 5(2): 160–167.

Enright, Mary K. and Thomas Quinlan. 2010. Complementing Human Judgment of Essays Written by English Language Learners with E-rater Scoring. *Language Testing* 27(3): 317–334.

Ericsson, Patricia F. and Richard Haswell (eds.). 2006. *Machine scoring of student essays: Truth and consequences*. Logan, UT: Utah State University Press.

Foltz, Peter W., Lynn A. Streeter, Karen E. Lochbaum and Thomas K. Landauer. 2013. Implementation and applications of the Intelligent Essay Assessor. In: Mark D. Shermis and Jill Burstein (eds.). *Handbook of automated essay evaluation: Current applications and new directions*, 68–88. New York, NY: Routledge.

Franco, Horacio, Harry Bratt, Romain Rossier, Venkata Ramana Rao Gadde, Elizabeth Shriberg, Victor Abrash and Kristin Precoda. 2010. EduSpeak®: A speech recognition and pronunciation scoring toolkit for computer-aided language learning applications. *Language Testing* 27(3): 401–418.

Hinton, Geoffrey, Li Deng, Dong Yu, George Dahl, Abdel-rahman Mohamed, Navdeep Jaitly, Andrew Senior, Vincent Vanhoucke, Patrick Nguyen, Tara Sainath and Bria Kingsbury. 2012. Deep neural networks for acoustic modeling in speech recognition. *IEEE Signal Processing Magazine* 29(6): 82–97.

Ivanov, Alexei V., Patrick L. Lange, David Suendermann-Oeft, Vikram Ramanarayanan, Yao Qian, Zhou Yu and Jidong Tao. 2016. Speed vs. accuracy: Designing an optimal ASR system for spontaneous non-native speech in a real-time application. *Proceedings of the 7th International Workshop on Spoken Dialogue Systems, IWSDS 2016*, January, 12–16, 2016, Saariselkä, Finland.

Just, Marcel Adam, Patricia A. Carpenter and Akira Miyake. 2003. Neuroindices of cognitive workload: Neuroimaging, pupillometric, and event-related potential studies of brain work. *Theoretical Issues in Ergonomics* 4(1–2): 56–88.

Kane, Michael. 2012. Validating score interpretations and uses. *Language Testing* 29(1): 3–17.

Landauer, Thomas, Darrell Laham and Peter Foltz. 2003. Automated scoring and annotation of essays with the Intelligent Essay Assessor. In: Mark D. Shermis and Jill Burstein (eds.). *Automated essay scoring: A cross-disciplinary perspective*, 87–112. Mahwah, NJ: Lawrence Erlbaum Associates.

Leacock, Claudia and Martin Chodorow. 2003. C-rater: Automated Scoring of Short-Answer Questions. *Computers and the Humanities* 37(4): 389–405.

Nayak, Sunita, Sudeep Sarkar and Barbara Loeding. 2009. Automated Extraction of Signs from Continuous Sign Language Sentences using Iterated Conditional Modes. Paper presented at IEEE Conference on Computer Vision and Pattern Recognition, June 20–25, Miami Beach, Florida.

Norris, John M. 2001. Concerns with computerized adaptive oral proficiency assessment. *Language Learning and Technology* 5(2): 99–105.

O'Loughlin, Kieran J. 2001. *The equivalence of direct and semi-direct speaking tests*. Cambridge, UK: Cambridge University Press.

Page, Ellis B. 1994. Computer grading of student prose, using modern concepts and software. *Journal of Experimental Education* 62(2): 127–42.

Page, Ellis B. 2003. Project Essay Grade: PEG. In: Mark D. Shermis and Jill Burstein (eds.). *Automated essay scoring: A cross-disciplinary perspective*, 39–50. Mahwah, NJ: Lawrence Erlbaum Associates.

Pearson. 2009a. *Versant English Test: Test description and validation summary*. Menlo Park, CA: Pearson. http://www.versanttest.com/technology/VersantEnglishTestValidation.pdf (accessed 20 June 2014).

Pearson. 2009b. *Official guide to Pearson Test of English Academic*. London: Longman.

Pearson. 2013. *English for Professionals exam*. Menlo Park, CA: Pearson. http://www.eproexam.com/pdfs/epro_validation_report.pdf (accessed 22 October 2013).

Reckase, Mark D. 1974. An interactive computer program for tailored testing based on the one-parameter logistic model. *Behavior Research Methods and Instrumentation* 6(2): 208–212.

Roever, Carsten. 2013. Assessment of Pragmatics. In: Antony John Kunnan (ed.). *The Companion to Language Assessment*, 125–139. New York, NY: Wiley-Blackwell.

Schmidtke, Jens. 2014. Second language experience modulates word retrieval effort in bilinguals: evidence from pupillometry. *Frontiers in Psychology* Feb 21; 5: 137.

Shermis, Mark D. 2014. State-of-the-art automated essay scoring: Competition, results, and future directions from a United States demonstration. *Assessing Writing* 20: 53–76.

Tepperman, Joseph, Abe Kazemzadeh and Shrikanth Narayanan. 2007. A text-free approach to assessing nonnative intonation. *INTERSPEECH* 2007, 2169–2172.

Tepperman, Joseph and Emily Nava. 2011. Long-distance rhythmic dependencies and their application to automatic language identification. *INTERSPEECH* 2011, 1061–1064.

TIRF. 2009. *The impact of English and plurilingualism in global corporations*. The International Research Foundation for English Language Education. http://www.tirfonline.org/wp-content/uploads/2010/09/TIRF_KeyQuestionsWorkforcePaper_Final_25March2009.pdf (accessed 22 September 2014).

Van Moere, Alistair. 2012. A psycholinguistic approach to oral language assessment. *Language Testing* 29(3): 325–344.

Weber-Fox, Christine M. and Helen J. Neville. 1996. Maturational constraints on functional specializations for language processing: ERP and behavioral evidence in bilingual speakers. *Journal of Cognitive Neuroscience* 8(3): 231–256.

Weigle, Sara Cushing. 2010. Validation of automated scoring of TOEFL iBT tasks against non-test indicators of writing. *Language Testing* 27(3): 335–353.

Whithaus, Carl. 2013. Foreword. In: Mark D. Shermis and Jill Burstein (eds.). *Handbook of automated essay evaluation: Current applications and new directions*, vii–ix. New York, NY: Routledge.

Xi, Xiaoming. 2010. Automated scoring and feedback systems: Where are we and where are we heading? *Language Testing* 27(3): 291–300.

Xi, Xiaoming, Derrick Higgins, Klaus Zechner and David M. Williamson. 2008. Automated scoring of spontaneous speech using SpeechRater v1.0. RR-08-62. http://origin-www.ets.org/Media/Research/pdf/RR-08-62.pdf (accessed 20 June 2014).

Yang, Yongwei, Chad W. Buckendahl, Piotr J. Juszkiewicz and Dennison S. Bhola, D. S. 2002. A review of strategies for validating computer-automated scoring. *Applied Measurement in Education* 15(4): 391–412.

Young, Steve. 2001. Statistical modeling in continuous speech recognition (CSR). *Proceedings of the Seventeenth Conference on Uncertainty in Artificial Intelligence*, 562–571. San Francisco: Morgan Kaufman.

Yuko Goto Butler
22 Assessing young learners

1 Introduction

The number of children learning a second language (L2) or a foreign language (FL) has been on the rise for some time now. This fact, coupled with increasing globalization, has heightened the need to better understand the role of assessments in children's language learning processes and degrees of attainment (McKay 2006). Researchers, however, have only relatively recently begun to investigate assessments for young language learners (YLLs). Alderson and Banerjee's (2001) seminal review article on assessment was the first of its kind to include assessment for YLLs. At around the same time, *Language Testing*'s special volume on assessment for YLLs in 2000 addressed a number of important issues primarily from FL learning contexts in Europe (Rea-Dickins 2000). In the last two decades or so, a growing number of studies on this topic – both from L2 and FL contexts – have been published. This chapter draws on this recent literature to highlight the key issues related to assessing young language learners – issues that may be distinctly different from assessing adult learners.

I begin by describing the characteristics of young learners, including their needs and learning contexts, followed by a discussion of the major age-related characteristics that researchers need to consider. Next, I discuss how we should conceptualize the constructs of assessment among young learners so that they target the appropriate knowledge and skills. As I detail below, defining constructs for assessing young learners' language is a highly complicated business, and we are a long way from having a clear picture of it. The next section covers key issues related to practices and consequences for classroom-based and large-scale assessments. Subscribing to the notion that validity should include assessment consequences (Messick 1996), I consider the washback of assessment in teaching and learning as well as societal impacts, including ethical issues, related to assessing children. I conclude this chapter by suggesting topics for future research.

The overwhelming majority of studies on assessing young learners deals with English language, either English as a second or additional language (*ESL* or *EAL*, typically immigrant children and other non-heritage speakers of English learning English in an English-speaking community) or English as a foreign language or as a lingua franca (*EFL* or *ELF*, children learning English in a context where English is not spoken primarily in the given community). Therefore, the following discussion is largely based on cases of English assessment. That being said, much of what I discuss in this chapter should, in principle, be applicable to the assessment of languages other than English, but more research on other languages is definitely needed.

2 Characteristics of the target populations

What the phrase "young learners" refers to differs slightly depending on regions and learning contexts. However, by and large, young learners are defined as children from age 5 to either age 12 or the end of their primary school education (Alderson and Banerjee 2001).

2.1 Learning contexts

There is tremendous diversity in terms of types of programs and instruction that these young learners receive. Inbar-Lourie and Shohamy (2009: 84) place different language programs for young learners on "a language-content continuum" depending on the degree of emphasis on language and content. In this model, the programs can range from those that have more emphasis on language components (language awareness, language-focused, language and content/embedded) to those that are more content focused (language across curriculum and immersion). Although the classification is primarily meant to describe programs of English as a lingua franca, the notion of the language-content continuum applies to other contexts. Such variation in focus across young learners' programs brings substantial variability with respect to the needs of learners and other stakeholders (such as teachers, parents, administrators, and policy makers), and the learning goals that the learners and/or the programs set.

2.2 Age-related characteristics

In addition to the varying learning contexts, a number of age-related characteristics of young learners require special consideration when it comes to defining constructs, designing and implementing assessments, and using the assessments. Major characteristics include a) developmental factors; b) variability (individual differences); c) learning-centrality; and d) vulnerability.

2.2.1 Developmental factors

Young learners are still in the process of cognitive, socio-cognitive, linguistic, and affective development. Regarding cognition, their information-processing speed follows nonlinear developmental patterns, showing a rather drastic improvement until children reach their mid-teens. Memory and attention span show a similar non-linear development. Preschoolers' memory span is considered to be one-third the capacity of adults, on average. We also know that young children's memory differs from the memory of older children and adults not only quantitatively but also qualitatively; until around age 6, young children use different mnemonic strategies than older children do. In addition, children develop their analogical abilities, self-regulation abilities, and metacognitive-abilities throughout their school years (e.g., Fry and Hale 2000). While most children are able to manipulate their thoughts by the time they finish elementary school, hands-on experiences (i.e. contextualized tasks) still help them facilitate thinking. As social animals, human beings develop various socio-cognitive and communication abilities from birth, including having joint attention, making eye contact, and understanding intentionality (understanding other people's intention) (e.g., Tomasello 1999). Children learn to cope with others in tasks and to take turns by the time they are 5 to 7 years old. Although recent developmental literature indicates that children as young as 4 years old are much more sophisticated in assessing their own competency than researchers had long believed, young children still have "difficulty with some kinds of standards, such as information about prior knowledge, and cannot integrate information from multiple sources or standards" (Butler 2005: 216). When assessing young learners, all these developmental factors greatly influence and regulate assessment formats (e.g., age-appropriate items and task choices), modalities and procedures of assessment (e.g., one-to-one assessment vs. paired or group assessment; multiple-choice tests vs. alternative assessments), and the degree of contextualization and autonomy of assessment (e.g., self-assessment).

Another critical developmental aspect of young learners, being vastly different from most adult learners, is that they are still developing their first language (L1) and their literacy skills in L1 while they are learning an L2/FL. Depending on their age and learning context, children can have different degrees of knowledge of written language as well as skills and strategies to process written information in their L1. Some L2 learning-children may have relatively few chances to develop literacy skills in their L1 and yet need to develop literacy skills in their L2. Although there is substantial research indicating a close relationship between bilingual children's L1 and L2 literacy development (for reviews of such research, see Cummins 2000, and Genesee et al. 2006), we still have only very limited knowledge regarding the precise mechanisms of bi-directional cross-linguistic influences in different linguistic domains between children's L1 and L2. Because young learners' L1 is not yet fully developed, the nature of transfer from their L1 to L2/FL may be very different from that among adults. In phonology, for example, Flege's (1995) Speech Learning Model predicts that young learners' L2 sound perception would be different from adult learners, who rely on their firmly established phonological categorization in their L1. Moreover, we can speculate that, under certain conditions, young learners may have a greater cross-linguistic transfer from L2/FL to L1 than adults. In any event, young learners' acquisition processes both in their L1 and L2/FL have not yet been uncovered fully. Given the nonlinear and dynamic nature of the processes, capturing children's linguistic development certainly challenges the traditional assessment practice in which monolingual native-speakers' performance is set as the stable norm for learners.

2.2.2 Individual differences

The developmental factors addressed above all yield substantially varied developmental profiles among individuals. Different age groups show different developmental characteristics, but we also see tremendous individual variation among children within the same age groups. A child may be more advanced in a certain cognitive domain but may be less advanced in a social domain. In L2-learning contexts, teachers usually have children with various degrees of literacy foundation in L1 and a wide range of familiarity with decontextualized (or academic) language. Some children have little experience taking assessments, while others may be more familiar with assessment practices. Thus, giving young learners individual attention is often critical when assessing them. Substantial variability in the development among young learners makes it difficult to standardize assessment criteria and procedures.

2.2.3 The centrality of learning

A third age-related characteristic of young learners that requires special consideration is the centrality of learning in young learners' lives. Young learners are in the midst of acquiring not only language *per se* but also various types of knowledge in content areas. Meaning making through language, rather than developing accuracy and fluency, should be considered primary. Obtaining information on a child's performance at one point is meaningful only if it can help further develop his/her abilities. Thus, a recent emphasis on the notion of *assessment for learning* is particularly relevant to assessment for young learners. Theories of learning shifted the view from learning being individually based, universal sequential construction of knowledge (e.g., Piaget 1930) to a more socially oriented view of learning where learning is considered to take place through social interaction with others via cultural tools such as language (e.g., Vygotsky 1986). If we practice *assessment for learning* based on the social-constructionist view of learning, central concerns for assessment include issues such as how best to create dialogues between the learner and skilled partners (e.g., teachers and peers) in order to promote children's learning and to provide feedback and diagnostic information during and after the assessment.

2.2.4 Vulnerability

Children are vulnerable to adults' attitudes towards assessment. It is often reported that young learners of FL who initially exhibit excitement about learning a new language tend to quickly lose their motivation to learn the language during the primary school years (e.g., Carreira 2012; Lopriore and Mihaljević Djigunović 2011). According to Kim and Seo (2012), part of the reason for Korean children's *demotivation* came from their assessment results and their teachers' practices, along with pressure from stakeholders (e.g., teachers, parents, and school administrators) as a result of the assessment. Assessment results may have a long-lasting impact on young learners' affective components – such as their motivation, anxiety, and self-esteem – which in turn influence their learning. We should remember that in *assessment for learning*, children are not merely objects being measured, but are active participants in the assessment, making inferences of their performance and taking actions accordingly with the help of teachers and other adults (Brookhart 2003). Unfortunately, however, assessment results are often interpreted and used by stakeholders based on their own agendas. As I discuss below, given the vulnerability of young learners and the trend toward high-stakes testing, we should be cautious about how much "stake" we attribute to these tests.

3 Constructs to be measured

Varying goals of L2/FL programs and the age-specific characteristic discussed in the previous section all influence the way we define and understand constructs of assessment for young learners. In this section, I focus on two major construct-relevant issues that are frequently addressed in many L2/FL programs for young learners: namely, *communicative language ability* and *academic language ability*.

3.1 Communicative language ability

Communicative language ability (CLA) in L2/FL or one's ability to successfully communicate meaning for a variety of purposes in various social and academic contexts, is one of the most important targeted abilities for young L2/FL education. However, defining and operationalizing CLA turns out to be very challenging. This is in part due to the fact that CLA consists of multiple components (Purpura 2008). Major theoretical models of CLA, such as those developed by Canale and Swain (1980), Celce-Murcia, Dörnyei, and Thurrell (1995), and Bachman and Palmer (1996, 2010), have identified different components. Making matters even more complicated, we still know very little about the relationship among components for young learners or how each component develops; nor do we know how the components differ between young children and adults.

As an alternative to a theory-driven approach to CLA, young learners' assessment is often based on knowledge and skill descriptions derived from experts' judgments and on standards developed from such descriptions. One such example is the Common European Framework of Reference for Languages (CEFR) (Council of Europe 2001)[1], which has influenced curriculum development, instruction, and

---

1 Note that the CEFR is a framework, or a general guideline, rather than a standard.

assessment for young learners in Europe and other parts of the world. It is important to note, however, that the CEFR was not originally designed to serve the needs of young learners. Thus, if it is implemented with young learners, major adaptation is necessary; it not only needs to be localized to fit a given educational context but also must be made age appropriate for young learners (Little 2007). Researchers have made various adaptations, including creating additional divisions at the lower levels of CEFR and modifying descriptors to better fit a given primary school education (e.g., Figueras 2007; Hasselgreen 2005, 2012). Although such adaptation strategies may work at lower proficiency levels (e.g., A1 and A2 levels), the descriptors of tasks at higher levels (e.g., C1 and C2 levels) require higher degrees of cognitive maturity and are not suitable for young learners (Little 2007)[2]. Major international standardized proficiency tests of English for young learners, such as Cambridge Young Learners English (YLE), Pearson Test of English Young Learners, Oxford Young Learners Placement Test, and TOEFL Primary Tests, all link their test scores to CEFR as well. However, while there has been some preliminary effort to verify the linkage (e.g., Papp and Salamoura 2009 for a case of Cambridge YLE), the validity of the linkage between the major international tests for young learners and CEFR is far from clear.

3.2 Academic language ability

For children who receive schooling in their L2, conceptualizing and operationalizing the interactions between language knowledge and content knowledge is a big challenge. Educators in the United States, for example, have been concerned that what is measured in content-area assessments such as math and science is different for L2 learners and non-L2 learners; this is of particular concern given the widespread adoption of rigorous accountability systems in the United States. To address the ethical problems posed by these differences for L2 and non-L2 learners, Bailey and Butler (2004) proposed a test of *academic language* for L2 learners as a prerequisite for taking content-area tests. Academic language can be considered as "the vocabulary, sentence structures, and discourse associated with language used to teach academic content as well as the language used to navigate the school setting more generally" (Bailey and Huang 2011: 343). However, there are various definitions of *academic language* and yet few empirical investigations for justifying the suggested constructs. For example, if we were to accept that academic language includes discipline-specific language (Bailey and Heritage 2008), we first need to identify and specify academic language in each content-area at each grade

---

2 The requirement of a high degree of cognitive maturity is a potential problem when the CEFR is used for assessments of young learners who have received schooling in their L2 and/or in content-language integrated learning (CLIL) programs (Little 2007).

level before we develop a test of academic language. The relationship between the development of academic language and content-knowledge needs to be better understood as well. Furthermore, if we should wait to assess students' content knowledge until the students develop a certain level of academic language, as suggested by Bailey and Butler, how should we determine the level? And assuming that academic language is important for everybody regardless of his/her language status, do we need a test of academic language for non-L2 learners as well? English language development (ELD) standards developed by the Word-Class Instructional Design and Assessment (WIDA) consortium[3] can be considered a promising step. They defined ELD standards by grade level while linking five content area domains: namely, languages of socializing and instruction, language arts, mathematics, science, and social studies. By defining these standards by grade level and domain, they are "better representing the construct of academic English" (Llosa 2011: 377).

4 Key issues in assessment for young learners

In addition to the difficulty of defining constructs for assessment, there are a number of challenges when it comes to actually assessing young learners.

4.1 Identifying age-appropriate tasks and formats for assessment

Young learners' maturational constraints regulate what tasks should be used in assessment. Tasks that are used regularly in assessment for adults may not work well for assessing young learners, depending on the learners' cognitive and socio-cognitive developmental levels. For example, information-gap tasks may be inappropriate for young learners if they have not yet developed their direct attention in ways that the tasks require (Pinter 2011). Cognitively demanding tasks can penalize less-proficient young learners more heavily than more-proficient learners (Traphagan 1997).

We know that topics that catch children's interests and tasks that use concrete objects facilitate comprehension and elicit more responses (Carpenter, Fujii, and Kataoka 1995; McKay 2006; Traphagan 1997). Importantly, however, tasks that are supposedly developmentally appropriate and that work well in class may not necessarily be workable as assessments. Young learners may have a hard time exhibit-

---

3 The information about the WIDA ELD standards can be obtained through http://www.wida.us/ (accessed 15 July 2013).

ing in an assessment what they are able to do in a non-assessment context, or they may simply focus on completing the task without worrying about the language. Butler and Zeng (2014, 2015) argue that children need to be socialized into the world of assessments in order to perform well on them. They need to understand what they are expected to do during the assessment, which requires experience as well as a certain degree of cognitive and socio-cognitive maturity.

Similarly, Carpenter, Fujii, and Kataoka (1995) warned us about children's sensitivity to the pragmatic roles of participants during oral interviews, a popular format of oral assessment for young learners. For example, when being asked to name a picture, children age 5 to 10-may wonder if the assessor (teacher) also sees the picture (which is usually the case). Such sensitivity often results in avoidance or shyness. Carpenter, Fujii, and Kataoka stated that "this phenomenon of avoidance is quite problematic for assessment, since silence in a child is much less diagnostic than silence in adults" (1995: 160).

Although the child-adult interview is a popular oral assessment format, this format was found to be limited in its ability to elicit a variety of language functions, such as questioning and requesting from young learners. This may be due to the fact that children tend to want to please adults and so rarely challenge or show disagreement with what teachers say during the interview (Butler 2015; Carpenter, Fujii, and Kataoka 1995). On the other hand, the paired-assessment format, which has gained popularity in adult assessment, was found to be "extremely problematic" for use with children younger than 10 (Carpenter, Fujii, and Kataoka 1995: 168). Butler and Zeng (2014, 2015) found that by the age of 11 or 12, children could do better at working collaboratively (mutually developing topics and taking their partner's perspective) than younger children during the paired assessment, which resulted in their exhibiting a wider range of interactional functions. However, Butler and Zeng (2011) found that the child-adult interview format can be more beneficial than the paired-format for certain types of children, such as those who are less proficient and/or shy children, even if they are relatively older, because the teacher-child interview format allows the teacher to stretch such children's abilities.

4.2 Understanding the role of teachers in classroom-based assessment

The centrality of learning, one of the characteristics of young learners mentioned above, highlights the importance of classroom-based assessment. Classroom-based assessment is integrated in teaching and primarily used for a formative purpose. Despite the critical role that teachers play in classroom-based assessments, however, primary school teachers' insufficient training to conduct and interpret assessments has been reported repeatedly both from the L2 and FL contexts (e.g., Bailey and Drummond 2006; Brumen, Cagran, and Rixon 2009; Butler 2009a; Hild and Nikolov 2011; Hsieh and Hsiao 2004; Llosa 2005).

Edelenbos and Kubanek-German proposed the concept of "diagnostic competence," which they defined as "the ability to interpret students' foreign language growth, to skillfully deal with assessment material and to provide students with appropriate help in response to this diagnosis" (2004: 260). One can assume that the same concept should apply to L2 classrooms as well as FL classrooms. After observing how primary school teachers practice "assessment" in foreign language classes in the Netherlands and Germany, Edelenbos and Kubanek-German identified teachers' skills in performing a series of activities that manifested their diagnostic competence. Such skills include recognizing children's silence and other non-verbal expressions and behaviors that indicate their comprehension, grouping children according to their proficiency levels, and providing concrete examples of individual children's language development over time (see Edelenbos and Kubanek-German 2004: 279 for the complete list of such skills).

Developing such diagnostic competence appears to be quite difficult. Based on an observation of primary school teachers' practice of classroom-based assessment in the United Kingdom, Rea-Dickins and Gardner (2000) described a few instances of teachers' inconsistent (and sometimes inaccurate) record-keeping of children's language use and behaviors, and they also identified various factors that potentially threatened the validity and reliability of the assessment. The initiation-response-feedback (IRF) exchange, a teacher-student discourse pattern frequently used in classrooms, helps teachers determine if students know what the teacher has in mind, but it does not successfully elicit information about what the students do know, nor does it provide students with diagnostic information to facilitate their learning (Torrance and Pryor 1998). Similarly, classroom observation in primary EFL classrooms in Italy led Gattullo to conclude that "teachers seem to make little or no use of some types of questioning and negotiations that could be fed into formative assessment and enhance the learning processes" (2000: 283). Butler (2015) found substantial variability in the way that primary school teachers in China engaged in their students' task-based paired-assessment and in the language that they elicited from the students as a result of their engagement. As these findings demonstrate, we need more research that examines how teacher-student discourse can validate classroom-based assessment, but it should be based on a paradigm different from that of standardized testing (Davison and Leung 2009; Leung and Mohan 2004; Rea-Dickins and Gardner 2000).

Finally, Butler (2009b) addressed differences in the ways that primary and secondary English teachers in Korea holistically evaluated students' performance through observation. Primary and secondary school teachers differed with respect to their use of assessment criteria, how much they valued confidence and motivation as part of assessment constructs, and their beliefs about how students' potentiality should (or should not) be gauged as part of their communicative competence. Such differences may be largely due to the differences in the specific cultural and educational contexts in which these teachers taught. However, substantial gaps in instruction and assessment between primary and secondary schools' language classrooms are not unique to Korea, and a prevailing concern among educators and researchers across regions is how best to narrow such gaps.

4.3 Considering influences of assessment

Due to the vulnerability of young learners, it is vital that we understand the influence of assessment on teaching and learning (washback effects) as well its impact on the educational policies and societies at large (McKay 2006). One aspect of washback effects that needs more attention is how assessment/testing affect young learners' motivation and other affective domains. Although research on this topic is limited, it is undeniable that "young learners are extremely sensitive to criticism" (Hild and Nikolov 2011: 57). Using an interview and a picture-drawing technique, Carless and Lam (2012) elicited perceptions of assessments among lower grade students at primary schools in Hong Kong. While the assessment had the potential to bring a sense of satisfaction, negative feelings about assessments such as anxiety, sadness, and unhappiness were already present at a very early stage of their schooling. Importantly, the students' parents and teachers seemed to play a significant role in the development of both negative and positive feelings. Aydin (2012) found that factors that were known to be triggers for test anxiety among adult learners, such as insufficient instruction about the assessment, learners' distrust of assessment validity, and time limitations, also provoked test anxiety among young EFL learners in Turkey.

Washback effects are complicated phenomena; multiple factors are involved, and it is usually hard to predict the direct effects of assessments/tests and the intensity of these effects (Wall 2012). Researchers often find that tests do not uniformly affect teachers and other stakeholders. After examining Chinese primary school teachers' perceptions of the influence of exams on a new pedagogical innovation (i.e. implementing task-based instruction, TBLT), Deng and Carless found that teachers' perception and practice varied; they argued that exams influenced the implementation of TBLT in China but that "teacher beliefs mediated through societal values are even more powerful factors" (2010: 300).

In ESL contexts, an increasing number of standard-based educational policies include L2 learners in their high-stakes assessments (e.g., No Child Left Behind Act in the United States, the National Curriculum in the United Kingdom, and the National Literacy Benchmarks in Australia). In response, numerous studies have looked into test biases and various negative effects on L2 students as a result of high-stakes assessments. Among the biases that researchers have found are concerns about the validity of content-knowledge assessments for L2 learners with insufficient academic language proficiency, biases against culturally and socio-economically disadvantaged students in assessment items and procedures, and mismatches between instruction and assessment (McKay 2006). Scholars have proposed various test accommodations to address these biases (Rivera and Collum 2006); however, they have had mixed results (e.g., Abedi, Hofstetter, and Lord 2004; Kieffer et al. 2009).

In EFL or ELF contexts, commercial international proficiency tests for young learners have become increasingly popular. Chik and Besser (2011) examined the perceptions among stakeholders (including both teachers and parents) of the Cambridge YLE in Hong Kong. At a less-privileged primary school that they observed, the school could not afford to have all the students take the YLE test; rather, only a handful of students were chosen and allowed to take the test. The result was that only those students who took the YLE test were in a better position to be admitted to English-medium secondary schools, which were considered to be more prestigious than Chinese-medium schools. At a more privileged primary school, students who felt pressure (or were pressured by their parents) not to be left behind by their classmates tried to take every possible test, and then they compared the results among themselves. Chik and Besser found that the YLE served as a powerful means to gain additional advantage in the educational system but, importantly, they concluded that "it only empowers the group that has the resources to take the test" and "systematically disadvantages other groups" (2011: 88).

Rea-Dickins and Gardner (2000) indicated that classroom-based assessment, which is usually considered a type of low-stakes assessment, is often used for high-stakes decisions. International proficiency tests for young learners, regardless of the test developers' intention, appear to be increasingly used for high-stakes decisions (at least in certain contexts) and may contribute to widening achievement gaps between the rich and poor. In the assessment literature, there is no systematic criterion for deciding the degree of "stakes" of assessments, and the determination is often based on conventions and assumptions. Considering the high vulnerability of young learners, we need to be extra careful when making such decisions. One could argue that assessments for young leaners are potentially all high stakes.

5 Future directions

Assessment for young learners is an emerging field, and as the preceding discussion illustrates, much more research is needed.

5.1 Identifying clear trajectories of young learners' L2/FL language development

In order to identify what we should measure through assessment at each age group as well as to provide appropriate diagnostic information to the students and teachers, we need to have clear trajectories of young learners' L2/FL language development. As discussed above, we still don't know what exactly constitutes communicative competence or proficiency in L2/FL among young learners or how such components are related and developed over time. We are in danger of pushing standardization without having either trajectories of young learners' language development that are grounded in empirical evidence or sound theories of second language acquisition (SLA) and learning. While we have started seeing more empirical studies of young learners' SLA (e.g., Nikolov 2009; Philip, Oliver, and Mackey 2008), we need many more. Efforts to validate standards should go hand in hand with SLA research among young learners.

5.2 Enhancing our understanding of assessment for learning

Considering the centrality of learning for young learners, we need a better grasp of how to connect assessment with instruction and learning. Although the recent attention being given to diagnostic assessment in language testing is promising, Jang reminds us that "not all formative assessments are diagnostic" (2012: 120) and "[d]iagnostic tasks require a micro-analysis of learning behavior, level of cognitive difficulty, and learner background characteristics" (2012: 125). We need more research focused on improving and validating the quality of diagnostic information, and teachers and learners have to play central roles in this process – not just as source providers but also as active users of diagnostic information. Methodological challenges to understanding how children use diagnostic information may be resolved through triangulation – employing multiple perspectives and eliciting methods and instruments to confirm the validity of data with children (Pinter 2014).

We also need to know more about helping young learners develop autonomy. Self-assessment is increasingly being incorporated into standards and frameworks, as in the European Language Portfolio (ELP) in Europe (Little 2009) and Can-do descriptors in WIDA. While researchers are working to validate such can-do statements, we know little about how these statements are used to enhance instruction and students' learning. Butler and Lee (2006) compared an off-task self-assessment (a holistic self-assessment that is commonly observed across contexts) and an on-task self-assessment (a contextualized self-assessment design to assess one's performance in a specific task or a lesson) in a Korean primary school. They found that, in the on-task self-assessment, the young learners could self-assess their performance more accurately and were less influenced by their attitudinal and personality factors. There was an age effect as well: the sixth-graders (11–12 year-olds) self-assessed themselves more accurately than the fourth-graders (9–10 year-olds) relative to a general proficiency test and their teachers' evaluation. Butler and Lee (2010) examined the effect of implementing a self-assessment in Korean primary schools longitudinally and found that the effect differed depending on the students' learning contexts as well as their teachers' perceptions of the assessment.

We still know little about cognitive and socio-cognitive processes that children use when self-assessing their L2/FL competence across age groups, the interplay between such processes and environment, and the long-term effect of self-assessment practice on the learners' development of autonomy.

5.3 Collecting more information about various influences of assessment on young learners

A substantial amount of research has been devoted to examining the effect of standards and assessments that are implemented as part of standard-based educational policies on young L2 students' outcomes, teaching practice, and school policies. Teachers' assessment practices in classrooms and their assessment literacy (i.e. their understanding of sound assessment practice and the use of the assessment results) are getting more attention in both L2 and FL contexts. However, we still have limited information about long-term effects of assessment for young learners and its effects in a larger societal context. If the target language is powerful, either as a language of schooling or as a lingua franca (such as English), we need to pay closer attention to the impacts of assessments on learners' long-term career development and life goals as well as their impacts on socio-economic and linguistic disparities. In other words, we need to pay particular attention to fairness and ethical issues. We also know little about the effects of assessment on young learners' affective domains such as motivation and anxiety and the role of parents and teachers in the process. Considering the vulnerability of young learners, children's opinions need to be heard and taken more seriously. In this respect, we should embrace Pinter's (2014) suggestion to work with children by inviting them to be active agents in research rather than seeing them as mere subjects of research.

5.4 Using computers, multimedia, and games for assessment

Despite the increasing prominence of computer-assisted language learning (CALL) and computer-based assessment, we know surprisingly little about how technology can be used to assess young learners and how the learners interact with technology in L2/FL assessment. According to a review by Macaro, Handley, and Walter (2012), although the direct impact of technology on young learners' L2 development is not fully known, technology seems to have a positive influence on young learners' attitudes and behaviors with regard to learning L2. There are a number of possible advantages of using technology in assessment that are particularly appealing for young learners, among them 1. it creates a greater linkage between assessment and instruction (because technology is increasingly used in instruction); 2. many young learners are growing up with technology; they are so-called *digital natives* and are familiar with using technology in their daily lives; 3. technology can incorporate sensory stimuli and animated objects, which help children to keep their attention and motivation; and 4. technology can provide students with instant feedback to promote their learning and possibly even provide individualized assessment operations. However, we still know little about how technology is best utilized in assessment for young learners and the possible limitations and concerns that we may need in developing and administering computer-based assessment to children. We need validity and reliability checks as well as investigations into the impact of computer-based assessment on teaching practice. Technology in assessment for young learners is definitely an important topic for future inquiry.

In conclusion, although we have made significant advances in what we know about assessing young learners in the past decade or so, we still have many more questions than answers. Young learners have unique characteristics that require special consideration in assessment. These characteristics challenge some existing notions in the literature that are based on adult learners and may force us to take new approaches to assessment.

6 References

Abedi, Jamal, Carolyn H. Hofstetter and Carol Lord. 2004. Assessment accommodations for English language learners: Implications for policy-based empirical research. *Review of Educational Research* 74(1): 1–28.

Alderson, J. Charles and Jayanti Banerjee. 2001. Language testing and assessment (Part I). *Language Teaching* 34(4): 213–236.

Aydin, Selami. 2012. The effects of young EFL learners' perceptions of tests on test anxiety. *Education 3–13 International Journal of Primary, Elementary and Early Years Education* 40(2): 189–204.

Bachman, Lyle F. and Adrian S. Palmer. 1996. *Language testing in practice: Designing and developing useful language tests.* Oxford, UK: Oxford University Press.

Bachman, Lyle F. and Adrian S. Palmer 2010. *Language assessment in practice: Developing language assessments and justifying their use in the real world.* Oxford, UK: Oxford University Press.

Bailey, Alison L. and Frances A. Butler. 2004. Ethical considerations in the assessment of the language and content knowledge of U.S. school-age English learners. *Language Assessment Quarterly* 1(2–3): 177–193.

Bailey, Alison L. and Kathryn V. Drummond. 2006. Who is at risk and why? Teachers' reasons for concern and their understanding and assessment of early literacy. *Educational Assessment* 11(3–4): 149–178.

Bailey, Alison L. and H. Margaret Heritage (eds.). 2008. *Formative assessment for literacy, grades K-6: Building reading and academic language skills across the curriculum.* Thousand Oaks, CA: Corwin/Sage Press.

Bailey, Alison L. and Becky H. Huang. 2011. Do current English language development/proficiency standards reflect the English needed for success in school? *Language Testing* 28(3): 343–365.

Brookhart, Susan M. 2003. Developing measurement theory for classroom assessment purposes and uses. *Educational Measurement: Issues and Practice* 22(4): 5–12.

Brumen, Mihaela, Branka Cagran and Shelagh Rixon. 2009. Comparative assessment of young learners' foreign language competence in three Eastern European countries. *Educational Studies* 35(3): 269–295.

Butler, Ruth. 2005. Competence assessment, competence, and motivation between early and middle childhood. In: J. Elliot Andrew and Carol S. Dweck (eds.). *Handbook of competence and motivation*, 202–221. New York: The Guilford Press.

Butler, Yuko G. 2009a. Issues in the assessment and evaluation of English language education at the elementary school level: Implications for policies in South Korea, Taiwan, and Japan. *Journal of Asia TEFL* 6(2): 1–31.

Butler, Yuko G. 2009b. How do teachers observe and evaluate elementary school students' foreign language performance? A case study from South Korea. *TESOL Quarterly* 43(3): 417–444.

Butler, Yuko G. 2015. Task-based assessment for young learners: Old meets new cultures. In: Michael Thomas and Hayo Reinders (eds.). *Contemporary Task-Based Language Teaching in Asia*, 348–365. London: Bloomsbury.

Butler, Yuko G. and Jiyoon Lee. 2006. On-task versus off-task self-assessment among Korean elementary school students studying English. *The Modern Language Journal* 90(4): 506–518.

Butler, Yuko G. and Jiyoon Lee. 2010. The effect of self-assessment among young learners. *Language Testing* 17(1): 5–31.

Butler, Yuko G. and Wei Zeng. 2011. The roles that teachers play in paired-assessments for young learners. In: Dina Tsagari and Ildikó Csépes (eds.). *Classroom-based language assessment*, 77–92. Frankfurt am Main: Peter Lang.

Butler, Yuko G. and Wei Zeng. 2014. Young foreign language learners' interactions during task-based paired assessment. *Language Assessment Quarterly* 11(1): 45– 75.

Butler, Yuko G. and Wei Zeng. 2015. Young learners' interactional development in task-based paired-assessment in their first and foreign languages: A case of English learners in China. *Education 3–13 International Journal of Primary, Elementary and Early Years Education.* 43(3): 292–321.

Canale, Michael and Merrill Swain. 1980. Theoretical bases of communicative approaches to second language teaching and testing. *Applied Linguistics* 1(1): 1–47.

Carless, David and Ricky Lam. 2012. The examined life: Perspectives of lower primary school students in Hong Kong. *Education 3–13 International Journal of Primary, Elementary and Early Years Education* 42(3): 313–329.

Carpenter, Kathie, Noriko Fujii and Hiroko Kataoka. 1995. An oral interview procedure for assessing second language abilities in children. *Language Testing* 12(2): 158–181.

Carreira, Junko M. 2012. Motivational orientations and psychological needs in EFL learning among elementary school students in Japan. *System* 40(2): 191–202.

Celce-Murcia, Marianne, Zoltán Dörnyei and Sarah Thurrell. 1995. Communicative competence: A pedagogically motivated model with content specifications. *Issues in Applied Linguistics* 6(2): 5–35.

Chik, Alice and Sharon Besser. 2011. International language test taking among young learners: A Hong Kong case study. *Language Assessment Quarterly* 8(1): 73–91.

Council of Europe. 2001. *Junior European Language Portfolio.* http:// www.primarylanguages.org.uk/resources/assessment_and_recording/european_languages_ portfolio.aspx (accessed 1 July 2013).

Cummins, Jim. 2000. Language, power and pedagogy: Bilingual children in the crossfire. Clevedon, UK: Multilingual Matters.

Davison, Chris and Constant Leung. 2009. Current issues in English language teacher-based assessment. *TESOL Quarterly* 43(3): 393–415.

Deng, Chunrao and David R. Carless. 2010. Examination preparation or effective teaching: Conflicting priorities in the implementation of a pedagogic innovation. *Language Assessment Quarterly* 7(4): 285–302.

Edelenbos, Peter and Angelika Kubanek-German. 2004. Teacher assessment: The concept of 'diagnostic competence'. *Language Testing* 21(3): 259–283.

Figueras, Neus. 2007. The CEFR, a lever for the improvement of language professionals in Europe. *The Modern Language Journal* 91(4): 673–675.

Flege, James E. 1995. Second language speech learning theory, findings, and problems. In: Winifred Strange (ed.). *Speech perception and linguistic experience: Issues in cross-linguistic research*, 233–277. Baltimore: York Press.

Fry, Astrid F. and Sandra Hale. 2000. Relationships among processing speed, working memory, and fluid intelligence in children. *Biological Psychology* 54(1–3): 1–34.

Gattullo, Francesca. 2000. Formative assessment in ELT primary (elementary) classrooms: An Italian case study. *Language Testing* 17(2): 278–288.

Genesee, Fred, Kathryn Lindholm-Leary, William M. Saunders and Donna Christian (eds.). 2006. *Educating English language learners: A synthesis of research evidence*. Cambridge, UK: Cambridge University Press.

Hasselgreen, Angela. 2005. Assessing the language of young learners. *Language Testing* 22(3): 337–354.

Hasselgreen, Angela. 2012. Assessing young learners. In: Glenn Fulcher and Fred Davidson (eds.). *The Routledge Handbook of Language Testing*, 93–105. London: Routledge.

Hild, Gabriella and Marianne Nikolov. 2011. Teachers' views on tasks that work with primary school EFL learners. In: Magdolna Lehmann, Réka Lugossy and József Horváth (eds.). *UPRT 2010: Empirical studies in English applied linguistics*, 47–62. Pécs: Lingua Franca Csoport. http://mek.oszk.hu/10100/10158/10158.pdf (accessed 1 August 2013).

Hsieh, Li-hsueh and Ya-ping Hsiao. 2004. On the background and assessment perception on elementary school English teachers in Kaohsiung County. *Journal of National Taiwan Teachers College* 38(1): 237–261.

Inbar-Lourie, Ofra and Elana Shohamy. 2009. Assessing young language learners: What is the construct? In: Marianne Nikolov (ed.). *The age factor and early language learning*, 83–96. Berlin: Mouton de Gruyter.

Jang, Eunice Eunhee. 2012. Diagnostic assessment in language classrooms. In: Glenn Fulcher and Fred Davidson (eds.). *The Routledge Handbook of Language Testing*, 120–133. London: Routledge.

Kieffer, Michael J., Nonie K. Lesaux, Mabel Rivera and David J. Francis. 2009. Accommodations for English language learners taking large-scale assessments: A meta-analysis on effectiveness and validity. *Review of Educational Research* 79(3): 1168–1201.

Kim, Tae-Young and Hyo-Sun Seo. 2012. Elementary school students' foreign language learning demotivation: A mixed methods study of Korean EFL context. *The Asia-Pacific Education Researcher* 21(1): 160–171.

Leung, Constant and Bernard Mohan. 2004. Teacher formative assessment and talk in classroom contents: Assessment as discourse and assessment of discourse. *Language Testing* 21(3): 335–359.

Little, David. 2007. The Common European Framework of Reference for Languages: Perspectives on the making of supranational language European policy. *The Modern Language Journal* 91(4): 645–655.

Little, David. 2009. Language learner autonomy and the European Language Portfolio: Two L2 English examples. *Language Teaching* 42(2): 222–233.

Llosa, Lorena. 2005. Assessing English learners' language proficiency: A qualitative investigation of teachers' interpretations of the California ELD Standards. *The CATESOL Journal* 17(1): 7–18.

Llosa, Lorena. 2011. Standards-based classroom assessment of English proficiency: A review of issues, current developments, and future directions for research. *Language Testing* 28(3): 367–382.

Lopriore, Lucilla and Jelena Mihaljević Djigunović. 2011. Attitudinal aspects of early EFL learning. In: Gábor Szabó, József Horváth and Marianne Nikolov (eds.). *UPRT 2009: Empirical research in English applied linguistics*, 3–11. Pécs, Hungary: Lingua Franca Csoport. http://mek.oszk.hu/10000/10042/10042.pdf (accessed 18 July 2013).

Macaro, Ernesto, Zöe Handley and Catherine Walter. 2012. A systematic review of CALL in English as a second language: Focus on primary and secondary education. *Language Teaching* 45(1): 1–43.

McKay, Penny. 2006. *Assessing young language learners*. Cambridge, UK: Cambridge University Press.

Messick, Samuel. 1996. Validity and washback in language testing. *Language Testing* 13(3): 241–256.

Nikolov, Marianne (ed.). 2009. *Early learning of modern foreign languages: Processes and outcomes*. Bristol: Multilingual Matters.

Papp, Szilvia and Angeliki Salamoura. 2009. An exploratory study into linking young learners' examinations to the CEFR. *Cambridge ESOL Research Notes* 37: 15–22.

Piaget, Jean. 1930. *The child's conception of physical causality*. London: Routledge and Kagan Paul.

Pinter, Annamaria. 2011. *Children learning second languages*. London: Palgrave Macmillan.

Pinter, Annamaria. 2014. Child participant roles in applied linguistic research. *Applied Linguistics* 35(2): 168–183.

Philip, Jenefer, Rhonda Oliver and Alison Mackey (eds.). 2008. *Second language acquisition and younger learner: Child's play?* Philadelphia: John Benjamins.

Purpura, James E. 2008. Assessing communicative language ability: Models and their components. In: Elena Shohamy and Nancy N. Hornberger (eds.). *Encyclopedia of language and education*. Vol. 7: *Language testing and assessment*, 53–68. New York: Springer.

Rea-Dickins, Pauline (ed.). 2000. Assessment in early years language learning context. *Language Testing* 17(2).

Rea-Dickins, Pauline and Sheena Gardner. 2000. Snares and silver bullets: Disentangling the construct of formative assessment. *Language Testing* 17(2): 215–243.

Rivera, Charlene and Eric Collum (eds.). 2006. *State assessment policy and practice for English language learners: A national perspective*. Mahwah, NJ: Lawrence Erlbaum Associates.

Tomasello, Michael. 1999. *The cultural origins of human cognition*. Cambridge, MA: Harvard University Press.

Torrance, Harry and John Pryor. 1998. *Investigating formative assessment: Teaching, learning and assessment in the classroom*. Buckingham: Open University Press.

Traphagan, Tomoko W. 1997. Interviews with Japanese FLES students: Descriptive analysis. *Foreign Language Annals* 30(1): 98–110.

Vygotsky, Lev. 1986. *Thought and language*. Cambridge MA: MIT Press.

Wall, Dianne. 2012. Washback. In: Glenn Fulcher and Fred Davidson (eds.). *The Routledge Handbook of Language Testing*, 79–92. London: Routledge.

Lynda Taylor and Natalie Nordby Chen

23 Assessing students with learning and other disabilities/special needs

1 Introduction

Consideration of ethics and equal access is currently a dominant focus within both education and broader society. It is not surprising, therefore, that in recent years the task of making appropriate arrangements for assessing language learners with learning and other disabilities or special needs has received increasing attention from test developers as well as language educators. This can be seen in the regular discussion on this topic that now takes place at academic language testing conferences and in the published literature, as well as in the concerted efforts made on the part of institutional language test producers, i.e. examination boards and testing agencies, to offer a range of tests that have been modified or adapted to suit the specific requirements of language learners with diverse needs and expectations.

Improved access to education and widening participation at all levels has led to a significant growth in the number and diversity of students with disabilities who are learning a second or additional language. This includes not only learners with physical disabilities (e.g., hearing or visual impairment) but also those with cognitive or learning difficulties (e.g., Down syndrome or dyslexia). As a result, demand for appropriate language testing and assessment provision has steadily increased in recent years. Making appropriate assessment provision for learners with disabilities typically entails some degree of modification to standard testing material and administration. A standard test format or test delivery method that has been modified or adapted to make it accessible to such learners is sometimes referred to as a "testing accommodation", though there are varying views as to whether the terms "test modification" and "test accommodation" are synonymous or whether they apply to different sets of circumstances. Fleurquin (2008) for example, distinguished between the term "modification", used when referring to changes in the way a test is administered or taken that may change the construct being measured, and the term "accommodation" as the tools and procedures that provide equitable instructional and assessment access for students with disabilities (see also Randall and Engelhard 2010: 80). Koenig and Bachman (2004: 1) defined the term "accommodation" more broadly, to include not only tests modified for test takers with disabilities but also tests modified for English Language Learners (ELLs) in the United States' context (e.g., tests that use bilingual or L1 instructions): "Accommodation is used as the general term for any action taken in response to a determination that an individual's disability or level of English language development requires a departure from established testing protocol."

However the term is defined, the general principle underlying the provision of language testing accommodations is that standard test content, format or administration should be modified to meet the specified needs of an individual test taker or group of test takers. This is done in the interest of test fairness and equitable access. The primary aim of modifying a standard test format is to provide optimal opportunities for candidates to demonstrate, to the best of their abilities, their current level of language proficiency. Providing such arrangements typically involves departing from established testing protocol, modifying test content, format or administration so as to minimise the impact of those test-taker attributes that are irrelevant to the construct being measured. For example, a test taker with a broken wrist may need the assistance of a scribe to record her listening test answers or to complete the writing part of a test. Similarly, a visually-impaired candidate may need a specially-prepared braille or enlarged print version of a reading test for him to demonstrate his reading ability. By offering testing accommodations, test providers seek to make appropriate adjustments or arrangements so that, as far as possible, all test takers can take the test on an equal footing (or level playing field) with their fellow students and thus receive formal or informal accreditation of their proficiency.

This chapter considers the ethics, principles, and practice of test modifications or testing accommodations as they relate to tests of language proficiency. It discusses key test-taker characteristics to be considered when designing a language test, specifically factors associated with a permanent or temporary disability and the consequent nature and extent of any modifications that may need to be made to standard language test content and delivery. The chapter reflects upon the ethical, logistical, and measurement challenges involved in meeting the special requirements of learners with disabilities whilst ensuring that the assessment objectives are suitably met, and it also explores the role that can be played by research in this area.

2 History

Making provision for a language learner with a disability to take a language proficiency test is nothing new. An entry in a set of examination board committee minutes dating from 1947, from the archives of Cambridge English Language Assessment (a provider of English language proficiency tests since 1913), describes the provision of modified versions of the English Literature and Reading components for a visually-impaired student taking the high-level Cambridge Proficiency in English Examination:

> It was decided that a blind student at St Mary's Convent, Rome, should be allowed to offer two texts instead of three in the Certificate of Proficiency English Literature paper; the candi-

date would, however, be required to answer three questions on these two books. In the reading test, the candidate would be required to read a prepared passage from Braille, but would not be required to take the 'unseen' reading test, which would be replaced by an extension of the conversation test.

It seems likely that, in the past, provision for candidates with disabilities who wanted to take language proficiency tests tended to be somewhat ad hoc and unsystematic, largely dependent on the sympathetic and creative response of the test producers, as the above example might suggest. Over recent decades, however, as social attitudes and public policy within education and wider society have changed, there has been a development towards a systematic and sustained commitment to providing appropriate testing accommodations for language learners with disabilities, whether such disabilities are permanent or temporary in nature. There may be several reasons for this shift in attitude and practice.

2.1 Growing awareness of ethical issues in language assessment

The expansion in the range of language assessment opportunities available to test takers with special needs can be seen against a broader and growing awareness of ethical issues within the language testing profession. "Ethics" normally refers to a set of accepted beliefs and practices intended to constrain human behaviour and promote the common good. In western society at least, the second half of the 20th century was characterized by a quest for social ethics; there was increasing endorsement of the notion of a "social contract", according to which rules constraining individual and institutional behaviour are accepted as part of the social cooperation needed to achieve advantages and benefits for all (see Davies 2004, 2008).

Ethics in language testing can be directly associated with traditional concerns for test validity and reliability, and it seems reasonable to suggest that language testers have always acknowledged the important, often high-stakes, role played by language tests, with their potential to influence people's life choices in education and employment. For this reason, test developers have traditionally made strenuous efforts to ensure fairness in their language tests and the use of scores from their tests. From the early 1990s, however, interest in the ethics of language assessment grew, both within the language testing community and beyond, and language testers sensed a need to articulate the ethics of their field more explicitly, not only for themselves but also for wider society.

During the 1990s and 2000s, the field responded by steadily professionalizing itself and by developing explicit values and standards for its beliefs and behaviour as a community, influenced in part by the growing professionalization of social practices more broadly. In 1997, for example, the international language testing community's annual conference, the Language Testing Research Colloquium

(LTRC), took as its theme "Fairness in Language Testing", reflecting the growing focus on matters of test standards, test bias, equity and ethics for testing professionals (Kunnan 2000). Two years later, LTRC 1999 included a symposium entitled "Rights and responsibilities of testers and test takers in language testing settings: ethics, policy, practice and research." In 2002 a Language Assessment Ethics Conference was specially convened, leading in 2004 to a special issue entitled "The Ethics of Language Assessment" of the new international language testing journal *Language Assessment Quarterly*. In little more than a decade, therefore, the subdiscipline of ethics in language assessment had become well-established within the professional language testing community. The professional ethics of the field of language assessment continues to evolve, informed by the wider literature in ethics and moral philosophy (Kunnan, 2008).

2.2 The professionalization of language testing

As organisational bodies and work domains underwent a process of increasing professionalization, so they began to develop their own domain-specific codes of ethics and guidelines for good practice (Davies, 2004). The emerging language testing profession was no exception, developing for itself professional membership associations such as the Association of Language Testers in Europe (ALTE) and the International Language Testing Association (ILTA). As they reflected upon what it means to behave ethically, these new professional associations typically set about drafting for themselves quality standards, ethical codes and professional guidelines, in the expectation that such statements would help promote socially- and ethically-responsible behaviour among their members and could be used to communicate to others the fundamental principles and processes underpinning responsible test development and use. Their efforts built upon earlier work undertaken in the United States to produce *The Code of Fair Testing Practices in Education* (Joint Committee on Testing Practices 1988, 2004) and the AERA/APA/NCME *Standards for Educational and Psychological Testing* (1999), both of which set out technical, industry standards for test development, production and delivery, as well as guidance on matters of equity. For example, in Section C on "Striving for Fairness", *The Code of Fair Testing Practices in Education* (Joint Committee on Testing Practices 1988) states: "Test developers should strive to make tests that are as fair as possible for test takers of different races, gender, ethnic backgrounds, or handicapping conditions."

The new professional codes for language assessment sought to address matters extending well beyond a test's technical qualities. Not surprisingly, a key area for ethical consideration in language assessment was the extent to which the particular needs of candidates in certain minority groups or with special requirements, e.g., "handicapping conditions" or disabilities, are acknowledged and properly addressed. Examples of such professional codes include the ALTE *Code of Practice*

(1994), the ILTA *Code of Ethics* (2000), the EALTA *Guidelines for Good Practice* (2006) and the ILTA *Guidelines for Practice* (2007). A broad theoretical distinction can be drawn between a code of ethics and a code of practice. A code of ethics typically articulates a set of universal and foundational principles, sometimes amplified with a series of annotations for clarification or elaboration. A code of practice, on the other hand, usually seeks to instantiate these high-level principles in some detail, and it may reflect the requirements of local practice and the demands of particular cultures. In practice, however, this distinction is not always as clear-cut as either the theory or the labels would suggest: some codes of practice tend to read more like a code of ethics, and what are essentially codes of practice are often instead labelled "guidelines for (good) practice."

2.3 Concerns surrounding the washback and impact of language testing

The increasing professionalisation of language testing and the field's concern for its ethics coincided with a second developing trend: namely, a deepening understanding of the complex influence of assessment in language education and in wider society. Discussions about test washback and test impact gathered pace during the late 1990s and early 2000s reflecting growing awareness of the consequences of testing and assessment – both intended and unintended, both positive and negative (Hamp-Lyons 1997). This paved the way for an in-depth exploration and analysis of the socio-political dimensions of language assessment, with some in the field focusing on the potential for tests to serve as instruments of power and social control (Shohamy 2001; McNamara and Roever 2006), while others examined the diverse individuals and agencies who could be identified as stakeholders in relation to language testing (Rea-Dickins 1997; Taylor 2000). A major aspiration of the codes of ethics and practice which developed during the 1990s and 2000s was to ensure that test washback onto the learning curriculum and classroom and the impact of test use in wider education and society would be as positive and beneficial as possible.

2.4 Recognition of key stakeholders in language testing

A third reason for increased attention to the language assessment needs of learners with disabilities arises from a growing awareness of the multiple stakeholders involved in a language test. This helped to highlight the central role of the test taker in the language assessment event together with the importance of any specific characteristics on the part of the test taker, or group of test takers, that might need to be taken into account. Khalifa and Weir (2009) noted a relatively recent shift in the assessment literature away from the traditional focus on the actual test instrument and its various qualities, and instead towards a greater focus upon the features of the test taker, including any special needs due to short-term or long-term disability: "physical/psychological test-taker characteristics focusing mainly on longer term disabilities which require special modifications to be made to administrative arrangements or sometimes even to the tests themselves ... have only recently come into prominence in the assessment literature" (2009: 19). In their examination of the assessment of second language reading ability, Khalifa and Weir explored the practical application of a socio-cognitive framework of test development and validation to a suite of large-scale second language reading tests across several proficiency levels. This theoretical framework was first explicated by Weir in his 2005 volume *Language testing and validation: An evidence-based approach* and it brought together six core components associated with test development and validation. One of the six components – and to some degree the starting point for any test development or validation activity – focuses on the Test Taker (i.e. the intended population of test takers). It aims to help identify the relevant test-taker characteristics which need to be well described, understood and accounted for, not only in the test development process but also in the building of a sound validation argument to support claims about the usefulness of any test and the scores it generates.

2.5 The centrality of the language learner and test taker

Improved access and widening participation at all levels in education has led to a significant growth in the number and diversity of students with disabilities who are now learning a second or additional language. This includes not only learners with physical disabilities, e.g., hearing or visual impairment (and such disabilities may temporary or permanent), but also those learners who have cognitive or learning difficulties (e.g., Down syndrome or dyslexia). In some countries, e.g., the United Kingdom and the United States, the majority of learners with disabilities are no longer educated in separate "special" schools designed to cater for groups of students sharing the same disability (e.g., a school for the blind or a school for children with autism-spectrum disorders, such as Asperger syndrome). Nowadays, many students with disabilities receive their primary and secondary education within mainstream schools alongside their peers, attending routine lessons in addition to receiving support from a specially-trained learning support assistant or resource teacher. The steady integration of students with disabilities into mainstream primary, secondary, and tertiary education has led to the opening up of assessment as well as learning opportunities, often facilitated through the assistive technology that has been developed in recent years, e.g., screen readers or voice recognition software. Of course, the potential population for any test may include not only increased numbers of learners with permanent disabilities but also those who suffer some form of temporary incapacity, e.g., a broken arm following an accident, or wheelchair use due to a recent operation.

Given the multiple factors outlined above, it is hardly surprising that demand for appropriate language testing and assessment provision has increased significantly in recent years and that test providers have been challenged to respond by developing appropriately-modified tests.

3 Defining special needs populations and determining appropriate accommodations

This section will define the challenges of some special needs populations, as well as the accommodations most often offered on high-stakes standardized language tests by major testing organizations (for a more extensive list, see Taylor 2012). Thurlow, Thompson, and Lazarus (2006: 658) summarize examples of accommodation policies in the United States according to five main categories, which are presented in Table 1: presentation of the test stimuli (for the purpose of language testing, textual presentation is distinguished from audio presentation); response conventions; timing and scheduling; setting; and linguistic accommodation. The final category, which may employ the use of simplified English or allowing test takers to respond in their first language, is deemed an inappropriate accommodation for a test of language proficiency and thus will not be considered here. [See Li and Suen (2012) for discussion of this type of accommodation with English Language Learners (ELLs) in relation to maths, science or other content-focused tests.]

Tab. 1: Categories of special needs and typical accommodations.

For test takers with	Presentation		Response conventions	Timing and scheduling	Setting
	text	**audio**			
Visual impairments	– large print – colored paper – magnifier		– amanuensis or scribe – enlarged score sheets	– extended response time	– larger desk surface – special lighting
	– braille – graphics adapted to text – reader – screen reader		– amanuensis – keyboard (braille or other)	– extended response time – additional breaks	– larger desk surface

Tab. 1: (continued)

For test takers with	Presentation		Response conventions	Timing and scheduling	Setting
	text	audio			
Hearing impairments		– amplification – headphones – face-to-face – video mediated – sign language interpreter for instructions	– adjust paired speaking test format	– extended response time – additional breaks	– seating near audio source
Learning difficulties (dyslexia; dysortho-graphia; ADHD)	– colored test books or overlays – text marking device, such as a ruler		– keyboard – scribe	– extended response time – additional breaks	– seating away from distraction
Physical challenges (paralysis; diabetes; broken arms)			– amanuensis or scribe – keyboard	– extended response time – additional breaks	– special seating or furniture

3.1 Visual impairments

There is great variation among those who request accommodations to address visual impairments. Some test takers may have partial sight, and require a large-print test book, magnifier, and large-print response sheet, keyboard, or scribe to record their answers. Others may request braille versions of test materials and an amanuensis or keyboard. Still others may not be proficient braille readers. The National Foundation for the Blind (2013) reports a braille literacy rate of only 10 %. As a result, these test takers may seek either exemption from, or an aural presentation of, the reading comprehension section of the test.

3.1.1 Read aloud

The test taker who is visually impaired, but not a proficient braille reader, poses a particular challenge for testing organizations. Some organizations allow the use of a Reader – a professional adhering to a code of practice who has been formally appointed to read the test material aloud (Khalifa and Weir 2009: 23). Allowing a reader to present the content of a reading comprehension test arouses some debate, as doing so does not permit the test taker to demonstrate "reading ability" per se; however, if the test taker regularly employs the services of a reader when engaging with printed text in a professional or educational context, then this is indeed how he or she "reads." Banerjee, Chen, and Dobson (2013: 264) summarize thus:

> [...] the use of read-aloud in tests of reading comprehension is debated. This is largely because of differences in opinion over the construct being tested. Some test providers do not consider text decoding to be part of the construct of reading comprehension, while others do (Laitusis 2010: 154) ... Even if text decoding is relatively unimportant in a test of reading comprehension, when text is presented orally, test takers' listening ability presents a confounding factor to the measurement of reading comprehension.

Laitusis (2010: 154) explains the read-aloud debate as it stands with United States' state-mandated assessments – though these are not presented with regard to test takers with visual impairments, but to those with learning disabilities:

> States are not in agreement, however, on whether to consider the audio presentation of test content (i.e. read aloud) on reading assessment to be an accommodation or a modification. Some states consider decoding to be a primary construct being assessed and therefore do not permit audio presentation or read aloud in any form. Other states consider read aloud to be a secondary construct and thus allow some forms of read aloud on tests of reading (e.g., some test sections but not others or test items but not passages); and a few states do not consider decoding part of the construct and therefore consider read aloud of all test content to be an accommodation.

3.1.2 Braille

In preparing a test to be presented in braille, the test developer must recognize that due to the manner in which braille is read, braille is quite different from any other font. It is important to first understand the manner by which braille is read. Typically, a person reading braille uses both hands – the right hand will read a line while the left hand moves to the next line to make a smooth transition from one line to the next. If both hands are lifted from the text, the braille reader requires some time to find his or her place – more time than a sighted reader would require to skim or scan. This may affect both the presentation of the stimuli and the skills which can be tested appropriately in a braille test version (Banerjee, Chen, and Dobson 2013: 258).

In addition, where visuals are not central to the task design, they should be eliminated altogether or the information provided textually. In the latter case, it is critical that the description does not provide language that the sighted test taker would be expected to produce unprompted.

The difference in reading speeds for both text and braille must also be considered. Khalifa and Weir (2009: 21–22) note that although proficient readers with and without visual impairments employ similar cognitive processes when decoding a text (Koenig 1992), on average, braille readers read at about half the speed of print readers – about 150 words per minute (Pring 1994). As a result of this difference, accommodation in terms of extra test time is both appropriate and necessary. Additional breaks may also be necessary to combat test taker fatigue as a result of the lengthened testing session.

To accommodate braille-reading test takers in the production of written constructed responses to a prompt, they may be allowed to dictate their essays or short answers to an amanuensis (or scribe), spelling out content words and indicating punctuation if these are among the criteria by which the response will be scored. The amanuensis can read back the text to allow for editing by the test taker. Alternatively, test takers may type their responses on a keyboard or braille-writer (Banerjee, Chen, and Dobson 2013: 263).

For a paired speaking task, if the prompt is provided textually, it can be presented in braille for the blind test taker, and in print for a sighted partner at the appropriate level of proficiency whose performance is not being scored. Additional time would be provided to allow for the pace of reading the braille input (Banerjee, Chen, and Dobson 2013: 263).

3.2 Hearing impairments

Like the spectrum of visually-impaired test takers, those who are deaf or hard of hearing also present a range of needs depending on the severity of the disability.

During the listening comprehension section of a test, those test takers who are hard of hearing may benefit from the use of headphones, rather than listening to "broadcast" audio. This allows test takers to monitor and adjust the volume according to their own needs. Others simply request to be seated near the broadcast audio source. The needs of the profoundly deaf, however, are not met by either of these accommodations.

To accommodate those test takers who process the spoken language of others by employing lip-reading skills, some testing programs will present the stimuli visually. This can be accomplished by presenting the stimuli either as a face-to-face interaction or via video recording. The former approach requires that the script of the audio recording be read aloud by live interlocutors, allowing candidates to use lip-reading to process the input (Elliot 2013: 69–70). In preparing the test script, the test developer may need to modify the stimulus to limit the number of interlocutors while still trying to tap the same skills as originally intended, such as vocabulary knowledge or identifying important detail. Elliot (2013: 70) describes the challenge of this modification is that live delivery of the stimulus: "… inevitably leads to a certain degree of non-standardisation. Although the content of the script is the same for all candidates taking the same form […] different interlocutors will naturally deliver the script with different rhythms, speeds and emphasis, and with different clarity of lip movements."

An alternative approach is to present the input in a video-mediated format. Again, this may require adaptation of the script, and efforts must be made to ensure that the input is presented in a natural manner, with the speakers' mouths clearly visible, and without providing any context clues that would not be afforded to the unaccommodated test taker.

Some may suggest that a sign language, such as American Sign Language (ASL) or British Sign Language (BSL), be employed to test the "listening and speaking" skills of test takers who are deaf or hard of hearing. However, given the potentially differing constructs of signed and spoken English languages, competence in signing is best evaluated and certified in a separate test designed for that purpose rather than within the context of a conventional oral/aural test (Elliot 2013: 65). Gallaudet University, a leader in education and career development for deaf and hard of hearing students, located in Washington, DC, attracts a number of English as Second Language learners to its English Language Institute (ELI). The ELI provides the Michigan English Test (MET), without the Listening and Speaking sections, to assess the English proficiency of its students; in addition, they administer other tests of communicative effectiveness, including an American Sign Language Placement test and an ASL Proficiency Interview (ASLPI).

For those test takers who are hard of hearing and are able to speak, a challenge may arise when participating in a paired speaking test, such as is offered in the Examination for the Certificate of Proficiency in English (ECPE), or in many of the Cambridge English examinations. In this case, the test format may be adjusted to allow the test taker to take the test with a familiar partner who is not a test taker, which may help the test taker to lip-read more easily, or the test format may be revised to allow the test taker to take the test without a partner (O'Sullivan and Green 2011: 48).

A less obvious area of required accommodation for the deaf and hard of hearing is in the presentation of the reading components of the test. Goldin-Meadow and Mayberry (2001: 222) report that most profoundly deaf children read poorly, although a small minority do learn to read fluently. They note that within the United States, "the median reading level of deaf high school graduates is the fourth grade (Allen 1986; Trybus and Karchmer 1977)." Further, even children who have only mild to moderate hearing losses, read at lower median levels than do normally-hearing children. The root cause resides in the fact that reading requires familiarity with a language and an understanding of the mapping between that language and the printed word. This is not simply a result of deaf children being unable to "sound out" words, as hearing children are instructed; after all, children are able to learn to read logographic languages such as Chinese, which is not a phonetically-representative text. Rather, the difference goes deeper as neither ASL nor BSL map systematically onto English. In fact, each possesses its own grammar, quite different from that of written English. Goldin-Meadow and Mayberry (2001: 223) emphatically write, "ASL is *not* English."

As a result of these challenges, deaf and hard-of-hearing language learners – especially early readers – process text differently, and at a slower pace, than their hearing counterparts. Extended response time, and concomitant additional breaks to combat test-taker fatigue, are accepted accommodations.

3.3 Learning challenges

"Learning challenges" encompass a wide array of disabilities. Although research in the area of learning disabilities has been ongoing for more 50 years, the conceptual definition used within the United States is the same one introduced into federal law in 1968 (Sparks 2013: 47):

> Specific learning disability means a disorder in one or more of the basic psychological processes involved in understanding or using language, spoken or written, which may manifest itself in an imperfect ability to listen, think, speak, read, write, spell, or to do mathematical calculations. The term includes such conditions as perceptual handicaps, brain injury, minimal brain dysfunction, dyslexia, and developmental aphasia. The term does not include children who have learning problems which are primarily the result of visual, hearing, or motor handicaps, of mental retardation, of emotional disturbance, or of environmental, cultural, or economic disadvantage. (U.S. Office of Education 1968: 34)

Testing organizations should not try to match a "one-size fits all" accommodation to these takers who have disparate experiences and needs. Rather, they are encouraged to consider each applicant individually, noting the types of accommodation that best allow the test taker to demonstrate proficiency in the language tested without altering the construct tested or the meaning of scores as far as is possible or reasonable.

Test takers with dyslexia, dysorthographia, or other cognitive processing disorders may require extra time to process the input presented in the test and to respond accordingly. Additional breaks may also be beneficial, as might taking the test in a quiet, distraction-free environment set apart from other test takers (Khalifa and Weir 2009: 22). In addition, test takers whose disability affects their capacity to hand-write may benefit from the use of a keyboard or computer when composing their responses to writing prompts, or with the assistance of a scribe to record their answers, including the completion of sequentially-numbered answer sheets (Taylor 2012: 310). An alternative testing environment, such as a private room, will be needed to facilitate such accommodations.

3.4 Physical challenges

Test takers' physical challenges range from short term disabilities, such as a broken arm, to permanent disabilities including paralysis and paraplegia. Accommodations provided must address the specific nature of each test taker's challenges.

This may require specialized furniture, such as adjustable chairs or desks that can be raised to accommodate wheelchairs, or the use of a scribe to record the test taker's responses. Additional time, additional breaks, and an alternate testing environment may or may not be required depending on the nature of the disability and the accommodations provided.

3.5 Need for individual consideration

Even as each test taker's challenges are unique, the accommodations afforded each should be determined on a case-by-case basis. For example, although the deaf and hard of hearing are often grouped together, a very broad spectrum of hearing loss exists: ranging from those who have never heard, to those who have lost hearing, and from those who can hear (perhaps distortedly) with amplification, to the profoundly deaf. Therefore, it is important to note that individuals with similar disabilities will not necessarily all benefit from the same accommodations (Taylor 2012: 311). Likewise, it may be necessary to make several different accommodations for test takers with multiple special needs.

Each test taker's situation must be examined individually, and the best accommodation – the accommodation that best levels the playing field for each test taker – must be implemented. After all, "it is important to remember that the test-taker, rather than the test task, is at the heart of the assessment event" (Khalifa and Weir 2009: 18; Shaw and Weir 2007: 17).

4 Key Issues

4.1 Unfair advantage

As Section 3 demonstrates, modifying a test or adjusting administration conditions to accommodate the needs of test takers with disabilities is an important part of promoting fair testing practices (Khalifa and Weir 2009: 20). However, since test takers may have differing degrees of disability, and some may have more than one type of disability or need more than one type of assistance, selecting the appropriate accommodation(s) for each test taker is a challenge of utmost importance to the testing organization. Furthermore, given that the goal in selecting and implementing an accommodation is to level the playing field for the test taker requiring special needs, it becomes equally important to neither advantage nor disadvantage the test taker disproportionately. As Elliot (2013: 62) explains: "... candidates with special requirements should be provided the opportunity to demonstrate their true level of ability – removing any unfair disadvantage due to their circumstances – without being marked more leniently than other candidates or otherwise put at an unfair advantage, and without changing the construct being tested."

In other words, the accommodations are intended to remove the effect of the disability on the test taker's ability to demonstrate his or her true level of language proficiency while ensuring that the accommodation does not provide test takers with disabilities an unfair advantage over their counterparts (Shaw and Weir 2007: 18). Banerjee, Chen, and Dobson (2013: 254) note that concern must remain with regard to the extent to which accommodations achieve the aim of leveling the playing field without unwittingly tipping the balance in favor of the test taker who seeks the accommodation. They quote Sireci, Scarpati, and Li (2005: 458): "... if the accommodation leads to an unfair advantage for the students who get them, for example, if everyone would benefit from the accommodation, then the scores from accommodated exams may be invalidly inflated, which would be unfair to students who do not receive accommodations."

With this is mind, the testing organization responding to test taker requests for accommodation has to carefully balance meeting the test taker's needs without being more lenient to that test taker than to his or her unaccommodated counterpart. Likewise, they must ensure that the score remains meaningful and comparable, and that the underlying construct remains unaltered (Randall and Engelhard 2010: 80).

4.2 Assistive technology

Additional challenges surround the growing availability of specially designed electronic equipment to enable learners and test takers with disabilities to read, write, listen or speak as well as to access standard technology (e.g., a computer). The terms "access" or "assistive" technology are often used to refer to such equipment which includes video magnifiers, braille note-takers and screen-reading software. For a test developer or provider, the use of access technology raises some important issues relating to technological support and test security, as well as to equity and construct operationalization.

4.3 Test-score meaning

Ethical considerations pertain equally to the interpretation and use of scores from accommodated tests since adaptations to test content, format and delivery risk changing the ability construct, and thus the meaning of the test scores. Clearly, it is important that sufficient and relevant information about test-score meaning is properly communicated to test users (such as university admissions officers or employers) who will have to interpret and make decisions based on test outcomes. In some cases, it may be appropriate to add an endorsement (or "flag") to a test taker's certificate indicating that some objectives of the test could not be assessed due to the candidate's disability in some respect. However, this approach raises other ethical issues and needs careful handling to ensure that it does not unduly or un-fairly label test takers as having taken a modified test and thus lead to them suf-fering subsequent discrimination. The example of language test provision for test takers with disabilities conveniently highlights the complex challenges that can confront language testers as they seek to work out in practice a commitment to behaving ethically.

5 Research

Interestingly, there exists relatively little published research, either theoretical or empirical, in the area of testing accommodations for English language learners with disabilities. There are two main reasons for this. Firstly, the overall population of test takers is very small indeed (e.g., fewer than 1% of CaMLA test takers overall request special accommodation); and secondly, the diversity of the disabilities in-volved often means that conducting research into any particular area of test accom-modations is extremely challenging. Studies are often difficult to design, carry out and interpret. For this reason, decisions about the nature and extent of modifica-tion to language test content and delivery tend to be based largely upon profession-al judgment informed by ethical values and practical considerations.

Nonetheless, it is clearly essential that relevant issues are investigated in the interests of ensuring fair access to assessment opportunities. It is also important that test-score users can place confidence in the meaningfulness of scores from accommodated tests and test providers therefore need to bring forward evidence in support of any claims they make about the usefulness of scores from their modi-fied tests. Examination boards and testing agencies are often in direct contact with test candidates and testing centres requesting accommodated tests and may there-fore be well-placed to undertake some of this much-needed research, perhaps in the form of small-scale but well-designed case studies.

Examples of the sort of research that can be conducted in this area include two pieces of research undertaken by Cambridge English Language Assessment. Shaw and Weir (2007) reported a multi-phase case study that investigated provision for test takers with dyslexia. Taylor and Khalifa (2013) conducted an impact-focused case study with four groups of stakeholders involved in accommodated tests; they included not only test takers, but also test writers, test administrators, and test raters. Both qualitative and quantitative data were gathered and analyzed using document review, questionnaire, and semi-structured interviews. The aim was to explore the perspectives of the four groups in order to investigate the match be-tween existing policy and current practice and to identify any areas meriting fur-ther attention. The data revealed a number of recurring themes, including: the extent and nature of special arrangements information provided to stakeholders; the importance of sustained and comprehensive training; the complex logistics of implementation; the challenge of achieving a consistent and professional approach; and possible avenues for future research. The particular value of this study lay in the way it explored the impact of assessing students with disabilities through the voices of stakeholders directly involved in the process.

6 Future directions

In conclusion, educational, employment, and social opportunities for people with disabilities have clearly increased significantly in recent years. Combined with a greater awareness of individual human rights and associated legislation, this has led to increased demand for access to testing and assessment provision. Anti-discrimination legislation and developments in English language pedagogy worldwide mean that greater attention has focused on meeting the specific needs of growing test-taker populations seeking access to assessment opportunities, including test takers with disabilities. In addition, attention has focused upon the responsibilities of institutional test providers, and there have been attempts to develop appropriate structures of accountability and systems of quality assurance (Van Avermaet, Kuijper, and Saville 2004). Over the last couple of decades, the provision of testing accommodations has become an important measure of the social responsibility or ethical standing of any language test provider. The principle applies whether the test provider is an individual classroom teacher devising a local test for her own students or an examination board offering high-stakes international tests on a large scale. Test takers with disabilities, whether of a temporary or permanent nature, constitute a significant and much more visible group in education and civic life nowadays, and language testing organisations thus have a responsibility to provide appropriately for their specific needs (Elliott 2013).

There remains much work to be done, however, to develop research in this area and to increase our understanding of the nature and value of testing accommodations, especially in some of the key areas highlighted above, e.g., the potential effect of accommodations on the underlying construct being assessed, the likely role of assistive technology in future testing accommodations, and the proper interpretation of scores resulting from accommodated tests.

7 References

AERA, APA, NCME (American Educational Research Association, American Psychological Association, and National Council on Measurement in Education). 1999. *Standards for educational and psychological testing.* Washington, DC: American Educational Research Association.

Allen, Thomas E. 1986. Patterns of academic achievement among hearing impaired students: 1974 and 1983. In: Arthur N. Schildroth and Michael A. Karchmer (eds.). *Deaf children in America*, 161–206. San Diego, CA: College Hill Press.

Association of Language Testers in Europe (ALTE). 1994. *Code of practice*. http://www.alte.org/ setting_standards/code_of_practice (accessed 28 May 2014).

Banerjee, Jayanti, Natalie Nordby Chen and Barbara Dobson. 2013. Special needs test forms: Levelling the playing field for test takers with disabilities. In: Dina Tsagari and George Spanoudis (eds.). *Assessing L2 students with learning and other disabilities*, 253–270. Newcastle upon Tyne: Cambridge Scholars Press.

Davies, Alan. 2004. Introduction: Language testing and the golden rule. *Language Assessment Quarterly* 1(2–3): 97–107.

Davies. Alan. 2008. Ethics, professionalism rights and codes. In: Elana Shohamy and Nancy H. Hornberger (eds.). *Encyclopedia of language and education* (2nd ed.) – Language testing and assessment 7: 429–443. New York: Springer Science + Business Media LLC.

European Association for Language Testing and Assessment (EALTA). 2006. *Guidelines for good practice in language testing and assessment*. http://www.ealta.eu.org/guidelines.htm (accessed 28 May 2014).

Elliott, Mark. 2013. Test taker characteristics. In: Ardeshir Geranpayeh and Lynda Taylor (eds.). *Examining listening: Research and practice in assessing second language listening*. 36–76. Cambridge, UK: UCLES/Cambridge University Press.

Fleurquin, Fernando. 2008. *The challenges of testing candidates with disabilities: Guidelines for stakeholders*. Poster presented at European Association for Language Testing and Assessment (EALTA), Athens, Greece, 9–11 May, http://www.ealta.eu.org/conference/2008/ docs/posters/DisabilitiesPost.pdf (accessed 31 July 2014).

Goldin-Meadow, Susan and Rachel I. Mayberry. 2001. How do profoundly deaf children learn to read? *Learning disabilities research and practice* 16(4): 222–229.

Hamp-Lyons, Liz. 1997. Washback, impact and validity: ethical concerns. *Language testing* 14(3): 295–303.

International Language Testing Association (ILTA). 2000. *Code of ethics*. http://iltaonline.com/ index.php?option=com_contentandtask=viewandid=57andItemid=47 (accessed 28 May 2014).

International Language Testing Association (ILTA). 2007. *Guidelines for practice*. http:// iltaonline.com/index.php?option=com_contentandtask=viewandid=122andItemid=133 (accessed 28 May 2014).

Joint Committee on Testing Practices. 1988. *Code of fair testing practices in education*. Washington, DC: Author.

Joint Committee on Testing Practices. 2004. *Code of fair testing practices in education*. Washington, DC: Author.

Khalifa, Hanan and Cyril J. Weir. 2009. *Examining reading: Research and practice in assessing second language reading*. Cambridge, UK: UCLES/Cambridge University Press.

Koenig, Alan J. 1992. A framework for understanding the literacy of individuals with visual impairments. *Journal of visual impairments and blindness* 86(7): 277–284.

Koenig, Judith. A. and Lyle K. Bachman (eds.). 2004. *Keeping score for all: The effects of inclusion and accommodation policies on large-scale educational assessments*. Washington, DC: National Academy Press.

Kunnan, Antony J. 2000. Fairness and justice for all. In: Antony J. Kunnan (ed.). *Fairness and validation in language assessment. Selected papers from the 19th LTRC, Orlando, Florida*, 1–14. Cambridge, UK: UCLES/Cambridge University Press.

Kunnan, Antony. J. 2008. Towards a model of test evaluation: using the Test Fairness and Test Context Frameworks. In: Lynda Taylor and Cyril J. Weir (eds.). *Multilingualism and Assessment: Achieving transparency, assuring quality sustaining diversity – Proceedings of the ALTE Berlin Conference May 2005*, 229–251. Cambridge, UK: UCLES/Cambridge University Press.

Laitusis, Cara Cahalan. 2010. Examining the impact of audio presentation on tests of reading comprehension. *Applied Measurement in Education* 23(2): 153–167.

Li, Hongli and Hoi K. Suen. 2012. Are test accommodations for English language learners fair? *Language Assessment Quarterly* 9(3): 293–309.

McNamara, Tim and Carsten Roever. 2006. *Language testing: The social dimension.* Malden, MA and Oxford: Blackwell.

National Foundation for the Blind. 2013. https://nfb.org/braille-general (accessed 9 November 2013).

O'Sullivan, Barry and Anthony Green. 2011. Test taker characteristics. In: Lynda Taylor (ed.). *Examining speaking: Research and practice in assessing second language speaking,* 36–64. Cambridge, UK: UCLES/Cambridge University Press.

Pring, Linda. 1994. Touch and go: learning to read braille. *Reading Research Quarterly* 29(1): 66–74.

Randall, Jennifer and George Engelhard, Jr. 2010. Performance of students with and without disabilities under modified conditions: Using resource guides and read-aloud test modifications on a high-stakes reading test. *The Journal of Special Education* 44(2): 79–93.

Rea-Dickins, Pauline. 1997. So, why do we need relationships with stakeholders in language testing? A view from the UK. *Language Testing* 14(3): 304–314.

Shaw, Stuart D. and Cyril J. Weir. 2007. *Examining writing: Research and practice in assessing second language writing.* Cambridge, UK: UCLES/Cambridge University Press.

Shohamy, Elana. 2001. *The power of tests: A critical perspective on the use of language tests.* Harlow: Longman/Pearson.

Sireci, Stephen G., Stanley E. Scarpati and Shuhong Li. 2005. Test accommodations for students with disabilities: An analysis of the interaction hypothesis. *Review of Educational Research* 75(4). 457–490. http://www.jstor.org/stable/3516104 (accessed 11 December 2012).

Sparks, Richard L. 2013. Students classified as learning disabled in L2 courses: The "special" case of the United States. In: Dina Tsagari and George Spanoudis (eds.). *Assessing L2 students with learning and other disabilities,* 45–68. Newcastle upon Tyne: Cambridge Scholars Press.

Taylor, Lynda. 2000. Stakeholders in language testing. *Research Notes* 2. University of Cambridge Local Examinations Syndicate – English as a Foreign Language (EFL). 2–4. http://www.cambridgeenglish.org/images/22642-research-notes-02.pdf (accessed 8 September 2014).

Taylor, Lynda. 2012. Accommodations in language testing. In: Christine Coombe, Peter Davidson, Barry O'Sullivan and Stephen Stoynoff (eds.). *The Cambridge Guide to Second Language Assessment,* 307–315. Cambridge, UK: Cambridge University Press.

Taylor, L. and H. Khalifa. 2013. Assessing students with disabilities: Voices from the stakeholder community. In: Dina Tsagari and George Spanoudis (eds.). *Assessing L2 students with learning and other disabilities,* 292–252. Newcastle upon Tyne: Cambridge Scholars Press.

Thurlow, Martha L., Sandra J. Thompson and Sheryl S. Lazarus. 2006. Considerations for the administration of tests to special needs students: Accommodations, modifications, and more. In: Steven M. Downing and Thomas M. Haladyna (eds.). *Handbook of test development,* 653–673. Mahwah, NJ: Lawrence Erlbaum, Inc.

Trybus, Raymond J. and Michael A. Karchmer. 1977. School achievement scores of hearing impaired children: National data on achievement status and growth patterns. *American Annals of the Deaf* 122(2): 62–69.

University of Cambridge Local Examinations Syndicate and the British Council. 1947. Joint Committee minutes, 19 March 1947, Item 5.

U.S. Office of Education. 1968. *First annual report of the National Advisory Committee on Handicapped Children.* Washington, D.C.: U.S. Department of Health, Education, and Welfare.

Van Avermaet, Piet, Henk Kuijper and Nick Saville. 2004. A code of practice and quality management system for international language examinations. *Language Assessment Quarterly* 1(2–3): 137–150.

Weir, Cyril J. 2005. *Language testing and validation: An evidence-based approach.* Basingstoke, Hampshire: Palgrave Macmillan.

Cecilia Guanfang Zhao

24 'Authorial voice' in the assessment of writing

1 Introduction

The concept of voice in written discourse has received considerable attention from academics and practitioners in the fields of composition studies, second language (L2) writing, and language assessment. Although researchers and teachers all agree that this concept is almost too slippery to be captured in any simple definition, and many find it especially challenging to explain and teach this concept to student writers, voice nonetheless remains one of those highly-valued and indispensable elements in writing instruction and assessment at both secondary and postsecondary levels (DiPardo, Storms, and Selland 2011). In the U.S.A., for example, voice has been a prevalent concept included in various state English Language Arts (ELA) learning standards (Zhao and Llosa 2008), statewide direct writing assessment rubrics (Jeffery 2009), and freshman composition textbooks (Ramanathan and Kaplan 1996). The concept of voice is therefore viewed by many as a key element that defines good writing.

Recently, however, as the student population in English-speaking countries becomes increasingly more diverse, the viability of teaching voice to L2 students has gradually come under scrutiny. Many researchers argue that such a slippery concept, laden with the Western mainstream ideology of individualism, is probably incomprehensible to L2 writers, especially those from a collectively-oriented cultural background. Hence, the relative importance of voice in L2 writing instruction and assessment also becomes a topic of debate among scholars and practitioners. Perhaps due to the elusive nature of this concept, much of such debate is still at the abstract and theoretical level. Empirical research that systematically investigates whether and how the strength of an authorial voice may affect the perceived text quality is scarce in the literature. And even fewer studies exist that explore how authorial voice in written texts might be precisely captured and reliably measured.

This chapter will seek to provide an overview of the issues associated with the assessment and instruction of this subtle dimension of the construct of writing competence. It will start with a review and synthesis of the existing literature on voice, which includes the many different theoretical conceptions of voice and empirical studies on voice-related issues in various educational contexts. Based on such a review, I will identify the gaps in the literature and discuss the major issues often associated with voice research. Next, the chapter will present a most recent empirical study that addresses some of such issues and offers new evidence on the nature and relative importance of voice in L2 writing. Finally, the chapter will highlight avenues for future research, with a particular focus on the potential challenges and opportunities for the inclusion of subtle constructs such as voice in the assessment of second/foreign language proficiency in general, and L2 writing competence in particular.

2 Theoretical conceptions of voice

Since the early 1970s, researchers across the fields of composition studies and L2 writing have made quite a few attempts to formulate a satisfactory definition of voice. Within the L1 composition community, for instance, voice is often seen as a reflection of an author's identity in writing. Many scholars believe that the presence of an individual voice in a written text is a key feature of successful writing. Elbow (1968, 1981), for example, defines voice as "the sound of the individual on the page" (Elbow 1981: 287). Similarly, Stewart (1972) argues that each writer has a particular voice of her own, and this "authentic" voice is what makes a piece of writing unique and powerful. To him, hence, voice is a "fundamental quality of good writing" (Stewart 1992: 283). Many researchers also believe that this authentic voice is something innate, something that writers can discover from within and through practices of expressive writing (e.g., Elbow 1968, 1981; Graves 1994; Stewart 1972, 1992). Consequently, this particular view of voice is often also referred to as the expressivist view.

More recently, however, such an expressivist conception of voice has been challenged by a social constructivist perspective, which holds that an authorial voice in written discourse is not innate or static, but socially and culturally constructed. This focus on social and cultural context then opens up new discussions about the nature of voice among researchers and practitioners. Ede (1992: 171), for example, presents a "situational voice" and argues that "just as people dress differently for different occasions, so too do writers vary their style depending upon the rhetorical situation." Similarly, Bowden (1999) and Yancey (1994) also believe that writers adopt different voices for different purposes, and therefore a writer is able to have "multiple voices" instead of just one generic voice. Such a notion is endorsed by many other researchers and echoed in L1 composition literature (e.g., Farmer 1995; Harris 1987; Kumamoto 2002; Lensmire 1998), L2 writing research (e.g., Hirvela and Belcher 2001; Ivanič and Camps 2001), as well as scholarship on general academic writing (e.g., Hyland 2008a). Drawing on works of Voloshinov and Bakhtin in particular, Prior (2001) further complicates the definition of voice from a sociohistoric perspective and argues that the concept of voice is simultaneously personal and social.

Yet another alternative conception of voice is Cummins's (1994) notion of "voicing." As pointed out by Hirvela and Belcher (2001), Cummins's "voicing" captures the nature of voice not as an inherent feature, but as an activity and a process. According to Cummins (1994: 49), this voicing is "a process of continually creating, changing, and understanding the internal and external identities that cast us as writers, within the confines of language, discourse, and culture." If these aforementioned theoretical conceptions of voice all seem to be somewhat loosely presented, Matsuda (2001: 40) for the first time offers a relatively more formal definition. According to him, "voice is the amalgamative effect of the use of discursive and non-discursive features that language users choose, deliberately or otherwise, from socially available, yet ever-changing repertoires." Even such a definition, however, is too ambiguous and vague to assist our understanding of the concept. Researchers are therefore still finding ways to better capture and articulate this notion in more precise and explicit terms.

Hyland (2008a: 5), for example, proposes a new interactional model of voice that can be used to explore "how the [linguistic and discourse] choices writers make ... construct authorial voice" in academic writing in particular. Hyland (2008a: 6) argues that "we do not sacrifice a personal voice by writing in the disciplines," and "we achieve a voice through the ways we negotiate representations of ourselves and take on the discourses of our communities." This notion of voice in academic written discourse is therefore closely related to the concept of interaction and is composed of two major dimensions, according to Hyland. One is what he calls "stance," which refers to writer-oriented features that explain how writers present themselves, their opinions, and their arguments. It is realized through the use of four linguistic elements: hedges, boosters, attitude markers, and self-mention. The other dimension, "engagement," mainly concerns reader-oriented features, and is realized through the use of five other language features: reader pronouns, personal asides, references to shared knowledge, directives, and (rhetorical or audience directed) questions.

Hyland's (2008a) interactional model of voice, hence, sees voice as essentially social and embraces a dialogic approach that many believe is a valuable way of looking at the issues of voice in writing (e.g., Farmer 1995; Prior 2001). By incorporating both authorial stance and reader engagement into the model, Hyland's (2008a) theory emphasizes not only the individualistic aspect of voice but also the interdependent aspect of it. In a sense, this model successfully "embraces contraries" (*Reconsiderations: Voice in writing again: Embracing contraries,* Elbow 2007) and makes clear that these two aspects of voice are not at odds, but are two sides of the same coin. Moreover, while acknowledging the elusiveness of the concept, Hyland's (2008a) model at least offers a systematic way of looking at the construction of voice in academic writing through the use of specific linguistic- and discourse-level elements available in the English language. It will therefore also help to demystify the admittedly very complex concept for L2 writers and writing researchers alike.

3 Empirical studies of voice

Just as scholars formulate different theories about what voice is, researchers and teachers also debate the relative importance of voice in writing instruction and assessment. Some, particularly those in rhetoric and L1 composition studies, tend to attach great importance to the development of an authentic voice in writing, and thus support the teaching of voice in writing classrooms (e.g., Easton 2005; Hickey 1993; Holding 2005; McHaney 2004; Romano 2004). Others, mainly in the field of L2 writing research, often challenge, from different perspectives, the viability of teaching voice in either L2 writing classrooms or L1 composition classrooms where the student population has become culturally and linguistically diverse (e.g., Helms-Park and Stapleton 2003; Ramanathan and Atkinson 1999; Ramanathan and Kaplan 1996; Stapleton 2002). Based on their analysis of ten widely used freshman composition textbooks in US colleges and universities, Ramanathan and Kaplan (1996), for instance, point out that the concept of voice is of itself a product of the Western society and culture, and the teaching of voice in US writing classrooms is essentially inductive and heavily dependent on students' inherent knowledge of American culture, ideology, and tradition. The authors hence argue that voice is a problematic concept for L2 students, since they often have no access to such cultural knowledge. Similarly, Ramanathan and Atkinson (1999) also point out that prevalent concepts in L1 writing instruction, such as voice, peer review, critical thinking, and textual ownership, are problematic for L2 students, as these concepts are too closely associated with the US mainstream ideology of individualism.

Empirical research results, as well as anecdotal evidence, seem to support this observation that L2 writers would usually have difficulty learning to write with a voice of their own in a different culture and for a different audience. Several well-known autobiographical studies, for example, show how learning to develop a distinctive personal voice in writing is closely related to the development of a new writerly self or identity. Of such studies, the most widely cited is Shen's (1989) narrative of how he struggled to reconcile his old "Chinese Self" that always emphasizes the notion of "we" with a new "English Self" which glorifies the "I" in his English composition classes. Similar experiences can be found in many other reflections on or studies of writing issues faced by L2 learners (e.g., Canagarajah 2001; Connor 1996; Gale 1994; Li 1996), and sometimes even L1 writers (e.g., Fecho and Green 2002; McAlexander and Marston 1994; Schwartz 2003).

As more L2 students enter mainstream classrooms, and more begin to notice and articulate their difficulty grappling with the concept of voice, the issues associated with the teaching and learning of voice also becomes more salient in the field of L2 writing research. The Journal of Second Language Writing (JSLW) even published a special issue in 2001 (Vol. 10, Issues 1–2) on the topic of voice in L2 writing. In that issue, researchers again tend to link the discussion of voice to that of identity construction and self-representation in L2 writing. Hirvela and Belcher (2001), for instance, describe the struggles three mature multilingual writers experience when learning to write with a voice that is appreciated by the mainstream audience and yet foreign to their own ears. Through in-depth interviews with these writers, the authors conclude that the struggles these mature multilingual writers experience are tied to the identity conflict that they encounter while writing to enter the North American academic community as graduate students. The authors argue that L2 writing researchers and teachers should not view voice only as a pedagogical focus in writing classrooms; instead, we should seek to better understand multilingual writers themselves through discussions of voice in L2 writing.

Similarly, Ivanič and Camps (2001) also explore how L2 graduate students negotiate a proper voice and self-representation when writing in a different culture. The authors' analysis of 6 Mexican graduate students' writing samples points to three major channels through which L2 students voice and position themselves, i.e. ideational representation of the world, interpersonal positioning in relation to the intended audience, and textual construction of meaning. Like Hirvela and Belcher (2001), the authors believe that L2 writers can have multiple voices and identities and that the negotiation of identity and voice is "an integral part of any act of writing" (Ivanič and Camps 2001: 4). However, they do not view the concept of voice as problematic and troublesome to L2 writers as many researchers do; instead, they argue that the inclusion and proper treatment of the topic in L2 writing classrooms can raise L2 writers' awareness of self-representation and help them gain better control over voice and identity projection in their writing.

Likewise, Matsuda (2001) also argues that voice is not something completely foreign and inaccessible to L2 writers. Through analysis of a Japanese female writer's web diary, Matsuda (2001) demonstrates how L2 writers, even those from a so-called "collectivist" cultural background, are able to write with a strong personal voice using their L1. Results from this case study counter the argument that the concept of voice is exclusively tied to the Western ideology of individualism and is, therefore, beyond the comprehension of L2 learners. If evidence shows that L2 writers are able to construct a strong individualistic voice in their L1 writing, then we have reason to believe that with proper instruction and help, L2 writers may well be able to understand and construct an equally strong personal voice in their L2 writing. The more critical question here is probably how writing researchers and teachers might go about helping students to develop their voice in L2 writing.

Immediately following the publication of the JSLW special issue on voice, researchers begin to shift their focus from discussions about the nature and "teachability" of voice (to L2 students) to investigations of the relative importance of voice in L2 writing instruction and assessment. Stapleton (2002) first argues conceptually that the notion of voice has been given more attention than it really deserves in writing classrooms and the L2 writing community. He calls on the field to "return the spotlight to ideas" instead, as he believes that it is "ideas" that are "the most important aspect of writing" (Stapleton 2002: 189). The rising debate among scholars and teachers about the relative importance of voice in L2 writing classrooms thus leads to a need for not only theoretical speculations but, more importantly, also empirical evidence on the relationship between authorial voice strength and text quality.

Although Yeh (1998), in his validation of a rubric that scores argumentative writing along the dimensions of development, voice, and conventions, indirectly offers some insights into the role voice plays in argumentative writing, intentional empirical probing into the relationship between voice and writing quality remains few and far between in the literature. The first study that directly and purposefully looked into such a voice-writing quality relationship is probably Helms-Park and Stapleton's (2003) investigation of the importance of voice in the context of undergraduate L2 argumentative writing. In this study, an analytic Voice Intensity Rating Scale was developed to measure voice intensity through dimensions of assertiveness, self-identification, reiteration of the central point, and authorial presence and autonomy of thought. Meanwhile, Jacobs et al.'s (1981) ESL Composition Profile was adopted to evaluate text quality. Subsequent correlation analysis indicated that overall voice intensity and text quality were unrelated, and there was also no significant correlation between any of the individual voice dimensions and text quality. Based on such findings, therefore, the authors question the value of voice instruction in L2 writing classrooms and programs.

While Helms-Park and Stapleton's (2003) study is the first to have offered some empirical evidence on the relative importance of voice in L2 writing, the validity of their conclusion about the lack of association between voice and text quality has been challenged. Some critics, for example, argue that Helms-Park and Stapleton's (2003) voice rating scale is a "skewed representation" of the construct of voice (Matsuda and Tardy 2007, 2008). Viewed from a social constructivist perspective, an authorial voice, particularly one in academic discourse, is realized through both the representation of the writerly self and the author's interaction with other members of the discourse community (Cumming et al. 2005; Hyland 2008a; Palacas 1989). Hence, a voice rubric that captures only the presence of the writer in the text is by all means limited. Consequently, the conclusion about the unimportance of voice in L2 academic writing is probably still premature.

To further investigate the importance of voice in academic writing, Matsuda and Tardy (2007) focus on examining the role voice plays in the process of a blind peer review of an article submitted for publication in an academic journal. Close analysis of the manuscript itself, reviewers' comments, as well as interviews with reviewers and the manuscript author, showed that reviewers frequently construct an authorial voice and identity based on various textual features while evaluating the quality of the manuscript. Evidence from this case study therefore indicates that voice may indeed play an important role in professional academic writing practices. However, as the study is of small scale and is confined to the context of rhetoric and composition studies for professional academic writers, the generalizability of such results across different writing and assessment contexts remains uncertain.

Zhao and Llosa (2008), hence, further explored the role voice plays in academic writing. Situated in the context of a high-stakes L1 writing assessment at the high-school exit level, Zhao and Llosa (2008) replicated Helms-Park and Stapleton's (2003) study and examined the association between voice intensity, as measured by the Voice Intensity Rating Scale, and text quality, as defined by the scores on the 42 anchor essays from the New York State Regents Examination in English Language Arts. Analysis from this study showed that voice intensity was a statistically significant predictor of writing quality, at least in L1 argumentative writing. Zhao and Llosa (2008) argue, therefore, that if voice is considered to be a critical element in mainstream educational assessment, and if the ultimate goal of any ESL program is, after all, to prepare L2 students for the mainstream educational setting, then voice should be treated as an important concept in L2 writing classrooms as well.

4 Salient issues and gaps in the literature

Based on the above review, we can see that while theoretical discussions and conceptualizations of voice abound in the literature, this concept remains an elusive one that is at once intriguing and vexing for both researchers and teachers (Dipardo, Storms and Selland 2011). The construct is certainly difficult to define in theory, but it is even more challenging to operationalize in practice. Consequently, although abstract conceptions of voice proliferate, few have been successfully translated into research-friendly instruments or pedagogically useful tools that can facilitate empirical studies as well as the teaching of voice. While writing rubrics that contain voice as a criterion for evaluation do exist, voice in those rubrics is either holistically evaluated in rather broad terms based on a reader's general impression (e.g., mature/immature in Yeh 1998; absent/distinctive in DeRemer 1998; lifeless/compelling in various versions of the Six-Trait Scoring Rubric), or considered as a subcomponent under other analytical dimensions on a rating scale (e.g., Wolfe et al. 1996; NYSED 2010). Except for Helms-Park and Stapleton's (2003) Voice Intensity Rating Scale, there is no analytic rubric that measures exclusively the presence and intensity of authorial voice in written texts. Moreover, the Voice Intensity Rating Scale is criticized for its construct under-representation and lack of formal validation (Matsuda and Tardy 2007; Zhao 2013). Hence, a reliable and validated analytic voice rubric is much needed. The presence of such a scale could not only open the way to more empirical studies on the relative importance of voice in various writing contexts, but it could also inform writing pedagogy. Writing teachers can use such an analytic rubric to demystify the seemingly "unlearnable" concept of voice and break it down to its components, when helping students to develop an individual voice and teaching them to use that voice effectively.

A related issue, as evidenced in the literature, is the heated and as yet unresolved debate about how important voice is in writing instruction and assessment, particularly L2 writing instruction and assessment. Probably due to the lack of an accurate and reliable voice measure in the field, little empirical research exists that systematically investigates the nature and characteristics of the relationship between voice and writing quality in authentic academic settings. Instead, most of the existing empirical studies on voice have focused on describing the struggles writers go through while learning to develop a voice of their own and construct a writerly identity in their writing. Such troublesome experiences can be found among basic or beginning writers (e.g., Cappello 2006; McAlexander and Marston 1994; Young 1996), L1 or L1 minority writers (e.g., Fecho and Green 2002; Schwartz 2003), and especially L2 writers (e.g., Canagarajah 2001; Gale 1994; Hirvela and Belcher 2001; Li 1996; Shen 1989). Methodologically speaking, almost all these studies are qualitative in nature, and are ethnographic or case studies, if not autobiographical accounts.

Another line of research has focused on exploring how voice is constructed through the use of various linguistic features in written discourse (e.g., Hyland 2008a, 2008b; Ivanič and Camps 2001; Matsuda 2001; Matsuda and Tardy 2007). This type of research is mostly qualitative in nature as well, and often takes the form of either case studies or discourse analysis of a particular person's writing. Additionally, researchers have also examined the use of individual voice elements in student and expert writing. These voice elements include first person pronouns (e.g., Hyland 2002a, 2002c; Tang and John 1999), modifiers such as hedges and boosters (e.g., Hyland 1998, 2000a, 2000b; Hyland and Milton 1997), as well as directives, connectives, questions, and references (e.g., Barton 1995; Hyland 2002b, 2002d; Palacas 1989). Typically, these studies are done quantitatively using corpus-based linguistic analysis. Frequencies of these language features are often explored and compared between different writer groups. A few other empirical studies have examined the prevalence of the concept of voice in writing textbooks (e.g., Ramanathan and Kaplan 1996) and the effectiveness of voice instruction in ESL academic writing classrooms (e.g., Aghbar and Chitrapu 1997). But they are limited in number and are either criticized for or self-evaluated as lacking a rigorous research design (e.g., Raimes and Zamel 1997; Aghbar and Chitrapu 1997).

Empirical studies that have actually examined the relationship between voice and writing quality are scarce (Helms-Park and Stapleton 2003; Zhao and Llosa 2008). Results from these few studies, however, can be best characterized as inconclusive, if not downright contradictory, which therefore warrants further scrutiny of the role voice plays in various writing classrooms and assessment settings. Until such empirical evidence is available, all the debate among researchers and practitioners about the importance, or lack thereof, of voice in writing instruction is at best only theoretically assumed. Since issues of voice are particularly prevalent and salient in the L2 writing community, and the debate about the viability of voice as a pedagogical tool is mostly associated with the L2 student population, more research probably needs to be done to further explore the importance of voice in L2 writing instruction and assessment.

5 New evidence from the most recent empirical study

As an attempt to address the above identified issues and fill the gaps in the literature, Zhao (2010, 2013) investigated the nature of voice in L2 academic writing, developed an analytic rubric that measures voice strength in L2 written texts, and explored the relationship between voice strength and L2 text quality. Since academic writing, especially academic writing at the post-secondary level, is predominantly argumentative in nature (Helms-Park and Stapleton 2003; Ramanathan and Kaplan 1996), the study is situated in the context of a high-stakes L2 argumentative writing assessment (i.e. TOEFL iBT independent writing test). In addition, given the theory that a writer's L1 or cultural background often influence their L2 writing (e.g., Connor 1996) and that certain groups of L2 writers, particularly those with a collectivist cultural background, are more likely to have difficulty "voicing" themselves in writing (e.g., Ramanathan and Atkinson 1999; Ramanathan and Kaplan 1996), Zhao (2010) also set out to investigate, for the first time, the potential effect of key writer background factors on the construction of voice in writing and on the relationship between voice and writing quality.

Based primarily on Hyland's (2008a) interactional model of voice, Zhao (2010, 2013) first developed a preliminary voice rubric. Ten prevalent linguistic and discourse elements identified in the literature as being relevant to the concept of voice were translated into ten analytic categories on the rubric. Each category was evaluated on a scale of 0–4, representing the range from the absence of a particular voice feature to extensive use of that feature in a writing sample. Factor analysis of such voice ratings from 200 TOEFL iBT writing samples pointed to three major dimensions that together capture the strength of an authorial voice in an L2 argumentative written text. These dimensions included the presence and clarity of ideas in the content, manner of idea presentation, and writer and reader presence. The quantitative analysis results were also corroborated and supplemented by rater think-aloud and interview data, which looked into the reliability, validity, and applicability of the preliminary voice rubric. Based on all the analyses, the rubric was restructured and revised to capture voice from the three identified dimensions and with more concrete and precise qualitative descriptors derived from rater think-aloud and interview data.

This revised rubric was then applied to another 200 L2 writing samples for validation purposes. Confirmatory factor analysis and other statistical analysis further suggested that the three voice dimensions tap into the underlying construct of voice. Subsequent analysis of the relationship between overall voice strength and text quality showed that voice is a statistically significant predictor of L2 writing quality; specifically, voice accounted for about 25 % of the variance in the TOEFL iBT independent writing scores. And of the three voice dimensions, while each appeared to be strongly and positively associated with text quality when examined in isolation, only the presence and clarity of ideas emerged as the most significant predictor of text quality, when the effect of other voice dimensions was controlled for. Moreover, analysis of the potential effect of writer background factors suggested that key writer background factors such as their age, gender, and native language rarely, if at all, affected the construction of voice in L2 written texts, nor did they affect the relationship between voice and text quality. In other words, the relationship between voice and writing quality does not vary as a function of any of these writer background variables.

Zhao's (2010, 2013) empirical study hence not only offers a new three-dimensional model that characterizes the nature of voice in L2 argumentative writing, but it also provides the field with a rubric that can be used to measure this nebulous construct. Unlike the few existing measures of voice that are mostly holistic and impression-based, this theoretically grounded and empirically validated analytic voice rubric, with its clearly identified dimensions and explicitly defined descriptors, is the first of its kind that can be used to both facilitate empirical research on the topic and inform writing pedagogy. Writing teachers, for example, can use this voice rubric in their instruction to demystify the concept for their students, especially L2 students, and support the effective teaching and learning of this construct.

Results from this study regarding the close association between voice and writing quality also provide further evidence on the relative importance of voice in L2 argumentative writing, which in turn contributes to the ongoing debate in the literature about whether voice should be treated as a worthy pedagogical focus in various L2 writing classrooms and programs. Additionally, findings on the relationship between individual voice components and text quality also offer us a more nuanced interpretation of the role voice plays in L2 writing. After controlling for the effect of other voice dimensions, the content-related voice dimension was the only significant, strong, and positive predictor of L2 argumentative writing quality. This could bear important implications for L2 writing instruction.

Stapleton (2002: 177) argues that L2 writing researchers and practitioners should pay less attention to voice and "return the spotlight to ideas." What Stapleton implies in this statement is that voice and ideas are two separate and unrelated constructs. Zhao' (2010) study, however, not only empirically identifies this dimension of idea and content as an integral part of the concept of voice, but it also shows that it is indeed this dimension that is most critically related to writing quality. Consequently, writing instructors should not teach voice in isolation, nor treat it purely as a matter of expression; rather, they should explicitly link idea and content development to the concept of voice for their students in their instruction. Finally, results from this study about the lack of association between overall voice strength and writer background variables also counter the popular argument in the literature about the inaccessibility of voice to L2 writers from a non-Western cultural background. We have reason to believe that, with proper instruction, L2 writers too will be able to write with a strong voice of their own.

6 Future directions

Recent scholarship in the fields of composition studies and L2 writing has evidenced a strong interest in topics related to voice in written discourse. Writing researchers and teachers in Western educational systems are particularly attracted to this notion due to their emphasis on the value of individualism that is deeply embedded in their cultural and political traditions. It follows, therefore, that despite the complexity and difficulty of capturing voice in written texts, many have been endeavoring to formulate theories and definitions that can help elucidate the nature and the core characteristics of this construct. Although recent research on voice has shed more light on what voice is and what it does in both student and expert writing, there are still many unresolved questions and issues that await our further investigation.

First of all, further validation and refinement of existing theories and measures of voice is needed. For scholarly discussions of voice to be useful and meaningful, especially for educational purposes, we should not always dwell on abstract and theoretical conceptions of this notion. More research needs to be done to transform complex theories into "simpler" instruments and tools that are, hopefully, more readily understandable and useful to researchers, teachers, as well as student writers. Of course, existing voice measures in the literature also need to be further validated before they can be widely applied. As DeVellis (2003: 159) and many other researchers point out "validation is a cumulative, ongoing process;" scale or rubric developers and users need to consider "the extent to which the validity of the scale generalizes across populations, settings, or an assortment of other dimensions." Hence, there is undoubtedly a need for further validation and revision of existing voice rubrics, or perhaps even the development of new voice measures for different contexts and purposes.

Secondly, the debate about the relevance, or irrelevance, of voice in L2 writing classrooms in the literature has been inconclusive. More empirical evidence, therefore, needs to be gathered if we want to determine exactly how important voice is for L2 writing programs and student writers. In addition, such evidence should go beyond idiosyncratic reflections and theoretical speculations; rather, future research should consider more direct inquiries into the association between voice and writing quality in order to provide decisive evidence on the relative importance of voice in various writing assessment contexts. Currently in the literature, such empirical inquiries are still few and far between (Helms-Park and Stapleton 2003; Zhao and Llosa 2008; Zhao 2010), and results from these few studies are not sufficiently consistent or generalizable.

Another direction for future research is to look into the types of challenges L2 writers encounter when learning to write with a strong voice that is deemed acceptable by the mainstream English-speaking audience, and the strategies successful L2 writers employ to overcome such challenges when writing in different educational settings and discourse communities. Much of the existing literature has focused on arguing and describing how this concept of voice, laden with the mainstream Western ideology of individualism, may be difficult for L2 writers to understand; yet, the more important piece that is missing in this body of literature is exactly how to help L2 writers better understand, develop, and maneuver their voice. As discussed earlier, if the mainstream audience and readership expect and value a notable authorial voice when they read and evaluate written texts, then L2 writers will inevitably have to face and deal with the challenges of constructing a clear voice in their writing, if ever they want to be heard and accepted by that community. So, it would be more constructive and fruitful if future research could focus more on finding and presenting ways that can help L2 writers successfully project their voice into their writing.

Of course, research may also want to further examine the role voice plays in L1 versus L2 writing assessment and instruction, in high-stakes versus classroom-based assessment settings, and in different genres of writing. Only with such additional evidence can we have a more precise understanding of the nature, characteristics, and functions of voice across various educational contexts. And such an understanding, in turn, can not only help inform L2 writing pedagogy, as discussed earlier, but also contribute to the development of L2 writing assessment theory and practice in the long run. As some applied linguists also argue (e.g., Connor and Mbaye 2002), in addition to the linguistic aspect of writing that is traditionally focused on when evaluating L2 student writing, the sociolinguistic and communicative aspects of writing also deserve our attention when assessing students' writing competence. Admittedly, it will be rather challenging to define and operationalize subtle constructs such as voice, yet it also opens up opportunities for researchers, teachers and L2 students to learn about and attend to such critical aspects of writing competence that has long been undervalued in L2 writing assessment and instruction.

7 References

Aghbar, Ali-Asghar and Devi Chitrapu. 1997. Teaching for voice in ESL writing from sources. *Maryland English Journal* 31(2): 39–47.

Barton, Ellen L. 1995. Contrastive and non-contrastive connectives: Metadiscourse functions in argumentation. *Written Communication* 12(2): 219–239.

Bowden, Darsie. 1999. *The mythology of voice.* Portsmouth, NH: Heinemann.

Canagarajah, Suresh. 2001. The fortunate traveler: Shuttling between communities and literacies by economy class. In: Diane Belcher and Ulla Connor (eds.). *Reflections on multiliterate lives*, 23–37. New York: Multilingual Matters.

Cappello, Marva. 2006. Under construction: Voice and identity development in writing workshop. *Language Arts* 83(6): 482–491.

Connor, Ulla. 1996. *Contrastive rhetoric: Cross-cultural aspects of second language writing.* Cambridge, UK: Cambridge University Press.

Connor, Ulla and Aymerou Mbaye. 2002. Discourse approaches to writing assessment. *Annual Review of Applied Linguistics* 22: 263–278.

Cumming, Alistair, Robert Kantor, Kyoko Baba, Usman Erdosy, Keanre Eouanzoui and Mark James. 2005. Differences in written discourse in independent and integrated prototype tasks for next generation TOEFL. *Assessing Writing* 10(1): 5–43.

Cummins, Gail Summerskill. 1994. Coming to voice. In: Kathleen Blake Yancey (ed.). *Voices on voice: Perspectives, definitions, inquiry*, 48–60. Urbana, IL: National Council of Teachers of English.

De Remer, Mary L. 1998. Writing assessment: Raters' elaboration of the rating task. *Assessing Writing* 5(1): 7–29.

De Vellis, Robert F. 2003. *Scale development: Theory and applications.* 2nd ed. Thousand Oaks, CA: Sage Publications.

DiPardo, Anne, Barbara A. Storms and Makenzie Selland. 2011. Seeing voices: Assessing writerly stance in the NWP Analytic Writing Continuum. *Assessing Writing* 16(3): 170–188.

Easton, Lois Brown. 2005. Democracy in schools: Truly a matter of voice. *English Journal* 94(5): 52–56.

Ede, Lisa S. 1992. *Work in progress: A guide to writing and revising.* 2nd ed. New York: St. Martin's Press.

Elbow, Peter. 1968. A method for teaching writing. *College English* 30(2): 115–125.

Elbow, Peter. 1981. *Writing with power: Techniques for mastering the writing process.* New York: Oxford University Press.

Elbow, Peter. 2007. Reconsiderations: Voice in writing again: Embracing contraries. *College English* 70(2): 168–188.

Farmer, Frank. 1995. Voice reprised: Three etudes for a dialogic understanding. *Rhetoric Review* 13(2): 304–320.

Fecho, Bob and Aaron Green. 2002. Madaz publication: Polyphonic identity and existential literacy transactions. *Harvard Educational Review* 72(1): 93–120.

Gale, Xin Liu. 1994. Conversing across cultural boundaries: Rewriting "self". *Journal of Advanced Composition* 14(2): 455–462.

Graves, Donald H. 1994. *A fresh look at writing.* Portsmouth, NH: Heinemann.

Harris, Joseph. 1987. The plural text/the plural self: Roland Barthes and William Coles. *College English* 49(2): 158–170.

Helms-Park, Rena and Paul Stapleton. 2003. Questioning the importance of individualized voice in undergraduate L2 argumentative writing: An empirical study with pedagogical implications. *Journal of Second Language Writing* 12(3): 245–265.

Hickey, Dona J. 1993. *Developing a written voice.* London: Mayfield.

Hirvela, Alan and Diane Belcher. 2001. Coming back to voice: The multiple voices and identities of mature multilingual writers. *Journal of Second Language Writing* 10(1–2): 83–106.

Holding, Mark. 2005. Liberating the student's voice: A teacher's story of the college essay. *English Journal* 94(4): 76–82.

Hyland, Ken. 1998. *Hedging in scientific research articles*. Amsterdam: John Benjamins.

Hyland, Ken. 2000a. Hedges, boosters and lexical invisibility: Noticing modifiers in academic texts. *Language Awareness* 9(4): 179–197.

Hyland, Ken. 2000b. 'It might be suggested that …': Academic hedging and student writing. *Australian Review of Applied Linguistics* 16: 83–97.

Hyland, Ken. 2002a. Authority and invisibility: Authorial identity in academic writing. *Journal of Pragmatics* 34: 1091–1112.

Hyland, Ken. 2002b. Directives: Argument and engagement in academic writing. *Applied Linguistics* 23(2): 215–239.

Hyland, Ken. 2002c. Options of identity in academic writing. *ELT Journal* 56(4): 351–358.

Hyland, Ken. 2002d. What do they mean? Questions in academic writing. *Text* 22(4): 529–557.

Hyland, Ken. 2008a. Disciplinary voices: Interactions in research writing. *English Text Construction* 1(1): 5–22.

Hyland, Ken. 2008b. 'Small bits of textual material': A discourse analysis of Swales' writing. *English for Specific Purposes* 27(2): 143–160.

Hyland, Ken and John Milton. 1997. Hedging in L1 and L2 student writing. *Journal of Second Language Writing* 6(2): 183–205.

Ivanič, Roz and David Camps. 2001. I am how I sound: Voice as self-representation in L2 writing. *Journal of Second Language Writing* 10(1–2): 3–33.

Jacobs, Holly L., Stephen A. Zinkgraf, Deanna R. Wormuth, V. Faye Hartfiel and Jane B. Hughey. 1981. *Testing ESL composition: A practical approach*. Rowley, MA: Newbury House.

Jeffery, Jill V. 2009. Constructs of writing proficiency in US state and national writing assessments: Exploring variability. *Assessing Writing* 14(1): 3–24.

Kumamoto, Chikako D. 2002. Bakhtin's others and writing as bearing witness to the eloquent "I.". *College Composition and Communication* 54(1): 66–87.

Lensmire, Timothy J. 1998. Rewriting student voice. *Journal of Curriculum Studies*, 30(3): 261–291.

Li, Xiao-Ming. 1996. *"Good writing" in cross-cultural context*. Albany, NY: State University of New York Press.

Matsuda, Paul Kei. 2001. Voice in Japanese written discourse: Implications for second language writing. *Journal of Second Language Writing* 10(1–2): 35–53.

Matsuda, Paul Kei and Christine M. Tardy. 2007. Voice in academic writing: The rhetorical construction of author identity in blind manuscript review. *English for Specific Purposes* 26(2): 235–249.

Matsuda, Paul Kei and Christine M. Tardy. 2008. Continuing the conversation on voice in academic writing. *English for Specific Purposes* 27(1): 100–105.

McAlexander, Patricia J. and Jane Marston. 1994. Writing and suppression of self: A case study of a basic writer. *Research and Teaching in Developmental Education* 11(1): 75–83.

McHaney, Pearl Amelia. 2004. Let every voice be heard: Focus essays create democratic classrooms. *English Journal* 93(5): 72–76.

New York State Education Department. 2010. *Information booklet for scoring the Regents comprehensive examination in English, January 2010*. http://www.p12.nysed.gov/ assessment/hsgen/110/541e.pdf (accessed 5 August 2014).

Palacas, Arthur L. 1989. Parentheticals and personal voice. *Written Communication* 6(4): 506–527.

Prior, Paul. 2001. Voice in text, mind, and society: Sociohistoric accounts of discourse acquisition and use. *Journal of Second Language Writing* 10(1–2): 55–81.

Raimes, Ann and Vivian Zamel. 1997. Response to Ramanathan and Kaplan. *Journal of Second Language Writing* 6(1): 79–81.

Ramanathan, Vai and Dwight Atkinson. 1999. Individualism, academic writing, and ESL writers. *Journal of Second Language Writing* 8(1): 45–75.

Ramanathan, Vai and Robert B. Kaplan. 1996. Audience and voice in current L1 composition texts: Some implications for ESL student writers. *Journal of Second Language Writing* 5(1): 21–34.

Romano, Tom. 2004. *Crafting authentic voice*. Portsmouth, NH: Heinemann.

Schwartz, Tammy A. 2003. Urban Appalachian girls and writing: Institutional and 'other/ed' identities. *Pedagogy, Culture and Society* 11(1): 69–87.

Shen, Fan. 1989. The classroom and the wider culture: Identity as a key to learning English composition. *College Composition and Communication* 40(4): 459–466.

Stapleton, Paul. 2002. Critiquing voice as a viable pedagogical tool in L2 writing: Returning spotlight to ideas. *Journal of Second Language Writing* 11(3): 177–190.

Stewart, Donald C. 1972. *The authentic voice: A pre-writing approach to student writing*. Dubuque, IA: Brown.

Stewart, Donald C. 1992. Cognitive Psychologists, Social Constructionists, and Three Nineteenth-Century Advocates of Authentic Voice. *Journal of Advanced Composition* 12(2): 279–290.

Tang, Ramona and Suganthi John. 1999. The 'I' in identity: Exploring writer identity in student academic writing through the first person pronoun. *English for Specific Purposes* 18(Supplement 1): S23–S39.

Wolfe, Edward W., Sandra Bolton, Brian Feltovich and Donna M. Niday. 1996. The influence of student experience with word processors on the quality of essays writing for a direct writing assessment. *Assessing Writing* 3(2): 123–147.

Yancey, Kathleen Blake. 1994. Introduction: Definition, intersection, and difference – mapping the landscape of voice. In: Kathleen Blake Yancey (ed.). *Voices on voice: Perspectives, definitions, inquiry*, vii–xxiv. Urbana, IL: National Council of Teachers of English.

Yeh, Stuart S. 1998. Validation of a scheme for assessing argumentative writing of middle school students. *Assessing Writing* 5(1): 123–150.

Young, Morris. 1996. Narratives of identity: Theorizing the writer and the nation. *Journal of Basic Writing* 15(2): 50–75.

Zhao, Cecilia Guanfang. 2010. *The role of voice in high-stakes second language writing assessment*. New York, NY: New York University dissertation.

Zhao, Cecilia Guanfang. 2013. Measuring authorial voice strength in L2 argumentative writing: The development and validation of an analytic rubric. *Language Testing* 30(2): 201–230.

Zhao, Cecilia Guanfang and Lorena Llosa. 2008. Voice in high-stakes L1 academic writing assessment: Implications for L2 writing instruction. *Assessing Writing* 13(3): 153–170.

Luke Harding and Benjamin Kremmel

25 Teacher assessment literacy and professional development

1 Introduction

In this chapter we discuss the notion of "language assessment literacy" (LAL) and its related issues, with a particular focus on language teachers and their professional development in this area. We will begin with a historical view of the term "language assessment literacy", charting its emergence in the field of language testing, before discussing the different definitions and conceptualizations which have been employed in LAL research. In the second section we provide a survey of current views on what LAL for language teachers should entail, covering both componential and developmental models. We then consider current issues in pre- and in-service training in language assessment across a range of international contexts, focusing on key surveys of the provision of language assessment instruction, and innovations in the delivery of instruction. Finally, we outline some pressing challenges which exist for fostering LAL among classroom teachers and suggest directions for future research and approaches to professional development which might address them.

2 The emergence of LAL

A number of "new" literacies , such as media literacy, computer literacy, and science literacy, have appeared in academic and public discourse in recent years (Taylor 2013), in effect broadening the traditional scope of literacy as pertaining solely to reading and writing skills or practices. Among these, the concept of "assessment literacy" has emerged in the literature of educational measurement. First introduced by Stiggins (1991) as "the knowledge assessors need to possess" (Inbar-Lourie 2013: 301), assessment literacy is generally viewed as "the knowledge and skills required for performing assessment-related actions" (Inbar-Lourie 2012: 1). However the term has undergone both an expansion and fragmentation in meaning, much like the concept of "literacy" itself in the fields of education and linguistics. Assessment literacy is now also frequently associated not only with a skills-based "know-how", but with a multilayered set of competences such as the awareness of, and ability to draw on, a deep knowledge-base of assessment for critical reflection on one's own assessment practice and the practices of others (Taylor 2013).

Within the umbrella term assessment literacy it has been argued that language assessment literacy (LAL) is a research and training area which might need to be considered separately due to the unique complexities that are entailed in the testing and assessment of linguistic skills, knowledge and communicative competence (see Inbar-Lourie 2008; Taylor 2013; Jeong 2013). Nevertheless, it was not until the early 2000s that LAL began to be explored in earnest in the language testing literature, with Brindley remarking that "although there has been a considerable amount of research in general education into teachers' assessment practices, levels and training and professional development needs [...], there have been relatively few investigations of these questions in the context of language teaching programmes" (2001: 126). The past decade, however, has seen rapid growth in research and commentary on LAL, with symposiums, handbook and encyclopedia entries, and recently a special issue of *Language Testing* (see Inbar-Lourie 2013) devoted to the topic.

While recognized now as a distinct entity, LAL has been conceptualized in various ways across the literature. O'Loughlin defines language assessment literacy as "the acquisition of a range of skills related to test production, test-score interpretation and use, and test evaluation in conjunction with the development of a critical understanding about the roles and functions of assessment within society" (2013: 363). Inbar-Lourie (2008: 389) sees it as "having the capacity to ask and answer critical questions about the purpose for assessment, about the fitness of the tool being used, about testing conditions, and about what is going to happen on the basis of the test results." Malone (2013: 329) states that LAL "refers to language instructors' familiarity with testing definitions and the application of this knowledge to classroom practices in general and specifically to issues related to assessing language." Similarly, Scarino (2013) maintains that, apart from a knowledge-base of some kind, LAL must also entail the development of self-awareness as assessors, particularly for teachers who are often trapped in a highly-complex dual role of teacher and assessor. Scarino (2013: 310) claims that "not only do teachers need to understand the conceptual bases of different approaches [to language assessment], they also need to relate such knowledge to their professional practice in their particular context." Only in this way will teachers be able "to explore and evaluate their own preconceptions, to understand the interpretive nature of the phenomenon of assessment and to become increasingly aware of their own dynamic framework of knowledge, understanding, practices and values, which shape their conceptualizations, interpretations, judgments and decisions in assessment and their students' second language learning" (Scarino 2013: 311). Pill and Harding (2013) provide a somewhat broader definition of LAL attempting to encompass the various stakeholders involved with test-score use. They state that LAL "may be understood as indicating a repertoire of competences that enable an individual to understand, evaluate and, in some cases, create language tests and analyse test data" (Pill and Harding 2013: 382). Fulcher (2012: 125) offers perhaps the most detailed working definition of LAL to date:

> The knowledge, skills and abilities required to design, develop, maintain or evaluate, large-scale standardized and/or classroom based tests, familiarity with test processes, and aware-

ness of principles and concepts that guide and underpin practice, including ethics and codes of practice. The ability to place knowledge, skills, processes, principles and concepts within wider historical, social, political and philosophical frameworks in order understand why practices have arisen as they have, and to evaluate the role and impact of testing on society, institutions, and individuals.

Fulcher's (2012) definition is much more aligned with the end-goal of expertise than, say, Inbar-Lourie's (2008) definition which describes a level at which someone may participate in an informed way in discussion on assessment matters. In fact, these differences in definitions point towards other divergences concerning the scope of LAL: what should be taught, and what level of expertise should be expected of stakeholders. These issues are addressed in the next section.

3 Describing and prescribing LAL for language teachers

While recent studies have demanded that appropriate levels of assessment literacy, however that may be defined, be nurtured among a wide variety of stakeholders and possibly even among the general public (see O'Loughlin 2013; Pill and Harding 2013; Taylor 2009), it is first and foremost language teachers who are considered to need "a dose of assessment literacy" (Popham 2006: 84). This is echoed by the fact that the majority of research into LAL carried out so far has focused on teachers, a situation which is also reflected in the many definitions of LAL that refer specifically to teachers (e.g., Malone 2013; Scarino 2013). Language teachers are regularly confronted with assessment issues as they make decisions about the design, administration, scoring and feedback mechanisms of language assessments. They are also often the users of test scores; making decisions not only about who will pass or fail, but also about who will move up a level, who needs additional help, whether the class is progressing well, and whether their own teaching has been effective.

LAL for teachers is therefore fundamental (Popham 2009) and should form an integral part of teachers' professional development. In a time where language tests are gaining increasing influence on decisions of all kinds worldwide, whether at the macro level (i.e. societal) or at the micro level (i.e. the classroom), there is an urgent need for language teachers to be conversant and competent in the principles and practice of language assessment (see also Brindley 2001). But despite the consensus view that LAL is necessary for language teachers, there has been little agreement in the research literature concerning what components should be taught and prioritised. An influential early attempt at setting standards for teacher competence in assessment literacy, mostly transferable to the LAL context, can be found in The American Federation of Teachers, National Council on Measurement in Education and the National Education Association's list of standards from 1990. These seven standards are shown below:

1. Teachers should be skilled in choosing assessment methods appropriate for instructional decisions.
2. Teachers should be skilled in developing assessment methods appropriate for instructional decisions.
3. Teachers should be skilled in administering, scoring, and interpreting the results of both externally produced and teacher-produced assessment methods.
4. Teachers should be skilled in using assessment results when making decisions about individual students, planning teaching, developing curriculum, and improving schools.
5. Teachers should be skilled in developing valid pupil grading procedures which use pupil assessment.
6. Teachers should be skilled in communicating assessment results to students, parents, other lay audiences, and other educators.
7. Teachers should be skilled in recognizing unethical, illegal, and otherwise inappropriate assessment methods and uses of assessment information.

(American Federation of Teachers 1990)

More recently, Popham (2009), one of the most enthusiastic proponents of assessment literacy in the general education field, has provided what he sees as the thirteen content points that should be covered in professional development programs for general assessment literacy. These are presented below as they represent one of the most expansive sets of goals for an assessment literacy "syllabus", and might be usefully applied to the language assessment context (2009: 8–10):

1. The fundamental function of educational assessment, namely, the collection of evidence from which inferences can be made about students' skills, knowledge, and affect
2. Reliability of educational assessments, especially the three forms in which consistency evidence is reported for groups of test takers (stability, alternate form, and internal consistency) and how to gauge consistency of assessment for individual test takers
3. The prominent role three types of validity evidence should play in the building of arguments to support the accuracy of test-based interpretations about students, namely, content-related, criterion-related, and construct-related evidence
4. How to identify and eliminate assessment bias that offends or unfairly penalizes test takers because of personal characteristics such as race, gender, or socioeconomic status
5. Construction and improvement of selected-response and constructed-response test items
6. Scoring of students' responses to constructed-response test items, especially the distinctive contribution made by well-formed rubrics

7. Development and scoring of performance assessments, portfolio assessments, exhibitions, peer assessments, and self-assessments
8. Designing and implementing formative assessment procedures consonant with both research evidence and experience-based insights regarding such procedures' likely success
9. How to collect and interpret evidence of students' attitudes, interests, and values
10. Interpreting students' performances on large-scale standardized achievement and aptitude assessments
11. Assessing English Language Learners and students with disabilities
12. How to appropriately (and *not* inappropriately) prepare students for high-stakes tests
13. How to determine the appropriateness of an accountability test for use in evaluating the quality of instruction

Popham's (2009) view is quite broad, incorporating what some might see as tangential issues such as appropriate test preparation practices and knowledge of ways to collect and interpret data on students' attitudes, interests and values. This, however, is quite in line with the broader view of validity proposed by Messick (1989) which highlights the importance of both consequences and values within the social context in which all assessment takes place.

Within the field of language testing there have also been efforts to map out the types of content that are crucial for establishing LAL. Brindley (2001), for example, determines five components of LAL, two of which he sees as core to any stakeholder involved with assessment, and the other three optional, taking into account that "different levels of expertise or specialization will require different levels of literacy, and different needs will dictate the type of knowledge most useful for stakeholders" (Pill and Harding 2013: 383; see also Brindley 2001; Taylor 2009). For language teachers, however, all five areas identified by Brindley might be understood as mandatory. He suggests that all teachers, as part of their professional development, need a firm knowledge about 1. the social context of assessment, including educational and political aspects and issues of ethics, accountability and standardization, 2. the definition and description of proficiency, i.e. discussing theoretical bases of language tests but also fostering familiarity with key terminology and concepts such as validity and reliability, 3. constructing and evaluating language tests, providing teachers with "skills in test development and analysis" (Brindley 2001: 129) including a basic introduction to statistics, 4. the role of assessment in the language curriculum, focusing on criterion-referenced language learning and assessment and alternative assessment options such as portfolios, journals and self-assessment techniques, and 5. putting assessment into practice, following-up the previous modules in action with concrete test construction or assessment research projects. We can see here some overlap with elements of Popham's list, although with the key point of difference that language testers need to know about language and language development in order to understand the theoretical constructs they are measuring.

Taking a somewhat broader view, Davies (2008) proposes three core elements language teachers should be equipped with in their pre- or in-service training: skills, knowledge and principles. According to Davies, "[s]kills provide the training in necessary and appropriate methodology, including item-writing, statistics, test analysis, and increasingly software programmes for test delivery, analysis and reportage. Knowledge offers relevant background in measurement and language description as well as in context setting. Principles concern the proper use of language tests, their fairness and impact, including questions of ethics and professionalism" (2008: 335). These three areas roughly correspond to what Inbar-Lourie (2008) considers the three key questions to be addressed in LAL: the "how-to" (skills), the "what" (knowledge) and the "why" (principles) of assessment. Taylor (2009: 27) presents a view of LAL which synthesizes, to some extent, the views put forward by Davies (2008) and Inbar-Lourie (2008), stating that "training for assessment literacy entails an appropriate balance of technical know-how, practical skills, theoretical knowledge, and understanding of principles, but all firmly contextualized within a sound understanding of the role and function of assessment within education and society."

Fulcher (2012) attempted to identify the assessment training needs of language teachers empirically, gathering online survey responses of 278 teachers involved in language teaching in a variety of contexts. He reports that practicing language teachers, as opposed to testing specialists, would regard the following components pivotal in developing LAL among their profession: 1. knowledge, skills and abilities concerning the practice of language testing at both classroom as well as standardized large-scale level, 2. familiarity with the processes, principles and concepts of assessment and thus an awareness of what guides best practice, and 3. an understanding of the historical, social, political and philosophical frameworks within which language assessment can be placed, i.e. a solid grasp of its origins, reasons and impacts in order to be able to critically evaluate the wider societal dimensions of language testing. Fulcher's (2012) tripartite model of 1. the practice of language testing (practical knowledge), 2. the guidance for practice (procedural/theoretical knowledge), and 3. origins, reasons and impacts (socio-historical understanding) appears, content-wise, to correspond with Taylor's (2009) view outlined above. Fulcher's approach, however, represents a valuable expansion of the way in which LAL may be conceptualised in two key ways. First, it acknowledges that not all of these components will be required for all stakeholders. Although Taylor (2009) had made this point explicitly in an earlier paper, Fulcher implies a hierarchy in his model of LAL, where practical knowledge appears as the bedrock, with principles and then contexts at higher levels. Second, it acknowledges the importance of the practicing teachers' experience, involving them in attempting to define the main

Tab. 1: A continuum model of language assessment literacy (Pill and Harding, 2013: 383).

Illiteracy	Ignorance of language assessment concepts and methods
Nominal literacy	Understanding that a specific term relates to assessment, but may indicate a misconception
Functional literacy	Sound understanding of basic terms and concepts
Procedural and conceptual literacy	Understanding central concepts of the field, and using knowledge in practice
Multidimensional literacy	Knowledge extending beyond ordinary concepts including philosophical, historical and social dimensions of assessment

components of LAL and, by extension, LAL training courses, instructional materials and so on. Importantly, Fulcher (2012) proposes that theoretical concepts in testing textbooks and courses should be presented within the context of practical test construction, using the test development cycle as the scaffold and introducing principles and core terminological knowledge along the way rather than merely introducing them as decontextualised components of LAL. An implementation of this approach can be found in Fulcher's (2010) textbook *Practical Language Testing*.

Other research has attempted to describe how LAL might develop. Pill and Harding (2013) – in a recent study of the LAL exhibited by policy makers in an Australian federal parliamentary inquiry into the accreditation process for overseas-trained health professionals– suggested that LAL should be viewed as a continuum rather than a modular concept. Based on the work of Bybee (1997) and Kaiser and Willander (2005) in the fields of scientific and mathematical literacy respectively, Pill and Harding (2013: 383) suggest a cline of LAL from "illiteracy" to "multidimensional language assessment literacy", with brief descriptors given across five levels (see Table 1).

This approach can be contrasted with the component models described above (Brindley 2001; Davies 2008; Fulcher 2012; Inbar-Lourie 2008; Taylor 2009) in that it attempts to place different aspects of language assessment literacy on a progressive scale. However the scale is limited in some respects. First, it is not clear from the scale itself what levels of LAL different stakeholders should or must achieve, although it seems sensible to expect that classroom teachers would require at least a procedural and conceptual literacy, and that this would hopefully become a multidimensional literacy as experience was gained and teacher education programs were undertaken. Second, the descriptions at each level are not entirely consistent, referring only sporadically to practice (i.e. "methods" and "knowledge in practice") with, perhaps, an overemphasis on procedural/theoretical knowledge. Finally, the trajectory of literacy development in the scale is at odds with what Brindley (2001) and Inbar-Lourie (2008) have recommended in their modular approaches. While they see the socio-historical contextualization of language assessment as fundamental, and Brindley includes it as the first of the two core modules, suggesting

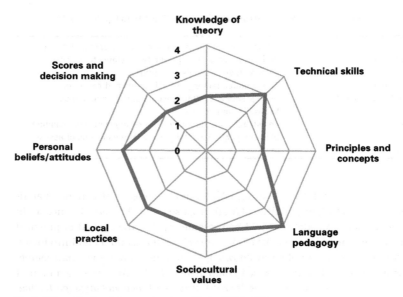

Fig. 1: LAL profile for classroom teachers (Taylor 2013: 410).

that it is a competence which should be obtained by virtually everyone involved in learning about language assessment, Pill and Harding's continuum places this type of knowledge at the highest level, a position which suggests that it is only of importance for those who are developing advanced levels of expertise in LAL (for example, graduate students taking language testing courses). There may be a need to incorporate the importance of knowledge of the social dimension of assessment at the procedural/conceptual stage in future incarnations of these levels, as well as to flesh-out what might be expected in the development of practical skills.

Nevertheless, in a recent summary paper for a special issue of *Language Testing* on language assessment literacy, Taylor (2013) helpfully blends the most recent insights and models into a set of LAL profile models for four different groups of stakeholders in language assessment: test writers, classroom teachers, university administrators, and professional language testers. The profile for the types and level of LAL required for classroom teachers is shown in Figure 1 above. This diagram illustrates that, for classroom teachers, the most important component of LAL is knowledge of language pedagogy, and the least important are knowledge of scores and decision making, and principles and concepts of language assessment.

Taylor's diagram is valuable because it accounts for the depth of knowledge required on eight dimensions of LAL gleaned from the research literature by mapping these onto the five levels of LAL (0–4) proposed by Pill and Harding (2013) (0 = illiteracy; 4 = multidimensional literacy). There is a conceptual difficulty, however, in applying the term "multidimensional" to a deep knowledge of one specific content area, as Taylor does here, because multidimensional denotes a broad understanding of many content areas. A more appropriate term for the purposes of constructing such profiles might be "comprehensive literacy" or "expert literacy" to indicate a depth of knowledge on a particular component which weaves together various aspects of understanding. While the LAL profile for classroom teachers accounts for some shortcomings of previous models, integrating a depth of knowledge dimension, and providing different profiles for different stakeholder constituencies, Taylor's dimensions remain speculative. They do, however, provide a rich theoretical basis for further research in the area.

4 Pre- and in -service instruction in language assessment

While there have been advances in describing and prescribing LAL, it seems to be the case that pre- and in-service instruction is still not as effective as it could be (if, indeed, such instruction happens at all). Bachman states that most "practitioners who develop and use language tests, both in language classrooms and as part of applied linguistics research, still do so with little or no professional training" (2000: 19–20). Brindley (2001: 127) has also argued that language teachers in general do not hold sufficient levels of LAL, suggesting two reasons for this: the low profile of assessment on teacher training courses, and the inaccessibility of much of the testing literature. It is difficult to know the true extent to which assessment is covered on teacher training courses for language educators because we have little data on the multitude of degrees, diplomas, short-courses and in-house courses which are delivered worldwide to language teachers at any one time. For entry level English language teacher training certification courses such as the Cambridge CELTA (2010) and the Trinity CertTESOL (2013), publicly available syllabus documents show either very basic or no discernible coverage of assessment techniques or issues. Assessment issues are, however, covered in more depth at Diploma level courses offered by the same organisations such as the Cambridge DELTA (2010) and the Trinity Diploma in TESOL (2006), both courses designed for in-service teaching professionals.

There are a number of standalone introductory courses on language testing offered worldwide (as summer schools or short-courses). For example several professional testing associations such as the European Association of Language Testing and Assessment (EALTA), the Association of Language Testers in Europe (ALTE) and the International Language Testing Association (ILTA) have offered pre-conference workshops and low-threshold regional training events for interested practitioners. Organisations such as the International Association of Teachers of English as a Foreign Language (IATEFL) and TESOL are branching into the delivery of virtual seminars for in-service teachers, some of which have had assessment themes. Recently, some large-scale projects designed specifically to promote LAL have also been launched: 1. ProSET (Promotion of Sustainable Excellence in Testing and Assessment of English), a teacher training programme across 18 universities for Russian secondary school teachers set up by the Russian Ministry of Education and Science in cooperation with the European Union's TEMPUS programme (Green 2012); and 2. the British Council's Language Assessment Literacy Project, which aims to enhance LAL for British Council staff, as well as others, through a four-phase process, graded in detail and depth, which is mostly delivered online (Berry et al. 2014).

More extensive modules concentrating on language testing and assessment are also prevalent on university degrees in Applied Linguistics and TESOL, particularly at the postgraduate level. The most extensive review of introductory language assessment programs of this kind thus far is Brown and Bailey's (2008) study of the characteristics of "basic" language testing courses, itself a partial replication of an earlier study (Bailey and Brown 1996). In this study, Brown and Bailey (2008) administered an electronic questionnaire to 97 instructors working in a range of international contexts. Brown and Bailey found that the topics with the highest levels of coverage on these programs were "Classroom testing practices", "Testing in relationship to curriculum", and "Measuring the different skills." Topics that received little coverage on these courses were "Aptitude testing", "Measuring attitudes" and "Language program evaluation" – perhaps not surprising as the last two have only peripheral connection with the field. According to the survey, some topics received at least *some* coverage on *all* of the courses (suggesting that these are in some sense "standard" topics); these were "Criterion referenced testing", "Achievement testing" and "Washback." Brown and Bailey also collected data on the types of practical skills which were developed on language testing courses, reporting that "Test analysis" and "Test critiquing" received the most coverage. Despite these useful findings, Brown and Bailey call for further research at the very end of their paper, stating, "[a]ll in all, there is still much that we do not know about how language testing is being taught in language teacher training programs around the world, and how it should be taught. We hope that our 1996 study and this 2007 replication will at least provide a starting point for better understanding our language testing sub-specialization in applied linguistics" (2008: 373).

There have, however, been some concerted efforts to collect data of this kind. Fulcher's (2012) study – discussed above – is essentially a needs analysis, as too were earlier studies conducted by Hasselgreen, Carlsen and Helness (2004) and Huhta, Hirvalä and Banerjee (2005). The latter are valuable snapshots of the needs of language teachers in Europe, but they are now approaching the 10 year mark and may no longer represent the needs of the next generation of language teachers in this region. Vogt and Tsagari's (2014) large-scale survey of EFL teacher assessment literacy in seven European countries refines and updates the study by Hasselgreen et al. (2004) by attempting to describe the assessment practices of regular in-service EFL teachers, and to identify their training needs. The results of surveys and interviews showed that there is a considerable mismatch between the language testing and assessment training teachers believe they need and the training they actually receive. The majority of teachers had received little or no training at all in language testing and assessment, and those who had felt that this training was inadequate for the demands of the job (echoing earlier findings from a national survey in Greece – see Tsagari 2011). The study concludes that teachers often rely on their own testing experience, or on learning on the job from their mentors; a situation which makes the perpetuation of traditional testing approaches more likely, and which leaves little room for innovation or critical questioning of the quality of existing assessment methods. While similar surveys appear to have been conducted in the USA (e.g., Malone 2008, cites an unpublished presentation authored by Swender, Abbott, Vicars and Malone), there have been fewer studies from contexts in Asia, Africa, and South America. One exception is Jin (2010) who conducted a survey study similar in scope to Brown and Bailey (2008) among language testing instructors in China.

There is much discussion in research of this kind of the types of books that are suitable for teachers who are embarking on a program of LAL. There have, in fact, been numerous introductory texts published in the last few years which provide a useful "way in" to what might sometimes be perceived as a technical and forbidding field for training teachers. Malone (2008) has examined a range of popular coursebooks used to deliver what was considered the assessment basics at their time. Her findings, however, suggest that psychometric concepts feature heavily in many of these, rendering them technical and of limited accessibility to a broader audience and thus often only partly useful for the professional development of classroom teachers. Since the time Malone was writing, language testing instructors have been treated to a number of additional texts to choose from including Bachman and Palmer (2010), Carr (2011), Douglas (2010), Fulcher (2010), Fulcher and Davidson (2007), Brown and Abeywickrama (2010 – a revised edition of Brown, 2003) and Green (2014). These books might be understood as tipping the balance back, providing, in each case, a range of skills, knowledge and principles, though with obvious differences in the weighting of these three components. Combined with other well-established introductory texts such as Alderson, Clapham and Wall (1995), Brown (2005), Hughes (2003), McNamara (2000), and Stoynoff and Chapelle (2005), for an instructor who knows his/her learners' needs, there is now more choice and more diversity among introductory texts than there has been in the past.

5 Challenges for fostering teacher LAL and future directions

If LAL is to be enhanced and improved across the language teaching profession, there needs to be a cascade from the theoretical to the practical. In other words, conceptual advances concerning the components of LAL need to be translated into syllabuses, and these syllabuses need to be taught effectively and, in turn, evaluated and improved. However there remain stumbling blocks. As can be seen in the discussion of LAL concepts in the first part of this chapter, a major challenge for promoting LAL among teachers will be to come to grips with what LAL should comprise. Inbar-Lourie suggests that this "difficulty of reaching an agreed-upon definition [of LAL] reflects the lack of consensus within the professional testing community as to what constitutes the assessment knowledge that will be disseminated to future experts in the field" (2013: 304). However, it may be that the need for a clear consensus is over-emphasized. Rather, as the literature has yielded a repertoire of possible competences which may comprise LAL (and, in fact, the review above finds that there is more agreement than disagreement between scholars) it is then in the hands of the curriculum designer to determine what he/she chooses to select and to sequence these according to the needs of learners, environmental constraints, and pedagogical principles (see Nation and Macalister 2010). As cultures of language assessment differ globally, we can also imagine that the requisite knowledge required to operate within those assessment cultures would also vary. A teacher in Hong Kong may need a very different type of training in assessment from a teacher working in Austria.

This is not to say, however, that assessment experts should not recommend a "core inventory" of content which can act as guidance for course designers across various contexts. In arriving at a core inventory of this kind, Fulcher's (2012) research, as well as Scarino's (2013) and Malone's (2013: 343) has emphasized the need for involving practitioners in this process in conjunction with testing experts, as "what interests language testing experts may not be of interest to language instructors." As a case in point, the focus prescribed by many language testing professionals on the social context of assessment may arguably be less urgent for teachers than it is for language testing professionals themselves. Teachers in many contexts may be highly aware of the social consequences of assessment, and the limitations in fairness of various testing decisions, as they prepare, counsel and ultimately congratulate or console the students who go through various assessment processes (see Pill and Harding 2013, for evidence of the critical position towards the IELTS and the OET taken by test preparation instructors). What teachers may be less aware of, even from a critical position, is the way in which the technical quality of tests (whether their own or those produced by others) can strengthen or weaken claims of fairness, for example. Meanwhile, language testing professionals well versed in the technical aspects of measurement may need reminding that the instruments they design have real world consequences.

Even within the stakeholder group "language teachers", individuals will have different needs depending on the teaching/testing context they are operating in, and this type of "negotiated syllabus" – selecting from a core inventory and adding contextually specific material – would arguably work best if it is conducted at the local level. By reaching an agreement on the core components of LAL, research into the development of LAL among individuals and groups as well as evaluations of LAL instructional programmes could be facilitated. Inviting teachers and other stakeholders to take part in this process will also help to overcome unnecessarily complex terminology and the perception by "outsiders" that language testing is a highly technical and specialized field best left to professionals (Taylor 2009).

Establishing an agreed-upon base of component areas of LAL, charting a realistic trajectory of development, and ensuring that LAL is tailored to the needs of different stakeholders (including the different needs of those within stakeholder groups) might thus present the greatest challenges to be faced by those involved in promoting LAL. Teacher development in LAL will ultimately require cooperation between teachers, teacher trainers, testing and assessment experts and educational administrators and policy-makers in addressing these points of course design. A further challenge concerns the mode of delivery for LAL instruction. Although several modes of delivery have been suggested and set up, little research effort has gone into the evaluation and comparison of the effectiveness and accessibility of these. Brindley (2001) suggests traditional forms of promoting LAL such as short courses and seminars or workshops, but current trends increasingly focus on the potential of new technologies in making educational material available. Fulcher's (2013) language testing resources website, online since 1995, provides an invaluable resource of accessible information on language assessment issues allowing for self-study of a range of key topics. This type of self-study has also been advocated by Malone (2008), who in a more recent publication reported on the development of an online tutorial for US foreign language teachers (www.cal.org/flad/tutorial/). Low-cost, non-technical low-threshold web-based learning tools could be crucial in making professional development in LAL more attractive for in-service teachers.

6 References

Alderson, J. Charles, Caroline Clapham and Dianne Wall. 1995. *Language test construction and evaluation*. Cambridge, UK: Cambridge University Press.

American Federation of Teachers, National Council on Measurement in Education and National Education Association. 1990. Standards for teacher competence in educational assessment of students. *Educational Measurement: Issues and Practice* 9(4): 30–32.

Bachman, Lyle F. 2000. Modern language testing at the turn of the century: Assuring that what we count counts. *Language Testing* 17(1), 1–42.

Bachman, Lyle F. and Adrian S. Palmer. 2010. *Language assessment in practice: Developing language assessments and justifying their use in the real world*. Oxford, UK: Oxford University Press.

Bailey, Kathleen M. and James D. Brown. 1996. Language testing courses: What are they? In: Alistair Cumming and Ron Berwick (eds.). *Validation in language testing*, 236–256. Clevedon, UK: Multilingual Matters.

Berry, Vivien, Barry O'Sullivan, Diane Schmitt and Lynda Taylor. 2014. *Assessment literacy: bridging the gap between needs and resources*. Symposium presented at The 48th Annual International IATEFL Conference and Exhibition, Harrogate, UK, 2–5 April.

Brindley, Geoff. 2001. Language assessment and professional development. In: Cathie Elder, Annie Brown, Kathryn Hill, Noriko Iwashita, Tom Lumley, Tim McNamara and Kieran O'Loughlin (eds.). *Experimenting with uncertainty: Essays in honour of Alan Davies*, 126–136. Cambridge, UK: Cambridge University Press.

Brown, H. Douglas. 2003. *Language assessment: principles and classroom practices*. New York: Longman.

Brown, H. Douglas and Priyanvada Abeywickrama. 2010. *Language assessment: Principles and classroom practices*. New York: Pearson Education.

Brown, James D. 2005. *Testing in language programs: A comprehensive guide to English language assessment*. New York: McGraw-Hill.

Brown, James D. and Kathleen M. Bailey. 2008. Language testing courses: What are they in 2007? *Language Testing* 25(3): 349–383.

Bybee, Rodger W. 1997. *Achieving scientific literacy: From purposes to practices*. Portsmouth, NH: Heinemann.

Cambridge English. 2010. CELTA: Syllabus and assessment guidelines. Cambridge: University of Cambridge ESOL Examinations.

Cambridge English. 2010. DELTA: Syllabus specifications (from 2011). Cambridge: University of Cambridge ESOL Examinations.

Carr, Nathan T. 2011. *Designing and analyzing language tests*. Oxford, UK: Oxford University Press.

Davies, Alan. 2008. Textbook trends in teaching language testing. *Language Testing* 25(3): 327–347.

Douglas, Dan. 2010. *Understanding language testing*. London: Hodder Education.

Fulcher, Glenn. 2010. *Practical language testing*. London: Hodder Education.

Fulcher, Glenn. 2012. Assessment literacy for the language classroom. *Language Assessment Quarterly* 9(2). 113–132.

Fulcher, Glenn. 2013. Language testing resources website. http://languagetesting.info (17 August 2013).

Fulcher, Glenn and Fred Davidson. 2007. *Language testing and assessment*. London and New York: Routledge.

Green, Anthony. 2012. *Promoting Sustainable Excellence in Testing and Assessment of English*. Paper presented at the EALTA Classroom-based Language Assessment Special Interest Group Meeting, Innsbruck, Austria. 31 May.

Green, Anthony. 2014. *Exploring Language Assessment and Testing: Language in Action*. Oxon: Routledge.

Hughes, Arthur. 2003. *Testing for language teachers*. Cambridge, UK: Cambridge University Press.

Hasselgreen, Angela, Cecilie Carlsen and Hildegunn Helness. 2004. *European Survey of Language Testing and Assessment Needs*. Part 1: *General findings*. http://www.ealta.eu.org/ documents/resources/survey-report-pt1.pdf (accessed 17 August 2013).

Huhta, Ari, Tuija Hirvalä and Jayanti Banerjee. 2005. *European Survey of Language Testing and Assessment Needs*. Part 2: Regional findings. http://www.ealta.eu.org/resources.htm (accessed 17 August 2013).

Inbar-Lourie, Ofra. 2008. Constructing a language assessment knowledge base: A focus on language assessment courses. *Language Testing* 25(3): 385–402.

Inbar-Lourie, Ofra. 2012. Language Assessment Literacy. In: Carol A. Chapelle (ed.). *The Encyclopedia of Applied Linguistics*. Oxford, UK: Wiley-Blackwell. DOI: 10.1002/ 9781405198431.wbeal0605

Inbar-Lourie, Ofra. 2013. Guest Editorial to the special issue on language assessment literacy. *Language Testing* 30(3): 301–307.

Jeong, Heejeong. 2013. Defining assessment literacy: Is it different for language testers and non-language testers? *Language Testing* 30(3): 345–362.

Jin, Yan. 2010. The place of language testing and assessment in the professional preparation of foreign language teachers in China. *Language Testing* 27(4): 555–584.

Kaiser, Gabriele and Torben Willander. 2005. Development of mathematical literacy: Results of an empirical study. *Teaching mathematics and its applications* 24(2–3): 48–60.

Malone, Margaret E. 2008. Training in language assessment. In: Elana Shohamy and Nancy Hornberger (eds.). *Encyclopedia of language and education.* 2nd ed., Vol. 7. *Language testing and assessment*, 225–239. New York: Springer Science + Business Media.

Malone, Margaret E. 2013. The essentials of assessment literacy: Contrasts between testers and users. *Language Testing* 30(3): 329–344.

Nation, Paul and John Macalister. 2010. *Language Curriculum Design.* New York and London: Routledge.

McNamara, Tim. 2000. *Language testing.* Oxford, UK: Oxford University Press.

Messick, Samuel. 1989. Validity. In: Robert L. Linn (ed.). *Educational Measurement*, 13–104. New York: Macmillan.

O'Loughlin, Kieran. 2013. Developing the assessment literacy of university proficiency test users. *Language Testing* 30(3): 363–380.

Pill, John and Luke Harding. 2013. Defining the language assessment literacy gap: Evidence from a parliamentary inquiry. *Language Testing* 30(3): 381–402.

Popham, William James. 2006. All about accountability / Needed: A dose of assessment literacy. *Educational Leadership* 63(6): 84–85.

Popham, William James. 2009. Assessment literacy for teachers: Faddish or fundamental? *Theory into Practice* 48(1): 4–11.

Scarino, Angela. 2013. Language assessment literacy as self-awareness: Understanding the role of interpretation in assessment and in teacher learning. *Language Testing* 30(3): 309–327.

Stiggins, Richard J. 1991. Assessment literacy. *Phi Delta Kappan* 72(7): 534–539.

Stoynoff, Stephen and Carol A. Chapelle. 2005. ESOL tests and testing: A resource for teachers and program administrators. Alexandria, VA: TESOL.

Taylor, Lynda. 2009. Developing assessment literacy. *Annual Review of Applied Linguistics* 29: 21–36.

Taylor, Lynda. 2013. Communicating the theory, practice and principles of language testing to test stakeholders: Some reflections. *Language Testing* 30(3): 403–412.

Trinity College London. 2006. *Licentiate Diploma in Teaching English to Speakers of Other Languages (LTCL Diploma TESOL): Course Summary and Bibliography.* London: Trinity College London.

Trinity College London. 2013. *Certificate in Teaching English to Speakers of Other Languages (CertTESOL): Syllabus – from June 2013.* London: Trinity College London.

Tsagari, Dina. 2011. Investigating the 'assessment literacy' of EFL state school teachers in Greece. In: Dina Tsagari and Ildiko Csépes (eds.). *Classroom-based Language Assessment*, 169–190. Frankfurt am Main: Peter Lang.

Vogt, Karin and Dina Tsagari. 2014. Assessment literacy of foreign language teachers: findings of a European study. *Language Assessment Quarterly* 11(4): 374–402.

Biographical notes

Philippe Anckaert is Head of the teaching and research department Languages & Cultures at the Francisco Ferrer University College Brussels. He teaches legal translation courses at Francisco Ferrer and at the Catholic University Leuven. His main research domain concerns the assessment of translation competence. He is consultant for the scientific committee of the Belgian governmental recruitment agency (SELOR).

Jayanti Banerjee is a language assessment professional and researcher with 18 years' experience in teaching the principles of language testing, designing and evaluating language tests, and conducting research into testing and assessment issues. She has delivered workshops on the assessment of listening, the assessment of speaking, research methods, and qualitative approaches to data analysis. She has published in the areas of language testing and English for academic purposes and presented papers at a number of international conferences. Her recent research foci have been a review and revision of a writing rating scale and investigations into the differential item functioning of listening items.

Tineke Brunfaut teaches and researches language testing at Lancaster University, UK. Her main research interests are reading and listening in a second language and the assessment of these skills. Her publications include investigations on the relationship between test-task and test-taker variables and second language reading and listening performance. In addition, she is interested in standard-setting practices and procedures and the use of judgement in reading and listening research.

Yuko Goto Butler earned her Ph.D. in educational psychology from Stanford and is Associate Professor of Educational Linguistics at the Graduate School of Education at the University of Pennsylvania. She is the Director of the TESOL program at Penn. Her research interests include second and foreign language acquisition among young learners and language assessment.

Natalie Nordby Chen serves as CaMLA's Director of Assessment, guiding activities that create, support, and strengthen CaMLA testing programs. Her professional assessment experience includes developing a wide range of testing products, conducting item writing and rater training workshops, serving on professional review panels, mapping test specifications to governmental standards, and participating on research teams for both organizational and grant-funded projects. She taught ESL/EFL in the United States and Taiwan.

Larry Davis is an Associate Research Scientist at Educational Testing Service, where he is involved in research and development of English language assessments. His interests focus on various aspects of speaking assessment, including task design, interaction among speakers, automated scoring of spoken responses, and rater cognition and the nature of rater expertise. He has also worked in program evaluation, where he has consulted on the evaluations of a number of university language programs.

Ryan Downey is Director of Assessment Product Management at Pearson. Prior to his current position, Ryan led the creation of an end-to-end assessment program at Rosetta Stone, Inc. Previously, Ryan worked in Pearson's Knowledge Technologies group, leading development of a range of automatically scored high-stakes spoken and written assessments, including a Dutch Literacy and Reading Comprehension exam for immigration purposes and a four-skills test of

Business English. Ryan holds a PhD in Language and Communicative Disorders from San Diego State University and the University of California, San Diego.

Thomas Eckes is Head of the Psychometrics and Research Methodology Department at the TestDaF Institute, University of Bochum, Germany. He has taught and published widely in the field of language testing, educational and psychological measurement, and multivariate data analysis. His research interests include rater effects in performance assessments, many-facet Rasch measurement, item response theory, standard setting, and web-based testing.

June Eyckmans is Professor in Applied Linguistics and Translation Studies at Ghent University. Her research interests include the methodology of interpreting and translation assessment and cognitive approaches to foreign language vocabulary learning. She publishes in national and international journals and she is often consulted by national and international organisations for the improvement of language assessment procedures. She is invited as an external jury member in PhD boards dealing with translation studies and foreign language acquisition.

Glenn Fulcher is Professor of Education and Language Assessment in the School of Education, University of Leicester. He has served as president of the International Language Testing Association and is currently co-editor of the Sage journal *Language Testing*. He has published widely in the field of assessment. His most recent books include the edited Routledge *Handbook of Language Testing* and the monograph *Practical Language Testing* from Hodder Education.

Kirby C. Grabowski is Lecturer of Linguistics and Language Education in the Applied Linguistics and TESOL Program at Teachers College, Columbia University. She was a Spaan Fellow in 2007 and the Jacqueline Ross TOEFL Dissertation Award recipient in 2011. Kirby currently serves on the Editorial Advisory Board for *Language Assessment Quarterly* and was the ECOLT conference co-chair in 2014. Her research interests have a particular focus on grammar and pragmatics assessment, as well as applications of discourse analysis in language test validation.

Liz Hamp-Lyons is Visiting Professor of English Language Assessment at CRELLA at the University of Bedfordshire, UK, and Guest Professor at Shanghai Jiaotong University, China. Her recent research and development projects have focused on school-based assessment at the secondary school level in Hong Kong, very large-scale test reform in China, and academic literacy assessment for tertiary education. She is Editor of *Assessing Writing* and the *Journal of English for Academic Purposes*.

Luke Harding is a Senior Lecturer in the Department of Linguistics and English Language at Lancaster University, UK. His research interests are in language testing, particularly in the areas of listening assessment, pronunciation and intelligibility, assessor decision-making, assessment literacy, and the challenges of English as an International Language for language assessment and teaching.

Ari Huhta is a Professor of Language Assessment at the Centre for Applied Language Studies, University of Jyväskylä, Finland. He has participated in several research and test development projects, such as the EU-funded DIALANG and the National Certificates in Finland. He has been an external advisor to the European Commission on the European Survey of Language Competences and a member of the TOEFL Committee of Examiners.

Paolo Infante is a Doctoral candidate in the Department of Curriculum and Instruction at The Pennsylvania State University with a primary focus on English language learner education. His research interests focus on Vygotskian-based approaches to L2 teaching and learning, paying particular attention to the use of Dynamic Assessment and Concept-Based Instruction with individual learners and small groups to support their L2 development.

Talia Isaacs is a Senior Lecturer in Education in TESOL/Applied Linguistics at the University of Bristol and co-coordinator of the Centre for Assessment and Evaluation Research. Her research broadly examines influences on listeners' judgments of second language speech in academic and professional settings where the stakes for achieving successful communication are high. Current projects center on developing an empirical basis for more clearly operationalizing key constructs in L2 oral proficiency scales.

Nivja H. de Jong earned her PhD from Radboud University Nijmegen and is Assistant Professor in the Dutch Department at Utrecht University. She is currently principal investigator in a research project on second language fluency. Previous research includes investigations of morphological relations in the mental lexicon at the Max Planck Institute for Psycholinguistics, speech error repairs at the University of Edinburgh, and second language speaking proficiency at the University of Amsterdam.

Hanan Khalifa's expertise lies in the fields of language testing, educational evaluation, standard setting, alignment to CEFR, and impact assessment. Her co-authored book with Cyril Weir was a runner-up for the 2009 Sage/ILTA award for Best Book on Language Testing. It is used as course book for ALTE programs and MA modules in UK universities. Together with Anne Burns and Katherine Brandon, Hanan is the recipient of the 2013 IEAA award for innovation in international education.

Ute Knoch is the Director of the Language Testing Research Centre at the University of Melbourne. Her research interests are in the areas of second language writing assessment, writing development, and assessing languages for academic and specific purposes.

Benjamin Kremmel is a Researcher at the University of Innsbruck, Austria, where he is also teaching courses on language testing and assessment for pre-service teachers. He holds an MA in Language Testing from Lancaster University, UK, and is currently a PhD student at the University of Nottingham, UK. His research interests are in language testing, particularly in the areas of testing lexical knowledge, the assessment of L2 reading, and language assessment literacy.

Fabiana MacMillan is a Test Development Manager at Rosetta Stone. She has focused her research on the interface of language assessment, particularly reading assessment, and written discourse analysis. She has taught ESL in Brazil and Canada, and has been involved in the development of language tests and ESL instructional materials for over ten years.

Susy Macqueen is Research Fellow at the Language Testing Research Centre at the University of Melbourne. Her research interests are language assessment for specific purposes, communication in healthcare contexts, language assessment for younger learners, and formulaic sequences.

Anika Müller-Karabil is a Test Validation Officer at the TestDaF Institute, University of Bochum, Germany. She is in charge of the unit providing special arrangements for test takers with disabilities and handles test development and quality assurance issues for the TestDaF reading component. Anika's special field of interest is in new developments in reading assessment, with a focus on integrated tasks and online testing.

Spiros Papageorgiou is a Managing Research Scientist at Educational Testing Service in New Jersey, where he conducts research related to English-language tests, such as TOEFL iBT. Spiros has published in *Language Testing* and *Language Assessment Quarterly* and has also been an active member of the language testing community, serving as Member-at-Large of the Executive Board of the International Language Testing Association.

Karmen Pižorn is Associate Professor of English Language Teaching Methodology at the University of Ljubljana, Faculty of Education, Slovenia. She has been actively involved in setting up and running national English language assessment schemes. She has also been a member of the Advisory Board to the European Commission on the European Survey of Language Competences.

Matthew E. Poehner is Associate Professor of World Languages Education and Applied Linguistics at The Pennsylvania State University. His research is organized around the use of Vygotskian theoretical perspectives to understand processes of instructed L2 development and also as a basis for L2 educational practices, especially Dynamic Assessment. Publications include *Dynamic Assessment: A Vygotskian approach to understanding and promoting L2 development* (2008), *Addressing issues of access and fairness in education through Dynamic Assessment* (2013, co-edited with P. Rea-Dickins), and *Sociocultural theory and the pedagogical imperative in L2 classrooms* (to appear, with J. P. Lantolf).

James E. Purpura is Associate Professor of Linguistics and Education in the TESOL and Applied Linguistics programs at Columbia University. His research interests include grammar and pragmatics assessment and learning-oriented assessment. He is author of *Strategy use and L2 test performance* (CUP) and *Assessing grammar* (CUP). He is co-editor of *New Perspectives in Language Assessment* (Routledge), and associate editor of *Language Assessment Quarterly*. He is Past President of ILTA and currently serves as expert member of EALTA, member of the TOEFL Committee of Examiners, and member of the U.S. Defense Language Testing Advisory Panel.

Kerry Ryan has a background in Applied Linguistics having worked and studied for many years at the University of Melbourne's Language Testing Research Centre (LTRC). He completed his PhD on the Australian citizenship test at Swinburne University of Technology's Swinburne Institute for Social Research (SISR) and currently researches refugee resettlement policy in Australia.

Nick Saville is Director of Research and Thought Leadership for Cambridge English Language Assessment where he is responsible for coordinating the work of highly-qualified research staff. He holds degrees in Linguistics and TEFL, and a PhD in language testing with a thesis on the impact of educational assessment.

Yasuyo Sawaki earned her Ph.D. in Applied Linguistics at the University of California, Los Angeles and is Associate Professor of English Language Education at Waseda University in Tokyo. Her current research interests include validity and use of high-stakes language assessments, reading and writing, diagnostic assessment, and the relationship between assessment and instruction. She is a past Member-at-Large of the International Language Testing Association and current associate editor of the *Language Assessment Quarterly* journal.

Gila Schauer is Professor of English and Applied Linguistics at the University of Erfurt, Germany. She received her PhD from the University of Nottingham, England. Her research interests include intercultural communication, cross-cultural pragmatics, interlanguage pragmatics, linguistic impoliteness, and gender and language. She is the author of *Interlanguage pragmatic development: The study abroad context* (Continuum, 2009) as well as of several articles and book chapters.

Winibert Segers teaches translation theory and translation from French into Dutch (administrative, cultural and medical texts) at the Catholic University Leuven and at the Université Catholique de l'Ouest (France). His research focuses on translation evaluation, translation didactics, and translation theory. He wrote a doctoral dissertation on the untranslatability of and in the texts of the French philosopher Jacques Derrida. Together with Jean Yves Le Disez he organizes international symposia on translation theory and reality called "Théories et Réalités en Traduction" (Brest, Antwerp, Naples).

Lynda Taylor is Senior Lecturer in Language Assessment at the Centre for English Language Learning and Assessment (CRELLA), University of Bedfordshire, UK. She has a long-established background in language learning, teaching and assessment as well as extensive experience in language testing research and validation. She regularly teaches, writes and presents on language assessment matters, including the area of test accommodations, and she has provided expert assistance for test development projects worldwide over the past 25 years.

Dina Tsagari is Assistant Professor in Applied Linguistics/TEFL at the Department of English Studies, University of Cyprus. Her main research interests are language testing and assessment, teaching/learning, teacher training, materials design, and evaluation. She has taught and conducted research in Hong Kong, Cyprus, Greece, and other European countries. Dina is the editor and author of several volumes, journal papers, and book chapters. She is also the coordinator of the Classroom-based Language Assessment SIG – EALTA and currently principal investigator in a research project on second language assessment literacy.

Carolyn E. Turner is Associate Professor of Second Language Education in the Department of Integrated Studies in Education at McGill University. Her research examines language testing/ assessment in educational settings and in healthcare contexts concerning access for linguistic minorities. She is Past President of ILTA and served until recently as associate editor of *Language Assessment Quarterly* since its inception (first issue in 2004). Her work has been published in journals such as *Language Testing, TESOL Quarterly, Canadian Modern Language Review,* and *Health Communication*, and in chapters in edited collections concerning language assessment. She currently serves as the ILTA representative on the ICAO Aviation English Language Test Endorsement Steering Committee.

Alistair Van Moere is President of Pearson's Knowledge Technologies, a group which pioneers artificial intelligence techniques to automatically assess essays, spoken language, and math performances. Alistair has an MA in English Language Teaching, a PhD in Applied Linguistics, and an MBA. He has worked in various language training and assessment roles over the last 20 years and has published 20 research articles in peer-reviewed journals.

Xiaoming Xi is Director of the Center for Language Learning and Assessment in ETS's Research & Development Division in Princeton, NJ. Her areas of interest include validity and fairness issues in the broader context of test use, validity of automated scoring, and speaking assessment.

Sonja Zimmermann is a Test Validation Officer at the TestDaF Institute. She has many years of experience in providing operational and quality assurance support for the TestDaF writing component and has published in this field. Sonja's current research interests include assessing productive skills with specific reference to the testing of speaking and the impact of technology on testing.

Cecilia Guanfang Zhao received her MA in English from The Ohio State University and PhD in TES-OL from New York University. Currently she is Assistant Professor at Shanghai International Studies University. Her research interests include language assessment and second language writing in general, and second language writing assessment in particular.

Index